DEVON AND CORNWALL RECORD SOCIETY

New Series

Volume 64

JAMES DAVIDSON'S EAST DEVON CHURCH NOTES

EDITED BY

JILL COBLEY

DEVON AND CORNWALL RECORD SOCIETY

THE BOYDELL PRESS

First published 2022

A publication of the
Devon and Cornwall Record Society
published by The Boydell Press
an imprint of Boydell & Brewer Ltd
PO Box 9, Woodbridge, Suffolk IP12 3DF, UK
and of Boydell & Brewer Inc.
668 Mt Hope Avenue, Rochester, NY 14620–2731, USA
website: www.boydellandbrewer.com

ISBN 978 0 90185 302 8

Series information is printed at the back of this volume

A CIP catalogue record for this book is available
from the British Library

The publisher has no responsibility for the continued existence or accuracy
of URLs for external or third-party internet websites referred to in this book,
and does not guarantee that any content on such websites is,
or will remain, accurate or appropriate

This publication is printed on acid-free paper

CONTENTS

ILLUSTRATIONS

The editor and publisher are grateful to all the institutions and persons listed for permission to reproduce the materials in which they hold copyright. Every effort has been made to trace the copyright holders; apologies are offered for any omission, and the publisher will be pleased to add any necessary acknowledgement in subsequent editions.

PREFACE

This volume contains the hitherto unpublished 'Church Notes for East Devon' ('Church Notes', vol.I), recorded by James Davidson (1793–1864) which are stored in the Devon Heritage Centre (DHC). These notes are an eyewitness account of East Devon's churches in the mid nineteenth century before Victorianisation brought about irreplaceable change. Davidson's factual notes highlight what has been lost from the archaeological record of the churches' fabric and fittings, and allow us to make comparisons with the churches today, showing the effects of changes in liturgy and fashion which took place during the late nineteenth century.

This edition provides material for further studies of topics ranging from details of furnishings that did not survive nineteenth-century reordering. The information about memorials and their inscriptions (some of which have been destroyed) provides material for tracing family histories (for the wealthy who could afford a memorial) and for studying the causes of death in Devon from the fifteenth to the early nineteenth centuries.

ACKNOWLEDGEMENTS

Thanks must go to the archivists and in particular the help and assistance of Devon Record Office for which I am most grateful. The project owes its inauguration to Dr Todd Gray and John Allan who suggested that Davidson's 'Church Notes' should be transcribed for publication, therefore making them available to a wider audience. I am grateful for their continuing support. Thanks must go also to Stuart Blaylock for his helpful suggestions and to my editor, Professor Catherine Rider.

Abbreviations

DHC   Devon Heritage Centre

Pevsner, *Devon*   B. Cherry and N. Pevsner, *The Buildings of England. Devon*
(London: Yale University Press, 1991)

Editor's Note

Davidson paginated his 'Church Notes' in the original manuscript volume, and these reference numbers are given at the beginning of the description of each church. The headings in the index correspond to Davidson's original index but his page numbers are not used, and instead the page numbers refer to the pages in this volume.

INTRODUCTION

The remarkable, although little known, Devon antiquarian James Davidson left a wealth of seldom referenced manuscript records on many subjects, ranging from archaeology to heraldry to Devon's churches, from the 1820s until his death in 1864. This volume considers the unique documentation that Davidson made of East Devon's 110 churches. Another four volumes, covering South, West, and North Devon and Exeter, respectively, are written in an identical style, giving the same amount of detail about the churches. It is hoped that the publication of Davidson's 'East Devon Church Notes' will provide a picture of Devon's nineteenth-century churches and highlight what has been lost through the Victorianisation of these 110 churches.

Davidson's descriptions are an observation of Devon churches in the mid 1800s. The breadth of coverage and vividness of detail provide a unique picture of churches on the brink of change because of both economic and social factors. The 'notes' were written in the field, as far as can be ascertained, the same as those of the Rev. Jeremiah Milles (1714–84), who visited and recorded churches in the mid 1700s (see below for a fuller discussion). Davidson's practice of writing in the field is in contrast to John Swete (1752–1821), who wrote up his journals in the comfort of his library; they have been published as *Travels in Georgian Devon* (1789–1800).[1] As well as building on the work of earlier antiquarians based in Devon, Davidson was also part of a wider set of nineteenth-century observers who were interested in recording the styles and fittings of parish churches. If we look at the surrounding counties, there were others recording churches in similar ways; in Cornwall we have C.S. Gilbert, who published *A Historical Survey of the County of Cornwall* (1820)[2] and in Dorset John Hutchins (1698–1773) catalogued churches and their monuments in *The History and Antiquities of the County of Dorset* (1774), which was updated in subsequent editions.[3] Edmund Rack carried out extensive surveys of Somerset churches, details of which can be found in *The History and Antiquities of the County of Somerset* (1791), published by John Collinson after Rack's death.[4] Sir Stephen Glynne (1807–74) visited and recorded details of churches in Cornwall,[5]

[1]   T. Gray and M. Rowe (eds), *Travels in Georgian Devon: The Illustrated Journeys of the Reverend John Swete, 1789–1800*, 4 vols (Tiverton: Halsgrove, 1997–2000).

[2]   C.S. Gilbert, *An Historical and Topographical Survey of the County of Cornwall, to which is added a complete Heraldry of the same* (Plymouth-Dock: J. Cogdon, 1817–20).

[3]   J. Hutchins, *The History and Antiquities of the County of Dorset*, 3rd edn, 4 vols (London, 1861–73).

[4]   J. Collinson, *The History and Antiquities of the County of Somerset, collected from authentick records and an actual survey made by the late Mr. Edmund Rack* (Bath: R. Cruttwell, 1791).

[5]   T. Cann-Hughes (ed.), 'Sir Stephen Glynne's Notes on the Churches of Cornwall', *Notes and Queries* 167 (1934) 363–6, 400–2, 438–9; 168 (1934) 5–7, 42–5, 74–7, 111–13, 151–3, 182–4, 219–20, 255–60, 295–7, 329–31, 366–8, 399–41, 437–9; 169 (1935) 6–8, 43–5, 78–81, 112–15. An edition by Paul Cockerham of some of Glynne's church notes relating to Cornwall is in progress.

Devon,[6] Dorset[7] and Somerset.[8] Up to 1851 Glynne used the preferred terminology of the Ecclesiological Society (First Pointed, Middle Pointed and Third Pointed). After 1851 he switched to Thomas Richman's (1776–1841) definitions, which were also those used by Davidson. Richman had attempted to discriminate the styles of English architecture as Norman, Early English, Decorated and Perpendicular.[9] In part this interest in recording information about churches may be because the nineteenth century was an age of narrative history and these antiquarians sought to record empirical evidence of churches before they were destroyed or altered. In doing so, they provided an observation of that period of time with authentic references and facts collected in the field.

On Davidson's death his extensive library passed to his son, James Bridge Davidson, and was subsequently donated to the Plymouth Institute on the son's death; by 1908 it was part of Brooking Rowe's library and was then transferred from there to the Exeter City Library. We know this because of the *ex libris*, pasted on the endpapers of all the 'Church Notes' volumes. The books of church notes were then relocated to the West Country Studies Library in central Exeter and finally to the Devon Heritage Centre at Great Moor House, Exeter. They comprise five seminal volumes, and remain unpublished. Davidson's first dated entry of visiting a church is in 1826 and his last is in 1844, although all are dated in the DHC catalogue as 1843. All the notes are hand written (it can be assumed by Davidson, as the handwriting matches that of his other manuscripts in DHC) on white (sometimes blue-ish) paper, paginated and indexed alphabetically, recording the name of the hamlet, the people buried there and unusual church features. In Volume 3 an unnamed newspaper cutting dated 1857 states that 'a gentleman of this county has accomplished an arduous but interesting task of recording all the churches and Episcopal chapels in the County of Devon', concluding with, 'five quarto volumes of manuscripts, a work perhaps does not exist for any other county in the Kingdom.'[10]

Davidson's other hand-written books and papers, also in DHC, consist of the notes which he used to write about both the history and archaeology of Axminster where he lived. Parts of these were published as *British and Roman Remains in the Vicinity of Axminster* (1833),[11] *The History of Axminster Church* (1835),[12] and *The History of Newenham Abbey* (1843).[13] Geoffrey Chapman has suggested that

[6]   T. Cann-Hughes (ed.), 'Sir Stephen Glynne's Notes on the Churches of Devon', *Notes and Queries* 163 (1932) 328–31, 363–5, 400–2, 437–41, 471–5; 164 (1933) 21–6, 57–60, 95–6, 130–2, 169–71, 200–4, 236–9, 277–80, 313–15, 348–51, 416–17, 454–6; 165 (1933) 20–2, 63–5, 96–8, 130–2, 168–70, 204–6, 241–3, 274–7, 314–16, 349–51, 382–4, 420–2, 456–8; 166 (1934) 24–7, 63–5, 93–5, 131–3, 168–70, 200–3.
[7]   J.M.J. Fletcher (ed.), 'Sir Stephen Glynne, "Notes on some Dorset Churches"', *Proceedings of the Dorset Natural History and Antiquarian Field Club* 44 (1923) 86–104; 45 (1924) 12–74.
[8]   M. McGarvie (ed.), *Sir Stephen Glynne's Church Notes for Somerset*. Somerset Record Society 82 (Taunton: Somerset Record Society, 1994).
[9]   H. Colvin, *A Biographical Dictionary of British Architects 1600–1840*, 3rd edn (London: Yale University Press, 1993).
[10]   J. Davidson, 'Church Notes', DHC, G2/11/15/2, Vol. 3, opp. p. 1.
[11]   J. Davidson, *The British and Roman Remains in the Vicinity of Axminster, in the County of Devon* (London: J.B. Nicholls and Son, 1833).
[12]   J. Davidson, *The History of Axminster Church in the County of Devon* (Exeter: W.C. Pollard, 1835).
[13]   J. Davidson, *The History of Newenham Abbey in the County of Devon* (London: Longman and Co., 1843).

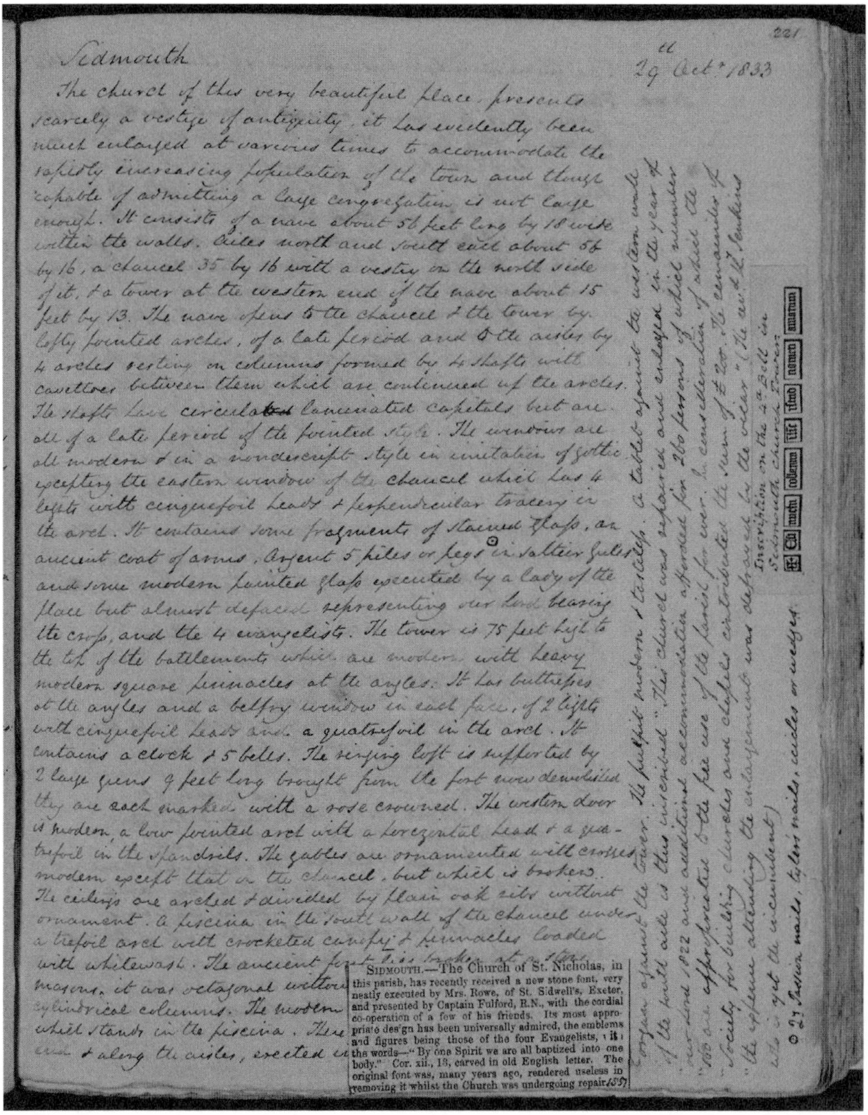

Fig. 1. Page of Davidson's handwriting recording details of Sidmouth church (Davidson, 'Church Notes', vol. 1, p. 221). Reproduced by kind permission of Devon Archives & Local Studies.

Davidson had also intended to write and publish the complete history of Axminster, although in practice this did not happen.[14]

James Davidson (1793–1864)

James Davidson was born on 15 August 1793 at Tower Hill (London), the son of James Davidson, a London stationer and deputy-lieutenant of the Tower of London, and Ann, daughter of William Sawyer of Ipswich. It has been suggested that from his father he inherited a fortune which absolved him from the necessity of earning a living.[15] In the 1820s Davidson bought Secktor House, Sector Lane, Axminster (Devon) where he carried out extensive restorations to the property and enlarged the surrounding parkland to sixty-four acres.[16] Davidson's research led him to discover that the Secktor estate formerly belonged to Newenham Abbey (Axminster) and was mentioned in the abbey's cartulary as the property of Thomas Stede, which in 1279 was valued at 100 shillings.[17] Davidson reported that a boss found in Secktor House was said to have come from the ruins of the abbey, which had been used as a building site, as had a 'plain elegant pointed arch of the thirteenth-century'.[18] This was drawn by W. Spreat, *in situ* as an Axminster shop doorway, which Davidson used to illustrate his *History of Newenham Abbey*. Today the arched doorway of Axminster bookshop opposite the church is evidence of this.

Davidson married Mary, the daughter of Thomas Bridge of Frome St Quinton (Dorset), in 1823 and they had two sons and three daughters. His eldest son, James Bridge Davidson (1824–85) became a barrister and also published articles in the *Reports and Transactions of the Devonshire Association* on the sites of Devon's antiquities. As noted above, Davidson's considerable library was given to the Plymouth Institution on the death of his son in 1885. It was destroyed in the bombing of Plymouth in the Second World War and therefore much of his original research has been lost (although we have no details of how much).[19] As stated above, the 'Church Notes' volumes and two further sets of notes relating to Axminster are in the collections of the DHC where they can be consulted. Little is known about Davidson's private life, but we do have written accounts of the part he played in Axminster affairs, as he was a churchwarden of Axminster parish church.[20]

In the 1820s, furthermore, Davidson became a trustee of the Axminster Turnpike Trust which was established in 1754 to implement the Turnpike Act.[21] The importance of turnpike roads is hard to understand today but in the eighteenth century they were crucial for the movement of goods and people. The inception of the Trusts was characterised by a focus on linking local market hubs rather than creating long-distance highways. The Devon and Dorset Trust was created in 1754

---

[14] G. Chapman, *A History of Axminster to 1910* (Honiton: Marwood Publications, 1998), p. 3.
[15] W.P. Courtney, revised by I. Maxted, 'Davidson, James (1793–1864)', *Oxford Dictionary of National Biography* (Oxford: Oxford University Press, 2004); *Pulmans Weekly News,* 8 March 1884, p. 3 col. 5.
[16] Chapman, *History of Axminster*, p. 20.
[17] J. Davidson, *A History of the Town of Axminster*, DHC, DAVCOL, 1832, p. 369.
[18] Davidson, *History of Newenham Abbey*, p. 152 and Plate 6.
[19] Courtney and Maxted, 'Davidson, James'.
[20] Chapman, *History of Axminster*.
[21] The source for this paragraph is Chapman, *History of Axminster*, esp. p. 22.

but fragmented into independent trusts centred on market towns such as Axminster, which had twenty-two miles of turnpike roads with six toll gates. In 1822 these were described as being in a ruinous condition, narrow and incommodious for carriages, and so the Trust was instructed to carry out maintenance and widen the road. By 1840 this had been completed. These turnpike roads would have been familiar to Davidson, and close to his own property. The turnpike road now called Sector Lane ran east from Axminster, past Davidson's estate, across Hawkchurch common onto the Crewkerne road and on to Lyme Regis at Blackpool Corner; all these places are still traceable today. There was a toll gate on Sector Lane at NGR 3042 9832 but nothing remains of it today.

Davidson's expertise in Devon's antiquities was also well known. In an obituary of his son James Bridge Davidson, Davidson senior is described 'as having an intimate knowledge of all matters relating to Devon, ranging from architectural to heraldic, to ancient manorial divisions of property and antiquities, to which he devoted 40 years of study'.[22] Before we look at Davidson's senior's oeuvre recording Devon's churches, we need to assess his published and unpublished manuscripts to help understand the man. Davidson compiled two commonplace books, all hand written, titled and referenced with footnotes and newspaper cuttings, and indexed. The books contain the drafts of his published work on Axminster.

In addition to these unpublished notes, in the 1830s and 1840s Davidson published the three books on Axminster listed above. Later, in 1861, he published *Notes on the Antiquities of Devonshire which Date before the Norman Conquest*, after his articles on this subject had first appeared in Trewman's *Exeter Flying Post* in the 1850s.[23] The book comprised an alphabetical compilation of all the known or suggested archaeological sites in Devon, as recognised by him and seventy-eight other writers, ranging from Tudor antiquarians, Donn's maps, Camden's *Britannia* and Polwhele's *History of Devonshire*. Davidson catalogued the different types of sites, such as barrows and hillforts, and made suggestions regarding their use and who occupied them, something no other Devon antiquarian had attempted to carry out.

Davidson's writing reflects the conventions of the day, quoting known 'experts' and his observations but not his personal opinions. Thus, in the introduction to his *A History of the Town and Parish of Axminster in the County of Devon*, Davidson describes his work as follows: 'the following has been the agreeable occupation on many an interval of leisure amidst the duties and enjoyments of domestic and rural life. It makes few pretentions beyond a faithful compilation of facts gleamed [gleaned] from local information and labours of previous writers.'[24]

Examining Davidson's Possible Rationale for Recording Churches

Before we look at Davidson's recording methods for churches, we need to establish why he undertook such an enormous task of documenting 499 Devon churches and some Dorset churches. He could possibly have been planning to write a history of Devon, including details of all the churches. Devon's antiquarians had been

[22] Anon., 'Obituary of James Bridge Davidson', *Reports and Transactions of the Devonshire Association* 18 (1886), p. 58.

[23] J. Davidson, *Notes on the Antiquities of Devon which Date before the Norman Conquest* (Exeter: W. Roberts, 1861).

[24] Davidson, *History of the Town and Parish of Axminster*.

preoccupied with the aim of writing a history of Devon since John Hooker (1527–1610) undertook a topographical survey with a view to writing the county's history. However, Hooker made few references to churches and their memorials, and neither did his fellow Devon antiquarians of the sixteenth and seventeenth centuries, as they principally focused on the genealogy of Devon's gentry.

Devon's Georgian antiquarians, again while collecting material to write Devon's history, provided the first documented record of the churches and their memorials. Possibly the first documented evidence is provided by the Rev. Jeremiah Milles, dean of Exeter Cathedral, who visited 318 Devon churches between 1747 and 1762; he included sixty-seven East Devon churches and documented the memorial inscriptions in thirty-two of them.[25] These are recorded in what is now known as 'Milles Parochial Collection', held by the Bodleian Library.[26] Milles' records are hand written on brown paper and contain details of the exterior and interior of each church, the painted glass and some memorials. Davidson makes no mention of Milles' research, possibly because he did not know of Milles' undertaking. As noted above, Davidson carried out empirical research and did not rely on the findings of earlier writers. By making comparisons between Milles' documentation from the 1750s and Davidson's, it is possible to ascertain what was lost in the intervening ninety years. For example, in Woodbury church the north side aisle had been removed, the wainscoting (wooden panelling) had gone, as had the painted glass in the north aisle, a brass memorial plate, a memorial of a man and his daughters kneeling at a desk, and the black marble altar within the altar rails.

Other Georgian antiquarians had also documented Devon churches. Between 1769 and 1779, the Recorder of Barnstaple, Benjamin Incledon (1730–96), visited 179 Devon churches of which fifty-one were in East Devon. He made pen-and-ink drawings of the church monuments and their inscriptions, giving a brief description of each church.[27] Incledon recorded the memorials in two volumes, noting in 1774 that because of failing eyesight he could not continue.[28] In 1831 Davidson tried to purchase Incledon's manuscripts but George Oliver (1781–1864), who was acting as

---

[25] East Devon churches visited and recorded by Milles: Forde Abbey, Church Stanton, Axmouth, Beer, Bicton, Branscombe, Broadclyst, Broadhembury, Buckerell, Budleigh Salterton, Clyst Hydon, Clyst Honiton, Clyst St George, Clyst St Lawrence, Colaton Raleigh, Colyton, Combe Raleigh, Combpyne, Cotleigh, Dunkeswell, Farringdon, Farway, Gittisham, Harpford, Honiton, Littleham, Luppitt, Lympstone, Membury, Monkton, Musbury, Northleigh, Offwell, Otterton, Payhembury, Plymtree, Rockbeare, Sidbury, Sidmouth, Southleigh, Sowton, Talaton, Whimple, Withycombe Raleigh, Widworthy, Bampton, Bickleigh, Bradninch, Burlescombe, Butterleigh, Calverleigh, Clayhanger, Clayhidon, Cullompton, Halberton, Holcombe Rogus, Huntsham, Kentisbeare, Moorbath, Sampford Peverell, Willand.

[26] Oxford, Bodleian Library, MSS. Top. Devon b.1–6; 'A Parochial History of Devonshire 1747–1762', DHC 193 (microfilm copy of Bodleian ms.).

[27] Churches visited and recorded by Incledon: Thorncombe, Church Stanton, Axminster, Axmouth, Aylesbeare, Beer, Bicton, Branscombe, Broadclyst, Broadhembury, Buckerell, Clyst Honiton, Colaton Raleigh, Colyton, Combe Raleigh, Combpyne, Cotleigh, Dunkeswell, Escot, Exmouth, Farway, Feniton, Gittisham, Harpford, Honiton, Kilmington, Luppitt, Membury, Musbury, Northleigh, Offwell, Otterton, Ottery St Mary, Payhembury, Plymtree, Salcombe Regis, Seaton, Shute, Sidbury, Southleigh, Uplyme, Upottery, Venn Ottery, Whimple, Widworthy, Bradninch, Burlescombe, Calverleigh, Clayhanger, Clay Hydon, Halberton, Hemyock, Kentisbeare, Morebath, Tiverton, Washfield, Willand.

[28] B. Incledon, 'Monumental Inscriptions', North Devon Athenaeum d2 929 5/NC.

a go-between, stated in a letter that a Mr Strong wanted the princely sum of £250 and Oliver thought that was four times their value.[29] There is no further reference by Davidson to buying Incledon's manuscripts. In 1904 Wainwright published in the *Reports and Transactions of the Devonshire Association* a full list of all Incledon's memorial inscriptions because the originals had either been destroyed or were now becoming illegible and lost from memory.[30] He hoped this would be useful to antiquarians. In East Devon Incledon recorded 310 inscriptions of which 206 had been removed by the time Davidson recorded the memorials.

By Davidson's time there were also published descriptions of some East Devon churches. The Rev. Richard Polwhele (1760–1838) was the only Devon antiquarian to publish a *History of Devon* (1793–1806) that contained information on churches.[31] Polwhele made observations of the church fabric of forty-two East Devon churches, and recorded the memorials in twenty-three and their inscriptions in nineteen.[32] The brothers Daniel (1762–1834) and Samuel Lysons (1763–1819) wrote *Magna Britannia: Being a Concise Topographical Account of the Several Counties of Great Britain* (1806–22); and published *Devon* (vol. 6) in 1822. This work also contains information on Devon churches, listing the architectural periods, rood screens and rood lofts, pulpits, fonts and effigies; although there is no mention of any monuments and their inscriptions. The Lysons provide detailed information about Devon's gentry and their heraldic devices. Davidson owned a copy of *Magna Britannia* and could have used it to ensure he had correctly assigned the heraldic devices to the right families, but we have no proof of this.

Davidson was the contemporary of a number of other nineteenth-century writers on Devonshire churches. He corresponded with George Oliver, who as we have seen tried unsuccessfully to help Davidson purchase Benjamin Incledon's manuscript. Oliver published articles on 'Ecclesiastical Antiquities' in Exeter's newspapers, where he documented twenty-eight East Devon churches and mentioned the memorial inscriptions in sixteen.[33] Lieutenant-Colonel William Harding of North Devon (1792–1886) bought Oliver's papers on his death, and also visited seventy-nine East Devon churches; however, the two sets of papers became muddled together so it is difficult to know which churches Harding recorded and which were recorded by Oliver.[34]

[29] J. Davidson, 'Collection for Axminster', DHC, Z19/12/1.

[30] T. Wainwright, 'An Index to the Names of Persons Found on the Monumental Inscriptions in Devonshire Churches', *Reports and Transactions of the Devonshire Association* 36 (1904), 522–42.

[31] R. Polwhele, *The History of Devonshire*, 3 vols (London: Cadell and Davies, 1793–1806).

[32] Churches visited and recorded by Polwhele: Axminster, Aylesbeare, Bicton, Branscombe, Broadclyst, Broadhembury, Buckerell, Clyst Honiton, Clyst St George, Clyst St Lawrence, Colyton, Dunkeswell, East Budleigh, Farringdon, Farway, Gittisham, Honiton, Kilmington, Littleham, Membury, Musbury, Ottery St Mary, Plymtree, Rockbeare, Rousdon, Seaton, Shute, Sidmouth, Southleigh, Talaton, Widworthy, Woodbury, Burlescombe, Clyst Hydon, Cullompton, Holcombe Rogus, Kentisbeare, Morebath, Sampford Peverell, Tiverton, Heavitree.

[33] Churches visited and recorded by Oliver: Awliscombe, Axminster, Axmouth, Broadclyst, Budleigh Salterton, Clyst St George, Colyton, Combe Raleigh, Farringdon, Honiton, Kilmington, Littleham, Lympstone, Membury, Otterton, Sidmouth, Woodbury, Bampton, Bradninch, Butterleigh, Cullompton, Tiverton, Heavitree.

[34] W. Harding, Athenaeum NDHC hrd/H.

Davidson also knew William Spreat (1816–73), who provided the engravings for his *Newenham Abbey* (1843) and published *Picturesque Sketches of the Churches of Devon* (1842) with lithographs showing the exteriors and interiors of twenty-one East Devon churches among a total of seventy-four lithographs of Devon churches.[35] Spreat wrote in his introduction that the book 'was to fulfil the increased interest in Ecclesiastical Edifices' and cater for the societies that had been formed to look at church architecture. It was not his intention to enter into architectural discussions or to recall the good and the great under the pavements 'where nothing remains except a tablet'.[36] Spreat's lithographs provide a pictorial record which allows comparisons to be made with the churches today.

Two other projects to record Devon's churches were also underway at the time Davidson was writing. The Exeter Diocesan Architectural Society was founded in 1841 whose aim was to report on the churches' fabric and approve the design of new churches. Davidson referenced their work and produced the index. Then in the 1850s the Devon and Exeter Institution began collecting material on ecclesiastical antiquities for a planned 'County History', sending a questionnaire to all Devon churches asking who built the church, the ground plan, whether it was pewed [had box pews] and if it had a library. There is no evidence of any questionnaires being returned, however, and by the 1850s Davidson had completed his survey, so he could not have used the information they collected.

In addition, Davidson may have been responding to social and economic changes which were affecting the Church, with changes to the liturgy and consequently the internal layout of churches. Between 1800 and 1900 the Church of England was simultaneously in a state of transition and continuity with the past. It underwent a transformation more rapid than any that had been experienced since the Reformation. The Church, which had been closely linked to the political and legal systems, now became a denomination, powerful and legally recognised as the established Church. Alongside these political changes came calls to change the liturgy and the layout of parish churches. The John Keble Assize Sermon of 1833 called for the reinstatement of the altar as a focal point for worship and a change in theological thinking away from the auditory church of the eighteenth century which had focused on the word and preaching. This linked to the requirement of the Cambridge Camden Society and the Tractarians for a change in the whole layout of the church. The Tractarians and the Cambridge Camden Society wanted the church to return to becoming central to daily life as it had been in the medieval period, focusing on the symbolism of the sacrament.[37] They opposed social divisions of rich and poor and wanted Christian equality within the church building, without having the poor relegated to the galleries.[38] They gave precise guidance as to the layout of the church with a return to a focus on the nave, and sought the removal of pew ownership and the comfort

---

[35] W. Spreat, *Picturesque Sketches of the Churches of Devon* (Exeter: W. Spreat, 1842). East Devon churches visited and recorded by Spreat: Awliscombe, Aylesbeare, Bicton, Broadclyst, Buckerell, Cadbury, Clyst St George, Combe Raleigh, Cullompton, Littleham, Feniton, Honiton, Killerton, Lympstone, Otterton, Ottery St Mary, Sidbury, Silverton, Sowton, Thorverton, Withycombe Raleigh.

[36] Spreat, *Picturesque Sketches of the Churches of Devon*, p. 1.

[37] C. Webster and J. Elliot (eds) '*A Church as it Should Be': the Cambridge Camden Society and its Influence* (Stamford: Shaun Tyas, 2000), p. 349.

[38] G. Oliver, 'Common Place Book', NDA, Athenaeum, File H43 (1828), p. 187.

of domesticity in the box-pews. They also wanted the return of a raised altar visible from all parts of the church, a move away from the focus being on the pulpit as it had been during the Georgian period.[39] In Devon John Hayward (1807–91), the official architect for the Exeter Diocesan Architectural Society, was a member of the Cambridge Camden Society, and he was influential in restoring or rebuilding seventeen East Devon churches in the Gothic Revival style.

Whether a church needed rebuilding or restoring in response to this guidance was a matter decided by the parishioners or a reforming vicar. The suggested date for the start of the Tractarian influences on church restoration is 1840,[40] although in Devon there are examples of rebuilding from as early as 1826, as at All Saints (Culmstock), and restoration from 1838, as at St Mary and St Giles (Buckerell). This may not have been carried out for ecclesiological reasons, though, and may have been more a case of the deterioration of the church buildings. Davidson must therefore have been aware that churches were changing even as he wrote his notes.

East Devon Churches

In the early 1800s East Devon consisted of 110 parishes. In 2021 two of these are in Dorset and one in Somerset, and East Devon consists of sixty-nine parishes; the remaining thirty-five are in Mid Devon and three in Exeter. These changes happened after the Great Reform Act of 1832 which introduced extensive changes to the parliamentary constituency boundaries. In particular, the detached parts of Devon were annexed, and Thorncombe was transferred to Dorset. Forde Abbey was transferred to Dorset under the Counties (Detached Parts) Act of 1844, while Church Stanton was transferred to Somerset under the 1894 Act which abolished sanitary districts and replaced them with rural districts.

Davidson started visiting East Devon churches in 1826, which must have been an arduous physical task at that time. He visited only one church in 1826 and one the following year. In the September of 1828 he visited twenty-eight churches, then fourteen in 1829, ten between 1830 and 1840; in July of 1840 he visited eighteen, subsequently in July and August of 1843 he visited another twenty-nine. For a further nine churches we have no date for his visit. If the numbers are looked at as they stand, however, they do not give the correct picture of Davidson's research, as during this time he was also visiting and recording other Devon churches – as detailed in the additional four volumes of 'Church Notes'.

When we look at Davidson's catalogue of East Devon churches the following facts appear. Of the 110 East Devon churches, five were built during Davidson's lifetime and have not been altered since.[41] Just two – Forde Abbey and Widworthy – have not been restored or rebuilt since Davidson's day. Davidson could walk into them today and recognise them as he saw them. Whilst the chapel at Forde Abbey was altered from the former Cistercian monastery's chapter house, it is still as Davidson recorded it, as are the memorials.

---

[39] Webster and Elliot, 'A Church as it Should Be', p. 353.

[40] G.K. Brandwood, 'Anglican Churches before the Restorers. A Study from Leicestershire and Rutland', Archaeological Journal 144 (1987), 383–408 at 392.

[41] Chevithorne, Countess Wear, Escot, Killerton, Tipton St John.

Fig. 2. The exterior of the bomb-damaged Clyst St George church painted by Leighton Hall Woollatt in 1940. Exeter, Royal Albert Memorial Museum and Art Gallery, 27/2012/10. © Royal Albert Memorial Museum and Art Gallery, Exeter.

Fig. 3. The east end of the destroyed Clyst St George church painted by Leighton Hall Woollatt in 1940. Exeter, Royal Albert Memorial Museum and Art Gallery, 27/2012/11. © Royal Albert Memorial Museum and Art Gallery, Exeter.

Of the remaining 102 churches, forty-four were rebuilt[42] and fifty-eight have been restored to various degrees, some twice.[43] The best example of a church altered to fit classic Tractarian principles is Sowton, which Davidson visited in 1840, four years before the changes were made. Seven churches have been totally rebuilt since Davidson visited them, including Musbury church which has been both restored and rebuilt.[44] Therefore Davidson is frequently painting a picture of churches interiors which have largely been lost.

There are two examples of East Devon churches where Davidson's records provide a unique picture of church interiors that have since been destroyed. At Honiton a fire in 1911 completely gutted the interior of the church, with only the outer walls remaining, destroying the fittings that Davidson had recorded. The rood screen, galleries, desk, pulpit and font were all lost in the fire, and some fourteen memorials were destroyed. A note of caution needs to be sounded, however, as the church had been restored in 1896, so possibly alterations had already been made. At Clyst St George the church was destroyed by enemy action in August 1940 when an incendiary bomb set fire to the church, although the tower and parts of the walls survived. The church had been restored in the 1850s by the Rev. H.I. Ellacombe, who set out to 'modernise' the church to Tractarian principles: he removed the screen, replaced the inscribed floor memorials with Minton tiles and removed the box pews. All of these were lost with the font in the bombing of the church, along with ten memorials. When the church was rebuilt in 1952 it was as a simpler version of the original.

These figures underline that the great majority of East Devon churches no longer exist in the form that Davidson recorded, and his record is therefore a unique picture of the ecclesiastical fabric during the early nineteenth century. Since then, these churches have undergone a series of transformations because of changes to the liturgy and a desire to venerate, improve and adapt the buildings in new ways. From Davidson's accounts it is possible to trace these changes and identify what has been lost from the archaeological record. We now need to look at Davidson's records in more detail, starting with the churches' fabric and fittings, and lastly the memorials.

---

[42] Thorncombe, Axmouth, Broadclyst, Broadhembury, Clyst Hydon, Clyst Honiton, Clyst St George, Colaton Raleigh, Cotleigh Dunkeswell, Farringdon, Harpford, Honiton, Kilmington, Lympstone, Monkton, Newton Poppleford, Northleigh, Otterton, Rockbeare, Sheldon, Sidmouth, Southleigh, Sowton Whimple, Withycombe Raleigh, Withycombe Raleigh (St John), Yarcombe, Ayshford, Bickleigh, Burlescombe, Butterleigh, Calverleigh, Cove, Hemyock, Hockworthy, Loxbeare, Petton, Shillingford, Uffculme, Topsham, Heavitree.

[43] Church Stanton, Awliscombe, Axminster, Axmouth, Aylesbeare, Branscombe, Broadclyst, Broadhembury, Buckerell, Clyst St Mary, Colyton, Columb David, Columbjohn, Combe Raleigh, Combpyne, East Budleigh, Farway, Feniton, Gittisham, Kilmington, Littleham, Luppitt, Membury, Nether Exe, Offwell, Ottery St Mary, Payhembury, Plymtree, Salcombe Regis, Seaton, Shute, Sidbury, Talaton, Uplyme, Upottery, Venn Ottery, Widworthy, Woodbury, Bampton, Bradninch, Cadbury, Clayhanger, Clayhidon, Cullompton, Culmstock, Halberton, Holcombe Rogus, Huntsham, Kentisbeare, Morebath, Sampford Peverell, Silverton, Thorverton, Tiverton, Tiverton St George, Uplowman, Washfield.

[44] Beer (1876), Bicton (1850), Budleigh Salterton (1891), Cove (1855), Exmouth (1905), Musbury, Rousdon (1872).

Davidson's Method of Recording

Davidson recorded the date he visited a church and the distance in miles from the nearest large town, but not the church's dedication, except at Kilmington. Occasionally he gave a brief description of the surrounding landscape. At Salcombe, he noted that 'the church of this romantic little village stands nearly at the head of the narrow valley or combe which opens to the sea – it is a very pleasing object when viewed from either of the roads to the place or from the surrounding hills'.[45] At Broadhembury he observed that the parish church of this village was 'a very interesting edifice as it contains several curious relics of antiquity and seems to have been adorned with some liberality of expense'.[46] There is evidence that the pages on which Davidson wrote his record had been folded into three, with the name of the village on the reverse, and possibly kept in a box before being bound together. His inventory is not a set of questions but a description that follows a similar pattern each time.

The internal fixtures and fittings, as catalogued by Davidson, start with a description of the nave giving its measurements, then the same for the chancel, side aisles and tower; these have not been checked but they do seem broadly accurate. Davidson noted the arches and the capitals and their frequently being coated in 'whitewash', and the architectural features of the windows and roof arches and whether they had been altered or repaired. Davidson makes no mention of the construction of the exterior of the church, only the location of the tower. There follow details of the wall paintings, bells, piscina and sedilia, rood screen, altar, pulpit, pews, gallery, font and plate. The most notable record was of the memorial inscriptions and their heraldic devices, which is the area where the biggest loss has occurred, though occasionally Davidson wrote that he did not copy all the 'laudable verses' nor all the Latin verses. This detailed catalogue of contents allows us today to ascertain what is missing or has been moved or removed from a church, almost two centuries later. We now look at how Davidson documented these features in Devon churches.

(a) Wall paintings

In AD 604 St Gregory the Great decreed that the walls of parish churches were to become '*biblia pauperum*' (Bibles of the poor) and by the Middle Ages they became like picture books, with the plaster painted for the edification of the illiterate, illustrated with the lives of saints and Judgement Day to instigate reverence, obedience and fear. In 1547 Parliament ordered the obliteration of these 'superstitious' images, and again during the Civil War paintings were whitewashed, removed or covered with biblical texts.[47]

Nonetheless paintings remained in a number of the churches Davidson visited. Davidson detailed in 1850 a mural in Ayshford chapel as 'very gaudy similar to those in Burlescombe church [which Davidson did not record, or possibly it had already been removed] – on the south corner near the communion Table – richly ornamented

[45] J. Davidson, 'Church Notes', DHC G2/11/15/2 vol.1 (1843), pp. 217–20.

[46] Davidson, 'Church Notes', pp. 397–403.

[47] S. Friar, *A Companion to the English Parish Church* (Frome: Alan Sutton, 1996), pp. 486–7.

with armorial bearings and cherubs', which remains today.[48] The following five wall paintings have been destroyed but it is interesting to read how Davidson described them. In 1843 at Calverleigh church he saw on the plaster above the chancel screen

> a rude painting but executed with great spirit representing in the centre a tree laden with fruit and below it the text "Herein is my father glorified that the bear much fruit" On each side of it is a painting of another tree, one living but without fruit and two men cutting it down – with the text "Every branch in me that bear not fruit he takes away and every branch that bear fruit he fungith it that it may bring forth more fruit" while in the other a dead tree has an angel cutting it down and the devil pulling at it with a rope, with the words "Cursed be the tree that bear no fruit" Another text reads "Every tree that bringeth not forth good fruit is hewn down and cast into the fire".[49]

A newspaper cutting dated 26 November 1843 in Davidson's notes regarding Cullompton church stated that when workmen were scraping the mortar off the walls they laid open many paintings of landscapes, buildings and figures, all of them sacred subjects, and emblems of the Passion, surrounded with interlaced borders, and explained by scrolls in black letters. The vicar immediately had them whitewashed over as he thought they would distract the congregation.[50]

In 1843 Davidson stated that the walls of Columbjohn church had been covered with texts of scripture painted in English letters on the plaster, within large panels bordered with scrolls.[51] In Combe Raleigh church, on the north wall of the aisle above the windows, Davidson noted there were some ancient paintings which extended about half the length of the aisle and represented a range of columns ornamented with angular and other devices having a sort of Ionic capital and supporting semi-circular arches. Under the arches were representations of a variety of human figures but these have been so much defaced since Davidson's day that their occupations cannot now be ascertained.[52] The walls of Membury church in 1826 had been adorned with texts of scripture in old block letters but many of them were obliterated with whitewash.[53] Davidson occasionally missed wall paintings if they were not on show. The Sidmouth antiquarian Peter Orlando Hutchinson wrote a book on the rebuilding of Sidmouth church (1859) where he detailed the destruction of a small wall painting, which Davidson had not seen in 1833 as it was then hidden.[54] Nonetheless there is a positive note on which to end: the inscriptions and text Davidson documented in Sidbury church are still there.

[48] Davidson, 'Church Notes', vol.I, pp. 569–71.
[49] Davidson, 'Church Notes', vol.I, pp. 657–60.
[50] Davidson, 'Church Notes', vol.I, pp. 417–29.
[51] Davidson, 'Church Notes', vol.I, p. 461.
[52] Davidson, 'Church Notes', vol.I, pp. 100–3.
[53] Davidson, 'Church Notes', vol.I, pp. 61–9.
[54] P. Hutchinson, *The History of the Restoration of Sidmouth Church*. DHC (1880) DRO 4584, p. 3.

(b) Church Bells

Davidson's recording of church bells shows the thoroughness of his observations, since it takes more than a casual visit to climb a tower, enter the belfry, and scrabble around to record the inscription in poor light. He documented the inscriptions found on thirty-five bells, and noted another 241 bells found in ninety-three East Devon churches. There were only seventeen churches where he did not record any bells.[55] Not all the bells were medieval, as many had been recast, with their ancient inscriptions copied by means of wax or clay impressions, to transfer the inscription to the new mould. Bells of the seventeenth century can be found in Axmouth (1612), Payhembury (1635), Seaton (1633) and Sheldon (1628) (Table 1). By the late 1600s the inscriptions were written in a mixture of Latin and English, which by the 1700s had become solely English. The inscriptions changed over the years from religious mottoes to the names of the church-wardens and the people who had cast the bells. For example, Davidson documented fifteen churches where bells had been cast by the Bilbie family of Cullompton between 1715 and 1815.[56] Five bells were catalogued as cast in London,[57] but for another fteen bells we have no indication where they were cast.[58] There was a bell foundry operated by Thomas and John Pennington in Exeter, from 1618 to 1752, but perhaps surprisingly Davidson made no record of any bells cast by them in East Devon.

Some bell inscriptions were popular across East Devon. The inscription 'I to the church the living call and to the grave do summon all' can be found in Musbury, Upottery, Hemyock, Broadhembury, Burlescombe and Bampton churches. 'Mr Treble your head rejoice' could be found in Kilmington, Shute and Widworthy churches. Others were unique; 'Health and Delight' could be found in Widworthy church, and one bell at Church Stanton has this unusual inscription: 'I was made in hope to ring at the coronation of our King 1660' (Charles II). The bells Davidson recorded date from 1612 to the late 1850s. Whether they had been recast is not something that Davidson documents.

Table 1. Periods in which bells found in East Devon churches were cast.

Year	No. of bells
1600–1649	19
1650–1699	15
1700–1749	37
1750–1799	32
1800–1849	39
1850–1899	14

[55] Beer, Budleigh Salterton, Cotleigh, Countess Wear, Columbjohn, Cullompton, Escot, Exmouth, Forde Abbey, Honiton Clyst, Killerton, Plymtree, Rousdon, St John Exmouth, Silverton, Thorncombe, Withycombe Raleigh.

[56] Bampton (1800), Broadhembury (1767), Clayhidon (1810), Hemyock (1811), Hockworthy (1808), Holcombe Rogus (1763), Musbury (1785), Otterton (1777), Shute (1761), Talaton (1792), Tiverton (1791), Topsham (1778), Uffculm (1801), Uplyme (1805), Widworthy (1722).

[57] Farrington (1815), Halberton (1851), Harpford, Otterton (1864), Upottery (1818).

[58] Burlescombe, Dunkeswell, Farway, Feniton, Kentisbeare, Luppitt, Morebath, Nether Exe, Payhembury, Rockbeare, Kilmington, Southleigh, Sowton, Uplowman, Yarcombe.

Further details about these bells and their inscriptions can be found in *A Detailed Account of the Bells in the Old Parish Churches of Devonshire*, by the Rev. Henry Thomas Ellacombe (1790–1885) who became the vicar of Clyst St George in 1850. Ellacombe climbed and recorded some 452 church towers in 1864 and 1865, commenting on the poor state of repair of their ringing lofts, and documented the inscriptions of forty-one East Devon churches.[59] *A Detailed Account of the Bells in the Old Parish Churches of Devonshire* was published by subscription in 1872. Ellacombe informed his subscribers, of whom James Bridge Davidson (Davidson's son) was one, by letter that the book would cost 31s 6d and an extra 3s for the supplement. Ellacombe's book gives a brief history of church bells, stating that they were unmistakably of 'Christian origin' and the earliest bells were named 'Nola' and 'Campanae' in the fifth and sixth centuries. After this bells were given saints' names. He suggested that the majority of Devon bells were date-stamped. Sometimes by comparing the records of Ellacombe and Davidson we can guess when bells were recast. For example, Davidson recorded five bells in Hemyock church as dated 1621, yet Ellacombe documented them as 1811, suggesting that they had been recast between the two visits.[60]

(c) The Piscina and Sedilia

A piscina is a niche containing a stone bowl with a drain, built into the south wall of the chancel near the altar, used to wash the sacred vessels. They are sometimes seen today where there is no obvious sign of an altar, as at Widworthy church in the south wall of the south side aisle. Davidson documented eighteen piscinae which are still *in situ*.[61] A further four have since been removed: at Clyst St George during rebuilding in 1955, at Thorncombe in 1867, and during restorations at Salcombe in 1869 and at Sidbury in 1884.

A sedilia is a set of three stepped stone seats recessed into niches in the south wall of the chancel, often decorated and canopied. During Victorian restorations chancel floors were frequently raised to elevate the altar with steps, which makes the sedilia seats appear uncomfortably low. This happened in Axminster when it was restored in 1870. Today sedilia can still be found as Davidson recorded them at Ottery St Mary and Plymtree churches.

(d) The Rood Screen

Before the fifteenth century the chancel screen served as a division between the secular nave and the ecclesiastical chancel, supporting images of the Virgin Mary. Devon screens are distinctive and were the property of the congregation

---

[59] H. Ellacombe, *A Detailed Account of the Bells in the Old Parish Churches of Devonshire* (Exeter: W. Pollard, 1872), pp. 15–16.

[60] Mention must be made of John G.M. Scott (et al.), *Towers and Bells of Devon* (Exeter: The Mint Press, 2007), which is a survey of Devon bells and their towers and is comparable to Ellacombe's *A Detailed Account of the Bells in the Old Parish Churches of Devonshire* (1872) published some 140 years before. How much Scott used Davidson's or Ellacombe's work is not known.

[61] Aylesbeare, Bampton, Burlescombe, Combe Pyne, East Budleigh, Halberton, Harpford, Hemyock, Northleigh, Petton, Rockbeare, Sampford Peverell, Seaton, Sidmouth, Yarcombe, Widworthy, Whimple, Uffculme.

who wanted to beautify the church with the work of local carvers. Their display elements faced the parishioners and were seen as a status symbol as well as part of the cult of the saints. The side of the screen facing the parishioners was often painted with images of saints, while the back facing the altar was often plain. During the fourteenth century the use of the screen became more complex and by the late fifteenth and early sixteenth century its role changed. Services were now held in front of the screen, and the focus was on the pulpit rather than the altar. The destruction of the rood screen and its images started as early as the seventeenth century, although this was not universally complied with and during the Reformation they were used by musicians. One suggestion why so many screens disappeared at this time is because they were decaying.[62] Prejudice against medieval ornament and a disinclination to incur the expense of repair may also have played a part, especially as the changes to the liturgy favoured an open church where the screen was seen as an impediment to worship. In East Devon Davidson noted forty-six churches with screens or parts of screens,[63] and sixteen churches where the screens were removed in his lifetime.[64] He stated that Axminster's had been removed in 1660. At Church Stanton Davidson recorded no screen, but a new one was built c.1910. Another eight screens were removed after Davidson's death in 1864.[65] During the nineteenth century the screens were viewed with indifference by the county clergy as superstitious and survivors of papal domination that would be better swept away.[66] Bligh Bond records the years some of these screens were removed, noting that the screen at Broadhembury was burnt in a shed, whereas at Culm Davey it was burnt in the church and at Woodbury removed by a 'modernising vicar'.[67] At around the same time John Stabb published information on Devon's church architecture, giving further details of the destruction of rood screens.[68]

---

[62] F. Bligh Bond, 'Devonshire Screens and Rood Lofts', *Reports and Transactions of the Devonshire Association* 24 (1902), 531–50, at 547.

[63] Church Stanton, Awliscombe, Bampton, Broadhembury, Broadclyst, Buckerell, Colyton, East Budleigh, Farway, Feniton, Honiton, Kilmington, Littleham, Luppitt, Northleigh, Ottery St Mary, Payhembury, Plymtree, Rockbeare, Rousdon, Sheldon, Sowton, Venn Ottery, Whimple, Woodbury, Yarcombe, Ayshford, Bampton, Bradninch, Burlescombe, Calverleigh, Collumpton, Culmstock, Halberton, Hemyock, Hockworthy, Holcombe Rogus, Huntsham, Kentisbeare, Morebath, Petton, Shillingford, Uffculme, Uplyme, Washfield, Willand.

[64] Bampton (1860), Broadhembury (1851), Church Stanton (1830, new screen built c.1910), Culmstock (1825), Heavitree (parts made into pews c.1830), Hemyock (1847), Holcombe Rogus (1828), Huntsham (1859), Kilmington (1846), Luppitt (1828), Northleigh (partly removed 1829), Ottery St Mary (c.1800), Shillingford (decaying when Davidson visited in 1828), Sowton (end of eighteenth century), Whimple (1822, a few painted panels remain), Yarcombe (1829).

[65] Broadclyst (1867), Farway (no date), Hockworthy (no date), Honiton (1911, in a fire), Morebath (no date), Rockbeare (1887), Uplyme (twentieth century), Venn Ottery (1884).

[66] Bligh Bond, 'Devonshire Screens and Rood Lofts', 531.

[67] Bligh Bond, 'Devonshire Screens and Rood Lofts', 549–50.

[68] J. Stabb, *Devon Church Antiquities: Being a Description of Many Objects of Interest in the Old Parish Churches of Devonshire* (London: Simpkin, Marshall, Hamilton, Kent, and Co., 1908–16). For a recent discussion of this, see M.A. Williams, 'Medieval English Roodscreens (with special reference to Devon)', Unpublished Ph.D. Thesis, University of Exeter, 2008.

Fig. 4. The screen at Clyst St Lawrence church, just as described by Davidson (T. Gray, 2021).

(e) The Altar

With the introduction of the first English prayer book in 1549 a new form of liturgy developed that increased the laity's participation in the service, and movable wooden communion tables were introduced. These tables were kept in the chancel or as required against the east wall in the sanctuary except during the communion service when they were placed in the nave. These tables replaced the stone altars which had been common in medieval times but were regarded from the Reformation onwards as popish.[69]

Communion tables were heavy and difficult to move, and were left in the nave where they were frequently used by the laity. Their use continued to be debated during the religious changes of the late sixteenth and seventeenth centuries. On the one hand, the Puritans wanted to take communion to the congregation in their pews, rather than have them kneeling round the table; on the other hand, Archbishop Laud wanted the altar returned to the east wall. A compromise was reached with the altar remaining in the nave surrounded by wooden rails at which the congregation knelt.[70] The movement of the altar continued into the seventeenth century with Charles I decreeing that it should be against the east wall, but by 1643 this was forbidden.

With the Restoration the altar was returned to the sanctuary with a surrounding rail. This changed with the auditory church (and the focus on the pulpit) and the

[69] Friar, *Companion to the English Parish Church*, p. 10.
[70] G.W.O. Addleshaw and F. Etchells, *The Architectural Setting of Anglican Worship* (London: Faber, 1948), p. 127.

altar located as it was in the sanctuary became hidden away. Davidson documented free-standing altars at Branscombe, Woodbury and Broadhembury, where they can still be seen today. Other altars he recorded cannot be identified because they are covered and there is no accurate description.

(f) The Pulpit

With the advent of preaching the need for a pulpit arose. The post-Reformation liturgical changes resulted in a greater emphasis being placed on direct communication with the congregation and the pulpit became central to this form of worship.[71] From the sixteenth and seventeenth centuries pulpits and reading desks were combined as 'double-decker' or in some cases 'triple-decker' pulpits, which towered over the box pews, complete with sounding boards often decorated with a trumpet-blowing angel. The only recorded example of a pulpit on top of a screen was at East Budleigh, since removed.

In the nineteenth century changes to the liturgy and the accent being placed once more on the sacrament resulted in the removal of the multi-decker pulpits. From Davidson's documentation we have evidence of 'double-decker' pulpits at Lympstone and Venn Ottery, and triple-deckers at Axminster, Tiverton and Uplyme. All have since been removed, although such a pulpit survives at Branscombe. At Ottery St Mary a sounding board complete with an angel was removed and the angel is now above the south transept. The sounding boards at both Burlescombe and Morebath have been removed since Davidson recorded them.

(g) The Pews

The history of church seating has been one of evolution and change with a need for flexibility in response to liturgical transformations of the day. Originally stone benches around the church were used, but these were too remote from the symbolic presences to witness the potency of imagery within the service, such as the altar and the sacrament.[72] After the Reformation, the emphasis moved from the Eucharist to the 'word' and fixed seating became the norm.[73] The replacing of the mystery of the Mass by the word in the seventeenth and eighteenth centuries required an 'auditory' layout with simple doored bench pews facing the pulpit; although this greatly underestimates the variety of seating possibilities in the post-Reformation centuries. In the nineteenth century the Cambridge Camden Society and the Tractarians became obsessed with box-pews because they thought they encapsulated all that was wrong with the Church of England. They wanted them removed because they desired a uniformity of seating, and sought to abolish inappropriate seats, which belonged to the gentry, as well as the practice of renting seating and the stigma of free seating for the poor, which was usually in the gallery.[74]

---

[71] Friar, *Companion to the English Parish Church*, pp. 367–8.

[72] P.S. Barnwell, 'Seating in the Nave of the pre-Reformation Parish Church', in T. Cooper and S. Brown (eds), *Pews, Benches and Chairs* (London: Ecclesiological Society, 2011), pp. 69–70.

[73] S. Brown, 'Introduction: Pews – Understanding Significance, Recognising Need', in Cooper and Brown, *Pews, Benches and Chairs*, p. 2.

[74] C. Webster, 'Patterns of Church Seating from Waterloo to 1850, and the Role of the Cambridge Camden Society', in Cooper and Brown, *Pews, Benches and Chairs*, pp. 197–8.

Fig. 5. The box pews at Clyst Hydon church as recorded by
Davidson (T. Gray 2021).

The importance of access for all to the church was another aspect of the Tractarian
policy and this was achieved in some cases by grants provided for 'Commissioners'
churches' under the Church Building Act 1818 which provided grants towards
free extra seating, and the box-pews found in many churches were phased out, or
the doors removed.[75] With the Victorian restorations, criteria were laid down: all
free seats had to be east-facing and bench ends were to be carved using medieval
patterns; in Devon it was found that the layouts of many churches could not be
improved upon as the pews already faced east.[76] The Society for the Enlargement
and Building of Churches and Chapels provided grants for free seating and we have
evidence for this on boards often still found in churches, which will be discussed in
the next section detailing galleries. These changes were sometimes (but not always
or inevitably) responsible for the destruction of irreplaceable historic fabric. In his
'Church Notes' Davidson's identified the type of seating in thirty-one churches, and

---

[75] Webster, 'Patterns of Church Seating from Waterloo to 1850', pp. 204–8.
[76] T. Cooper, 'How Many Seats in Church?', in Cooper and Brown, *Pews, Benches and
Chairs*, p. 221.

in eight of these it has since been removed. At Church Stanton the bench ends were carved with men and angels, at Yarcombe the bench ends terminated in fleurs-de-lis, at Huntsham three carved bench ends were converted into the pulpit and at Tiverton the carved pew doors were removed.[77] Davidson noted that in fifteen churches the pews were 'modern', as at Thorverton, Bicton, Broadclyst, Calverleigh, Exmouth and Sampford Peverell. This modernisation happened between 1828 and 1844 when Davidson was visiting these churches.[78] At East Budleigh, Clayhanger, Burlescombe and Silverton, however, the pews retained their carved bench ends.[79]

(h) The Gallery

The gallery was usually situated at the west end of the church and originally built to accommodate the choir and musicians, but was later used for family pews, servants and the poor.[80] In the eighteenth century, with the advent of the auditory church, galleries were built on the west, north and south walls to accommodate the growing population. During the Victorian restorations many galleries were removed. Davidson provides evidence of seventeen churches where galleries can still be found, for example, at Gittisham where the gallery was erected in 1827; at Kentisbeare where the gallery is dated 1632; at Uffculme (dated to 1631); and at Axminster (dated 1735). These were single galleries located on the west side of the church.[81] Davidson documented six churches which had another gallery besides one on the west end. At Topsham there were galleries on the north and south sides, at Budleigh on the north side, Clyst Hydon on the south side. At Clayhanger the front of the gallery was supposed to have been built from the screen. Broadclyst church had evidence of galleries one above the other on the west-side, as did Silverton above the choir (dated 1734). Silverton also had one at the east end of the south aisle. At Axminster the east and north galleries were reduced in size in 1824. The remaining thirty galleries that have been removed since Davidson's day were situated on the west side of the church.[82] The gallery at Ottery St Mary was dated 1606, Tiverton 1659, Membury 1713, Uffculme 1721, Bampton 1731, Woodbury 1740, Offwell to 1754, Hockworthy 1822, and Honiton 1911 (the rebuilt one). At Clayhanger, Davidson suggested the gallery was Elizabethan and had been made from the old rood screen.

---

[77] Pews recorded by Davidson which have been removed: Church Stanton, Cullompton, Harpford, Huntsham, Netherexe, Tiverton, Whimple, Yarcombe.

[78] Pews recorded by Davidson as 'modern': Bicton, Broadclyst, Bradninch, Butterleigh, Cadeleigh, Calverleigh, Cullompton, Exmouth, Halberton, Sampford Peverell, Silverton, Thorverton, Uplowman, Tiverton, Willand.

[79] Pews recorded by Davidson which are still *in situ*: Bickleigh, Burlescombe, Clayhanger, Chevithorne, Clyst Hydon, East Budleigh, Loxbeare, Venn Ottery.

[80] Addleshaw and Etchells, *Architectural Setting of Anglican Worship*, p. 98.

[81] Galleries Davidson recorded that are still *in situ*: Axminster, Bicton, Bradninch, Broadhembury, Buckerell, Cadbury, Clayhanger, Cullompton, Exmouth, Gittisham, Kentisbeare, Payhembury, Rockbeare, Sidbury, Tipton St John, Uffculme, Uplyme.

[82] Galleries that Davidson recorded that have been removed: Axminster, Axmouth, Bickleigh, Bradninch, Cadeleigh, Calverleigh, Clyst St Lawrence, Colaton Raleigh, Cotleigh, Culmstock, Farrington, Harpford, Heavitree, Honiton Clyst, Loxbeare, Lympstone, Moorbath, Newton Poppleford, Offwell, Otterton, Salcombe Regis, Sampford Peverell, Southleigh, Sowton, Talaton, Thorverton, Uplowman, Washfield, Willand, Yarcombe.

All have since been destroyed, as have the memorials that were positioned on the walls before the galleries were erected, for which we have no record.

In both the gallery and the main body of the church, additional seating was added in many of Devon's churches. Some of this work was funded by the Society for the Enlargement and Building of Churches and Chapels (now Incorporated Church Building Society). This was established in 1818 to keep England religious following the turmoil of the Napoleonic wars and the rapid expansion of industrial towns. The Society's aim was to provide free seating in contrast to the then customary provision of private (fee paying) pews. Davidson records details of East Devon churches that received grants. Sidmouth church was rebuilt in 1822 and 260 free seats were added with a grant of £200; Axminster had a grant of £500 in 1826 for ninety-seven free seats in the body of the church; and in 1827 Southleigh had a grant to provide an extra 156 seats, of which 143 were to be free. Topsham's free seating was increased by 180 in the galleries in 1827. Colyton had a grant of £100 in 1818 and added 220 free seats. Newton Poppleford church was enlarged in 1826 and 120 seats made free, plus another 160 given by H.W. Marker, the minister. Similarly at Uplyme church in 1827, the gallery was built to provide an extra 100, of which fifty were to be free, paid for by a grant from the Society, and another forty-two free seats were given by the Rev. C.W. Ethelston, the minister.

Besides the Society's grants, churches expanded their seating thanks to private benefactors and voluntary contributions from the congregation. Although Buckerell was 'newly' seated in 1774 no mention is made of free seating. Culmstock in 1825 increased its seating by 250 of which 170, in the north aisle, were free. The number of seats at Honiton was seen as inadequate and seating was increased to 500 of which 300 were free. The original Beer church increased the number of free seats by the addition of galleries, but Davidson gave no number. At Exmouth 380 seats were free out of the 2000 seats. At Shute church the north aisle was enlarged by voluntary contributions to provide extra seating.

(i) The Font

The font was traditionally found at the western end of the nave or adjacent to the porch at the symbolic start of a Christian journey,[83] although at the Savoy Conference (1661) it was agreed that it could be placed wherever it was most convenient for the congregation.[84] Towards the end of the Reformation it became fashionable to have the font, reading pew and pulpit combined in a group near the altar.[85]

Davidson recorded the fonts in ninety-six churches, of which fifty-one were octagonal: forty-three were carved[86] and eight were plain.[87] Nine fonts Davidson

---

[83] N. Yates, *Buildings, Faith and Worship* (Oxford: Oxford University Press 2000), p. 159

[84] Addleshaw and Etchells, *Architectural Setting of Anglican Worship*, p. 66.

[85] Addleshaw and Etchells, *Architectural Setting of Anglican Worship*, pp. 63–7.

[86] Awlescombe, Axminster, Aylesford, Bampton, Buckerell, Budleigh, Burlescombe, Calverleigh, Clyst St Mary, Clyst St George, Cullompton, Culm Davey, Combe Raleigh, Cotleigh, Culmstock, Escot (1840), Farway, Feniton, Gittisham, Harpford, Heavitree, Kentisbeare, Kilmington, Littleham, Loxbeare, Monkton, Musbury, Offwell, Otterton, Payhembury, Plymtree, Rockbeare, Shillingford, Sidbury, Tipton St John, Uffculme, Uplowman, Venn Ottery, Whimple, Widworthy, Withycombe Raleigh, Woodbury, Yarcombe.

[87] Clyst Hydon, Dunkeswell, Littleham, Membury, Sheldon, Thorverton, Tiverton, Uplyme, Willand.

noted were circular,[88] five were 'modern',[89] six 'ancient',[90] four square[91] and one oblong.[92] From Davidson's 'Church Notes' we have evidence of twenty-two churches where the fonts have since been changed or are otherwise noteworthy.[93] For example, Davidson wrote in 1850 that Ayshford chapel's plain circular font had been restored to the chancel, after lying in the adjoining farmyard. Sometime before 2021 it was removed. At Branscombe the 'modern' octagonal font that Davidson recorded in 1829 was replaced by a new font brought from Teignmouth in 1911. The Gothic font at Broadclyst was changed and Davidson wrote in 1843 that a new font was in preparation. The font was also changed at Colyton possibly because it had been re-carved and in consequence was smaller. Exmouth's font was changed when the church was enlarged, Honiton was presented with a new font after the fire in 1911, and Huntsham's font dated 1856 has since been changed. Salcombe Regis was presented

Fig. 6. Drawing of 'ancient' font at Sampford Peverell church (Davidson, 'Church Notes', vol.I, p. 546). Reproduced by kind permission of Devon Archives & Local Studies.

with a new font by Teignmouth church. At Upottery the font was moved from the west end to the east end of the church then back to the west end.

Other fonts for which Davidson provided details include those at Chevithorne, which was made of Caen stone, and Hembury, which was made of marble covered in whitewash. At Sowton, Davidson noted that the old octagonal font was in the vestry and the new one was made of marble. Sidmouth's old font was broken and the modern font was in the piscina. Seaton's old font was in the belfry and the new one was black marble, whereas at Sampford Peverell the old font was lying in the garden and the modern one was in the Grecian style. Ottery St Mary's font was encased in oak (possibly like the font at Swimbridge in North Devon), but has now been replaced by one of marble. At St John's chapel, Withycombe Raleigh, the oval font had a wood canopy dated 1668, now removed. Some fonts were much simpler. The font at Holcombe Rogus was a pewter basin kept in a cupboard, and at Southleigh it was a wooden bowl.

At Church Stanton Davidson stated the font was 'Anglo Norman'. At Luppitt Davidson recorded a 'primitive' font ('Norman of the most barbaric 'native kind'). This was removed some time after his visit in 1828; in 1890 it was found in a hedge

---

[88] Butterleigh, Clayhanger, Clayhidon, Clyst St Lawrence, Cove, Farrington, Petton, Topsham.

[89] Axmouth, Beer, Bicton, Cadbury, Countess Wear.

[90] Colaton Raleigh, Hockworthy, Littleham, Luppitt, Lympstone, Northleigh.

[91] Halberton, Hockworthy, Honiton Clyst, Washfield.

[92] Membury.

[93] Aylesford, Branscombe, Broadclyst, Chevithorne, Church Stanton, Colyton, Exmouth, Hembury, Holcombe Rogus, Honiton, Huntsham, Luppitt, Morebath, Ottery St Mary, Salcombe Regis, Sampford Peverell, Seaton, Sidmouth, Southleigh, Sowton, Upottery, Withycombe Raleigh (St John).

and reinstated. At Morebath Davidson recorded another 'Anglo Norman' font, but there is now one of black marble.

Kate M. Clarke carried out a survey of Devon fonts between 1913 and 1922 and her findings can be found in the *Transactions of the Devonshire Association*, but she makes no mention of Davidson's recordings.[94]

(j) Church Plate

Davidson documented the church plate in eight East Devon churches; the details are set out below. On the subject of church plate, Davidson's 'Church Notes' were supplemented in the early twentieth century. In 1900 the Devonshire Association formed a committee to determine the amount of plate held by each Devon church, which was to be achieved by sending a form to all the clergy. This proved to be unsatisfactory, and showed discrepancies, as, for instance, the clergy respondents failed to mention if the hallmarks were the same on the chalice and its cover. The Rev. John Frederick Chanter (1853–1939) took over the recording, visiting a selection of churches and providing evidence of the hallmarks and photographing the plate.[95] In 1911 Chanter visited four churches in East Devon detailing the plate Davidson had catalogued and noting the additions. Below is Davidson's catalogue with Chanter's additions.

> *Bampton*, visited in 1828: a chalice and paten dated 1664, a plate and a small cup; also a magnificent silver service presented by Miss Davey the sister of the present vicar in 1832, comprising a flagon, chalice, plate and paten, weighing more than 9 pounds. This was not recorded by Chanter so presumably had since been removed.
>
> *Burlescombe*, visited in 1828: two large silver flagons, two plates, and a chalice inscribed 'Donum Philippi Culme', and a small chalice inscribed 'The parish of Burcome'. On the destruction of Canonsleigh's chapel (an Augustinian priory) a flagon bearing the Ayshford arms was given to Burlescombe church. Chanter in 1919 verified this plate was still there.
>
> *Clayhanger*, visited in 1828: a cup and small-sized paten dated 1574. In 1919 Chanter recorded the addition of a flagon to the set.
>
> *Hemyock*, visited in 1828: a flagon weighing 38 oz 15 dct, inscribed 'Hemyock 1763', and a chalice marked 'I.W. 1651'. This was not recorded by Chanter.
>
> *Honiton*, visited in 1829: a large flagon, chalice, two plates, and a paten all silver without date. This was not recorded by Chanter.
>
> *Huntsham*, visited in 1828: a chalice and paten both inscribed 'Huntsham 1734'. This was not recorded by Chanter.

---

[94] K.M. Clarke, 'The Baptismal Fonts of Devon', *Reports and Transactions of the Devonshire Association* 45–54 (1913–1922).

[95] J.F. Chanter, 'Fifth Report of the Church Plate Committee', *Reports and Transactions of the Devonshire Association* 45 (1913), p. 93.

Morebath, visited in 1828: a small Charles I paten dated 1593, and a large paten dated 1698. In 1919 Chanter recorded the addition of a chalice, flagon and alms dish.

Uplyme, visited in 1828: a small silver cup with no date, paten dated 'Uplyme 1685', small paten for alms dated 1721. This was not recorded by Chanter.

The above record of East Devon's church plate shows that Davidson recorded five sets that Chanter did not. There is the possibility that these churches had sold their plate. This once again proves the value of Davidson's recording. Chanter's research also identified the additions of plate to two churches.

(k) Memorial Monuments

Antiquarians' records are a primary source for later historians and archaeologists as their descriptions are often all that survives of monuments and their inscriptions.[96] The first assault on tomb monuments took place under Henry VIII with the destruction of the monasteries which frequently were the burial sites of nobility and those who had the means to be memorialised. Doctrinal changes between 1533 and 1580 began with the Henrician religious insurrections and the break with Rome, and by 1540 there was a growth in iconoclasm of religious images and the destruction of the rood which has been discussed above.[97] The Dissolution and Reformation were disastrous for the churches' material heritage of religious imagery, and also for their memorials. The seventeenth century again saw an assault on tomb monuments, especially during the Civil War (1642–51) with many being destroyed. In 1641 Parliament legislated against tomb inscriptions and monuments, which were seen as idolatrous, with the Puritans wanting the church cleansed of such things. Then with the church restorations and rebuilding in the 1800s more monuments were destroyed or moved.

Davidson recorded ledger stones, brasses, effigies and tombs, all memorials to the dead showing the changes in the fashion of the day alongside social and political influences.[98] One form of popular memorial in the medieval period was a floor inscribed stone, often with engraved coffin-shaped lid. By the seventeenth century these had evolved into ledger stones which remained popular into the mid-nineteenth century. These developed into chest tombs with or without effigies and armorial devices.

Another popular form of medieval monument was an engraved brass attached to the wall, floor or tomb-chest. These brass memorials were made of latten, a copper alloy. During the Reformation they were seen as popish and torn down, but were often reused, with new inscriptions engraved on the reverse of the original. For example, Milles in the 1750s documented a fragment of brass of a knight and a lady in Luppitt church.[99] By the time of Davidson's visit in 1828 it was missing, but in 1906 it was found in a hedge bank, with engraving on both sides. The female figure

---

[96] P. Lindley, *Tomb Destruction and Scholarship: Medieval Monuments in Early Modern England* (Donington: Shaun Tyas 2007), pp. 1–4.

[97] 000 [around note 65].

[98] K.A. Esdaile, *English Church Monuments 1510–1840* (London: Batsford, 1946), p. 5; S. Roffey, 'Deconstructing a Symbolic World', in D. Gaimster and R. Gilchrist (eds), *The Archaeology of Reformation 1480–1580* (Leeds: Maney Publications, 2003), p. 343.

[99] J. Milles, 'A Parochial History of Devonshire 1747–1762', DHC (microfilm), p. 193.

Fig. 7. Drawing of monument at Widworthy church (Davidson, 'Church Notes', vol.1, p. 160), possibly Sir William Prouz (d. 1316). Reproduced by kind permission of Devon Archives & Local Studies.

has brooches bearing the shields of Sir William Bonville (1408) on her shoulders.[100] This destruction of brasses continued during the Civil War and with the restoration and rebuilding during the eighteenth and nineteenth centuries. Davidson recorded monumental brasses in eleven churches which have since been removed.[101] At Kentisbeare church the brass effigy of John Whyttne dated 1529 was stolen from the chest tomb in 1857 and, in spite of a reward of £10, it was never recovered. The floor brass memorials of the Sherman family (1542 and 1583) in Ottery St Mary can still be seen; although the wall brass dedicated to the Duke family dated 1641 in Otterton was lost, probably during the rebuilding of the church in 1869.

The later chest tombs were often decorated with carved effigies, which changed in the fifteenth century to become free-standing canopied chest tombs with stylised figures, and then mural monuments or entablatures with kneeling figures and rows of children; these later evolved into mural monuments with busts or half effigies of the deceased.[102] They were modified to include the deceased's coat of arms, which did not provoke hostility to religious imagery and only stressed the honourable lineage of the dead.[103] An example of a chest tomb can be found in Honiton church, for Thomas Marwood, physician to Elizabeth I, while a large mural monument to the Drake family can be found in Musbury, and to the Aclands in Broadclyst. At Gittisham there is a small composition of kneeling figures in profile of the Beaumonts and at Widworthy is an example of a draped female that adorns a pair of richly-draped urns as a memorial to the Marwoods.

Davidson suggested that the effigies in the chancel of Axminster church were of Alice de Mohun and a priest, both removed from Newenham Abbey. At Woodbury he argued that the effigies of the Prideaux family had been removed from the private chapel at Nutwell Court, Lympstone and placed in the chancel. He also made the suggestion that an effigy had been removed from beneath the chancel arch in Luppitt church but no proof has been found to support this.

In East Devon and indeed throughout Devon it is possible to trace the development and changes that occurred to memorials by examining the ones that have not been destroyed but have been moved since Davidson's day. From Davidson's accounts we

[100] B. Cresswell, 'Notes on Devon Churches. The Fabric and Features of Interest in the Churches of the Deanery of Honiton', vol.1, DHC S726.5/Dev/cre (1920b), p. 121.

[101] Broadclyst, Clyst St George, Cullompton, Dunkeswell, Honiton, Kentisbeare, Otterton, Ottery St Mary, Sidbury, Thorncombe, Washfield.

[102] M. Aston, *England's Iconoclasts. Volume I: Laws Against Images* (Oxford: Clarendon Press, 1988), p. 21; Roffey, 'Deconstructing a Symbolic World', p. 346.

[103] Aston, *England's Iconoclasts. Vol. I*, p. 34.

know of three large monuments which were moved within churches. At Branscombe the Wadham monument was moved from the north wall of the chancel to the south wall of the south transept. During the rebuilding of Clyst St Mary church, the wall tablets were moved from the south aisle to the north aisle, and at Otterton church a chest tomb was removed from the church and lost.

(l) Missing Memorials

In the 110 churches he visited in East Devon, Davidson catalogued 1,748 memorials and their inscriptions. This has to be an underestimation of the memorials that Davidson saw, however, as he frequently mentions that the inscriptions were illegible or hidden under pews, so we can only guess at the correct numbers that were extant in his day. The same applies to the other 389 churches that Davidson visited throughout Devon. Of the 1,748 memorials recorded, 749 are now missing, but this number needs some qualification, as it is not possible to give an average number of memorials missing from a church. In some of the churches the number of memorials (or the lack of memorials) extant today is similar to in Davidson's day. As Table 2 shows, we know that six churches were built in Davidson's lifetime and had no memorials. One was rebuilt after his death and also had no memorials. Seven churches were rebuilt and twelve churches were restored after Davidson visited and recorded the memorials but no memorials have been removed since Davidson's day. In another four churches Davidson visited, the memorials are still the same number as he recorded. A further two churches have been converted into private dwellings and no access was possible. This overall accounts for thirty-two churches (Table 2).

Table 2. Churches with no missing memorials.

Churches built and visited in Davidson's lifetime with no memorials	Chevithorne 1843, Countess Wear 1838, Escot 1843, Killerton 1838, Petton 1846, Tipton St John 1839
Churches built after Davidson's death with no memorials	Exmouth 1905
Churches rebuilt after Davidson visited with no memorials removed	Ayshford 1847, Calverleigh 1883, Cotleigh 1867, Sheldon 1871, Shillingford 1856, Newton Poppleford 1826, Thorncombe 1867
Churches restored after Davidson visited with no memorials removed	Aylesbeare 1896, Buckerell 1838, Cadbury 1856, Clayhanger 1879, Columb David 1860, Columbjohn 1851, Gittisham 19th century, Morebath 1875, Payhembury 1895, Shute 1869, Washfield 1875, Woodbury 1846
Churches Davidson visited that are unaltered	Forde Abbey, Gittisham, Tiverton, Widworthy
Churches Davidson visited that have been converted to private dwellings	Cove, Monkton

This leaves a further seventy-nine churches where memorials have been removed between the time Davidson recorded them and the present. The greatest loss of memorials from any church is 135, lost when Sidmouth church was rebuilt, followed by thirty-one from Salcombe Regis and thirty from Littleham, both of which were restored. In total 339 memorials were removed from thirty-three churches which were built or rebuilt, but the biggest loss was the loss of 410 memorials from the forty-five churches which were restored. This could suggest that the restoration of churches had a greater impact than total rebuilding, which often did retain some memorials. For example, we know that the rebuilding of Sidmouth church caused Peter Orlando Hutchinson (1810–97) the Sidmouth antiquarian heartache, but he did manage to ensure that some of the memorials were kept intact and replaced. It is worth noting that Davidson recorded 890 floor memorials and 858 wall memorials but, as noted above, this has to be an underestimation of the total number of memorials found in East Devon churches because Davidson stated he was unable to decipher or gain access to all the memorials. The conclusion has to be that antiquarians' records are frequently the only evidence we have of the former furnishing, fabric and memorials within a church.

Conclusion

The evidence provided by Davidson shows what has been lost due to both zealots who wanted to sweep away the old and the Victorianisation of churches, while (on a lesser very much more localised scale) bombing during the Second World War and fire have also altered Devon's churches. Whilst we think we see the church as it has always been, in the majority of cases this is a fallacy. Over the years churches have gradually changed. In particular Davidson's work shows how the history of the church is linked to its monuments. Records lost from memory cannot be replaced, but Davidson's records allow us to reconstruct the lost churches of the early nineteenth century.

Editorial Method

Davidson's East Devon 'Church Notes' (1826–44) have been transcribed with no attempt to alter Davidson's structure. They have been transcribed in full, except for some of the additional documents collected by Davidson relating to the churches, where these do not include details on the fixtures and fittings of the churches themselves: for example, a short biography of Ezra Cleaveland, rector of Honiton, copied by Davidson from George Oliver, on pp. 93–4. The records have been kept in the order in which they are bound in the volume, which is not organised alphabetically or by date order as to when Davidson visited the church. They are paginated and correspond with Davidson's index. The spaces Davidson left in his descriptions have been compacted, and to this end the spacing of the opening lines such as place and date have been standardised. I have included the modern church dedication which Davidson did not include, the number of missing memorials, and the dates when a church was rebuilt or restored, as defined by Pevsner.[104]

The newspaper cuttings that Davidson pasted into the 'Church Notes' next to the description for several of the churches have been transcribed and placed at the end of the respective accounts. Where Davidson wrote additional notes in the margins, these have been included at the end of an appropriate section in his text in parentheses. Square brackets have been used to signify that a fitting Davidson recorded,

---

[104] B. Cherry and N. Pevsner (eds), *The Buildings of England: Devon* (London: Yale University Press, 1991).

such as a gallery, is no longer there, for example: [missing] or [moved]. As noted above, Davidson did not always copy what he called 'laudatory' inscriptions, so these have been lost in many cases from the archaeological record.

Place names have been modernised but otherwise Davidson's original spelling, use of capitalisation, and likewise his punctuation have been retained, as has his use of D° for 'ditto', with variations characteristic of the eighteenth century. Davidson's use of a Roman font and numerals to number heraldic lists and his spaces and dashes in the text have also been retained. Abbreviated words (English and Latin) have not been expanded where the meaning is clear. Paragraphs have not been modernised, and where Davidson used a dash to indicate a break in the text this has been retained. Davidson's original index has been reproduced at the end of the text.

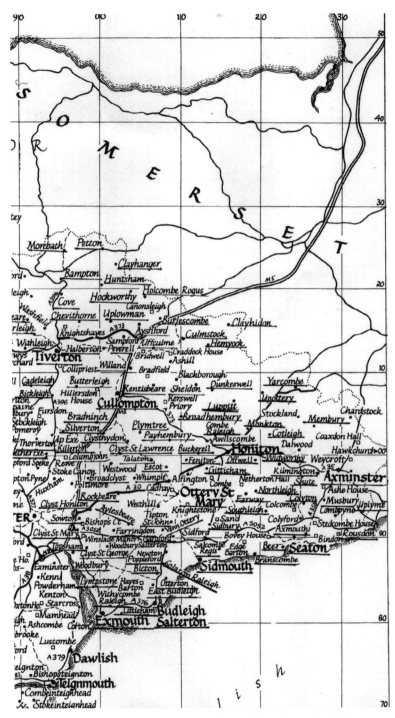

Fig. 8. Map of East Devon churches visited by Davidson (underlined) between 1828 and 1844, adapted from B. Cherry and N. Pevsner, *The Buildings of England. Devon* (London: Yale University Press, 1991), frontispiece.

TEXT OF DAVIDSON'S EAST DEVON CHURCH NOTES

Forde Abbey Chapel

Davidson (pp. 1–6) visited Forde Abbey chapel on 17 August 1843, where he noted the 'many alterations' that had taken place to the Cistercian abbey and that it was 'doubtful to which part of the original structure the eastern part of this chapel belonged'. Davidson suggested the chapel was formerly part of the chapter house. Pevsner (Pevsner, *Devon*, 208–9) thought this was correct and possibly the work of Edward Carter who preserved the twelfth-century ribbed vaulting and the perpendicular style of architecture of the window above the altar which Davidson recorded.

There is a very large semicircular arch ornamented with a chevron moulding in the Anglo Norman style and beyond it in the eastern face of the wall a large window in the perpendicular style of architecture, but whether erected in this situation before or since the dissolution is questionable. There is nothing else worthy of notice in this neglected chapel except the monuments and armorial bearings which convey the following particulars.

Against the north wall a white marble tablet thus inscribed
Hic jacent vir honoratissimus hujus fundi olim dominus aediumque restaurator Edmondi Prideaux filius natu secundus Edmondi Prideaux de Netherton Bart (obiit Aug 18° AD 1659) et Margareta uxor ejus unaquinque filiarum et cohaeredum Gulielmi Ivory de Cothay armigeri (obiit April 25° 1683) nec non Edmundus Prideaux Edmundi filius unicus haeresque (obiit Oct 16 A.D. 1702)
et Amia uxor ejus filia et ex dimidia parte haeres Johannis Fraunceys de Combe Flory armigeri (obiit Jan. 8. 1703/4) quorum omnium memoriam pie recolens omnibus superstes et ex asse haeres Margarita Edmondi et Amiae filia nupta Francisco Gwyn de Lansauor armo avo civiae patri matrique charissimae hoc monumentum posuit A.D. 1704

Arms 3 shields
I. (1) Argent a Chevron sable a label of 3 points gules impaling (Prideaux)
  (2) Or 3 Chevrons gules
II.(1) impaling (3) Argent a Chevron between 3 Mullets pierced gules (Fraunceis)
III.(4) per pale azure and gules 3 Lionesses rampant argent, on an escutcheon of pretence (Gwyn)
Quarterly 1 & 4 (1) 2 & 3 (3) (1 & 4 Prideaux, 2 & 3 Fraunceis)

North wall, a white marble tablet.
Juxta depositae sunt reliquiae Francis Gwyn de Ford Abbey necnon Lausaunor in com Glamorgan arm defuncti quarto die Nov. 1779 aet 80. et Frances uxoris defunctae 1780. Johannis Fraunceis de Combeflory arm. nuper cognomine Gwyn assito volens memoriam esse perpetuam et pie recolens H. M. A. D. 1808. Arms Quarterly.
1 & 4. as (4) 2 as (1) 3 as (3). (1 & 4 Gwyn, 2 Prideaux, 3 Fraunceis)
South wall. A small tablet with 2 figurines embracing one of a skeleton.

M.S. Fraunceis Prideaux bonae indolis et optimae spei iuvenis Edmondi Prideaux armigeri et Amia uxoris ejus (cuj: cognomen ante nuptias Fraunceis Combflorensis in Somersetensis) filius et haeres unicus academia nuperrime relicta Patre Matreque cum plurimis aliis magnopere renuentibus terras reliquit. Natus 3° die Aprilis An Dni 1659 et obiit 14° die Februarii Anno Domini 1679 et aetatis suae 19°. In cujus memoriam Edmondus Pater hoc erexit momentum. Arms (1) impaling (3) Prideaux and Fraunceis*

A tablet with a weeping figure and an urn.
Sacred to the memory of Elizabeth Fraunces Gwyn the wife of John Fraunceis Gwyn of Ford Abbey late of Combeflory in the co of Somerset esq, pious, charitable and humane, patient in her long sufferings excelling in her person and as amicable in her mind sincere in her affection towards her husband and resigned to the will of her creator she departed this life the 24 day of September 1807 aged 36 Her husband much lamenting her loss placed this monument Anno Domini 1808. *Hic restant cineres tumulo caelestibus umbra – Longum cara vale O Elizabetha vale.* Arms. Quarterly, 1 & 4 as (4) 2 as (1) 3 as (3) impaling 2 coats (1 & 4 Gwyn, 2 Prideaux, 3 Fraunceis) I In chief, (5) Argent a Fess sable & in chief 3 Fleur de lys of the last.
II in base, (6) Or 3 Bars sable

6 Hatchments
I. for widower – as (4) with an escutcheon of pretence (Gwyn)
Quarterly 1st & 4th as (1) 2nd & 3rd as (3) impaling (1 & 4 Prideaux)
Quarterly 1 & 4 as (1) 2 & 3 as (3) (2 & 3 Fraunceis)
II. for baron. Quarterly 1st & 4th as (4), 2nd & 3rd quarterly (1 & 4 Prideaux)
1 & 4 as (1) 2 & 3 as (3) impaling (2 & 3 Fraunceis, Gwyn, 1 & 4 Prideaux, 2 & 3 Fraunceis)
(7) Sable a fess checky argent and azure between 3 Torteaux.
III for widower – as (1) impaling as (3) (Prideaux)
IV for bachelor as (1) (Fraunceis)
V for baron. Quarterly 1 & 4 as (1) 2 & 3 or 4 Chevrons gules impaling as (3) (1 & 4 Prideaux, 2 & 3 Fraunceis)
VI for baron. Quarterly of 14.
1 as (4) ___ (Gwyn)
2 as (1) ___ (Prideaux)
3 as (3) ___ (Francisei)
4 Or a chough or raven proper (Corbet)
5 Gules 2 Bends or and argent (Fitzwalter)
6. Gules 5 Fusils conjoined in fess or. (Newmarch)
7. Argent on a Cross gules 5 Mullets or. (Broadspere)
8. Ermine a bend azure (Welsh)
9. Per pale gules and azure 3 fleur de lis or. (Gwering Dhun)
10. Argent a Lion rampant sable. (Morley)
11. Argent a Griffin's head erased vert holding in his mouth a gauntlet gules (Griffith Vaughan)
12. Sable a chevron between 3 Fleur de lys argent (Llynclin ap David)
13. Sable a Lion rampant argent (Mathew)
14. as (4) (Gwyn)
An escutcheon of pretence

Ermine 3 Lions passant in pale gules.

St Mary's Church Oxford. Against the east wall of the choir is a tablet thus inscribed "*M.S. Jacobi Fraunceis filii natu secundi Joannis Fraunceis Gwyn de Comb. Flory in comitatu Somersetensis armigeri. Obiit 6° die Maii. A.D. 1787 aetatis 19. Memoriam pie recolens frater Johannis nomen ejus in futurum recognosci voluit*".

Arms. Quarterly 1st and 4th per pale azure and gules three lions rampant argent. for Gwyn. 2nd Argent a Chevron sable, a pile of three labels gules for Prideaux: 3rd Argent a Chevron between three Mullets gules for Fraunceis. 14 Aug. 1857

THORNCOMBE

Davidson (pp. 7–9) visited [St Mary] Thorncombe during 1827. The present church was built in 1886–7 by J.M. Allen of Taunton and incorporates items from the former church Davidson described.[1] Thorncombe was in Devon until 1842.

The church of Thorncombe in the county of Devon consists of a nave chancel & two side aisles & though there is nothing peculiarly characteristic in the style of its architecture it appears evident that the south aisle is of greater antiquity than the other – it is divided from the nave by two pointed arches uprising from a low massy column with a circular seeded capital boldly executed – the access of this aisle is by a doorway within the church porch [now blocked] over which is a bracket formerly supporting as is probable an image of the virgin Mary, for tradition asserts what is very likely to be true that this part of the church was appropriated to the tenants under the abbey of Ford which was situated in the parish of Thorncombe – This aisle was probably erected at the expense of that religious community & apparently some time in the 14th century. The north aisle which is also separated from the nave by a low circular column seems to be of later date & was in all probability erected about the beginning of the 15th century perhaps by Sir Thomas Brooke who was the first of that family who populated the estate & mansion of Holditch in this parish & who with his lady lies buried here – That this north aisle was built by this gentleman seems also indicated by the corbel heads supporting a label over its eastern window which represent a man & woman the latter of which is attired in a head dress of peculiar shape (The horned head dress) similar to that on the brass of her monument. The son of this Sir Thomas Brook who was the first Lord Cobham of that name also chose this spot as the place of his interment. In the wall on the north side of the chancel is a locker or closet to hold the ampullae or cruets for the use of the altar [missing] and in one of the pillars on the south eastern end of the nave is a small & rude piscina [missing]. the wall is perforated to enable the occupants of the north aisle to witness the elevation of the host at the altar. In the chancel stands an ancient wooden lectern or reading desk [missing] upon which there still slumbers in dirt & mould a black letter copy of Fox's Martyrs chained to the desk – a chain also remains which once confined a bible on the opposite side but the book itself is gone. The vicar informs me that within a circular hole in this reading desk a robin redbreast once made her nest & hatched her brood.

The lectern as well as the table are of the period of Elizabeth & are no doubt the first which were placed in the church. The font is not remarkable for antiquity or elegance but there are some oaken seats in the nave of ancient date. It has been the custom here from time immemorial to commence the celebration of marriages in the

---

[1] J. Newman and N. Pevsner, *The Buildings of England. Dorset* (Harmondsworth: Penguin, 1972), pp. 420–1.

body of the church i.e. in the nave according to the strict letter of the rubric & not at the sacramental table. The living of Thorncombe is a vicarage endowed with the sectorial tithes, but not any copy of the endowment (*in the margin:* endowed by one of the Brasse family but a payment of £4 per annum reserved (Mr. B.)) nor indeed any papers relating to it have been discovered notwithstanding diligent search on the part of the present incumbent. – The chancel is kept in repair by John Brasse esq the lord of the manor of Thorncombe. (*in the margin:* 2 July 44 Elizabeth 1602 date of 2 Eliz. grant of the manor & advowson of Thorncombe to Matthew Brasse – who was a merchant of Lyme – it is described as having been in the tenure of Pollard – a rent of £9 p ann: reserved to the crown. Told me by John B. esq who has the original grant 16 Aug. 1828.)

The monumental inscriptions in this church are as follow and on floor of the chancel is a flat stone which has borne a cross betokening the burial place of either an incumbent of the parish or one of the religious of the neighbouring abbey.

About the centre of the north aisle is a flat stone on the floor about 7 feet 8 in long & 4 feet wide bearing 2 brass figures a man & his wife with a dog at the feet of each. the man is clothed in the civil habit of the period & the women in an appropriate dress – the armorial bearings on four brass shields have been removed but the inscription also on a margin of brass remains & is nearly perfect - it is this. † Here lyth Sir Thomas Brook knight the which dyed of January the yere of oure lorde MCCCCXXIX and the fifte yere of Kinge Harry the V. Also here lyth Dame Johan Brook the wyfe of the sayde Thomas the which dyed the X day of Apryll the yere of our Lorde MCCCCXXXXIJ and the XV year of King Harry the VI on whose soules God have mercy & pite that for us dyed on the rode tree amen [now moved to the east end of the north aisle and raised off the ground].
In the north aisle is a mural monument inscribed Here lieth the body of the revd. Thos Cook late vicar of Thorncombe who departed this life on the 26 day of Jan. AD. 1747 in the 80 year of his life having been minister of this place 44 years - also Mary relict of the above Thos. Cook who died 30 Dec. 1767 aged 87
Arms in stone a chevron engrailed between 3 lions rampant impaling on a chief 3 martlets. [missing]
At the east end of this aisle is a mural monument bearing the following inscription – Sacred to the memory of William French MA. late vicar of this parish & rector of Wambrook in the county of Dorset. He departed this life the 13 Nov. 1760 in the 44 year of his age. – Mural tablets in this north aisle also record some female members of the revd. Mr Cooks family and a -- Hood esquire. –
On the south side of the chancel is a large oval mural tablet in marble the work of Kendall of Exeter with this inscription
Filiae unicae carissimae desideratissmae Lucy Dolphin indole matris suae ingenuam singulari suavitate formamque eximiam praeditae pater viduus et superstes p. ob. cal aug. XVI. AD. MDCCCII aet IIII phthisis perempta. Neque
voluit selese marmor te Lucy Anne mater optime conjux dilectissima, domi forisque et decus et deliciae cheu! nimium brevis aevi gemellorum puerperio cum prole occidit cal Julii VIII AD. MDCCCI aet XXIX olim de Sadborow ex stirpe Brazze per octo annos uxor T.U. Dolphin armigeri de Eyford in agro Glocestriensi nunc apud Slaughter procul hinc sepulta.

Arms in stone Quarterly 1 & 4. vert 3 dolphins in pale 2 & 3. Or a fess stable betw: 3 gryphons heads erased impaling Brazze –
Three hatchments hung in the chancel exhibit the following armorial bearings –
1. Or a chevron quarterly between 3 bulls passant sable for Brazze.
2. Brazze impaling sable a chevron: between: 3 cherubs Argent:
3. Quarterly 1 & 4. Ermine: a chevron: between: 3 bulls passant gules 2 & 3 Sable 3 swords in pile argent: hilted Or. a crescent for difference argent: (Poulett) Impaling Argent. a chevron: gules between. 3 ravens or choughs proper. 27 Coade

The parochial registers which are in the care of the vicar commence with the 7th 1552 they are all in good preservation & very legible –
The following are the later vicars of this parish
Thomas Cook 1703 to ob: 1747
William French 1747 – ob 1760
Samuel Hood 1760 to ob 1776 or 1777
George Gibbs 1777 to 1789 he left it for his successor
William Brazze 1789 to ob 1790
Charles Egerton 1790 living 1829
In digging among the ruins at Holditch court in 1829 4 keys of ancient form were found lying together 2 of them large without pipes & having merely notches for the wards of the lock – some years after a large gilt spur was found here.
Lease 1674 – Matthew Brazze of Thorncombe gent
Abraham Richard & William his sons – Frampton papers
1692 – Abraham Brazze of Newenham Abbey clothier – sr -

Copied by the revd Chas. Egerton from the original in the parish church of Thorncombe 1827 – the seal is entirely destroyed. [There follows a Latin letter dated to '9th December 1239 – 24 Henry III'.]

For Thorncombe see
Bibl. Harl. 5827 fo. 80. For right of presentation to the church of Holdich in Thorncombe see Placitorum Abbreviatio 10 Joh. Rot 9. in d. extracted in Collections for East of Devon page 29.
For deeds relating to the church of Thorncombe & abbey of Ford see Coll. for East of Devon page 35.
Robert Gomersall vicar of Thorncombe in Devon inscribes some verses "To his worthily deare friend Thomas Fuller B. D. upon his excellent work. The Holy Warre." Prefaced to the first edition in 1639.

Extract from 'Recommendations of the Ecclesiastical Commissioners' approved and ratified by an Order in Council dated 5 October 1836.
[copy of extract concerning the transfer of the parish of Thorncombe to the archdeaconry of Dorset in the diocese of Salisbury]

UPLYME

Davidson (pp. 11–14) visited [St Peter and St Paul] Uplyme on 2 September 1828 and described the church as being 'about 4 miles south east of Axminster and 1 mile north-west of Lyme Regis, co. Dorset'. The church was restored and the chancel floor altered in 1875 by G.L. Bather of Shrewsbury (Pevsner, *Devon*, 882). There are two memorials missing from the twenty that Davidson recorded.

Uplyme church is situated on a rising ground on the northern side of the village. It consists of a nave chancel north aisle south porch and a tower square & embattled at the western end of the nave to which it opens by a lofty pointed arch. The nave is 38 feet long by 18 wide within the walls and is divided from the N. aisle by 2 columns & 2 halves octagonal with plain laminated capitals supporting 3 pointed arches the columns have square bases of unusual shape & are of an early date [missing], in the south wall close to the door on the eastern side is the rather uncommon relic in this neighbourhood a niche for holy water. the pulpit which is of carved oak is at the SE end of the nave. The N aisle is 54 feet long by 11ft 6 in wide, its eastern extremity appears to have been used as a chapel or chancel, it is separated from the other part of the aisle & from the chancel by oaken screens of open work [missing]. The chancel is 29 feet long by 16.6 in wide – the tower is 14.6 in long & 11 wide it is 47 feet high to the top of the battlements & is adorned with pinnacles at the corners it contains 6 bells all cast during the rectory of Nicholas Vere by Billbee in 1805. One of them bears the motto "When I begin let all strike in," another "God preserve the church and King." The windows of this church are various tracery the lights with cinquefoil & trefoil heads, the window of the chancel is of 3 lights large & of rather elegant tracery. the principal part of the building may be assigned to the 14th century – A gallery erected over the north aisle is panelled with pointed arches. A tablet affixed to the N wall records as follows. This gallery was erected in the year 1827 by which means 100 additional sittings were obtained & in consequence of a grant from the Society for promoting the building & enlargement of churches & chapels 50 of that number are hereby declared to be free & unappropriated for ever in addition to 42 formerly provided C W Ethelston Minister. Charles Wickstead Ethelston Curate whose wife is a daughter of Robert Peal esq. of Ardwick Lancashire
The font which stands near the western end of the nave is of stone octagonal modern small – The church plate consists of a small silver cup without date – a paten for the bread with the date Uplyme 1685 & a smaller one for alms having the following inscription engraved underneath it. Mr Charles Hutton formerly rector of this parish gave £1.1 towards this plate Uplyme 14 April 1721.
The monumental inscriptions in this church are as follows. On a flat stone in the chancel floor has been a small brass figure with an inscription but both have disappeared –
A flat stone. Here lieth the body of Thomas Ashford Minister of this parish who departed this life 6 July 1676 [missing]
On a brass plate Here lieth the body of Elizabeth the wife of Charles Hutton rector of this parish who dyed in childbed 2 July 1683 in the 21 year of her age. Against

the S wall of the chancel a tablet in memory of the Rev. Nicholas Vere Rector of this parish 39 years prebendary of the cathedrals of Winchester & Wells obit 16 Jan 1800 aged 78 leaving a widow & 2 daughters. Here also are deposited the remains of Frances relict of the Rev. Nicholas Vere who died 11 March 1810 aged 75 years

N wall a tablet exhibiting a sarcophagus inscribed to the memory of Frances Catherine Ann Vere who in the 50 year of her age died 17 Sept 1823. This tablet inscribed by an affectionate and only surviving sister. –

On the chancel floor "*Hic jacet Gilbertus Budgell DD expectatione diei supremi Qualis erat dies iste indicabit Obiit anno Dom 1710*".

A brass plate against N wall of the chancel Catherine Collyer died 1 Jan 1799 aged 9 weeks daughter of the Rev Thomas Collyer Rector of Gislingham in the co: of Suffolk and Sophia his wife then sojourners at Lyme [missing]

On the floor of the nave – a defaced stone – Mr John Hayne ob: – 1747 – Mary mother of the said John Hayne – arms appear to have been a chevron between 3 martletts. Another defaced stone ----- sister to Mr Alexander Jermyn. Against N wall of nave a tablet with an urn Sacred to the memory of Ann wife of Robt. Williams esq, of Rhode Hill in this parish & eldest daughter of Thos. Leigh esq. of Iver in the co. of Bucks who departed this life 25 Nov 1804 aged 54. Arms Gules a demi wolf Argent issuant from a rock on the sinister side proper; impaling Gules a crop engrailed Argent, in the dexter chief point a lozenge of the second – underneath this a tablet Here also are interred the remains of Lieut. Col. Robert Williams who died 6 Jan 1827 aged 81.

Against the S wall of the nave over the door a tablet, In memory of William Alfray 1st Lieutenant RN who died 26 Sept 1827 aetat 80.

N aisle – a brass plate. John Jones of Cannington gentleman dyed 26 Jan 1651 in the 66 y" of his age. Arms – a lion passant gardant between 3 crofes patee fitchee a chief – an esquires helmet Crest on a wreath a lion rampant holding an anchor

N aisle a brass plate – Grace widow and relict of John Jones of Canington in this parish gent (who living and dying at Islington near London anno 1646 lyes interred in that parish church) being the daughter of Edmund Fortescue late of Winston in the parish of Modbury in this county esq. dyed anno 1663 & lyes here interred

We'el not presume her vertue to relate

a theme for angells well to celebrate

Grace their granddaughter the wife of Charles Hutton Rector who dyed 12 Sept 1703 in the 36th year of her age is likewise here interred

Here lye three children by their mothers side

a fourth at Moreton where he lived and dyed

The branches thus lopt off the tree at last

Was quickly overthrown by a strong blast

The mother went to Heaven to see her babes in haste.

N aisle a brass plate – Martha wife of John Jones of this parish ob: 7 Sept 1703 aged 63. Mary their eldest daughter died 1688 in the 26 year of her age.

D⁰ D⁰ – John Jones of Ware gent ob: 11 June 1718 in the 87 year of his age. Arms as above impaling the same.

D⁰ D⁰ Martha wife of Stephen Thorpe rector of Wootton Fitzpaine late relict of John Forrester gent ob: 12 Aug. 1719 in the 50 year of her age.

E end of north aisle a brass plate. Under this seat are deposited the remains of John

Forrester gent. grandson of John Jones of Ware who died 2 Feb. 1721 aged 23 years. Also Bridget his wife sister to Henry Seymer esq. of Hanford in the co: of Dorset who died the 10 July 1745 aged 46 years, their issue were a son and daughter John Jones Forrester the son who died the 23 Feb 1738 aged 18 years and is buried in Folk church near Sherborne in the co: Dorset and Bridget their daughter widow of John Foot of Charlton in the co: of Wilts gent: who has inscribed this plate to their memory 1789.

Against one of the pews in the chancel is nailed a shield carved in oak with the arms of Drake of Ash Bart a wyvern – [missing]

N wall of N aisle a tablet "In the aisle opposite to this monument are deposited the mortal remains of Mrs. Ann Stuart a native of America & wife of the rev. James Stuart formerly rector of Georgetown and All Saints South Carolina and Chaplain to the Kings Rangers in the North America. She departed this life the 12 July 1805. In the same grave is interred the body of the above-named Rev James Stuart born in 1743 at Boyndie near Banff in North Britain and died 1809 at Newbury Berks"

In the church yard is a stone enclosed by an iron railing. Hic jacet Ludovicus Jovenne obiit 3. Decembris 1821 aetatis suae 77.

Here are the remains of a very ancient yew tree. South of the church tower [missing]

'Phelippo Lowys psona ecclie de Uplyme' occurs as witness to a deed dated 14 Hen 6. See Harleian charter in British Museum 53 D. 23 under Wycroft

Charles Hutton Rector of Uplyme in his native county MA 1676 (2 Woods Ath. 874)

For value of tithes of Uplyme see Coll. for East of Devon p.59 & for notices as to the advowson see idem p 77.

AXMINSTER

Davidson (pp. 15–30) visited [St Mary] Axminster in March 1835 and noted it was 9 miles east of Honiton and 25 miles east of Exeter. The church was restored in 1870 by Edward Ashworth and in 1928 by William Weir (Pevsner, *Devon*, 142). There are twenty-four memorials missing from the thirty-one that Davidson recorded.

The parish church of Axminster stands on the south western side of the town & its lofty embattled tower is an interesting & conspicuous object. The most ancient part of the building appears to be an Anglo-Saxon doorway formerly the entrance on the south of the nave, now at the east of the south aisle. It is formed of piers with attached shafts on which rest a series of semicircular arched mouldings enriched with the billet zigzag & triple-indented ornaments & bounded by a border of flowers in the centre of which was a crowned head of Athelstan the Anglo-Saxon King. This central stone was mislaid on the re-erection of the doorway & was afterwards fixed over the eastern door of the north aisle. The church measures in length within the walls 112 feet in breadth at the western end 49 feet, & at the eastern end 47 feet. The chancel which is an addition to the ancient choir is 19 feet long by 16 wide. The whole comprises a nave with a large square tower between it & the chancel, an aisle with a porch on the north & an aisle on the south. The nave was probably built at the same time as the chancel about the beginning of the 14th century. The ceiling which was removed in 1834 for a new roof, was coved & divided into compartments by ribs crossing each other & their intersections were adorned with quatrefoils & devices of foliage. The western window is formed by a pointed arch & is divided into five cinquefoil headed lights by mullions which are ornamented on their outward faces by shafts with circular moulded capitals. From the central mullions spring two subarches enclosing tracery in quatrefoils & trefoils & having a transom between them supporting four cinquefoiled arches with tracery above & a quatrefoil in the apex. This window was erected in 1834 & was intended to be a facsimile of the ruinous one which it superseded in the style of the early part of the 15th century. The heavy but venerable looking tower may be assigned to the early part of the 13th century. Its embattled parapet is 72 feet from the ground. At the southwest corner an octagonal turret with a newel stair to the belfry & the roof, rises 5 feet higher & is finished with battlements pinnacles & a vane representing a cock – The chancel has been extended by half its length. It is lighted by three windows. Those on the sides are small but of beautiful design. They are divided by a mullion into two lights having trefoil heads with a quatrefoil in the point of the arch & are finished externally by a label resting on corbels of human heads of both sexes in the attire of the 14th century. Internally the openings for these windows are feathered in the upper part with cuspid mouldings which give them the appearance of cinquefoiled arches. The eastern window is large – made by 3 mullions into 4 lights which having been despoiled of their trefoiled sweeps now appear with plain arched heads [altered]. The mullions branch into several subarches enclosing trefoils and quatrefoils. The head is ornamented with modern stained glass put up about 1802 consisting of 5 figures intermingled with devices in gaudy colours The figures were painted by an amateur & presented to the church by Dr. Monkhouse once curate of the parish. The central figure at the top represents St John the Baptist & the other ecclesiastics two of whom have shields at their feet charged with armorial bearings incorrectly blazoned and having no reference to any families connected with this vicinity. Those designs being only painted on the surface are gradually disappearing from the glass [no longer there] – In the south wall is an elegant piscina & 3 stone stall seats. The piscina consists of a recess under an acutely pointed arch ornamented with several mouldings which form a trefoil canopy surmounted by a label resting on corbels of human heads. A projecting lip resting on a sculptured bunch of vine leaves & fruit. The stalls for the priest deacon & subdeacon are of unequal height & consist merely of seats in the wall under trefoil headed arches. The rood loft seems to have extended across the western arch of the tower as a doorway walled up in the turret appears to have led into it. The chancel appears to have added to the ancient choir about the reign of Edward 2nd at which time also additional height was probably given to the tower. The north aisle with its porch must be referred for its erection to various periods of time – the first when only the transept stood a part of the church of the 12th century, the next when a small aisle or chantry was added to its eastern side in the 15th & the last when the aisle was extended the whole length of the nave in the 16th century. Traces of the chantry or Yonges aisle may be observed. It was erected by the Yonge family about the year 1480 & several members of it lie buried in the vaults beneath. The western part of the north aisle is separated from the nave by three columns & two halves formed of four shafts with a deep hollow between each, supporting arches struck from four centres the archivolts of which are moulded to correspond with the columns. The capitals were originally ornamented with sculpture consisting of groups of angels with expanded wings holding scrolls & shields but the columns now exhibit wooden capitals of angular form put up by the builder of the opposite aisle who was actually permitted to destroy the carved stone capitals & replace them with wood in a shape of his own design & this for the sake of producing uniformity of appearance. The half column against the western wall exhibits shields bearing the knots or badges of the families of Stafford & Wake. The porch which is large & comprises an upper story is entered by a pointed arch with several mouldings. The floor above was formerly a small room with a chimney & was entered by a narrow staircase in the wall of the aisle but it was opened to the church in 1823 & now forms part of a gallery to which access is gained by a flight of steps on the outside. The aisle is lighted by 6 windows which are formed by arches struck from 4 centres & are divided into three lights which were originally finished with cinquefoil heads. The tracery above was also subdivided into lengthened quatrefoils but the whole in common with that of the chancel have been defaced & present a mutilated appearance. The two windows towards the eastern end which belonged to the Yonges aisle & are of earlier date are more highly finished & the weather cornices by which they are surmounted rest on corbels of human heads. The piers & quoins both of the aisle & porch are supported by buttresses & a highly ornamented parapet extends the entire length and breadth of the aisle and porch. It is constructed of Ham Hill stone & is elaborately sculptured. It comprises a range of open quatrefoils, having their centres enriched with roses foliage & devices & relived at intervals by shields exhibiting coat-armour & heraldic badges e.g. the cross engrailed the ancient coat of Reginald de Mohun lord of the manor of Axminster in the 13th century & the fleur de lis the subsequent bearing of that family, the three torteaux of the Courtenays & knots or badges of the noble families of Harrington & Stafford & other devices which are probably those of the cloth & other manufacturers of the town who were numerous in the 16th century & who contributed to the erection of the aisle. In that part of the parapet which stands at the front of the porch are introduced three pieces of sculpture of very ancient date & probably relics of the building of the 13th century. These represent St John the Baptist with the lamb & a book, St Catherine of Alexandra with a wheel & a sword the instruments of her martyrdom & 2 keys in saltire connected by a chain having reference perhaps to the metropolitan church of York to which this church is an appendage. The horizontal line of the parapet is broken by several square pinnacles faced with trefoil headed panels & adorned with canopies crockets & finials, some of them bearing in front the often-repeated Stafford knot. The water is conveyed from the roof by gargoyles of uncouth figures executed in the spirited style of the period. Some of the devices introduced among the ornamental features of this aisle will decide the date of its erection. There are the Harrington & Stafford knots & a monogram formed by the letters J.C. – Cicily only daughter & heiress of Lord Bonville & Harrington of Shute, was married first to the Marquess of Dorset, & after his death in 1501 to Henry Lord Stafford, second son of Henry Duke of Buckingham, who was created Earl of Wiltshire & whom also she survived. This lady contributed to the erection of many churches in the neighbourhood of her large estates & as the manor of Uphay in the parish belonged to her, she probably assisted in the enlargement of the church. She was married to Lord Stafford about 1503 & died in 1530, having borne at once the titles of Marchioness of Dorset, countess of Wiltshire, Lady Ferrars of Groby, Bonville, Harrington, Astley & Stafford. The adoption of the Stafford knot therefore in addition to the badge of Harrington proves that the aisle was erected within the last mentioned period – But the monogram formed by the letters J.C. refers in all probability to John Cabell who was abbot of Newenham in this parish from 1525 till 1530 & who with his convent being lords of the manor of Axminster contributed doubtless to the building of the new aisle & thus recorded the date of its erection. The south aisle was erected in 1800 – it is open to the nave by columns & arches similar to those of the north aisle & is lighted by 6 windows copied from the mutilated windows of the opposite aisle – the whole is a miserable specimen of 'carpenters gothic'. The erection of this aisle caused the destruction of the west transept which was occupied by the Drake family of Ash House for their estate of Trill in this parish – In a hole under the pulpit I found the remains of a stone monument with a slab bearing this inscription –

"This monument in Trill Ile is the monument of Sir John Drake knt & bart & Jane his first wife ye daur of Sir John Yong of Culliton knt & bart by whom he had 2 sones & 1 daughter, viz John Walter & Elizabeth. His said wife died 31 of July Anno Dom 1652." Two escutcheons bore the arms of Drake viz Argent a wivern gules and Yonge viz Ermine on a bend cotised sable 3 Griffin's heads erased or, and a large shield displayed their alliances in this coat.

Quarterly of 8. (the colour defaced)

1 (argent) a wivern (Gules) (Drake)

2 (argent) on a chief (gules) 3 cinquefoils (of the field) (Billet)

3 Gules on a Fess argent 3 Mullets (sable) (Hampton)

4 Ermine on a Chief indented 3 Crosses fitchees (Orwey)
5 Ermine 3 Bars azure (Offwell)
6 (azure) 6 Lioncels rampant (argent) 3. 2 & 1 – crowned (gules) (Forde)
7 (argent) 2 Chevrons (sable) (De Esse or Ash)
8 (argent) a wivern (Gules) (Drake) [missing]
In other corners of the church were found oak shields which had ornamented the roof
& walls with the arms of Drake in alliance with (Impaling)
Gules 3 Horseman's rests or – (Grenville)
– a Fess checky between 6 Cup croplets (Botteler)
Azure a Bend party per Bend indented Argent & gules between 6 Escallops of the
second --- (Cruwys)
Ermine, on a Bend cotised sable 3 Griffins heads erased or. – (Yonge)
Per pale or & sable 2 Chevrons between 3 Griffons passant countercharged (Eveleigh)
Ermine a Fess gules. (Bitton)
Argent a Chevron between 3 Conies sable – (Strode)
Argent 2 glaziers-irons in saltier sable between 4 Pears pendent or. (Kelaway)
This aisle was dismantled of its furniture & decorations after the sale of the estates
on the death of the last Lady Drake in 1782.
There are galleries in each aisle & at the western end of the nave, the latter was an
old heavy structure was reduced in 1824 to its present dimensions to accord with
those in the aisles [removed]. The organ purchased by subscription at the cost of
£225 was placed in it in the year 1800. The gallery is the north aisle has been erected
at four several periods [removed]. The eastern end of it over Yonges aisle bore the
following inscription on its front "This gallery was erected for the use of the charity
children AD 1735, the contributors to which charity were the Lady Drake of Ash,
the revd. Mr Thomas Cook of Thorncombe and Thomas Saffin of Exon gent." The
western and formerly called Liddon's gallery was erected by private subscription as
was also the outermediate part in 1826 & the following year by several families who
were unprovided with seats with the assistance of a grant of £50 from the Society
for the enlargement & building of churches & chapels; 97 additional free sittings
being thereby gained in the body of the church & elsewhere. In the same year the
gallery in the south aisle was erected at the cost of £78 which was defrayed by the
parish [removed]. Near the middle of the nave & fronting the east stand the pulpit
& desk which were erected in 1633 as appeared by a date formerly at the back of the
pulpit. They are formed of oak, the panels enriched with arches & devices of foliage
& scrolls which are carved with considerable effect though in point of style totally
at variance with that of the building. Before the south aisle was built they were
fixed against the south-western pier of the tower. In its appropriate situation before
the western door stands the font a large heavy octagonal basin carved in stone &
lined with lead, resting on a plinth of similar form adorned with several mouldings;
judging from the form its style & proportions it may be assigned to the 14th century.
The communion plate consist of a handsome silver flaggon & cup presented by S.
Bunter esq. in 1768 2 chalices & 2 salvers to which may be added a small silver cup
and paten presented for the use of the sick by a benevolent individual on the 6 Sept
1732 as appears by an entry in the register to that effect. The words "Deo Christo et
Ecclesiae Axminsteriensi, in usum infirmorum" are engraved on both.
The tower contains a peal of 6 bells which have been recast at several times – there
is also an ancient clock & a set of chimes which were in existence in 1660 – The

brass chandelier of 24 lights which hangs below the tower was purchased by the parishioners in 1750.

A Tablet against the south wall put up in 1759 thus records the benefactions to the poor of the parish of Axminster.

Alexander Every Citizen of London Clothworker by will dated 25 Dec. 1588 – £100 the interest thereof to be laid out yearly in corn or bread & given to the poor of the parish at such times as the parson & churchwardens shall think proper and also £50 to be lent unto so many poor young men for their better maintenance for any time not exceeding three years as the churchwardens shall think proper; the persons to whom lent paying yearly fourty shillings towards repairing the church.

Donations the parish of Axminster.

The ancestors of the Yonge family at Eastcott 40 shirts to the poor of Axminster for ever to be distributed yearly

Leonard Peream by will dated the 20 Feb 1710 – £100 the interest thereof to be laid out in 20 shirts of 5 shillings value each & given by the churchwardens & overseers yearly at Christmas to 20 poor persons – Persons once nominated to the charity are to have it for life.

Ann Scriven by will dated 13 Feb 1727, £5 the interest thereof to be laid out in 10 loaves of bread & given yearly on St Luke's day by the vicar & overseers to ten poor widows not receiving pay of the parish

Thomas Whitty, Mercer, by will dated 11 May 1713, 20 shillings a year to the poor of Axminster to be paid out of a piece of ground called Willhay.

Penelope Saffin by will dated 28 Sept 1742, £164.18.3 to feoffees for ever for the charity school of Axminster for educating in reading & writing 12 poor children

Thomas Cook clerk by conveyance to trustees one messuage with its appertenances in Axminster part of the manor of Prestaller for the benefit of the said charity school. Simon Bunter. Amos Liddon churchwardens 1759

There are two ancient sepulchral monuments here, one of a female in the wall of the north aisle, the other that of a priest in the north wall of the chancel. They consist of whole length effigies each recumbent under an arch rudely formed in the wall & exhibiting the style of the thirteenth century. The female figure which reposes under a low pointed arch relieved by two unequal cuspid mouldings is attribute with a whimple on her head an article of dress which came into fashion in the twelfth century & I have no hesitation in appropriating this monument to Alice the daughter of Lord Briwere & wife of the Reginald de Mohun to whom the manor of Axminster belonged as coheiress of her brothers estates who died in the year 1231. This lady is represented as holding between her hands which are uplifted in the attitude of prayer an image of the blessed virgin to who the church of Axminster is dedicated. It is therefore highly probable that to this lady the people were chiefly indebted for the erection of their church as well as that of Membury for in the latter which was built about the same time & was then a chapel to Axminster appears a facsimile of this monument placed in a corresponding situation within the wall. The decease of Lady Alice de Mohun took place shortly before the year 1257 – The corresponding monument which occupies a low pointed arch has been considerably defaced but is evidently that of a priest, as may be seen by his habit & the maniple suspended from his left arm, a fact which may account for the more than common injury done to it by the iconoclasts of the seventeenth century. This is in all probability the effigy of

Gervale de Prestaller chaplain & steward of Lord Briwere, as he held the living of Axminster at the time abovementioned, & may well be supposed to have assisted in building the church. The names dates & essential particulars of the monumental inscriptions will now be recorded.

Chancel walls.
Mary wife of Mr John Butler. Died 12 Feb 1783 aged 31 [missing]
William Drake of this town. Dd 28 July 1775 aged 48 [missing]
Mary his relict. Dd 8 Nov 1808 aged 77. – William his son Dd in Jamaica 18 Aug 1809 aged 58 [missing]
Near the remains of her infant son, Charles William Steer, lies interred Jane, wife of the Rev. Charles Steer who died 28 April 1809 aged 50.
Edward Kennet Dawson, youngest son of Benjamin K.D. Esq of Wakefield co York & nephew of the Rev C Steer vicar of this parish, dd at Sidmouth 15th May 1830 aged 24.
Newspaper cutting, no name of newspaper:
'Aug. 30, at Sidmouth in her 85th year, Catharine, relict of the late Benjamin Kennet Dawson, Esq., of Sandal Magna, Yorkshire.'
John Ellard of this town gent Dd 25 May 1816 aged 68. Hetty his wife Dd 29 Sept 1821 aged 70 – Rev John Ellard AM their son Dd 20 May 1812 aged 35. Harriet their daughter Dd 14 Sept 1795 aged 16. A family now extinct. Mr. E. gave by will £100 for the benefit of the poor of the parish.

Chancel Floor.
Rev. John Pester, vicar of this parish Dd 22 March 1767 aged 65.
Pollard Lewis of this town surgeon, Dd 13 April 1764 aged 32.
Eliz. King. Dd 28 June 1806.

Nave Wall
In memoriam
Dilectissimi patris
Bernardi Prince Gen"si
Nuper de Abby & Mariae Crocker
Uxoris ejus 1mae de Lyneham oriundae
Et Janae Drake uxoris ejus 2dae ex longo
Stemmate natae; Hoc monumentum pie-
tatis ergo Joh'es Prince, A.M. olim
vicarius de Totnes, nunc de
Berry-Pomroy, d'ti Bernardi
et Mariae filius, mae-
rens posuit.
1709.
(John Prince author of the "Worthies of Devon")

North Aisle Walls.
Sarah, wife of Ozias Upcott, only child of Rev Matthias Swallow, rector of Hawkchurch. Dd 1 May 1705 – Sarah Swallow, widow of Rev. M.S. Dd 16th June 1718 – Elizabeth Henly her sister Dd 9 July 1726.
Giles Lawrence of this town grocer. Dd 13 May 1746 aged 40. Ann & Sarah his infant daughters by Meliora his wife [missing]

North Aisle floor.

Orate pro anima magist'i Joh's Waty olim hujus ecclie vicar's q. obiit die m'cii a'o d'ni MCCCCCXIX cui's a'i'e p'piciet d'us. (Black letter) [missing]
Here lieth the body of John Yonge esq. late of this parishe, buried IX Feb 16-8. Arms (Ermine) On a Bend cotised (Sable) 3 gryffons heads erased. (or) [missing]
Thomas Fry Dd 8 April 1754 aged 53. Mary wife of William Drake & widow of Thomas Fry Dd 6 Oct 1759 aged 40 [missing]
Mr. Willian esq 1825 [missing]

South aisle
AD 1774. Meliora wife of S. Bunter & surviving sister of the Hon. Nathaniel Gundry esq. one of the justices of the court of Common Pleas. Arms, gules, a chevron between 3 unicorns heads erased argent impaling Or. two lions passant gardant in pale azure (Gundry) [missing]
Nicholas Brazze esq. of this town, surgeon Dd 17 Sept 1809 aged 85 – Sarah his wife Dd 4 Feb 1805 aged 77. – William their son Dd an infant – Sarah their daughter wife of Henry Sealy esq. Dd 14 Sept 1793 aged 31. – Denzel B. their son Dd 14 July 1794 aged 37. – Betty their daughter, wife of Henry Weare esq. Dd 20 May 1803 aged 44. – Mary B their daughter Dd 10 Oct 1822 aged 67 – William their son Dd 26 Feb 1825 aged 59 – William Domett Tomkins their grandson Dd 3 Sept 1826 aged 23 – Arms. Or a Chevron gules between three Bulls passant sable [missing]
James Alexander esq of Newham London, & of Cloakham house in this parish. Dd 28 Oct 1823 aged 64. [missing]

Church Yard
Mary daughter of John Symes & Prudence his wife Dd 7 Dec 1732 aged 26 – John Symes attorney of this town Dd Nov 1774 aged 80 – Prudence his wife Dd 16 Aug 1760 aged 58 – Prudence their daughter Dd 24 July 1772 aged 47 – Thomas their son Dd 23 Oct 1779 aged 47 – Ann his wife Dd 11 Jan 1780 aged 39 – Samuel Short Symes Dd 16 April 1824 aged 62 – Harriet his daughter Dd 6 April 1828 aged 32 –
Bridget daughter of William & Elizabeth Brooks, descendant of the revd John Verchill rector of Jacobstow in Cornwall. Buried 26 April 1745 aged 24.
William Pear of this place Surgeon Dd 1 July 1749 aged 29.
Thomas Whitty of this town Tanner & Mercer. Dd 3 May 1756 aged 62. Sarah his wife Dd 8 June 1741 aged 51 – Amelia their daughter Dd 25 April 1758 aged 21.
Dorothy wife of Matthew Liddon Dd 19 Jan. 1749 aged 66 – William their son Dd – Jan 1734 aged 36 – William Pratt Liddon their grandson Dd 4 Jan 1754 aged 3 – Ann daughter of ---
John Keate son of revd James Keate vicar of Chardstock Dd –- July 1761 aged 90 – Elizabeth his first wife Dd 1724 aged 50. – Sarah his second wife Dd 1763 aged 84
Mary wife of David Willmott esq Capt RN Dd 23 July 1797 aged 33. –
Walter Oke Smith Dd 25 May 1820 aged 44
Mack Daniell, Wesleyan Minister Dd 21 Feb 1821 aged 55.
Francis Deght Dd 10 July 1822 aged 70
Jane Miller Dd 10 April 1823 aged 87.
The revd Henry Hayman of Halstock Dorset Dd 17 Dec 1825 aged 50.
Thomas Clarke of this town attorney at law – Hannah his wife – Thomas, Johanna & Bridget, his son & daughters [all are missing as the headstones have been removed].

The following are the extreme dates of the entries in the parochial registers which are in a poor state of preservation

Baptisms – 1 May 1566 to 2 April 1580
One entry in 1610
10 Oct 1648 to 11 Oct 1653
One entry in 1658
One entry in 1659
16 Dec 1660 to the present time

Marriages 11 July 1695 to 16 Nov 1705
16 Aug 1708 to 26 Nov 1723
7 April 1724 to 28 Sep 1741
25 June 1754 to the present time

Burials 10 Dec 1559 to 17 Oct 1569
16 Oct 1648 to 4 Oct 1653
6 Jan 1660 to the present time

The number of sittings in the church allowing about 18 inches in width to each is not less than 1000, of which 185 are free, both exclusive of galleries for children which will admit about 130. –

In consequence of interment during so many centuries the soil of the church yard has greatly accumulated & its area is considerably higher than the level of the road by which it is surrounded on three of its sides. It is therefore supported by a wall which has been kept in repair from time immemorial by the tenants of several estates in Axminster & Kilmington, according to a scale which is entered in one of the register books & recorded on a tablet in the church, as follows "The bounds of the church-yard wall, & particulars concerning its repair, beginning at a house formerly called John Rawling's & ending at the vicarage

For Trill – 6 feet
Wick chapel - 20
Axminster manor - 96
For Haccombefee - 32
Prestaller Tenants - 73
Hills' Farm - 13
Gamons' Hill - 6
Kilmington Parish - 84
Axminster Parish Tenants - 3
Uphay farm - 34
Westwater - 75
Smallridge - 107
Weycroft & Stratford - 33
Beer Hall farm - 30
Umfraville - 14
Wick Tenants (late Sir R. Strodes') - 13
Axminster Parish - 30
The vicar – 13

The church yard was formerly surrounded by rows of Cornish elm & lime trees which were planted about the year 1760 by the revd John Pester then vicar of the parish, but many of those on the north side were cut down in 1832 & others at various times. A very handsome yew tree stands north west of the church, & on the south side another, which last was given & planted by Mr Hallett when churchwarden in 1794.

The stained glass window at the east end of the chancel, attempting to represent some of the principal events in the history of our Lord, was put up at the expense of Mrs W Conybeare in August 1860. A brass plate below it bears the following inscription *"In memoriam Gulielmi Joannis Conybeare hujusce parochiae olim vicarii, necnon filii infantis. Eliza Conybeare Uxor. Mater. Anno Domini MDCCCLIX."*

The following inscriptions are on plain tablets of black marble against the north wall of the nave of Axminster church.–

Sacred to the memory of Thomas Northmore Esq of Cleve, Devon and Magistrate for the county, who died May the 29th 1851 in the 85th year of his age. An attached husband an affectionate father a sincere friend – beloved and respected by all around him. Possessed of extensive knowledge and great acquirements, yet led to feel that only faith in Christ could impart real peace in life and death. What things were gain to me, those I counted loss for Christ. Phil 3.7.

Sacred to the memory of Emmeline Northmore the beloved wife of Thomas Northmore of Cleve in this county and daughter of sir John Eden Bart of Windlestone in the county of Durham who departed this life on the 21 July 1850 in the 70 year of her age. Her family mourn the loss of a devoted wife and tender mother. "Them which sleep in Jesus will God bring with him" 1 Thess 4.14. Also of her son Eden Shafto Northmore who died at sea June 1. 1838 aged 26 years.

MUSBURY

Davidson (pp. 31–4) visited [St Michael] Musbury in 1828 and noted it was '3 miles south of Axminster on the road to Axmouth'. He observed the church was 'situated on a rising ground at the eastern end of the village'. The church was partly rebuilt in 1874–6 by John Hayward (Pevsner, *Devon*, 581). Two memorials are missing from the fourteen that Davidson recorded.

It consists of a nave, 2 side aisles, a south porch now converted into a vestry [changed] and a square tower at the western end of the nave, embattled & having an octangular stair turret at the SE corner, the height of the tower to the top of the battlements is 51 feet, & it contains 5 bells which were formerly 3, but according to the inscription on one of them the 3 were cast into 5 in 1785 by Thos. Bilbee of Collumpton – One of them bears the inscription "I to the church the living call and to the grave I summon all" another "When I call, follow all" the others bear the names of the churchwardens of the time. There is also a clock in the tower.

The nave is 31 feet long by 17 wide within the walls, the north aisle which is 29 feet long by only 6 wide is a specimen of the ancient pentices attached to churches of ancient date & which formed the aisles it is separated from the nave by one octangular column & 2 half columns supporting 2 plain pointed arches & having plain capitals, the whole evidently of very early date. The south aisle is 48 feet by 10 & is parted from the chancel by 1 arch & from the nave by 2 clustered columns supported by 3 pointed arches with plain capitals, these appear to be of an earlier date than the aisle itself which may be assigned to the 16 century & This is called Drake aisle. The principal windows of the church are large comprising 3 lights & the eastern one of the chancel has 4 lights, their erection of the church may be considered to be about the end of the 15 or being of the 16 century – The font is of stone small, octangular & lined with a circular basin of lead, it bears the date 1662.
(*In the margin*: The manor of Musbury was purchased of the Rev. George Tucker of Coxden William Payne esq. residing at Colyton House in 1827. The advowson was purchased of Mr John Wills who brought it of the rev. S. Tucker by Wm Payne esq. (then residing at Seaton) on the 29th Sept 1828, sold me by Mr Payne at Axminster 2 Oct 1828)

The registers which are kept in an iron chest in the chancel begin in 1653 & are continued to the present time, at the commencement of that beginning in 1653 is the following mem. "There is an older register bearing date from the 28th April 1622 & continued down to this time. Mr Salter Rector" but the book to which this note applies is now lost. In the chest is a terrier of the plate goods furniture &c belonging to the church of Musbury dated 26 June 1744 it mentions with other articles of inferior note the following. One large quart silver flaggon with the arms of Sir William Drake engraved in the front & underneath this inscription "This flaggon was

given to the parish church of Musbury by Sir Wm Drake Bart Nov 10th 1730." One
silver salver for the bread with the arms of Sir Wm Drake & a similar inscription
round it – One silver salver for the alms with the same inscription arms & date –
One silver pint cup or chalice inscribed Musbury Dec. 10th 1730. No weight marks
on either of them. The terrier further states that the fences of the church yard are
kept on the east north & part of the west sides by the owners of the land adjoining,
the hedge on the upper part of the south side is repaired by the rector, the chancel is
repaired by the rector, the church & tower by the parishioners. The office of clerk &
sexton are united in one person who is chosen by the rector at a salary of 40/ a year
paid by the parish – signed Wm Salter Rector –
A memorandum on the back of the terrier states the quantity of land in Musbury
parish to be 1490 acres.

The monuments and inscriptions in this church are as follows.
In the chancel on the floor a stone with two inscriptions in the old letter very much
defaced "Here lieth John Ganarecke gentleman" only visible – another stone to the
memory of one of the rectors, the name & date gone – against the north wall is a
tablet inscribed "*Gulielmus Salter AM hujus ecclesiae per annos 44 pastor vigilantissimus mortalitate valedixit Mar 17 1770 an aetat 75. Memoriae optimi patris hoc
marmor sacrum voluit Carolus Salter*" –
A mural tablet "In memory of Mary Salter wife the rev Mr Salter descended from
a respectable family in the city of Bath died 27 March 1754. Anne Salter their only
daughter died 21 Dec 1755"
A stone on the floor Here lieth the body of Frederick Salter who died 5 Sept 1740 –
M.S. 1754. A.S. 1755 [missing]
At the eastern end of the south or Drakes aisle against the south wall are the remains
of a very large & beautiful monument of stone painted & gilded it has consisted
of an entablature supported by columns & underneath the figures of 3 knights bare
headed but otherwise in complete armour with 3 ladies by their sides as large life
all with large ruffs round their necks kneeling with books before them. On the base
are shields bearing the coat armour Argent a wivern gules – The inscriptions are
as follow
Here lieth the body of John Drake of Aish esq and Amie his wife whoe was the
daughter of Sir Roger Graynefeild Knt by whom he had issue six sonnes whereof
lived three at his death viz. Barnard Robart and Richard. He died the 4th Oct 1558
and she died the 18 Feb 1577.
Here is the monument of Sir Barnard Drake Knt who had to wife Dame Garthrud
the daughter of Bartholomew Fortescue of Filly esq. by whom he had 3 sonnes and
3 daughters whereof whear five living at his death viz John Hugh Marie Margaret
and Helen. He died the 10th April 1586 and Dame Garthrud his wife was here buried
the 12 Feb 1601. Unto the memory of whom John Drake esq his sonne hath set this
monument Anno 1611.
John Drake esq buried here the 2 of Aprill 1628 Dorothy Drake his wife buried here
the 13 of Dec 1631 Sir John Drake knight buried here the 26 of Aug 1636 Dame Mary
Rosswell wife of Sir Henry Rosswell kt was buried here the 4th Nov. 1643.
(*In the margin:* Musbury advowson in the hands of E of Devonshire Harl. MS
1074. 119. Fo. 141. Wills. Mychell persona ecclesiae de Musburye 1377. Deed for
Axminster advowson title. See Coll. for East of Devon page 77.)

A tablet part of another monument also remains inscribed to the memory of Walter Drake second son of Sir John Drake kt Bart by Jane his first wife daughter of Sir John Yonge of Colyton. He was born at Trill 14 Feb 1649 died at Exon unmarried April 5 & was interred here April 9 1674.

Sir John Drake Bart eldest son of Sir John Drake by Jane his wife He was born at Lyme in Dorset 13 Jan 1647. died at Ash unmarried 9 March & was interred here 13 March 1683

Elizabeth the only daughter of Sir John Drake by Jane his wife. She was born 15 Jan 1648 & was married to Sir John Briscoe of Boughton in Northamptonshire and of Amberley castle in Sussex knt. She died at Boughton 9 Nov & was interred here 17 Nov 1694.

Dame Judith wife of Sir Wm Drake Kt Bart. She was the second daughter of Wm. Eveleigh of Holcombe in Ottery St Mary esq. by Anne his wife. She was baptized 10 March 1669 married to Sir William Drake 5 April 1687 Died at Ash 8th May & and was interred here 14 May 1701. She left 2 sons John & William & 2 daughters Elizabeth & Anne. She had another daughter named Judith born 25 Dec 1690 died the same day & was interred here.

This monument was erected by an affectionate grateful brother & a sincerely tender husband

On the floor of the nave a stone much defaced the following only to be traced
---Ellen daughter & coheiress of John Lord Boteler Barron of Bramfield was buried here --- of August 16 ----------

Arms Drake impaling a fess checky between six cross crosslets

A stone on the floor of the nave to Bunston of this parish gem. Ellen Knight grandchild of the Rd. Wm Bunston died 2 July 1669 at 4 – Elizabeth his wife ob. Dec. 167-

Against the wall of the south aisle a tablet inscribed to Nathaniel Gundry one of the justices of HM Court of Common Pleas Died on the western circuit at Launceston 30 March 1754 aged 53 Arms Or 2 lions passant gardant in pale Azure impaling argent 2 glaziers irons in saltier sable between 4 pears pendant or [missing]

A mural tablet to John Anning late of Colyton gent ob. 16 April 1793 aged 73 & another to some of a family named Warren.

The rev George Tucker is the present rector (1828). He resides at Coxden in Chardstock co: Dorset. 5 miles distant. Now residing at Musbury – 1831

(*In the margin:* Against the wall of the aisle a hatchment Arms. Drake. Crest a spread eagle Gules Motto Aquila non capit mures.
See Roberts Hist. of Lyme Regis (Kelloway))

COMBEPYNE

Davidson (pp. 35–7) visited [St Mary the Virgin] Combepyne in 1827. The church was restored in 1878 by George and Peto (Pevsner, *Devon*, 285). One memorial is missing from the eight that Davidson recorded.

The rector of the parish church of Combepyne holdeth as in right of his said church 4 closes of land with an orchard cont by est 30 acres of glebe &c. The lord of this manor is patron of the church of Combepyne being esteemed to be worth per ann £50. From a survey of 1704.

The church of Combe Pyne consists only of a nave & chancel, & its tower, unlike perhaps any other, has neither battlements nor a spire but is covered with a slated roof like that of a dwelling house. There are not any memorials within the church of the ancient possessors of the manor, the monumental inscriptions being only a small tablet in the chancel to the memory of the revd Nicholas Pinney who was buried in December 1693, & two others in the nave to persons of the family of Oke the representative of whom, Miss Mary Oke still resides at the age of 70 in the principal house of the place. The font seems to be ancient & coeval with the church & appears to have some ornament or inscription upon it but it is covered by a thick inscrustation of successive coats of whitewash. There is a piscina in the south wall of the chancel.

The registers begin in 1685. The earliest is very legible & in good preservation from it I gather the following names of rectors.
Nicholas Pinney 1690. ob 1693
Robert Cheek 1693 1696
Thomas Upham 1700 to 1738. Richard Gerrard curate 1747
John Rendall 1785 1791 1802
Edward Cook Forward 1807

William Launce rector of Combe Pyne exchanged with William Langerigg rector of Charmouth & was instituted to the latter living 9 April 1392. Hutchins' Dorset

Combe Pyne – Churchyard on the south side an altar tomb. "This tomb is erected in memory of Mr Henry Cheek gent of Axmouth, who died May the 12th 1673 aged 65. Also to the memory of Mrs Ann Bartlett who departed this life 2nd July 1826 aged 83 years" [missing]
1843 Chancel East wall. Stone tablet
Here under lyeth Nicholas Pinney rector of this parish who was buried December 1 1693
Nave. East wall, a white marble tablet
To the memory of William Oke esq son of John Oke esq of Combe Pyne by Mary his wife daughter of R Bridge

This monument was erected by his affectionate sisters Elizabeth Buckland and Mary Oke. He died 17 Nov 1817 in the 47th year of his age.

South wall, a white marble tablet

Sacred to the memory of Walter Oke late of Pinney in this county who departed this life 18 July 1763 aged 60 years also of Frances Oke his widow who died 2nd day of March 1806 aged 94 years both of whose mortal remains are deposited under this tablet.

Floor. Mary Oke died Oct. 14 1830 aged 72.

E. Buckland obiit Oct 24 A.D. 1812 aetatis 57.

Here lieth the body of Susan Crow wife of Richard Crow who was buried 13 day of Aprill Ano. Dom. 1671.

Here lyeth the body of William Hooke who was buried 21 day of April An. Dom 1644. Here lyeth also the body of Anne Hooke his wife who was buried the 18 day of May A.D. 1660.

In the register book are the following memoranda

March 21.1802 Planted yew tree. Rev John Rendell rector

1811 Feb. 12 Miss Mary Oke had a yew tree planted – the one nearest the road – in the church yard. R.C. Forward rector.

In the tower of Combe Pyne church are 3 bells – one very ancient date with an inscription round the crown rudely cast in the monkish black letter, a second without any inscription and a third which is cracked bearing this inscription "Mr Collins Warden – Wroth fecit 1732." This bell was taken down, while the church was under repair in May 1857, to be recast. It weighed 2 cwt 1qr 5 lbs.

The inscription on the ancient bell was copied in December 1859 by Mr Newbery, Drawing Master, of Axminster who found it to be as follows

SALVET NUNC ACAM QUI CUNTA CREAVIT ET ADAM

Salvet nunc Acam qui cun(c)ta creavit et Adam.

The letter D in the first "Adam" has been accidentally reversed. It will be observed that the same type served both for C and D, as the letter E turned partly round formed an M. The letters are in the forms of what are termed both the Saxon and the monkish character, indicating a bell inscription of very early date.

AXMOUTH

Davidson (pp. 38–48) visited [St Michael's] Axmouth in 1828, observing that Axmouth was an ancient village. The church was restored in 1882–9 by John Hayward and Son with carving by the stone mason Harry Hems (Pevsner, *Devon*, 145). Nineteen memorials are missing from the twenty-eight that Davidson recorded.

The parish church of the ancient village of Axmouth exhibits the remains of an edifice of very early date. It consists of a nave chancel & side aisle which is separated from the nave on the south side by 4 low massy cylindrical columns 4 feet 10 high & 6 feet round resting on heavy square plinths & surmounted by plain circular laminated capitals, they support arches acutely pointed & such as would be formed by the intersection of semicircles struck from the respective columns. The aisle is very narrow only 6 feet wide & its roof is supported by semicircular arches springing on the inside from rude piers resting against the columns already mentioned & on the outside from plain corbels in the outer wall – the roof is immediately supported by buttresses above the arches resting against the wall of the nave; the whole is in Anglo Norman style & is well worthy of observation as affording a perfect specimen of the ancient "appenticia" appendages or pentices which were attached to the churches of that period & formed the aisles – This indeed with its sloping roof which is a continuation of that of the nave, realizes in every respect the idea of a penthouse –
(*Added between lines into the margin:* There are heavy buttresses between the windows on the outside which are now reduced in size but seem formerly to have extended into the church yard far enough to have formed recesses or small rooms in the pentice – Qy were they confessionals or anchorites cells? On examining this aisle again the inner arches of semicircular form appear to be more modern & to have been erected to strengthen the side wall of the church which leans from the perpendicular. There seems no doubt of the ancient date of this aisle as respects the upper buttresses of the south wall of the church 1830.)

To the same period may in all probability be assigned the north door way which is highly enriched with ornamental mouldings & is in tolerably good preservation having been protected by a large porch erected at a subsequent date. It consists of a semicircular arch resting upon plain impost mouldings & supported by 2 columns of which that on the eastern side is cylindrical with a capital hatched in the most usual style of the period; that on the west is octangular & its capital consists of ornaments of a bold character greatly resembling the Ionic volute – The arch itself exhibits a series of the chevron moulding surmounted by a sweeping cornice bearing the billet ornament while the lintel within the arch is ornamented with a bold specimen of the embattled fret. The entrance is 4 feet wide by 6 feet 6 in high & is under a flat pointed arch. No other part of the church presents any appearance of the same style which we may very safely assign to a period very near the conquest if not anterior to it.

The remaining part of the nave & the chancel appear to have been erected in the 15th cent but have undergone various subsequent alterations and as far as respects the windows some very tasteless ones. (Added lower down page, with insertion mark here: the eastern window is large & divided by mullions into 4 lights but there are not any remains of painted glass.)

(*In the margin:* New roofs which were raised 2 feet higher than before were placed to the nave & chancel in 1829 & the church otherwise repaired.)

A lofty pointed arch reaching to the roof opens from the nave into a heavy square tower of the same date at the western end embattled & having an octagonal turret at the north eastern corner for the staircase – it contains 3 bells dated respectively 1612. 1671 1755 One bears the motto "Soli Deo Gloria".

– So: of the chancel & adjoining the pentice or aisle is a chapel or aisle of later date wherein the monuments of the Erles hereafter m- perhaps it was erected them = Qy is it dedicated to St Leonard?

The length of the church within the walls is 67 feet 6 in the nave is 38 feet long by 22 wide the chancel 29.6 long by 15.6 wide – in the north wall at the junction of the nave & chancel is a low recess which perhaps has been a confessional (or more probably a closet) – the font is modern –

The monumental remains & inscriptions in Axmouth church are these.

In the north wall of the chancel under a low arch ornamented with a cinquefoil moulding resting on two corbel heads of priests is a monument with the recumbent figure of a priest who lies on his back with his hands crossed on his breast – he wears the maniple over his left arm and there is a lion dog or some other animal at his feet but it is much defaced as is also part of the figure – this monument may be assigned to the 13th century –

(*In the margin:* On the repair of the church in 1829 & 1830 this wall was rebuilt- underneath the effigies was a rude stone coffin not of one piece & within it the bones of a man at full length – on one of the legs was the remains of a leathern boot which appeared to have been made to lace up half way of the calf)

On the pavement of the chancel

John – 1654 Arms. Party per pale – 3 bees apparently displayed 2 & countercharged within a bordure [missing]

Hercules Pyne gent 1610 Arms a chevron between 3 pine apples pendant – crest, a horse's head erased [missing]

Capt. Hercules Pyne of Whitlands nephew of the above died 19 Nov 1670

Mrs Joane Pyne widow ob 27 Aug 1719 aet. 91 [missing]

Thomas brother of John Seward of Downelands gent bur 30 Dec 1693

Jasper Pyne gent 1613 [missing]

Elizabeth Wright 1658. William Wright an infant 1654 [missing]

Sarah wife of John Dore of Axmouth gent 1665 arms in a lozenge 3 spread eagles [missing]

John Tucker vicar of this parish ob. 25 Sept (year gone) [missing]

Edward Rowe vicar ob 1706 aet 66 Catherine his wife ob 1707 aet 67 [missing]

Edward Rowe vicar ob. 1723 aet. 32. [missing]

Mrs Honor Sugar wife of Mr John Sugar of this parish formerly the wife of the rev Mr Edward Rowe late vicar of this parish deceased ob. 1758 [missing]

An inscribed stone to "William" another vicar defaced [missing]
Thomas Seward the elder ob 1622 [missing]
Thomas Seward the son ob 1639 [missing]
John Seward of this parish gent; ob: 1710 aet 91. [missing]

In the south aisle
On the floor – Anna (query Susan) wife of John Mallack of Axmouth gent the
daughter of John Willoughby of Hembury esq ob: 1651 (query 14 March)
Gideon Mallack her son ob (27 March) 1704 [missing]
John (query William) Mallack her grandson & son of William Mallack esq. of
Farway ob. 1702. [missing]
South aisle – a plain mural monument "Heere lye the bodyes of Dame Anne Erle
wife Sir Walter Erle and of Thomas Erle their only sonne and heire two rare patterns
the one for her pietie the other for his wisdome & abilityes – she was heires, to
Francis Dymmock of Erdington in the county of Warwick esquire. The sonne dyed
June the 1. 1650 the mother the 26 of June 1653". [missing]
(*In the margin:* The principal estate of the Erles was at Charborough in co:
Dorset – they sold Axmouth to purchase lands there – The house of Erle was
married to Grosvenor.)

A mural tablet
Juxta hic jacet corpus Gulielmi Serle nuperrime de Bradford in comitatu Somerset
armigeri cujus proavi olim et avi jamdudum de Godford in Aliscombe in comitatu
Devon fuerunt. Qui obiit 7mo die Aprilis 1726 aetat: suae 71.
(*In the margin:* William Searle esq. was the owner of Downelands a considerable
estate in Axmouth worth about £600 a y. It was formerly part of the manor but
was sold in fee by the Erles.) The coat of arms on the top has been defaced with
whitewash but it appears to have been. Quarterly 1 & 4 Party per pale or azure & 2
& 3 Gules a bend argent
Crest – a tower Or.

In the nave – on the floor See page 48
Mallack – as appears only by the arms [missing]
Mallack ob 1617.
Anna wife of Thomas Seward ob 1622
Gertrude wife of Thomas Pyne ob 1626
Anne (Qy Agnes) daughter of Robert & Anne Dening first the wife of Richard
Mallack esq. of this parish and late the wife of Mr Robert Cheek of Roestdown ob
(Feb 18) 1744 aet 67.

Against the south wall of the nave next the chancel a marble monument consisting
of a pediment supported by flutes Corinthian columns & surmounted by angels – in
the middle is the following inscription. –
Juxta hunc locum sepulta jacent corpora Richardi Hallett de Stedcombe Armigeri
filii natu minoris Johannes Hallett de Bridge-town in insula de Barbados armigeri
et Meliorae uxoris sue filiae Hothersall de Giddy Hall in agro Essexie armigeri.
Ex qua suscepit plures liberos qui omnes praeter Johannem hic etiam sepultum
sine prole obierunt. Johannes Janam Thomae Southcott de Dulcis armigeri filiam
unicum duxit de qua duos filios reliquit Southcott Hallett et Richardum Hothersall

Hallett qui majorum suorum memoriam pie respicitentes hoc monumentum posuerunt anno 1749
Meliora ob Nov 1733
Richardus ob Dec secundo Cal Jan 1746
Joh: ob Oct Iduum Maii 1749
Arms in a shield on top of the monument
Quarterly 1 & 4 Or a chief engrailed sable over all a bend gules changed with 3 bezants
2 & 3 or on a fess indented Azure 3 stars of the first on a canton azure a tiger's face Or. impaling Azure a tiger rampant Or spotted sable (Hothersall)
Crest on a wreath a lion rampant issuant Argent holding a bezant.
Arms on a smaller shield below
Per fess engrailed sable & Or a bend engrailed Gules charged with 3 bezants – for Hallett impaling Argent a chevron gules between 3 coots sable for Southcott
Against the walls of the church are 4 hatchments viz:
Per chevron engrailed Or & sable in chief 2 pellets each
Charged with a fleur de lis of the first in base a bezant charged with a fleur de lis of the second – Mallack
Sable 3 holy lambs passant 2 & 1 argent Crest on a wreath a bulls (bucks or grus) head sable attired Argent very rudely & badly painted
Hallett impaling Southcott. Crest – a demi tiger rampant sable collared & langued Gules holding a bezant.
Azure on a bend engrailed Or 3 pellets

Bindon in the parish of Axmouth fell to 3 heiresses at a date unknown – It is now the property of Dare who farms the estate Mr Bartlett & Mr Hallett of Stedcombe. Mr Dare is owner of about half of it – Mr H has the smallest portion of it. There is an old mansion house there –
The house formerly inhabited by the Mallocks near the village is now pulled down. No – a part remains though very ruinous – it is now called "Steps" or "Steps house" windows with several lights – in a room up stairs with an ornamental cornice in plaster are the letters R M S and the date 1617

The name 'William Malek' is mentioned in the court rolls of the manor of Axmouth dated 23 Henry 7th

In the possession of J.H. Hallett esq. of Stedcombe is the original grant of K Edward 6 dated at Westminster the 11 July in the 6th year of his life (1552) by which he gives to his faithful servant Walter Erle esq. one of his grooms of his privy chamber the manor of Axmouth with the rectory & the advowson of the vicarage with all its members liberties franchises & appurtenances & including fisheries lately part of the possessions of the monastery of St Saviour, St Mary the virgin & St Bridgett of Sion in Middlesex & afterwards part of the lands of the lady Catherine late Queen of England being portion of her dower & jointure to hold to the idem Walter Erle as of the manor of East Greenwich in the county of Kent reserving an annual rent of £53.13.5½ (which appears to have been the clear annual value) to the crown expecting also the annual payment of 4/5½ to the hundred of Axmouth – & the fee or salary to the steward & bailiff of the manor (Axmouth not mentioned) also 3/4 annual rent arising from the manor payable to the Bishop & archdeacon of Exeter for Procuration & synodals –

Mr H has also the original grant by Philip & Mary with their signs manual dated 22nd day of Dec. 1 & 2 of their reign by which referring to the grant of Edward. 6 in consideration of the sum of £600 paid to Sir Edward Peckham Kt their chancellor the grant to Walter Erle lately groom & now gentleman of the privy chamber the manor of Axmouth and the rent of £53.13.5½ to him & his heirs for ever.

In consequence of a writ of "Quo warranto" (27) 6 May 32nd Elizabeth (1590) The lordship & manor of Axmouth was granted & confirmed to Thomas Erle & his heirs – this deed signed "Sandes" is also with Mr Hallett. It is very long – reciting all the providers & appurtenances –

Thomas Erle conveyed the manor &c to Sir Walter Yonge Bart 18 March 1679.

Sir. Walter Yonge sold it 1691 (Manor of Axmouth & farm of Stedcombe) to Richard Hallett esq. 12 June (merchant of Barbados). Mr Hallett has some original rolls of the manor & hundred of Axmouth dated in the reigns of Henry 7th & Henry 8 down to the 37 Henry 8

Mr H has a ms vol. dated 1710 "Manor of Axmouth." with the following memorandum at its commencement.

"The id. manor was anciently as appears by the old court rolls in the reign of Henry 7 called the hundred & manor of Axmouth but through disuse by the irregular Keeping of the courts thereof the inhabitants did of late times repair on occasion to the hundred court of Axminster & joined with them in all the public taxes.

The vicarage house formerly stood on the east side of the churchyard till the year 1817 when J.H. Hallett esq exchanged some lands with his brother the rev. Rich Hallett for others of the glebe & built the new vicarage in its present situation.

The registers of Marriages, baptisms & burials commence in 1603 are uninterrupted to the present time & are in good preservation.

Edward Rowe vicar 1710-Richard Hallett 1828

The tithes of Axmouth are the property of J.H. Hallett esq excepting part of Bindon belonging to Mr Dare

Stedcombe estate was anciently part of the manor. The mansion house was erected in 1695 by Hallett esq. the great-grandfather of the present owner (1828) & is believed to have been built from a design by Inigo Jones. Buckland Trill is in Axmouth & was part of the manor. Another Buckland also part of Axmouth was sold by J.H. Hallett esq. to Lord King

Charlton a vill in the manor of Down Umfraville supposed to be a subinfeudation from Axmouth – (Qy is not in Domesday see Axminster) as Mr Hallett has the manorial rights there, & wreck found on the coast is divided between him & and the freeholders there – Part of the Glebe of Axmouth lays at Charlton (Qy whether the chapel of St. Leonard was there) (*in the margin:* yes – see note of Down Umfraville). Down Umfraville was sold by Lord Petre to John Mountstephen How esq. who afterwards sold part to Mr Doune – part to Mrs Eady & subsequently the remaining part to Mr Northmore of Cleeve near Exeter.

The manor of Axmouth anciently paid a fee farm rent of 5d. a year to the duchy of Lancaster – Several of these rents round the county were purchased by one of the Palk family of whom Mr Hallett redeemed that of Axmouth at about 60 a year purchase – Enquire further of Mr H about this & see if deed if any

William Wright vicar of Axmouth was witness to the will of John Mallack of that place dated 3 August 1669. It was proved at Exeter the 7 Sept. following.

Nicholas Goudwayne vicar of Axmouth 47 Edw. 3 1373 Frampton papers (Goudwayne 1387 DD 1369 See Combpyne deeds)

Thomas Earle one of the Commiss. of Milita in 1648. See the order of appointment among Axminster papers.

For mention of the family of revd Thomas Lewes vicar of Axmouth see notice of Chumleigh church

Axmouth church yard. The soil on the south side of the church yard is raised to a considerable height above the level of the church floor perhaps 3 feet & it seems to have been avoided as a burial place for only one tomb-stone stands there – In digging the grave for that burial as also on forming a deep gutter along that side of the church a stratum of bones was found of about a foot or 18 inches thick, mixed in a mass & extending almost the length of the church. This fact may be accounted for by this spot having been made the common burial place of the neighbourhood during the plague & this will account for no other burials taking place there during many years. – But if the mass of bones were as extensive as is said & as the ground seems to point the number must have been very great of persons buried here – Is it possible that any of the slaughtered Danes were thrown into a common grave here after the first days fight in the year 937.

At a little distance perhaps 200 feet west of the church there was formerly a small chapel some of the walls of which were standing within the memory of man, near it on its south western side was an ancient yew tree the trunk of which still remains & yet exhibits signs of life. – It was this St Leonards chapel which Mr Oliver somewhere mentioned to me at Axmouth – No it cannot be for Mr Olivers communication is as follows.

"I find St Leonard's chapel is described in a deed of no importance dated 24 March 1417 fol. 238 vol 1 Staffords Register as situated "in villula de Dona infra parochiam de Axemuth." It therefore was probably within Down Umfraville perhaps at Charlton. Yes. See notice of D. Umf.-

"Libera capella Sci Pancratii in parochial de Axmuth" is mentioned in Bishop Bothes' register 14 April 1473. From Mr Oliver.

Now visible on the floor of the nave.

Here lieth the body of Elizabeth second wife of Richard Mallacke & daughter of Sir Richard Strode of Newnam who died 20 May 1693 Also the body of Richard Mallacke gent who died the 8th day of September in the 49 year of his age 1744

Axmouth Church: Newspaper cutting from Exeter Lancet *dated 2 December 1856*
A work of considerable architectural interest has been recently carried out in this ancient Church by the restoration of the old Norman doorway in the North wall. To this doorway a porch was subsequently added, probably in the 15th century, and to

the same date may be assigned the insertion of a sub-archway into the old Norman work. The rich mouldings of the doorway, which are in good preservation, were disfigured by successive coats of whitewash, the sub-arch was in a crippled and dangerous state, and the porch, which in modern times has been converted into a vestry, had fallen into a state of grievous decay. There were settlements in the walls, and the oak roof with a richly ornamented wall plate had been plastered internally, and had become perfectly rotten from long exposure to wet. The door-way has now been carefully cleaned from whitewash and pointed, without any attempt at over-restoration, and the crippled sub- arch made good, when the following inscription, in black letters of bold character and quaint abbreviations, was discovered under the whitewash on the tympanum of the arch:- "I had rather be a door-keeper in the house of my God than dwell in the tents of wickedness -1698" The letters, which had become almost obliterated in places, have been carefully touched in. A new outer doorway of Beer stone, with folding gates of oak, have been inserted in the end wall; the internal jambs and arch of the doorway into the Church have also been renewed in Beer stone, and a new oak door provided with ornamental strap hinges; a new oak roof has been fixed, of precisely similar design to the old one. With carved bosses at the intersections of the moulded ribs, boarded at the back of the rafters, and covered with slating, together with new coping stone and cross, the latter on the old saddle stone, whilst the walls have been thoroughly made good, strengthened by the addition of two buttresses, and pointed both inside and out. The floor of the porch has also been lowered 6 inches to suit the original level of the Church, and laid with Maw and Co's tiles in plain colours, and the stone benches at the sides have been newly seated with oak. The restoration has been carried out by Messrs. Hayward and Son, of Exeter, who were also the architects for the restoration of the roof and windows, of the south aisle of the Church, recently completed, and the work has been very satisfactorily executed by the builders, Messrs Luscombe and Son, also of Exeter. The newly restored porch was opened to the parishioners on Christmas Day. The Vicar of the parish, the Rev. S.C. Davis, is very anxious to proceed with the further restoration of the Church, which possesses many interesting features, but is now in a very dilapidated condition; and a Bazaar, to which very influential items has been promised, will be held at Seaton during the ensuring summer in aid of the building fund.

ROUSDON

Davidson (pp. 49–50) visited [St Pancras] Rousdon and noted it was '3 miles west of Lyme and 3 miles east of Axmouth'. He observed that the church or chapel of St Pancras was 'about a furlong west from the farmhouse of Rousdon, and was desecrated [by] being used as a lumber room'. The present church was built in 1872 (Pevsner, *Devon*, 706) to replace the church Davidson described. A photograph of the church Davidson described can be seen in Combpyne church.

It is a low building 26 feet long by 17½ feet wide outside the walls & is without any bell turret. It has at the eastern end a window with two lights which seem to have had cinquefoiled heads. There is also a small oblong window & a door in the north side – a door also on the south, but the heads of the doorways have been removed, as the roof which is thatched, is much lower than the original one. There is not any floor or fitting up. Under the east window is a small plain tablet with the following inscription. "Near this place lies buried Robert Cheek esq of this parish who died Oct the 14th 1758 aged 60" This gentleman was the owner of the estate & question whether his name was not Chick. Two children of Robert Chick Bartlett esq of Axminster the present owner are also buried here. In the south wall near the east end is a small square closet.

KILMINGTON

Davidson (pp. 53–60) visited St Giles's, Kilmington, in 1826 and noted it was '1½ mile west of Axminster, 23½ east of Exeter'. The church was restored by C.F. Edwards in 1862 (Pevsner, *Devon*, 519). Three memorials are missing from the fifteen that Davidson recorded.

The church of this village is dedicated to St Giles. It consists of a nave with a south porch, an aisle on the north, a chancel & a tower at the western end. – The nave is about 38 feet long by 17 wide – the windows are under pointed arches & are divided into 2 cinquefoil-headed lights with a quatrefoil in the arch. The aisle is of later date, its windows have horizontal architraves & are divided into 3 lights with trefoil heads – It is about 54 feet long by 12 wide – a doorway with sculptured mouldings [missing] under a low pointed arch, & the eastern window of the aisle probably belonged to the nave before the aisle was erected. The chancel is 14 feet by 13 & is lighted by an eastern window of 3 lights with cinquefoiled heads & 2 narrow single lights in the south wall [missing] – It opens to the nave by a pointed arch beneath which are the remains of a carved oak screen with folding doors above which was formerly a rood loft, the steps leading up to it remain in a large buttress against the north wall [missing] – In the north wall of the chancel is a small locker for the altar cruets, under a pointed arch [missing]. The nave open to the aisle by 3 semi circular arches of 9 feet 9 in span resting on 2 columns & 2 halves each formed of 4 shafts with alternate hollow mouldings & having quadrangular capitals enriched with foliage apparently well executed but filled up with whitewash [missing]. The roof the aisle has wooden ribs the intersections of which are ornamented with sculptured roses & knots the device of Lord Stafford & among 2 which appear to be meant for crests, representing a bird pecking a wheatsheaf [missing]. Mr Oliver thinks that this aisle was the chapel of St Christina which Thomas Vyvyan bishop of Megara & Prior of Bodmin blessed on the 10th Jan. 1509.

The tower at the western end of the nave is 48 feet high to the top of the battlements, there is a pinnacle at each corner and a large grotesque figure of an animal as a gargoyle, carved in stone but much decayed. At the south east corner is a circular turret with stairs to the roof & to the belfry which contains 5 bells, bearing the dates of 1672, 1677, 1759, 1759 & 1776 – one of them has also this inscription "My treble voice your hearts rejoice"

The pulpit is quite plain of painted wood [changed] – The font is handsome, of stone lined with lead – in shape octagonal 3 feet 4 inches high & 2 feet 2 in. diameter having a small projection on one side of the cage, perhaps for the hinge of a cover. The sides are sculptured in quatrefoils & foliage & the pillar is formed into trefoil headed panels each alternate one having a flower.

In the western window in the tower & in one of those of the north aisle are some fragments of stained glass – [removed]

In the church yard on the SE side is a venerable yew tree which at 6 feet from the ground girths 14 feet 6 inches, the interior of the trunk is considerably decayed & several of its branches have been torn off by the winds.

The monuments & mortuary inscriptions are as follow
North wall of the aisle at the east end a monument of black & white marble sculptured & gilt, bearing the following inscription
Juxta positae sunt exuviae Thomae Southcott de Dulcis ar. ex antiqua et numerosa familia de Southcott oriundi in qua emicuit Michael Southcott de Southcott Anno. Dom.1243.
Haec stirps non in hoc comitatu radices suas antiquitus agendo
Magis quam in exteros feliciter ramos extendendo celebranda.
Prefatus Thom. Southcott filius secundus fuit Thomae Southcott & Marie filiae Thomae Shapcott de Shapcott armigeri
Nepos autem Georgii Southcott qui uxorem duxit Joanan filiam et Haeredem Bernardi Fry de Dulcis armigeri
Qui filius fuit secundus Thomae Southcott de Calverly ar. ex. Maria filia Johannis Croker de Lynham armigeri
Ille vita cessit 31 Dec' 1715 aetatis suae 71
Patria amicus suorum amans
In cujus et majorum memoriam Georgius Southcott de Dulcis ar. filius natu maximus hoc monumentum posuit Anno Dom 1735.
From Michael Southcott a foresaid descended
Judge Southcott who lived in the reign of Queen Elizabeth
Sir George Southcott of this county knight & Barronett
Sir Popham Southcott of Mohuns Ottery & Judelo knight
Sir John Southcott of Bliborrow in Lincolnshire &
Sir Edw. Southcott of Witham in Essex knight"
On the top of the monument is a shield bearing Argent a chevron gules between 3 Coots sable (Southcott) impaling on the dexter side Sable on a chevron between 3 birds (query ducks) argent 5 guttes de sang from the sinister side Sable two swords in saltire, points downwards argent, hilted or.
Other shields exhibit
Southcott impaling Croker of Lynham
Southcott impaling Fry of Yartie
Southcott impaling Sable 3 Dovecots argent (Shapcott) (query Sheepcote)

Floor of chancel a black marble – the arms of Southcott in a lozenge – Here lieth the bodies of Elizabeth and Joan the daughters of George Southcott of Dovileheis jour gent 1671 [missing]

North wall of aisle – west end a marble tablet with an urn in bas-relief & the following inscription
Sacred to the memory
of Mrs Agnes Tucker
the fifth daughter
of Wm Tucker esq of Coryton
and Mary his wife the only daughter
of Thomas Marwood esq of Widworthy

(parents blessed & happy in themselves
and in a numerous offspring!)
Esteemed and beloved through life
For every moral social and Christian virtue
She exchanged this transitory state
for a better
November 21st 1788
aged 60 years
Her youngest brother the rev W. J. Tucker AM
Rector of Widworthy
Erected this monument to the memory
of a sister not more endeared to him
by the ties of blood
than by those of esteem & friendship

On the floor are some stones inscribed to the memory of a family named Hore who appear by the parish books to have long occupied Hill's farm & on the south wall are two tablets to the name of Anning [missing]

On the floor of the aisle a free stone about 7 feet 2 in long by 2ft 8 in wide has on it a cup with a circle at the foot which is thus inscribed as far as can be decyphered Here lyeth John C ... ... whose so ... have mercy Anno Domi 1567. [missing]
The names John Rowe and John Bowe appear as churchwards in 1556.

Near the south east corner of the church yard is a stone sarcophagus tomb within iron railings & thus inscribed – Sacred to the memory of Mary Anne daughter of William Symons of Hatt in the county of Cornwall esq the beloved wife of the rev Charles Tucker, who rests beneath humbly confiding in the merits of her redeemer Jesus Christ. She died 29th June 1825 aged 67.

Against the wall over the north door of the church is a tablet thus inscribed –
In the year 1780 a parcel of waste lands or common within the parish of Kilmington adjoining Stone's ground containing by estimation 2 acres was by the unanimous consent of the freeholders & tenants annexed to the charity lands belonging to the school of Axminster on condition of educating & instructing for ever under the limitations of & according to the provisions of the Axminster trust-deed, two poor children inhabitants of the parish of Kilmington

1849. Over the north door of the aisle a tablet of white marble has been erected bearing the following inscription.
Sacred to the memory of William Tucker esq of Westwater in Axminster who was buried at Dalwood March 9 AD. 1691 aet 73.
William Tucker esq of Westwater in Axminster son and heir of the above who was buried at Dalwood March 15. A.D. 1733 aet. 70.
William Tucker esq of Coryton Hall in this parish son and heir of the above who was buried in this church Nov. 11. A.D. 1748 aet. 57
William Tucker esq son of the above who was buried in this church April 8. A.D.1740 aet. 19.
Benedictus Marwood Tucker esq of Coryton Park in this parish brother of the above

and heir of the late William Tucker esq who was buried in this church Sept 17. A.D. 1779 aet 48.

Sacred also to the memory of William Tucker esq of Coryton Park in this parish son and heir of the above who departed this life Sept 2 and was buried within these walls Sept 10 1841 aet. 79.

This tablet is erected as a mark of respect to his high character both as a Christian a magistrate and a man by his only child William Tucker of Coryton Park.

"Insignem pietate virum"

For Tucker Arms Quarterly 1&4 Barry of six argent and azure on a Chevron or between three Sea Horses per pale of the first and second finial gules five guttes de poix. 2nd & 3rd Azure on a Chevron embattled or between three Sea Horses per pale Argent and of the field finials gules five guttes de poix.

A Hatchment

For Tucker Azure on a Chevron embattled or between three Sea Horses naiant argent as many hearts gules – impaling

question Cossrat. Argent a Chevron between two Mullets in chief and a heart in base gules the heart pierced with a Arrow azure.

Crest a Demi Sea Horses argent holding in his fins a heart gules

Newspaper cutting, no name of newspaper, dated 1 October 1862:

Axminster: Re-Opening of Kilmington Church –

Kilmington is a chapelry held with the living of Axminster, from which town it is about a mile and a half distant, and on Wednesday last the Church, which has been renovated at a cost of £1,300 was re-opened. The whole of the Church has been rebuilt with the exception of the tower, which only needed reparation. £400 was left by Mr C. Tucker, of Honiton, £400 was raised on the rates, to be repaid, two-thirds by the landlords and one-third by the tenants. C. Tucker, Esq., the Rev. M. Tucker, Rev. Mr Heberden, and W. Anning Esq., gave £50 each, F. Hewson, Esq., £10, and grants were obtained from the London and Diocesan Societies. The church has been considerably enlarged in the 16th century style of the old church. Some fine stained glass windows have been supplied by Mr. Beer, of Exeter. The pews are low and open and afford accommodation for 410 persons. The reading desk is given by C. Tucker Esq., and M. Tucker, Esq., jun.; the altar cloth by friend of the curate, the Rev. H.G. Southcomb; and the altar books by the Rev. T.F. Tucker. Mr C.F. Edwards of Axminster.

Newspaper cutting, no name of newspaper, dated 1863

Axminster – A very beautiful stained glass window has recently been erected in Kilmington Church, a daughter church of this parish. It has an appearance of antiquity and a reverent subject is the Crucifixion. All the figures, but especially that of the Virgin, are excellently drawn, and the colouring is deep and effective. We may add that the cost of the window is much below average. It is the gift of the Misses Wynne, sisters of the Rev. George H. Wynne, late curate of the parish, and is the work of Messrs. Horwood Brothers of Well, near Frome [window missing].

MEMBURY

Davidson (pp. 61–9) visited [St John the Baptist] Membury in 1826 and noted it was 3 miles north of Axminster. The chancel arch was restored in 1892 by George Vialls (Pevsner, *Devon*, 567). Three memorials are missing from the nineteen that Davidson recorded.

The parish of Membury is a chapelry to that of Axminster and a chapel evidently existed here early in the 13 century. The annexation of a cemetery & the addition of a baptistery or font took place on the 22 July 1316 when the whole was consecrated by Stapleton Bishop of Exeter. It is dedicated to St John the Baptist. The building with its lofty tower presents a respectable & interesting appearance externally. It consists of a nave & chancel a projecting aisle on the north and a side aisle on the south with a tower at the western end of the nave. The total length within the walls including the tower is 96 feet, its breadth 30. The nave & chancel are the most ancient parts of the edifice. They are separated by a pointed arch without ornament. The chancel has an eastern window of three lancet-shaped lights & 2 small loop-hole lights on the sides all of which designate the early part of the 13 century as the date of its erection. The interior of the eastern window is surmounted by an arched moulding supported on each side by two shafts with capitals of various designs in the style of the period just mentioned. One of the lights contains a few fragments of stained glass – In the south wall of the chancel is a small & rude piscina

The north aisle is called S. Catherine's or Brinscombe aisle which latter is the name of an estate in the parish. It is of small & irregular dimensions & not at all worthy of notice but under a low semicircular arch in the north wall is placed the recumbent monument of a female habited in a long gown with veil & whimple her head resting on a cushion & her hands uplifted before her breast holding between them an image of the blessed virgin & child. This is a facsimile, though of inferior execution, of a monument in Axminster church. It may be assigned to the 13 century & may be most probably considered as the effigy of Lady Alice de Mohun who is believed to have principally contributed to both the structures at Axminster & Membury.

The south aisle opens to the nave by four low pointed arches supported by columns formed of 4 shafts with intervening hollow mouldings, their capitals rudely ornamented with foliage [removed]. This aisle was formerly called "Our Lady ile" & was erected by one of the family of Fry of Yartie House. It is lighted by 6 windows with horizontal heads & appears by the style of its ornamental parts to have been built some time in the 16 century. The seat formerly appropriated to the family opens to the chancel by an arch of similar style to the others & is separated from the other part of the aisle by a light screen carved in oak, over the folding doors of which is a coat of arms Quarterly 1 & 4 Gules 3 Horses courant in pale, or (Fry) 2nd & 3rd Quarterly Sable & or a Bendlet argent (Langton) with the following inscription "This monument & seats were repaired & beautify'd by Robert Fry of

Yearty Esq. Anno Domini 1718." The corner of the wall of the church which could not be removed without endangering the edifice has been perforated at the time of the erection of the aisle to allow the occupants of this seat a sight of the preacher. The tower of Membury church though of disproportionate size & elevation is the handsomest part of the edifice & appears by the style of the belfry windows, for it is devoid of ornament, to have been erected in the 14 century. It is 68 feet high to the top of the battlements & 7 feet more to the summit of a semi-octagonal turret on the south side which contains a newel stair. There are 5 bells.

The font which stands near the western end of the aisle is large & heavy, made of stone, octagonal in form & resting on a column & base of the same shape. It is adorned with panels of quatrefoils with foliage in the centre & a range of shields in the moulding below. There is a gallery across the western end of the nave on which appears the following notice "This gallery was erected A.D. 1713." [removed].

The walls have been formerly adorned with texts of scripture in the old block letter but many of them are obliterated with whitewash [removed].
The king's arms affixed to the north wall of the nave are those of George I & have this motto "*In recto decus*" with the date 1715.

The several monuments & achievements are in a state of dilapidation – the inscriptions as far as practicable & as appear of any consequence are here transcribed. Against the south wall of the aisle over the Fry's seat are the remains of a mural monument painted & gilt but now ruinous & much defaced with whitewash. It exhibits an entablature & cornice supported by columns & ornamented with angels cherubs & coats of arms; beneath are the effigies of a man & woman kneeling opposite to each other with a desk & books between them, they are habited in the costume of the 17th century, each with a large ruff, & their hands are uplifted in prayer. Beneath the figures is a tablet with the following inscription which was decyphered with great difficulty –
'Here lie the bodies of -- las Fry -- eartie esq. who died the 25 of October 1632 in the 79 yeare of his age, and of Ely -- his wife the daughter of John Britt of Whitstaunton in the county of Somerset esq. She died the 28th March 1619 in the -- the yeare of her age they lived in wedloocke 37 --- yeares and had issue 4 sonnes and 6 daughters, Willyam theire eldest sone who married Mary the youngest daughter of John Yonge esq. Henry their second sonne who married Elizabeth the youngest daughter of Richard Parrett of -- Bucking gent. Nicholas their 3 sonne who dyed an infant John their 4 sonne who yett liveth unmarryed Margaret theire eldest daughter who marryed Robert Ashford of -- Newell esq. Elizabeth theire second daughter who married Henry Worth of Worth esq. Bridgett their third daughter who marryed Edward Pyne of East down esq. Ann theyre fourth daughter who dyed an infante Alice there fifth daughter who marryed Henry Luscombe of Luscombe esq. Agnes theire youngest daughter who married Gydes Sherman of Knightston -----"
At the top of this monument is a coat of arms in stone & painted. Quarterly – 1st gules 3 Horses courant in pale or (Fry) 2nd Sable a Fess engrailed between 3 Mullets argent (Yartie) 3rd --- a Lion rampant -- 4 -- 3 birds (apparently swans) ---- Crest a horse's head erased argent
In front of the desk between the kneeling figures a shield with their arms viz. Fry, impaling Argent semee of Cross crosslets gules a Lion rampant of the last (Brett).

Beneath the brackets which support the monument & on each side of the tablet is a shield, but the arms are defaced excepting one coat which appears to have been gules a Chevron between 3 leaves (or cups) --- impaling --.

In the south east corner of the aisle is a large mural tablet of black & white marble ornamented with sculpture & the following inscription in gilt letters on the tablet
In memory of Robert Fry of Yearty Esq who married Frances the daughter of Joseph Langton of Newton Park in the county of Somersett esq by who he had issue 1 son 6 daughters who all died young save Elizabeth who was married to John Lord King baron of Ockham she died 28 Jan -- aetat 23 who lies also here interred without issue. The said Robert Fry descended from John Fry of Yearty and Agnes his wife the only daughter and heiress of Yearty of Yearty esq and which said John was the son of John Fry of Fenniton esq & Jane daughter of Edmond Duke of Somersett the grandson of John of Gaunte Duke of Lancaster who was the son of King Edward the third. Robert Fry obiit <u>--</u> Jan 1725 aetatis suae <u>--</u> Frances Fry obiit 24 Dec 1730 aetatis suae 50. From John Fry afore-mentioned descended Henry Fry now of Deer park esq. Gilbert Fry late of Wood in this county esq. Bernard Fry yett afore of Dulcis esq whose daughter & heiress was married to George Southcott second son of Thomas Southcott of Calverly esq & great grandfather George Southcott now of Dulcis esq. This monument was erected pursuant to the directions of the last will & testament of the said Frances Fry by Reymundo Putt Richard Hallett & George Southcott esq. executors in trust therein named <u>by</u> Margaret Joane Elizabeth daughters of John Fry <u>uncle</u> to the aforesaid Henry Fry esq. Anno 1742.
(Mem. the words & figures above underlined are not distinctly legible. I was informed by an old and respectable inhabitant of the parish that this inscription was purposely defaced some years ago in consequence of a law suit then pending as it conveyed unwelcome testimony)
Above the tablet is a shield with the coats of arms Fry impaling Quartly Sable & or, over all a Bendet argent (Langton)

Against the eastern wall of the aisle is an elegant mural monument consisting of the bust of a young female surrounded by flowers very well sculptured in white marble & a tablet beneath this inscribed "Frances daughter of Robert Fry of Yearty Esq by Frances his wife died 18 of March 1718 aetat suae 17 who disconsolate for her loss erected this monument to her dear memory Anno D. 1723" Then follow some verses in the highest strain of adulation – Above the monument is a lozenge with the arms of Fry

There is lying in a window of the aisle an oaken frame about 15 inches by 12 enclosing a shield with helmet crest & mantle cast in plaster & painted – The arms of Fry impaling Argent a wivern gules (Drake of Ash) [missing]

Of 4 hatchments affixed to the walls two are entirely defaced, the others exhibit
I. a shield supported by angels with the arms Argent a Saltire engrailed between 4 Roses gules leafed vert, & beneath it *In memoriam Dominae Annae uxoris Johannis Fry de Yearty Devoniense armig. quae unica fuit filia Roberti Naper de Puncknole Dorcestriensi armig. Obiit 25 die Martii Anno Dom. 1683 aetat 39.*

Chron.
CaeLVM VXorI pIa De Vo paraVIt

Hac Annae corpus dilectae conditur Vrna
Quae vivens laeta prole beata fuit
Felicis paucas natura ac nomine cernes;
Anna fuit nomen, Gratia signat idem [missing]

II. The arms of Fry impaling Langton with the motto
CI ΟΥΤΩ ΤΡΕΧΕΤΕ ΙΝΑ ΚΑΤΑΛΑΒ'ΗΕ
(*Ita currite ut comprehendatis.* So run that ye may obtain)

On the chancel floor a stone bearing the arms of Fry in a lozenge & the following inscription
In memory of Mrs Ellinor Fry youngest daughter of William Fry esq of Yearty who dyed Aug 27 An Dom 1705 aged 83.
Who whilst shee liv'd a virgin pure
Desir'd her dust might rest secure
With the grave beneath this stone before
The last trump soundeth the time's no more.

Against the north wall of the chancel is a small stone monument with a tablet thus inscribed. 'In Memory of Shilston Calmady knight who dyed the 13 day of Feb. Ano Dni 1645.
This toomb's sublimed to a shrine, & doth containe
An holier saint than could all legends faine
Whose virtues supersede our spice and baulme
Whose name perfumes ye breath yt sounds the same
As when a fly's involved in amber t'were
Less gaine to live than finde such sepulchre
So life's not worth such honor as to have
Fame write his epitaph, hearts afford his grave
Above it a shield with arms azure a Chevron between 3 Pears pendant or. [missing]

On the chancel floor.
Here lieth the body of Walter Tucker late of Lime Regis in the county of Dorset Marchant who died in Lime the 24 of July Ano Domini 1644. He was in his life time five times maior of the said town of Lime Regis.

Nave floor before the chancel
"Here lyeth the body of James the son of Arthur Broughton and Elizabeth his wife who departed this life the -- day of July -- In all thy -- Memento mori." At foot a shield with arms (Argent) a Chevron between 3 mullets (gules) impaling -- a Saltire engrailed -- in chief a leopard or a lion passant gardant. (*In the margin:* Baker. See page 346.)

Nave floor a large stone with the following letters only visible along the edge
THE BODY OF W--M PERY
Here lieth the body of Walter Weston of Rokey gentleman who dyed the 5 day of July An Dom 1621
-- Harv -- Rokey decess -- XIX day – Februarie 1697.
Here lieth the body of Mr Samuel Harvey of Roakhey in this parish who departed this life September 1-- 17.8 aged 8- years
The remains of two stones with crosses on them

Here lyeth the body of Mary Sampson the wyf of John Sampson of Ford gentlemane who dyed the 1 daye of January AD. 1618.

South aisle wall. A plain white marble tablet. Sacred to the memory of Joan, wife of John Hoyle of Manchester & daughter of Thomas and Martha Newbery of this parish who departed this life May 1 1811 aged 22 years -- This tablet also records the death of Martha the only child of the above named John & Joan Hoyle who departed this life Feb. 27 1812 aged 22 months.

The pavement of the south aisle has a number of stones which have inscriptions but now so much worn as to be unintelligible. The lower part of one of them shews the words 'gentelman who departed thys' and what appears to be the base of a cross with the name 'Jesus' – The upper part is again inscribed thus. 'Here lyeth the body of Henery Marwood of Land gentleman who dyed 21 d– of March 1678.'

-- Sampson of Ford gen --- -no dom 1618 --

Here lieth the body of Edward Holwell of Lowsele who dyed the 13 day of May Anno Domini 16—
-- *generosus -- uxor – obitus dies -- videlicet xx -- dom MCCCCCXXXIII*
(on the same stone) Here lyeth ye body of William Marwood of Land gent who dyed August ye 27th Anno Dom 1692.

The registers of Baptisms in the parish of Membury begin with the year 1637, those of Marriages at the same time & those of Burials within a few years after that date.

YARCOMBE

Davidson (pp. 73–6) visited [St Andrew] Yarcombe on 1 September 1829 and noted it was in Devon and 'about 5 miles west of Chard, co. Somerset'. The church was restored in 1888–9 by Gould and Webb (Pevsner, *Devon*, 293). The two memorials Davidson recorded are missing.

This village is situated in a rich & beautifully wooded part of the county & the church with the parsonage house nearly adjoining it forms a pleasing object from the high road. This building although part of it may be called ancient has evidently superseded one of earlier date for the corbel stones which support the roof of the north transept are parts of an erection (perhaps the jambs of a doorway) adorned with a lozenge moulding. The church consists of a nave 54 feet 3 in long by 16.6 wide a chancel 25ft 9 by 14.6. South transept 23 feet long by 16ft 3 wide North ditto 14ft by 13. South aisle (with a porch) 36ft long by 7.8 wide – North aisle 40½ft by 9½ a tower at the west end of the nave 12 feet by 11 wide contains 4 bells & a clock. The measurements above are all taken within the walls – The nave & chancel are divided by a triangular pointed arch resting on 2 shafts with capitals of several laminae or mouldings but it is doubtful whether these or any part of the existing building are of so early date as the eastern window which seems disproportionately large to the chancel – this is under a lancet pointed arch resting inside on 2 shafts which have had circular capitals it is surmounted by a label. Four mullions divide the windows into 5 lights with acutely pointed heads & intersect one another above leaving only a 4 foil in the point of the arch – This window may be given to the 13th cent. The others are of recent date – The nave is divided from the tower by a lofty pointed arch partly hidden by a modern singing gallery of incongruous style [removed] – 3 columns & 2 halves open to the aisles on each side these are formed of 4 shafts with alternate hollow moulding & support pointed arches of similar character – These aisles are embattled on the outside & were evidently built in the 15 century the windows have cinquefoil heads lights with tracery in the heads – The transepts appear to be of about the same date as the aisles at least the windows are similar that on the north has 3 foil headed lights, that on the south cinquefoil headed lights with perpendicular tracery – the arches of the aisles against the transepts rest on large corbels representing angels with expanded wings holding labels & having crosses on their heads – The ceilings of the nave & chancel are coved & have intersecting ribs without ornaments those of the aisles have small bosses of foliage – The chancel has a door in the south wall under a pointed arch & in the north wall is a low recess with a square head but for what purpose does not appear – an ancient piscina under a trefoil arch is in the south wall – There has been also an altar in the south transept as a similar piscina exists in the south wall. These have been openings from both transepts through the walls to afford a sight of the high altar – Several fragments of a chancel screen remain, these consist of panels forming niches with cinquefoil heads painted & gilt against the reading desk & the pulpit stairs are 4 well carved oaken panels which have been removed

from some other places, these are about 3 feet long & 1 foot wide & represent each a figure standing under an ogee arch surrounded by foliage –
1st the virgin crowned & holding the child on her left arm both with an apple in their hands. 2nd St John the Baptist with the lamb. 3rd St Peter with a key
4th St James as a palmer with a staff an escallop & a pilgrims staff on his hat.

The pulpit is adorned with 3 foil headed panels [removed] – The font which has been removed from its original situation & stands between the nave & the north aisle is of stone 3½ feet high by 2½ in diam. Octagonal & lined with lead – five of the sides are panels carved into quatrefoils with foliage in the centre 2 other have plain shields & the 8th is without ornament having been against a wall or column, it rests on an octagonal column adorned with trefoil headed niches. The base & other moulding is spotted with vine leaves & other foliage [now at west end of south aisle]. Several ancient benches remain in this church their ends terminating in a fleur de lis carved in oak [removed].

Some of the windows are enriched with stained glass, the east window of the chancel among several fragments ancient & modern exhibits the following coats of arms – Gules 3 lions passant gardant in pale Or (England) – Azure semee of fleurs de lis Or (France) these are ancient – The following are modern –
1. Sable a fess wavy between 2 stars argent (Drake) Crest on a wreath Argent & Sable a hand from a cloud proper with the words 'auxilio divino' drawing a ship round the globe both proper, by a cord Or – 2. Argent a chevron between 3 palmers scrips sable. 3. Argent 3 Chevrons Gules –

In the north window of the north transept at the point of the arch is a piece of modern glass exhibiting a shield bearing Argent a cross Gules but query whether it be a coat of arms – below this are 4 ancient figures very well executed & except the first is in good preservation.
1. a crowned head – 2nd St Peter with a book & keys 3rd St Paul with a book & sword 4th a pedlar with a pack on his back supported by 2 staves one over each shoulder – this mans dress seems to be of the style of the 16th century.
there are some other old fragments in this & other window of this transept & in the window of the south transept intermixed with some modern specimens – The exterior view of this church is rather interesting, the tower is embattled with buttresses at the angles, large gargoyles at the corners of the roof & half an octangular turret on the north side for the stairs – The door of the north aisle is under a low pointed arch with a rectangular label supported by corbel heads & foliage in the spandrels rude & fantastic gargoyles convey the water from the roofs of the aisles & the windows are surmounted by labels which rest on corbel heads of various character 2 of them a king & an abbot seem to be facsimiles of 2 at Axminster & it will be remembered that the tithing of Yarcombe is an appendage to the hundred of Axminster once the property of Newenham abbey. A vestige of an ancient cross remains on the gable of the chancel. The few memorials of death in this church are as follow –

Against the north wall of the chancel is a hatchment with the arms of Baron Heathfield the gallant defender of Gibraltar, viz Quarterly – 1&4. Gules on a bend Or a ships bolt Azure, on a chief of the last an embattled castle with 2 round towers at the angles between 2 Ionic columns Argent, beneath, the words "plus ultra" 2nd &

3$^{rd.}$ Sable a fess wavy between 2 stars Argent (Drake) A barons' coronet – Crest on a wreath Or & Gules a dexter arm armed Azure charged with a key Sable holding a scimitar proper hilted & pommelled Or. Supporters, on the dexter side a ram on the sinister a goat rampant Argent each wreathed round the neck with a garland of leaves Azure, a foot of each rests on a mural crown Or on the summit of a rock Argent.

In the floor of the north aisle at the west end is a flat stone to the memory of the revd Thomas Hare ob: Dec. 15 1819 aet 65. [missing]
Chancel – a flat stones Samuel S-- apothecary late of Bow Street Covent Garden London ob: June -- aet 71 years. – 2 other stones apparently to members of the same family defaced [missing]
In the churchyard on the south side is an ancient altar tomb with a plain cross on the slab.

A wooden tablet in front of the gallery is thus inscribed
A list of the charity money given to the poore of the parish of Yarcombe in the co: of Devon. Made the 20th daye of Jany 1714 as followeth. Imprimis. given by Mr Giles Martin ye sum of £10 a year for ever to be paid by the Honorable company of Mercers in London unto the vicar & church wardens for the time being for distribution – Given towards the meadow called Longcraft purchased to the use of the said poore viz. by Same. Newberry senior. £5 by Henry Newbery £5 who also put in £10 given to the poore of Robert Newbery his father – By William Vincent senior. 2 £5. By Robert Vincent senior £1 who also put in £10 given to the poore by William Pavey – Put in towards the said purchase by Samuel Newbury junior. The trustee of High Northam £20 – given by Alice Fursey widow £5 – by Dorothy Matthew widow £5 – by Elizabeth Legg £1 – By Richard Stevens £1 – by Nicholas Knight £1. – by Eliz. Barnes 10/- By Joan Stoakes widow 10/- By Samuel Cosens 5/- By Samuel Hall 5/- By James Vincent 5/- the residue of the purchase money for the said meadow was anciently given to the poore by persons whose names at present are unknown – James Stevens & John Shark churchwardens.

UPOTTERY

Davidson (pp. 77–9) visited [St Mary the Virgin] Upottery on 3 September 1828 and noted it was 'about 5 miles north east of Honiton'. Davidson noted that the church had been repaired in 1827 'in characteristic style' by J. & W. Lee of Honiton; this was lost when St Mary the Virgin was insensitively restored 1875 by B. Ferrey (Pevsner, *Devon*, 883). Six memorials are missing from the eight Davidson recorded.

This parish is beautifully situated in a very picturesque valley watered by the river Otter, it comprises about 7000 acres & consists of one Manor called Upottery the property of the Viscount Sidmouth, who has a cottage residence in the village on the west side of the church. The cathedral church of Exeter are the rectors and present to the vicarage which is now held by the revd John Gaius Copplestone rector of Offwell. The church is a very interesting structure & much superior in its style & architecture to the generality of village churches – it was repaired throughout in the year 1827 in characteristic style. It consists of a nave 44 feet 6 in long by 18ft 6 in wide a north aisle 56.6 by 11.6 a chancel 23 feet long by 13.6. a south porch converted into a vestry and tower at the western end of the nave 10 feet square. The nave is divided from the aisle by 2 columns & 2 half columns clustered & having capitals ornamented with vine leaves and grapes they support pointed arches & the whole are of early date perhaps in the 14 century. The windows are of coeval period large wide divided by mullions into 3 lights (that at the east end of the aisle into 4 lights) with cinquefoil heads, their pointed arches adorned with tracery. The eastern window in the chancel contains some modern stained glass with 3 ancient coats of arms Argent on ships rudder Or which is false heraldry but perhaps time has faded one or other of the colours [removed] –

The western window i.e. that of the tower has also some remains of ancient painted glass. The tower which is 58 feet high to the top of the battlements contains 5 bells which were cast from 4 ancient ones by Mears of London in 1818.

The font which has been removed from the western end of the nave to the eastern end of the aisle is octagonal ornamented with quatrefoils & resting on a column adorned with niches [now at the west end of south aisle]. The south door has a flat pointed arch with numerous mouldings supported by ancient detached shafts having circular laminated capitals. The west door has a pointed arch with several mouldings the outer one hollow & adorned with foliage – The chancel door has a flat pointed arch finished with a square head the corners filled up with foliage – plain crosses adorn the gables of the chancel & porch. –

The inscriptions in the church are these –
On the floor of the north aisle at the eastern end is a stone having two inscriptions in the gothic letter but of various periods it is much defaced & the following can only be traced

--- *pauperibus Till mors abstulit -- extulit ipsum* ---- [missing]
Here lieth the body of Henrie Tillie gentleman deceased the 15 day of Aprill anno Dom 1624.
On the floor of the north aisle – Here lyeth the body of John Marwood son of Thomas Marwood gentleman of Blamphain in the parish of Culliton & Joan his wife daughter of John Hutchins gent of Allor in this parish who died 25th Oct 1705 aged 14. Here also lieth the body of Thomas Marwood brother of the aforesaid John Marwood who died – Feb 7 1711 aged 14 [missing]

Against the N wall of the aisle a tablet. Here lye the bodies of John Hutchins of Allor gent who dyed April 8, 1709 aged 77. Katherine his wife who dyed March 8. 1707 aged 75. Joan his wife the daughter of Thomas Marwood esq. of Sutton in the parish of Widworthy who dyed 1 April 1741 aged 82. Also of John & Thomas sons of the said Thomas Marwood esq & Joan his wife John dying 18 Oct 1705 aged 14 Thos 3 Feb 1711 the same age. Arms above, those of Marwood Gules a chevron between 3 goats heads erased ermine Crest a goat passant proper. (*In the margin:* Mem: The crest of the Marwoods in Widworthy church is a goat couchant [missing]).

At the west end of the aisle on the floor a stone much defaced --- --- aged 60 years also Ann his wife -- Moly A.D. 1727. [missing]

Against the N wall of the chancel a tablet. Sacred to the memory of the rev. Nicholas Gay who died 26 April 1815 aet 63. at St Thomas' in this county where his remains are interred – above 19 years the affectionate pastor of this parish. [missing]

Against the W wall of the N aisle a table of Benefactions. [missing]
1715 Henry Preston esq of this parish by his will dated 15 Nov 1623 bequeathed to the churchwardens of the same an annuity of 40 shillings for ever issuing out of his lands in this parish called Crinehays to be paid yearly on Christmas day or within 10 days after (if demanded) to be employed either for repairing church or relieving the poor of this parish as the said churchwardens shall judge most needful.

Mrs Ann Palmer daughter of Mr Joseph Newbery of this parish by a deed dated 30 August 1714 settled a parcel of land called House-close and the north part of Great Oxen-close (being part of Greenhays lately possessed by Joseph Davy of Stockland) in the hands of 7 trustees who are to distribute the clear profits of the said estate to such poor of this parish as by their industry shall keep themselves and families from monthly relief. But in such manner as none shall have more than 10 shillings in one year, and the said trustees are to enter in the parish book every Easter how and to whom they have distributed the said charity.

Under the will of Mr William Ham Warren of Upottery gent who died at Upottery AD. 1825 £100 of which £10 were paid for the legacy duty to be laid out in security by the minister and churchwardens of this parish and the interest to be given at their discretion yearly on old new year's day to persons having no relief from this parish.

A tablet also records – The accommodation in this church enlarged in the year 1827 by which means 150 additional sittings were obtained and in consequence of a grant from the Society for promoting the enlargement and building of churches and

chapels 100 of that number are declared to be free and unappropriated for ever in addition to 150 formerly provided.
J.G. Copplestone Vicar
G.T. Smith Curate.

There is an old established Baptist meeting house in this parish called Newhouse.

The communion plate belonging to this church is of pewter excepting a chalice of silver without date.

See notice of the death of Prebendary Copplestone vicar of Upottery in Gents' Mag. April 1831 page 378.

Abbreviatio Placitorum Trin 17 Edw. 1 r. 24.
Advowson of the chapel of Rovrigg. & chapel of Gerliston, parcels of the church of Upottery, belongs to the Dean & Ch. of Exeter which in process of Quare imf. Between John de Hardington & Felicia his wife (Plts) & the said D & Ch (defts) said John recovered. But now said John *hic remiss. dictis decan. & cap. in perpet.*

HONITON

Davidson (pp. 81–100) visited [St Michael and All Angels] Honiton on 3 September 1829. The church was restored by E.H. Harbottle in 1896, but a fire in 1911 destroyed much of the church, which was rebuilt by C.E. Ponting and then restored in 2000 after an arson attack (Pevsner, *Devon*, 494). Forty-three memorials are missing from the fifty-four that Davidson recorded.

The church of this parish is situated on the side of the hill about a mile from the town on the south & it is a pleasing object from the hills on the opposite side of the fertile & beautiful vale in which the town is built. It is difficult to say with certainty that any part of this building is of earlier date than the 15th century but it seems probable that the nave the transepts & the chancel were so, the eastern window of the chancel although it has received modern additions retains the form used in the 13th century in its intersecting mullions of the lancet style & the rude bosses at the intersections of the torus in the ceiling which represent human heads may be considered of an early date. – It seems evident however that the present church consisted originally of a nave chancel & transepts only & that on the erection of the aisles & tower in the 15th century the present large windows of the transepts were inserted. The nave is 50 feet long by 18½ wide within the walls the chancel 26 by 15 the north aisle 76½ by 9½ the south aisle 74 by 10½ the tower at the west end of the nave 14ft square & the only porch on the north side 8ft 9in square: with an addition to it on the west side 7ft 9 long by 4½ wide, this porch with its addition now form a vestry – The nave & chancel are separated from the aisles by columns consisting of 4 shafts with intervening mouldings which support pointed arches of similar character, the capitals are quadrangular & are formed of foliage well executed in various devices one of these on each side viz on the west side of the transept against the aisle bears a shield with the Courtenay arms (viz 3 torteaux but without a label) (*in the margin:* See Cleaveland f. 281) the capitals of the two columns nearest the eastern end of the chancel against the 2 aisles are inscribed in the old letter 'Pray for ye soul of John Takell & Jone hys wyffe' & another of the capitals next the south aisle bears the letters JHD & a shield with a cross. It seems therefore not improbable that the two aisles against the nave were erected in part if not wholly at the expense of the Courtenay family then lords of the manor of Honiton or perhaps by Courtenay at the same time bishop of Exeter while the aisles east of the transepts & adjoining the chancel were built by John Takell at the latter end also of the 15th century. The east window of the chancel already mentioned has 5 lights & has received some modern additions in a style not corresponding to its ancient character, it is finished above with a circular compartment adorned with a Calvary cross in stained glass. below it are other portions of glass in gaudy colours & among them 4 shields with these bearings but query whether they are coat armour of any families –
1 Argent 3 bends sinister Gules
2 Gules 3 chevrons Azure.
3 D°. – 4 Argent 3 bends sinister Az.

The windows of the transepts and aisles are in uniform style with cinquefoil headed lights & perpendicular tracery as is also that of the tower except that it has a transom. The tower appears to have been built at the same time & it opens to the nave by a lofty pointed arch with panels in its soffits – The nave is also lighted by 4 clerestory windows 2 on each side, of concave triangular form enclosing foliated tracery of sweeps – The church has an interesting appearance on the outside in consequence of the uniformity of its spacious windows – the tower is 65 feet high to the top of the battlements which are ornamented with quatre-foils, it is strengthened by buttresses at the angles & adorned with gargoyles of rude figures at the corners of the roof; a square turret on the south side contains the staircase – The west door is under a pointed arch the moulding of which is ornamented by a series of hops & leaves cut in bold relief – the roofs of the aisles are embattled & the doors on the north side to the chancel & the rood loft have foliage in the spandrels of the arches, a door in the south wall has been converted into a window – The most interesting object in the interior of the church is the screen which divides the chancel & it its aisles from the nave & supports the rood loft – It is said to have been presented by one of the Courtenay family perhaps the Bishop, it is of oak beautifully carved forming a range of open pointed arches their heads filled with perpendicular tracery, the shafts which rise between them spread into a beautiful projecting canopy richly adorned with panels quatrefoils & foliage. the lights into which the arches are divided by mullions are finished in cinquefoil heads & above the canopy are 3 mouldings elaborately carved in vine leaves & other foliage. the whole is painted in imitation of marble & occasionally gilded but this seems to have been a recent addition – some rails have been added at a subsequent period in a dissimilar style on the top & the ancient rood loft now forms a gallery for the singers & contains an organ which is placed in the centre, the access to it is by the old staircase in a demi octagonal turret projecting from the north wall of the church with a door on the outside [screen destroyed in the fire of 1911] – Portions also of screens of an inferior design but about the same date remain between the chancel & the aisles & against one of the columns are fixed carved panels which perhaps formed part of a reading desk or pulpit with letters IL & the date 1632. The present desk & pulpit are of modern erection [destroyed in the fire]. Galleries have been placed (about the year 1820) over the aisles & across the western end of the church, the panels of which have mouldings in an appropriate style [missing] – The font which stands under the tower is a modern octagonal stone lined with lead 1 foot 2in high & 1.10 in diam. but it stands on an old octangular pedestal which has the appearance of a font inverted [present font dated 1912]. The communion plate consists of a large flaggon a chalice 2 plates & a paten all of silver without date but perhaps about a century old – Two small brass chandeliers hang from the roof of the nave [missing] – There is a large & handsome altar screen of white & black marble against the east wall of the chancel but it is a modern style quite incongruous to that of the building [destroyed in the fire] – The tower contains 5 bells with the following inscriptions on them. "Mr Matthew Hilson Rector. God save the church. Mr Ezra Cluel and Mr Joseph Tooze Warden 1719"

2 "Mr Charles Bertie rector 1749" 3 "Let me most sweetly close the strain likewise the death of all proclaim Bilbee 1749" – 4 "Health plenty and peace to this neigh-bourhood John Blagdon esq. Joshua Salter church wardens 1753" – 5 – "1761"

This church which is said to be very inadequate in size to the number of the parishioners who would attend it will accommodate about 500 with seats, in addition to about 300 charity & other school children: –

The monumental inscriptions in this church are as follow beginning with those in the chancel. –
Floor – *Hic jacet magist. Johes Ryzze qudam* (hidden by a pew) *--ne ppiciet deus amen.* [missing]
Floor – A long Latin inscription defaced except the following words at great intervals. – *Guilelmo – Septimo 1740 – Elizabetha – filia – Jonathan W --- mercatori nupta – quorum ille obiit --- 1739 Haec autem 20 die Julii Anno Domini 1749".* [missing] –
Tablet north wall with an urn – To Sophia the faithful & affectionate wife of the rev. Edward Honiwood LLD. Rector of this parish who died 17 Feb 1795 aged 35 – Arms Argent a chevron between 3 eagles heads erased Azure a mullet for difference of the second – impaling Sable semee of a lion rampant Argent. –
Nave floor – Here lieth the body of Katharine Brown widow of Amos Browne late of this parish merchant who died the 27th May AD 1663 – Here lieth also the body of Gabriel Ais-te – merchant who -- 16 -- [missing]
Floor. Here lieth the body of Rachell the wife of Mr Richard Gill of Honiton apothecary who was here interred 26 Sept AD 1721 aged 58 yrs also Susanna Christopher & Rose 3 of their children – Arms defaced – a bend – Crest – a squirrel holding a sprig – also Elizabeth the daughter of Richard Gill & Rachel his wife born 20 June 1701 & buried 9 Nov 1725 – Also the above Mr Gill who died 7 Oct 1742 in the 88th year of his age.

North aisle beginning at the eastern end –
A marble tablet with figure in relief of a sailor weeping over a tomb around him several implements of naval warfare executed by Peter Rouw of London – In memory of George Blagdon Westcott esq. Capt. Of his Majesty's Ship Majestic who fell in the glorious battle of Aboukir on the 1st of August 1798 aged 45 years His services as a naval commander are recorded by his country in a national monument erected in St Paul's Cathedral – this monument is dedicated in the place of his nativity by a truly grateful sister.
A marble tablet between 2 fluted Corinthian pilasters Here lyeth the body of John Blagdon esq. buried 10 Dec 1714 aged 46. – Margaret his wife buried 20 April 1733 aged 64 – Margaret their daughter buried 13 May 1720 aged 23. John their son buried 18 August 1727 aged 28 Sarah his wife buried 5 Oct 1724 aged 21 Rachel daughter of Henry B esq. buried 25 March 1733 aged 6 weeks Elizabeth daughter of the said Henry B. buried 1 April 1733 aged 12 months. Elizabeth Maunder his sister buried 30 Aug 1736 aged 34 – The said Henry B, buried 25 Jan 1737 aged 32 Rachel his wife buried Nov 15 1743 aged 39. Arms Azure 3 trefoils slipped Arg. On a chief indented or. 2 annulets Gules (Blagdon) impaling – Gu: on a chevron between 3 trefoils slipped Argent as many pellets (2) Blagdon impaling Per fess Azure & Argent, a fitched & an eagles head erased in chief the same in base counter charged on a bend over all Sable 3 cinquefoils Argent (Gill) (3) Quarterly – 1 & 4 Blagdon 2 & 3 Argent: on a chevron Azure 3 bezants between: as many Gules, An escutcheon of pretence the arms of Gill. –

A white marble tablet with a medallion portrait – This tablet is erected by the inhabitants of Honiton as a mark of their attachment affection & regard to the memory of the rev. Edward Honywood clerk LLD who was rector of this parish upwards of 24 years & died 1 Dec 1812 aged 50 years – As a preacher he was eloquent & persuasive as a magistrate he was just & humane His remains were interred on the north side of the altar on the Monday after his death & on that solemn occasion the shops in the town were kept shut all business was suspended and the parishioners at large of every denomination flocked to this sacred place to bid a last adieu to their beloved pastor – Arms Argent a chevron (*in the margin*: Quart. 1 & 4 Gules Argent: Crest on a) engrailed Azure between 3 eagles heads erased proper, impaling 3 roses Argent. barbed & seeded proper. 2 & 3 Azure: 3 mural crowns wreath Argent & Azure: a wolf's head couped proper. [missing]

A white marble tablet – 'To the memory of James Basleigh of this place who died 15 Feb. 1823 aged 68 yrs & of Ann his wife who died 1805 aged 52 yrs. In grateful recollection of whose virtues this tablet is erected as a tribute of sincere affection by their surviving family' [missing]

A marble tablet Ann Baker died July 24 1770 aged 23 years she was the daughter of the late rev. Thos. Baker vicar of Hungerford Berks: Under the gallery in the same vault are deposited the remains of Susan B. her mother who after supporting with fortitude & resignation a long & painful illness died universally lamented 25 Oct 1785 aged 74. [missing]

A hatchment the arms of Blagdon in a lozenge [missing]
Flat stones – *Hic jacet + Johan Takell vidua que obiit XIV die Julii anno Dom MCCCCCXXIX cuius anime propiciet Deus Amen.*

John Searle gent of Heathfield died 19 Dec 1728 --- [missing]
John Blagdon of this towne gent died 23 July 1694 aged 59 yrs
Margaret the daughter of John B. esq & Margaret his wife and granddaughter of the above named J.B. gent died 8 May 1720 aged 23 years. Arms (Blagdon)

North transept – a marble tablet. Under the great tombstone by the church door in the same repository with her great grandfather Thomas Marwood gent. physician to Queen Elizabeth lies interred Bridget Ford relict of Edward F of this town bachelor of physick she died 3 March 1746 aged 78 years. Mary wife of William Tucker of Coryton esq her niece & executrix has caused this monument to be erected to her memory as well in obedience to her aunts will as a testimony of her own gratitude to her worthy benefactress – Arms defaced – a castle in a fess impaling a chevron between 3 goats heads erased ermine for Marwood –

A white marble tablet with an urn. Near this spot are deposited the remains of Samuel Lott esq. late of this parish who died in the city of Bath 23 March 1819 aged 71 years this monument is dedicated by his only son to the memory of a beloved father. [The Lott memorials were destroyed in the 1911 fire and a single monument on the south wall has been erected to the Lott family.]

North Aisle close to the door – an altar tomb of stone painted black with the letters in old English form gilt. Here lies the body of Thomas Marwood gent who practised physick & chirurgery above 75 years & being zealous of good works gave certain houses & bequeathed in his will to the poor of Honiton £10 & being aged above 105 departed in the catholick faith. Sept. 18. 1617. Here also lies Temperance the wife of the above said Thomas Marwood who died 9 Oct 1644.

South transept – white marble mural monument by Rouw of London. A weeping figure an urn & a medallion portrait – To the memory of John Watts esq late of this parish who died 12 Jan 1800 aged 40 years, this monument erected by his afflicted & disconsolate widow. [missing] Arms Azure on a fess 3 blackamoors heads couped in profile between 6 arrow points downwards Or impaling Or a stag springing proper. Crest on a wreath a hound sitting Sable Motto Honestas de --- suis praestat. (Memorandum: Mrs. M is said to have been a Prussian lady)

Flat stone – John Richard merchant died 3 May 1673 aged 70 Mary his wife died 15 June --- aged 73 Daniel R. Doctor of Physick died 7 March 1709 aged 55. Elizabeth the wife of Hugh Serle gent & daughter of the above John & Mary R. died 27 July 1695 aged 38. [missing]

South aisle of Chancel. On a grey marble pedestal surmounted by a funereal urn. H.I. Jacobus Sheppard de Lawell eques auratus et serviens ad legem domini Regis Georgii in expectatione diei supremi qualis erat dies iste indicabit ob. aetat 49 1730 against the wall 2 fluted pilasters with foliated capitals supporting a broken entablature & the arms quarterly 1 & 4 sable a fess Argent: 3 battle axes erected barwise in chief of the 2nd – 2 & 3 Argent: a lion rampant within a bordure of 7 gules – An escutcheon of pretence Ermine on a canton Gules an owl Argent. Crest on a wreath a buck sejant gardant Argent:

A white marble tablet with an urn – Sacred to the memory of John Guard esq a much respected inhabitant of Honiton he died May 4 1800 aged 64. Susan his wife survived him 22 years passing the days of her widowhood at Ottery St Mary & at the advanced age of 82 was buried in the same vault with him in the middle aisle of this church where also lie Susan their eldest daughter & Richard youngest son both taken from them to their great sorrow in the prime of life.

A marble tablet. H.M.S. in mem: Elija Blampin gen: qui a famulo per merita provectus et amicus inde magistro fidelissimus ob: 4 Dec 1787 aet 59 [missing]

A white marble tablet & urn. – To the memory of John How of this town gent – died 28 Dec 1775 aged 47 also underneath this monument are interred the remains of Rebecca H. wife of the above. J.H. who died 14 Dec. 1801 aged 74. also of Elizabeth H. daughter of the above J. & R. H. who died 4 Oct 1786 aged 22. also Mary daughter of J. & R. H. who died 17 Aug 1798 aged 37. also of Rebecca Gould daughter of the above J. & R. H. who died 20 Aug 1804 aged 44. also of the rev Jasper H. son of J. & R. H. who died 13 Feb 1810 aged 44. This monument was erected by the rev. Samuel How rector of Southleigh in this county also of Winterbourne Stickland in the co: of Dorset the only surviving son of the above J. & R. H. Feb 1822. [missing] –

A marble tablet with a medallion portrait and a shield with the arms of Gill as before – In a vault underneath are deposited the remains of John Gill gent: who was interred 1 Dec 1736 aged 27 years also William Gill esq. Barrister at law who died 2 Nov 1744 aged 32. Susanna mother of the said John & William Gill died 2 April 1748 aged 68 years. William Gill esq. father of John & William & husband of Susanna died 4 Dec 1756 aged 72 years. This monument erected to their memory by Susanna Duke (the only surviving child of the said William Gill & Susanna his wife) relict of John Duke late of Otterton esq: deceased who was one of the representatives in parliament for this borough 14 years. [missing]

On the floor is an old stone with the inscription defaced but enough of the coat armor remains to show – a fess & in chief 3 spears erect impaling 3 bulls heads caboshed.

The inscriptions in the church yard are these
Stone – East end – William Hodge gent died June 1784 aged 33 erected by his mother. – D°. D° Matilda relict of Major Thomas Murphy formerly of the 44th regiment of infantry died 21 Feb 1828 aged 60.
Altar tomb D° – John William Pfeil esq late of London merchant died 8 Jan 1809 aged 60 also Henry Thomas his infant son died 9 April 1808 aged 4 weeks.
D° North side – Elizabeth Ann only daur of Col. George Elliott Vinicombe & Dorothy his wife died 17 Sept 1826 in her 33rd year.
Stone D°. – G Doddington Lee esq. died Feb 19 1799 aged 44 yrs only son of Samuel L. esq. late an eminent surgeon in London descended from a family long known in this neighbourhood –
Altar tomb D°. John Knott son of Thomas K & Honour his wife died 23 July 1724 aged 20. In memory of John K malster who died Oct 7 1800 aged 70 years. Nathaniel K son of the above J. K died in 1772 aged 5 yrs. Elizabeth daur of the above J. K died July 11th 1805 aged 35.
Stone D°. – George Humphrey & Elizabeth his wife both of this parish. He died July 19. 1759 aged 45 years & she Jan 30th 1790 aged 80 years they left 2 surviving sons Ozias & William the former was a painter in crayons to his Majesty a royal academician & F.A.S. he died March 9. 1810 aged 68 years & the latter is the present vicar of Kemsing cum Seal & Birling in Kent by whom this stone was ordered to be erected.
D° D°. – Thomas Lisle gent died 5 Aug 1729. aged 90.

An altar tomb against the north wall of the chancel with a brass plate on the slab thus inscribed – Here lyeth the body of James Rodge of Honinton in the county of Devonshire (bone lace siller hath given unto the poore of Honinton parishe the benyfitt of 100 L for ever) who deceased the 27 of July A°. Di. 1617 aetate suae 50 Remember the poore.
D°. North side Here lieth the bodie of Edward S--ark of this parish --- day of April 1607.
Stone – D° – In memory of George Russell esq. of St Mary Abbots terrace Kensington Middlesex who died 10 Aug: 1828 aged 36 years
D°. D°. – William Flood died 12 April 1820 aged 80 years
Grace relict of the above died 24 Oct 1824 aged 89 years
D°. D°. – Daniel Flood died 19 Sept 1823 aged 59 years.
Tomb altar – Edward Tyrrell esq. Captain in the Royal navy died 4 June 1789 aged 30 years.
Altar Tomb north side – Inscribed in one compartment on its north side – *Caleb Pierce nuper in hoc oppido rei satis amplae ac bonae existimationis Acnopolae hic situs est vixit annos XLIV obiit a nato Christi CIƆ IƆCCXVIII XII Kal: Julias.*

Una obdormit nunc denuo thalami consors. – On the other compartment – *Mariae Thomae Courtenay eodem de oppido Acnopolae filia bene merita proli facilis non male indulgens pauperibus larga, pietatis modestiae morumque comitate paucis admodum amore erga Maritum nulli prorsus secunda quae dum illum ereptum et se superstitem plus nimius defleret ipsa omnibus flebilis suis desideratissima extremum clausit diem. Prid: Id: Octobris CIƆIƆCCXVII aetatis suae XLII.*
On the south side *Hic pariter requiescit pariter in parentum complexu filia natu minima Elizabetha Quae annum iam egressa VIII priusquam per aetatem scire potuerat quod sit vivere e vita decessit prid: non: Junias CIƆIƆCCXIII*
At the east end *Caleb P. superstes cognatis cineribus hunc tumulum posuit maerens.*

A stone west side of the church yard – Samuel Pierce esq. died Oct 22 1718 aged 50. Elizabeth his wife died Oct 28 1739 aged 53 – John their son died 27 May 1724 aged 12. Edward their son died 28 May 1724 aged 10.

A tomb west side of the church. George son of John & Sophia Betts born at Calcutta in Bengal 4 Sept 1821 died 30 Jan 1827.
A tomb so: side here lieth the body of William Leuermore (Qy as to name) Apothecary who dyed the 6 daye of October AD. 1624 aetat: suae ----
Dº. Dº. – Eliza the wife of William Seaman of Honiton gent died 4 March 1769 aged 44 also Catherine second wife of the said W S. -- died 8 Aug 1779 aged 56. Also the said W. S. died 10 May 1785 aged 60. William S. only son of the said W. S. by Elizabeth his wife died 5 July 1789 aged 28 years. Edward Carter gent died 25 March 1807 aged 35 years.

Dº. Dº. – John Colesworthy gent. Jane his wife & 5 of their children. John died April 10 1759 aged 61. Jane Sept 9. 1747 aged 43. Rebecca their daur April 10 1751 aged 21. John, John Richard & Mary died all in their infancy.

Stones So: side – Thomas Isaac died Dec 11 1824 aged 80 years Katherine wife of T.I. died 7 June 1800 aged 56 years also 10 of their children – also Amy his second wife died 6 Oct 1813 aged 50 years.
William Hodge gent died June 1784 aged 33. erected by his mother Susanna wife of Thomas Jeffery daughter of Peter Gibbons gent: of Honiton died 30 Aug. 1807 aged 57 also Catherine the daughter of Thomas & Catherine I his first wife aged 10 yrs.
Joseph Thompson esq died 26 Oct 1820 aged 42
Manston Teed Surgeon died 5 Feb 1780 aged 54 also Anne T granddaughter of the above & daughter of Henry Manston T. died 22 June 1815 aged 19.
Against the wall of the aisle south of the chancel a hatchment. – The arms of Gill impaling Or a fess gules between 3 escutcheons of the last each charged with a bend vairy between 2 cinquefoils of the field all with a bordure Azure bezant of 8. – (Passmore).

John Southdon rector ecclesie de Honiton 1365.1368. See deeds for La More in Colyton.

Biography of Cleaveland author of the History of the Family of Courtenay [There follows on pp. 93–4 a short biography of Ezra Cleaveland (d. 1740), author and rector of Honiton.]

The above is transcribed from a MS addition to a copy of Mr Cleaveland's work belonging to the ref Geo. Oliver of Exeter lent me by him – 16 Feb 1830. JD.

The following copy of the inscription on the floor of the chancel in Honiton church to the memory of the revd Ezra Cleaveland is taken from a collection of Monumental inscriptions made by Benjamin Incledon Esq of Barnstaple.

Hic jacent Exuviae mortales Reverendi admodum visi Ezrae Cleaveland S.J.B. Collegii Exon. Apud Oxonienses quondam Socii, et deinde Cita volente perhonorabili viso Dno Gulielmo Courtenay de Powderham Baronetto hujus Ecclesiae quadraginta per annos Rectoris Per id omne tempus studiis graviter incubuit. Animoque, omnigena fere Scientia imbuto, tum Ethica necnon Christianae Fidei articulos peculiari quadam perspicuitate Concionibus enucleavit.
Uno contentus Sacerdotio alterum non ambivit Oblatum etiam recusavit
Vitam prorsus innocuam duxit, et quamplurimis Benefecit
Moribus --ierat severitas, Sermoni Gravitas, ut decuit Ministram Dei: Idem vero cum tempus posceret, Comes mire festivus, multo Permaduit Sale.
Completis tandem octoginta annis. Senio potius
Quam morbo confectus, quasi obdormivit beatae
Resurrectionis spe septimo die Augusti AD 1740"
Elizabetha Jonathani Wood Exonii haud obscuro Mercatori nupta (quam unicam habuit) Filia Testamento legavit, ut nomen ejus memoriae Traderetur superimposito hoc saxo. Hanc vero Inscriptionem putatis ergo dictitavit Ricardus Lewis A.M. Scholae Honitonensis praeceptor Juxta etiam requiescit Henricus Waad praedictae Elizabethae filius natu maximus et ipsa pariter Elizabetha Quorum ille obit ---- 1739. Haec autem vicesimo die Julii anno Dni 1749.

Newspaper cutting, no name of newspaper, dated 28 October 1835:
Honiton New Church –
On Wednesday last, the foundation stone of the New Parish Church, intended to be erected in this town, was laid by Christopher Flood Esq. [Details follow of the procession and dinner to mark the occasion.] We understand that the edifice thus happily begun is intended to accommodate 1500 persons, of which 500 sittings are to be free. The designs are by that eminent Architect Charles Fowler, Esq., of Gordon Square, London, and are universally admired. We cannot omit to mention that it is intended to erect this building by subscription, and the inhabitants of the Town have, by their subscriptions, manifested a zeal which is highly creditable to them. There is, however, at present a considerable deficiency in the Funds requisite to complete their undertaking, and, therefore, we hope that the appeal which the Committee have felt it necessary to make to the public for aid, will be responded to in such a manner as to enable them to execute their work according to the original design.

Press release, no name of publication, dated 1848:
HONITON NEW CHURCH
There is at last a total suspension of divine service at this church, owing to the unsafe state of the roofs. Plans have been taken during the past week by Messrs. Carver and Giles, architect, who we understand are to make a report thereon immediately. We have no doubt a church rate will have to be made, to meet the expenses of a new roof, although the present church has been built only 10 years. Divine service is to be

performed at the old church on Sunday next, and already a number of the inhabitants have removed their books, hassocks &c. We trust while the alterations are going on, the tower will not be forgotten, and that a new clock will be put up, either by the rates or subscription, that the public may no longer be puzzled as to the *real time*, and thus confer a benefit on the inhabitants at large instead of the unsightly dial face now attached to this church.

Honiton

The chapel of Allhallows in the town of Honiton stands on the site of a former building as does the school room adjoining to it – The master of the school the rev. R. Lewis knows of no record of the foundation but it seems not improbable that the chapel & the school were coeval in their origin for it appears that the former building consisted of a tower & in the area beneath it were the doors of the chapel & the school room opposite to each other. It does not seem probable that the tower would have been placed at the eastern end unless the school which it connected to the chapel was part of the original structure – The present chapel is a most unsightly building of quadrangular form in a debased Roman style, it is 62 feet long 24 wide within the walls & has 2 doors opposite to each other in the north & south walls. A tablet over the south door inside is thus inscribed literatim "This chapel being ruinous was taken down AD 1712 was begun to be rebuilt from the ground AD. 1743 was completely finished & opened July 6th AD 1769. The rev. Charles Bertie Rector, the rev. Richard Lewis Rob. Gidley Gent. Churchwardens." There is a gallery at the western end and a wooden altar screen of Ionic design against the eastern wall. The font is a plain black marble basin on a wooden pedestal. There are no burials here – Prayers are read twice a week & a sermon is preached on Sunday evenings by the master of the school. – The tower is a large square erection at the eastern end of the chapel between it and the school room, it contains a clock with chimes & 6 bells thus inscribed respectively. –

1. *Corripuit me flamma vorax depressa resurgo aucto didici grandius ore loqui.* The rev. Richard Lewis and Robert Gidley Gentlemen churchwardens 1769. cast by Thos Bayley Bridgewater
2. I lead in the melodious round T.B. fecit 1780
3. Destroyed by fire in 1765 reinstated 1780 Charles Bertie Rector. Thomas Bilbie fecit
4. D^{o}.
5. The rev Charles Bertie Rector 1780 T.B. f.
6. John Tooze & Samuel Salter churchwardens 1780 T.B.f.

The tower is 65 feet high to the top of the battlements at each of the 4 corners is a pinnacle with a vane. The roof of the chapel has a deplorable appearance being partly slated & partly thatched.

The authority of the rector of Honiton in this chapel does not seem to be clearly defined, he does no duty in it nor does the master of the school receive any regular stipend, the evening lecture seems to be paid by voluntary contributions & it seems extraordinary that the greater number of the parochial baptisms should take place here. –

The school room which is at the eastern end of the chapel (the base of the tower only intervening) stands on the site of the former one but is larger the old one was 24 feet long the present is 44½. – the eastern window is large containing 5 lights with cinquefoil heads & upright tracery in the arch – It belonged to the former building & seems to be of the 15th century – There does not appear to be any other vestige of antiquity about the place (except that the lower part of the tower exhibits on the north side vestiges of a former building – the base of the tower is perhaps the ancient one altered & added to on the western side is a small niche containing a whole length stone figure in a gown & hood & bearded – it is probably a saint or perhaps a schoolmaster). The present school room was built about 1818 or 1820. The school house adjoining is also a modern erection.

St Margaret's Hospital about ½ a mile west of Honiton – 22 Sept 1829

This foundation is now the residence of 9 poor unmarried people 3 men and 6 women. The oldest man who is the governor and who if he lives till Christmas will be 90 years of age and another man who assists him have each 3 shillings a week, the others only 2/- & they have each an additional gift of 10 shillings at Christmas this amounts to £56.10 a year. The lands which form the endowment are said to be 6 fields in the neighbourhood & the management is in the hands of Mr Gidley attorney of Honiton. The people are nominated to the charity by the parson churchwardens & overseers of Honiton. The chapel is 32 feet long by 13 wide within the walls but 12 feet are parted off at the west end which forms a lumber room, a bell hangs in the west gable – two windows under low arches have trefoil headed lights – in the east wall is a small locker. The structure appears to be of about the 15 century – A common deal desk stands at the eastern end and prayers are read on Wednesdays & Fridays by the Governor assisted by another who reads the lessons. The inmates attend sermon & the sacrament at Honiton church nearly 2 miles off a great distance for these aged & infirm people.

COMBE RALEIGH

Davidson (pp. 100–3) visited [St John the Baptist] Combe Raleigh on 25 September 1828 and noted it was about 1½ miles north of Honiton. The chancel roof was replaced in 1886 (Pevsner, *Devon*, 285). Two memorials are missing from the six that Davidson recorded.

The church of this village consists of a nave 43 feet long by 16 wide, a chancel 22 by 15 with a modern vestry on its south side, a north aisle 55 feet long by 13 wide & a tower at the western end 8½ long by 9½ wide having a turret with three sides at the south eastern corner for the staircase. The nave and chancel are separated from the aisle by 5 columns & 2 halves composed each of 4 shafts at the angles with intervening hollow mouldings the shafts have small circular laminated capitals & these support pointed arches. The roof is arched & ribbed. The windows have all cinquefoil headed lights & are flat on the top excepting those at the ends of the aisle & nave there which have pointed arches. The porch at the south door has windows with trefoil headed lights. The font is of stone large & heavy octangular in shape & 2½ feet in diameter. The sides are adorned with quatrefoils it is lined with lead & rests on an octangular column ornamented with niches having trefoil heads. There are some ancient benches in the nave & the floor has several old ornamented tiles. The screen & rood loft between the nave & the chancel have been removed but the door remains in the north wall & the staircase in a large buttress, which led up to the roof loft. In the north wall of the chancel is a square locker for the ampulla & in the opening between the chancel & the aisle extending between the 2 columns is a large stone slab which seems to have been the side of an altar tomb it is ornamented on the north side with quatrefoils having shields in the centre & pinnacles between them but it is much defaced & is coated with whitewash [removed]. – On the north wall of the aisle above the windows & immediately beneath the roof is some ancient painting it extends about half the length of the aisle & represents a range of columns ornamented with angular & other devices having a sort of Ionic capitals & supporting semi circular arches – under the arches are represented a variety of human figures but these have been so much defaced that their occupations cannot be ascertained. A gallery at the western end of the nave conceals the opening to the tower which is a pointed arch resting on large corbels representing lion's heads and foliage [removed]. The tower is 48 feet high to the top of the battlements 51 to the top of the stair turret & contains 3 bells one of which is ancient & is thus inscribed in the gothic letter "*Plebs ois plaudit ut me tam sepius audit*" another T.P. Exon 1671 & the third. T. Bilbee 1758.

Against the N wall of the aisle at the eastern end is a marble tablet thus inscribed. In the family vault underneath are deposited the remains of the revd. James Bernard rector of Stoodley in this county & of Combe Flory in the county of Somerset lord of the manor of Combe Raleigh & principal proprietor of lands within the parish. He died at Sidmouth 20 Nov. 1823 aged 70 Also of Henry Richard Bernard 4th son of the above by Mary his wife a lieutenant in his Majesty's navy who served with distinction until the peace of 1814 after which he became owner & commander of a West India merchant ship. He died at Sidmouth 1 Nov 1821 aged 29. Arms a bear rampant. Or an escutcheon of pretence a cross vairy between 4 mullets. Crest on a wreath a demi bear rampant muzzled. Motto "*Nec sinit esse feros*".

Against the south wall of the chancel is a marble tablet to the memory of Ann wife of J.B. Sweeting of Honiton Surgeon &c & daughter of the revd. Wm Palmer late rector of this parish and Ann his second wife, who died 23 March 1790 aged 36 years. Also of Mary wife of the above named Revd. Wm Palmer who died 16^(th) Sept 1742. John Bacon Sweeting died 23 March 1803 aged 54 years.

South wall of chancel a marble tablet erected by his widow to John Sheldon esq. surgeon F.R.S. & professor of anatomy in the royal academy who died 8 Oct 1808 aged 56 years. Arms. Sable a fess between 3 geese argent beaked & legged Or. impaling Argent a chevron between 3 purses sable stringed Or.

On the floor of the nave. Pertesa Crossing daughter of Nicholas Crossing of Staverton in this county gent: buried 5 Oct 1680 aged 66.
On the floor of the nave. Elizabeth wife of Samuel Pulman of this parish gent: died 16 August 1725 aged 54.
An altar tomb in the church yard records James Petty esq. of Woodhayne in this parish died 4 July 1822 aged 74.
Against the south wall of the nave is a hatchment displaying the undermentioned heraldic bearings erected for the husband.
Gules an eagle displayed Or in chief a naval crown between 2 fire balls fused on the 2^(nd) on an escutcheon of pretence Quarterly 1&4 Per bend Or azure an eagle displayed countercharged 2&3 Azure a chevron between 3 mullets Or (Graves query) The shield surrounded by the ribbon bearing the motto to which is suspended the jewel of the order of the Bath. A knight's helmet bears the crest. On a wreath Or & gules an eagle displayed Or holding a pennon Gules staff. Inscribed "*Per sinum Codanum*". The supporters are dexter An eagle Sable, beaked & armed & charged on the breast with an anchor Or, sinister. A female draped Argent & azure crowned with laurel behind her an anchor prostrate Sable. On the dexter side of the hatchment above the support is a shield bearing Per pale Argent & Sable on an escutcheon of pretence impaling Argent a pile in bend wavy Sable.

Combe Raleigh is a rectory held by the rev. C.E. Band who is the patron & resident here – Mr Bernard who lives at Sidmouth is lord of the manor.

Book extract pasted into the manuscript
Spreats Churches No. 19: Combe Raleigh [1842]
Combe Raleigh is one of the many fertile parishes that lie within the luxuriant vale of the Otter, being situate on the right bank of that river, and opposite to the borough of Honiton; it abounds in most delightful rural scenery, well dressed with forest trees and woodland.
The name of "Come", "Cume", "Combe" frequently occurs in the Domesday Survey, being the Saxon term for a small upland valley stretching into the hills in an oval form, and spreading wider as it opens upon the larger vale; it is common in all

parts of Devonshire. "Ralegh" or "Raleigh" is an adjunct derived from its possessor, Sir John Ralegh, in the reign of King Edward the 2nd: it was in early times called Comb Baunton. And Comb Matthew from Sir Matthew de Baunton, in the time of Henry III., and John de Baunton after him.

The church is rather spacious, and is pleasantly situated on a gentle knoll, nearly in the centre of the parish; it is built of stone, but possesses no architectural features of much interest; the tower at the west end of the nave is low – it contains three musical bells. The eastern window of the north aisle is of good decorated work, those on the north side are of the latest Tudor, being square headed and filled with good tracery. The chancel window is of the earlier Tudor, when the pointed arch had become much depressed, but before the square-headed window prevailed; the south porch has a neat unglazed window of this kind. The monuments are, one to the memory of John Sheldon, F.R.S. and professor of Anatomy, who died in 1808: one to the memory of the Bernard family, and some others. A yew tree of considerable age, size, and beauty, ornaments the church-yard. The Church is stated in the Thesaurus to be dedicated to St Nicholas, but in some authorities, the Patron Saint is said to be St. Erasmus. The registers are perfect from the year 1655 to the present time. The living is a rectory in the deanery of Dunkeswell, and in the arch-deaconry and diocese of Exeter. The parish is in the hundred of Axminster; its population in 1831 was 296.

The parsonage, the residence of the present rector, Rev. Charles Edward Band, who was instituted in 1827, is in a lovely situation, backed by fine woods and the towering hill of St. Cyre, and commanding luxuriant vale scenery, but is at some distance from the church. The family of Drewe of the Grange are the possessors of the advowson.

LUPPITT

Davidson (pp. 105–7) visited [St Mary's] Luppitt on 3 September 1828 and noted it was about 6 miles north of Honiton. He observed the church was 'situated on an elevated spot on the north side of the village and overlooking it'. The large building Davidson thought presented 'few architectural beauties', and was 'almost devoid of ornaments within and without'. The chancel was rebuilt in 1880–1 by C.F. Edwards, and re-seated and re-floored in 1923 by Harbottle Reed (Pevsner, *Devon*, 543). Four memorials are missing from the eight that Davidson recorded.

The church consists of a chancel 34 feet long by 17 wide a nave 50 feet by 19.6in: transept 46.6 in their whole length by 19.6. with a tower at the western end 11 feet square opening to the nave by a lofty pointed arch and containing 4 bells. The eastern window has 4 lights with cinquefoil heads & the pointed arch is enriched with tracery – the N window of the N transept has 3 lights with lancet shaped cinquefoil heads, exhibiting a specimen of the style of the 13 century, the other windows are not remarkable – In the wall on the N side of the chancel is a low flat cusped arch beneath which on each side is a corbel head, perhaps formerly a slab but for what purpose is only conjectural (*in the margin:* for the sepulchre at the festival of Easter) – at the bottom of the tower lie the remains of a beautiful stone screen which once crossed the south transept, it appears to have been of an early date the arches equilateral & the lights with three foil heads [missing]. The roof at the crossing of the nave & transepts is relieved with groining of oak which at their central intersection are adorned with a boss carved in the representation of a savage human head & painted – The font situated close to the door is a curious specimen of Anglo Norman sculpture it is 2 feet square having a circular leaden basin and 2ft 10in. high, its base is circular resting on a square plinth – the sides of which (two only are visible as it is fixed in a corner) are rudely carved one of them apparently representing two monstrous animals, the other has 2 whole length figures of men one of them holding a stake or a large nail which seems resting on a human head below & which is between the men's feet, the other figure is partially defaced but was perhaps in the act of striking the stake (*in the margin:* This perhaps represents a martyrdom) but the whole is so loaded with successive coats of whitewash as almost to defy investigation. [now free standing]

(*In the margin:* For the endowment of St Nicholas chapel in the south aisle of Luppit church by Dame Elizabeth relict of Sir Thomas Carew Baron of Carew on 8 Feb. 29 Henry VI See fo: 496 of Bishop Lacey's Register. Note by rev Geo: Oliver in his account of Newenham Abbey in the Western Times newspaper.)

The inscriptions in this church are these
On a stone in the floor of the south transept. *Hic jacet Johane uxor Wille Wenard & filia Johis Bebyle cui. aie propiciet Ds*

On the same floor – *Mors mihi lucrum – Sub hoc lapide resurrectionem expectans quiescit quicquid terrestre erat reverendi necnon omni literarum genere peritissimi viri Humphridi Johnson nuper ecclesiae pastoris vigilantissimi. Obiit 28 Decembris anno Dom 1639 aetatis 73.*

Chancel floor – here lyeth the body of Mary the wife of Mr Humphrey Johnson some time the reverend vicar of this parish and daughter of John Wollaston esq. who was buried 26 Sept AD. 1650 Here also lyeth the body of Mary Johnson daughter of the said Humphrey Johnson and Mary his wife who dyed March the 30th AD. 1690 aet 70. [missing]

On the floor of the nave. Edward Pearse of Greenway in this parish Doctor of Physick Ob 31 Dec. 1729 [missing] aet: – Here also – Mary wife of Edw. Pearse gent ob.4 Jan. 1753 aged 44. [missing]

Floor N transept. Elizabeth wife of William Lee. Ob – May 1735 – Grace daughter of William and Elizabeth Lee of this parish who died 5 Sept 1739 aged 37.

Abigail Hewet wife of William Hewet. [missing] –

In the church yard on the south side of the church is an altar tomb inscribed "In memory of James Hawker gent who died 9 Sept 1727 aet. 62 also of William Hawker gent who died 28 Jan 1738 aet. 37. James son of William Hawker who died 11 Feb 1736 aged 9 months – Mary daughter of William Hawker who died 29 Dec 1740 aged 6 years." A shield the coat armour gone – Crest a bird, a martlet or perhaps a hawk.

Taxatio eccles. P. Nicholai p.143.
Exon dioc. Decanat de Donkeswell
Ecclia de Louepath (Loisepeate) Taxatio 10.0.0 *Decima* 1.0.0

Incumbents presented to the vicarage of Luppit by the Abbot & Convent of Newenham.
Baldwyn de Moun Rector by Abbot J. de Northampton
Walter de Spekyngtone vicar by Abbot de la Hous in 1344.
Richard de Kyngiston vicar by the same abbot.
Robert de Farmannystone vicar by the same abbot in 1351.
Vincent at Hill Vicar by Abbot John de Legga about 1401.
Richard Hicks was vicar in 1531.

For the augmentation of the vicarage in 1385 by the Archbishop of Canterbury – see Gibson's Codex vol.2 page 1490 & the deed transcribed at length in my collection for the East of Devon page 183.

COLYTON

Davidson (pp. 109–24) visited [St Andrew's] Colyton on 23 September 1828 and noted it was in Devon and about 5 miles south west of Axminster and 6 miles west of Lyme Regis in Dorset. He observed that 'the church of this ancient town is [a] handsome and very interesting structure', which originally consisted of a nave, chancel and transept with tower, 'but this edifice has received additions and alterations at various periods which though necessary for its increased accommodation have taken from the uniformity of its style and character'. The galleries were removed in 1897, and a fire in 1933 caused more renewing (Pevsner, *Devon*, 280). Nineteen memorials are missing from the forty-seven that Davidson recorded.

It seems that chapels or aisles were first erected on each side of the chancel & these have now been lengthened into aisles extending the whole length of the building. The extreme length of the church within the walls is 116 feet. The nave is 52 feet long by 21 wide & is divided from the aisle on each side by 3 columns & 2 half columns composed of alternate shafts & hollow mouldings these are crowned by quadrangular laminated capitals in a sort of Grecian style & support semicircular arches relieved by mouldings these were erected on the south side when the aisle was built and on the north when that aisle was erected in 1769 in order to correspond with the other, but the whole are in an incongruous & tasteless style. The nave is lighted by a large & beautiful window at the western end nearly as wide as the body of the church & having its apex reaching almost to the roof it is divided by mullions & transoms into numerous (27) lights with flat arched heads turned from 4 centres of which there are 9 in its width. the lower tier of these are adorned with sweeps highly enriched which form Cinquefoil heads and it is apparent that the whole window with the tracery in its head has been adorned in a similar manner, but has been most barbarously mutilated by the removal of all the enrichments. This window is very similar in its construction & proportions to specimens at Winchester and Gloucester cathedrals & may safely be attributed to the commencement of the 15 century – the western door as in the instance of that at Winchester is in the centre of the window which has a part of its mullions brought nearly to the floor. The chancel is 41 feet in length by 16 wide and is divided from the lateral aisles or chapels on each side by a column & 2 halves composed of clustered shafts having quadrangle capitals highly enriched with foliage leaves & grapes these support acutely pointed arches with numerous mouldings & the hollow mouldings of the half columns towards the altar are adorned with detached pieces of foliage. The eastern window is beneath a pointed arch of early date resting on 2 large corbel heads of a priest & a nun. The window itself of smaller dimensions has a circular head & is divided by mullions into 5 lights terminating except the central one in lancet shaped heads without sweeps but it is not improbable that this window has been defaced similarly to the others. This window is enriched by ancient & modern painted glass consisting of coats of arms devices & borders, the head of the central light shows an ancient specimen of painted glass representing the taking down from the cross or the entombment from a picture by Annibal Caracci this was purchased at Exeter by the parish at the cost of £5/- 5d. (*in the margin:* This window was repaired in 1829 and the coats of arms preserved. See page 123) [missing] An ancient coat of arms with numerous quartering cannot be deciphered from below – 2 modern coats are Argent a Salter gules and Argent a crop sable (*in the margin:* These are not coats, mere devices of the glazier) – The altar screen is of varnished oak in the Grecian style & bears the inscription John Sampson Senior Esq donor *anno Domini* 1795 with the arms a crop moline or & crest a demi lion rampant holding a sprig of oak. The aisle or chapel on the South of the chancel called the Pole aisle & containing the monuments of that family is 34 feet long by 16 wide & has an entrance from the church yard consisting of a pointed door way enriched with foliage the roof is divided by ribs of oak into angular compartments with knots of foliage at their intersections the whole painted & gilded. The monuments of the Poles which occupy its eastern end were formerly enclosed by a wooden screen which became ruinous & was removed & they are now protected by a beautiful stone screen which formerly enclosed a chapel or perhaps a monument at the extremity of the south transept but which was removed when some alterations were made in the church. The space which it enclosed being now occupied as a vestry. This screen is elaborately carved in stone with openings having trefoil heads & various tracery above them the arches are pointed in the best style & that of the door which is in the centre is enriched by sweep & pendant ornaments: enclosed by these are two shields one of these bears the letters FR the other TB with a briar which is a punning representation of the individuals name to whom the letters refer Thomas Brerewood (Vicar of Colyton, according to Mr. Anstis, at the time of the valuation of first fruits in 1292) this screen may therefore be dated about the commencement of the 14th century.

At the western end of this aisle or chapel remains part of an ancient oaken lectern or reading desk with chains attached to it which formerly confined the Bible & the Book of Martyrs, to the back of this desk was affixed the alms box as appears by following inscription carved in the frame in the gothic letter. "This is the chest for the poure and he that hath pitie upon them lendith unto the Lord, Pro:19" [missing] In this aisle also stands the font which has been removed from the western end of the church, it is of stone small and ancient but has been newly sculptured & conse- quently reduced in size. it is octagonal each panel adorned with a quatrefoil & it stands on a column ornamented with panels [now different font] –

This aisle is lighted by 2 windows of early date having lancet arches & divided into 4 lights with cinquefoil heads. –

The aisle north of the chancel or as it is called Yonges' aisle is 34 feet long by 15ft 6in wide – it is lighted by windows similar in form to the Poles aisle and its eastern end is enclosed by a lofty & heavy screen without openings ornamented on the top with a sort of pinnacles in the Elizabethan style & bearing the Yonges arms in stone with the crest a boar's head erased & looking forward – this aisle is kept in repair by a charge upon some lands in the parish – & the enclosed part is used as a parish vestry room (See further next page but one.) [now has an opening]

The south aisle is comparatively modern it is 73 feet long by 16.6in in width, it is lighted by pointed windows of 4 lights having heads turned from 4 centres in imitation of the old windows of the church omitting at the same time the sweeps which have been barbarously removed from the latter. A porch protects a door way into this aisle under a pointed arch & this porch is lighted by a square headed window of 2 lights which also seem to have been despoiled of their ornamental sweeps. The north aisle was erected in 1769 & has been subsequently enlarged, it is lighted by windows similar on all respects to those of the south aisle & is 73 feet long by 19.6in wide. Against the wall is a tablet with the following inscription AD. 1818. This church was enlarged by voluntary contributions by a loan to be repaid by a church rate in 20 years & by a donation of £100 from the society for enlarging churches given upon condition that one half of the area added containing 240 sittings should for ever be left open and free for the general use of the inhabitants of which this tablet is a record. James Lile George Beed Churchwardens.

The roof of the nave is intersected by rectangular ribs of oak ornamented by stars at the intersections. Two brass chandeliers with numerous lights hang from the roof of the nave – The pulpit & desk are situated at the western end & are of oak in a Roman style of erection & ornament. The front of the pulpit bears the arms of Pole with crest & supporters well carved in oak [now stone] –

A heavy tower 23 feet square outside the walls, rises at the intersection of the nave chancel & transepts to all which it opens by narrow pointed arches but these although of ancient form are modern erection for the base of the tower being found ruinous a stone mason of the town named [blank] Robins in the year [blank] undertook to rebuild it which he did in a masterly style having suspended the tower & restored the base from its foundation with complete success. This tower rises in a square form to the height of 61 feet to the top of the battlements being open on each side to the belfry by a pointed arched window divided by a mullion into 2 lights, on the summit of the tower is an octangular lantern supported by flying buttresses springing from the corners which are ornamented with pinnacles, the lantern is also lighted by 4 windows pointed & divided into 2 lights, it is finished on the top by battlements & is itself 22 feet high from its base or 19 from the battlements of the tower making the total height from the floor of the church 80 feet. A large vane forms an apex to the tower.

The tower contains 6 bells which bear the following inscriptions

"O Lord how glorious ar thy works Ano Di 1611"

"William Drake gent: churchwarden J.M.F. 1667"

"When I call follow me all. John Abbot 1667"

"NAF. *Annae Regi Mag. Brit. Decimo. Sum. Vitae Mortis Temporis atque Tubae* A.D. 1711. Mr William Salter Vicker. John Reed. John Spiller Churchwardens"

"John Bilbee fecit 1772 This bell was put up at the expense of the parish"

"Thomas Bilbee fecit 1775 Mr. William Vicary and Mr. James West Churchwardens" (*in the margin:* The largest bell recast 1837)

The window of the Yonges aisle or chapel is adorned with some modern stained glass & at the eastern end in the south wall are the remains of an elegant piscina – its opening is square & it seems to have been finished with an arch and ornamented pinnacles, behind which at the top are panels with 3 foil heads – the bottom of the hollow has a leaf carved in the stone beneath which is the hole for the discharge of the liquid poured into it. On the floor is part of a stone, what remains of the inscription is only "of September 161-". Arms in the centre Yonge with helmet & crest [missing]. Three hatchments are affixed to the walls & they are in a perishing condition. The 1st shews the arms of Yonge viz Ermine on a bend cotised (Yonge) sable 3 griffins heads erased Or in a canton the arms of Ulster impaling Gules a lion rampant reguardant Or. No crest as this (Morice) hatchment was placed for the femme.

2nd Azure on a chevron Or between 3 foxes? passant Argent as many roses Gules. On a chief of the 3rd 3 griffins heads erased Sable. Impaling Azure on a chevron Or between 3 eagles heads erased Argent 2 cross crosslets Sable. Crest a bull? Passant proper winged Or.

3. Quarterly of 6. 1&6 Yonge. 2 defaced 3 Argent a saltier sable (3 Coriton) 4 defaced 5 Barry wavy of 8 Argent & Sable. Impaling Quarterly 1&4 Argent a chevron Sable between 3 mullets (1&4 Davie) pierced Gules. 2nd & 3rd Azure 3 cinquefoils Or, on a chief of (2&3 Davy) the last a lion passant Gules. Crest defaced. Motto. *Fortitudine et Providentia.*

The eastern window of the Pole's aisle has some modern stained glass intermixed with some ancient coats of arms viz. Argent a fer de Moulin Sable (2nd) – sable 6 mullets Argent 3. 2&1 (Bonville)

Bonville – Argent 2 chevrons Sable (Esse-De Esse or Ash) Argent 2 bars wavy Sable The monuments coats of arms & inscriptions in the Pole's aisle are these. Viz. In the centre with one end against the east wall is a heavy stone altar tomb 8 feet 6in long 3.9 wide and 4 feet high consisting of a thick slab supported by Ionic pilasters between which are large shields with the arms painted and on the top a brass shield with the arms engraved. Resting on the end of the slab against the eastern wall are 2 Roman Doric columns supporting an entablature beneath which is a coat of arms and a brass tablet with the following inscription in the gothic letter. "Here lieth the body of William Pole late of Shute esq. deceased who married Kateryn daughter of Alexander Popham of Huntworth esq: the said Wm was sonne of Wm & of Agnes daughter of John Drake of Ashe which Wm was sonne of John & of Edith daughter of Rychard Tytherleigh of Tytherleigh which John was sonne of John and of Joane his wife daughter of Robert Code of Cornwall which John was sonne of Arture & of Johan daughter; and heire of John Pole whiche Arthur was second sonne of Sir Wm Pole of Pole in Wirral in the county of Chester knight & of his wife daughter of Sir William Manwaring of Pyver. He hath left behind only on sonne named William & on daughter named Dorothy married to Thomas Erle of Charborough esquire he dyed the XV of August *Anno.* 1587 being of the age of lxxii yeares and VI dayes."

Arms on the sides and at the end of the tomb

(1) Pole viz. Azure semee de lis Or a lion rampant Argent impaling

(2) Drake viz. Argent a wyvern Gules

Pole impaling (3) Ermine 2 irons in saltier Gules (Qy Tytherleigh)

Pole impaling (4) Argent a chevron Gules between 3 Cornish choughs sable (Code)

Pole impaling (5) gules 3 cocks Argent (Qy Manwaring)

Pole impaling (6) Argent 2 bans Gules (Martin)

Pole impaling (7) Argent (Qy or) a Sable face Gules (Pole)

Pole impaling (8) Argent on a chief Gules 2 bucks heads caboshed Or. (Popham)

Arms against the wall under the entablature

Quarterly of 14

1 & 14 Pole

2 (9) Argent a lion rampant Gules (Nonant Baron of Totnes)

3 (10) Argent a chevron sable between 3 bucks heads caboshed Gules
4 as (5) above
5. (11) Or a stags face Gules (Pole)
6. (12) Vairy 3 fishes Hauriant
7. (13) Per pale Ermine and Gules
8. (14) Gules 3 escallops Argent (Keppel)
9 (15) ermine on a chief indented Sable 3 cross crosslets fitchees Or.
10 (16) Argent 4 bars Azure between 15 trefoils Sable
11 (17) Argent 2 chevrons Sable (De Essa or Ash)
12 (18) sable 6 mullets 3.2 & 1 Argent a label of 3 points Gules
13 (19) Sable a tree eradicated fructed of 5 apples Or (De la Ford)
Three crests 1 On a wreath Or & Azure a lions paw Or. (*in the margin:* Sable poppy
with roots and fruit Or. De la Ford of Musbury See Polwhele 3. 297)
2 On a wreath Or & Azure a bucks head caboshed Gules attired Or
3 Out of a ducal cornet. A wyvern's head Azure beaked Or. Motto *Pollet virtus* 1587.
On the front of the entablature 5 shields – Pole impaling Drake
Pole impaling (6) Pole impaling (11) Pole impaling (4) Pole impaling (3)
On the slab a brass shield quarterly of 12
1 Pole
2 Two chevrons between 3 bucks heads caboshed (20)
3. as (5)
4. as (7)
5. as (12)
6. as (13)
7. as (14)
8. Ermine 4 Bars
9. as (15)
10. as (17)
11. as (18)
12. as (19)

Against the eastern wall on the north side is a monument of stone painted, consisting
of an entablature supported by 4 Corinthian columns beneath which is the effigy of
a female kneeling on a cushion with her hands in the attitude of prayer before her
kneel 5 sons behind her 2 daughters all are dressed in black with large white ruffs
round their necks. A tablet below bears the following inscription
Here lieth the body of Katherin daughter of Alexander Popham of Huntworthi in the
counti of Somerset esquire the sister of Sir John Popham knight Lord chief justice of
England lately the wief of William Pole esquire the elder unto whom shee brought
foorth William Pole knight and Dorothe the wife first of Thomas Erle esquire secondly
of Walter Vaughan Knight which were living and Alexander Hugh Richard Arthur
and Amy which died younge. Shee died the 28 of October 1588 unto the memorie of
whome Sir Wm Pole knight. her son hath set this monument. Arms 8 coats.
1 Pole
2 Pole impaling (8)
3 In a lozenge (8)
4 In a lozenge (8)

5 (8) impaling (21) Argent 3 pales Azure over all a bend Gules charged with 3 cinque-foils Or

6. (21) impaling (22) Sable 6 Martletts 3.2 & 1 Argent

7. (8) impaling (23) Gules on a bend Argent 3 escallops Sable

8. (23) impaling (24) Argent a saltire Gules between 4 eagles displayed Sable.

Against the eastern wall on the south side is a mural monument of stone painted representing the effigies of a female kneeling on a cushion with her hands in prayer before her 4 sons & behind 5 daughters all dressed in black with white large ruffs on their necks a tablet below inscribed.

Here lieth the body of Mary late the wife of S Wm. Pole of Shute Knt. being the eldest daughter and one of the 4 heires of Sir W. Periham of Fulford Knight. Lo. Chief Barron of the Kings Majesties exchequer. She left behind her 4 sones & 5 daughters unto her said husband viz. John Periham Will & Francis sones Mary Katherine Elizabeth Anne & Elionor daughters. She brought unto him also 2 others sones viz. Wil her first child and Arthur being on of the 3 sones which she brought at on birth & perished by an unfortunat fall. Shee dyed the 2nd of May in the yeere of our Lord 1605 being then of thage of 38 and on moneth and maried unto her husband 22 yeares tenn moneths. Arms coats

1. Pole

2. Gules a chevron engrailed between 3 leopards faces Or (Periam)

3. 1 impaling 2.

4. In a lozenge Quarterly 1st & 4th as 2 above 3rd Argent a chevron azure between 3 pears pendant Gules (Periam) 3rd Argent 2 bars wavy between 3 billets Sable

2 crests. 1 On a wreath Or & Azure. 2 arms embowed, attired azure, cuffed argent, hands proper holding a lions face Or 2. on a wreath Or & azure a lions paw erased Or.

Against the eastern wall a wooden tablet. To the pious & beloved memory of Mrs Grace Pole the second daughter of Sir Thomas Trenchard knt and late wife of William Pole esq whose body lies interred in the church of Charminster in the county of Dorset while her soul lives in the felicities of heaven and her honoured memory in the register of fame. – Arms 3 coats. 1. Pole. 2 Argent 3 pales on the dexter side Sable. 3. 1 impaling 2. 2 crests 1 Pole. 2 dexter arm holding a dagger. Mottoes both to the last coat. *Pollet virtus. Nosce teipsum.* –
On the same tablet. *Memoriae Johannis et Gulielmi filiorum Gulielmi Pole armigeri et Gratiae uxoris ejus* – then follow – some laudatory verses.

On the north side of the aisle opening to the chancel is an altar tomb surmounted by an entablature & an elevated canopy supported by 8 Corinthian columns, the whole of stone painted in gaudy colours beneath the canopy upon the tomb lie the effigies of 2 recumbent figures – on the south side a knight in full black armour except that his head is bare, with spurs & a large ruff round his neck, he lies on his right side with his head on his hand & his elbow on a pillow, a clasped book in his left hand – On the north side a female with her back to her husband in a black dress with a tippet of lace having a ring on the thumb of her left hand which rests upon a skull – A tablet on the north side of the tomb bears the following inscription. *Hic jacet Elizabetha uxor Johis Pole Baronetti & unica Rog. How mercatoris Londiniensis filia obiit 16 die Aprilis 1628 tres filios totidemq filias vivent reliquit duobus insuper & filio & filia defunctis* – Some Latin verses on another above second that the monument was erected by William Pole her eldest son – The inscriptions if there have been any on the south side are no longer legible – Arms in 6 coats viz

On the south side (1) Pole 4. Pole impaling (2) Gules a chevron engrailed Argent between 3 lions faces Or – (3) Argent a fess engrailed between 3 wolves heads couped Sable (How) impaling (4) Azure (3 How 4 Symmes)

3 escallops in pale Or – On the north side in a lozenge (3) – Pole Bart impaling (3) – Pole Bart impaling (3)

Against the south wall a large tablet of white marble adorned with flowers and cherubs inscribed. Sir William Pole Bart: (of Shute) Master of the household to her late majesty Queen Anne of ever glorious memory dyed 31 Dec. 1741 aged 63 Arms Pole Bart impaling – (not painted, or has been destroyed).

A hatchment – Pole impaling Templer – as in Shute church

On the north side of the chancel against the screen of the Yonges' chapel stands a very beautiful monument which has lately been removed from the western end of the chancel & has been repaired & cleaned – It consists of an altar tomb upon which lies the effigies of an interesting female child with her hands in the posture of prayer, her hair is long & curling & her head which is encircled by a coronet rests upon a pillow which is supported on each side by an angel, and her feet rest upon a dog. (*in the margin:* Margaret daur of Wm Courtenay E of Devon by the Lady Catherine daughter of K Edw. IV died at Colcombe castle, choked with a fish bone.) – From the side of the tomb against the wall rise shafts which spread into fan work & tracery terminating in pendant ornaments & supported in the intervals by angels forming a canopy the face of which is enriched in front by the most beautiful tabernacle work – in a panel at each end of the tomb beneath the canopy is the figure in relief of a priest dispersing odors from a censer and on the outside at the western end is an angular shaft upon the capitals of which rests a pedestal supporting a sitting female figure under a richly ornamented canopy holding in her left hand a reversed sceptre & supporting with her right a female child which is resting on her knee – The front of the tomb is adorned with panels having trefoil heads within each of which is a shield, one only of these bears coat armour. That of Courtenay 3 torteaux up a label of 3 points – Between the shafts at the back of the monument & above the effigy are 3 shields 1 Courtenay 2 Quarterly France & England 3 in the centre, Courtenay impaling Quarterly France & England

This beautiful specimen of art has been & still remains considerably defaced but it has been partially & not very judiciously repaired & is now surrounded by a good fence of wood & iron – The cornice of quatrefoils at the top is modern – its whole length is about 4 feet 6 inches. [fence removed]

(*In the margin:* This beautiful monument formerly ornamented on the top with a highly enriched canopy of tabernacle work carved in stone a brass plate with an inscription has recently been affixed to it. 1834. thus inscribed "Margaret daughter of William Courtenay Earl of Devon and the Princess Katherine youngest daughter of Edward. IV king of England died at Colcombe choked by a fish bone A.D. MDXII & was buried under the window in the north transept of this church")

On the south side of the chancel a mural monument of stone an entablature supported by 2 Corinthian capitals beneath which are 1 male & 2 female figures kneeling – they represent William Westofer who is stated to have died in 1622 with his wife and daughter A tablet below is inscribed – Here lies the body of William Drake of Yardbury son of William Drake of Yardbury who lies buried in the Temple church in London and was the son of John Drake of Ash esq: The mother of the said William Drake the son was Margaret the sole daughter & heir of William Westofer of Yardbury gent: & Elizabeth his wife. He died 6 March 1680 in the 51 year of his age. Here also lie Richard, Letitia & Dorothy three of his children – Arms in 4 shields 1 Argent (1) 3 lions rampant Gules? within a bordure engrailed Sable impaling (2) Azure fretty Or within a bordure Argent (Kirkham) 2 Drake a crescent for difference impaling Argent 3 torteaux a chief Gules? 3. as the first coat (1) 4. Drake impaling the first coat (1)

On the chancel floor is a stone to the memory of one of the Marwoods (*in the margin:* – de Ham -- Elizabeth -- obiit 4" et sepultus -- an 169--) the inscription gone but the coat of arms remains – A chevron between 3 goats' heads erased impaling a chevron between 3 swans or pelicans (Qy Mitchel or Cary) Crest on a wreath a goat couchant. [missing] In the floor N aisle. James Marwood of the parish of Widworthy in the co: of Devon gent who died 28 Feb. 1607. [missing] On the floor of the N aisle Geo: Sampson gent buried 7 Jan 1610 aged 33 John Sampson gent his elder brother buried 9 ---1639 aged 67. [missing]

Wall N aisle a marble tablet *M S. Thomae Sampson armigeri. T.S. et Annae uxoris ejus filii unici nati undecimo Calendas Maii CIƆIƆCXLII (1642) denati quarto iduum novembris CIƆIƆCC (1700). Hoc posuit maerens pentissima affectionis ergo illius unica coniux Eleanora.* Arms Azure (Qy Argent) a cross Moline Argent (Qy Azure) impaling Azure a pallet crenelle Argent N aisle a mural tablet – In memory of John Sampson esq who died 18 July 1780 aged 87 also Mary his wife (daughter of Samuel Taner of Crealey in the parish of Farringdon in this county esq) who died 5 Feb 1764 aged 74; Anne their daughter died 7 Oct 1749 aged 21. Anne the wife of Samuel Sampson of the borough of Chard in the co: of Somerset gent their son died 4 Feb 1780 aged 49. The said Samuel Sampson died 11 Dec 1788 aged 62. This monument was erected by the said Samuel Sampson the executer of the said John Sampson anno 1781. Arms. Or a cross Moline Azure impaling Argent 2 bass Gules on a chief of the last 3 mullets of the field

N aisle a mural tablet – In a vault near this place lieth the body of John the eldest son of John Sampson the younger esq. who died 12 March 1792 aged 14. This monument was erected by John Sampson esq his grandfather. Also by his side with the body of the said John Sampson esq. that of his grandfather who died 17 March 1796 aged 76. Arms & crest Sampson – Azure a crop Moline Or

North aisle a mural tablet with an urn. – In memory of Mary Callard widow of John Callard esq; of Ford in the parish of Stockland in the co: of Dorset & daughter of John Sampson esq: who died 11 March 1803 aged 87. Arms. Gironny of 6 Or & sable 3 blackmoors heads proper impaling Argent a crop patinee Gules within a bordure Sable. – [All 13 memorials listed below are missing]

Under the tower on the north side a mural tablet – Sacred to the memory of John Sampson esq. late of this parish Barrister at law & many years one of his Majesty's justices of the peace for this county. He died on the 18 Dec. 1814 aged 59 years. His remains are interred in the vault of his ancestors near this place. – Arms Or a crop Moline Sable. Crest on a wreath a demi lion rampant Argent a sprig of oak

S wall S aisle mural tablets – Sacred to the memory of Mary Warmington 2nd wife of John W. of Colliton gent & daughter of Thomas Wells esq of Southampton who died 17 July 1800 aged 69 & lies interred in a vault underneath. Arms Azure within a bordure Or an inescutcheon. Argent on a chevron bent between 3 martletts sable 5 ermine spots Or a bordure of the fourth – the shield surmounted by an esquires helmet with the crest An a wreath Argent and Vert Out of a ducal coronet Gules an unicorns' head Argent crined & armed Or. –
In memory of John Warmington gent late proctor of this parish who died 15 Nov 1783 aged 61

N wall of chancel a mural tablet. Sacred to the memory of the revd. Geo: Rhodes late vicar of this parish who departed this life on the 15 March 1798 aged 54 he left a widow with six sons & seven daughters. –

S. wall S: aisle a marble tablet and urn inscribed to John Paumier esq. who died 3 March 1798 aged 24. The tablet erected by Sir John William De la Pole Bart; Arms Azure on a chevron 2 locks of hair Sable between 2 roses in chief and an apple leafed in base Or. Crest a demi lion rampant Azure.

Against a column S side of Chancel a tablet to the memory of Joseph Chapman of Cornwall MA erected by his pupil William Walrond of Bradfield esq: died 8 July 1663. Arms above. Or on a chevron gules 3 trefoils & slipped of the field – Arms below - Argent 3 bulls heads caboshed Sable (Walrond) (*in the margin:* see page 124 for this inscription at length)

Chancel floor – Here lieth the body of Elizabeth Long the wife of Joseph Long gent: who died 1 April 1624. Arms a griffin segree between 4 cross crosslets. Impaling a chevron engrailed between 3 garbs a mullet for difference 2 crest 1. Out of a ducal coronet a demi griffin segreant. 2 on a wreath a dove with wings expanded holding in her beak a trefoil slipped

N aisle. Mural tablet Sacred to the memory of Mr Philip Mitchell late of Barrishays in this parish who died 26 June 1800 aged 67 also of Elizabeth Mitchell wife of the above who died Jan 18th 1814 aged 75.

N aisle Mural tablet of marble – Near this place lieth the body of Capt. Henry Wilson who commanded the Honorable East India Company Packet the Antelope when wrecked on the Pelew Islands in August 1783 and was wonderfully preserved with the ship's company amongst strangers in a land unfrequented and unknown. He died 11 May 1810 aged 70. years. –

S. aisle tablet – To the memory of Captain John Batut late of the 14 regiment of foot. This monument is erected by his faithful friend John Piper esq of Colyton with whom he came from London to end his days and died the 2nd Jan 1788 aged 50

S. aisle a tablet with an urn. In memory of John Piper esq. Captain in His Majesty's 6 regiment of foot who after a residence of 14 years died here the 17 June 1801 in the 62nd year of his age. This monument is erected by his disconsolate widow.

S aisle a mural tablet To the memory of the late Mrs Elizabeth Bours of Newport Rhode island North America eminent for her goodness and misfortunes. She died on the 27 Feb. 1806 aged 76 years. This stone was erected by her affectionate grand Nephew Lieutt Col John Piper

In various parts of the floor [all missing] –
Sub hoc lapide reconditae fuerunt reliquiae Edwardi Clarke senioris 30 Maii MDCX.
Here lieth the body of Elizabeth Gye daughter of Edward Clarke buried 22 Nov 1610.
Here lieth the body of Agnes Clarke late wife of Edward Clarke who died 2 July 1616.
--- Stover gent: buried 23 Jan 1610
Edward Croft gent died 27 April 1680
Edward Pratt died 22 Sept 1690
Henry Parsons died 1653 Mary Parsons died 1666. Sarah wife of Thomas Parsons died 1690.
Sarah daughter of Richard Hallaway died 19 July 1661.
MS Annae Mri. Antonii Bartlett uxoris charissimae quae vitam immortalem amplexura mente placida animam suam Deo reddidit. Calendis Octobris 1726 aet. suae 29.
Eleanor Buckland late wife of Hugh B. died 2 Jan 1615
Jane Vye died 9 May 1655. Walter Vye buried 28th August 1672

A tablet against the north wall of the chancel records the following. "Benefactions to the poor of this Parish AD 1812. Extract from the will of Mr Isaac Grigg late of London native of this place "I give and bequeath to the minister and churchwardens of the town of Culliton in the county of Devon for the time being the sum of One Hundred Pounds stock in the 3 per cent Console to be distributed to the poor house-keepers and others of the said town (not receiving alms of the parish) in bread at Christmas for ever. Which sum was first transferred on the 3rd December 1812."

See mention of the revd Geo: Anstis (I think vicar of Colyton) in Dr Stephens will – in Carwithens Exeter charities p 117.
14 Oct 1819 To be sold. Manor of Down Umfraville &c. in the par. of Axmouth – Manor of Ottery &c – manor of Northleigh &c – Mansion called Colyton house late the residence of John Mountstephen How esq. His property. Meriv: coll: mem: book 1.
To be sold in fee. – Estate called Kingsdown in the parish of Colyton. 4 m from Sidmouth. 6 from Honiton 16 from Exeter now & for several years in the occupancy of the owner – Farm house cottages &c. – 220 acres of arable meadow pasture & orchard & about 80 acres of coppice wood & plantations
Mr. White solicitor Yeovil – Sherborne Mercury 26 Oct 1829

Colyford Havene – See deed of 1381 in Comb Pyne & other deeds for Colyton among those for Combe Pyne

(*In the margin:* In Colyton church yard an altar tomb recently erected & thus inscribed "In memory of Frances Camilla Payne who died Nov 28. 1826 aged 40 years." – "To the memory of Georgina Maria Payne daughter of William Payne esq. and Frances Camilla his wife who died June 23 1844 aged 17 years.")

Mr Stirling has also the following notes of inscriptions in Colyton Church –
South Aisle a flat stone "*Johis Trethelke qui obiit – die iiis Januarii ano Dni M° CCCCCXIV*"
In the robing room. A flat stone "Here lies John Wilkins minister of this place from Sept. 19. 1647 until the 24 of Aug. 1667.
Such pillars layd aside
How can the church abide
He left his Pulpit, he
In Patmos God to see
This shining light can have
No place to preach but i' grave
Left wife, 2 sonnes & 4 daughters
Mary layd here 8 weeks after. [missing]

"Richard Wykesland vicair delglise de Colyton" Deed of 1383 – See Collections p. 106 – Deed for Combe Pyne
Richard Buller, vicar of Colyton, son of William Buller. Bishop of Exeter –

Arms and inscription in the east window Colyton church.
I Lozenges or & vert on a bend azure 3 Bezants. Impaling
1. Ermine on a bend cotised Sable, 3 Griffins heads erased or. langued gules Yonge
2. Argent a Saltier couped Sable, on a chief gules a Leopard's face or.
II Argent on a Chevron azure 3 Fishes Hauriant of the field (qy or) impaling Fissacre.
Argent 3 eagles displayed gules Doddiscombe or Newenham
III The Royal arms
VI. Or 3 Torteaux Courtenay
VII. A coat evidently made up of fragments: partly Yonges.
IX. Or 3 Torteaux (Courtenay) impaling
Argent a Chevron between 3 Conies sable. (Strode)
On a label at the bottom "*In honorem Dei et Domini nostri Jesu Christi, ecclesia prius auctor et restaurata fenestram hanc. dat dedicat. Fredericus Barnes. S.T.P. vicarius A.D. MDCCCXXIX.*" [missing]

Chancel floor, *Exit vias hic suas Henricus et Maria Parsoniics ille anno 1653 haec anno 1666 utrique spe firma resurrectionis futurae vitae aeternae deposuerunt. Hic suas denique viz ano 1690 Sara uxor Thomae Parsonii eadem spe deposuit.* [missing]

On the wall of the tower a hatchment put up lately (1843) for Wedriver Quarterly creneled or and ermine an eagle displayed sable beaked gules. (Piper) impaling Azure 2 chevrons or.

(*In the margin:* In a window in the passage at the vicarage house is this coat & date. Gules a fess within a border engrailed ermine 1635. In a window of the dining room among other devices that of Thomas Arcrurrel and one of W Herm the letter W & a heron. The arms of Bishop Veysey and a figure of St Andrew with his cross & the words Sancta Andrea ora pro nobis. The porch with its little study over it looking onto the garden walk has a motto in front *Meditatio totum pedicatio totum'* and the date 1529.)

At Colcombe house or castle near Colyton, the few windows which remain in the ancient part of the building now rapidly falling to decay are large, comprising each 3 lights the heads of which form flat arches – they are each surmounted by a rectangular label or weather moulding which rests at either side on a carved corbel, those which remain represent, one an eagle with wings displayed, one a shield – one a female head and three of them seem to designate a faggot or bundle of sticks bound together – Query, whether this had any reference to armorial bearings or a cognizance. I think something similar is represented on one of the shields of the parapet which surmounts the north aisle of Axminster church. This part of the building is said to have been erected by Sir W Pole the distinguished antiquary who died in 1635 & such devices would scarcely have adorned a building under his superintendence without a meaning.
See notice of the families of Basset & Courtenay with mention of Colcombe in History of Cachampton p. 342

Tablet on the pier south of the chancel Colyton church – some words doubtful
Memoriae sacrum viri moribus admodum imbuti et uiter acutioris literaturae
proceres olim insignis Josephi Chapman generosi Cornubiensis et artium magistri
gui tam cum qeneri planctu quam amicorum singultu plurimo tantillus ad huc annis
a terrenis hisce nexibus expeditus spiritum cretis famam saeculis et exuvias hic
alieno reliquit sole mense
Ita interioris observantiae et amoris
Ergo posuit ejus maxime dilectus
Sic et minime dignus quondam pupillus
Gulielmus Walrond de Bradfield armiger
Qui sopitos debitus dudum nec inmerito
Sparsit tandem cineres lachrymantis mense Iulii 8 1663 [missing]

SHUTE

Davidson (pp. 125–30) visited [St Michael] Shute in 1828 and noted it was 'about 3 miles west of Axminster 1 mile south of the high road to Honiton'. He observed the church of this hamlet was a chapelry dependent on Colyton, and was 'situated within the boundaries of Shute Park and ¼ mile west of Shute House the residence of Sir William Templer Pole Bart. The ancient residence of the Bonvilles is near the church on the south side & and the western gate of Shute Park is close to the church yard.' The church was restored in 1869 by Edward Ashworth (Pevsner, *Devon*, 731).

This church consists of a nave chancel N & S transepts a north aisle & an aisle or chapel adjoining the chancel on the N side which is appropriated to the monuments of the Pole family & beneath which is the vault for their interment a tower which is 14 feet 6in square outside the walls is placed at the intersection of the nave & transepts & it is 43 feet high to the top of the battlements of which the corners are surmounted by pinnacles & each of these by a vane.

The nave is 41 feet long by 20 wide and is divided from the N aisle by 2 columns & 2 halves consisting of alternate shafts & hollow mouldings & having a sort of non descript laminated capitals it is lighted by a window at the W end with a lancet arch & divided into 3 lights. The font which stands at the western end is octangular & is adorned with quatrefoils it rests on a plain modern column. The pulpit is of mahogany ornamented in the Grecian style [now stone] & a brass chandelier of several branches hangs from the roof.

The chancel is 24½ long by 14½ wide & is separated from the adjoining aisle by a clustered column & 2 halves supporting 2 pointed arches of early date & having angular capitals adorned with foliage and shields at the corners apparently of the same date as those of the chancel in Colyton church.

The eastern window is modern though in the pointed style having 3 lights with cinquefoil heads & is adorned with modern painted glass as are also parts of the other windows of the church which appear to be new & of similar design.

The Pole aisle or chapel adjoining the chancel is 20 feet by 12 & is enclosed by an iron railing being exclusively appropriated to the monuments of the Pole family is lighted by a window of 3 lights with cinquefoil heads at the western end & opens to the N transept by an arch resting on 2 half columns similar in date & design to that against the chancel.

The north transept is 13 feet long by 15 wide & is occupied by pews, the south transept is 17 long by 15 wide & is occupied part of it by a vestry & the remainder a large pew for the Pole family over which is a carving of the Pole arms painted & gilded [removed], the transepts have windows at the ends of 3 lights with pointed heads & tracery but their ornamental sweeps have been destroyed.

The north aisle is 36 feet long by 13.6 wide & appears to have been recently enlarged to which perhaps this inscription against the gallery across the western end of the church refers. "This church was enlarged by voluntary contribution in the year of our Lord 1811". The openings to the tower are 4 lancet shaped arches supported in front by 8 cylindrical columns with plain circular capitals having a slight hatched ornament. There are 5 bells all dated 1761 3 of them having inscriptions as follow "The rev George Anstis vicar T.B. fecit" – "My triple voice your hearts rejoice" "Thomas Bilbee Cullompton fecit" –

The exterior of the church presents no remarkable feature, a porch protects the south door & there are plain crosses at the eastern gables. –

The monuments and inscriptions are these.
On the floor of the chancel
--- Penelope the second daughter of Sir Courtenay Pole Bart: the wife of the Honourable Francis Roberts of Lampydrick in Cornwall esq. she died ---- elsey in the Lord Radnor's house 2 July and was interred here the 31st of the same month 1680. Arms 3 stars 2 & 1 on a chief wavy a mullet impaling Pole. –

In the Pole aisle
A whole length statue capitally executed in white marble holding the wand of office & habited in a rich court dress the ornamental pedestal which supports it is thus inscribed "Sir William Pole Bart Master of the household to her late majesty Queen Anne of ever glorious memory Dyed 31 Dec 1741 aged 63"

N Transept A white marble mural tablet & urn
MS. Elizabethae (Amicarum optimae) Georgii Anstis Clerici vidua Johannis Gulielmus de la Pole Baronettus Animo Hoc Marmor gratissime posuit Vitam Aug. 11. 1780 Aet 52
Humanam reliquit vivere. Teste caelo.
Arms in a lozenge. Argent a cross saguly Gules between 4 larks or doves Azure impaling Pole.
East end of Pole aisle a mural tablet "Memoriae sacrum Jacobi Templer Armigeri Johannes Gulielmus Pole Baronettus Hoc Posuit Ob 4 March 1782"
E end of the same aisle. A tablet with a medallion representing a shipwreck surmounted by an urn.
Consurgunt naute et magno clamore morantur fractosque legunt in gurgite remos"
Virg:
Sacred to the memory of Charles Bickford Templer who on the 6th night of January 1786 perished in the Halsewell East Indiaman in Studland Bay. This monument in testimony of mutual regard between the unhappy victim and his tributary friend and brother is erected by Sir John William Pole Bart: Obiit Aº aet: 16 Arms Templer

South wall of the chancel a white marble tablet with an urn at the top & fascis at the sides the work of P. Rouw sculptor London
"Sacred to the memory of Sir John William de la Pole Baronet of Shute House in the county of Devon Lieutenant Colonel of the Royal last Devon Cavalry who departed this life on the 30 Nov 1799 in the 42nd year of his age"
--- He was educated at the collage of Winton & Corpus Christi in Oxon. His ancestor obtained an hereditary title for his family from the hands of King Charles the first. -
--- he rebuilt the dilapidated mansion of his forefathers &c."

In the Pole aisle a tablet – "To the memory of John George Pole who was suddenly attacked with a violent fever on the 26 Aug 1803 which carried him off in the 16th year of his age."

Against the S wall of the chancel. A white marble tablet with a sitting infant figure the work of R Westmacott RA sculptor London inscribed.

Within this chancel lie the remains of Anne widow of the Honorable Reginald Cocks he was the youngest son of Charles Lord Somers by Anne daughter of Reginald Pole esq. of this county. She was the second daughter of James Cocks esq by Martha daughter of Vice Admiral Watson. A fatally rapid decline deprived her (when but lately a wife) of a beloved husband he died under her tenderest care at Flushing in Cornwall Nov 20th 1805. and after a short interval of patient affliction the same disorder united her to him in death. She died at Sidmouth in this county March 19th AD 1810 aged 28 years leaving one orphan son Henry Somers Cocks. – As a record of the exemplary discharge of conjugal and maternal virtues and in gratitude for the exertion of them towards a beloved son and grandson Anne dowager Lady Somers has caused this stone to be inscribed to the memory of a lamented daughter.

North side of the Pole aisle a beautiful monumental tablet of white marble representing in relief an angel conveying a female to heaven. inscribed to

Sophia Anne wife of Sir William Templer Pole Bart only daughter of George Templer esquire who in the flower of her youth aged 20 years departed this life 17 March 1808. She had issue 1 daughter and 2 sons Sophia Anne born 11 June 1805 died 12 June 1806. John George born 21 Jan 1808. Her disconsolate husband consecrates this monument. There follows some excellent verses.

Chancel floor – Abigail Purse wife of Daniel Purse died 3 Jan 1734 aged 38.

South wall of nave. Underneath this stone are interred the remains of John Clapp of Hampton in the parish who died 6 July 1788 aged 27.

D[o] – Stephen Smith son of Francis Smith born at Smittens Pit in this parish died in St Martin's le Grand London the 8 Jan 1815 aged 83 and gave by will dated the 14 Nov 1802 £20 the interest thereof to be laid out in 20 threepenny loaves of bread to be given four times a year to 20 poor persons of the parish of Shute such as the minister and churchwardens shall deem proper.

The armorial bearings in Shute church are as follows

A hatchment for Lady Pole – Pole impaling Templer. Supporting Dexter a buck attained Or. Sinister a Grey Heron armed & gorged with a ducal coronet Or eyed & lanqued gules. –

Over the family pew in the S transept – the Pole arms.

The E window of the NE aisle is richly ornamented with painted glass & contains three coats. –

In the centre a coat with the date 1808 viz.

Pole. Quarterly 1&4 Azure semee of fleurs de lis Or, a lion rampant Argent. 2&3. Ermine a per de Moulin in pale Sable, an escutcheon of pretence the arms of Ulster impaling Templer. Viz. Quarterly Azure and Gules on the first quarter an eagle displayed Or, on the second a buck trippant Or. M base on a mound bent a temple Argent with a crop on the summit Or.

Crest on a wreath Argent and Azure a lion's paw Gules. Motto Pollet virtus. beneath its coat as follows

Quarterly of 19

1. Pole
2. Argent a chevron sable between 3 bucks heads caboshed Gules
3. Gules 3 cocks 2&1 Argent
4. Or a stags face 2&1 Gules (Pole)
5. Barry of 11 Argent & azure
6. a Maunche a label of 3 pointed Gules
7. Argent 3 Saltier Sable 2&1 (Tracy)
8. Argent a saltier Gules within a bordure sable. bezanted
9. Argent a fess between 3 bears passant Sable (Okebere)
10. Sable 6 mullets. 3. 2&1 Argent a label of 3 points Gules (Bonville)
11. Sable a Poppy with roots and fruit Or (Dela Ford)
12. Argent on a chief indented Sable 3 crop crosslets fitches Or, (Orivey)
13. Argent 2 chevrons sable (Esie, de Esme or Ash)
14. Ermine 3 Bars Azure (Offwell)
15. Argent a lion rampant Gules (Nonant)
16. Gules a chevron engrailed between 3 leopards faces Or (Periam)
17. Argent a chevron Sable (27 Azure) between 3 pears pendant Gules (Periham)
18. Argent 2 bends wavy between 3 billets in fess Sable
19. Argent a fess engrailed between 3 wolves heads erased Sable langued Gules.
Motto *Pollet virtus*
On the north side of the window appears an ancient coat Pole Bart. Impaling Sable a chevron (or) between 3 doves – cots Argent (Shapcott)
Baronet helmet Crest on a wreath Argent and Azure a lions' paw Or. Motto *Pollet virtus*.
On the So: side of the window an ancient coat.
Azure 3 stars 2&1 Or. on a chief wavy of the second a mullet sable. Crest On a wreath Or & azure a lion rampant or holding a sword Argent hilted of the first broken & from it a flame issuant also of the first. A mullet sable for difference

1845: In the east window of the south transept is a Coat of arms in stained glass which appears to have been recently erected viz. Quarterly azure and gules, on the 1st quarter a Spread eagle or, on the 2nd a Stag al gage gules, in base of 3&4 a Templer argent – impaling.
Argent two bars sable a Canton of the last.
On a quarter round the coat the inscription "Templer esq. Shapwick co. Somerset 1794" For grant to the church of Shute see Collection for East of Devon p 267

The church of Shute is a chapelry of ease annexed to the vicarage of Colyton but now burials are used here. Survey of 1704 penes I A Frampton esq

MONKTON

Davidson (pp. 131–2) visited [St Mary Magdalene] Monkton on 14 September 1829. The church was rebuilt by John Hayward in 1863 (Pevsner, *Devon*, 574). It is now a private dwelling, so it is not possible to ascertain if the two memorials Davidson recorded are missing.

This chapel consists only of a nave & chancel with a tower at the western end – the length inside is 39 feet of which the nave is 23 the chancel 16, the width 16 feet. The eastern window has 3 lights with cinquefoil heads & the tracery of the arch is of the perpendicular style, the other windows have 3 lights without sweeps under flat heads. a pointed arch divides the nave & tower panelled in its archivolt, the pulpit is modern. The ceiling is coved & ribbed with foliage at the intersections – In the south wall of the chancel is a square locker – The porch has a holy water basin in a square niche on the eastern side. The font is of stone octagonal 2 feet in diameter 3 feet 4 in: high it is carved in quatrefoils & foliage & rests on an octagonal column adorned with panels forming trefoil headed arches: In front of a singers gallery at the western end of the nave is the arms of Southcott Argent Gules between 3 coots proper On a wreath Argent & Gules a coot. – The east window contains stained glass with the following devices in shields but query whether they represent the coat armorial of any families.
Argent a saltier Azure
Azure 2 chevrons Or
Quarterly &4 Or a bend Azure 2&3 Argent a fess Azure
Quarterly 1 & 4 Barry of 4 Argent & Gules 2 & 3 Argent a crop vert.
Arms painted on one of the panels of a few against the south wall. – Azure semee of fleurs de lis Or a lion rampant Argent (Pole) impaling sable on a crop quarter pureed Argent 4 eagles displayed on the fifth. (Buller)
an esquire helmet Crest on a wreath Azure & Gules
a lion paw erected & erased Or – Supported Dexter side
a stag gules. Sinister a griffon argent gorged to a ducal Coronet Or – Motto Toied virtus (for *Pollet virtus*)

On the chancel floor. Thomas Southcote late of Mohun's Ottery esq died 19 Sept 1699. Arms a chevron between 3 coots impaling Ermine on a bend cotised 3 Griffons heads erased (Yonge)
Nave floor. William Southcote esq. died 7 May 1679 Prudence his wife died 2 Feb 1676 Katherine their daughter in 1688.
The tower is embattled, with half an hexagonal turret on the south side for the stair case, it contains 3 bells & appears to be about 35 feet high.

SEATON

Davidson (pp. 132–41) visited [St Gregory] Seaton in 1828. The church was partly demolished in 1817 for an extension to the west gallery, and then restored in 1868 by Edward Ashworth with further restoration in 1901, with a new roof, pulpit, font and clergy desk (Pevsner, *Devon*, 721). Two memorials are missing from the sixteen that Davidson recorded.

The parish church consists of a nave chancel & 2 side aisles but it has undergone various additions & alterations at different periods – The nave is about 50 feet long by 20 wide but it was evidently at one time as wide as the chancel which is about 25 feet long & 13ft.6in wide, these as well as both aisles appear to have been erected about the same period perhaps the middle of the 15th century. The north aisle is called Walrond aisle & was built by that family as their arms appear on a shield held by an angel forming a corbel to one of the windows – the entrance to this aisle was by a door at the east end now walled up but visible on the outside, above it is a window which appears to be of earlier date than any others in the church & perhaps was removed thither when the aisle was built it may be referred to the 13 century – from this aisle there is an opening made through the wall of the church to view the altar. The south aisle is called Starrs' aisle & was no doubt built by an individual of that family which was one of considerable opulence in the place but it is now extinct. From this aisle also an opening has been made through the walls to gain a sight of the altar – on the south side of the chancel is a plain piscina under a pointed arch & in the window on the north side two relics of stained glass representing a lamb & an eagle both with the nimbus [missing] – At the western end of the nave is a low & inelegant tower of the same date embattled & having at the south eastern corner an octangular stair-turret – there are 4 bells. –
A large font which appears to be coeval with the present church has been removed & lays in ruins in the belfry – it consists of a heavy square basin of stone & was supported by an octangular column ornamented with cinquefoil headed arches – it has been replaced by a small dish of black marble [now an octangular font] –

The living of Seaton & Beer is a vicarage the present incumbent the revd R. Cutcliffe. –The registers of baptisms marriages & burials commence in 1583 are in tolerable preservation & are almost uninterrupted to the present time. – Sir Isaac Heard, Garter, had there to London such extracts such as he thought proper. It is at present in contemplation to enlarge the church by lengthening the north aisle at the eastern end an addition has been made of this north aisle at the western end as is thus recorded on a stone fixed in the wall "This aisle and gallery were built at the expense of Lord and lady Rolle for the accommodation of their Beer tenants AD 1817." Against the wall hangs a board with a piece of parchment upon it but torn & in decay with the following. Memorandum "A list of part of the seats and sittings in Seaton church taken this day of Dec. 1817" – then follows the names of persons
The following are the monuments & monumental inscriptions in Seaton church.

North aisle

In the north eastern corner a mural monument probably of marble but much defaced with whitewash – it consists of a pediment supported by two Corinthian columns between which is the kneeling figure of a man in half armour with trunk hose in the attitude of prayer at a desk an open book at a desk beneath him is the following inscription

Epitaph on the death of Edmund Walrond of Bovey esq. who was buried Sept 19 anno Domini 1640 aetat suae 48 Composed and set up by Anne Walrond his wife.

Here lieth the body of my husband deare
Whom next to God I did both love and feare
Our loves were simple we never had but one
And so I'll bee although that thou art gone
And you that shall this sad inscription view
Remember it allwaies that deaths' your due.

On the top are 3 coats of arms the principal one is

Walrond impaling what appears to be a lion rampant but this with the other two are so buried in whitewash as not to be deciphered. Crest seems to be some animal head erased. As not to be deciphered.

North aisle
On the north wall a tablet

"Sacred to the memory of William Walrond esq who died at Bovey in 1762 aged 45 years and his first wife and infant son, also of Sarah Oke his second wife by whom he had issue Sarah, Courtenay – William, and Judith – Maria, of these the last and only surviving one wife of John Rolle esq. MP for Devon erected this monument in respect to the best parents and at the request of her mother who departed this life Feb 1st 1787. aged 67."

Arms above in stone – (Walrond) impaling Oke –

A hatchment – Argent 3 bulls heads caboshed Sable 2&1 attired Or, Walrond impaling Sable a chevron between 3 oak slips acorned Or. (Oke) Crest a wolf sejant tenny langued Or.

On the north wall a tablet

Sacred to the memory of William Henry Paulson Midshipman of His Majesty's Ship Queen Charlotte who with eight seamen all volunteers perished in a gale of wind off Sidmouth whilst cruising in a galley for the prevention of smuggling on the 13 June 1817 in the 23rd year of his age.

It was God's high will that in the prime of youth
The hand of death should whelm him in the wave
His will be done! But know the eternal truth
Redeeming mercy triumphs o'er the grave.

On the floor – "Anna Francklyn" date etc gone.

Chancel
On the north wall a tablet

To the memory of W Jonathan Bawden Salt officer, he was born at West Lowe in Cornwall of which he was several times mayor. He was a person very pious honest and generous. He died to the great grief of his friends Dec 24 1726 aetat: sue 66 and was buried near this wall.

On the south wall a tablet

Near this place lieth interred the body of Abraham Sydenham of this parish Salt officer which office he enjoyed 40 years. He died Nov 12th 1748 aged 69. Also body of Sarah Sydenham his wife she died Nov 15th 1748 aged 64.

On the floor a defaced stone.

-- "who was unfortunately drowned 22nd day of Oct 1646."

South aisle

On the south wall a tablet

Sacrum memoriae of Capt Timothy Head aged 26 years whose remains were deposited in this church on the 19 Feb 1806. This marble is erected by his relations Joseph Horsford esq of Weymouth as a mark of esteem and regard for his worth.

The following are in the nave but were removed from the south aisle –

A stone with part of an inscription covered by a pew. At the top is represented a star & then "John Starr Anagram Starr on here should be yet underneath A Starr doth sleeping in yet shall he more glorious. The starres in A^{o}. aetat 49 & January. Jann Haec 1633 for his sep 12. 9bris, A 16. conjugalis a ergo pose Elizabetha St

Robert sonne of --- Starr died 30 June 1651 [missing]

Susanna wife of Robert Starr bur 30 March 1643, Mr Henry Starr her son who died 17 April 1659."

In the south aisle – on the floor Jane Starr buried 27 Sept 1670 Priscilla Starr buried 4 May 1653 also her sister – Twigges Dec 1689 [missing]

Nave on the south wall a tablet

"In memory of Richard Kettle late of this parish who died 14 Feb 1787 aged 35 years Beneath from all the pains of life and care lies the kind husband and a father dear ennobled by the virtues of his mind. Constant in goodness and to death resigned"

On the floor

"--- wife of Edward Maston"

The pew in the nave formerly occupied by the family of Waldron had an entrance from the north aisle and is surmounted by a kind of canopy carved in oak with foliage of vines & coats of arms – which are as follows commencing at the western end [missing, now two pieces of carved wood in two glass cases]

1. Arg. 3 bulls heads caboshed 2&1 sable armed Gules a crest gules for difference Waldron impaling Azure: a lion rampant Argent lanqued & armed Gules
2. Gules a pair of couples Argent
3. Waldron as before
4. Sable 3 fishes lanqued in fess Argent
5. as N° 1
6. Waldron impaling Azure a stags head caboshed Argent
7. Waldron impaling – party of a chevron gules in chief Waldron & in base Azure a stags head caboshed Argent.
8. Waldron impaling Gules 2 demi lions passant gardant in pale sable.
9. Argent a spread eagle Sable (2nd Worth)
10. Waldron
11. Argent a knot azure

Above is a hatchment Waldron impaling vert. 3 trefoils slipped argent on a chief indented Gules 2 annulets

Or. – crest a wolf segant argent langued Gules.

Among the inscriptions in the churchyard are the following

A stone with the representation of a vessel well carved on it underneath are the words "The Fly" & as follows

"Sacred to the memory of Robert Lippen late Seaman of his Majesty's sloop Fly Zachary Mudge esq. Commander who departed this life the 12th May 1799 aged 41 years

Tho' Boreas blasts and Neptune's waves
Have tossed me too and fro
Yet now am I by Gods' decree
At anchor here below
And thus at last am safely moored
With many of our fleet
Yet once again I must set sail
My admiral Christ to meet

In remembrance of and to shew respect to British Seamen this stone is erected at the sole expense of his shipmates."

Henry Brown died 1 Sept. 1823 aged 41.
If I had virtues imitate them – if vices reject them
Thou art gone to the grave and it's wrong to deplore thee
Since God was thy ransom, thy guardian thy guide
He gave thee and took thee and soon will restore thee
Where death hath no sting since the Saviour hath died.

Originalia. 38 Hen 8. 64. 10 Aug. (1546) (From the Merivale MSS)
Rep concess. John Frye gent. Maria de Maynbowe et (query Membury)
Seaton & rest. De Seton &.

See Beare.
11 Jac I. P5. 48. *Hic. Waltero Yonge gen alien rect & eccl de Seaton & Beere Wmo Fry sen Gen & Marie ux.*

Calend: inquis p. m: sive escaet: Vol. 2.
Page 119. 18 Edw 3. (1344) no 18. *Gilbertus de Umfrevill feoffavit Adam de Tetbourn psonam eccl de Coumbe pyne Toryton manor 5ta pars. – (Combe pyne manor' Doune – Umfrevill & Seton terr & ten' &c remanent eidem Gilberto.)* – Devon.
21 Sept 1450 (29 Hen 6) Bishop Lacy granted 40 days indulgence to true penitents who should contribute to the works *"in novu portu in littore maris apud Seton"*

Memorandum: by rev: Geo: Oliver
The remains of a harbour may still be traced at Seaton in the form of a ditch which runs from the beach about ¼ mile inland as far as the church & is called "Merchants roads." – On sinking a well near this towards the beach several successive layers of beach & mud were penetrated which seems to prove that the harbour was choked by successive irruptions of the sea beach covering the preceding deposit of alluvial soil –

For several deeds relating to Seaton see those of Combe Pyne. –
"Ada capno de Setum qui hunc carta composuit" deed without date for Upottery.

BEER

Davidson (pp. 143–4) visited [St Michael] Beer on 20 February 1829 and noted it was 1¼ mile south west of Seaton. He observed that this was a chapelry to Seaton parish church and 'of a very early date & of small dimensions'. A new church was built 1876–7 by Hayward & Son and paid for by Mark Rolle (Pevsner, *Devon*, 161). Therefore Davidson's record is a unique account of what was there in 1829 and the two memorials.

The chapel consisted only a nave & chancel, the former 27 feet long by 12 wide the latter 17 by 12 within the walls, but there have been aisles added on the north & south sides both of which are more than twice the size of the original structure & with the galleries will accommodate perhaps 10 times the number of people, these aisles are evidently of modern date as the columns & arches are in an incongruous style not agreeing with that of the nave & chancel which seem to have been built in the 13th or 14th century – the windows east & west & the arch dividing the chancel & nave are lancet shaped, the east window has 3 lights acutely pointed & has modern stained glass the arch is supported by shafts with circular capitals. The pulpit is modern as is the font which is a basin on a column of stone both fluted & of small size. The communion plate consists of a flagon cup & plate of silver presented by Lady Rolle & dated 1784. In the wall at the east end of the north aisle is a tablet inscribed "John the fifth son of William Starr of Beer gent and Dorothy his wife which died in the plague was here buried 1646."
West wall of the chancel – "Near this place lie the remains of Edward Good late an industrious fisherman who left to the vicar & churchwardens for the time being and their successors for ever Twenty Pounds in trust for the poor of this parish the interest to be distributed annually at Christmas in the proportion of two thirds at Beer and one at Seaton. He died Nov 7th 1804 in the 67th year of his age" [missing] Against the east wall of the south isle is a hatchment for the late Lady Rolle – the arms of Rolle with those of Waldron in an escutcheon of pretence [missing].

Worship is performed at this chapel by the vicar of Seaton – & there is a Sunday evening lecture founded by the late Lady Rolle and now supplied by the revd. John Medley curate of Southleigh (afterwards Bishop of Fredericton.)
On the top of the water conduit at the head of the principal street is an ancient stone cross which was perhaps brought from the church.

Originalia (from the Merivale MSS.)
7.E.6. 22. 3rd Mar: (1553) R. con Johe & Niclo Hassard man' de Bere.
12. Eliz. P. 3. 137. (1570) Pdon alien mess &c in Beer &c. quam Andreas Willoughbie gent fecit William Pole ar.
33. Eliz. 52. (1591) Lic Willo Poole ar & Marie ux alien ½ 20 mess in Beere Johe Walrond gen.

33. Eliz. P.2. 123 Lic Willo Poole ar & Marie ux alien mess in Beer & Seaton John Younge & hs.

9 Jac.1 P4. 86. Perd. alien tr in Beere Seaton & Colyton Johes Walrond ar & Jana ux Johi Natch ar & al.

The fisheries & saltponds at Beer & Seaton belonged to the abbey of Sherborne. See Hutchins II. 375.

NORTHLEIGH

Davidson (pp. 147–9) visited [St Giles] Northleigh on 15 September 1829. The chancel was rebuilt 1858 and restored in 1868–9 with new windows and roof by C.F. Edwards of Axminster (Pevsner, *Devon*, 601). One memorial is missing from the five that Davidson recorded.

This church consists of a nave 30 feet long by 15 wide, a chancel 17½ by 13 a north aisle 45 by 10 & a tower at the western end of the nave 8 feet long by 9 wide. The total length of the church within the walls is 80 feet The nave & chancel appear ancient, the south door is under a plain semicircular arch resting on an impost moulding supported by 2 capitals one of them plain the other ornamented with a sort of Ionic volute, the shafts have been removed but the circular bases remain – This is no doubt a vestige of the 11th or 12 century – The eastern window of the chancel is formed into 3 lancet pointed lights by mullions which intersect each other in the heads of the arch, the whole is without sweeps & is a specimen of the style of the 13 century. – The side windows of the chancel are also of early date they have 2 lights with trefoil heads & a quatrefoil in the arch. The nave opens to the aisle by 3 low pointed arches resting on columns formed by 4 shafts with intervening hollow mouldings the capitals are quadrangular & ornamented with sculptured foliage. The chancel opens to the nave & to the aisle by pointed arches having panels in their archivolts but the upper part of that next the nave has been destroyed, a lofty pointed arch opens to the tower. The east & west windows of the aisle have 3 lights with cinquefoil heads & perpendicular tracery in the arches which are low, that of the tower is similar but the arches of the lights are of the ogee form – the windows of the nave & the side of the aisle have flat heads & are divided into cinquefoil headed lights, there are some fragments of stained glass in the windows of the aisle & in one of them the lower parts of the figures of St Peter with the keys St James with a book & staff & between them an abbot or bishop with a crosier in his left hand his right uplifted with one finger erect in the attitude of benediction. There are 2 rings on his fingers, these figures have been done in capital style & the colours are rich – The tower is embattled & has half an octagonal turret at the north east corner for the staircase it is 43 feet high to the top of the battlements It contains 4 bells all of ancient date & bearing inscriptions in relief in the old letter one of them is "✝" *Sce Petr* e *"ora pro nobis"* another something like this "✝ *Est ---- collatum nomen amatum –*"

The remains of a beautiful screen stand between the nave & chancel it was formed by a range of pointed arches but their tracery is wholly destroyed, the upper is richly spread into tracery & foliage & the front is adorned with mouldings of rich foliage & quatrefoils this seems to have been an early specimen of screens & to have been beautifully executed, a screen of later date parts the eastern end of the aisle its arched openings have cinquefoil heads & it is adorned with mouldings of foliage but much inferior to the other design & execution. – There is a piscina in the south wall of the chancel with a trefoil head under an ogee arch. The font is ancient a square block of stone with two of the corners cut off 2 feet in diameter standing on a heavy square column with 4 cylindrical shafts at the corners having circular capitals & bases, it is 4 feet high & the cavity is lined with lead. The pulpit is modern of oak – some oaken benches remain in the nave their ends carved in trefoil headed panels & roses.

On the floor of the aisle are the following inscriptions
Here lieth -- of -- Marwood gent who died the 2nd day of July Anno Dom 16-- in the old characters Frances M. relict of John Marwood of Blamphayne gent died 5 April 1700 aged 71 [missing]
John Marwood of Blamphayne gent died 9 Aug, 1671
Edward Searle jun. buried Feb 3.1680.
A marble tablet against the wall. Robert Underdown esq. of this parish died 2 April 1811 aged 57 yrs.
A tomb in the church yard. Samuel Underdown esq. of Widworthy Barton died March 28 1812 aged 51 years also Thomas Sarah Abraham Henrietta sons and daughters of the above died in their infancy.

Against the south wall of the nave is a wooden label thus inscribed
Donations given to the parish of Northleigh
Eight acres of land in the parish of Northleigh vested in feoffees the rents of which are to be distributed among the industrious poor of the said parish under the directions of the feoffees
The rev. James How gave by will the sum of £200 stock in the 4 percent consols for ever since transferred to the 3 percents vested in the rector churchwardens & overseers of the poor (for the time being) the interest of £100 for the establishment & support of a Sunday school in the parish aforesaid and the interest of the other £100 to be distributed in bread and money every year on Christmas day to the poor of the parish only £25 of the above £200 were sunk in the payment of the legacy duty the expenses of the transfer &c. –

Newspaper cutting, no name of newspaper, dated April 1828:
The Perpetual Advowson of the Rectory of North Leigh, in a beautiful part of the County of Devon, to be sold by Private Contract.
North Leigh is three and a half miles from Honiton and Colyton, and seven from Sidmouth. House quite new, but small; Incumbent in his 70th year. The Glebe consists of 47 acres, and with the Tithe is worth 270l. Taxes, &, About 30l.
Apply, if by letter, post paid, to N.L., care of Mr. Hatchard, 187 Piccadilly, from whom further particulars may be known.

Stephanus psona de Northleghe 1381. See deed of this date for Sparkhayes in Colyton. The lord of this manor is patron of the church of Northleigh valued at £80 per ann: Survey of 1704 penes I.A. Frampton esq.

SOUTHLEIGH

Davidson (pp. 151–4) visited [St Lawrence] Southleigh on 15 September 1829. The chancel was rebuilt in 1852–4 by T.T. Bury, and general restorations were carried out in 1880 by Hayward (Pevsner, *Devon*, 747). Five memorials are missing from the six that Davidson recorded.

The church of this sequestered and beautiful parish consists of a nave 29 feet long by 16 wide a chancel 10½ by 16 and a tower at the western end 9.9in: by 10.3 wide the wall between it & the nave is 2.3 in thickness so that the total length inside is 51 feet 6 inches – An aisle recently built on the south side is 42 feet long by 16 wide & is separated from the nave & chancel only by wooden pillars without arches which support the roof [now stone]. The nave chancel & tower seem to have been erected in the 15 century the east & west windows have each 3 lights with cinquefoil heads & perpendicular tracery in the arches, the other windows have been modernized – those of the new aisle have each 2 lights with rounded heads but seem wholly deficient in taste. The pulpit is modern as is also a gallery extending across the western end of the church this latter has a clock in front of it [both removed]. The east window is entirely blocked up by a wooden altar screen & by a large picture over it representing the wise men's offering to the infant Jesus – This painting seems well executed but is rapidly going to decay in consequence of the damp [removed], it was the gift of Mr How of Wiscombe park as was also a brass chandelier of 24 lights hanging from the roof – this gentleman is said to have been an attorney & to have previously resided at Chard. – The font is a small wooden bowl on a pedestal [changed]. The ancient one an interesting relic stands in its primitive position in the north east corner of the basement of the tower, it has a bracket immediately over it perhaps for an image, it is cut from a block of stone, square & 2 feet in diameter each side adorned with a range of 4 semicircular arches on plain columns without capitals, it is lined with lead & rests on a circular column with a square base adorned with a moulding, and a step – its total height is 3½ feet of which the step is 9 inches. The church plate consists of 2 silver patens and a silver chalice all without date on the largest paten is the cipher b13 well engraved with motto *Omne solum forte patria* – The register of Baptisms Marriages & Burials all commence in 1718 – The following names & dates of incumbents are therein mentioned John French rector 1721-1725 G Blagdon rector 1726. Richard Priest rector 1748-1772. The present rector is the rev Henry William Marker who resides at Aylesbeare. The tower is 40 feet high to the top of the battlements it contains 4 bells one of which is broken the inscription on the 3 are "† *Sancto Michael*" ---- "1663" ---- "God save the church Mr John French Rector" ---

A modern cross stands on the gable of the south porch and over the south door inside is a wooden tablet thus inscribed "This church was enlarged in the year 1827 by which means 156 additional sittings have been obtained and in consequence of a grant from the society for promoting the enlargement and building of churches and chapels 143 of that number are hereby declared to be free & unappropriated for ever in addition to 30 formerly provided." Henry William Marker Minister – [missing]

The monuments & inscriptions here are as follows.
Against the north wall of the chancel a tablet under a pediment supported by 2 Doric columns inscribed "*Armiger auratus Robertus nomine Dracus hic jacet ille pius pauperibusque bonus septem gnatos ERVGIET gnatas quinque venustas parturit coniux Elizabetha sibi 1600 obiit 30 Mar*: Arms on 5 Shields.
1. Argent a wyvern Gules (Drake) impaling An a chevron surmounted of a fleur de lis between 3 crescent 2 roundels.
2. Drake impaling Grenville.
3. Drake impaling. On a chevron in base a mullet a label of 3 points.
4. Drake impaling ermine 3 pickaxes
5. Drake impaling a fess between 3 fleurs de lis - all whitewashed.

East wall of chancel a marble tablet – *Marmore sub hoc inhumatur corpus Johannis Rose arm: Richardi Rose ar: et Elizabethae ux: ej: filii primo geniti nati apud Leigh de Winsham in agro Somerset 1626 denati vero apud Morganshay in Southleigh Devon Dec. 7. 1705 aet 79 S.T.T.L. Rebecca Rose conjux unica et foecunda ut tesseram affectus maerens posuit hoc M.S.* Arms On a pale 3 roses leafed & slipped impaling Barry of 6 escutcheons of pretence Gyronny of 8 --- & Ermine [missing]

East wall of chancel a marble tablet. – In memory of Thomas and Cholmondeley Vickers Elizabeth the disconsolate widow the afflicted mother offers this monument of her affection to them and her gratitude to her brother Stanbroke Cholmondeley whose tender generosity bequeathed this manor to her which she wished to have dedicated to the happiness of the two brothers but alas can only consecrate its now vain produce to her grief for all of them. Arms Or on a cross flory Stable 5 mullets of the first; on a chief Gules 3 roses Or impaling Gules in chief 2 esquires helmets Argent in base a garb Or.
On the floor – Beneath this sepulchral stone lie interred the bodies of the otherwise above monumentally named Thomas Vickers esq. and Cholmondeley son and only child of Thomas and Elizabeth his surviving wife. The father died May 25 1753 aged 53 years and the son April the 5th 1774 aged 19. (*in the margin:* A hatchment with this coat.) [missing]

East wall of chancel A white marble mont. with an urn. John Mountstephen How esq late of Wiscombe park in this parish died March 21 1813 aged 57 – The rev. Thomas How AM formerly fellow of Balliol college Oxford and rector of Huntspill in the county of Somerset died March 15. 1819 aged 61. The revd James How AM. Formerly fellow of Hertford College Oxford died Feb 4 1817 aged 58. This monument erected by the revd Samuel How AM, rector of this parish also of Winterbourne Strickland in the co: of Dorset to the memory of his most dear and much lamented brothers.
Chancel floor – Here lieth the body of Amy wife of -- Starr -- ton gent -- deceased -- day of December 1640 [missing]
Aisle floor. Here lieth the -- Edmund Clode of -- Goldsmith who -- 5 day of Dec buried the 13 Anno Dom 16-- [missing]

In the church yard on the east side a tomb with an inscription some of the letter reversed – here lieth the body of Henry Willoughby who dyed the 28 day of Sept 1610. Arms outlined at the end. Quarterly 1&4 a crofs 2&3 a cross couped. –
Church yard western side 2 tombs – Andrew Ham buried 10 Sept 1667 Amy wife of Andrew Ham died 18 April 1675. Bridget wife of John Ham died 24 Oct 1717. John Ham died 18 Feb 1720. John Ham son of Edward Ham of this parish gent. Died 11 Aug. 1748 aged 22. Edward Ham of this parish gent died 5 Oct 1782 aged 69 years. This family are said to have been owners of Tattickshays farm and other lands in this parish now the property of Charles Gordon esq. of Wiscombe park,

A wooden tablet against the north wall of the nave records Donations to the parish of Southleigh Devon. [missing]
The rev. Thomas How rector of Huntspill Somerset gave by will to his trustees the sum of £200 to be invested in 5 percent consolidated annuities and the interest thereof to be laid out in blankets and necessary clothing and distributed yearly at Christmas to the poor of this parish in such manner as his trustees (with the advice of the rector and the churchwardens) shall think proper
The rev. James How gave by his life will £200 stock in the 5 per cent consol for ever, the interest of £100 thereof to be applied towards the support of the Sunday school and the interest of the other £100 to be distributed in bread and money every year on Christmas day to the poor of the parish and appointed the rector & churchwardens & overseers for the time being trustees thereof. The above sums after deducting the legacy duty were invested in the names of the respected trustees in the 5 percent consol dated annuities since converted by Government into 4 percent. Present annual produce of each donation £7.5.0 –

For deeds relating to the advowson of Southleigh see Coll. for East of Devon page 333 & seq,

The registers of Southleigh begin 25 March 1718. The previous books were destroyed with the rectory house by fire on the Wednesday in Whitsun-week 1783. The present rector (1846) The rev H.W. Marker also vicar of Aylesbeare the resident rev J.H Marker.

(*In the margin:* From a survey dated 1704 penes I A Frampton esq
The lord of this manor is patron of the church of Southleigh valued at £120 per annum 15 Nov. 1705. Thomas French cl. Being the present incumbent of the living of Southleigh the next presentation thereof is granted unto Thomas French the younger of the city of Exon apothecary £75.5.0.)

FARWAY

Davidson (pp. 155–8) visited [St Michael] Farway on 17 September 1829. The church was restored in 1874–6 along with a new pulpit by C.F. Edwards (Pevsner, *Devon*, 447). Four memorials are missing from the sixteen that Davidson recorded.

This church consists of a nave 38 feet long by 15 wide a chancel 19½ by the same width an aisle on the north side 37½ feet long by 14 wide a tower at the western end of the nave 10½ feet square, the total at the western end of the nave 68 feet. – the nave opens to the aisle by 3 pointed arches and a half one at the western end of the earliest date resting on heavy low cylindrical columns, their capitals seem to have been square & to have had the corners cut off. They are adorned with a sort of rude hatched moulding – The arches which divide the nave from the chancel & the tower are pointed. The eastern window of the chancel has 3 lights with ogee formed heads & 3 quatrefoils in the arch the west window 3 lights with perpendicular tracery in the arch the other windows have each 3 lights with flat architraves. The aisle which has superseded a more ancient one has a porch at the eastern end which forms the entrance to the sort of chapel or space enclosed by a screen for the pew & the burial place of the Prideaux family of Netherton, beneath it is the vault – The ceiling is coved & ribbed with oak & there are remains of a chancel screen gilt & adorned with moulding of foliage [removed]. The pulpit is modern formed of oak. – There is a locker in the south wall of the chancel. The font is of stone octagonal in form resting on a plain pedestal of similar shape it is 3½ feet high & 2ft 2in in diameter [now square]. – The tower is embattled & contains 3 bells.
The church plate is a large flaggon the weight of which is marked at the bottom 47.16.0. In the front is the coat of arms Prideaux impaling On a Saltier 5 fleurs de lis - & an inscription. The gift of the lady Prideaux wife of Sir Edmond Prideaux of Netherton in Devon 1720. A Plate dated 1826 with a chalice & paten of older date. –

The registers commence in 1653. In the centre of the north wall of the aisle is a niche with a stone bust in relief of a man dressed in a close jacket with a double ruff round his neck & below it is the following inscription. "This part of the church was new built in the year of our Lord 1628 by the benevolence of Humphrie Hutchins of this parish" (This man is said to have found a large sum of money in an earthen pot on the hill above the village which he appropriated to the purpose of building this aisle). Against the north wall also hangs loose a brass plate fixed upon a piece of wood thus inscribed. *In piam memoriam Richardi Bucknoll de Pedhill qui moritur ano Dom 1632 aetat: suae 70mo Epitaph Tho: Foster hujus eccles: Rector:*
He that procured this sacred edifice
To be erected here now here he lies
His zealous care was th'efficient cause
To build this fabrick for the use of Gods lawes
In life a saint in death a happie soule

None but the envious can this controule
He lov'd our nation and hath built us a Synagogue Luc. 7.
Viuit post funera vertus.

At the east end of the aisle against the north wall is a large stone monument in the Roman style consisting of an altar tomb upon which under an arch lies the effigies of a man draped in a gown & trunk hose, he has no hair but wears a scull cap & his hands are uplifted in the attitude of prayer he is on his back with his head & shoulders on a large pillow – Below on a level with the floor is the figure of a knight in half armour resting on his right side with his head on his helmet which is ornamented with a large plume of feathers his sword is in his right hand and on his left arm is a small shield bearing the arms of the Prideaux. Under the arch is a small tablet thus inscribed "In memorie of Sr. Edmund Prideaux Baronets who dyed the 28th day of March Anno Domini 1628. aetatis suae 74" Above the monument is a shield surmounted by an esquires helmet & bearing the following coat but without the baronets escutcheons. – The whole is bedaubed & defaced with whitewash.
Quarterly of 9.
1. (azure) A chevron (sable) in chief a label of 3 points (gules) (Prideaux)
2. A fess between 3 roundels
3. as 2
4. (Doubtful) On a bend 4 keys endorsed two & two.
5. Per fess dancette – 2 barrullets
6. 3 lozenges in fess
7. 2 chevrons
8. A lion rampant debruised of a bendlet
9. Barry of eight

Crest on a wreath a man's head couped – capped. –
Against the east wall a marble tablet To the memory of Sir Peter Prideaux baronet son of Sir Peter Prideaux baronet by Susannah his wife sister of Lord John Poulett baron of Hinton St George which Sir Peter P. married Elizabeth eldest daughter of Sir Neville Granville of Stow in Cornwall Kt and sister to the right honourable: John late Earle of Bath by whom he had 4 sons and 6 daughters. This monument was erected at the sole and proper cost of Susannah P. eldest daughter of Sir Peter P. his sole executrix. Obiit 22 Nov. 1705 aet 79. Arms. Argent a chevron Sable in chief a label of 3 points Gules on an in escutcheon the arms of Ulster impaling Gules 3 horseman's rests Or. On a baronets helmet the crest On a wreath a mans head couped in profile proper capped Argent. (Grenville)

Tablets in the chancel.
The rev Richard Blake rector of this parish 31 years died 22 Sept 1788 aged 66 erected by his affectionate relative Hannah Atkinson.
Hannah Atkinson of the city of Exeter died Dec. 6. 1796
She established a school by her will for educating poor children of the parish.
Mrs. Frances Alford relict of the rev. Mr Thomas Alford late vicar of Curry Rivall in the co: of Somerset & daughter of Samuel Powell esq. of the same place died 20 Sept. 1738 aged 61.
Johannis Gould A. M. fil: Henrici G. de civit: Lond: merc: & hujus ecclesiae per 28 ann: rect: ob: an: 1757 aet 69 [missing]

Letitia G. vid: J.G. supradicti ob: Nov: 1. 1768 aet 70.
Chancel floor – in the old letter – *Hic jacet Georgius Haydon Armiger q -- ultimo die Augusti Anno Domini 1558.* defaced [missing] –
Nave floor – an inscription in the old letters defaced [missing]
Aisle floor – an inscr: in the old letters defaced & on the same stone -- body of Mary Nut- ---m who died the 4 day of Jan. AD. 1659 [missing]

Tombs in the church yard
In the old letter – Here lieth the body of John Haydon sonne of -- of -- the 18 of March 1604.
Here lieth the body of Thomas Haydon of Poltimore who deceased the 13 of Sept. 1610.
William Wheaton gent late of this parish died 24 May 1794 aged 81. Jenny wife of the above died 13 Nov 1805 aged 77. William W. gent son of W. & J.W, died by the accidental discharge of his gun 1 Nov. 1803 aged 36.
Mr. Nicholas Carter son of Mr William C. died 7 April 1812 aged 26. also at an advanced age William Guppy esq. buried 20 May 1726 also at D° – Mrs. Joan G. sister of the above N.C, buried. 23 Nov 1750 also at D° --- Wm Guppy esq. son of the above WG. & husband of Mrs Joan G. died 10 July 1766. also Jonas G. esq. son of W.& Joan G. died 2 Sept 1787 aged 64. Mrs Mary G. daughter of Edward & Elizabeth Haine of Southleigh & wife of the above Jonas Guppy died 10 Nov. 1801 aged 70 years.
William Wish gent of this parish died 29 Jan 1767 aged 62
Susanna his wife died 22 Aug 1778 aged 75 William their son died 30 Jan 1788 aged 51. On a wooden tablet against the south wall of the nave this inscription Donations bequeathed to the parish of Farway – Hannah Atkinson late of the parish of St Paul's Exeter spinster gave by will dated Feb 10 1797 the sum of £250 in the 3 percent reduced annuities towards supporting a charity school in this parish for teaching 12 poor children to read and to be instructed in the principles of religion and for supporting them with Bibles and other religious books, the rectors of Farway Northleigh and Offwell are the appointed trustee for the above donation. – Also Elizabeth Cox late of this parish gave by will dated Feb 15 1782 the sum of £20 unto the minister & churchwardens of this parish upon trust for the time being to be put out at interest and the produce thereof to be by them yearly for ever paid applied & disposed of in bread unto and amongst the poor inhabitants & families of the same parish. – 1825. – [missing]

In the church chest is an old book in a state of decay containing notices of the parish affairs in the time of Queen Elizabeth – Timothy Shute appears to have been rector 12 Car: 2.

WIDWORTHY

Davidson (pp. 159–62) visited [St Cuthbert] Widworthy on 1 October 1828 and noted that Widworthy was about 5 miles from Axminster and 4 miles from Honiton and half a mile south of the village of Wilmington. The church was refitted in 1785–7 (Pevsner, *Devon*, 910).

Widworthy church consists of a nave chancel & transept with a square embattled tower at the western end of the nave 41 feet high to the top of the battlements. The nave is 30 feet long by 15. feet 6in; wide within the walls it is divided from the chancel & transepts by pointed arches the latter supported by columns clustered & having rudely foliated capitals, the hollows of the columns are adorned with leaves & roses, the transepts extend to 35 feet by 10 feet wide & are lighted each by a pointed window of good proportions at the end, divided by a single ramified mullion into two lights, these & the general appearance of the building seem to fix its date at about the end of the 14th century. The Chancel is 20 feet long by 13 wide, in the south wall is a piscina with a trefoil head & a moulding round it – a similar but smaller & less ornamented is in the wall of the south transept towards the eastern side which proves the former existence of an altar there. The font which stands at the western end of the nave is octagonal of stone, ornamented with quatrefoils & supported by a column adorned with trefoil headed niches. The tower which is 13 feet long by 10 wide contains 5 bells of these 4 were cast by Bailey Street & Co. in 1756 & the 5th by Bilbee of Cullompton. One of them bears the motto "Health wealth and peace to the neighbourhood" another "Health and peace ringing yield" a third "My treble voice your hearts rejoice"

Over the door which opens into the tower at the western end is a kind of shallow niche or recess with a pointed top in which are represented in relief 3 shields hanging but the bearings if any have been destroyed as has also some sculpture which shows the traces of figures & which perhaps represented the crucifixion, a small rude cross adorns the gable end of the chancel. This little church is in the whole a well proportioned & not inelegant structure & the beautiful monuments which ornament the interior are worthy of inspection –
(*In the margin:* Over the porch is a small sun-dial with the motto "Tempus fugit")

These and the other monuments inscriptions are as follow.
In the wall under the window of the north transept is an altar tomb beneath a low flat arch finished above with a square moulding, the soffits of the arch is enriched with roses and quatrefoils. Upon the tomb lies the effigy of a knight in full armour, his head wearing a plain helmet without a crest rests on a pillow supported by 2 angels, his feet rest upon a couchant lion – his coat of mail reaching from his head to his hips is covered by armour & his hands by gauntlets are lifted in the attitude of prayer, his legs are protected by greaves & he has spurs upon his heels, on his left side is his sword & his left arm is hidden by a long triangular sheet which displays

in bold relief his armorial bearings 3 lions rampant 2 X 1 on a field semee of crop crosslets. (Q[uery] Prous)

The next in order of date is a flat stone in the floor of the chancel which though much defaced & broken the coat of armour may be traced, vair & may be allotted to one of the family of Chichester, the date 1661 appears on the stone but this is probably a subsequent inscription. –

Against the wall of the chancel on the N side is a tablet inscribed 'Beneath lie the bodies of three brothers James Marwood of Sutton esq. MD who died 27 Oct 1722 aetat 66. Benedict's Marwood of Hornsey's esq. who died 18 Aug. 1745 aetat 82. Thomas Marwood of Sutton esq who died 21 March 1748 aet. 88. eminent for piety & good economy'. Arms. Gules a chevron between 3 goat's heads erased Ermine.

On the E side of the transept is a mural monument of marble consisting of an urn & a sarcophagus inscribed "In Memory of Robert Marwood of Cookshays esq. who died 13 July 1733 aged 57 also Mrs Bridget Marwood his sister of the same place who dyed the 9 Dec. 1756 aged 79. *Sua praemia Virtus*" The coat armour having been painted is obliterated

On the E side of the N transept is a handsome monument executed by Bacon of London in 1781 consisting of a pedestal supporting an urn encircled by a wreath of flowers, on side stands a full length figure of affection holding a pelican's nest, on the other one of justice or honesty with the scales and mirror the figures are of white marble in relief on a ground of scagliola marble. Inscription "James Marwood esq. died 3 April 1767 aged 65. The memory of the just is blessed"

On the W side of the N transept is a monument of grey marble with figures of white marble in relief a female with 2 children inscribed – "Sarah Marwood relict of James Marwood esquire and daughter of Samuel Sealy esquire of Avishays in the county of Somerset. She died on the 4th April 1797 aged 85 years"

On the W side of the S transept is a large & beautiful monument of white marble executed by P. Rouw of London 1815 consisting of an ornamented sarcophagus with a medallion & portrait supported on one side by a female figure kneeling with an open book on the other by a sitting figure having another recumbent female reclining on her knees. On the base is the inscription "In memory of James Thomas Benedictus Marwood esquire of Avishays House in the co: of Somerset and of Sutton in the co: of Devon who departed this life on the 20th Feb. 1811 in the 64th year of his age". Above the figures are the words "Thy will be done" and the coat of arms a chevron between 3 goats heads erased Crest a ram couchant.

In the N transept is a hatchment with the Marwood arms Gules a chevron between 3 goat's heads erased Ermine. Crest on a wreath Gules & Sable a goat or ram couchant proper

On the N side of the chancel a mural tablet "Mrs Alice Sack the wife of Sebastian Sack esq was interred the 3 May 1685 their children Mr Sebastian Sack was buried 14 Aug. 1681 Mrs Elizabeth Sack buried 31 Jan. 1677 Mr Thomas Sack buried 16 April 1683." Arms sable a bend Or on a canton Argent a leopards face of the field impaling Ermine on a bend cotised Sable 3 griffins heads erased Or (Yonge). This family are said to have resided at Ford in Wilmington now the house called Wilmington cottage the residence of Robert Wrey esq. –

On the S side of the chancel a mural tablet "*Spe beatae resurrectionis subter conditae sunt reliquiae Jacobi Somaster viri probi et rei medicae periti. Quam*

Honitoni novem per annos feliciter exercuit. Ob: Aug: 28 1748 Aet suae 34° Juxta etiam requiescit Anna praedicti soror quae ob: Mar 9° 1755 aet: suae 39°.
Suae memor mortalitatis Hoc praeeuntium Fratris et Sororis dilect: M.P. Jos. Somaster hujus Eccles: Rector. Arms a tower of 3 turrets between 5 fleurs de lis. Crest a portcullis.

In the church yard on the S side of the tower is an altar tomb inscribed to John Dewbury gent who died 20 March 1642 & Ellen his wife who died 7th October 1644. Against the N wall of the nave is "A table of benefactions" with the name & date Mr. L. Tucker Rector 1789.
"A particular of the charities belonging to the parish of Widworthy
AD. 1733 Robert Marwood esq gave 20/ charged on a field called Stone Burrows in this parish to be distributed to the poor on St Luke's day for ever.
1742 Benedictus Marwood esq gave £100 the profit thereof to be given to the parish & schoolmaster yearly for ever
1767 James Marwood esq gave a school room & 40/ yearly to the schoolmaster for ever
1769 The rev Jos: Somaster rector gave £100 the profit thereof to be given one half to the parish schoolmaster the other half to the poor in bread on Christmas day for ever" [missing].

The registers of this parish commence on the 25th March 1540. At one end of one of the books is a memorandum dated 1630 relative to the bounds of the parish at a certain point which seem to have been disputed.
The following information is also noted there.
Rectors of Widworthy, the names of those who stated to have been buried at Widworthy are entered in the registers.
Roger Slade buried here 11 March 153-
Robert Coyle deprived 1556
Bartholomew Cowde instituted 23 May 1556
Bartholomew Palmer instituted: 12 July 1575. buried: 24 Aug
Robert Perry instituted 22 Nov. 1610.
John Chichester inst. 26 April 1644 buried 14 Jan
Samuel Periam inst. ---1650 buried 19 April
John Bury. Canon of St Peters Exon inst. 1659
Benjamin Dukes inst. 1663 buried 22 Oct 1695
Robert Cole inst. 1695 buried 26 March 1728
Peter Sheely inst. 1728
Joseph Somaster inst. 1736
William John Tucker inst. 1769 living 1828

Geo: Franklyn of Widworthy delinquent 1651 See Axminster Papers of this period for particulars.
Williamus de Wydeworthy – mil. – 1258 See deeds for Whitford in Colyton
Ricus psona de Wydeworthy – 1361 See Sparkleghes in Colyton –

The lingering remains of a revel, fair or feast may be observed in the village of Wilmington on the 28th September.

Newspaper cutting, no name or date of newspaper:
Widworthy co: Devon
6137 Plain Old Manuscript; _ The Roman Emperors, and the ten persecutions, 169 +
(Sermon) By Mr. John Bull att the funeral. Of Anne Pint, April 27, 99, + A Godli and
Comforting letter of Mr. Dukes, Minister of Widworthy, (Devon), sent to an Antiente
frinde of his in trouble and Weakness, + (an Address) Sent to Mrs. Huish of Sand on
a faire 1710, R.N. = folio, old binding, 7s Reserved

COTLEIGH

Davidson (pp. 163–5) visited [St Michael] Cotleigh on 14 September 1829. The chancel was partly rebuilt in 1867 (Pevsner, *Devon*, 291).

This church consists of a nave 36½ feet long by 14½ wide, chancel 15½ by 12½ a north aisle 46 by 11½ & a tower at the western end of the nave 10 feet by 9 & as the wall between the nave & chancel is 2 feet thick & that between the nave & tower 2½ the total length within the walls is 66½ feet. –
The nave opens to the aisle by 4 pointed arches which rest upon quadrangular columns composed each of 4 shafts with intervening hollow mouldings their capitals are angular & carved in foliage, the windows have flat heads are formed into 3 lights each with trefoil heads there are apparently with the columns of the 16th century the east window of the chancel seems to be of the 13th century, it has 3 lights in the easily pointed lancet style the centre one higher than the others & without an arch the east window of the aisle seems to be an imitation of that in the chancel but its moulding betrays its more recent date. – The ceiling is covered, divided by ribs which are adorned with heads & foliage at their intersections. The pulpit modern. The font is ancient, a block of stone of octagonal form 2 feet in diameter & 3 feet 1 inch high resting on a circular column surrounded by 8 shafts with circular capitals each of the 8 sides is formed into a panel some representing quatrefoils encloses a shield another 2 pointed trefoil headed arches a third an eagle in a ring. – There is a modern gallery at the west end of the nave [removed]. – The tower is 51 feet high to the top of the battlements, it has square diagonal buttresses at the corners & half an octagonal turret on the south side for the stairs and rude figures at the angles of the roof for the gargoyles. The north door is under a pointed arch surmounted by an angular label with foliage in the spandrels the west door way has a pediment arch similarly ornamented
The tower contains 3 bells thus inscribed "1664" "1734" – "Rev. Wm. Mitchell rector 1828". –

There are not any monumental inscriptions in the church or any in the church yard worthy of notice. On the floor of the nave is a stone marked with a cross bottom [now learning against the south wall by the door]
In the centre light of the chancel window is a small coat of arms well executed in good colours & apparently about a century old –
Azure 3 ships of 8 masts in full sail Or sails and flags argent with a crop Gules. On a chief Or between 2 roses Gules leaved vert a pale quarterly 1&4 Gules
A lion passant gardant Or 2&3 Azure a fleur de lis Or and esquire helmet mantled Gules doubled Argent
Crest on a wreath Or & azure a celestial sphere Or Between 2 pennons Argent each charged with a cross & pointed Gules handles Or points Azure Supported 2 sea lions proper manned & armed Or. Motto. *Deus indicat* [missing]. –

Against the wall of the nave a wooden tablet. Parish of Cotleigh John Hobbs by his grant or deed dated 16 July 1571 gave granted & confirmed unto John Hunt & eleven others therein named their heirs & assigns for ever all that manage lands and premises with its appurtenances commonly known by the name of Lydeates containing by estimation 12 acres or there-about were the same more or less situated in Cotleigh in trust to pay the annual profits thereof unto the hands of the church-wardens of the said parish of Cotleigh for the time being who shall employ the same for and towards repairing such parts of the parish church of Cotleigh aforesaid as the parishioners of the said parish used heretofore to repair and that the said churchwardens should give annual account of such monies unto the said trustees and parishioners to be perused past and signed by them with such power as is therein contained for the appointment of new trustees when necessary – Wm Clapp & Wm Burrow churchwardens 1826.

The Southcotts were patrons of the living of Cotleigh about 1600
See "a discourse of Devon & Cornwall" In Bibl. Harl 5827. Other particulars there also.

OFFWELL

Davidson (pp. 167–70) visited [St Mary the Virgin] Offwell on 14 September 1829. Eight memorials are missing from the ten that Davidson recorded.

This church consists of a nave 37 feet long by 15 wide chancel 17½ by 13 North aisle 51 by 10 & tower at the west end 8½ by 9 wide, allowing therefore 4½ feet for the thickness of the intervening walls the total inner length of the building is 63 feet – a semicircular arch resting on piers divides the nave from the chancel but it does not appear to be of ancient date. The north aisle seems to have been built in the 14th or early in the 15 century it opens to the nave by 3 low pointed arches supported by columns composed of 4 shafts with intervening mouldings & having quadrangular capitals carved in foliage & figures amongst which latter are some which were better defaced – a pointed arch divides the chancel from the aisle & is ornamented in its archivolt with panels finished at either end in trefoils, the south door of the chancel is under a pediment arch. The windows throughout have 3 lights with trefoil heads & are without arches, except the east & west windows of the aisle which were perhaps removed from the nave when this addition was made to the church, they have cinquefoil headed lights with perpendicular tracery in their pointed arches & may be assigned to the 15th century one of them contains some fragments of stained glass – of this last mentioned period is probably the south door & porch the arch of the latter is pointed & rests on shafts with circular capitals it is finished with a square head & is adorned with foliage in the spandrels and what is unusual has a series of foliated ornaments in the hollow mouldings on both sides of the arch inside & outside – In the east wall of this porch is a holy water basin. A lofty pointed arch opens from the nave to the tower but its effect is hidden by the gallery for singers bearing the follows inscription on the front. This gallery was erected to promote the glory of God at the sole charges of John Ford gent of this parish in the year 1754 [removed]. The pulpit is of oak & modern upon its panels are figures of the four evangelists carved in relief – The ceilings are coved and ribbed with oak The font is of stone of octagonal form adorned with quatrefoils & foliage resting on an octagonal column with panels forming trefoil headed arches, it is 3 feet high & 2½ in diameter – The tower is embattled with a turret for the stairs on the north side it is about 45 feet high & contains 5 bells – 3 of them are ancient with inscriptions in the old letters one of them has a legend somewhat like the following
† *Protege virgo pia quos co--- co sancta ---*
The other two are dated 1709 & one of them informs us *"Huic ecclesiae me donarunt amici aliquot liberales quorum largitiones sedulo collegit Mr Guil. Bendle 1709 T.W. –"*

The monumental inscriptions are these
Against the north wall of the chancel a tablet
Dorothea uxor Henrici Southcott gen filia Gulielmi & Annae Collyns de Collwell arm. hoc etiam sepulchro una cum sorroribus suis et avis proavis sepulta. Ob: 16

Sep: 1698. Arms Quarterly 1&4 Argent a chevron Gules between 3 coots Sable, a mullet for difference 2&3rd. Azure a chevron Ermine between 3 birds close Argent Crests. 1 On a wreath a demi lion rampant holding a crown 2. On a wreath a bird – both on helmets

On the floor in the old letter – "died 30 day of February anno – [missing]

Nave. A wooden tablet. Underneath lyeth the remains of John Ford of this parish gentleman and Mary his wife daughter of Nicholas Fry of Wood in the parish of Cotleigh gent. Mary died in 1724 aged 61 John died in 1729 aged 75. Arms – Gules a tower with 2 turrets embattled Argent surmounted by a ducal crown Or impaling Gules 3 horses currant in pale Argent – The shield surmounted by a ducal crown Or [missing].

On the floor a long stone which has been ornamented with a cross in relief [missing]

Aisle – a mural tablet *"Joanna uxor Thomae Southcott de Kilmington gen fil: natu maxima Gulielmi et Annae Collyns de Collwell arm: ob: 14 Dec.1696."* Arms as before described [missing]

On the floor – Here lyth Thomas Collyns of -- mor of Offwell & Gra -- the 15 day of May *Anno Dni 1598 annoq. aetatis suae 74.* [missing] –

Here lieth the bodie of Johan Collyns the wife of Thomas Collyns gent who died the 1 day of May anno dni 1610 [missing]

Here lieth the body of William Collyns gent who died the 31 day of October Anno Domi 1657. [missing]

--- --- *Anno Dni 1612 annoq. Aetatis sue 23* [missing]

In the church yard appears the following inscription John Ford died 20 Oct 1770 aged 71. Mary wife of Richard Upham and sister of the above died 10 April 1770 aged 74 John Ford Upham died 23 Feb 1810 aged 67.

A farm house of the south side with the estate were the property of John Ford Upham but were brought by Dr. Copplestone the Bishop of Llandaff brother of the present incumbent of Offwell & the house was rebuilt by him in the year 1828 in the style of the late period of the pointed order of architecture.

In the north wall of the church is a niche with a trefoil head perhaps for the image of a saint.

A tomb near the east end of the church is inscribed Sacred to the memory of Elizabeth wife of Emanuel Dommett who died 7 March 1809 aged 62 years also of the said Emanuel Dommett who died 4 Dec. 1827 aged 88 years.

A wooden tablet against the south wall of the nave Charities belonging to the parish of Offwell Devon.

1st a field of 4 acres called Parish Close near Gray stone in the said parish the income of which is to be given at the discretion of the feoffees to the most deserving poor labourers not receiving parish relief. This field was brought AD 1725 for £60 of which sum Dorothy Southcott bequeathed £20 Henry Southcott bequeathed £20 a charity called Raddon's money was applied in part £10 The parish raised by the poor rate £10. Total £60

2nd a field about 4 acres called School Close situated in the said parish near Honiton Hill brought AD 1824 with the timber thereon for £99 part of a sum of money given by Emmanuel Dommett of Offwell amounting to £120 and vested by him in feoffees the income from the land to be applied to the education of the poor. The remainder of the sum now secured by note from the rev. I.G. Copleston to be expended if the feoffees hereafter think fit in building a school room or house for the residences of the schoolmaster or minister the interest if not wanted for the current expenses of the school to accumulate for the poor house of such building.

3rd A cottage for the present use of the charity school situated in the village of Offwell also given by the said Emmanuel Dommett. –

A school house in the pointed style of architecture is now building at the north eastern entrance of the village.

Henric. psona de Offewell 1361 See deed for Sharkehayes in Colyton

BRANSCOMBE

Davidson (pp. 171–7) visited [St Winifred] Branscombe on 16 September 1829. He noted 'the church of this sequestered village forms a highly picturesque and interesting object in the romantic scenery of the valley in which it stands, the difficulty of access to the place arising from the steepness of the hills and roughness of the roads is amply repaid by various points of rural beauty approaching very nearly to the character of Welsh scenery – The approach to the church from the east, brings to mind the fact that churches were anciently parochial fortresses for the heavy square tower with its corbel table resembling machicolations and its circular turret the appearance of a strong hold rather than a temple of peace – This building is evidently very ancient & the tower may be reasonably assigned to the 12 century if not earlier.' The church was restored by W.D. Carõe in 1911 (Pevsner, *Devon*, 204). There are three memorials missing from the thirty-one that Davidson recorded.

The whole is of unusual form as it consists of a nave & chancel with the tower between them & 2 projecting aisles forming s transept west of the tower & this seems to have been the form of the original structure – The nave is 56½ feet long by 19 wide, the tower 15ft .3 square the chancel 31 by 15.3 the north aisle 15½ by the same width & the south aisle 16.9 by 16ft wide – these measurements are within the walls & as the piers of the tower are 3 feet wide the total length of the church inside is 108ft 9 in The tower is built upon rectangular piers with a heavy impost moulding in lieu of capitals supporting pointed arches in the earliest style, on its north side is a circular turret for the stairs as high as the roof & upon this has been erected at a later period an octagonal addition which is embattled & rises higher than the parapet of the tower – all the windows or rather loopholes of the tower have semicircular heads & the parapet (which is not embattled) is supported with a corbel table, the corbels are carved in rude representations of heads & as the parapet projects beyond the face of the tower in the form of machicolations the whole has much the appearance of a fortress or the tower of a castle. – It is 50 feet high to the top of the parapet. – That the nave is of the same date in its origin with the tower is evident as a similar range of corbels rudely carved run round the roof on the outside below the eaves – The north & south aisles seem to be of the same early date they open to the nave by early pointed arches resting on angular overarching imported mouldings supported by shafts with circular capitals
These if not [as] early a date as the tower may be safely ascribed to the 13th century the windows of the church have been altered & enlarged at various periods, one of the ancient narrow loop like windows remains in the north aisle & parts of the openings for similar ones remain in the walls of the chancel. The existing windows of the chancel are still of early date, they have each 2 lights with trefoil heads & a quatrefoil in the points of the arch The east window is large being five lights in width divided by a transom & having cinquefoil heads the head of the arch is divided

by tracery in the perpendicular style & the inner arch rests on shafts having angels for their capitals holding labels. The labels over this window on the outside rest on corbels formed of shields, that on the south side bearing the arms of the see of Exeter (at that time) viz. A sword in bend surmounted by 2 keys adorned in bends sinister. The shield on the north side bears a Saltier, the arms of George Neville who was bishop of Exeter from 1458 to 1465 which determines the date of this window – The window of the south aisle has 3 trefoil headed lights with a cinquefoil in the arch – one of the windows of the nave is in the style of the 15 century but it has been despoiled of part of its tracery, a door way under a pointed arch at the west end has been formed into a window & close to it stands the font a modern octagonal stone basin fluted on the sides as is the column on which it stands it is 3ft 5in high & 1.4 in diameter [the present font came from Teignmouth in 1911]. The ceiling is coved & ribbed with oak having small knots of foliage at the intersections – A gallery with a front of oak erected in the 17 century crosses the west end of the nave & is approached by steps on the outside – The pulpit also of oak is modern. The tower contains 5 bells inscribed "1635" – "When I call follow all 1669" – "T.P. Exon 1671" – "Ellis Bartlett gent church warden 1696" – "Wroth fecit 1747" –

The monuments & inscriptions are as follow. In the chancel a stone tablet under an entablature supported by Corinthian columns "Here lyeth entombed the bodie of a virtuous and godly gentlewomen named Anne one of the daughters of John Mychell of the Wrow in the countye of Cornwall gent – she was marryed to Ellis Bartlett of Branscombe gent and had issue by him one child she lived the age of 47 years and died the last day of Jan. 1606" Arms Argent 2 bars between 3 cinquefoils sable
A wooden tablet also against the north wall "In memory of Mr Ellis Bartlett and of An his wife the daughter of Richard Duke of Otterton esq. and of Margaret the daughter and heire of Mr Henry Ellicot of Exminster wife of Ellis Bartlett the younger he was buried 4th of Oct. 1623, An was buried 22 April 1654. Margaret was buried 4 July 1640" Arms on 2 shields – Bartlett, impaling Argent a fess between 3 lozenges sable each charged with a bird of the field – Bartlett, impaling Lozenge or & Azure a bordure Gules. (Ellicott)
East wall a mural tablet – "*M.S. hon. patris hujusce sub introitum inhumatur corpus Elizei Bartlett gen: Elizei & Anna uxoris ejus filii unici nat: in hanc parochiam de Branscombe Feb. 15. 1615 denati ibidem Feb. 26 1691 aet 76. hic eodem obdormivit sepulchre Oct 4. 1623 aet 75.*" Arms Bartlett.
A tablet – "*Elizei Bartlett de Hole gen: et Gulielmi filii ejus unici: ob. ille 22 Maii aet 65 hic 17 Dec aet 25. 1744*"
In memory of Mrs Dorothy Bartlett who died 11 April 1749 aged 64" – Arms Bartlett.
Tablet – "*Georgius Woodward arm. Georgii Woodward de Hinton sr Georgii in agro Somerset eler filius ob. 1 Junii 1741 aet 33.*" Arms, argent a saltier between 4 birds close vert impaling sable a fess wavy between 2 stars of eight points Argent (Drake of Buckland)
Tablet – Mr John Leigh died May 28 1732 aged 52 Mrs Mary L. died 7 August 1746 aged 58.
Tablet – Mrs Ann Churchill died Nov. 7 1741 aged 23.
Tablet William Bampfield of Beer esq. & Agnes his wife he died May 8 1754 she March 13 1753 aged 85 years also their two sons William and Edward B: both of

Beer esquires William died Nov. 19 1747 & Edward 12th May 1753 each in the 49th year of his age. This monument erected the grandson & nephew William Carslake of Beer gent

Flat stones – Edward Pynn A.M. & vicar of Branscombe buried – June 1650 [missing] William Clarke bur. July 12 1710 [missing]

Mary wife of George Channon 2 June 16-- Abigail wife of Thomas Channon -- June 7 1706 aged 72 [missing]

Under the lower Mural tablets – John Bampfield buried 16 July 1719 aged 86 –

"*Ellis Bartlett gen: Elizei & Mariae ux ejus fil. primogen exuvias suas caducas spe firma resurrectionis futurae & vitae aeterna deposuit Ap. 14. 1711.*" Arms Bartlett – impaling Barry of 6 Argent & Sable in chief 3 cinquefoils of the last.

Samuel son of Ellis Bartlett of Hole gent & of Edith his wife died 29 Oct 1704 aged 16 years. Arms. Bartlett with a crescent for differences

Mrs Eadith Bartlett died 6 Nov 1737

Mary wife of William Bartlett gent of Hole in this parish & daughter of William Beere gent of Honiton died 8 Feb1751 aged 26. Arms as above

In the north aisle against the north wall are two tombs both of which are hidden by pews but the superstructures are visible – upon the tomb on the eastern side is a tablet under an entablature & pediment supported by 2 Doric pilasters upon the tablet is a shield with the arms covered with whitewash (Azure) a chevron (Argent) between three blackamoors heads couped filleted impaling three rams passant a crescent for difference (Holcombe). No inscription visible –

On the west side a tomb upon which also is a tablet under an entablature & pediment supported by 2 Doric pilasters fixed against the wall – Upon the tablet are represented in relief 2 kneeling figures of men facing each other with their hands in the attitude of prayer. He on the dexter side is the elder & is habited in a loose gown, the younger is in armour & his helmet & gauntlets are before him – On the dexter side behind the man kneels a women with 14 children 5 sons & 9 daughters, behind the other women with 5 children 1 son & 4 daughters – A smaller tablet below held the inscription but it is entirely defaced – the tomb seems to have been erected by a women to the memory of her two husbands for above the figure are 3 coats the centre on a lozenge which is impaled with each of the others on shields: –

Arms in a lozenge (1) Quarterly of 6
1. Two [drawing of a cross] in saltier – query dipping irons crosiers or crooks
2. A chevron between 3 escallops query Trenchard, Pollard, Farway, Norton, Westcot or Shapleigh
3. Semee of escallops a lion rampant
4. A lion rampant within a bordure bezant, a label of three points (Cornwall)
5. On a bend 5 roundels
6. Or chevron 3 fleur de lis

Shield on the dexter side (2) Quarterly of 4. 1&4 Two glaziers irons in saltier between 4 pears pendant within a bordure engrailed – Kellaway
2. A bucks head caboched
3. A chevron between 3 escallops impaling the arms in a lozenge (1) above Shield on the sinister side (3) Quarterly of 9.
1. A chevron between 3 roses. (Wadham)

2. On a chevron 3 birds (query martlets)
3. Or a chief 2 stags heads caboched
4. a chevron between 9 roundels in chief 3.2. in base 1.2.2
5. Six lioncels rampant Or 3.2.1.
6. Per fess indented a bend
7. Barry of 8 an eagle displayed
8. A lion rampant Or
9. A bend lozenge each displayed with an ermine spot Impaling the coat in a lozenge (1) above, –
Under the pediment is a rose argent leaved vert seeded Or, the crest of the Wadhams of Edge & Merrifield. –

On the floor of the south aisle is a stone on which is represented a cross [small drawing on page], & beneath it in old letter the words *"Orate pro anima John Hedraunt (or Hedmunt)"* on another in Roman letters "February Anno Dom 1600"

Nave. North wall, a mural monument of marble representing a sarcophagus with a tablet above it with a long inscription of which the follows is the substance "Sacred to the memory of Robert Stuckey esq. Mary his wife and family of Weston in the parish." a magistrate. He died 9 Dec. 1768 in his 79th year. Mrs. S. died 26 Nov. 1763 in her 82nd year. In this vault also William Stuckey esq. youngest son of the above – learned in the law – died in London 2 Oct 1775 aged 54.
Arms Quarterly 1&4 Per bend sinister dovetailed Or & Azure a lion rampant double queue Ermine
2nd & 3rd Sable 2 bars between 3 cinquefoils Argent (Bart) Crest on a wreath Or & azure A demi lion rampant double queue couped Ermine. An esquire's helmet.
Motto *Fortitudine et fidelilate.*
On the north wall also a similar monument:
Sacred to the memory of John Stuckey of Weston esq. the only surviving issue of Robert S. & Mary his wife the sole daughter & heiress of William Bartlett of Hole in this parish gent – a magistrate --- died unmarried 26 Jan. 1810 aged 91 years – Erected by Barnaby John Stuckey Bartlett his relation & sole executor – Arms
As above. – a hatchment exhibits the same coat
On the floor – here lieth the body of Mary Stuckey wife of Robert Stuckey of Weston esq. who died 26 Nov. 1763 aged 83. Arms as above.
Here lieth -- Jone the wife of Robert Lee of Branscombe who dyed 25 Dec. 1638.
Dorothy wife of Henry Carslake of Sidmouth died 17 July 1698.
-- Sonne of -- Lee who died 21 Feb 1642
--- Body of -- Lee of B---combe -- the -- July -- Dom 16--

In the churchyard are 2 rude blocks of stone which if turned over would perhaps bring inscriptions to light – One of them said to belong to a family named Payton
Among the inscriptions are these –
On the edge of a large stone John Taylor buried the 10th April 1586
Joan Bartlett of Weston died 24 March 17-- aged 75
Charity Lee Wm Lee her husband & Robert Lee her only son were both buried together in one grave 2 Oct 1658
Sarah daur of John Carslake by Ann his wife did 1 April 1705
William Carslake gent of this parish died 12 Dec 1774

Elizabeth wife of John Sampson the younger of Culliton in this county esq daughter & only child of Mr Anthony Braddick late of Bulstone in this parish and of Elizabeth his wife died 2 April 1770 aged 53.

For an inscription in verse to one Joseph Braddick who died 27 June 1673 see Hutchinson's Guide to Sidmouth p. 94.

OTTERY ST MARY

Davidson (pp. 179–200) visited [the church of St Mary] Ottery St Mary on 14 August 1834. Before his own notes we find several pages of printed material on the history of Ottery pasted into the manuscript [pp. 178 (1)–(5)]. The church was restored in 1826 (Pevsner, *Devon*, 618). Thirty memorials are missing from the fifty-seven Davidson recorded.

A cursory view of the very interesting church at this place will exhibit at once the traces of at least three distinct periods of the pointed style of architecture. Portions of a building erected in the 13th century have been evidently applied to a much later structure in the 14th and one of the aisles stands alone a beautiful specimen of the style which prevailed in the latter part of the 15th century.

On entering the principal gate of the church yard on the south, a stone inserted into the pier on the west exhibits the arms of Bishop Oldham who died AD. 1519 viz a chevron between 3 owls on a Chief as many roses [missing]. –
The building consists of a nave with aisles a chapel north of the north aisle porches north and south, a transept with a tower at each end, a chancel or choir with aisles, an eastern or lesser transept, and a Lady Chapel east of the Chancel.
The nave is divided from its aisles by 5 pointed arches on each side resting on piers & shafts from which spring the stone ribs of the roof forming triangular compartments with bosses of foliage at the intersections, and shields bearing the arms of Grandisson (I) Paly of 6 Argent & Azure on a Bend gules a mitre between 2 Eagles displayed or, & of Montacute (II) Argent 3 Fusils in fess gules. The clerestory windows are 5 on each side having 3 lights with cinquefoil heads. The aisles are similar in style & ornament. The south door is ancient & heavy with a remarkably large & rude lock & key. The old handle of the latch is marked JH. 1575 for John Haydon. The south porch appears to be of later date than the aisle. The door way is a low arch with roses in the spandrels, above it is a tablet with the kings arms & supporters having columns at the sides & above the inscription "He that no ill will do, do no thying yt lang yt to. Anno Domini 1571". Below the text *"In te Domini speraui non confunder in eternum"* with the letters J.H probably for John Haydon who seems to have erected the porch as his coat armorial appears in stone over the outer entrance. – Doors under pointed arches open to the church yard from the aisles in the western wall. – The transept is lightened by narrow lancet lights except on the western sides in each of which is a large window of 5 long narrow lancet lights, highest in the centre, which are parts of a building of the 13th century. The towers are of 3 stories with narrow lights, the angles have buttresses of several stages & the tops are finished by embattled parapet pierced with trefoil headed openings below which is a range of gargoyles in figures of monstrous heads. On the north tower is a low leaded spire with a vane & at the corner of each are low pinnacles. The towers are 65 feet high to the top of the battlements & contain 6 bells with an ancient clock & chimes.

The roof of the transept is divided by stone ribs into lozenge-shaped compartments with bosses of foliage & arms as before (I) & (II) & those of Courtenay (III) Or Forteaux, a label of 3 points azure. – In the centre appears the figure of a Bishop in full pontificalibus, probably intended for Grandisson.

The Choir is divided from its aisles by 5 pointed arches of the same character as those of the nave with intervening shafts from which spring the stone ribs which ornament the roof with flowing tracery including quatrefoils at the intersections are bosses of foliage & other others with well sculptured figures of the virgin and other saints & the coats (I) & (II) as before. The clerestory windows have each 3 lights the centre highest with plain arched heads but these appear to have been despoiled of their sweeps. At the eastern end of the choir is an altar screen beautifully executed in the Beer free-stone under the directions of Mr. Blore and said to be as nearly as possible a facsimile of an ancient one much defaced found to be covered with plaister. It is formed into 3 principal divisions of which the lower exhibits a central compartment consisting of 5 separate foil headed niches, the sides of 6 cinquefoil headed niches the whole ornamented with pediments crockets & finials. The central or principal division is also occupied by a range of niches with pedestals for statues highly enriched in the style of the 15th century with canopies pediments crockets finials and pinnacles. The upper part of the screen is a portion of the ancient one & comprises a range of shields and foliage surmounted by an embattled cornice. (Sir Otho de Grandisson Brother of the founder). The shields exhibit the following bearings. (IV) Paly (argent & azure) of 6 on a Bend 3 Buckles (or) (V) Ermine a cross engrailed (Arms of Sir John de Northwood Knt) (VI) Barry of 6 on a chief pales between as many bar esquire (Mortimer) dexter & sinister
In the fess point an escutcheon. (VII) Four barrulets or 2 Bars in (See p 203) (Sibill daur of Lord Teagoz & wife of Will Lord Grandisson) chief a Lion passant gardant. (VIII) Ancient France Semee de lis (IX) Ancient France & England (X) Grandisson (XI) Montacute (XII) Courtenay the Label charged with 9 plates
(XIII) Paly of 6 (Argent & azure) on a bend 3 Eaglets displayed (or) (Grandisson). At the back on the eastern side of this screen are 2 ranges of arches in which have been anciently painted the figures of saints but they are nearly defaced – The coat (XII) above mentioned being according to Westcote the arms of bishop Courtenay it is not improbable that the screen was erected during his episcopate between the years 1478 & 1487 – This screen though highly ornamented & beautifully finished seems to want variety & appears in consequence rather flat & tame. (*in the margin:* The renovation of this screen cost nearly £300) On the south side of the altar are 3 sedilia of different height having open canopies with cinquefoil heads surmounted by crocketted pediments & finials, with crocketed pinnacles between them, the whole presenting a bold & elegant appearance. The choir aisles are lighted by windows formed of narrow lights in pairs divided by a pier & shafts. The roofs are ribbed with stone having bosses at the intersections of foliage and the arms (I) & (II) as before. The eastern end of the north aisle appears to have been a chapel: there is an ambry in the north wall – In each aisle is a range of ancient oaken seats with arms against the walls. The seats turn up & present carvings of Grandisson arms and masks. The eastern or smaller transept is in the same style as the ailes the windows like & the roofs ribbed with bosses of foliage. It comprises 2 stories in height the north side is used as a lumber room, the south side a vestry.

The Lady Chapel is entered by a doorway [now removed] behind the altar screen of the choir. It is lighted by 4 windows, 2 on each side, of 3 lights with cinquefoil heads & the centre higher than the others. The eastern window occupies nearly the whole breadth of the wall & is formed of 8 narrow lights with cinquefoil heads. The roof is divided into quadrangular compartments & quatrefoils by ribs having bosses at the intersections of foliage & the coats of arms (I) & (II) as before and sculptured figures of the virgin & other saints.

(In the margin: Newspaper cutting, no name of newspaper, dated March 1856
During the past week a very handsome stained glass window has been erected in the Lady Chapel, of our church, by Mr. Hardman, of Birmingham, in pious memory of the late F.G. Coleridge, of this town. The execution of the work is very chaste, and it is much admired.)

In the South wall are 4 niches for seats with trefoiled canopies. There is a pedestal for a piscina or an image & at the western end a gallery formed of stone & approached by stairs in the north wall. It is supported by shafts and the front is pierced into quatrefoils, the whole is painted. In the walls appear an ornament which occurs in various parts of the exterior of the building, a sunk quatrefoil in which is an angel holding a cross. Against the east wall of the chapel is a wooden screen in the paltry style of King James I [removed]. The floor is boarded & probably covers some inscribed stones [now tiled]. This chapel is now proposed to be put into a state of repair & to be used for occasional prayers.

The highly elegant chapel or aisle in the NW side of the church opens to the north aisle by 5 low pointed arches resting on piers of clustered shafts with capitals enriched with scrolls and foliage. It is lighted by 4 windows under low arches of which that to the west is large having 6 lights the others have 3 lights each, all with cinquefoil heads & trefoil headed perpendicular tracery. These windows on the outside are shielded by labels resting on corbels of angels holding shields. The roof is formed into elaborate & highly enriched fan tracery in cinquefoils and quatrefoils with large open pendants terminating in roses. The ribs spring from corbels in the walls & angels representing angels beautifully designed some bearing plain shields & others shields with the coats viz Courtenay - & (XIV) (argent on) On a cross, (sable) a bucks head couped between 4 doves (of the field) On a chief (azure) a cross fleury between 2 roses (or) (By Veysey). The north porch is entered from the chapel by a massive oak door in small square panels (appears to be of the same date as the chapel). It comprises 3 stories, the second lighted by single lights with low arched head & having labels resting on corbel heads. The roof of the entry is ribbed with a head in the central boss – against the walls are pedestals for images & over the door the remains of sculptures defaced – Two angels remain holding shields I Quarterly 1&4 loaded with whitewash 2 & 3 Courtenay II Bp Oldham over the door on the inside wall is painted the arms of the see of Exeter impaling Argent a Bend azure. This is not the coat of either of the bishops of Exeter & has probably been painted incorrectly. The walls of this chapel & porch are ornamented with buttresses Battlements pinnacles & gargoyles of heads & beneath the parapet runs a cornice ornamented with rosettes and the knots of the Harrington & Stafford families. Over the doorway of the porch are 2 niches one above the other with canopies, shafts on the sides & pinnacles. The lower one contains a shield with supporters which appear to be dexter a lion sinister a bear. The arms are defaced but immediately above &

below the shields appears the Stafford knot. The actual date of the erection of this elegant chapel & porch has not been ascertained but the arms of bishops Oldham & Veysey seem to point to their episcopates between the years 1504 & 1551 while the ornaments on the outside refer to the family who were owners of Knightstone in this parish. Cecily Bonville Marchioness of Dorset Lady Harrington married secondly Henry Lord Stafford & as the devices of both those families appear, this lady probably contributed largely if not entirely to the erection of the porch. She died in 1530.

This church is an interesting object as viewed towards the western end. The entrance on this side is in a recess & is formed into 2 doors divided by a triple shafted column – on each side are niches under trefoil headed canopies & finials. Above is the western window of 5 narrow lights of which the centre is the highest & over it the remains of an image of the Virgin under a canopy & crocketed pediment with pinnacles & finials. The apex of the gable is ornamented with a highly ornamented cross.

The eastern end of the Lady Chapel is ornamented with a cinquefoiled niche under a canopy & finial, in each side of the great window. Above it are 3 similar niches, the central one highest, they have cinquefoiled heads with canopies adorned with crockets & finials. At the angles of the wall are modern square pinnacles ornamented with pediments & finials and on the apex of the gable is a plain cross.

To return to the interior. A gallery reaches across the western end of the nave ornamented with carvings in oak but in a heavy style [removed] – An inscription along the sculptured base at the end records thus "Ended the 10 day of October Anno Domini 1606. G.C. - W.C. - I.S." It contains an organ by Flight & Robson in an appropriate Gothic case, erected in the year 1828.

(*Newspaper cutting, no name of newspaper, dated July 1828.*
An organ, of which reports speak highly, and of magnificent exterior, erected in the church of Otter St. Mary, by Flight and Robson, London, is intended to be opened on Sunday next 27th inst., by Mr. Flight junior.)

A gallery over the south aisle fronted with square panels was "Erected by J.V. (Vaughan esq.) 1658" and a coat of arms in front Gules 3 Boars heads erased in pale argent armed or, a label of 3 points – Crest on a wreath a man's head affronte erased proper wreathed the temples argent & sable. [removed]
Galleries in the transept are occupied by the boys of the Free School of Ottery. [removed]
The pulpit is of oak hexagonal in form carved in panels four of which have the evangelists in high relief. The sounding board is in the same style large & heavy & both are ornamented with carvings of foliage & fruit. The upper part of the sounding board which gives it so heavy an appearance with the angel on top is evidently of more recent date [sounding board removed and the angel now resides on top of the clock]. An open book in front is inscribed "Richard Marker clerk MA Church warden 1722". At the foot of the pulpit is a low inscription "All this in every part was done by William Culme born in this parish". This man is said to have gone afterwards to Rome & on his return being ashamed of his work wished to have destroyed this pulpit [inscription no longer there]. The font is of stone octagonal & lined with lead, the body of it is encased in oak carved by the same W. Culme so that

it is not visible: it rests on a pedestal with panels of trefoil headed arches [changed to a square marble font].

The cloisters belonging to the College stood tall within a few years on the north side of the church yard.

Newspaper cutting, 8 June 1858: Exeter Devon Architecture Society
The Rev. J.L. Fulford read an able paper, written by Mr. Markland, of Bath, on certain apertures (100 in all) in the roof of the parish church of Ottery St. Mary. These crevices Mr. Markland, very clearly showed to have been, in all probability, used for suspension of lamps – and this also was the opinion of Mr. Butterfield, the architect, who had superintended the restoration. Another use might have been, in certain parts of the building, the drawing up of cages used by the workmen and others in reaching loft parts of the pillar and walls, as well as the roof.

The monuments & inscriptions in Ottery church are these.

In the Lady Chapel.
A stone formerly in the floor now against the N. wall.
Here lieth the body of William Eveleigh of Holcombe esq. well known and better loved for his piety loyalty and integrity. He died 15 Oct. 1679 in the 45 year of his age. Arms per pale 2 Chevrons between 3 Griffins passant impaling – 3 Leaves (Query Malkerbe)
On the floor a Brass plate. Ann King intd. beneath with 2 infant children 1793.

Choir & its aisles.
On the north side of the altar opposite the sedilia a stone altar tomb surmounted by a pediment, the table thus inscribed "*Hic jacet Johannes Haydon de Cadhay, armiger et Johanna uxor ejus consanguinea et haeres Johannae Cadhay quae fuit uxor Hugonis Grenvile generosi qui quidem Johannes fuit primus gubernator incorporatus hujus parochiae ac obiit sine exitu nono die Martii Anno Domini 1587. Dicta autem Johanna obiit sine exitu decimo nono die Decembris Anno Domini 1592 pro quibus laus sit Deo. J.H. 1587*" On the apex of the pediment "*1587. Ferme en foy*" and the coat of arms Quarterly.
1 & 4 Haydon, 2 & 3 per Saltire --- in pale & in fess as many
2 lions passant gardant Bulls passant. Crest a Lion vulning a bull, a crescent for difference. – Motto "*Ferme en Foy*" On the front of the tomb 2 shields 1. Arms of Grenville, 3. Rest. 2. Crest of Haydon. On the back of the tomb the same. On the tympanum in front "Here lyeth the body of Gideon Haydon esq of Cadhay son of Gideon Haydon esq who departed this life in the 41 year of his age 1706". On the tympanum at the back "Here lieth the body of William Haydon gent son of William Haydon esq of Cadhay who departed this life in the 80th year of his age 1722".
N. aisle – W. end – S. wall – A stone mural monument.
Two Corinthian columns supporting an arch & an enriched entablature. The figures if any & the tablet destroyed. Arms. 2 Shields. 1st Three Bulls heads caboshed impaling Per fess. – 3 Chaplets. – Crest a dog sejant. 2nd Fretty. 2nd Walrond 2nd Duke [missing]
S. aisle – E end – N. wall – A stone mural monument. Three Corinthian columns supporting 2 arches & an entablature the figures, if any destroyed. – Two tablets below, one blank the other inscribed with laudatory particulars of some female in inflated language without name or date. [missing] –

Several coats of arms about the monument, some defaced & the remainder, as follow.
I. Quart. 1 & 4 (1) Or a Lion rampant sable between 3 Holly leaves proper (Sherman)
       2 & 3. (2) Argent a Chevron between 3 Eagles displayed gules (Terront)
II. (3) Argent 3 Bar-gemels Azure On a chief gules a Barrulet dancetty or (Haydon)
III. – (4) Argent a Wyvern gules (Drake)
IV. (5) Gules 3 Horses courant in pale argent. (Frye)
V. – (1) impaling (6) Ermine on a Bend cotised sable 3 Lions passant gardant Argent.
VI – (1) impaling (2) – VII (1) impaling (7) Per chevron engrailed or & sable, in
       chief 2 pellets each charged with a fleur de lis of the first, in base a bezant
       charged with a fleur de lis of the second. (Mallock)
VIII (1) impaling (3). – IX (1) impaling (4) – X (1) impaling (5).
So aisle. E Wall. a stone Tablet fixed & thus inscribed. If wealth wit bewtie youth or
modest mirth, could him persuade intice prolong beguile
Death's fatall dart this fading flower on earth, might yet unquailde have flourished
awhile
But mirth youth bewtie wit wealth nor all, can stay or one delay when death doth call,
No sooner was she to a loving mate from carefull parents solemlie bequeathed
The new alliance scare congratulate, but she from him them all was straight bereaved
Slipping from bridall feast to funeral beere she soon fell sick expired lies buried heer
A death thou mighest have waited in the field, on murdring canon wounding sworde
and spear
Or there where fearful passengers doe yield, at everie surge each blast of wind
doth rear.
In stabbing taverns or infected townes, in loathsome prisons or in princes frownes
There not unlookte for many a on abides, thy direful summons but a nuptiall feast
Needs not thy grimm attendance; mayden brides, in strength and flower of age thou
might let rest
With winges so weake mortallitie doth fly, in height of flight death strikes we fall &
dy. – 1618. [missing]
(*In the margin:* On the wife of Gideon Sherman esq. daughter of Nich. Fry of Yarty
esq. who died the first week of her marriage. Prince: another monument by Prince to
John Sherman and his son who died both on the one day AD 1617)

So aisle – E. end – S. wall. A tablet fixed & thus inscribed
Within this monument doth also lie
A patterne true of or infirmitie
Whose infancie childhoode youth & age
Was still attended by the wrathfull rage
Of that which crept in by our parents fall
Her welcome entertainment end and all
Seemed all alike from first to latest breath
She always seemed to die on living death
Small griefs sometimes seem great
But hers were so as greater or never made lesse
These were her passions now her actions stoode
Like the Samaritans entitled good
Had she a respite from her proper woe
That day she'd respite others pains also

It was her custome and her comfort here
As soon as her owne rod did disappeare
The comfortlesse to comfort and restore
According to her talent sick and sore
Hence envious Death did slay without remorse
And pitiless to her no pity yielded
Cause others paines she pitily relieved
What need more words works shewe her life was action
Her dying words her death was contemplation
She died the XXVIIth of August 1620. [missing]

Against one of the piers South side of the choir, a marble tablet gilt & thus inscribed
M.S.
Carolos Vaughan armig
Qui veterem unde ortus est prosapiam
Suis insuper virtutibus
Exornavit
Vir erat
Vigens felici, probitate antiqua, humanitate singulari,
Cum paucis
Intimiori consuetudine conjunctus
Urbana interim officia praestabat
Omnibus,
Rei familiaris non aliam habuit rationem
Quam quae suis ac suorum sumptibus
Quantum par erat
Suppiteret.
Religione virtute et doctrina academica
Probe institutus
Ab academicorum moribus adeo non abhorruit
Ut vitam caelibem degere
Otioq. frui literato
Constanter decrevit
Hydrope demum confectus
Diem obiit supremum
Anno Aug Xne 1736 Aetat. sue 56
Maria Richardo Ducke armig conjux
Soror unica superstes et ex asse haeres
Amoris hoc munus extremum
P.
Arms. Gules 3 Boars heads erased in pale argent armed or. – crest a mans head &
shoulders couped proper wreathed about the temples argent & sable. – (Vaughan)
[missing]

Against the walls of the choir are four stone shields as hatchments exhibiting these
armorial bearings,
I. Quart. 1st & 4th Vaughan. – 2nd Gules a mans head erased proper wreathed about the
temples azure & sable. – 3rd Gules 3 snakes fretted in triangle argent. – Crest. Vaughan.
II. Vaughan impaling Ermine a Lion passant gules (Drewe) Crest Vaughan.

III. Vaughan impaling Argent a Crop Moline Sable (2nd Sampson) Crest Vaughan

IV. Vaughan impaling dexter Or on a Fess wavy sable 3 lozenges of the field (Ducke)

Sinister Argent a spread eagle gules debruised by a chevron or, on a canton of the last a chaplet vert.

Against one of the piers south Side of the choir, a white marble monument or tablet, adorned with foliage flowers & fruit & above it an urn executed by Bacon. 1794. [missing]

To the memory of William Peere Williams of Cadhay esq. and of Elizabeth Sugnoret his wife. He died in 1766 aged 63 years, and she in 1792 aged 83. His knowledge & integrity long commanded the respect of the county as a magistrate, her beneficent charities were of general relief to the neighbourhood. Arms. Quarterly 1 & 4. a demi wolf currant issuant from a rock 2 & 3 a wyvern (Drake of ash). An escutcheon of pretence. Azure a Fess between 3 Mullets. [missing]

Pier on the south – a Brass plate – *Infra reconduntur cineres reverendi Thomae Gatchell artium baccalaurii et hujus ecclesiae vicarii qui obiit decimo quarto die Julii Anno Dom 1713 aetat. suae 50.* [missing]

Against a north pier. A Tablet with an urn. Sacred to the memory of John Harrison Stapleton esq. Lieutenant Colonel. Of the South Devon Militia who lived in the hearts of his brother soldiers and died most feelingly lamented by all. On the 20 July 1809 in the 40th year of his age. a tribute of sincere regard this tablet is erected by Colonel Lord Rolle. [missing]

Tablet, So. Aisle. To the memory of the revd. John Coleridge who died AD. 1781 aged 63. of Ann his second wife who died A.D. 1809 aged 83 & of their children John died in the East Indies AD. 1786 aged 31. William an infant. William at Hackney AD. 1780 aged 23. Luke Herman at Thorverton AD. 1790 aged 24. Ann at Ottery AD. 1791 aged 23. Francis in the East Indies AD. 1792 aged 22. George at Ottery AD. 1828 aged 64.

North aisle. A Tablet with an urn – Near this place are deposited the remains of Thomas Hopkins esq. who departed this life at Sidmouth the 5th October 1817 aged 76. This monument is erected to his memory by his affectionate wife. [missing]

On the floor behind the altar screen – *Hic jacet Oliverus Smythe quondam custos hujus collegii qui obiit IX die April Anno Dom M°DXCIIII* – in the middle of the stone a heart with the letters J.H.S. (This inscription has been lately renewed)

On the floor. *Hic jacet Johannes Enderby prebendarius hujus collegii qui obiit XX Decembris An Dom M°CCCCCXXXII.*

On the floor. Richard Chanon esq buried May 16 1668 in the 85 year of his age. Here lieth with Richard his son Katherine & Johanna his daughter and Mores Chaplin son of Johanna. Arms. A chevron embattled counter embattled between 3 Birds heads erased (Chanon) impaling a Chevron between 3 hands couped (2nd Maynard)

Floor N. aisle. Here lieth the body of --- Burwell of Waxway --- parish gent who died -- 1749. The only son of Thomas Burwell -- of the college of -- Anno Dom 1703. Elizabeth his wife who died April 22. 1736 [missing].

Here lieth the body of Catherine eldest daughter of Gideon Haydon of Cadhay esq and of Catherine his wife who decease 28 July A.D. 1643 aetatis suae die tertio. Arms of Haydon in a lozenge.

Here interred lie the Sonne and Margaret the daughter of William Euery esq and Margaret his wife who died the one 4 Aug. 1602 aet 1 die the other 31 Jan 1605 aetat anno secundo. Arms 3 or 4 Chevrons.

Some verses, then follows *"Sara Haydon filia Roberti Haydon armig ob. 24 die Aprilis An Dom 1602 et anno aetat suae --"*. Arms in a lozenge 3 Swords points downwards in the kile & the letters on the sides S.H. (These are not the arms of Haydon but of Poulett) (*In the margin:* Given by Polwhele III 246 27 AD. 1626)

Nocet posteris Hic sepultus est, Henricus Marker gen. obiit 9 Junii A.D. 1705 aetatis suae 83 etiam Henricus ejus filius unus e quatuor hujusce ecclesiae majoribus obiit dec. septimo Septembris 1708 aetatis suae 63. Etiam Elizabetha uxor Henrici Marker gent obiit --esimo primo Augusti Anno Dom 1711 aetatis suae 39. [missing]

Here lieth the body of Mary wife of Anthony Coplestone who died February. 22. 1754. [missing]

On the floor of the Choir. –

Here lie enshrined the ashes of James Burnard late of this parish gent. who died 27 June in the year of our redemption 1683 together with those of Rebecca his wife who followed him February. The 18th in the year 1704.

Isthoc sub marmore depositae sunt reliquiae Annae filia Henrici Trosse Exoniensis armigeri ex uxore Rebecca uxoris Nicholai filii Gideonis Haydon de Cadhay armigeri ex uxore Margareta quae obiit VII Februarii AD. CIƆIƆCLII Arms Haydon impaling 3 scimitars barwise in pale Laudles towards the sinister side. [missing]

Under this stone lieth the body of Samuel Taylor esq Capt. RN who departed this life February. 7. 1790 aged 68. As also the body of Mary his widow who died Nov. 24. 1798 aged 81 Also beneath this stone are deposited the remains of Thomas Hopkins esq who departed this life at Sidmouth 5 Oct. 1817 aged 76. [missing]

Marmor hoc a loco paululum inferiori quo Johannis Vaughan ar. uxorisque ejus natae Johannes Upton de Lupton ar. avi sui aviaque nunc restant reliquiae ad hunc quo Pater suus Materq Francisci Drewe de Grange ar. filia cum pluribus domus suae (de Penwyn in Cambria Boreali ortae) fuere sepulti transferri curavit Carolos Vaughan hujus parochiae ar. Anno aere Christiana MDCCXXIV. [missing]

Hic situs est Gilbertus Garde ar. unus sociorum Medii Templi London qui obiit XVIII die Augusti Anno Dom 1679 aetatis suae 79. Hic etiam jacet Janae uxor ejus quae obiit 2 August AD. 1688 aetatis suae 74. Arms. – On a chevron between 3 water bougets a roundel (Yarde) impaling a fess between 3 griffons or Lions heads erased. [missing]

In this vault are deposited the remains of Mr. Joseph Newberry of this parish and of St Stephen Coleman street in the city of London who died Dec. 1. 1830 in the 38 year of his age. [missing]

Nave.

On each side is an ancient altar tomb having upon it a full length figure, on the north side that of a knight in complete armour and on the south a female probably his wife, both in the costume of the reign of Henry IV between 1399 & 1413 – the tombs are surmounted by a cinquefoiled arch with a crocketed canopy & finials with a pinnacle on each side. These monuments are precisely alike and are richly adorned with foliage & shields but do not exhibit any armorial bearings. They are supposed to be the tombs of the Father & Mother of Bishop Grandisson. The female has a whimple on her head and two dogs at her feet, & her head is supported by angels-

On the floor a very large stone with a fragments of brass along the edge thus inscribed in old letters "*quondam doctor sacre theologie et cancellarius vniversitatis oxonie*" – Floor. Here lieth the body of Thomasine Baker relict of Charles Baker late of this place gent who departed this life the 20 day of January AD. 1742 aged 78 Here also lies Sarah their youngest daughter. [missing]

South Aisle
Over the south door a stone tablet – the arms of Haydon with a crescent for difference – *In obitum ornatissimi viri Johannis Haidoni armigeri vita defuncti carmen.* There follow some Latin verses & the date 1618. (*In the margin:* Given at length by Polwhele III.245)
Marble tablet. Near this place are deposited the remains of Frances Salter wife of Richard Salter of this parish who died May 21. 1833 aged 29 years also Flora her daughter aged 8 months. This tablet erected by her affectionate husband. [missing]

North aisle.
Floor. Here lieth the body of Edward Dryden gent who died May 27. 1742. [missing]

Chapel or additional North aisle.
East end. A mural monument of marble painted & gilt consisting of a pediment supported by 2 Ionic columns. Beneath it a whole length standing figure of a Knight in half armour with trunk hose, a baton in his right hand sword in his left and his helmet at his feet. On a tablet below The monument of John Coke of Thorne esq the son of Christopher Coke and Joan the daughter of Richard Copleston esq. He married Margaret the daughter of Richard Sherman gent and had issue Richard John William Jane and Jone He was of the age of 42 years and 7 months and dyed the 28 day of March 1632. (Then follow some Latin verse) – Arms on 3 shields.
I. Ermine on a Bend cotised Sable 3 Lions passant or. (Coke)
II. Or a Lion rampant sable between 3 leaves vert. (Sherman)
III. Quarterly of 9. 1 as I above.
    2. Argent a fess wavy gules between 3 Lions rampant sable (2nd Thorne)
    3. Gules a Chevron between 3 (grey owls) argent (27 Radway)
    4. Argent 2 irons in saltire between 4 pears pendent within a border engrailed
        Sable. (Kaleway)
    5. Argent a chevron gules between 3 (question bells) sable Exeter
    6. Azure semee of (question hearts) or, a Lion rampant of the last.
    7. Or, a lion rampant gules within a border engrailed sable (Pomeray)
    8. Argent on a bend sable 5 Bezants.
    9. Argent on a Chevron gules 3 (question Leopard faces) or Crest a demi lion
        rampant or.

On a small tablet below This was newly beautified by his grandson John Grandission gent. July 30. 1726 Arms Argent 3 cocks heads and necks erased gules impaling an anchor erect or. Crest on a wreath a cock's head & neck erased or. (Misson) (verses also given by Polwhele)

North West corner a marble monument with Corinthian pilasters at the sides which support an entablature & pediment. A tablet between them thus inscribed In a vault near this place lie the bodies of Anne the relict of Hugh Vaughan late of this parish esq (whose body lies in this church) and of Letitia his sister relict of Richard Carew late of Barly (near Exeter) esq daughter of John Goodall of Fowye in the county of Cornwall merchant who had one daughter more called Mary by Elizabeth his second wife married Malachy Pyne of Exeter merchant. Anne Vaughan died the 30 Jany 1730. Letitia Carew died the 5 February 1730 and was buried together the 10th of the same month by John Pyne their nephew. Also here lieth the body of Elizabeth the wife of Mr Richard Maker of this town gent. daughter of John Kestell of Kestell in the county of Cornwall MD. Who died June the 22nd 1772 aged 69 years.

Arms on 4 shields viz.

I (1) Gules 3 Boars heads erased in pale argent armed or. impaling 1st (2) Or On a Fess wavy sable 3 lozenges of the field. (Ducke) 2nd (3) Argent a Spread-eagle gules debruised of a chevron or, on a canton of the last a chaplet proper. Crest on a wreath a man's head & shoulders affrontee couped proper

II (4) Gules a chevron between 3 Pineapples slipped or, impaling (2) (Pyne)

III Or 3 Lions passant in pale sable langued & armed gules impaling (2) Carew

IV (1) impaling (2)

North wall a marble tablet.

Windsor Vaughan the descendant of two noble families but more ennobled by a blameless conversation and a Christian death died June 17. 1786 aged 70. His widow the eldest daughter of James Kestell of Kestell in the county of Cornwall died June 25. 1824 aged 93.

Floor. A large stone on which are 3 brass whole length figures of men with labels over the heads of two of them, the third removed. 1 *Johannes ob. 1542.* 2nd *Guilielmus ob. 1583.* – On a brass tablet below *Sac. Memoriae Johannis Sherman generosi Gulielmi filii eius et Richardi nepotis qui ex ipsorum voto una requiescunt.* Then follow some Latin verses: *Tres tegit hoc unum marmor virtutibus omnis, (ut tumulo) meritis, sanguine, laude, pares.*

Here lieth the body of Frances Walrond widow relict of John Walrond of Sidbury gent. and daughter of Robert Duke of Otterton esq who died 9th day of February 1714 in the 80 year of her age. Arms 3 Bulls heads caboshed impaling Duke. –

Charles Gellius Collins Born the 9th. August & died 30 Sept 1820 William George Collins Born 6 May 1833 died 1 Feb. 1825. [missing]

Underneath this stone lieth the body of Mrs Deborah Vaughan widow of William Vaughan of London gent who died the 9th May 1769 in the 75 year of her age, Also the body of Eleanor Vaughan her daughter-in-law who died 3 Aug. 1775 aged 65 And of Windsor Vaughan esq son of Mrs. Deborah Vaughan and husband to Mrs. Ann Vaughan who died June 17. 1786 aged 70 Also Betty Kestell widow of the above Windsor Vaughan esq who died June 25 1824 aged 93.

N Transept.
Against the east wall. The arms of Drake of Ash with helmet & mantle in stone.
On the floor. *Hic jacet Richard ----*

S. transept.
Floor. *Depositum Georgii Coleridge clerici hujusce eccles. capellani necnon et scholae Otteriensis pedagogi qui ob. Jan. 12. 1828 anno aetat. 64.*

Church yard. –

Stones at the west end of the north aisle.

In memory of Sarah Hathaway widow, daughter of the revd. John Coleridge formerly vicar of this parish, who died 16 Dec. 1832 aged 85.

Sacred to the memory of Francis George Patterson son of the Hon Sir John Patterson knight one of the Judges of the court of King's bench and Frances Duke his wife daughter of James Coleridge esq of Heaths court Ottery St. Mary who died 17 April 1831 aged 1 year & 18 days. Also of Henrietta Duke Patterson daughter of the same parents who died 10 April 1833 aged ten months & 12 days and was buried at Trinity church in the parish of St. Giles in the fields of London. [missing]

Tombs in various situations.

Subtus deponuntur Gul. Browne pii doctri integri relliquiae seu potius exuviae qui in omnibus vitae officiis tum in alios tum in se ita se praestit egregium ut Exemplar morum quasi pro testamento suis reliquerit. ob. die Junii 16. 1816 aet. 83. Here also are deposited the remains of Sarah Browne wife of the said William Browne to whom she bore 10 children & died April 18. aged 76. [missing]

In memory of Richard Denning of Pitt in this parish gent who died 10 Sept 1778 aged 79. Joan his wife died 3 July 1778 aged 86 Richard their son died 23 Feb. 1816 aged 83. [missing]

Sacred to the memory of Henry Palmer esq late of the island of Jamaica who departed this life 17 Nov 1814 aged 85 [missing]

In this vault are deposited the remains of James Kestell of Kestell in the county of Cornwall who died 21 March 1751. Elizabeth Marker his wife died 5 Sept. 1767 Also of John Kestell who died 24 July 1817 aged 79 and Bridget Kestell died 12 February. 1782 children of James & Elizabeth Kestell also the remains of Sarah Clapp of Salcombe Regis first wife of John Kestell who died 25 Sept 1777. [missing]

Here lieth the body of Mrs. Rebecca Bailey relict of the revd Mr Richard Bailey lately vicar of Portesham in Dorsetshire who died 1 Jay 1740 aged 65. NB. Rebecca Bailey was sister to John Burnard esq of this parish who died 15 Aug. 1721 and by her will bequeathed an estate to the vicar of Ottery of £12 per annum for preaching a monthly preparation sermon the Saturday before the administration of the holy sacrament [missing].

Sacred to the memory of Capt. Jeffery R.N. who died Nov. 26 1833 aged 53. Henry Jeffery his infant son buried 10 May 1823 aged 13 weeks also Eliza Jeffery died 11 Sept. 1827 aged 8 months. [missing]

Richard Johnson Surgeon died Sept. 5 1804 aged 81 years. Loveday Johnson wife of Richard Johnson died 2 March in the 25 year of her age. [missing]

Against the walls of the choir are 4 handsome modern wooden tablets varnished & gilt & thus inscribed.

I Ottery St. Mary 1832. Particular and rental of the lands and premises situated in this parish held in trust for the benefit of the necessitous persons of the parish not receiving parochial relief.

Three cottages adjoining each other and one behind with out-buildings & garden in Mill street held by John Perriman under a building lease. p.14 £2. 15s. od.

A dwelling house office and walled garden bounded by Silver street and back street held under a building lease heretofore granted to William Brooke p.23. £1.ov.ov.

The workhouse and garden in front occupied by the parish poor at the bottom of

Mill street without rent. The workhouse garden adjoining in which are two cottages r.2p.26. £6. 0s. 0d.

Three adjoining houses and gardens in Sandhill street called Almshouses occupied by poor people rent free ---- p.28. £0. 0s. 0d.

Two cottages and gardens in Jesue street – p.32. £7. 0s. 0d

Cottage and garden adjoining the last --- p.17. £4.0s. 0d.

(*In the margin:*

14 Oct 1819 To be sold – the manor of Down Umfraville etc. in the parish of Axmouth – manor of Northleigh in Colyton House etc & The manor Cordslip & Hundred of Ottery St. Mary in about 4000 acres of land of which 200 plantation – (Memo: collection: memorandum book I.) The property of John Mountstephen How esq. –

Andr. atte More custos ecclie Collegial. bte Marie de Ottery – Johes Tappehot protector (procurator) ecclie pdce --- See 2 deeds dated 1377 relating to Egleshughe & Clesewey in the hundred of Axm & one dated 1374 for Axminster.)

A dwelling house next the last with curtledge and buildings and garden, 2 orchards adjoining and behind the curtledge and a close of arable land at the south end of the south most orchard divided only by a lane. --- a.2. r.2. p.23. £18. 0s. 0d.

A house next adjoining the last used as a charity school on Bell's system and for the residence of the schoolmaster with a garden behind free ---- a.0. r.0. p.30. £0. 0s 0d.

Six adjoining houses called almshouses in Jesus street with gardens adjoining occupied by poor people rent free. p.34. £0. 0s. 0d.

II. A close of arable land in Heather Gerwell lane called John Land's close. a.1.r.3.p.13. £5. 10s. 0d.

A moiety of a close of land at Bradleigh adjoining the last mentioned close the whole whereof is 6 roods. --- a.0.r.3.p.0. £1. 0s. 0d.

Teap's meadow adjoining Little well. --- a.4.r.3.p.12. £21. 0s.0d.

The Rag arable land lying between Hang bow meadow and parish meadow & separated from Teap's meadow on the east of the water course. a.r.1.p.27. £1. 0s. 0d.

An orchard near Shute r.3.p.27. and one close of arable land adjoining a.2.r.2.p.22. in all a.3.r.2.p.19. £12. 0s. 0d.

Three adjoining closes of arable land called Four-acres and Higher & Lower closes near Shute on the south of Chineway road. a.7.r.3.p.28.

Two closes of arable land called Higher and Lower Thorns lying in the east of Great Well meadow and on the south of Chineway road. a.5.r.1.p.31. total for both lots £33. 10s. 0d.

Two closes of arable land called Three acres and Two acres next to the last mentioned Four acres on the south a.5.r.1.p.30. £15. 0s. 0d.

A close of land adjoining to the last mentioned Two acres 2.1.5. One other close adjoining on the east 2.1.8 and one other close adjoining on the north of the last close. 4.0.0. all arable a.8.r.2.p.13. £10. 0s. 0d.

A close of Pasture land called Haskins on the south adjoining the first of the last mentioned three fields. – a.3.r.3.p.3. £14. 10s. 0d.

Two closes of meadow and 5 acres of arable land adjoining each other with a barn lying on the east of Higher Thorns close and on the north adjoining to Leggeshayes. – a.26.r.2.p.13. £54. 0s. 0d.

III A close of land adjoining East Hill bounded on the north and south by Cold Harbour estate. – a.4.r.1.p.o. £8. 8s. od.

An orchard at Ridgeway about ¾ acre bounded on the east by an orchard belonging to Richard Coles. – a.o.r.3.p.o. £5. os. od.

A close of arable land lying at Rush lake near Redhill. a.1.r.1.p.16. £3. 5s. od.

A close of arable land at Cookman Hill. a.1.r.o.p.o. £3. os. od.

A cottage curtledge barn, one orchard & 6 closes of arable land and coppice and plot through which the river runs called Burnt-house estate at Woodford. a.17.r.2.p.15. £47. os. od.

Two cottages and gardens called Burnt-house occupied by poor people rent free. a.o.r.1.p.6. £0. os. od.

One meadow and 5 closes of arable land at Goveton a.19.r.1.p.38.

A farm-house farm buildings courtledge garden 2 meadows 1 orchard and 13 closes of arable land called Raxhays near Goveton. a.64.r.3.p.o. £120. os. od. for the two lots

An orchard at Fenny Bridges.   a.1.r.o.p.22. £1. 10s. od.

One close of pasture land and 7 closes or parcels of arable at Metcombe a.16.r.2.p.37. £45. os. od.

a chief rent payable at Lady-day annually out of Burcombe estate the property of the representative of the late Stephen Stocker of. £.o. 6s. 8d.

An orchard and 5 closes of arable land called Davy's Dole on which is a barn lately built a.12.r.2.p.19. £18. 6s. od.

A meadow near Tipton bridge called Labersash part of Davy's donation a.1.r.o.p.24. £3. 3s. od.

IV Ottery St. Mary 1832

A particular and rental of lands and premises situated in the co of Somerset held in trust for the benefit of the necessitous persons of this parish not receiving parochial relief.

A farm-house courtledge buildings garden orchard and 8 closes of pasture and arable land and one garden orchard called Rappa in the parish of Ilton also a chief rent of 4s/2d. payable out of lands adjoining these premises called Gunhams a.40.r.3.p.27. £83. 10s. od.

Two closes of land called Great Bonds and Little Bonds in the parish of Abbots Isle. a.10.r.2.p.5. £23. os. od.

A dwelling house courtledged garden one orchard 4 closes of arable and pasture land called Windmill hill in the parish of Ashill. a.13.r.2.p.15.

& Mullins mead in the parish of Abbots Isle. a.8.r.o.p.1. £40. os. od. for the two lots.

One close situated in Abbots Isle near the turnpike road leading from Ashill to Taunton being one entire allotment lately made under the Neroche forest enclosure act in lieu of the 4 rights of common thereon belonging to the aforesaid several lands in Somerset about. a.6.r.o.p.o.

Against the north wall of the north aisle a similar tablet.

Benefactions. – Mr William Woodrow of this parish yeoman by his will dated March 5. 1807 gave to the vicar & church Wardens for the time being in trust the sum of £100, one moiety of the interest to be applied towards the support of a Sunday school and the other moiety to be distributed at Easter among the most constant and deserving poor communicants as the vicar & churchwardens should think fit.

The revd James How of Colyton in this county clerk MA by his will dated Oct. 1st 1816 gave to the officiating ministers church-wardens and overseers of this parish for the time being in trust the sum of £300 stock in the 4 per cent Consol the interest of it to be applied towards the establishment and support of a Sunday school in this parish. The above sum of £100 has been laid out in the purchase of £120.4.3 Consolidated 3 per cent annuities which now stand in the names of the vicar & church-wardens of this parish.

The above sum of £300 now stands in the 3½ per cent reduced annuities formerly 4 per cent in the names of the vicar, church-wardens and overseers.

Wonford belonged to the Montacute Earls of Salisbury Lysons 263.

Oakford – Lysons 370

Poltimore belonged to the Simon Lord Montacute temp Edward 1272 to 1307 Lysons 419

Stokeham belonged to Sir John Montacute younger son of William U.E. of Salisbury temp Edward III. Polwhele 1. 258 & Lysons 482

Edward Courtenay eldest son of Edward earl of Devonshire married Eleanor daur. of Roger Mortimer Earl of March & left no issue. He died before his father in 1416 For seal of Cath. Countess of Devon with arms including those of Mortimer – AD. 1514. See Polwhele III. 346

Henry Tregos held lands at Stokeinteignhead 1274. in which he was succeeded in 1302 by John Bittlesgate Pole 250. Lysons 461.

Henry Tregos 2 Bars in chief a lion

Bronescombe 1257-1280

Grandisson 1327-1369

Wm. Montacute ob. 1344

E of Salisbury ob. 1344

Foundation 1334 Lysons 377

Destruction of church ornaments by Cromwell Polwhele 1. 307

For a grant by the abbot & convent of Newenham to the Custos & Cannons of the colligate church of Ottery of a yearly rent charge of 13/4 temp Edward 3 – see appendices to Oliver Historic collections of my Collections for east Devon page 379

Book extract inserted into the manuscript:
Restoration of the Parish Church of Ottery St Mary Devon

[The] Parish Church of Ottery St Mary is an ancient and venerable Structure of great size and beauty, first consecrated in 1260, but so enlarged and adorned by Bishop Grandissen in the early part of the Reign of Edward 3rd that it may be more properly considered as work of that period in our Architectural History of which it is a most interesting Specimen.

It is in tolerable substantial repair but has suffered by injudicious alterations made from time to time without and it is disfigured to an unusual extent within by numerous Galleries ill contrived and clumsily executed and by a system of pews as bad as can be conceived.

The Parishioners are sincerely desirous of removing a state of things which is not only very inconvenient to many among them especially to the poorer Classes, but which they feel to be disgraceful to themselves and very inconsistent with a true zeal for the honour of God, and the advancement of Christ's religion among men. They have resolved therefore to attempt the reseating of the Church on a uniform plan and this entire architectural restoration of the whole Fabric.

The Drawing which we have placed at the head of this Paper and which does not in the least exaggerate the size and character of the Church, will show better than any description in words that the object in view are beyond the un assisted means of the Parishioners. There are Circumstances too serious which diminish this ability, nearly all the larger Estates in the Parish are this property of Absentees who take less interest in the Condition of this Church than it is probable that they would, if it were before their eyes and they were daily or weekly enjoying the use of it from their tenants, persons in many instances of small capital less assistance can in reason be expected. At the Reformation the Sheaf Tithes were withdrawn and granted to the Dean and Chapter of Windsor, these have been commuted at nearly £1000 a Year, and if they were in the hands of a Resident Rector, there can be no doubt that very important assistance would be afforded from that source. The Small Tithes commuted at £250.12 are in the hands of a Corporation, created by Henry VIII, and charged with the repair of Vicarage and School House, and the payment of the Vicar Chaplain Priest, and Schoolmaster. Yet under these discouraging circumstances within a few years two additional Churches have been built and endowed with little help from individuals out of the Parish, and a third it is hoped will in a few weeks be ready for consecration; to one of these a Parsonage and a School House have been added. It is right to mention, that six Clergymen are at present engaged in the pastoral care of the Parish, and that the united Ecclesiastical Income of them all from every source, do not amount to £400. They however, and their flock and it is hoped will not be found wanting in the present work and five individuals, one a non resident owner of lands have each declared their intention of contributing one tenth of the whole outlay.

Under these circumstances we venture to apply for assistance beyond the limits of our parish, we trust that it will be felt that this is a work which aught to be done, and which it can sincerely be expected that the Parishioners alone will be able to do and that the maintenance of such a structure is not merely of parochial interest but may be considered as in some sense belonging to the County of Devon, and the Country at large. Buildings such as this have their use and interest not merely for the Architect and men of taste but sprinkled as they are through our Land they serve to remind our population at large of the pious magnificence of our Forefathers and tend to raise among them devout and unworldly feelings.

[Whatever] is contributed will be applied with a due feeling of the importance of the trust by a Committee formed for the purpose and under the direction of an eminent Architect. Any Donations will be thankfully received by the Revd Dr Cornish the Vicar the Right Revd. Bishop Coleridge Salston House near Otter St Mary. The Honourable Mr. Justin Coleridge Heaths Court Ottery St Mary or 26, Park Crescent, London, Members of the Committee and by the following Bankers. Messrs. Flood and Loss, Honiton and the National Provincial bank Exeter.

Signed for the Committee,

J.P. Coleridge.

August, 1846

GITTISHAM

Davidson (pp. 201–8) visited [St Michael] Gittisham on 22 September 1829. He noted that 'the church of this beautiful and sequestered village is an interesting object of attention not so much from its structure as for the good preservation of the ancient monuments it contains'.

The building consists of a nave 34 feet long by 18½ wide a chancel 18 by 44 An aisle on the south side 62 feet long by 12, & a tower at the western end of the nave 10 feet by 9. The total length within the walls is 66 feet. The nave is divided from the chancel and the tower by lofty pointed arches and from the aisle by 4 low pointed arches supported by quadrangular columns composed each of 4 shafts with intervening mouldings the capitals are well carved in foliage & exhibit shields with the follow coat armour & letters but the whole are thickly coated with whitewash 1 baring 3 bars (Beaumont) Barry of 6. baring & Gules. impaling two coats of 1st in chief a cross of lozenges. 2nd in base 3 bendlets sinister. II Beaumont, with 2 bears collard & chained for supporters. III the letters EH. IV 3 lioncels rampart V. the letter HB. The arch between the chancel & the aisle rests on pillars only without columns or capitals and is adorned with panels in its archivolt an opening is formed diagonally through the wall between the nave & chancel to enable the occupants of the aisle to view the altar. The eastern window of the chancel is divided into 3 lancet shaped lights & the mullions intersect one another in the arch above which is pointed, the side window of 2 lights is of similar style & they prove the erection of this part of the building to have been in the 13th century, the nave was probably of the same date but the windows here have been despoiled of their tracery for which has been substituted plain mullions rising perpendicularly to the top of the arch which have a very tasteless appearance, two windows of the aisle the eastern one & that next to it have escaped the demolition, the one has 4 & the other 3 lights with cinquefoil heads & perpendicular tracery in the arches in the style of the 15 century or soon after. – The north door of the nave is protected by a porch & is under a pointed arch adorned with numerous mouldings resting on 4 shafts with circular capitals – a beautiful specimen of the pointed style –
The doorway into the aisle is under a low pointed arch –

The tower is embattled & is about 40 feet high, it contains 3 bells & a clock the basement was converted into a vestry in 1829 & half the cost defrayed by the rev. H Marker the present rector. – The roofs are coved & ribbed with oak & adorned with foliage at the intersections of the ribs, a screen divides the chancel from the nave in a sort of Roman style as also the pulpit & a singers gallery at the western end of the nave, in this gallery is an organ erected in 1827 & contained in a case of appropriate design in the pointed style [organ now in the south aisle]. – The font is of stone octagonal, the sides adorned with panels formed into quatrefoils with foliage in their centres, below them are several mouldings & it rests on an octagonal column & base the former panelled in trefoil headed arches it is lined with lead & is 3 feet 4 inches in height & 2 feet 3in: in diameter – In the east window of the chancel are 3 shields of old glass, viz in the centre. France & England quarterly within the garter with the motto – on the north side Beaumont on the south P. fess in chief Gules a crop of lozenges Argent 3 bendlets sinister Azure impaling Beaumont – In the north window of the chancel are 2 circular pieces of painted glass in the Flemish style representing the taking down from the cross & the entombment of our Lord, these 2 windows have also several additions of modern stained glass in various colours. In the eastern window of the aisle is a shield with helmet & mantle in painted glass, the arms are Argent a lion rampant within a mascle Sable (Putt) impaling Or 4 chevrons Gules Crest a lions paw erased Sable holding an arrow point down

The monuments in this church are these. –

Against the south wall of the aisle a marble monument enclosed by an iron railing [missing], painted & gilt consisting of an entablature supported by 3 Corinthian columns beneath which are the effigies of a man & woman each kneeling on a cushion before a desk with an open book, the man in plated armour with a close ruff & his sword by his side. On his desk is inscribed *"Obiit Aprilis primo 1591"* the woman is in long & loose drapery with a ruff & cap on the side of her desk is carved in low relief the figure of an infant sleeping on a couch – below the figures is the following inscription. –

Enterred here in this tomb doth Henry Beaumont rest
A man of just and upright life with many graces blest
Who learned to know God's holy will all wicked waies defyed
And as he learned so did he lyve and as he lyed he dyed
What good he might he gladly did and never harmed any
Courteous he was in all his life and friendly unto many
But most of all his liberal gifts abounded to the poore
A worthy practice of that word that he had learned before
Borne of what honourable race is needless for this verse
Since French and English chronicles so oft his name rehearse
Which ancient bloud within himself by want of issue spent
The sinking line thereof he corckt by one of that descent
He lived thrice ten years and nine with his most godly wife
Who yielded him his honour due void of unkindly strife
And for true witness of her love which never was defaced
As dutie last this monument she caused here to be placed.

Arms I. 3 bars Gules (Beamont) impaling Or 3 piles pointes meeting in base Azure. (Brian)

II. Quarterly 1&4 Beamont 2nd & 3 Gules a saltier vairy (Champernown) Argent & Azure – An esquire's helmet & crest on a wreath Azure & Gules a stork Argent.

III Beamont impaling Gules 3 lions passant gardant in pale Or In chief a file Azure of 3 points each changed with as many crosses of the second.

IV Beamont impaling Or a lion rampant Gules

V. Beamont impaling Gules 4 Fossils in fess Argent

VI (Over the man) Beamont impaling Or a chevron between: 3 eagles displayed vert.

VII (over the woman) Beamont quarterly as II. Impaling Quarterly of 12.

I. Argent on a fess dancette Sable a crescent Or (perhaps) for difference

2. Gules semee of cross crosslets fitchee & a lion rampant Argent:
3. Azure 3 leopards each jessant a fleur de lis Or
4. Barry of 6 Or & Azure on a chief of the first 2 pales between 2 Bar squirrels dexter & sinister of the second. An escutcheon
5. Gyronny of 8 Argent: & gules a bordure Sable bezant of 10
6. Lozenge Gules & Vairy
7. Argent 3 mallets Gules
8. Gules 3 lioncels rampant Or within a bordure Argent:
9. Gules 3 horseman's rests Or (Grenville)
10. Argent: on a bend cotised Gules 3 mullets Or (2nd Bampfylde)
11. Gules 3 bendlets enhanced Or
12. Argent 10 escallops Sable 4.3.2.1
VIII. Beamont impaling Gules a cross of lozenges Argent (Stowell)
IX. Beamont impaling Argent 3 rams passant sable
X. Beamont quarterly as II impaling Quarterly of 8.
1. Or a chevron between 3 eagles displayed vert.
2. Bendy of 8 Argent: & Azure: a bordure Gules
3. Argent a chevron Sable in chief a file of 3 points Gules
4. Argent: a chevron between 2 crosses patees in chief and a saltier in base sable
5. Argent: 3 Cornish choughs Sable
6. Or on a chevron Gules 3 martlets of the field (Chiseldon)
7. Azure: a chevron between 3 chess rooks Or (2nd Rogers)
8. Azure: 2 bars between 9 martlets Or. (2nd Tantifer)
XI. Azure semee of fleurs de lis & a lion rampant Or (Beamont)

Against the north wall of the chancel – a tablet under a pediment supported by 2 Corinthian columns on the top 2 figures a skeleton in a shroud and an angel, the whole ornament painted & gilt – below in capital letters. Here lyeth the body of Joane the wife of Glidd Beaumont rector of this parish and daughter of Edmund Greene of Exon gent who dyed the 14 May 1627.
Arms – Azure semee of fleurs de lis & a lion rampant Or impaling Argent on a fess Gules between 3 bulls heads couped sable a mullet Or – Crest a (broken) Argent gorged with a ducal crown Or.
On the tablet in capital letters
Dilectissimae sorori suae
Epitaphi hoc
E.H
P.P
Amoris et Honoris
Ergo
This urne holds sacred dust each, pious ey
Here drop a teare and weep that she should dy
No one perfection of the femal kind
But lies with her within this tomb enshrynde
Here wants no epitaph ith' hearts of men
Writ are her prayers teares are now the pen
Only this proud stone needes would have it tolde
What pretious dost it doth here under holde

Holde it a while in peace till it shall be
Raysde to a better life and glory see.
Floor of the nave – here l. -- body of Bea --- died ---

Chancel floor north side an inscription in the old letters illegible.
Nave east wall a tablet – Underneath this seat lie the remains of the Honorable David
Stuart third son of James earl of Moray who departed this life 12 June 1784 aged
39 years and 4 months. Arms Quarterly 1&4 the arms of Scotland within a bordure
Gobony Argent & Azure
2 Or a fess checky Argent & azure 3. Or 3 cushions tasselled within a double tressure
flory counter flory Gules Crest a pelican in her piety (not coloured)

Aile south wall a tablet of marble gilt –
Adeste niuei candidiq. Lectores cum liliis ac hyacynthis libate lachrymas tales enim
deposcet Exequias mellitissimus ille Juvenis Johannes Fiennes Hosp: Grayensis
Armiger Johannes Fiennes de Amwell in agro Hartford arm. secundae sobolis a
patre suo Gul: vicecomiti Say et Seale et ipsius uxoris Susannae filiae et haeredis
Tho' Hobbes Hosp: Grayens: Armiger: Faelix filius speratusq. pater qui perillustre
Fiennorum genus perennaret posteris fuit nimirum adolescens ad naturae Normam
perpolitus Aque corporis ac animi Dotibus ornatissimus quibus vel a pueritia
prudentia senilis mores maritavit amaenissimos ut audiret saeculi par Decus, ac
Deliciae sed raro praecoces diurnant fructus, dum nimium festinus ille surculus
(futurum familiae columen) in aetatis vernantis anno vicessimo tertio MDCLXXI.
Caelebs, immatura morte praereptus est. Lugete lachrymulisq. cineres ejus irrorate
praeficae vos charites omnes et lugete Musae. Arms azure 3 lioncels rampant Or.

Floor aisle – here lyth the body of John Fiennes esq. son and heire of John F.
of Amwell in the county of Hartford esq. (second son of the right Hon. William
viscount Say and Seale) and Susannah sole daughter and heir of Thomas Hobbs of
Grays inn, esq: who died the 1st day of December 1671 in the 23rd year of his age to
whose memory the opposite monument is concreted –
Arms – 3 lioncel rampant.

Against the north wall of the aisle under a semicircular arch is a white marble altar
tomb covered by a black marble slab on which stand two large funeral urns of white
marble ornamented with festoons of foliage acorns & roses, the whole is enclosed by
an iron railing [missing] and on the front of the tomb is this inscription. Here lieth
the body of Sir Thomas Putt of Combe Baronet who departed this life 25 June AD.
1686 in the 43rd year of his age. *Libenter mortalis quia futurus immortalis.* Ursula
Lady Putt died 22 April 1674 possessed of as much beauty wit wisdom learning
virtue and piety as nature art and grace are produced excelling all in a generous
affection to her husband Sir Thomas Putt who dedicated this to her memory – Arms
I Putt with arms of Ulster II Putt impaling 2 esquires helmets in chief & a garb in
base. – Over the key stone of the arch a baronets helmet in white marble with the
crest on a wreath a lions paw erased holding an arrow point downwards. On each
side is suspended from the wall a banner with the arms on each viz.
Argent a lion rampant within a mascle Sable, on a canton the arms of Ulster (Putt)
impaling 1st per fess Gules & barry wavy of 6 Argent & Azure: in chief a demi

(Trevilian) horse issuant leaping Argent – 2nd Sable a lion rampant between 2 flanches Or. (Prestwood)

Five Hatchments exhibit the following coat armour

I. Putt with the motto. *Non est vivere sed valere vita* (Walker)

II. Putt impaling Azure a griffin segeant Argent within a bordure engrailed Ermine. Motto. *Lex est non paena perire.*

III. Putt impaling Argent 3 pheons Sable on a chief a dog courant (question to this coat)

IV. Quarterly 1&4 Putt. 2nd & 3rd Or 4 chevrons Gules an escutcheon of pretence Per pale Or & Sable.

V. Quarterly 1st & 4th Putt 2nd Or 4 chevrons Gules 3rd Gules two esquires helmets in chief & a grab in base Or an escutcheon of pretence Quarterly 1&4 Argent on a chevron Sable 3 garbs Or 2&3. A fess Gules between 2&3. 2nd Horton 3 lions rampant sable. An esquires helmet Crest on a wreath sable & Argent a lions paw erased sable holding an arrow point downwards Or barbed & feathered Argent, –

On the nave floor – partly hidden by a pew. -- ye. 15 day of December. 1690 in the 23 year of his age and also the body of Margaret the daughter of the said Nicholas Mitchell by Johanna his wife daughter of Richard Putt gent who died the 28 of August in the 2nd year of her age 1696.

Aile floor – here lieth the body of John Mitchell of this parish gent who died ----

Do – Here lyeth the body of Algee the widow of John Mitchell gent of this parish she dyed the 7 day of October and Ursula her daughter who died 6 day of February Anno: Dom: 1731.

Do – here lieth the body of William Sac--- er gent who died 6 of December 16--.

Do – Mary the daughter of William Isacke Dec 6th Feb. 1637.

Do --- body --- of Nicholas ---

Do Nicholas Blam --- of Gittisham bur 16 Feb. ----

In the churchyard are the following inscriptions –

On the north side – Margaret wife of Alex Brett esq of Witch Taunton (Whitestaunton) in the co: of Somerset dies 16 Dec 1774 aged 77.

Against the tower. Near this marble stone is the cave wherein lies interred the remains of Thomas Gibson esq. of Gittisham in Devon who departed: this life in hopes of a better 22 March 1768 aged 80

A tablet – Near this place lieth the body of William Paul MA rector of this parish & of Winfrith Newburgh in the county of Dorset who died 19 Sept 1736 aged 48.

A tablet in memory of Mary wife of Rich Holme rector of this parish & vicar of Ottery daughter of Mr William Putt by Mrs Mary Hanbury. She died 13 March 1747 aged 38, Richard Holme died 24 July 1759 aged 56 and Ann his daughter April 3rd 1768 aged 19.

A tomb – here lieth the body of the rev. Mr John Burrough above 9 years rector of this church who died March 2nd 1722 aged 62 years. Here lies the body of Clare his wife which died about seven weeks before him

Stone – Lieutenant Henry Ince late of the Royal Garrison Battalion Gibraltar. The works of which fortress bears lasting testimony to his skills industry and zeal – after serving His Majesty 49 years he retired full of honour to this place and closing in piety the remains of a useful life died 9th Oct. 1808 aged 72. –

A piece of ground was added to the eastern side of the church yard & consecrated in 1827.

A tablet against the south wall of the aisle is thus inscribed Charitable donations for the relief help and succour of the poor aged and impotent people of the parish of Gittisham

Henry Beaumont & Elizabeth Beaumont in 1590 & 1594 gave divers sums of money which were laid out in the purchase of the following lands

Counties & parishes	Lands	Tenants	No: of acres
Devonshire			
Kings Nympton	Wampford farm	George Luxton	92
	Wampford mills	James Rogers	16
Buckerell	2 closes called 2 lands	John Haycraft	4. 4
Luppitt	estate called great Bullock	Henry Symons	23. 4
Halberton	estate called Gunhill	Henry Bennett	11. -
Gittisham	Five cottages	Poor persons	
Somerset			
Abbots Isle	Three closes	Samuel Yard	20

1823

SIDBURY

Davidson (pp. 209–14) visited [St Giles and St Peter] Sidbury on 12 August 1834. He observed that 'the church of this village presents evident traces of a building of the 13th century, which has been altered & enlarged at later periods probably in the 15th & 16th centuries'. The church was restored in 1843 by John Hayward and again in 1884 by J.T. Micklethwaite and G.S. Clarke Jun. (Pevsner, *Devon*, 731). Two memorials are missing from the eighteen Davidson recorded.

The church consists of a nave about 50 feet by 15 within the walls N & S aisles, transept, chancel about 27 ft by 15, tower at the western end & a south porch with 2 embattled heavy turrets for stairs, one leading to the belfry & the other to a room over the porch. The nave is lofty with modern lights in the roof & 2 lights with cinquefoil heads in the eastern gable over the chancel. The roof is divided by carved oak ribs into quadrangular compartments with bosses at the intersections of foliage & shields bearing. 1. 3 leaves or fleurs de lis in bend. 2. The head of a pole axe. 3. a Trivet. 4. a mans hand and an axe. The nave is divided from the aisles & transept by 4 pointed arches on each side of early date, resting on cylindrical columns. The arches between the aisles & transept are highly ornamented with foliage but loaded with whitewash. The windows of the aisles & transept generally have 3 lights with cinquefoil heads & perpendicular tracery, three of the N aisle have labels on the outside supported by corbels of human heads badly executed. 3 windows in the transept are of the 13th century having 3 lancet lights the centre higher than the others. The nave opens to the chancel by an early pointed arch. – The chancel has 4 windows with cinquefoil headed lights with quatrefoils above, of earlier date than those of the aisles. There is a vestry on the north side, & some vestiges of a piscina in the South East corner of the chancel [missing]. At the western end the stones of the wall on the outside are worked into a sort of chequered ornament, & below the eaves on the North & South sides runs a corbel table of rude heads. The tower is not lofty, it has 2 belfry windows of 2 lights each on every side of early date, is embattled & surmounted by a low octagonal stone spire with a weather cock. It contains a clock with a face on the western side & 6 bells. The western door is under a pointed arch ornamented with knots of flowers & of a label supported by corbel heads. The windows above has cinquefoil headed lights with perpendicular tracery. The south door is surrounded by a sort of nebule moulding. The porch is in a heavy style, embattled, with buttresses against the corners & large rude figures for gargoyles. The roof below is groined, the ribs spring from shafts in the corners with circular capitals, a large boss in the centre seems to represent the virgin supported by angels, but it is heavily charged with whitewash. Over the entrance is a sun dial with the motto "*Ut hora sic vita!*"

At the west end of the nave is a large gallery, made still larger by addition of front seats in 1754 as appears by an inscription in front. It contains a small organ & a clock. A gallery which has been recently erected over the north aisle against the transept is entered by stairs from the outside. The pulpit is plain, of oak, & erected in 1715 by a date at the back [missing]. On the walls are several texts of scripture in gold with cherubs and flowers. The font at the western end of the nave is of stone painted, rather large, octagonal, lined with lead & having a lock still remaining upon it [lock missing]. The sides are carved in quatrefoils & foliage & the pedestal in trefoil headed arches.

The monumental inscriptions here are as follow

Chancel.
South wall. Tablet. – *Exuvias svas caducas juxta hanc parietem & uxorem suam unicam et charissimam Richardus Babingtonus clericus pene octogenarius hujus ecclesiae viginti annos plus minus olim vicarius spe firma resurrectionis futuvrae et vitae aeternae anno Dom 1682 deposuit.* Arms above. Argent 10 Torteaux 4.3.2.1 impaling Or 3 bars gules. (Bury)

South wall. Tablet. An epitaph upon the life & death of John Stone Freemason, who departed this life the 1 January 1617 and lieth here under buried.
On our great corner stone
This stone relied
For blessing to his building
Loving most
To build God's temples
In which workes he dyed
And liv'd the Temple
Of the Holy Ghost
In whose lov'd life is proud
And honest fame
God can of stones
Raise seed to Abraham.

South wall. Brass plate. "*1650 Hic jacet Henricus Roberti Parsonii filius qui exiit anno aetatis suo climacterico* ΔΕΥΤΕΡΟΠΡSLΤΩ" [missing] (*in the margin:* See Notes & Queries 2 Ser. IV. 148)

East wall. White marble tablet. "On the east side of the church are deposited the remains of Mrs Alice Gilbert Cheek widow of the late revd Nicholas Morley Cheek founder of St. Stephen's church Salford Manchester and daughter of the late Robert Banister esq of the island of Antigua. She died at Court Hall Sidbury Nov 14 1825. This tablet is erected to the memory of the best of mothers by her eldest son J.M.G. Cheek."

North wall. Tablet of black & white marble. – Beneath this stone in the burial place of their ancestors of Sand in this parish, are deposited the bodies of the four daughters of Francis Huyshe formerly rector of Clyst Hydon, and his wife Sarah daughter of Richard Newte, of Juval in the parish of Bampton who themselves closed the eyes of Elizabeth Nov 12 1731 in her 21st year. Sarah the eldest and widow of John Thomson rector of Mesey-Hampton co. Gloucester died Jany 2nd 1794 having completed 86 years. Frances followed her sister April 22nd 1797 at the age of 82 Jane the youngest ended that line of the family with her own blameless life Oct 23rd 1802 in her 83 year. Where now is the boast that they and their forefathers of Sand were a branch of

the family of Huyshe of Lud-Huyshe and Doniford co Somerset and that the blood
of the Plantagenets flowed in their veins through Joan daughter of the first Edward.
Nothing can now avail them. But their endeavours, through the grace of our great
God and Saviour Jesus Christ (Tit. II.13) to be prepared to meet that saviour as their
judge. Reader, the same judgement awaiteth thee.
Arms in a lozenge above.
Quarterly 1 Argent on a bend sable 3 Luces naiant of the field (Huyshe)
2. Argent 5 Fossils in Fess sable between 2 Barrulet gules (Avunel)
3. Argent a cross engrailed gules between 4 water bouget sable (Bourchier)
4. Masonry argent & sable a Chief indented of the last (Reynel)

On the floor. A stone inscribed in the old letters almost entirely hidden by pews –
Nave floor. – In old letters defaced – Here lieth the body of John Hack-- (Qy) --- 3
day of August Ano 1639 -- [missing]
West wall. – Stone tablet. – 'In memory of Nicholas Warren gent of Winscombe and
John his brother who were born at Musbury in this county August 25 1661. John dyed
June 3 1707. Nicholas departed this life Oct 29. 1737.'
Under the arch of the tower – a white marble tablet. – This tablet is erected to the
memory of Nicholas Warren of Winscombe esq in this parish who died 1 Jany 1760 and
Emily Warren his widow who died 1 Feb 1800. In the same vault is interred also their
third and last surviving daughter Mary Abell who died 4 January 1821 aged 79 years.

N Aisle. Floor. – Under this stone lie the remains of Catherine daughter of Thomas
Jackson of Cinningstone (Qy) in the co of Limerick esq by Helena his wife born
April the – 1808 died June 22. 1814. Beneath is the vault belonging to Thomas
Jackson esq.

Church yard. – In the south wall of the chancel is an old tomb under a low pointed
arch – A short inscription on a stone in front is defaced except – 168 ---
A tomb -- *Hugonis Gundry -- uxoris suae -- Octobris anno 167- --- die Decembris
Anno 1676.*
The remains of Mrs Judith Gundry aged 85 the last of a respected family were
deposited here with those of her worthy ancestors & beloved relatives Dec, 31. 1807.

A tomb 'Sacred to the memory of James Perry Bartlett of Topsham minister of
the gospel who departed this life 11 May 1788 aged 43 years. Also Jane his widow
who was afterwards the wife of Stephen Hayman of Honiton Devon attorney at
law who died 5 April 1809 aged 54 years. also Mary Tooze Hayman daughter of
the above named Stephen Hayman by Martha his wife who died 31 March 1816
aged 6 months also the above named Stephen Hayman who died on the 19 January
1826 aged 68 years.'
A tomb 'Sacred to the memory of Charlotte youngest daughter of the late Gill Slater
esq of Liverpool who died at Sidmouth July 27. 1832 aged 53 years.'
A tomb 'Sacred to the memory of the revd William Jenkins MA. Formerly vicar of
Upottery in this county who departed this life Oct 13. 1779 in the 63 year of his age.
Also Mrs Joan Jenkins his widow who departed this life April 27. 1803 in the 84 year
of her age. Also Thomas Jenkins esq son of the above named who dept. this life Oct.
18. 1814 aged 54 years. – Sacred to the memory of Joseph Jenkins esq who died Oct.
26 1821 aged 70 year.'

Tomb E side of porch door. – This tomb -- of Bovey esq. in memory of Jemima wife of Edward Searle (late of Peofordcombe gent) who departed this life 19 Dec 1744 aged 70 years.

Against the walls of the nave are wooden tablets thus inscribed.
Anthony Isaac gent of this parish gave Bull meadow, yearly value £2.11.0, to be distributed to the most aged impotent & poor people dwelling in Sidbury. The counts are to be settled on the 3rd May yearly.
1549 Henry Beaumont esq of Gittisham gave lands & livings the parish of Ashill and Abbots isle in the co of Somerset yearly value £13.5.6 high rent 16/ to be distributed yearly to the most aged impotent and poor people dwelling in Sidbury.
1637. Timothy Staple of this parish gave £1 to be paid out of lands yearly that he purchased of Thomas Clapp in Harcombe. the vicar and church wardens are to receive it at Michaelmas & to be distributed it to the poor of Sidbury on the day of All Saints following.
1665 Venottery estate purchased by the feoffees. yearly value £10, also one close of land near Sidford yearly value £1.10. – Anna Atleigh gave £5 a year to the poor of Sidbury to be paid out of Sand estate, - 1736. –

"To be sold by auction at the New London Inn Exeter on 30 Aug. 1834 in 17 lots by direction of Mortgages under power of sale. The manor of Sidbury with court leet and court baron --- Eligible residence Sidbury house, offices lawn-gardens, – excellent corn-mills – dwelling houses – cottages – nearly the whole village of Sidbury & about 3000 acres of land of which 2548 acres are divided into farms & upwards of 296 acres are expectant on the termination of one or more lives mostly aged --- a fair for cattle is held annually within the manor" --- (Substance of advertisement) The property of L Hunt Esq.

SALCOMBE REGIS

Davidson (pp. 217–20) visited [St Mary and St Peter] Salcombe Regis on 17 August 1829 and noted it was 1½ mile east of Sidmouth. 'The church of this romantic little village stands nearly at the head of the narrow valley or combe which opens to the sea – it is a very pleasing object when viewed from either of the roads to the place or from the surrounding hills.' The church was restored in 1869 by E. Christian (Pevsner, *Devon*, 710). Thirty-one memorials are missing from the forty Davidson recorded.

The building comprises a nave, chancel side aisles & a tower at the west end with a tower at the west end with a vestry room which has been added to the western end of the north aisle – the nave is 27 feet long by 13 wide within the walls, the chancel 24 by 11½ – the north aisle 26 by 12 & the south aisle 27 by 13. The tower is square embattled at the summit, it has a demi octagonal turret on the south side for the staircase & contains 3 bells. The nave is divided from the chancel & the side aisle by pointed arches, there are pointed arches, these on the sides rest on a column & 2 halves of which that on the north side is the most ancient, being heavy & of cylindrical form with a heavy square capital rudely carved into a sort of hatched moulding of the style of the 12th century & this aisle has probably suppressed one of more ancient date – the column against the south aisle has not any capitals – the windows do not any of them appear to be ancient, that at the east end is divided by mullions into 3 lights having cinquefoil & the label on the outside rests on corbels representing angels holding shields with 2 keys in Latin & a sword in pale – Below this window are inserted in the wall some fragments of fret work in stone in the Anglo Norman style & about it a circular open ornament, all of them no doubt relics of an earlier edifice – In the south wall of the north aisle at the east end is a piscina under a trefoil arch & in the corner a door formerly leading to the rood loft [missing] In the eastern window of this aisle are some fragments of ancient glass [removed]. – There is an uncouth singing gallery at the west end of the nave [removed] – The font is of stone large & heavy of octagonal form 2 feet 1 inch in diameter & resting on a heavy cylindrical column with a circular base – the whole is only 2 feet 9 inches in height & is certainly of ancient date [current font came from Teignmouth church].

The monumental inscriptions in & about this edifice are
Chancel floor. –
In the old letter "Robert" --- [missing]
D° Eleanor Spring died the 6th --- 1646 [missing]
Anne Hooper wife of John H. of Thorn of 21 Dec. 1695 [missing]
Juditha Avant Alani Belfield de –aunton generosi filia Philippi Avant hujus ecclesiae vicarii uxor que sepulta est 16 Decemb. 1672.
South wall a tablet. – *Joanna Avant Philippi Avant hujus ecclesiae vicarii filia ob. Exoniae 20 die Junii 1695*
Tablet north wall – Marcella --- here buried 30th of -- 1657

Tablet north wall. – Hannah relict of John Boniface of Chinking Sussex ob 10 April. 1827 aged 56. –

Tablet north wall – Honour wife of Joseph Hall vicar of this parish died Dec. 25. 1775 aged 75 Also Joseph Hall 63 years vicar ob. Dec 3rd 1791 aged 88.

Tablet south wall – William Creswell esq. late of Doctors Commons London ob: 6 April 1812 at 26 yrs.

Nave – a tablet against the north wall

Edmund son of Benjamin Mitchell ob. 5 Dec 1721 at 18 [missing]

William M. ob at sea on or upon 18 June 1734 at 17

Benjamin M. – ob. 19 Oct 1734 at 24

John M. – ob 17 August 1737 at 36 also their parents Benj. Mitchell ob: 1 Sept 1751 at 73 & Eliz. His relict daughter. & heir of Edmund Rowe gent ob 11 March 1760 at 83. Thos. M – gent son of Benj. & Eliz in whom concluded all the male issue of this most ancient & respectable family died without issue 8 Sept 1785 at 77. His sole nephew Isaac Heard Garter P.C. 1785 – Arms a shield above – 1 chevron Gules & Sable a chevron between 3 swords argent impaling Argent a bee hive beset with bees, diversely Volant sable (Rowe)

Between the nave & the north aisle – tablets

Eleanor relict of Robert Lee buried Dec 6 1729 at 83 [missing]

Robert grandson of Robert Lee died at sea & buried here Sept 1st 1761 at 24 – [missing]

Robert Lee ob 16 July 1726 at 84 [missing]

Nave floor – Hannah Boniface born 31 May 1771 ob: at Salcombe 10 April 1827

Nicholas --- Slade

Catherine Hooper

North aisle – floor – Nicholas Grigg ob, 4 Jan 1705 [missing]

Nicholas Son of Nicholas. G. ob: 21 February 1725 aet 64 – John son of Nicholas. C. ob December 1739 aet 49 [missing].

West wall – north aisle a marble tablet inscribed

Lector
Si quid boni habeant
Fidelitas virtus et pietas
Si morum suavitas
Et formae elegantia
Admiratione sint digna
Huic conditorio
Reliquias Aliciae Rogerson
De Salcombe tenenti
Reverentiam necesse est praestes
Vigint ferme annos nata
Aprilis 24 1795
Supremum diem obiit
Flebilis occidit
Nulli flebilior quam J.L. Gidoin [missing]

South aisle floor – Elizabeth Hooper widow of Nicholas H of Thorne ob 24 Oct 1633 – Grace wife of John H. of Thorne bur. 18 Feb 1638 – John H. – ob 1695 – others of the name [missing].

George Drake ob: 21 Aug 1645 – Katherine D his sister ob 31 Aug Philip D the father of George & Katherine ob 14 Sept 1668 [missing]
Jane wife of Philip D. buried 3rd 1676 – Arms, a wyvern [missing].

Tablet So: aisle –
Robert Lee ob 12 Nov 1785 aet 90 years
Mary his wife – ob -- Nov 1785 aet 77 yrs
James their son ob 6 Dec 1788 aet 42 years
Elias Lee ob June 1674
Dorothy his wife ob: 1 March 1684 [missing]
So: aisle – a tablet against the south: wall.
Hubert 8th son of James Cornish & Margaret Floyer his wife born 19 Sept 1757 died 16 April 1823 [missing]

Tombs in the church yard –
Jacobus Bryett AM ob 12 Jan 1812 at 75 – Eliz: B. his wife ob 19 Nov 1825 aet 82.
Helen wife of rev. Benj. Sandford vicar of Farningham Kent eldest daughter of Thos. Reed esq of Ewell in Surrey ob at Sidmouth 8 Aug. 1817 aet 23.
Charles Satterthwaite of Lancaster ob: at Sidmouth 7. Oct 1815 aet 29. also Frances Nannette Georgiana his widow eldest daughter of Charles Frances Sheridan esq. late secretary of war in Ireland ob 14 Oct 1816 aet 27.
William Mathews son of William Ffarington esq of Shawe Hall in co. Lancaster ob: at Sidmouth 24 April 1827 aet 17.
William eldest son of John Mitford Rees esq of the honourable EJ Comp Bengal civil service ob: 3 November. 1823 aet 12
William Creech Watson 3rd son of rev Chas. W. minister of Burntisland Fifeshire ob: at Sidmouth 1 April 1828 aet 19 months
Sophia daughter of rev. Thos. Best of Lufton Somerset. Ob 24b Aug. 1826 aet 9 weeks
Magdalene wife of Henry Harvey 20 March 1793 died 12 July 1822
Silena youngest daur of the late John Cooper esq of Ashburn Derbyshire ob: at Sidmouth: 24 July 1828
Maria wife of John Charles Purling esq. of Kingston Russell co: Dorset ob 20 April 1823 aet 29.
Sarah Cator widow of William C of Hon EJ Comp service ob: at Sidmouth: 21 Aug 1823 aet 68. erected by her only daughter. Also her son in law Major Gen Baynes late adjutant gent of the Canadians & Col. of the Glengarry fencibles ob: at Sidmouth. 6 Feb 1829 aet 58.
Mary youngest daughter of James O Brien esq of Woodfield co: Clare Ireland ob: at Sidmouth: 20 Nov. 1828 aet 18
Mary wife of Charles Sedgwick esq of this place ob: 24 Aug. 1828 aet 41.
Died of a decline at 19 on 20 July 1822 at Witheby cottage Sidmouth: Susanna Maria only daur of rev R Deverill of Castle Bytham co: Lincoln granddaughter of the late Walter Ruding esq of West Cotes Leicester
A tablet so: wall – Benj. Michelle gent bur. 4 April 1751 aet 73. Elizabeth: his relict buried 14 March 1760 aet 83. Thomas. M gent their sole surviving son buried 15 Sept aet 77
Isaac Heard Garter P.C. 1785.

SIDMOUTH

Davidson (pp. 221–35) visited [St Giles and St Nicholas] Sidmouth on 29 October 1833. He observed that 'the church of this very beautiful place presents scarcely a vestige of antiquity, it has evidently been much enlarged at various times to accommodate the rapidly increasing population of the town and though capable of admitting a large congregation is not large enough'. The church was rebuilt in 1859–60 by William White (Pevsner, *Devon*, 736–7). This would account for 135 memorials missing from the 152 that Davidson recorded.

It consists of a nave about 56 feet long by 18 wide within the walls. Aisles north and south each about 56 by 16, a chancel 35 by 16 with a vestry on the north side of it, & a tower at the western end of the nave about 15 feet by 13. The nave opens to the chancel & the tower by lofty pointed arches, of a late period and to the aisles by 4 arches resting on columns formed by 4 shafts with cavities between them which are continued up the arches. The shafts have circular laminated capitals but are all of the late period of the pointed style. The windows are all modern & in a nondescript style in imitation of gothic excepting the eastern window of the chancel which has 4 lights with cinquefoil heads & perpendicular tracery in the arch. It contains some fragments of stained glass, an ancient coat of arms, Argent 5 piles or pegs in a saltier Gules and some modern painted glass executed by a lady of the place but almost defaced representing our Lord bearing the cross, and the 4 evangelists. (*In the margin:* Qy Passion nails, Tyler's nails & icicles or wedges)
The tower is 75 feet high to the top of the battlements which are modern with heavy modern square pinnacles at the angles. It has buttresses at the angles and a belfry window in each face, of 2 lights with cinquefoil heads and a quatrefoil in the arch. It contains a clock and 5 bells. The ringing loft is supported by 2 large guns 9 feet long brought from the fort now demolished they are each marked with a rose crowned. The western door is modern, a low pointed arch with a horizontal head & a quatrefoil in the spandrels. The gables are ornamented with crosses modern except that on the chancel, but which is broken. The ceilings are arched & divided by plain oak ribs without ornaments. A piscina in the south wall of the chancel under a trefoil arch with crocketed canopy & pinnacles loaded with whitewash [now placed 6 feet up the wall]. The ancient font lies broken at a stone
masons, it was octagonal without ----
cylindrical columns. The modern ----
which stands in the piscina. There ----
end & along the aisles, erected ----

Newspaper cutting, no name or date of newspaper, with note '1851'.
Sidmouth. – The Church of St. Nicholas, in this parish has recently received a new stone font, very neatly executed by Mrs Rowe, of St. Sidwell's, Exeter, and presented by Captain Fulford, R.N., with the cordial co-operation of a few of his

friends. Its most appropriate design has been universally admired, the emblems and figures being those of the four Evangelists, with the words—"By one Spirit we are all baptised into one body." Cor. xii., 13, carved in old English letter. The original font was, many years ago, rendered useless in removing it whilst the Church was under repair.

(*In the margin*)
organ against the tower. The pulpit modern & tasteless. A tablet against the western wall of the south aisle is thus inscribed "This church was repaired and enlarged in the year of our Lord 1822 and additional accommodation afforded for 260 persons of which number are appropriated to the free of the parish for ever. In consideration of which the Society for building churches and chapels contributed the sum of £200. The remainder of the expense attending the enlargement was defrayed by the vicar" (The rev. H. Jenkins who is yet the incumbent)
Inscription on the 4th Bell in Sidmouth Church Tower [drawing]

The monumental inscriptions in the church are these

Nave Floor
Several stones to a family named Conant, partially hidden by pews. – "Here ly -- of Joan C -- who die -- of February.-- Here lieth the body of Henry Conant gent which died the 10 day of June AD 1684 -- here lieth the body of John Conant esq who died 13 January 1736 aged 38". Arms apparently – Paly of 6 --- in chief a demi spread eagle ---- impaling Per fess --- 3 wreaths or chaplets. –Crest effaced (perhaps, Per fess argent & azure 3 Garlands counter charged (Duke) [missing]
James Mansfield who died --- 1795 aged --- [missing]
In memory of Harriett and Elizabeth Mary Fulford [missing].

Tablets against the walls
Near this stone are deposited the remains of James Alexander Duff Lieutenant in the 3rd regiment of Foot guards son of Admiral Robert Duff, born at Logie in Aberdeenshire 3 March 1777 died at Sidmouth 16 Jany 1800 He was beloved by his friends & respected in his profession.
In memory of the revd Charles Hardy of Thorparch in the co of York who died Dec. 3. 1821 aged 41 years. God forbid that I should Glory save in the cross of our Lord Jesus Christ [missing]
To the memory of James Currie MD FRS. Late of Liverpool afterwards of Bath who died at this place Aug. 31. 1805 aged 49 years.
The milder virtues which the friend endear
The softened worth which wakes affection's tear
And all that brightened in life's social day
Lost in the shades of death may pass away
Fast comes the hour when no fond heart shall know
How lov'd Oh Currie! was the dust below
Here cease the triumphs which the grave obtained
The mass may perish but the sage remains
Freedom and peace shall tell to many an age
Thy warning counsels thy prophetic page
Art taught by thee shall o'er the burning frame

The healing freshness pour and bless thy name
And genius proudly while to fame she turns
Shall twine thy laurels with the wreath of Burns
Sacred to the memory of John Home esq of Edinburgh who died here on the 24 May
1799 aged 23 years. His body was interred in a vault near this place [missing]
Underneath lies buried Sarah Reynolds who died Nov. 24 1798 aged 81 years.
Here rest dear Saint and rest the 'Almighty's will
Then rise unchanged and be an Angel still [missing]
In memory of the late William Frederick Forster esq. late Colonel of the Somerset
Fencible Infantry who departed this life Aug. 26. 1801 in the 42nd year of his age
[missing]

Chancel
Floor. – Elizabeth Eaton died 22 April 1792 aged 61 years [missing]
George Bradshaw esq. died Dec. 26 1830 [missing]
George Armstrong esq. died 5 Jany. 1832 aged 22 [missing]
Tablets.
East wall. – a black & white marble mural monument a pediment supported by
2 Corinthian columns. Beneath a tablet inscribed *Juxta hunc locum insignissimi
Johannis Minshall hujusce ecc. vicarius dormiunt reliquiae viva et vera pietatis
charitatis spectata admodum erga pauperes liberalitatis necnon eruditionis
monumenta in perpetuam ejus memoriam prodita. Qui obiit ultima die Novembris
Anno Dom MDCLXIII.* Arms 3 coats I. Azure a star of 8 points Or within the form
of a crescent Argent. impaling Quarterly fess indented Gules & Or.
II defaced but appears to be. Ermine on a Bend Or an amulet Sable.
III Azure 3 pairs of Bar panels Argent, on a chief Gules a Barrulet dancette Or.
III Perhaps intended for Argent 3 bar gemels Az. On a chief gules a Barrulet dancette
or. (Haydon of Cadhay)

North wall – a stone pediment & tablet, whitewashed
Here lyeth the body of Walter Harlewyn esq who departed this life the 16 daye of
February Anno Dom 1631 (then some laudatory verse almost illegible) Arms.
3 apples or pomegranates, in chief a bar & above it an annulet, impaling – a bucks
head caboshed between 2 Flanches each charged with 2 pheons in pale. (Azure a Bar
argent, in base 3 apples erect or Gwillium Halewyn) (Query Parker? Sable a Bucks'
head caboshed between 2 Flanches or. Gwillim)
Beneath this place rests the mortal part of Samuel Cawley esq who departed this life
29 June 1811 aged 67 years.
Sacred to the memory of George Bradshaw esq whose remains are deposited in a
vault near this spot & who died at Cotlands in the parish of Sidmouth 26 Dec. 1830
aged 68 years.

South wall tablets.
Here lie the remains of the rev Mr Oliver Courtice vicar of this parish 22 years who
departed this life in March AD 1703 aetatis 49. Also the remains of the revd Mr John
his son vicar of this parish 57 years who departed this life AD 1766 aetatis 81: Both
of them much beloved reverenced and exemplary lives. [missing]
In a vault are deposited the remains of Maria Elizabeth second daughter and co-heiress
of the late Thomas Dyott Bucknall esq of Hampton Court in the county of Middlesex

who came to Sidmouth for the benefit of her health and after a long illness born with pious resignation and in exercise of every social virtue departed this life to the inexpressible grief of her family April 16. 1818. aged 25 [missing]. Early, bright transient chaste as morning dew she sparkled was exhaled and sent to heaven.

The memory of John Hunter esq of Clarges street London who died 2 June 1812 aged 25 years and whose remains were interred in the church yard adjacent

Floor – Theodosia Maria Rickards – (see Tablet) [missing]

John Doylas esq of Mains. Lieutenant Col. Stirlingshire Militia died 17 January 1810 aged 35 years.

Here lieth the body of Mary Dane -- and who departed this life the 20th January 1743 aged 26 who lived with Mrs. Sarah Wyatt ten year. She was a good servant and just before her death she repeated these words

Farwell my earthly parent dear
Christ caules for me I cant stay here
Weep not dear friends lament no more
I am not lost but gone before
T.B.R.M. [missing]

Tablets
† *I.H.L.*
Memoriae Sacrum
Mariae
Uxoris Francisci Addis
Londini
Quam tarda sed certa aegritudo consumpsit
Die XVI Augusti Anno Domini MDCCCXIV
aetatis vero suae XXV°
Charissima! quem coluisti luget
Te maritus tuus
Heu pietas! Heu prisca fides!
Ubi unquam invenient parem?
Requiescit in pace.

Near this spot are deposited the remains of Charles Watson esq. professor Saughton in the county of Mid Lothian who died here 2 June 1804 aged 66. *In te Domini Speravi.* [missing]

Near this place lie the remains of Nathaniel Marchant esq. a native of the island of Antigua where his ability as a physician a magistrate and a legislator & the many amiable qualities of his mind will be held in admiration while memory shall last. He died 23 February 1804 in the 49 year of his age and his disconsolate widow after receiving uninterrupted proof of his affection for 18 years caused this stone to be erected to his memory.

Sacred to the memory of Theodosia Maria Rickards eldest daughter of the late Peter Richards esq. and Catherine his wife of Evenjobb, county of Radnor aunt to the present Peter Rickards Mynors esq. of Evenjobb & Treago co Hereford. She departed this life 22 Oct. 1810 aet. 58 years. [missing]

In a vault underneath are deposited the remains of Ambrose Crawley esq late of Gloucester Place London who departed this place 13 Dec. 1810 aged 56 years.
Underneath are deposited the remains of Catherine wife of George Stacpoole esq of Grosvenor Place in the county of Middlesex who departed this life 28 Oct 1809 aged 37.

Underneath lie the remains of Christopher Norris esq many years of Lincoln's inn but last of Harpur street Red Lion Square London. Died Jany 17. 1805 aged 53 years [missing].

Inside this church and underneath lieth the body of William Henry Digby esq of Lauderstown co Kildare died at Sidmouth 10 Feb AD. 1809 aged 29 years.
Arms. Azure a fleur de lis Or. Crest an ostrich holding a wreath. Motto *"Deo non fortunae"*

Sacred to the memory of Catherine May eldest daughter of Sir John May bart who died 7 March 1813, aged 23 years.

Close to & underneath this stone are deposited the remains of Charlotte Temperance eldest surviving daughter of Thomas and Elizabeth Alston of Odell castle Bedfordshire. She died at Sidmouth 10 Nov. 1810 aged 19.

Near this stone lies Mrs. T. Swain wife of L. Swain justice Rochford in the co of Essex who died January 31. 1800 in the 31 age [missing].

Sacred to the memory of Margaret wife of Charles Bell esq of Bromley co Kent and eldest daughter of John St. Barbe esq of Blackheath in the same county. She departed this life 17 Dec. 1803 in the 30 year of her age and was interred in this church yard on the 23 of the same month [missing].

Near this pace are interred the remains of William Joseph Kemble eldest son of Thomas and Arabella Kemble of Mincing lane London who departed this life 12th Dec. 1804 aged 18 years [missing]

In memory of Catherine Thomson who died Jany 7 1801 aged 61 years. [missing]

Tablets.
Sacred to the memory of Caroline only child of L.M. Defflis of Blackheath in the co of Kent esq who departed this life on the 22 Jany 1824 aged 24 years. Her remains are deposited under this tablet.
Oh gone for ever lov'd lamented child
So young so good so innocent & mild
Never oh never yet a fairer bloom
Of opening virtues found an early tomb.

--ary wife of Robert Lisle of Acton house in the county of Northumberland esq died 21 February 1791 aged 39 years and by her own desire lies buried here
Blest with soft airs from health-restoring skies
Sidmouth to thee the drooping patient flies
Ah! Not unfailing in thy part to save
To her thou gav'st no refuge but a grave

Guard it mild Sidmouth and revere its stone
More precious none shall ever touch thy shore. [missing]

Below the above. Sacred to the memory of the Hon. M.J.B. Powlett daughter of the late Lord Bolton and niece to the above who died at Exmouth 24 February 1806 aged 24 [missing]. Also Mrs Ann Orde sister to the late Lord Bolton and Mr Lisle who died at Clifton Oct. 30. 1824 aged 76 [missing].

In memory of Henry Mayne Whorwood esq of Headington house in the county of Oxford who died 24 Oct 1806 in the 33 year of his age. Arms Argent on a chevron between 3 bucks heads caboshed. Sable 3 sprigs of broom? Or. Impaling Gules a cross patees Argent. On a chief vert 3 (animals with 6 legs, look like camels) passant in fess Or. [missing]

Against the walls of the church and chancel outside Tablets.
Sacred to the memory of Samuel Lyde of this parish who died 26 April 1780 aged 71 years. Also of Margaret daur of James and Mary Lyde who died 15 April 1783 aged 26 years
Sacred to the memory of James Lyde of this parish who died 8 February 1709 aged 74 years also Mary his wife dd 30 Aug. 1793 aged 71 years.
Here lieth the remains of Charlotte wife of John Storer MA rector of Hawksworth Notts. second daughter of Charles Wylde DD rector of St Nicholas Nottingham. She was a rare gift of God, soon taken away, rich in the faith of a crucified Saviour, and that faith enriched by its fruits a holy life, a flower early ripened by the eternal Sprit for immortal bliss. She left this present scene to her own joy but to the sorrow of her surviving relatives 29 January 1816 aged 25, leaving 3 sons. John Charles and George. [missing]
M. S. Frances Whitter died 24 March 1799 also her father Tristram Whitter esq captain RN. Died 22 June 1810. [missing]

The following are particulars of the several inscriptions in the church yard excepting such as appear to be of a humble description.
Colonel Gabriel Harper dd 14 Nov. 1800 aged 55 years.
George Curling esq late of Cleveland row St James London dd 20 Nov. 1809 aged 51 years.
Revd Charles Hardy, dd 3 Dec. 1821 aged 41, buried here.
Francis 5th son of the late Robert Dynsley esq of Bloomsbury square London died 3 April 1807 aged 22 years.
Anne eldest daur of Sir Henry Russell Knt Chief Judge in the supreme court of Judicature Calcutta dd 31 May 1808 aged 10 yrs.
Mary Mayhew by the memory of her Maker ceased to linger in wasting misery 14 Oct 1816 in the 23 year of her age. She was the (once beautiful) niece & adopted daur of William & Mary Lutwyche of Bath who inscribe this frail memorial of her.
Henry William son of the late Mr Henry Wm Hobbs of Sampson gardens St George's in the east Middlesex dd 27 Nov 1816 aged 18.
Sarah Law died 20 August 1825 aged 68.
Margaret Houlston late of Wellington Salop dd 24 June 1818 in the 40th year of her age.
Austin Paul Ternan dd at Sidmouth 22 Oct. 1821 aged 16. 3rd son of Lieutenant

Ternam RN & of Mrs Anne T. his wife – Also Lieutenant Ternam dd 14 February 1822 aged 73.

Robert Halls MD. Dd 10 February 1801 aged 33.

Elizabeth daughter of John & Sarah Barker dd 7 June 1891 aged 1 year & 7 months. John B father of the above & late of Amothereby in the N Riding of Yorkshire: dd 28 March 1822 aged 75 years. John Baker died 12 April 1829 aged 52.

Richard Wyatt dd 10 June 1802 aged 67. Eleanor his wife dd 18 Aug. 1800 aged 75.

Mr Richard Coles dd 21 May 1771 aged 62 also Mary Ann ---

Elizabeth Wife of Thomas W. Newman dd 17 June 1823 aged 31 Also John her son dd 9 Oct 1811 aged 6 weeks also James Drewe her son dd 5 Nov. 1815 aged 1 year & 13 weeks.

Elizabeth Wife of Nicho. Cawley dd 27 Dec. 1716 in the 85 year of her age

John Potbury of Broadway in the parish dd 30 Aug. 1790 aged 49 years also Sarah his wife died 18 Sept 1816 aged --

Wm Longman a native of Sherborne Dorset but for 9 years of Sidmouth chemist did 19 Aug. 1833 aged 34 years.

Elizabeth Foile dd 16 April 1831 aged 47 years.

William Jones formerly of Denbigh green Denbighshire North Wales dd at Sidmouth 12 Oct 1828 aged 97 years.

Charles Watson esq of Saughton co Mid Lothian dd 7 June 1804 aged 66 years.

Mr Ely Manning dd 16 February 1780 aged 28.

Richard Baker Maguire surgeon son of John & Mary Maguire dd 30 June 1828 aged 38. John son of Jd M.M did 20th Sept 1820 aged 33 yrs.

Josias Readshaw Morley esq of Marrick park York. Dd 7 February 1827 aged 56 years.

Letitia youngest daur of the late col. Wm Despard dd 13 Sept. 1824 aged 14 years.

John Caulfield Browne esq late Lieutenant of the 29 regiment Foot son of the late Hon John & Anne B. of the city of Bath dd 17 May 1824 aged 24.

Richard Steele esq eldest son of Sir Richard S. of the co of Dublin in Ireland Bart dd at Sidmouth 18 March 1825 the 22nd year of his age. Being early taught that there was a refuge for sinners he was led in his sickness to lay hold of the hope set before him and died in the faith of the Lord Jesus Christ. Blessed are the dead who died in the Lord.

John Morris esq of Glasgow dd at Sidmouth 16 February 1824 aged 21.

Sarah wife of Mr Daniel Shuttleworth of the New Kent road London did 16 June 1826 aged 40 years.

Hic situm est quicquid mortale fuit Georgii Sparkes, carus amicus carior propin-quuis 22 Dec 1824 e vita excessit anno aetatis 53. Nullius ille bonis flebilis recessi.

David Reid esq junior son of D.R. esq of Mill Bank in the county of Cork did 25 March 1828 aged 20 years.

Revd William Scott second son of Sir Joseph S. Bart of Barr Hall Staffordshire & rector of Aldridge in the same county died 3 February 1809 in the 34 year of his age.

Hoc sub sepulchro jacet quicquid mortale est Johannis Dennis arm. ex agro Dubliniensi qui obiit die XXII mensis Octobris Anno Domini MDCCCXXX aetatis nice LXVII quis desiderio sit pudor aut modus tam cari capitis?

Sacred to the memory of John Taylor of Todmorden Hall in the co of Lancaster second son of the late James Joseph Hague Taylor formerly of Whitworth in the same county surgeon. Dd at Sidmouth 12 April 1827 in the 24 year of his life.

Sacred to the memory of Charlotte the beloved third daughter of Robert Churchman

Long. clerk and Jane his wife of Dunstan Hall in the county of Norfolk dd 13 March 1828 aged 26.

John Christopher Ridout esq late of Baughurst Hants dd 21 Oct, 1817 aged 65.

Elizabeth wife of Richard Wilkins late of London died at Sidmouth 17 July 1829 aged 45,

E.P.F. 1830.

Samuel Blackhall B.D. Rector of Loughborough in Leicestershire sometime Fellow of Emmanuel College Cambridge second son of Theophilus Blackhall BD late Chancellor grandson of Offspring Blackhall DD formerly lord Bishop of this diocese, dd at Bristol Hotwells 6 May 1792 aged 54. He had a wish to be buried in this place in which he had taken great delight when living.

Christopher Newton esq third son of John Newton esq of Bulwell house in the co of Nottingham dd 21 March 1803 aged 35 years.

Daniel Ximenes esq late of Rose Mount in this parish died 21 August 1829 aged 68 years.

The revd --- Blanchard AB – Middleton Yorkshire died 30 Jany 1827 aged 25.

John Wyatt of Sidmouth Merchant dd 16 July 1735 in the 63 year of his age. Mrs Sarah Cooke relict of the above W J. Wyatt & wife of the revd w George Cooke dd Dec 19.1759.

Henry Blayney Martin esq died at Sidmouth 31 May 1827 aged 57.

Susanna Maria wife of Major Loftus Gray late of the Rifle Brigade dd 24 March 1823.

Sarah daughter of W G.E. Jackson of the Crescent Bir dd 5 February 1823 aged 15.

Jane youngest daughter of the late commissioner Hope of the Navy died at Sidmouth 11 Dec, 1822 in the 27 year of her age.

Patty Adey second daughter of the late George A. of Dursley in Gloucestershire died 16 Sept 1822 aged 65 years.

Elizabeth Sackville Gardiner relict of the late Sackville G. esq of the city of Dublin dd 24 February 1822 aged 73 years.

Anna Maria Reynolds dd 13 March 1821 aged 70 years also Joanna Gerrard Fulford dd 10 March 1823 aged 72 years.

Catherine daughter of W & E. Cuthbertson died 20 July 1826 aged 18 years.

Letitia wife of the revd James Hobson dd 28 July 1820.

Miss Susan Blyth dd at Sidmouth 9 February 1820 aged 20 years.

Catherine Pigou widow of the late Peter P esq dd at Sidmouth 30 Aug. 1822 aged 74.

Benjamin Wigglesworth of Leeds co York dd at Sidmouth 14 February 1821 aged 30 years.

Bridget Catherine Stuart widow of the late & mother the present Henry Stuart esq died 5 Aug. 1819 aged 80.

Henry Wigglesworth esq of Whitwell place nr Halifax co York dd here 9 January 1817 in the 26th year of his age.

William Hawkins eldest son of Anthony Mintonnier Hawkins MD. & Jane his wife of the Friars Newport Monmouthshire. Born 4 Oct 1801 dd 26 April 1815.

Mrs Caroline Gil dd 28th Dec. 1829 aged 26 years eldest daur. of Charles Widder esq of London & relict of John Francis Gil esq, Chargé d'affaires of the united provinces of Rio de la Plata at the court of St. James whom she survived 5 months.

Robert Cunningham esq of Moorhouse in East Lothian. Born Jan 11. 1781 dd February 13.1815

Eliza Lanfear of Woolley co Berks dd April 8. 1813 aged 24 years.

Miss Leticia Archer only daughter of the late Captain Benjamin Archer RN/ & W Jane Archer of the city of Dublin dd at Sidmouth 1 February 1818 aged 25 years.

Sarah widow of Higginson Johnston & 2 daughter of Henry Hutton esq deceased Lord Mayor of the city of Dublin dd 13 Dec. 1817 aged 26 years.

William Mackie esq of Sidmouth in this parish died 26 March 1831 in the 67th year of his age.

Jane Smyth widow dd 4 March 1820 in the 79 year of age.

Thomas Yeamans Eliot armiger obiit 7 die Marti AD. 1817 et aetatis suae 74

Sophia Johnstone dd Dec. 31. 1815 aged 19 years.

Revd William Spry dd 29 Oct 1815 aged 39 years.

Susanna daur of the late Samuel Welfitt esq of Manly Hall near Louth co Lincoln dd 6 Oct. 1814 aged 22 years.

Doctor James Clark MD. Late of Nottingham dd 12 April 1818 aged 39.

James John Wenys Clarke the infant son & treasured first born of James Clarke MD & Ellen C. his wife entered this world at Sidmouth 1 Sept 1811 quitted it 11 May 1812. also an infant son born 28 April 1813.

John Holden esq of London dd 7 Nov. 1811 aged 39.

Mary Anne Debruyn dd 20 Jany 1812 in the 32 year of her age.

Anna fourth daur of the late revd Mr Colton of Lancaster Ale & Vicar of Kirby Malhamdale in Yorkshire dd 27 Sept 1813 aged 20.

†Anne wife of Mathias Maher of Ballymullen in Queens' county esq dd 29 Nov 1813 in the 38 year of her age.

†Elizabeth Fitzherbert second daughter of Basil F. esq of Swynneton co Stafford esq & Eliza Heneage of Cadbury of Lincoln his wife. She dd 22 Jany 1812. aged 17. R.I.P.

Georgiana E.S. Giles dd 2 May 1820 aged 8 weeks.

John Hunter esq (as in the church)

William Woronzow Roberts dd 22 Dec. 1819 aged 2 months.

†J.H.S. Mary Addis (as in the church).

James Pickering gent late of the Middle Temple London dd 3 Oct. 1811 aged 28 years.

Richard Hammett son of the late revd Richard H. rector of Clovelly co Devon dd 4 July 1804 aged 23 years.

Barbara wife of Thomas Everard esq of Randellstown in the co of Meath & daur to the late James O'Riley esq of Ballonborgh co Westmeath Ireland dd 20 March 1806, on the day she attained her 49th year.

Captain T.B. Pearce son of Captain Pearce of the Halsewell East Midlands dd Oct 15th 1806 aged 30 years.

Emma Christian Nourse infant daur of Henry and Dorothy N, dd 4 March 1806 aged 7 months & 26 days.

Christopher Marriott esq dd at Sidmouth 9th March 1830 aged 58 years.

Captain T.B. Marriott esq dd at Sidmouth 9th March 1830 aged 56 years.

Henry Carslake gent of Cottinton in this parish dd 17 July 1757 in the 59th year of his age. Also Elizabeth his wife dd 20 June 1744 in the 35 year of her age also Joseph C their son dd Aug 6, 1757 in the 18 yr of his age. Anna Maria their daughter dd an infant.

Henry Carslake of Cottinton gent dd 20 Jany 1760 at 28.

Catherine wife of Capt Saul Elphinstone daur of Admiral Kruse both of the Russian navy. She was born in Russia 9 Jany 1767 died 6 March 1804.

Thomas Newbury surgeon of this place & late of the Hon E.I. Company service dd

6 Dec 1819 aged 47 years. also Frances Jane daughter of the above died 2 May 1819 aged 6 months.

Jane Cawley died 21 Jany 1826 aged 79 years also Ann Bartlett dd 9 Aug 1826 aged 75 years relict of the late Mr Ellis Bartlett of Branscombe.

M.S. Mrs Susan Morrish dd 29 Sept. 1823 in the 70th year of her age – erected by her sons.

Eliza daughter of the revd C.B. Massingberd of Nettlethorpe co Lincoln dd 8 Oct. 1832 aged 19 years.

Elizabeth wife of the revd Christopher Rigby Collins MA of the Fort fields dd 9 August 1827.

John Passemore of Tiverton, builder, late of Sidmouth dd 26 May 1827 aged 67 years John his son dd in Jamaica 18 Nov, 1829 aged 34 years.

Lieutenant John Willison RN. Late employed in the Coast guard service at Beer who was unfortunately drowned in crossing the river Axe on the 4 April 1829 aged 38 years leaving 5 young orphans to lament his untimely end. –

Margaret wife of Charles Bell esq of Bromley con Kent died 17 Dec. 1803 in the 30 year of her age.

May Georgiana Rigge eldest daur of Gray Rigge esq & Sarah his wife of Wood Broughton & Cark Hall in Lancashire dd at this place 25 Sept 1830 aged 13.

Samuel Tysoe of Broad Marston in Gloucestershire died at Sidmouth 7 August 1830 aged 36 years.

Robert P. de la Foss of Richmond Surrey 30 May 1802 aged 15 years.

James Beatty esq of the co of Longford Ireland died Sidmouth 8 Jany 1807 in the 30th year of his age (Then follow some verses). He was an advocate at the Irish bar. "This small emblem was erected by his mourning brother the revd Archdeacon Beatty"

Ann Gibson daur of John G esq of the island of Barbados died 10 May 1807 aged 25 years.

Sarah Gladstones (otherwise Ponsonby) wife of the Hon. George Ponsonby. Born 18 Sept 1787. Died 16 Feb 1809.

Louisa daur of Edward Lee esq of Tramore Lodge co of Waterford Ireland dd 16 August 1811 in the 8th year of her age.

John Davies Price of Newmead in the parish of Isserth co Radnor esq dd 20 February 1809 aged 25 years.

Elizabeth wife of Brigade Major Grove dd 29 Jany 1810 aged 31 years.

Lucy daughter of George Armstrong esq late of Dublin died in her 33rd year at Sidmouth 7th Feb. 1810. [all the above are missing]

OTTERTON

Davidson (pp. 237–40) visited [St Michael] Otterton on 22 September 1835 and noted it was 12 miles south east of Exeter and 3½ miles from Sidmouth. He observed that the church was 'situated on a hill at the western end of the village overlooking the river'. The church was rebuilt in 1869–71 by Benjamin Ferry at the expense of Lady Rolle (Pevsner, *Devon*, 614–15). All twenty-five memorials that Davidson recorded are missing.

It comprises a nave about 40 feet long by 24 wide, a chancel about 20 by 20, an aisle with porch on the south side 40 by 20, an embattled tower south of the chancel containing 5 bells & a clock, & a chantry or chapel south of the tower in the south wall of which is a piscina [missing]. The nave appears to be the most ancient part of the structure, beneath the roof on the north side runs a corbel table sculptured in the human heads & various devices. It opens to the aisle with two columns & two halves of angular form made by shafts & mouldings with capitals of foliage & shields supporting pointed arches in the style of the 15th century [missing]. The windows are of the same date as appears by their cinquefoil headed lights & perpendicular tracery. The chancel windows are of unusual design having 4 lancet lights under a low pointed arch. The south door is under a low pointed arch & retains its original lock & key which are very heavy & rude in their structure. The roof of the aisle is ribbed, the intersections ornamented with bosses of foliage among which appear the initials R.C. & CT [missing].
A gallery occupying the western end of the nave & a part of the north wall [missing] contains a hand organ [missing]. The font is of stone octagonal & carved in quatre-foils resting on a column of the same ornamented with trefoil headed panels. The pulpit is of oak but modern. In a window of the chancel lie fragments of an old copy of Fox's Martyrs [missing]. The monuments & inscriptions are as follow.

In the south chapel against the south wall a rude stone altar tomb, the tablet thus inscribed in the old letter.
Here lieth the body of Mr James Courtenay younger son of James Courtenay of Cheriton Esquire who departed this life the VI day of September An. Dom. 1591 [missing]
Chancel – Against the north wall a carved stone monument consisting of a pediment supported by 3 columns the whole coated with white-wash & no inscription. Except the date 1589 Above it a tilting helmet is suspended from the wall. [missing] –
On the floor a lose brass plate representing a kneeling figure 3 men & 5 women & inscribed *Sarah praecharissima uxor Roberti Duke ar. filia & cohaeres Rici Reynell de Creedy, ar. obiit 2 Feb. Ano. 1641. reliquit filios 3 filias 5.* Arms Per fess – 3 garlands impaling Masonry a Chief indented. Two crests, dexter a demi griffon segreant. Sinister a fess passant. (per fess argent & azure 3 garlands counter changed – Duke. Masonry argent & Sable, a chief indented of the last. Reynell). [missing]

A brass plate several kneeling figures – *Memoriae sacrum Rici Duke, ar. qui obiit 19 Apr. Ano Dni 1641 Reliquit filios 5 filias 2 omnis ear. faenum.* Arms (Duke). [missing] A brass plate – Here lyeth the body of Richard Duke Esq. who was buried 10 July 1740 aged 52. Arms (Duke) impaling 3 Base wavy [missing]

Nave floor – several inscribed stones worn & illegible
N wall Tablet Here lieth the body of William Summers who for 60 years was vicar of this parish. Died Oct 9 1782 aged 86. Mary his wife died 22 May 28. 1778 aged 87 and of their children William died Jan 1 1741 aged 18 Deborah died Feb. 11 1799 aged 64 Anne died May 22 1810 aged 82. Mary died Oct 23 1810 aged 84. [missing]

Aisle South Wall Tablet. Neare this place is laid to rest the body of Mr Richard Crossing together with his mother in hopes of a glorious resurrection who having been for 27 years the diligent pastor of this place departed hence to receive in heaven the happy reward of his labours the 5 day of January. 1688/9 in the 57 yeare of his age.
And while he from his labours rests let those
Who heard him see hee don't his labours loose
But practice what he taught so they shall bee
Happy with him to all eternity
Arms: On a chevron between 3 as many roundels (Or, on a chevron azure between 3 crosslets fitched gules, as many bezants) [missing]
Aisle. East wall. Tablet Here under lyeth expecting the second coming of Christ Jesus the body of Henry Dunstan who departed this life 2 day of May Ano Dom 1756 in the 73 year of his age. [missing]

Nave north wall a Tablet erected in 1745 Gifts given for the benefit of the poor of Otterton. Richard Duke Esq. deceased (& others) gave £100 the interest of there of given yearly at Easter Henry Austin deceased gave £100 the interest thereof given in bread the 1 Sunday in every month & Ten shillings yearly given by one Mr Chanon deceased out of a field in Credition called the poors field

Church yard tombs:
Here are deposited the remains of the rev Thomas William Shore MA 27 years vicar of Otterton. Died 17 Feb. 1822 aged 66 years [missing]
Simon Ramson of Northmostown in the parish died April 2. 1762 aged 83. Elizabeth his wife dies Oct. 2. 1787 in the 84 year of her life [missing].
James son of the revd. John Dennis of Budleigh Salterton AB. Born May 25 1816 Died Nov. 28. 1822 [missing]

Stones
William Richard Whyte second son of James W. Esq. of the Kingdom of Ireland died 23 Aug. 1793 in the 17 year of his age [missing].
R. Lawson Esq departed this life Aug. 1. 1823 aged 48 yrs [missing]
Anne wife of Richard Humphreys Esq. Capt. 1st Royal veterans died 1 March 1819 [missing]

A little west of the church is an ancient farm house which perhaps formed a part of the Priory buildings on the north gable is a stone crest, a bird seated on a globe – N.W of the church stands the remains the manor house now used as a school. Over the entrance of the porch is a shield with the arms – Quarterly 1 & 4 (Duke) 2&3 per pale wavy – Crest a demi griffon segreant holding a wreath (Per pale wavy or 1 azure (Poer))

For particulars at length inspecting the manor & priory of Otterton & the families connected with them see Polwhele, Lysons. Prince, Risdon & Oliver's Hist. Collections. See also Eccles Antiquity of Devon p. 129

From the Register book Otterton
Richard Duke   buried 27 Feb 1732 aged 81
Richard Duke   buried 10 July 1740
Robert Duke   buried 28 Sept 1750
John Duke   buried 7 Nov 1775
Lysons MSS Br. Mus. Add MSS 9430

NEWTON POPPLEFORD

Davidson (pp. 241–3) visited [St Luke] Newton Poppleford on 22 September 1835 and noted it was 11 miles east of Exeter. He observed 'the chapel of this hamlet, which is in the parish of Aylesbeare, stands on the south side of the high road from Exeter to Lyme Regis presents scarcely a vestige of antiquity though founded in the reign of King Edward III'. The chancel and lancet windows were added in 1875 by R.M. Fulford (Pevsner, *Devon*, 596).

It consists of a nave about 33 feet by 20 within the walls, a chancel which is formed only of half an octagon [altered], an aisle on the south about 33 by 15, & a tower at the western end, low embattled with pinnacles at the corners & containing 1 bell. On the north side of the tower is half an hexagonal stair turret & the remains of an ornamented window with a cinquefoil niche, these with the western window formed of 2 lights with cinquefoiled heads under a pointed arch, are probably the remains of the earlier structure. The nave opens to the tower by a pointed arch. The windows except that above mentioned are all modern as is also the pulpit & the font which later is of stone, octagonal in form carved into panels. There is a gallery across the western end of the nave [removed] & a clock in the tower. On one of the gables is an ancient cross.
Against the south wall of the aisle is a wooden tablet inscribed as follows 'This chapel was enlarged in 1826 by which means 120 additional sittings have been obtained & in consequences of a grant from churches & chapels for the Society promoting the enlargement & building of churches & chapels the whole of that number are declared to be free & un-appropriated for ever in addition to 160 formerly provided. Henry William Marker. Minister' [removed]

There is not a single monument inscription visible within the walls of this chapel & only two or three in the yard.

HARPFORD

Davidson (pp. 245–6) visited [St Gregory's] Harpford on 16 July 1840 and noted it was about 4 miles north west of Sidmouth. The church was rebuilt in 1883–4 by John Hayward (Pevsner, *Devon*, 471). All six memorials Davidson recorded are missing.

The church of this sequestered little village consists of a nave about 36 feet long by 15 wide with an aisle on the north and a porch on the south, a chancel and a tower at the western end containing 3 bells, one is dated 1668 & another 1839, low and embattled –There is a cross on the gable of the porch & below it a tablet thus inscribed "I.H.S. Anno Dni 1601" [missing].
The nave opens to the aisle by 3 pointed arches of early date resting on heavy octagonal columns with plain moulded capitals. The windows have 3 lights with cinquefoiled heads perpendicular tracery above. There is a gallery at the western end of the nave with a hand organ [both missing]. In the south wall of the chancel is a piscina with a shelf under a trefoiled arch. The font is a large octagonal basin of recent date set on the cylindrical column of an ancient one which had also 4 shafts at the angles of the square base which is moulded round the edge. The ends of some old benches remain carved in panels and foliage, 3 of them having the initials W.H. – M.B. – T.D. [missing] –

The monumental inscriptions record the following particulars

Chancel
Floor – a stone with a Latin inscription but illegible & 2 shields – I – A cross engrailed – and II a tower crowned with a ducal coronet [missing].
A flat stone – Catherine wife of the revd Thomas Martine late vicar of Seaton. died 5 April 1733 in the 63 year of her age. – Hannah wife of the revd. Joseph Gilling. died 29th April 1733 in the 74 year of her age. The revd. Joseph Gilling vicar of this parish who after he had served it near 37 years, and half that time in great pain and misery died 28 August 1733 in the 63 year of his age [missing].
Thomas Chanon vicar of this parish after he had faithfully discharged his ministry here 37 years departed this life 19 Feb. 1682 in the 62 year of his age. Arms – a Chevron embattled between 3 Birds heads & necks erased. – a crescent for difference [missing]
-- daughter of -- vicar of this parish -- Mary his wife -- day of -- 1670 -- weeks old [missing]

Nave
North wall. A tablet – Mrs Elizabeth Hoskyn died aged 94. Sydenham Peppin of Exeter Surgeon died 5 May 1816 aged 65. erected by his son & daughter [missing] Tablet Mrs Elizabeth Peppin widow died 1 Nov. 1836 aged 84 [missing].

TIPTON ST JOHN

Davidson (pp. 247–8) visited [the church of St John] Tipton St John on 16 July 1840. He observed that 'At this hamlet which is near the southern extremity of the parish of Ottery St. Mary a church has been erected by private & public subscription for the benefit of the increasing population near this spot which is about ---- miles from the parish church.' The church was built by John Hayward in 1839–40 (Pevsner, *Devon*, 807).

The building consists of an area about 54 feet long & 33 wide with a porch at the western end of the north side and a corresponding vestry on the south and a chancel about 10 feet by 16. The eastern window is formed by three lancet lights the centre one higher than the others in the style of the 13 century. The western window is circular formed by shafts into 10 openings furnished in trefoils. The side windows are formed by 2 lancet lights without cusps under a pointed arch each of which has inside a label resting on corbels of foliage and outside a similar label supported by corbels of heads or foliage. The roof is open & boarded under the rafters. 3 large Beams rest on spandrels supported by stone corbels in the side walls carved in foliage and shields with arms of See of Exeter. There is a gallery across the western end. The western door is under a pointed arch with various appropriate mouldings resting on clusters of shafts. Over the vestry door is a shield & supported with the Royal arms and the letters V.R in the old style and the date MDCCCXXXIX. The pulpit is of oak ornamented with cinquefoiled panels and mouldings. The communion table is of oak in the form of an altar, the slab inlaid with borders & devices. The sides are coloured black and ornamented with a range of trefoil headed niches with crocketted canopies and pinnacles carved in oak in high relief and in very good style. The altar screen below the window is of Beer stone & consists of a range of four panels under pointed arches ornamented with knots of foliage in their soffits and resting on clustered shafts with capitals of foliage. The font, also carved in Beer stone, is small, octagonal, the sides ornamented with trefoiled panels and the column which is also octagonal, with quaterfoiled mouldings. An open Turret on the western gable contains a bell – over each window in the outer wall is a trefoiled panel and over the door of the porch north, the inelegant though ancient device called the "vesica piscis". There is not as yet any monument or inscription either in the church or the church yard.

VENN OTTERY

Davidson (pp. 249–50) visited [St Gregory] Venn Ottery on 16 July 1840 and noted it was about 10 miles east of Exeter and 5 miles north west of Sidmouth. 'The church of this sequestered village [is] beautifully seated in a rich and fertile county.' The church was heavily restored in 1882 by Packham & Croote of Exeter (Pevsner, *Devon*, 886). Two memorials are missing from the five that Davidson recorded.

[The church] consists only of a Nave about 30 feet long by 18 wide a chancel about 15 by 18 and a low embattled Tower at the western end contains 3 bells of which one is dated 1657 & another 1669. It presents no remarkable features of antiquity. Two of the windows have 3 lights with cinquefoiled heads, in the perpendicular style – Some oaken benches remain very well carved in panels, quatrefoils & scrolls & devices, one of them bears the initials M.H. – there are some few remains of a chancel screen [removed]. The pulpit is oak & modern [now stone]. The font is not large, stone, octagonal in shape, on a column and base like form.

The monumental inscriptions present the following memorials.

Chancel.
North wall. A tablet. *H.S.E. Matthaeus Mundy A.M. hujus ecclesiae necnon de Plymtree rector qui obiit Julii 2. 1759. anno aetatis 71. Sic etiam Cecilia uxor Marshalli Ayer arm. filia et stirpis ultima que obit Junii 3. 1770 anno aetatis 83.*
Tablet. The revd Matthew Mundy MA. Vicar of Budleigh Died 15 Dec. 1793 aged 63. Dorothea Mundy spinster, Died 8 March 1808 aged 88. Dorothea Isabella daughter of Captain Mundy R.N. and Mary his wife. Died 23 Oct 1809 aged 3. Her youngest brother Gideon Ayre Died 17 Feb 1818 aged 12. Her second brother Thomas George Died 1 June 1818 aged 17. Her third brother William Terry Died 9 Feb. 1821 aged 18. Tablet. Matthew Mundy esq captain Royal Marines. Died 18 July 1821 aged 63. Erected by his wife.

Nave
Floor. James Yelverton of this parish Died 18 June 1795 aged 71. Mary his wife Died 8 Sept 1802 aged 76. Hannah wife of Thomas Yelverton of this parish Died 22 Nov. 1834 aged 65. Thomas Yelverton consort of the above Hannah Y. Died 26 March 1837 aged 80 [missing]
Elizabeth wife of Marshall Ayre gent and Luttrell --- Died 11 July 1715. Marshall Ayre esq husband of the aforesaid Elizabeth died 31 July 1720 in the 26 year of his age. [missing] Arms – on a bend between 6 Cross crosslets fitchee – 3 Mullets pierced --- impaling --- a bend between 6 Bends (query Sea mews) ---

Mary wife of William Taylor gent of this parish. Died 30 May 1798 aged 34. – William Taylor, Died 18 Feb. 1832 aged 62 – James son of William Taylor Died 10 June 1836 aged 32 [now to be found in the porch].

ROCKBEARE

Davidson (pp. 253–6) visited [St Mary] Rockbeare on 13 August 1834. He observed that 'the churchyard of this sweetly situated parish is entered by a Lichgate, a shed with a turnstile underneath it, but not of any great antiquity' [missing]. The church was rebuilt in 1887–9 by Hayward & Tait (Pevsner, *Devon*, 702). Nine memorials are missing from the fifteen that Davidson recorded.

The church comprises a nave about 33 feet by 18 within the walls, an aisle on the north about 55 by 12, Chancel 22 by 12, a tower at the western end and a south porch. The nave is divided from the aisle by 4 low arches resting on piers of shafts & mouldings having capitals sculptured in foliage but heavily whitewashed. The windows on the south have horizontal heads & are of late date, the north aisle may be assigned to the 15 century or perhaps later, its windows have 3 lights with cinquefoil heads perpendicular tracery & quatrefoils. The chancel windows have trefoil headed lights except that to the east which has cinquefoiled lights with perpendicular tracery. There is a plain piscina in the south wall. The basement of the tower is fitted up as a vestry [removed]. It is embattled, has buttresses at the angles, 4 quadrangular pinnacles & vane. There are 5 bells. The belfry windows have trefoil headed lights. A small portion remains of a screen between the nave & chancel carved in oak with foliage & cinquefoil headed arches. A gallery extends across the western end of the nave and aisle. The pulpit is modern. The font is of stone octagonal carved in quatrefoils & foliage, the pediment is trefoiled arches.

The monuments & inscriptions are as follow
Chancel. N wall. A white marble tablet with a sarcophagus veiled by a pall on which appears a crest, on a wreath a portcullis. In humble hope that his short life may have led to a blessed immortality beneath are deposited the remains of William Porter youngest son of the late Thomas Porter esq of Rockbeare house who died Dec 29 1820 in the 25th year of his age. His kind and affectionate heart deeply endeared him to his friends & relations and though that heart is now cold beneath as a testimony that he is still dear to those whom he loved on earth this marble has been erected.
Floor: Here lieth the body of Mr John Ducke minister of this parish who departed this life 24 Sept 1696/7 also Joyce his daughter aged 4 years also Joyce his wife who died August 2. 1730 aged 83. [missing]
Isto sub lapide jacet Georgius Churchill istius parochiae qui obiit vicessimo primo die Septembris ano Dom 1660 aetatis suae 61 Justi intuere et ingegri
Vitae statumque et ordinem
Videbis alto in otio
Laetam senectam degere. [missing]
Nave. South wall. Tablet. Sacred to the memory of Nicholas Reynolds Quick son of John & Juliana Quick of Tallaton & grandson of Nicholas & Thomazin Reynolds of this parish who departed this life Oct. 9. 1823 aged 13 years & 5 months.

Floor – here lieth the body of George Churchill yeoman of this parish who departed this life 7 April 1629. [missing]
Here lieth the body of Henry Baron of this parish yeoman who died 21 Aug. 1665 at age 43. also Lawrence son of Lawrence Colsworthy who dept this life 23 February 1698 aged 23. Also here lieth the body of John Eleap of this parish died 11 Sept 1726 in the 40 yr of his age Mary his wife who died 11 May 1743 in the 63 year of her age. [missing]
James Reynolds yeoman died 14 June 1757 aged: [missing]
James son of the above died 29 --- 1766 aged: [missing]
Juliana wife of the above J.R younger died 19 June 1796 aged 81 yrs. Thomazin wife of Nicholas Reynolds died 28 March 1828 aged 58 years. [missing]
William Patch of Alicombe died – April 1793 in the 68 yr of his age. [missing]
Elizabeth Norrish daughter of William Norrish died 17 Dec 1693. [missing]

North aisle. N wall. E. end. A handsome white marble tablet
M.S.
Thomae Porter armigeri
qui obiit die Octobris III A.D. UDCCCXV aetatis LXVII
Liberi hoc monumentum
D.D.D.
Maerentes quod hoc solum
Frigidum quidem et augustum
Pro tot beneficiis
Pro vitam datam excultam amplificatam
Pro bonis moribus virtute,religione
Et voce et exemplo inculcatis
Possint rependere
Sperantes autem quam erga liberos
Eadem cum fuisse erga Deum pietate
Deo, quod reliqui est, committunt
Juxta sepulta est
Sarah ejusdem Thomae Porter uxor
Obiit die Aprilis primo
A.D. MDCCCXXIII aetatis LXIV.
Arms. (no colours). 3 bells – a canton ermine. Impaling
On a chevron between 3 demi lions rampant 3 platen (Fishes of the island of Barbados) Crest a portcullis.

Tablet. Sacred to the memory of Charles Bidgood esquire who departed this life 6 Jany 1813 aged 63 also in memory of Ann his wife who died 24 Sept 1822. (*In the margin:* widow of Wm. Sloane of the island of Tobago)
Arms (I) Argent on a chief engrailed azure a Tortoise or. (Bidgood) impaling (II) (Fisher) Argent on a chevron between 3 demi-lions rampant gules as many plates.

Floor. Stones – to the families of Saunders & Radford Wilde.
Hatchments against the walls exhibit the coat armour following [missing].
1. Bidgood – 2. Bidgood. – 3. Bidgood impaling (II) above –
4. Bidgood impaling (II) above – Crest an arm embraced holding a serpent proper. – 5 sable 3 Bells argent, a Canton ermine (Porter) impaling (II) above. Crest a portcullis – 5. In a lozenge (Porter). –

A wooden tablet against the south wall of the nave [missing] is thus inscribed.
Benefactors in the parish of Rockbeare.

The sum of £58 principal money now in the public funds the interest of which to be given annually by 9 trustees the vicar always to be one bequeathed by the will of Mr. Style the deed of which is lodged in the parish chest.

The sum of £1.5.0 on an estate called Woodhouse belonging to Charles Bidgood esq. 10/ of which to be paid to the minister for a sermon & 15/ to the poor in bread both on Easter eve bequeathed by the will of Radford Wile of this parish gent.

12/ yearly paid by Charles Bidgood esq out of Farm estate that is 12/ penny loaves to 12 poor people the first Sunday in every month.

The sum of £4 to be applied by the minister church wardens & overseers to the support of two Charity schools chiefly in the east of the parish for teaching children the English tongue one of whom is also to be taught to write bequeathed by the will of the late Lawrence Colesworthy gent in quarterly payments from an estate called Allicombe now belonging to Mr Nicholas Reynolds.

The sum of 20/ to be paid to 20 labouring men on the second Sunday in March yearly from the aforesaid estate called Allicombe belonging to Mr Nicholas Reynolds by the will of the above Lawrence Colesworth gent. – 1810. –

One or more inscriptions to the memory of persons named Porter with the same coats of arms one in the church of St. Stephens near Launceston

Aylesbeare

Davidson (pp. 257–8) visited [St Mary] Aylesbeare on 15 July 1840 and noted it was about 8 miles east of Exeter. The church was restored in 1840 by E.H. Harbottle and the tower in 1924 by Harbottle Reed (Pevsner, *Devon*, 145).

This village Church consists of a Nave about 36 feet long by 18 wide with a porch covering the south door, a Chancel about 20 feet by 13, an aisle on the north about 48 feet long by 12 wide and a low embattled tower at the west end of the nave containing 3 bells. In the lead at the top of the tower is cast the names & date "S. Drake 1748" & above it a crest viz. a Lion rampant holding a branch. The nave opens to the aisle by 3 low pointed arches resting on columns formed of four shafts with intervening hollow mouldings & capitals carved in foliage. The windows of the aisle have 3 lights with cinquefoiled heads & perpendicular tracery above, there are some fragments of stained glass. – The windows of the nave & chancel are rectangular & formed into narrow lights with low arched heads. An arch between the chancel & the aisle is panelled in the soffits. The chancel has been newly fitted up, the ceiling ornamented with mouldings painted & gilded & the windows with borders of stained glass. In the south wall is a piscina with trefoiled head & across the east wall is a large brass rod to which hang tablets with the Lord's prayer & the belief [missing]. The pulpit is modern and the pews quite new. The font is of stone large heavy of octagonal resting on a column of similar shape – its sides sculptured in quatrefoils & foliage

The monumental inscriptions afford the following particulars

Chancel
North wall. A marble tablet. William Stokes gent of Minchin Court, Died 20 Oct 1766 aged 75. – Elizabeth his wife Died 18 Feb. 1784 aged 57. – Two sons – William died 30 Dec. 1771. aged 8 – Thomas Died 10 Jan 1772 aged 2 – Also with her infant son here buried Elizabeth daughter of the above W & E Stokes & wife of the revd. Henry Marker of Whitestone Died 19 Nov 1789 aged 24. Arms – Gules a lion rampant argent.
Tablet. The revd Henry Marker MA. 36 years minister of this parish – Died 2 Nov 1811 aged 76 – Mary his wife, Died 13 April 1812 aged 84 – Her unmarried sister Margaret Gandy, Died 6 Oct 1809 aged 81 – Arms Per pale argent & gules
A pale counter changed – impaling Gules 3 Saltier argent – On an (Gandy) escutcheon of pretence Per pale argent & sable a chevron between 3 Greyhounds courant all counter changed a chief gules 3 Leopards faces or.
Tablet. – The revd Henry Marker 21 years vicar of this parish son of Henry and Mary M. Died 9 April 1811 aged 45 – erected by his eldest son Henry William Marker the present vicar

Floor. – Thomas Stokes of Minchin Court gent. Died 27 March 1716 aged 65. Mary
S. his wife buried 10
Hic jacet Johannes Force gent qui obit 30 Marti AD. 1685.
-- daughter of George Drake -- Died 15 Nov 1585.
-- Jacob the son of --
Thomas Stokes of Minchin Court - buried -- day of May 1665 -- Charles Stokes
---- Thomas Stokes son of Thomas Stokes of Minchin Court gent, -----

Nave
North wall. Black marble Tablet. – The revd Hugh Bennett of Rosamond Ford in
this parish Rector of Treborough and Runnington Co. Somerset Died 21 Aug. 1797
aged 74. also his relative Samuel Walker of Rosamond Ford esq. descend from the
Walkers of Cobden in Whimple and formerly of Exeter Died 11 Oct 1834 aged 60 –
also Sarah his wife Died 22 Oct 1835 aged 56.

North aisle
Floor -- daughter of John Holwill of Colyton -- the daughter of Richard --vey gent.
Died 2 Oct.1623.
John -- of Aylesbeare yeoman. Died 17 April 1630.
Hic jacet corpus Marcie Dennett quae sepulta fuit vicessimo die ---
Here lieth the body of John Bennett of Aylesbeare gent who was buried

See my Allocations for Devon. History and Topography page 131.

Colaton Raleigh

Davidson (pp. 265–6) visited [St John the Baptist] Colaton Raleigh on 22 September 1835 and noted it was 11 miles 'east by south' from Exeter. The church was rebuilt in 1873–5 by R.M. Fulford (Pevsner, *Devon*, 273). All nine memorials that Davidson recorded are missing.

The village church comprises a nave about 36 feet long by 12 wide with a porch covering the south door [missing], a chancel 21 by 12, an aisle on the north side 56 by 12. & a vestry north of the aisle [missing]. A low embattled tower at the west end of the nave contains 3 bells. The nave is separated from the aisle by 4 heavy cylindrical columns and two halves, the remains probably of a former building they have moulded capitals without ornaments supporting pointed arches. The windows have cinquefoil headed lights with perpendicular tracery – The eastern window 3 lights – Those of the aisle have horizontal heads except two which have cinquefoiled lights with perpendicular tracery & are probably those of the nave before the aisle was erected. The ceilings are ribbed with bosses of foliage & devices, part of the cornice of the aisle has a range of angels holding shields which designates the date of its erection at about the end of the 15th century [removed]. A gallery at the western end of the nave contains a hand organ [both missing]. The pulpit is modern. The font is ancient & may be assigned to the 13th century. It is stone, low & heavy and lined with lead, octagonal in shape resting on a cylindrical column ornamented with a cable moulding & a circular base.

The monumental inscriptions are these – Chancel. Floor. A Brass – beneath are deposited the remains of Catherine wife of Henry Cutler Esq. above a Tablet. Near this place are deposited the remains of Catherine the wife of Henry Cutler Esq of Sidmouth and the youngest daughter of John Olive esq formerly of Oporto who died 3 Nov. 1816 aged 58 years. [missing]

Nave tablets.
Near this spot are deposited the remains of the revd James Hobbs who departed this life January 12. 1809 in the 74 year of his age, having been vicar of this parish & having resided among his parishioners nearly 50 years, also of Sarah the widow of the revd J. Hobbs who died April 1. 1803. This stone is erected as a mark of paternal regard by Thomas Hobbs Esq of Exmouth. Arms Gules a chevron engrailed between 3 fishes naiant argent, on a chief of the last 3 Cornish choughs proper. Crest. A Cornish chough [missing]
In a vault near this place are deposited the remains of Clementine Sobieski Allen the widow of Thomas Allen Esq of Blackmore Essex who died at Sidbury in this county Nov. 16. 1824 aged 86 years [missing].
Aisle floor – William Gould of the parish gent was buried. 18 April 1724. Here lieth the body of Grace Gould the daughter of Roger Gould who was buried 15 June 1678 [missing].

Tablets.

Sacred to the memory of Henrietta Grace Phillpotts wife of W. D. Phillpotts Esq. formerly of Hull 20th of Foot who departed this life 15 March 1833 aged 57 Her remains are interred in a vault near this tablet [missing].

Near this pillar lie the remains of Frances Greenwood wife of the revd Robert Greenwood Vicar of this parish who died Dec. 30 1824 [aged] 53 also Fanny Penny mother to the above F.G. who died Nov 21. 1825 aged 86. [missing]

A painted wooden tablet defaced except "Thomas Bellament was buryed the --- day of -- " [missing]

N wall a wooden tablet [missing] inscribed

Benefactors to the poor of Colaton Raleigh

	£	s	d
Thomas Bellament gave	42.	0.	0
John Abraham vicar	2	0.	0
William Webber.	10	0.	0
John Pearce of Sidmouth.	5	0.	0
Sir John Martin.	5.	0.	0
Nicholas Martin, gent.	10.	0.	0
Francis Hooper.	5.	0.	0
John Pitfield gent.	10.	0.	0
Mary Lane widow.	10.	0.	0
Jeffery Cross.	2.	0.	0
Thomas Elliott.	2.	0.	0
Charles Hart vicar.	10.	0.	0
Charles White	15.	0.	0.
William Reyner vicar.	2.	2.	0
Willam Reyner Junior vicar.	20.	0.	0
Revd James Hobbs, 50 years vicar.	21.	0.	0

BICTON

Davidson (pp. 269–72) visited [St Mary] Bicton on 22 September 1835 and noted it was 12 miles south east of Exeter, and 4 miles west of Sidmouth. 'This parish church, which was formerly a chapel to Otterton, is seated in a sequestered spot embowered with trees & shrubs adjoining the splendid gardens & domain of Bicton Lodge, the seat of Lord Rolle.' The church was built by John Hayward and consecrated in 1850. All eight memorials Davidson recorded are missing. The old church that Davidson visited was preserved as a ruin with the south east corner rebuilt and the monument of D. Rolle and family removed to what became the mausoleum designed by Pugin (Pevsner, *Devon*, 173–4).

It consists of a nave about 30 feet long by 15 wide a chancel 15 by 15 an aisle or chapel on the south about 12 by 12 and an aisle on the north about 45 feet by 12. The nave is separated from the north aisle by two columns & 2 halves formed by four shafts with intervening hollow mouldings, supporting pointed arches. It opens to the south aisle by a pointed arch without columns. The only trace of an ancient structure is the eastern window of the chancel which is formed by 3 lancet lights with as many openings above under a lancet arch & without sweeps or other ornament. The other windows may all be assigned to the 15th or 16th century, having cinquefoil headed lights with perpendicular tracery, but some of them have been defaced & altered. The walls & ceilings are quite plain [now wooden rafters]. The pulpit & pews modern & without ornament [pews now have carved ends]. A gallery at the western end of the aisle, the front of which is ornamented with foliage & flowers carved in oak, contains a hand organ [removed]. The font is a modern carved stone basin. A heavy oaken altar screen obscures part of the chancel window, which though handsomely sculptured in foliage flowers & fruit is an incongruous object in this place. It supports a good painting of our Lord sinking under the cross. At the west end of the nave is a small turret containing a bell –

(*In the margin:* The carved oak in this church was brought from Potheridge house the Duke of Albermarle's, on its destruction in 1734 see Lysons p. 602)

The funeral monuments & inscriptions here are as follows.
In the south aisle or chapel against the south wall is a large & handsome monument of black & white marble with effigies at the whole length of D Rolle esq his lady & child all richly habited, reclining on an altar tomb, with a pediment above on which is the following inscription, written by Dr. Fuller [missing].
The remains of Denys Rolle esquire
His earthly part within this tomb doth rest
Who kept a court of honour in his breast
Birth, Beautie, Witt and Wisdom sat as Peers,
Till death mistooke his vertues for his yeares,

Or else heaven envy'd earth so rich a treasure,
Wherein too fine the ware, too scant the measure.
His mournfull wife, her love to shew in part,
This tombe built here, a better in her heart.
Sweete babe, his hopeful heyre (Heaven grant this boon)
Live but so well, but oh! Dye not so soon.
Obit anno Dni 16 Aetatis 24
Reliquit filium unum filias quinque
Arms 3 shields
I. Or, on a fess dancetty between 3 delves azure each charged with a Lion rampant
of the field, as many Bezants, impaling sable, 3 swords in pile points downwards
argent, pomelled & hilted or
II. as I
III Quarterly of 10
    1. Rolle, as above
    2. Ermine 3 Dane axes gules
    3. Argent a Cross Moline azure, on a chief of the last 3 stars of 6 pointed or.
    4. Sable, 3 Fusils in fess ermine
    5. Gules, 2 bends wavy or.
    6. Sable, 2 Bucks trippant argent attired or, between 9 Bezants 3,3 & 3.
    7. Azure, a bend per bend indented or & ermine cotised argent & or.
    8. Sable a fess checky or & gules between 3 Crosses patees of the second.
    9. Argent on a Chevron between 3 Griffin heads erased sable, as many Acorns or.
    10. Azure semee of crosslets or, unicorn rampant of the last.
Crest on a wreath or and azure a hand cuffed or, trimmed azure holding a roll.
Motto. *Qui capit capitur*

Against the east wall a hatchment. The arms of Rolle & on an escutcheon of pretence
Argent 3 Bulls faces sable, horned or. a Barons coronet. Supporters Two wolves
proper, langued gules, bezanted & crowned or.

Nave floor. 2 stones inscribed to persons of the name of Cole of Colaton Raleigh
[missing].

Chancel.
South Wall a Tablet
On the south side of the communion table are deposited the remains of the revd John
Glubb thirty nine years rector of this parish. He died March 4. 1797 aged 68. This
monument is erected by his widow & children as a testimony of their affection &
gratitude. To the memory of Dinah widow of the revd John Gubb who died Jan 15th.
1800 aged 60 & of Emily Warren Palmer their daughter who died Nov 9. 1797 aged
34. – Arms Argent 3 Chevrons gules [missing]

Floor.
Here lieth the body of William Browne gent who departed this life 31 July AD. 1643
(the last figure altered to 4 thus 1644) [missing]

Nave. W. Wall a Tablet.
To the memory of Elizabeth Frances Hamilton daughter of John & Bridget Hamilton

who died Aug 28. 1794 in the 21 year of her life. This tablet is inscribed by an affectionate mother [missing]

Church yard.

Against the north side of the turret a carved stone tablet, utterly worn & defaced.

An altar tomb. Sacred to the memory of the revd Joshua le Marchant. He died at Sidmouth Aug. 12 1822 aged 58 years. This tomb is erected by his affectionate widow as a small tribute to his memory [missing].

North side a stone. To the memory of Chichester Wrey Bruton who departed this life Sept 29 1823 aged 53 years. Also daughter Charlotte Juliana who departed this life July 22. 1814 aged 13 years. [missing].

Stones inscribed to a family named Hallett. [missing].

On the south side of the church are the octagonal base & a part of the shaft of an ancient cross.

EAST BUDLEIGH

Davidson (pp. 273–5) visited [All Saints] East Budleigh on 14 July 1840 and noted it was about 10 miles south east of Exeter and 4 miles west of Sidmouth. He observed the church was 'situated on an eminence at the northern extremity of the village'. The church was enlarged in 1853 and further restorations carried out in 1884 by R.M. Fulford (Pevsner, *Devon*, 346–7). Eight memorials are missing from the nineteen that Davidson recorded.

It consists of a Nave about 48 feet by 18 wide with aisles north & south of the same length, a chancel about 30 feet by 15 which has evidently been lengthened about half its extent, and a Tower at the western end of the nave, 72 feet high containing 5 bells & a clock. The nave opens to the aisles by 4 low pointed arches on each side resting on columns formed of 4 shafts with intervening hollow mouldings & having octagonal capitals carved in foliage. On one of the columns is a projecting sculptured corbel for the support of an image. The ceiling is coved & ornamented with ribs having bosses of foliage at their intersections. The windows have been in the perpendicular style but all except 2 have been modernised by removing their mullions & tracery, three have 3 lights with cinquefoil heads. A gallery across the western end of the nave & the north aisle [removed]. A gallery across the western end of the nave & the north aisle contains a hand organ [removed]. The pulpit & chancel screen are not of ancient date – The font is of stone small and octagonal in shape, its sides ornamented with panels of quatrefoils & foliage and the column of similar shape on which it rests, with niches having cinquefoiled heads the whole remarkable for a great boldness of the sculptures. Many of the ancient oak benches remain the ends of them elaborately carved in panels figures angels, scrolls, devices & shields the latter exhibit the following bearings.
Three Battle axes erect impaling a unicorn rampant. – (Dennis)
Shield gone, helmet & suit a Pair of bucks horns. Supported 2 antelopes crowned – Date below 1537
A bend of 5 lozenges impaling 3 Horsemen's rests (Raleigh / (Greenville)
Quarterly 1 a star of 16 points – 2 Courtenay – 3 a bend regularly (1 2nd St Clere, 2 Courtney, 3 blank, 4 query Chiverston or Holwell)
Between 3 Mullets – 4 On a Bend 3 Goats passant.
Per Fess – In chief 1. 3 & 2 or the last in base 4 as last.
Per Fess – In chief a Talbot passant, in base an Owl within a Border engrailed. Crest a Dogs head & neck collard – (Ford)
Others of the carvings are rude figures e.g. a women with a jug, a man eating – a woman holding a dog's tail

There is a piscina in the south wall of the chancel under a trefoil headed niche, and in the eastern window some fragments of ancient stained glass which may trace the

Crucifixion, a head of the virgin, angels and 4 shields with the following coats of arms [removed].

I. Courtenay –
II. Azure 3 swans heads & necks argent – query Shoveltens heads
III. Argent a Cross gules
IV. Quarterly 1 & 4 Gules 3 Lions rampant or, 2 & 3. Sable 6 mullets pierced 3.2 & 1 argent.

The monumental inscriptions afford the following particulars.

Chancel.
Floor – Here lieth the body of the revd Philip Westcott -- [missing]
Arms – a Saltier engrailed between 4 Mullets impaling -- (defaced)
Here lieth the body of Mrs Mary Westcott 4th daughter of Henry Arscott gent of Tidwell in this parish late wife of the revd Mr Philip Westcott who died 20 August 1741 aged 78 also Mrs Hannah W. 5th daughter of Henry Arscott gent -- in this parish who died -- 1758 – aged 8- [missing]
Thomas Hooke. Died 10 May 1664 [missing]
Thomas Hooke student of Oxford. -- was buried 19 Sept [missing]
Mr Thomas Hearne vicar of this parish. Died 10th Nov. 1631 [missing].

Nave.
North wall. Tablet. Frances Elizabeth Yates wife of Matthew Ley Yates esq of this parish. Died 25 March 1811 aged 36.
Tablet Anna Maria daughter of the late rev. Robert Miller vicar of St. Nicholas Warwick, rector of Kimcote in the county of Leicester. Died 19 May 1817 aged 36.

Floor. A cross flory on 2 steps with a curious inscription round the border of the stone, the letters so placed that it could be read backwards the following may be traced. *Orate pro aia Johanne Ralegh uxoris Walt. Ralegh que obiit X die mens Augusti Anno domini MCC--*. See Oliver Ecclesias. vol. 2 p.64
S.M. William Jackson esq. Died 14 Nov. 1808 aged 84 [missing]

North aisle
East Wall. Tablet. Henry Frank. Died 28 March 1810 aged 70
Floor. Edward Dart. Died 4 Feb, 1813 aged 9 months. Frances Maria Dart. Died 16 April 1835 aged 14 years. [missing]

South Aisle
Tablet. – Edward Kendall Jones esq Merchant of London. Died 14 Nov. 1812 aged 55.
Tablet. Frances Maria daughter of Joseph Dart esq and Elizabeth Frances his wife. Died at Tidwell House 16 April 1835 aged 15. Edward their son died 4 Feb. 1831 aged 9 months
Tablet. Samuel Walker Esq of Winnards House in this parish. Died 20 Feb 1819 aged 73.
Tablet. John Palmer Barrow Esq Died 8 Sept 1836 aged 27 [missing].
Floor E.W. Sayword of Greenwich. Died 1 Sept 1815 aged 42.
Joseph Conner of Salterton Gent. Died 14 Oct 1755 aged 67
An old stone very rudely inscribed Roger Rowyez

WITHYCOMBE RALEIGH

Davidson (pp. 277–8) visited [St John in the Wilderness] Withycombe Raleigh on 14 July 1840 and noted it was about 10 miles south east of Exeter and 2½ miles north east of Exmouth. He observed that 'this parish church is partially destroyed and no longer used except for an occasional burial here. The only portions remaining are a low and venerable looking tower at the western end of the site of the nave and the north aisle.' The church was rebuilt in 1862–4 replacing the eighteenth-century church (Pevsner, *Devon*, 915–16). Ten memorials are missing from the twelve that Davidson recorded.

The north aisle which is about 52 feet long by 15 wide but which is of no great antiquity the windows being some in the perpendicular style having 3 lights, with cinquefoil heads and others of more recent date. The springing of the ribs of the roof which is open is ornamented by an oak cornice with sculptures of angels holding shields, one of which has the letters ID [removed]. – Some plain oaken benches remain. The font is of stone large octagonal, the sides ornamented with panels of quatrefoils and foliage resting on a column of similar shape with a moulding of foliage and panels having trefoiled heads.
The few monumental stones in this aisle afford the following records.

North Wall.
Tablet. Charlotte Frances Webber 2nd daughter of William Webber esq. Died at Exmouth 7 June 1809 aged 16. Edward William her youngest brother died at Llandilo in Wales 1 Jan. 1825 aged 19. [missing]
Tablet – Jane Peters Bourke daughter of Edmund Pearson Bourke esq late of Exmouth. Died 8 April 1815 aged 22. [missing]
Tablet. Anne Lydia wife of Ralph Rice Esq. Died 29 Dec. 1816 in 31 year of her life. Buried with her sister Jane P. Bourke. [missing]
Tablet. Jane Spencer daughter of Brent Spencer esq of Bell Hill co Down Ireland Born 31 July 1744. Died 27 Oct 1823. [missing]
Tablet. Joseph Hucks MA. Youngest son of the late William Hucks Esq of Knaresborough. Fellow of Catherine Hall Cambridge. Student of the Inner Temple London. Died 18 Sept 1800 aged 28
Tablet. Eleanor Hucks widow of William Hucks Esq of Knaresborough co York. Died 23 May 1807 aged 77.
Tablet. Penelope Woollan of Palmer Hill co Middlesex widow of the late Charles Woollan of Wrexham N. Wales. Died at Exmouth 13 March 1813 aged 63 [missing]

Floor. Beneath this stone lies what was mortal of the most modest chaste pious in a word most truly Christian, Mary Rix late of Newport Essex having watched like unto one that waiteth for his Lord's coming after a few days illness she at length gave up her soul to God. March 23. 1726 aged 22 years. Dying she lives.

Anna Maria Newton relict of John Leaper Newton. Died 2 Dec. 1830. [missing]

Marian Sophia Thompson first born child of George Nesbitt Thompson Esq & Catherine ----- in co Hants. Born 9 Oct. 1798. Died 3 Aug 1812. [missing]

Warren Hastings Thompson third son of George Nesbitt Esq & Catherine Maria his wife of --- Lodge co Hants aged 11 years. [missing]

Harriett Carter daughter of Thomas Richard Carter Esq of Bayford co Herts. Died 8 June 1798 aged 30. [missing]

William Hobbs Died 10 Dec. 1765 aged 64. Ann Hobbs his wife Died 6 Sept 1786 aged 69. Arms ------ a chevron between 3 fishes naiant ---- On a Chief --- 3 Cranes --- [missing]

Newspaper cutting, no name of newspaper, dated 1852
EXMOUTH. – We understand that the church of St. John in the Wilderness, has been renovated and restored, and that on Trinity Sunday divine service will be performed there for the first time for nearly 150 years.

Newspaper cutting, no name or date of newspaper
The parish chapel is undergoing repairs and decoration, by means of voluntary and liberal subscription of the parishioners and friends of the Church, to which Mr. Divett (the member for Exeter) has most liberally subscribed his residence (Bystock), being in the parish of Colaton Raleigh.

The ancient church of St. John in the Wilderness is the first church in the district. It was formerly the place of worship for east Budleigh, Woodbury, Lympstone, Littleham and Withycombe Raleigh. Having been repaired and temporarily seated, it was used for divine service on Sunday last, and will be used again the next three Sundays, when it is expected the chapel will be ready for use. 6 June 1852. The chapel was built upwards of 130 years since by voluntary subscription, and in the year 1841 it was enlarged and reseated by voluntary subscriptions, and it is now to be done by the same means, a worthy example to other parishes.

WITHYCOMBE RALEIGH,
CHAPEL OF ST JOHN

Davidson (pp. 279–80) visited the chapel of St John the Evangelist in Withycombe Raleigh on 14 July 1840 and noted it was about 10 miles south east of Exeter and half a mile north east of Sidmouth. He observed that 'here is a Chapel erected for the populous part of the parish of Withycombe Raleigh probably when a part of the old church of St John was taken down. It is a brick building with stone dressings in the Roman style with semicircular headed windows, with a porch covering the south door.' The church was rebuilt in 1864 (Pevsner, *Devon*, 915). All six memorials that Davidson recorded are missing.

The whole is an area of about 60 feet by 30 with a gallery at the western end. The altar screen is large and heavy of oak in the Roman style consisting of an entablature supported by Pilasters ornamented with angels and foliage in white plaster [missing]. The font is a small oval marble basin and cover standing on a wooden pedestal [missing]. A pointed wooden canopy for it is thus inscribed "This font was given by Gideon Haydon esq. 1668," [missing] a date which is much earlier than the apparent one of the building, which is said to have been erected about 1720.

The monumental inscriptions record the following particulars.

East Wall.
Tablet. With his parents Edward and Isabella Holwell are deposited the remains of the revd William Holwell vicar of Menheniot in the co of Cornwall. – Died in London 24 Dec. 1830 aged 73. – He married the Right Honourable Lady Charlotte daughter of James, 14th earl of Errol by who he had an only son whom he long survived. An accomplished scholar and possessing both taste and skill in painting he proved his excellent judgement by forming a collection of pictures of a very high class in art and munificence by bequeathing it to the National Gallery. Arms: Quarterly 1st & 4th. Gules on a Chevron argent 3 Mullets sable. 2nd & 3rd Or on a bend gules 3 Goats passant argent Holwell impaling Quarterly 1st & 4th as 1st above 2nd & 4th Argent Escutcheons gules. [missing]
Tablet. Edward Holwell esq. Died 28 March 1793 aged 66. [missing]
Isabella (Newte) his relict Died 4 May 1793 aged 73 their mourning offspring's William and Isabella erect this marble, &c. – Arms. Quarterly 1st & 4th. Or on a bend gules 3 Goats passant argent 2nd & 3rd Argent 3 Pilgrims staffs pike points downwards gules – impaling Gules a Chevron between 3 hearts argent transfixed with as many Swords sable hilted or. [missing]

North Wall.
Tablet. Philip Gedney of Marpool cottage. Died 8 July 1836 aged 73 years. [missing]

South wall.

Tablet. Edward Chippendell of Withycombe Cottage late of Manchester co Lancaster. Died 5 May 1822 aged 49. [missing]

Tablet & sarcophagus. The Honourable Alexander Abercromby one of the Lords of Council and session Lord Commissioner of Justiciary in Scotland. Died at Exmouth 17 Nov 1795. in the 51 year of his age. – *Amici R. D et W. C. Lune lapiden posuere.* Arms Argent a Chevron between 3 Boar's heads erased gules [missing].

LITTLEHAM

Davidson (pp. 281–6) visited [St Margaret and St Andrew] Littleham on 14 July 1840 and noted it was about 11 miles south east of Exeter and 2 miles east of Sidmouth. The church was restored in 1883–4 by R.M. Fulford (Pevsner, *Devon*, 537–8). Thirty memorials are missing from the fifty that Davidson recorded.

This parish church consists of a nave about 50 feet long by 24 wide with a porch covering the south door, a chancel with an aisle on the south, an aisle on the north about 65 feet long by 15 wide, and a Tower at the west end of the nave containing 4 bells. The chancel and the nave open to the north aisle by 5 low pointed arches resting on columns formed of 4 shafts with intervening hollow mouldings & having capitals carved in foliage 7 shields. The ceiling is coved & ornamented with ribs supporting a cornice relived with angels holding shields & the inter-sections with bosses of foliage. There are remains of a chancel screen in the perpendicular style consisting of a range of arches divided into openings with cinquefoil heads. The windows are of like date, with cinquefoil headed lights. The Pulpit is of oak but modern. In the chancel is an ancient chest with 3 locks & a hole in the top for deposits of money. The font is ancient & of unusual design. It is of stone large & octagonal, the sides carved in panels of quatrefoils each with a cross in the centre. It rests on a cylindrical column outside of which is a range of 8 detached angular columns the openings between them forming arches with trefoiled heads, the whole raised on 2 steps. In a window of the north aisle some pieces of stained glass – our Lord crowned with thorns – St. Michael or St. George with a sword and the dragon and a man in a red cap with a jewel in front resembling the portrait of K. Richard. 3. –

The monuments & inscriptions afford the following particulars

Chancel.
North Wall. Tablet. Major Gen. William Elliot of the Bengal Artillery in the Hon East India Company services & of Larrington co Roxburgh North Britain. Died at Exmouth 22 April 1803 aged 62.
Tablet. Mary Drake relict of the late Edward Holwell Drake late of Littleham – Erected by Hannah Park her nearest relative and Francis Festing clerk. Arms defaced [missing]
South wall tablet. Thomas Leventhorp Esq of Brunswick Square London. Died at Exmouth 30 July 1815 aged 39
Tablet. The revd John Rymer MA. Vicar of this parish Died 5 Jan. 1809 aged 52.
Floor. Thomas Reed rector of this parish 40 years. Died 28 March 1706 aged 66. [missing]
Elizabeth Daughter of Jo. & Eleanor Drake of Spratshays in this parish. Died 25 August 1768 aged 34. The revd Edw. Holwell Drake impropriate rector of this parish, Brother of the above. Died 20 Dec. 1797 aged 46. Also Mary his wife –

Thomas Warry vicar of this parish 16 years and a half Died 2 Oct 1722 aged 48.
George Drake of Bystock. --- Buried 21. [missing]
John son of John Humphrys then minister of this parish Died 15 March 1877/8 aged
1 month & 4 days [missing]
Grace Tailor wife of George T. of Ottery St. Mary. Died 4 Dec. 1645. John Tailor
their son Died 3 Dec in the same year [missing]
Drake of this parish gent. Died 16 May 1694 and Katherine his wife Died 10 Jan
169¾ – Philip D. son of the said John Drake gent. Died 19 Sept 1719 aged 53. Arms
a Wyvern
The revd Richard Prat BA. 27 years vicar of this parish. Died 6 June 1840 aged 76
[missing].

North Aisle
East Wall. Tablet. Mrs Jane Holwell of Spratshayes. Died 25 April 1751 aged 63. She
gave £5 to the poor of this parish.
Arms in a lozenge Per chevron --- & Ermine. In chief 3 Chess rooks.
North wall. Tablet. Frances Isaac wife of Isaac esq Died in December 1780 aged 44.
Her daughter Eve Caroline Died October of the same year aged 12.
Tablet. Robert Inverarity Captain in the Hon East India Company Madras army.
Died at Exmouth 16 Feb. 1833 in the 49 year of his age.
Tablet. Henry Stafford of this parish. Died 10 Aug 1746 aged 53. He gave to the poor
of this parish £50 [missing].
Tablet. – Henry Cholmley esq of Whitby & Howisham co York Died 24 Feb 1809
aged 61. Arms Quarterly. 1& 4 Gules, in chief 2 Helmets argent & in base a Garb or.
2 & 3 sable Chevron between 3 leopards faces or – On an escutcheon of pretence the
same coat quarterly [missing]
Tablet. Thomas Trevilian of Littleham gent. Died 7 April 1740 aged 66. Married
Elizabeth daughter of Henry Arscott of Tidwell esq. – Henry Arscott her brother
Died 28 Aug. 1754 in the 83 year of his age – he gave £6 to the poor of this parish
Arms. 2 Coats I. – in base 3 Bars wavy a demi seahorse issuant. – impaling per
chevron – & ermine in chief 2 Bucks faces. – II as the last coat.
Tablet. *M.S. Roberti Sutton armigeri qui morbo diutino affectus cruciatus indies
ingravescentes insigni patientia sustinuit vires sufficiente Christo ob. prid. non.
Martis A.D. MDCCCV aet. suae XXXIX. M. M. pos conx. Luctuosissima.*
Arms. Argent a Quarter sable impaling argent on a mound in base vert a tree proper,
over all a Bull passant sable collared argent.
Tablet. Dorothea wife of William Richardson MP. for the co of Armagh. Died 5 Sept
1793 aged 38.
Tablet. James Hodgson esq son of the rev. Jacob Hodgson late of Sea Bank terrace
Cosby near Liverpool. Died at Exmouth 9 Feb. 1827 in the 31 year of his age. Erected
by his widow [missing]
Tablet. Margaret Graham daughter of Thomas Graham of Edmond castle Cumberland.
Died at Exmouth 13 March 1794 aged 24
West wall. Tablet. Capt. Henry Vane of the Cold-stream Regiment of Guards. Died
at Exmouth 9 August 1829 aged 32. Erected by his parents [missing]
Floor – the revd John Williams Rector of St. Andrews co Glamorgan. Died at
Exmouth Aged 28 [missing]
Allis Howard wife of Robert Howard of this parish Died -- Dec. 1732. Mary daughter

of Robert & Mary Howard Died 22 July 1737 aged 16 months. Robert H. Died 15 Feb 1760 aged 75. Robert H. his son Died 12 April 1811 aged -- [missing]
Mary Ekins daughter of the revd Charles E. Canon residential of the cathedral church of Salisbury & Mary his wife. Died 28 April 1829 aged 21 [missing]
Hamlet Obins son of Michael Obins esq of Castle Obins in Ireland. Lieutenant in the 70 Regiment. Died 30 April 1786 aged 21 [missing]
Here lieth the body of Robert Drake gent who died 30 Sept 1628
Preachers and poor can say my death
Was ended in a lively faith
The yearly gift that I them gave
Till time be ended they must have.
Arms Drake impaling -- an anchor erect [missing]
--- day of March 1604 (Part hidden under a pew)
--- 1572 (Hidden under a pew)

South aisle
East wall. Tablet. – Joseph Warren of Green gent. Died 7 Oct 1772 aged 61. Elizabeth his wife. Died 3 April 1800 aged 88.
Tablet. – Elizabeth Baker of Green in this parish Died 5 June 1831 in the 85 year of her age. Robert Moalle Squire Died 5 Oct 1800 aged 10 weeks.
A marble mural monument consisting of a sarcophagus with a weeping figure. Sacred to the memory of Frances Herbert viscount Nelson Duchess of Bronti widow of the late admiral Lord Viscount Nelson and her son Joseph Nisbet esq Capt. Royal navy whom she survived 11 months and died in London 6 May 1831 aged 73. This humble offering of affection is erected by Frances Herbert Nisbet in grateful remembrance of those virtues which adorned a kind Mother in law and a good husband. Arms. Not coloured – 3 Boars heads couped – within a Bordure –
South wall. Tablet. – Sophia 3rd wife of Edward Cliff esq died 30 July 1812 aged 53. Edward Cliff esq died 17 June 1819 aged 91 [missing].
Tablet. – Frances Maria Cliff wife of Edward J. esq of Sacheverell Hall. Died 18 April 1776 in the 64 year of her age. Also Martha J his second wife died 9 July 1806 aged 56. Edward Cousin and Martha both children of the above Martha and Edward Cliff [missing]
Arms ermine on a Quarter gules a Spread eagle sable impaling Party per Bend sinister Ermine & ermine over all a Lion rampant gules.
West wall – A marble sarcophagus Tablet "Close to the south entrance within this church in the same grave with the remains of her sister Emily lies interred all that was mortal of Mary Peel daughter of Robert Peel esq and Elizabeth his wife late of Ardwick Lancashire. She died at Exmouth March 12. 1825 aged 25 years." (There follow some verses).
North Wall. Tablet. – Richard Turner esq RN. Harbour Master at Plymouth. Died 27 Aug. 1830 aged 67. erected by his widow [missing].
Floor – Deborah Hall. Died 4 March 1775 aged 66. – RUS. 1800. E. Baker 1831 [missing]

Nave
South wall. Tablet. Emily daughter of Robert Peel esq and Elizabeth his wife late of Ardwick Lancashire. Died at Exmouth 5 May 1824 aged 13. (Then follow some verses).
Black marble Tablet. – Elizabeth Wyatt Edgell. Died 28th Feb. 1826.

Tablet. Peter Middleton esq late of Hull born at Whitby co York. Died at Exmouth 24 Jan. 1803 in the 51 year of her age. Eliza Etheridge his youngest daughter. Died at Sidmouth 7 April 1840 aged 38 [missing].

Tablet. Jane Douglas of Cavers. Died 30 Dec. 1809 aged 18 years

Tablet. James son of James Hallwell esq and Elizabeth his wife of Broomfield Lancashire. Died at Exmouth 31 July 1827 aged 36

Arms --- 3 beavers (question) passant in pale --- (no colour)

Tablet. Esther Denis relict of W. R. Denis esq of London. Died at Exmouth 10 Dec. 1831 aged 37. Also Mary Ellen Blake grandchild of the above Died at Exmouth 29 Jan 1836 aged 6½ years.

Tablet. Frances wife of Hugh Lumsden esq of Pitcaple co Aberdeen Advocate in Edinburgh and daughter of Alexander Brebner esq of Glasgow forest in the same county Died at Alphington 12 Jan 1815 aged 25. Arms Azure in chief 2 Wolves heads (99) couped --- in base as Escallop --- in the Fess point a Buckle

West Wall. Tablet. – Joseph Austwick. Died 30 Jan 1837 aged 88 [missing].

Johanna his wife Died 9 June 1827 aged 72. Mary Lewer their daughter Died 20 Sept 1818 aged 28. – 3 Children died young [missing]

Tablet. Elizabeth Susanna Jordan of Gibraltar Died 21 Feb. 1788 aged 24. John Peter J. esq Died 1 Feb. 1795 aged 66. Peter J esq of the 69 Reg. Died at sea 19 Oct 1796. Frances J. Died 10 – aged 41. Hannah Maria J. Died at Exeter 1 July 1838. [missing]

Floor – John Stafford Died 10 July 1691 [missing]

William Lovett Henry D'Esterre Darby second son of John Darby esq of London merchant and Anne his wife Died 14 March 1790 aged 10 months [missing].

Janet Mansfield daughter of Capt. James M. of the 7th Dragons & Margaret his wife. Born 7 Jan 1779. Died 10th May 1809 [missing]

Thomas Rice youngest son of the late John Rice esq of Tooting co Surrey. Born 7 Nov 1783. Died at Exmouth 28 July 1818 [missing].

John Minyfy gent June -- Died 8 --17-- aged 4-- [missing]

BUDLEIGH SALTERTON

Davidson (p. 287) visited the chapel of St Peter, Budleigh Salterton on 14 July 1840 and noted it was about 11 miles south east of Exeter and 5 miles south west of Sidmouth. He observed that 'at this pleasant little seaside village is a Chapel of ease to the church of Budleigh [East] in which parish it is situated'. The church was built in 1891–3 by G.F. Prynne to replace the chapel of ease (Pevsner, *Devon*, 235). All three memorials that Davidson recorded are missing.

The building consists of an open area of three aisles with large and deep galleries one of which contains an organ [missing]. The windows are under pointed arches and are formed into lancet lights and there are crosses on the exterior gables but the structure though recent has no pretensions to architectural beauty. The only monumental notices are as follow.

Chancel
North wall. A tablet. – Emilia daughter of John Halsey esq wife of William Dunsford esq. Died 14 Sept 1829 aged 46 years – Erected by her sister Maria Elizabeth Budden [missing].
Tablet. Maria Elizabeth daughter of John Halsey esq relict of Major Richard Budden of the East India Company service. Died 26 April 1832 aged 51. Erected by her children [missing]. –
Tablet. Maria Elizabeth second daughter of Major Budden Honourable: East India Company service and Maria Elizabeth his wife Died 29 Dec. 1832 aged 21. Erected by her two sisters [missing].

Exmouth

Davidson (pp. 289–90) visited [Holy Trinity] Exmouth on 7 July 1830 and noted it was 10 miles south east of Exeter. He observed that the new church had been 'erected within a few years by Lord Rolle [and] is a conspicuous object and its tower has a good effect from many points of view. It is in the pointed style and the period adopted is generally that of the late 15th century.' The church was remodelled in 1824 by John Lethbridge, and the chancel was added in 1856 paid for by Lady Rolle, then remodelled again in 1905–7 (Pevsner, *Devon*, 443).

It consists of a nave with a chancel which is merely a continuation of the nave being of the same height and width – aisles & a tower at the west end. On each side of the tower is a lobby with a door which seems to be the entrance to the aisle or the gallery – the principal door is in the tower. On each side of the chancel is a small vestry. The windows throughout are divided by mullions & a transom into 6 lights with cinquefoil heads & the arches ornamented with tracery which as well as the arches of the windows lights is formed by arches turned from 4 centres – ogee arches. – The aisles & the angles of the tower are ornamented by quadrangular buttresses & the same are carried up between the clerestory windows – the whole of the parapets are embattled & the buttresses are crowned by heavy square crocketed pinnacles topped with foliage. Four large pinnacles crown the angles of the tower. The eastern end finished with an embattled gable, the apex disfigured with a pinnacle & below this the arms & crest of Lord Rolle carved in stone of a large size. The eastern window is large 10 lights of similar design to the others. The nave & chancel are about 82 feet long by 25 wide within the walls to open to the ailes by 5 arches on each side resting on a column formed of four shafts with intervening hollow mouldings & having moulded capitals. The ceiling is divided into compartments by ribs which are ornamented with bosses of foliage at their intersections [missing] – There are deep galleries & an organ. The pulpit & pews are of oak with appropriate mouldings. The font is of stone octagonal & sides ornamented with panels of quatre-foils& shields [the font has been changed and now has niches with statues]. The altar screen is of stone consisting of a range of panels finished with cinquefoiled heads, tabernacle work & an open parapet above.
This place contains 2000 sittings of which 380 are free.
There are not any sepulchral monuments or inscriptions.

TOPSHAM

Davidson (pp. 291–6) visited [St Margaret] Topsham on 15 July 1840 and noted it was 3½ miles south east of Exeter. The church was rebuilt in 1874–6 by Edward Ashworth (Pevsner, *Devon*, 820). Nineteen memorials are missing from the thirty-four that Davidson recorded.

The church at this place consists of 2 aisles thrown into a large area about 85 feet by 72 and capable of accommodating 2000 people. The whole has been modernised. The eastern window is formed by 5 lancet lights without cusps & the upper parts hidden by the ceiling. There are large galleries on three sides [removed] and an organ – In front of the gallery a tablet states as follows. The accommodation in this church was enlarged in 1827 by which means 180 additional sittings were obtained and in consequence of a grant from the Society for promoting the building & enlargement of churches & chapels the whole of that number are declared to be free and un-appropriated for ever. Henry Thorp perpetual curate [missing]. A tower on the western side contains 6 Bells. The pulpit is modern and in bad taste. The font is very ancient & curious a large circular stone basin on a rude cylindrical block ornamented by a sort of zigzag moulding & the rude figure of a dog with a collar of spikes around his neck.

The monumental inscriptions afford the following particulars.

East wall.
Marble Tablet. Sir Alexander Hamilton Knt Died 12 June 1809 aged 77 Buried here Dame Mary H. his wife died in London 18 Oct 1806 aged 65 Buried at St. Pancras church – Erected by their nephew Alexander Hamilton esq Arms. Quarterly 1 & 4 Gules 3 Cinquefoils argent 2 & 3 Or a gallery sable. On an Escutcheon of Pretence Argent a Chevron between 3 Torteaux. [missing]
Marble Tablet. John Palmer Died 13 May 1827 aged 81 Joanna his wife Died 10 April 1831 aged 77. Their children Elizabeth Veale Sheppard Died 5 Jan 1829 aged 49 John Veale Palmer Died 6 Nov 1807 aged 14. [missing]
Tablet with a figure & urn. Mary widow of the late George Farr esq of this parish Died 15 June 1818 aged 70 [missing] Their 2 sons Theodore Bere Farr esq Died 4 June 1812 aged 24 George Bere F. esq Died 30 June 1821 aged 41. Their only daughter Ann Bere Farr Died 20 Nov 1825 aged 42 [missing].
Tablet. Mr Elizabeth Cartside wife of Thomas Cartside of the co Lancaster Died 24 Oct 1813 aged 53 [missing].
Sarcophagus. – Charles Byrne Esq. Died 5 Oct 1815 in the 71 year of his age. His nephew – Richard Roche esq 1 Nov 1818 aged 47. Margaret Byrne spinster sister of the former Died 1 July 1829 aged 84 Arms Gules a Chevron between 3 Dexter Hands couped argent.

South Wall.
Sarcophagus. *Memoriae sacrum Guilelmi Spicer armigeri de Wear qui felicissime resurrectionis in expectatione pia subtus in hoc sepulchro conditus requiescit Monumentum*

hoc ex gratissimo ac piissimo animo curavit facundum ejus filius Gul. Franc. Spicer. Obiit 21 die Octobris A.D. 1788 aetat. sue 53. et Elizabethae uxoris ejus pietate non minus quam annis consummate obiit 31 die Decembris A.D. 1817 aetatis sue 84.

Arms. Sable a Chevron ermine between 3 Castles argent On an escutcheon of pretence sable a Buck's head cabeshed between 2 Flanches or.

Tablet *Memoriae sacrum Annae Spicer de Topsham pietatis egregie Obiit 16 die Maii AD 1791 aetatis 89.*

White marble Tablet. – Sarah Anne wife of Rear Admiral Sir Richard King Bart & K. C. B. Commander in Chief of Hill Squadron in the East Indies and only daughter of Admiral Sir John Thomas Duckworth Bart G. C. B. Died on board HMS. Minder at sea on her passage to Bombay 20 March 1819 aged 34. Interred in Bombay church. Arms. Sable a Lion rampant argent between 3 Crosses patees fitchee or, with an escutcheon for bart impaling Argent on a Chevron azure between 2 Ducks in chief proper and an Anchor erect in base Sable a Fire ball or, fire issuant there from Gules between 2 Crosses patees of the last, on a chief of the second a Naval coronet or between 2 stars of 6 points of the field.

A white marble Tablet with 2 whole length figures representing a military officer crowned by Fame. George Henry Duckworth late Lieutenant Col. Of the 4th Reg. of Foot who fell at the battle of Albuera 16 May 1811 at the head of the first battalion aged 28 years

Arms (no colours) – on a Chevron -- between 2 Ducks in chief and a naval cornet in base a Fire ball --- fire issuant there from. -- between 2 stars of 6 points, on a Chief --- 2 olive branches --- impaling Or a Chevron sable between 3 Fleur de lis

Tablet – Martha Woad Died 7 March 1778 aged 78- [missing]

Martha Woad her niece Died 24 April 1781 aged 60 [missing]

Tablet. Samuel Pyle gent Died 31 Oct 1815 aged 77 Sarah his widow Died 20 August 1818 aged 76 [missing]

Tablet. – Mrs. Read. Died 22 Sept 1823 in her 59th year [missing]

Tablet. Henry Sergeant Died 9 July 1813 aged 78. Erected by his widow.

West Wall.

Tablet. Ward Cadogan esq of Brenckburn Priory co Northumberland Died 18 Aug. 1833 aged 61. Arms Quarterly 1 & 4. Gules a Lion rampant reguardant. – 2 & 3 – 3 boars heads couped.

Tablet. James Patch esq Died 12 July 1829 in the 73rd year of his age. Lieutenant Charles Patch his son Died at Bartool in the East Indies Nov. 1818 aged 20. Three children buried in S. Lawrence church Exeter. Erected by Mary Elizabeth widow of James Patch. Francina Cornelia youngest daughter of the above died 21 Sept 1830 aged 18. Arms (no colours) – 3 Leaves slipped barwise in chief and a Hunting horn stringed and garnished in base. – A canton ermine impaling on a mound in base a Tree against it a Fox salient [missing]

Tablet. Rebecca relict of the revd Henry Philipps vicar of Gwennap co Cornwall & daughter of the late George Bent U.D. of Exeter Died 12 May 1801 aged 71 [missing] Henry Philips Died 13 Jan 1782 aged 70. Joanna Bent Died 26 Jan 1819 aged 84. Susanna bent Died 14 Dec. 1825 aged 86. [missing]

Tablet. Thomas Hole Esq of Southbrook in this parish. Buried Here. Died 20 Feb. 1788 aged 22 Arms. Quarterly argent and sable a Cross engrailed between 4 Escallops all counter changed [missing].

North Wall.
Tablet. – Hannah late wife of Mr. Henry Compton second daughter of Captain William Coggan of Lympstone Died 26 Dec. 1716 aged 37. Also 3 children – Henry Compton Died 9 July 1762 aged 88. Arms Sable a Lion passant between 3 Helmets or. [missing]
Tablet. Peter Pare Travers esq of Fairfield Lodge in this parish of the East India Company services at Bombay Died in London 26 May 1833 in the 65 year of his age. Arms Gules a Chevron – between 2 Escallops in a chief and a Boars head erased in base. [missing]
Tablet. Timothy Knight M.A. Died 10 August 1771 in the 73 year of his age. Arms Argent on a Canton gules a Spur of the field impaling Ermine on a Chief indented gules 3 Ducal coronets barwise or. [missing]
A very handsome white marble Monument being a large tablet representing in Bas relief a naval fight with several vessels in action, above it a Bust of the deceased with his sword and naval trophies – and on scrolls the words "HMS Orion 1 June 1794 – Minorca taken 15 Nov 1798 – Swedish & Danish West India islands taken March 1801 – Off St. Domingo French Fleet defeated 6 Feb. 1806" – On a tablet below To the memory of Sir John Thomas Duckworth Bart knight grand cross of the most honourable order of the Bath Admiral of the White squadron of his Majesties' Fleet who died in the chief command of his Majesties' Ships at Plymouth on the 31 August 1817 aged 69 years.
His private life was marked by benevolence too extensive and too effectual to be forgotten. To his country's services he was devoted from his earliest youth with a zeal that only death subdued and his achievements are recorded in the annuals of his country's glory – Arms not coloured --- on a Chevron --- between 2 Ducks in chief and an Anchor erect – in base a Fire Ball – fire issuant there out --- between 2 Crosses patees – On a chief --- a wreath of laurel within it the words St. Domingo between 2 stars of 6 points – On a separate escutcheon - Quarterly of nines (Sable) and (argent) on the 2nd 4th 6th & 8th Quarters an Eagle displayed of the first.
Tablet. William and John Fortescue sons of John Fortescue Deputy clerk of the peace for this county. William died 1754 in the 40 year of his age – John 1784 aged 69 having been pastor of this church 42 years.
Tablet. – John Goodrich esq a native of Virginia North America Died Nov 1785 aged 63. Margaret his wife Died 12 April 1810 aged 70 – Two of their children James G. Died 26 May 1707 aged 23 and Samuel G. Died 26 Oct 1807 aged 41. [missing]
Tablet. William Shapter Died 3 May 1806 aged 78. Ester his wife died 19 June 1792 aged 64. [missing]

Floor.
James Rodd esq late of Weare. Died 15 April 1782
Joanna Rodd his mother – Elizabeth Rodd his sister – James Fortescue R. – Emma R. & Maria R. son and daughter of James R. esq his son of Doddscombeleigh in this county. –
John Jonathan Lee esq late of Easthays near Bath. Died at Exmouth 23 Dec. 1796 aged 53.
Sub hoc lapide requiescit paulisper Benjamin Berry (query) Art Magister Christi fidelis -- Jesu – vicesimo quinto die Januarii Anno Redemptionis MDCLXXX.
--- Ricardus Duke quondam. –

Andrew Holwell & Elizabeth his wife buried 7 April 1687.
Henry Brand gent grandson of the above Henry Brand Died 23 March 1769 aged 55
Martha his wife Died 24 April 1810 aged 94. Mary Brand daughter of the above Died
5 Oct 1834 aged 79.
William Woolcombe. Died 17 April 1758 aged 73 [missing].

Hatchments exhibiting the following coats armorial are hung in different parts of
the church.
Sable a Chevron between 2 Escallops in chief and a Boars head erased in base argent.
Argent 2 Trefoils slipped in fess sable. A chief last with a crescent for difference
Bernard Argent a Bear rampant sable muzzled or.
The same as the last.
For Spicer as on the monument.
Vert a bend of 3 Lozenges within a Border engrailed a mullet for difference impaling
Gules 3 Horses courant in pale argent – for Baron.
For Sir John Duckworth as on the monument

Countess Wear

Davidson (p. 296) visited the chapel of St Luke, Countess Wear, on 29 May 1850 and noted it was 2 miles from Exeter. A chapel of ease to the parish of Topsham, it was erected in 1838. A plain neat building in the pointed style and there were no monumental inscriptions.

A chapel of ease about 64 feet long by 24 wide. The windows east and west are triplets, those on the sides lancet lights – a small chancel and a vestry on the south side of it – a turret on the west gable finished on the top by a fleur-de-lis contains one bell. – the roof is open – At the eastern end is a plain screen of stone [removed]. The font is of stone ornamented with quatrefoils and niches. There is no gallery – near the western door is a barrel organ [removed]. The front of the altar cloth is decorated with a large cross glory. There are no monumental inscriptions.

HEAVITREE

Davidson (pp. 297–304) visited [St Michael and All Angels] Heavitree on 15 July 1840 and noted it was one mile east of Exeter. He observed that 'this parish because of the large extent of building has become almost a suburb of the city of Exeter and the church stands a little south of the London road'. The church was rebuilt in 1844–6 by David Mackintosh and the chancel and tower extended in 1897 by E.H. Harbottle (Pevsner, *Devon*, 393). One memorial is missing from the forty-three that Davidson recorded.

The church consists of a nave about 57 feet long by 18 wide with aisles north and south of the same length, a chancel about 12 feet by 18, a Porch covering the south door, a vestry south of the chancel and a low embattled Tower at the western end containing 4 Bells. The windows are formed by lights with cinquefoiled heads and perpendicular tracery but most have been altered and the cuss removed. The ceiling is coved & divided by ribs of mouldings with bosses of foliage at their intersections. The nave opens to the aisles by 4 low arches on each side resting on columns formed by 4 shafts with intervening hollow mouldings & having their soffits ornamented with foliage and the capitals with rich carvings of angels, foliage & devices but the whole is loaded with whitewash. Two carved oak screens of the 16th century divide the eastern ends of the aisles from the nave and a portion of what was perhaps the chancel screen remains in one of the pews of the north aisle viz. three niches with cinquefoiled heads in which are painted as many figures of saints
1. St. Dunstan holding the devil by the nose with a pair of pincers
2. A female with a sword through her breast. question St. Agatha
3. D° with a sword through her neck. question St. Catherine of Alexandria
The altar screen is of oak modern heavy & in bad taste [changed in 1939], over it is a shield with the arms of the see of Exeter impaling Argent a Greyhound courant in fess sable on a chief dancette of the last 3 bezants [missing]. The gallery is perhaps of the 17 century [removed], the Pulpit has the date 1718 at the back [now on the stone steps]. The Font is of stone & ancient, octagonal, the sides ornamented with a range of small niches and panels with angles below them. It rests on a column the sides of which are cut in trefoiled niches [no longer used]. The gallery contains an organ [removed]. A brass chandelier the gift of Thomas Wright 1711 [removed].

The monumental inscriptions give the following particulars.

Chancel
North wall – Behind & above the top of the high panel line of the altar screen is seen the top of an arch which perhaps covers a tomb [removed].
Marble Tablet. Charlotte Cartwright relict of John C. gent of St. James Westminster died in Exeter 10 April 1800 in the 97 year of her age. Buried here near the remains of her daughter Mary wife of George Moore Vicar of this parish.

South Wall. Tablet. – Jane wife of Sir Henry Maturin Farrington Bart Died 8 Oct 1828 aged 38 leaving a large family. Sir H M Farrington Bart Died 4 Oct 1834 aged 56. Arms. Ermine on a Chevron gules between 3 Leopards faces sable as many Bombs or fired proper, an escutcheon for Bart, impaling Argent a Saltire couped gules.

Tablet. Elizabeth wife of William Hautenville esq of Dublin. Died 8 Jan 1827 in the 35 year of her age.

Tablet. Jane Cartwright. Died 25 Nov. 1814 aged 66.

Floor. The revd John Snell Vicar of this parish & Canon residentiary of the cathedral church of Exeter Died 4 Sept. 1728 aged 56. Susanna his wife Died 5 July 1754 aged 78. Several children – Wenman Colleton Dickinson great grandson of Wenman Nutt esq & only son of Richard Colleton Dickinson Colonel Royal Artillery and Ann his wife. Died 7 June 1811 aged 10 years.

Mary Nutt wife of Wenman Nutt esq daughter of the revd John Snell. Died 24 March 1800 aged 83. Wenman Nutt esq Died 8 August 1801 aged 88.

George Moore Vicar of this parish. Died Sept. – aged 31.

George Moore MA. Archdeacon of Cornwall Canon residentiary of the Cathedral church of Exeter Vicar of this parish. Died 12 March 1807 in the 76 year of his age.

Catherine wife of George Moore rector of Sowton Died 11 May 1810 aged 37.

A hatchment for Baron – Gules a Chevron ermine between 3 Pine cones or, impaling Sable a Talbot passant argent a Mullet for difference [missing].

Nave.

A Tablet against one of the south columns. Ambrose Rhodes esq of Bellair in this parish Died 1 March 1777 aged 72 Sarah his wife sole daughter of Solomon Andrew esq of Lyme Regis co Dorset Died 22 Aug 1783 aged 73. Mary their daughter Died 17 Nov aged 24. Ambrose Andrew Rhodes esq of Bellair son of the above Ambrose and Sarah gentleman of the Privy Chamber of His Majesty George 3rd Died unmarried 26 Nov. 1800 aged 71. Arms Argent a Lion passant gardant in bend gules between 2 acorns proper cotised ermine. On an escutcheon of pretence Sable a Saltier (e.g. argent) between 4 Cross crosslets or. – a Hatchment with the same coat.

Tablet. Captain J.T. Blunt Hon. E. India Company Bengal Engineers. Died 20 Oct 1834 in 68th year of his age. Arms -- 3 Bends wavy --

A white marble tablet in the form of a book & letters "*Virgilius*" inscribed. S. M. of Dudley son of Henry & Frances Wyatt of Brome in Suffolk. Died 14 Nov 1814 aged 13.

South Wall. Tablet. Martha wife of Robert Collins. Died 16 August 1814 aged 55.

Robert C. late of Islington co Middlesex esq. Died 1 April 1825 aged 69.

Floor. Roger Pyne jun. of this parish Died 28 Feb 1725 aged 25 – Anne his daughter Born 30 June 1723 Died 22 Sept 1723 – Roger Pyne the father of the above Roger Pyne Died 12 Nov 1737 aged 84. – Penelope relict of Roger Pyne jun. Buried 2 September 1784 aged 64 – The revd William Pyne son of Roger and Penelope P. Buried – April 1774 aged. –

Arms. – a chevron -- between 3 Fir cones -- impaling a Talbot passant. a mullet for differences (Burgoyne)

Hic jacet Hugh Legh qui obiit 2° die Augusti A.D. 1536 cujus anime propicietur Deus Amen. William Legh of Homeland Died 2 Nov. 1657 aged 82.

James Hamilton Esq of Blackheath. Died 7 Aug. 1801 aged 21.

Stackhouse Jeffrey esq Died 13 May 1807 aged 40. Diana his daughter Died 12 May

1800 aged 12. Stackhouse Edward Jeffrey Born 20 May 1797 Died 10 Feb, 1809. Frances Elizabeth T. Died 30 April 1812 aged 18.

Hic jacet Johannes Payne de Birchay qui obiit --- A.D. 1638 aetatis suae 77.

Jeannette Towne died 18 April 1808 in the 27 year of her age wife of Francis T. esq. Francis Towne- artist of great ability in landscape. Died 7 July 1816 aged 76.

Lucy Mary wife of William Goodhall of upper Guilford Street London. Died at Bellair in this parish 16 May 1804 aged 23.

North Aisle

North Wall, Tablet. Sebastian Isacke of Polsloe esq Died 6 Nov 1688. Arms. Sable a bend or, on a Canton argent a leopards face of the field impaling Barry of 6 or and gules.

Sarcophagus tablet. Elizabeth Rhodes widow of the late revd George Rhodes formerly Vicar of Colyton in this county and daughter of the revd John Sleech Archdeacon of Cornwall. Died 1 Aug. 1817 aged 62.

The revd Ambrose William Rhodes third son of the deceased Died 16 Feb. 1818 aged 36. Frances Bridgett Rhodes second daughter of the above Elizabeth Died 27 June 1832 aged 52.

Arms Rhodes as before.

Tablet. Master James Boyd. Buried here in his 8th year

Tablet. Maria Philippa Brereton late of Bellair in this parish oldest daughter of the revd John Sleech Archdeacon of Cornwall & relict of the revd Richard Brereton of Wotton House co Gloucester. Died 9 June 1807 aged 57.

Thomas Baker Rhodes nephew of the above and 6th son of the revd George R. vicar of Colyton & Elizabeth his wife Died 14 Aug. 1804 aged 9.

Arms in a lozenge Checky or and gules

Tablet. John Norman of Yatten & Swod House Congresbury esq one of His Majesty's Deputy Lieutenants for the county of Somerset Died 4 June 1837 aged 60. Erected by his widow and children. Arms Argent 4 Bars embattled counter embattled gules on a bend sable 3 Purses (or water bags or escallops) --- impaling Or 2 Chevrons sable between 3 Mullets in pale ---

Floor. John Wilcocks of this parish gent. Died 11 Sept. 1787 aged 65 Ann granddaughter of the above and daughter of Robert and Elizabeth W. Died 2 Sept. 1796 aged 4.

Abraham Payne gent Died 7 Feb. aged 46. Elizabeth his wife one of the daughters of Sebastian Isacke of Polsloe esq Died 11 Aug. 1765 aged 88. Elizabeth eldest daughter of Abraham and Eliz. Payne Died an infant. Mary their daughter wife of the revd John Simon Died 30 May 1792 aged 77.

Ann wife of Robert Mules esq Died 16 April 1840.

Thomas Wilde -- 1712 aged 88. Dorothy wife of Thomas W junior Died 24 May 1672. John Bragge gent Died 28 Feb. 1691. Dorothy wife of John B. Died 11 Dec, 1680. Arms – a Chevron between 3 Bulls passant -- impaling -- 3 Boars heads couped. -- within a border engrailed.

Orate p. an. John Legh.

South aisle.

East wall tablet. Joshua Loring Winslow esq. Died 22 Nov. 1820 aged 54. Elizabeth his wife Died 21 Sept. 1813 aged 40.

Against one of the columns a tablet – Robert Rookes Died 16 July 1821 aged 55. Mary his relict Died 4 July 1837 aged 74.

South Wall Tablet. Charles Sleech Rhodes Capt. Royal Engineers killed at the storming of St. Sebastian 31 Aug. 1813 in the 28th year of his age 4th son of the revd George R. Vicar of Colyton. Arms Rhodes

Tablet. Caroline youngest daughter of Col. Henry Vincent of the Bengal Establishment Died 22 March 1812 in the 24th year of her age.

Tablet. Hugh Somerville esq of Hamilton near Glasgow Died at his sons house in this parish 6 July 1805 aged 82. Arms defaced.

North Wall tablet – Major Thomas Edward of His Majesty's 6 Reg. of Foot Died 24 Aug. 1815 aged 82. Erected by his son.

Tablet Edward Swale Portbury esq late Secretary of the Marine Board Calcutta Died 1 March 1839 aged 71.

Floor. Charles Irish Lloyd son of Robert & Sarah L. of Kingsland co Middlesex Died 16 May 1796 in 18th year of his age.

John Blake MA. rector of Yeovilton & vicar of Pilton co Somerset. Died 21 Dec. 1812 aged 31. Buried here.

Richard Payne Died 25 March 1612.

William Leigh of Whipton in this parish Died 1 May 1616.

Thomas Salter gent Died 21 June 1797 aged 72. Mary his wife Died 3 Jan. 1823 aged 91.

Heavitree. Over the gateway to the Almshouses by the road side is a stone thus inscribed

"These almshouses were founded by Sir. Rob Dennis knight in March 1591 and finished by Sir Thomas Dennis his Brother in 1594"

Arms also in stone. Quarterly of 10.

   1. 3 Axes Dennis
   2. A crop patees on a chief 3 stars
   3. 3 Lozenges in fess ermine (Giffard)
   4. 2 Bends wavy (Brewer)
   5. 2 Bucks courant in pale (qu Buckerell)
   6. A Bend cotised (Beaupell)
   7. A Fess paly of 6 between 3 Crosses (or Mullets)
   8. On a Chevron between 3 Birds heads erased as wavy acorns (Chiderlegh)
   9. A unicorn rampant
  10. An eagle displayed

Copy
Grave stones in the Parish church of Heavitree.

Here lyeth the bodyes of Thomas George of Heavitree esq and Rose his wife. He departed this life the 17 of October 1670 and she the 14 day of April 1671

The loving turtell having mist her mate
Beg'd she might enter ere they shut the gate
Their dust here lies whose souls to heaven are gonne
And waite till angells rowle away the stone

Here lyeth the body of Susanna the wife of Rawlin Mallacke of Cockington esq & daughter of Thomas Gorges of Battcombe in Somerset esq who died 17 April Anno Dom 1673.

Enclosed with the above and the following letter are two rubbings on tissue paper of coats of arms which appear by the letter to belong to the inscription above.

1. Per fess – in chief (Mallock) – in base lozenge – a chevron --- for (Georges) – impaling
    – a Chevron between 3 Talbots heads erased – a crescent for difference – (Hall)
2. Mallock impaling Gorges (imperfect)

My Dear Sir,

I am very sorry I had not the pleasure of seeing you when you called at my son's office and I could not find you the next day. I beg to enclose you what I believe you required the arms and inscription of two grave stones related to your Family in Heavitree church; one part of the stone bearing the arms of Mallock & George has been broken and lost in the removal from the old to the new church.

Arms of Mallock of Axmouth Per chevron engrailed or and sable, on three Roundel, three Fleur de lis all counter charged Sir William Pole p. 492

Gorges Mascule or and azure a chevron gules 485.

Is the third coat that of Hall?

Do you know any thing of the Bearings on the Font in Colyton church?

There are no grave stones belonging to your family in the cathedral

If I can be of any further use pray do not scruple to ask it.

I am Dear Sir, Yours very truly, Pitman Jones, Heavitree 2 July 1847

Newspaper cutting, no name or no date of newspaper:

Heavitree Church of St. Michael, near Exeter

This new or rather re-erected parish church, was consecrated on Saturday by the Bishop of the diocese, supported by a strong corps of clergy. The architect is Mr. Mackintosh, the designer of several of the diocesan churches of Exeter. The contractors for the whole of the works was Mr. John Kenshole, of Heavitree, by whom Mr. Simon Rowe of Saint Sidewells, was engaged to execute the freestone work. The church has been built by subscription, assisted by grants to the amount of 500l, from the Church Building Societies. The amount of accommodation it affords is sitting for 1,220 persons, of which number 513 are free and un-appropriated. It is one of the largest churches in the county.

We extract the following abbreviated description of it from the *Exeter and Plymouth Gazette*:

The style is that of the 15th century, and all the peculiar characteristics of the ancient church have been carefully maintained and restored. The dimensions internally are as follows:- Chancel 25 feet by 16 feet ; nave, 86 feet by 22 feet; north and south aisles each, 94 feet by 13 feet 6 inches, with a southern porch and vestry at the eastern end of the north aisle. Externally it is faced in limestone from the quarries at Chudleigh, having the windows, string course, cornices, battlements mouldings, and other dressings of freestone from Caen in Normandy. A granite basement or plinth is carried round the building on all sides, and the gables are surmounted with floriated crosses. Internally, this church is remarkable for its altitude, and for all the high pitch of its open roofs, the principal timbers of which are oak, and in the chancel roof are some ancient carved bosses, coloured and gilt as they were in the former church. The columns and arches separating the nave from the aisles are a restoration in every point as regards detail of those in the old church; they are especially rich, and varied in their foliage and capitals. There is a fine chancel arch, richly moulded, and of good proportions, on the north side of which is situated the pulpit, carved in Caen stone, and somewhat similar to the ancient one at Harberton. On the southern side of the chancel arch are the reading desk and eagle, the latter carved in oak by Mr. Winsor, senior verger of the cathedral [missing]. At the eastern end of the chancel it was originally intended to have re-fixed the former window; but on inspection it being found much decayed, as well as of a somewhat debased architectural character; the Rev. Dr. Warren of Portview, liberally presented a new window of four lights carved in Caen stone; and the Rev. Arthur Atherley, the vicar, has filled the same with stained glass executed by Mr. Robert Beer, of Exeter, and comprising figures of the four Evangelists, Ec. The south window of the chancel has a figure in stained glass, of the Virgin. In the south aisle there is a specimen of a memorial window of three lights; the first and third bordered after a specimen in Exeter cathedral. The font in Caen stone, large and highly enriched. The bowl is octagonal, having each panel filled with ornamental tracery, and the sides of the shaft are likewise panelled with cinquefoil headed arches; springing from the shafts, to support the bowl, is a band of angels with expanded wings bearing shields. "We hope" adds the writer "to see ere long, an adequate tower and spire."

Newspaper cutting, no name of newspaper, dated May 1876
The erection has just been completed, in St. Michael's Church, Heavitree, of perhaps the most costly and chastely-designed mural monuments to be found in Devonshire. The monument, erected to perpetuate the memory of thirteen members of the Raleigh family, was designed and erected by the late J.M. Foley, R.A., and was one of the latest emanations from the chisel of that distinguished sculpture. It was at first intended to place the memorial in Exeter Cathedral but Sir Gilbert Scott objected, ruling that its style was not in harmony with the architectural features of that edifice. Hence the subsequent decision to place it in the parish church at Heavitree. The memorial, which is of the finest polished Italian marble, stands up-wards of Twelve feet high, is proportionately wide, and is fitted in a recess in the wall at the western end of the south gallery of the church. It is divided into three compartments. On the tablet of the centre compartment is the following inscription:-
In memory of
John Raleigh Esquire.,
Diplomatist and for a period of thirty-eight years,
And during six successive Governments,
Chief Secretary to Governments,
Buried in a vault within Kensington Church, Middlesex.
And also to Sarah his Wife,
And Dorothy Lipyeatt, their Daughter, buried at Heavitree.
And of their Four Sons,
Frederick Raleigh, Esquire., Diplomatic Service:
Francis Raleigh, Major H.M. 9th Regt, of Foot, and Town Major of Gibraltar;
And Edward Raleigh, Senior Major of H.M. 11th Regt. Of Foot,
Educated (with his brother) at Harrow School,
Served in the Peninsular War, in the West Indies, and on the Staff,
And died at Exeter, on the 27th February, 1819 aest. 50 years,
Buried in a Family Vault at Heavitree.
And also of
Ester Raleigh, relict of major Edward Raleigh;

Who died at Brighton, Sussex, on the 5th December, 1857.
In the 73rd year of her age.
And also of two Daughters of the above;
Emily Raleigh and Frances Raleigh,
Who died in their youth.
And in sacred Memory of
Frederick Raleigh
(Second son of Edward and Esther Raleigh).
A Major of the Bengal Army,
And for the last fourteen years of his life
Commandant of the Calcutta Militia;
Who Died of Cholera, at Calcutta. On the 25th April, 1856,
In the 45th year of his age,
And in the 29th year of his Military service.
And of his gallant Eldest Son,
Walter Frederick Keppel Raleigh,
Lieutenant of the 7th Regiment of Bengal Light Cavalry,
Who was killed at Lucknow,
On the breaking out of the India Mutiny at that Station,
On the 30th of May 1857,
At the early age of 17 years and 3 months.
And also in memory of
Edward W. Walter Raleigh, Esq., F.R.C.S.
Of the Bengal Medical Staff, &, &, &.,
Formerly surgeon to the Governor-General of India.
To the Calcutta Hospital and Eye Infirmary,
And "Professor of Surgery" at the Medical College of Calcutta,
Having held the above distinguished appointments for Seventeen Years;
He retired at a comparatively early age from active service, in 1845,
And died at London, 22nd January, 1865.

This compartment is surmounted by a cross of ecclesiastical design. The compartments on either side are recessed. That on the right contains a large sized and exquisitely-sculptured statue, emblematic of "Civil Law", while that on the left contains a companion statue, representing the military department of the British service. In the centre of the base the Raleigh arms have been inserted with the family legend, "A more at virtute". This splendid memorial of a distinguished Devonshire family has cost upwards of £1,000, and is said to have been erected in compliance with the terms of a recent bequest.

LYMPSTONE

Davidson (pp. 305–8) visited [Nativity of the Blessed Virgin Mary] Lympstone on 14 July 1840 and noted it was about 7 miles south east of Exeter. The church was rebuilt in 1889 by R.M. Fulford (Pevsner, *Devon*, 551). Eighteen memorials are missing from the thirty-three that Davidson recorded.

The church of this village consists of a Nave about 70 feet long by 22 wide an aisle on the north the same length and about 9 feet wide, a chancel and an embattled Tower at the western end 75 feet high to the top of the pinnacles, and containing 5 Bells. The nave is divided from the aisle by 5 low arches on columns formed by shafts & intervening hollow mouldings with capitals carved in foliage. The windows have been modernised. That on the west has 4 lights finished in cinquefoils with tracery, in the perpendicular style. The Pulpit is modern as are the galleries [removed]. The Font is very ancient, a large rude circular stone basin ornamented with a rude cable moulding round it resting on a pillar of nearly the same size [now situated in the porch]. At the south door, which is covered by a porch, is a niche for holy water [removed].

The monumental inscriptions are in substance as follows.

Chancel
North Wall. A small marble sarcophagus. Miss Mary Rolls daughter of the late John R. esq of the Kent Road Surrey. Died at Exmouth Jan. 1806 aged 25.
A marble monument a large Tablet and a Bust. In memory of Nicholas Lee esq patron of this church 3 times mayor, one of the aldermen & a guardian of the poor of the city of Exeter. Died 11 June 1759 aged 79 & buried here.

South Wall. Sarcophagus. Mary widow of John Lewis Gidoin esq Vice Admiral of the White. Died 16 Feb. 1803 aged 70. Erected by her son [missing].
Tablet. The revd John Prestwood Gidoin son of John Lewis Gidoin esq Vice Admiral of the White Died 18 Jan 1820 aged 57. having been rector of this parish 27 years. Erected by his brother – Arms – 3 Doves Volant --- on a chief azure 3 Mullets [now placed on the floor].
Tablet. To the memory of Sibyl Maria eldest daughter of the late revd John Tattersall (vicar of Harwood) Leyham in Yorkshire) and of Sibyl Christian his wife this tablet is erected by her mother sister & brothers. She was born 24 Oct 1790. Died 1 Jan 1812. Arms Sable a Chevron or between 3 leopards passant argent.
Sarcophagus. Robert Hunter esq jun. of Thurston in co Haddington Died at Lympstone 14 Jan 1808 aged 33.
Floor. Sarah Caroline Lee relict of the late Matthew Lee esq of Ebford Died 23 Nov. 1823 aged 36.
Rev. John Lee Rector of this parish Died 18 July 1786 aged 77.

Jane Smith second daughter of James Smith esq of Bideford Died 18 June 1823 aged 32.

James Reynolds Born 22 Dec. 18-- Died 14 May 1811.

Samuel Morgan Died 18 Dec. 1808 aged 9 days.

Richard Ussher son of the late revd Hemsworth Usher of Temple Aran co Westmeath. Died 22 Oct 1822 in the 22 year of his age.

Here lieth the body of Dorothea the daughter of Henry Drake of this parish gent. and of Frances his wife Born 18 Sept. 1705 Died 29 Dec. 1722. Arms in a lozenge Drake with a mullet for difference. Also Gertrude their daughter Born 31 March 1710 Died 7 Oct 1711 Also Frances their daughter Born 24 April 1711 Died 18 Jan 1711/2.

Henry Drake of this parish gent son of John Drake of Ivybridge in this co esq Died 4 May 1717 in the 46 year of his age. Arms (Wyvern) Drake impaling Drake. Motts. Sic parvis magna.

Nave.

South Wall. Tablet – Mary Ruth Glendining Died 31 Jan. 1817 aged 21. Eleanor Glending whose remains lie interred in the church of St. Michael Bassishaw Died 17 May 1814 aged 14 Daughter of Thomas and Mary G. of Burton Crescent London. [missing]

Tablet. Revd. Frederick Burgmann MA. Deacon of the Church of Christ & Curate of Morchard Bishop in the dioceses. Died 17 March 1833 aged 24. [missing]

Tablet. Sir George Burgmann Knt Died 15 Jan 1828 aged 67. [missing]

Tablet & urn. Egerton Filmore of this parish esq & Sarah his wife whose maiden name was Wyse, also Sarah their first daughter who was married to Mr John Filmore and Mary their second daughter who died unmarried. Erected in 1799 by Elizabeth their third and only surviving daughter who married Mr John Searle of this parish [missing].

Tablet. Ann wife of Mr Joseph Foy of Argyle street of London. Died 30 Jan 1813 aged 30. [missing]

Tablet. Eliza daughter of Joseph and Elizabeth Blisset Died 20 Oct 1814 aged 11. [missing]

Tablet. William Joseph Thomas esq second son of Richard Thomas esq of Code Helen co Caernarvon & Margaret his wife daughter of John Lloyd esq of Pentrehobyn co Flint Born 12 Sept 1780 Died 14 April 1806 aged 25. Also Thomas Lloyd Thomas brother of the above Born 10 Aug. 1786. Died 12 Nov. 1806. [missing]

Tablet. Caroline youngest daughter of -- Spurrier esq late of Yardleybury Herts. Died 2 Aug 1815 in the 18 year of her age.

Latin inscription – Richard Egerton descended from an ancient family in Cheshire Died 19 April 1689. Sarah daughter of Henry Ford of Nutwell esq and wife of John Egerton rector of this church. Buried 1728. Arms – a Lion rampant -- between 3 Pheons -- impaling 3 Lions rampant – crowned.

Timothy Curtis Esq. Post captain RN. Died 15 Oct 1834 in the 41 year of his age. [missing]

Amelia relict of the late Thomas Monteith of the Island of Jamaica esq and their third daughter of the late William Murray of Arbenne Perthshire Esq Died 26 April 1833 aged 67 [missing]

Mary Hoswill Died 22 Jan 1789 aged72. Robert Lovering Hoswill her son Died 17 August 1833 aged 81 [missing].

North aile

East wall. Tablet. Jane wife of Joseph Smith esq late of Bath. Died 31 Oct 1792 in the 61 year of her age. Also Joseph Smith esq Died 3 Sept 1793 in the 61 year of her age [missing].

Tablet. John Thomas Wright esq Died 14 Dec, 1838 aged 76 [missing].

North wall.

Tablet. John Bradfute of the City of Edinburgh son of the late revd James Bradfute Curate of Market Deeping Died 22 Nov 1807 aged 21. Erected by his Mother Mrs. Maria Bradfute. [missing]

Tablet. Richard Welland Lieutenant RN. Died 12 July 1820 aged 59. [missing]

Tablet. Elizabeth daughter of John Richard and Margaret Withall of Sowden Cottage in this parish. Wife of John Haddy James of Exeter Died 14 May 1839 aged 40. [missing]

Tablet. Margaret wife of John Sweetland esq Principal Commissary of Stores &c to HM Fortress at Gibraltar and daughter of John Richard and Margaret Withall of this parish. Born 1 Sept 1796. Died at Exmouth 17 March 1818 – Her infant daughter Harriet Bright Sweetland Died 26 Feb. 1817 aged 6 months. [missing]

Tower floor. A stone to the memory of several persons of the family named Black. [missing]

Henr. Andr. pson ecclie de Leueneston 1382. 1383. See deeds for Northleigh

WOODBURY

Davidson (pp. 313–16) visited [St Swithun] Woodbury on 14 July 1840 and noted it was about 6 miles south east of Exeter. The church was repaired and improved by the Rev. J.L. Fulford from 1846 to 1898 and major restoration took place in 1893 by R.M. Fulford (Pevsner, *Devon*, 917–18).

This parish church consists of a nave about 60 feet long by 25 wide with an aisle on the north side of the same length as it is to the chancel a Chancel about 33 feet by 16, opening to the aisle by a low pointed arch ornamented with numerous mouldings and panels in the soffits, a loft Tower at the western end of the nave, embattled supported by 2 buttresses on each face and containing 6 bells. The nave opens to the aisle by 5 low pointed arches resting on columns formed by 4 shafts with hollow moulding between them & having capitals carved in foliage. The windows are in various styles some have 3 lights with cinquefoiled heads and perpendicular tracery others of the lancet form & some of recent date. There is a gallery at the western end of the nave erected in 1740 & an organ [both removed]. There are the remains of a handsome chancel screen consisting of lights with cinquefoiled heads under pointed arches and above them several mouldings of leaves fruit etc. – The pulpit is modern. The reading desk of old oak carved but not remarkable. The font is ancient and handsome carved in stone and raised on 2 steps, its form is octagonal the sides cut in panels of quatrefoils and foliage and the column on which it rests in panels and foliage. There are some fragments of old stained glass in the eastern window representing bishops, abbots or saints. The Communion Table is remarkable for not being placed close to the east wall, but having a free passage around it except on the north wall where the rails are fixed to a Tomb hereafter mentioned [today against the east wall]. The rails are of oak very well carved in the Elizabethan style in the form of Corinthian columns supporting a heavy moulded & carved top rail the whole are said to have been brought from the Cathedral at Exeter. The Chancel is paved with chequered tiles of red & green [removed]. The tablet with the Kings arms over the chancel arch is thus inscribed "presented by Thomas K. Lee esq Captain of the Woodbury Volunteers 1799" [missing].

The monumental inscriptions give the following particulars.

Chancel.
Against the north wall is a large altar tomb --- has perhaps been removed from under the arch between the Chancel and the North aisle. Upon the tomb are the whole length effigies of a man in armour and his wife with dogs at their feet. There are panels on the sides and ornamented in the style of Elizabethan time or later not any inscriptions is visible. Above it on the east wall is the date 1610.
South wall a Tablet. – Mary wife of Thomas Heathfield esq of upper Nutwell in this parish. Died 4 March 1791 aged 38. also her husband. Died 28 Feb.1806. Arms Azure 5 garbs in saltire or impaling Azure a Chevron between 3 Garbs or.

Tablet, The revd John Davy Officiating Minister of this parish and a constant resident upwards of 50 years. Died 21 Sept. 1807 aged 74. Mary D. relict of the said revd J.D, Died 18 Sept. 1808 aged 75.

Floor. Underneath lies the dust of Sir Henry Pollexfen knt Lord Chief Justice of the Common Pleas who for his exemplary integrity & eminent knowledge in the learning of the laws liv'd highly esteemed & dy'd greatly lamented being a real ornament to the court wherein he sate to his country & the he liv'd in. He departed this life the 15 day of June in the 59th year of his age.

--- *Elizabeth ---- die Januarii A.D. MDCCCLXXXIII et.* ---
Louisa Graves wife of John Bacon Graves esq of Fort William in co Limerick. Died 28 May 1825 aged 25.

Nave
East Wall. Tablet. Philip Lempriere esq of the Island of Jersey Died 22 Feb. 1787 aged 69. Margaret his wife daughter of Charles and Margaret Weekes late of this parish Died 14 March 1799 in the 67 year of her age. Arms. Argent 3 eagles displayed sable. Supporters 2 men at arms holding spears.

Tablet. A weeping figure with an urn – Samuel Traugott Gruttner esq late of Elbing in Prussia. Died 6 April 1813 aged 55. Elizabeth Dorothea his wife Died 3 August 1816 in the 36 year of her age.

Floor. Elizabeth Hannah Gibbons second daughter of the late Sir John Gibbons Bart & K.B. of Stanwell Place co Middlesex. Died at Nutwell in this parish 24 Jan. 1830 aged 77.

Andrew Holwell of this parish Yeoman Died 20 July 1689 Andrew H. son of Andrew H. Died 18 July 1708. Elizabeth widow of Andrew H. Died 17 Nov. 1730 aged 74 [both memorials now on the floor].

Honour wife of Andrew Holwell Died 26 July 169- Ann wife of Nicholas Holwell Died 18 Jan. 1716. Arms – A Lion rampant between 3 Cross crosslets fitchee

Susanna wife of Andrew Holwell the younger. Buried 28 Oct. 1672. John Crockhey 1724. Thomas son of Thomas Crockhey of this parish Died 7 April 1711 aged 9 weeks Susanna Crockhey 1717. [memorials now on the floor]

North Aisle.
East wall. Tablet. Anna Maria wife of Comer Brande esq Died 25 Dec 1791 in the 46 year of her age. Arms Azure Swords in saltire points upwards argent impaling Gules 3 Falchions barwise in pale points to dexter side argent.

North Wall. Tablet. – Died at sea 3 March 1828 on her return from the East Indies aged 52 Mary Greir wife of Lieutenant Col. George Jackson of the Madras army and second daughter of the late Thomas Huckell Lee and Mary Greir Lee of Ebford Barton.

Tablet. Jonathan Greir Lee. Died 9 June 1798 aged nearly 10

Thomas Huckell Lee junior Died 14 Aug 1798 aged 17 near the Cape of Good Hope on his return from his third voyage to the East Indies. Thomas H.L. and Mary Greir Lee of Ebford in this parish erected this monument. Mary Greir Lee Died 20 Nov. 1815 in the 60 year of her age. Matthew Lee eldest son of T.H.L. and M.G.L. Died 12 Dec 1817 at Crowle in Lincolnshire aet. 40. Thomas Huckell Lee Died 4 June 1822 in the 70 year of his age. Arms Gules 2 bars or, in chief an eagle displayed of the last, over all a Bend engrailed vairy. A mullet for difference.

Tablet. Catherine Butter only child of Samuel and Joyce Farr of Budleigh wife of Jacob. B. esq of this parish Died 1 July 1837 aged 77. Jacob Butter esq Died 8 June 1838 in the 78 year of his age. Arms Argent a Cross azure between 4 Hearts gules.

Tablet – George Barons late of Colyton surgeon Died aged 72 Buried 11 Dec 1794 Erected by his cousin Robert Northcote of Buckerell.

Floor. -- Venn gent son --- George Venn --- merchant – 10 Dec --- aged 28.

Matthew Lee of this parish merchant Died 18 Nov. 1742 aged 60. Elizabeth Lee his wife Died 6 Sept 1767 aged 80.

Alexander Radford Hughes Captain 5 Reg. Madras Native Infantry. Died 22 June 1816 aged 34 Jane Brice Hughes his daughter Died 2 Oct 1817 aged 2½.

--- Venn gent son. --- Venn – Merchant --- 31 -- 28 aged 33.

George Venn, Merchant Died 8 April 1716 aged 66. Margaret relict of George Venn Died -- Feb, 1737 aged 77. Margareta – Died -- Sept. 1774 aged 56.

Dormitorium Guilielmi Martyn de Ebford generosi qui 220 die Februarii Anno Salutis 1670 aetatis suae 75 multum desideratus obiit – (Some Latin verses)

Arms (Argent) 2 bars (Gules) a Crescent for difference impaling – 2 Bars --- on a chief 3 cinquefoils

(In the old letter) Richard Haydon esq – (Arms defaced).

(In the old letter) Here lieth the body of John Terrie of this parish gent. who dep---
C.W.H. Trevillian. Died 29 Dec 1801 aged 8.

Printed extract, possibly newspaper cutting, not dated

The church is situated near the centre of the parish, and appears from Bishop Stafford's register, to have been new built and dedicated to St. Swithen in 1409 – it is 85 feet in length, by 40 in breadth. The tower is square and massive, supported by strong buttresses, it is 80 feet in height, and contains 6 deep toned musical bells. There is one monument without inscription to the memory of the ancestors of Sir Edmund Prideaux, who resided at Nutwell, which manor was purchased by Sergeant Prideaux, of the heirs of Dinham, who before possessed it; it is now the property of Sir T.T.F.E. Drake, Bart. There are besides, memorials of the families of Dinham and Haydon, much damaged, and of Philip Lempries, Esq. of Jersey, 1787; Anna Maria, wife of Comber Beard, Esq. 1791; and Thomas Heathfield, Esq. of Upper Nutwell, 1806. The vicars Choral of Exeter Cathedral are Appropriators of the tithes, and patrons of the perpetual curacy.

CLYST ST GEORGE

Davidson (pp. 317–19) visited [the church of St George] Clyst St George on 15 July 1840 and noted the church was 5 miles south east of Exeter. The church was extensively restored in 1854–5 by the Rev. H.T. Ellacombe and was gutted on 31 August 1940 by enemy action. It was rebuilt in 1952 in a plainer style by T.J. Rushton (Pevsner, *Devon*, 271). Ten memorials are missing from the thirteen that Davidson recorded.

This village church consists of a Nave about 45 feet long by 18 wide with an aisle on the north, a Chancel about 12 feet by 18 and a Tower at the west end containing 3 Bells. The eastern window is ancient formed of 3 lancet lights with the foiled heads and having some fragments of stained glass of early date representing The Crucifixion with the two Marias. The virgin & child St George with a cross on his shield – A priest at prayer with an inscription round him *"Ora pro nobis -- rector hujus ecclesiae"* – A shield bearing Argent on a Wyneard bend azure 3 Mullets of the field. There are other fragments in other windows – heads of bishops or abbots & that of a queen. The nave opens to the aisle by 3 low arches on columns formed of shafts & mouldings with circular capitals of about the 15th century. There is a plain piscina in the chancel south wall [not replaced when church rebuilt]. The pulpit is modern as is a gallery at the western end of the nave [not replaced when church rebuilt]. The font is of stone, octagonal, the sides formed into panels of quarter-foils of foliage & the column which supports it into trefoil niches [not replaced when church rebuilt]. The monumental inscriptions afford the following particulars:

Chancel.
North Wall. A mural monument a sarcophagus with a medallion portrait in bas relief. Richard Pidgley esq a native of this parish. Died 15 Oct 1802 aged 64 (many years a Banker at Falmouth) Arms. – a Lion rampant -- in chief 2 hearts. [missing].
South wall. Marble Tablet. – Jessica Catherine Rous Ellicombe youngest daughter of the revd. William Rous Ellicombe and Ester Harriet his wife Born 1 April 1815. Died 25 Oct 1830. Buried at Farringdon [missing].
Floor – (In Latin) Rev. John Hammat rector of this church Died 13 Jan. 1696 aged 39. Erected by his widow [missing].
(In Latin) Robert Buckland Rector of this church 50 years [missing].
(In Latin) Theophilus Eedes rector of this church buried here with 3 sons. Died 17 Sept. 1705 aged 37 [missing].

Nave.
Floor. Margaret Southcote widow of Fitzwilliam Southcott gent, of this parish of Sowton, daughter of Thomas Barrett late archdeacon of Exeter. Buried here 4 June 1663 aged 74 [missing].

North Aisle

East Wall. A Brass tablet female figure kneeling with a book before her inscribed below. To the memorie of Julian Osborne who deceased the 18th of Augustus Ao 1614
Bonifant a virgin, Osborne a loyal wife
For thirty yeares, a widow was fourty & more
A houndred yeares, almoste she lead her life
Kinde to the riche & good to all the poore
Here lyes her dust whose soules to heaven gone
Since she did live and dye a saint-lyke one.
Arms Ermine a Cross engrailed. – charged with a cinquefoil --- impaling Gules a Chevron (or) between 3 Reaphooks (argent) ----

North Wall – a large monument, a bust and various devices carved in marble. With a Latin inscription to Richard Osborn esq descended from an ancient family Died 5 Ides Sept. 1705 aged 52. Married to Kathleen. Jan 1686 Arms. Azure a cross or in the first & last quarters an ermine spot impaling Per chevron engrailed argent & gules 3 Talbots heads erased & counter charged A tablet underneath to Bridgett relict of the above Richard O esq. Died 18 Feb. 1738. [missing].

On the window sill of this aisle is an oak slab as a desk for books with the inscription under it "Fox's Martyrology in three volumes given to this church by the pious worthy and ancient family of the Osbornes of Keniford 1731." [missing]

A mural monument carved painted and gilded with a Latin inscription to the following effect.

This monument erected by George Gibbs of this parish 1708 in memory of his ancestors viz. John Gibbs his grandfather buried 15 July 1652 aged about 82 – Anstice his wife – George Gibbs his father buried 18 July 1683 aged 81 – Alice his wife. – Arms. Argent 3 Battle axes erect sable.

An oaken Tablet recording donations to the poor of the parish by Sir Edward Seaward of Exeter knt & Dame Hannah. S. his widow with their coat armorial viz. Gules on a Fess argent between 2 Chevrons ermine 3 Leopards faces azure impaling Argent a Fess wavy Broking between 6 Cross crosslets bar wise gules. [missing]

Floor. – Margaret Osborne daughter of Richard Osborne of this parish gent. Died 29 Nov. 1633 aged 14. [missing]

Mrs Johan Osborne of this parish widow Died 27 Feb. 1614. [missing]

Gideon Pearce son of Roger Pearce of this parish Buried 16 June 1660 in the 25 year of his age. Roger P. the elder of this parish. Buried 15 Sept 1662. Roger P Buried 11 Sept 1694 aged 64 [missing]

Newspaper cutting, no name of newspaper, dated 1853

The chancel of Clyst St George, which has lately been restored by the present rector, the rev. H.T. Ellacombe, in the style which prevailed in the 1300s, (with which date the original three-light east window accorded, and which has been copied in the restoration,) has been further improved by the addition of stained glass from the establishment of Mr. Ward, of Firth-street, London, in glass manufactured expressly by Messrs. Powell, of White Friars; after long and repeated experiments made by analyses of the glass of the 13th century, by Mr. Medlock, late of the Royal College of Chemistry, under the superintendence of Charles Winston, Esq., who has been indefatigable in his exertions to restore to its pristine celebrity, such a beautiful art, till lately to a great degree lost, through ignorance of the material anciently used.

Judging from this specimen, which is the fifth window yet made of the newly-discovered material, the efforts of all these gentlemen appear to have been most successful, as the glass equals in colour and sparkling brilliancy the old specimens remaining in many or our Churches. The tone of the whole is rich and harmonious – evidently arising from the use of materials different from those hitherto employed in modern glass. There is nothing flimsy or watery about it – it has a more substantial appearance even than "rolled glass", with-out any of its dullness, and its quite and rich, through brilliant appearance, presents a favourable contrast to the raw and flimsy though smudged glass of some modern manufactures. The blue, in particular, is soft and intense, and the white, the green, and pot-metal yellow, are in hue exactly like the old. The design of this very handsome gift to this chancel, consists of six groups of figures, dabbed on a running floriated buarry work, with a rich border by the sides, which also adorns the tracery heads. Each light has two of these metal-lions or groups. In the centre light, there is the Nativity of our Lord, with the Crucifixion over it (Christ healing the sick,) and over it the Resurrection – and in the right-hand light a Parable (the Sower), with the Ascension over. All the subjects are well treated, and have been designed and painted, as we are informed, by Mr. Hughes, in connexion with Mr. Ward.

Newspaper cutting, no name of newspaper, dated March 5 1846
The tower of the church of Clist St. George was struck by lightning in three places. The chief damage was done on the south side, against which a leaden pipe extended about half way down, and there terminated by an elbow, projecting about a foot from the wall. This is bearing out the theory of Mr. Hearder in his recent lecture before the Exeter Literary Society. After passing through the church and tearing the mortar from the joints in various places, the lightning struck a popular tree which is near the tower, about 25 feet from the ground, scored the bark in two lines down to the roots. It is conjectured that this tree being wet acted in some measure as a conductor, and saved the church from serious injury.

CLYST ST MARY

Davidson (pp. 321–2) visited [the church of St Mary] Clyst St Mary on 15 July 1840 and noted it was 4 miles south east of Exeter. He observed that 'this secluded parish church is situated nearly half a mile from the dwellings of the bulk of the population and immediately adjoins the beautiful gardens and grounds of Winslade House the property and residence of Mr. Porter. The building is now partially taken down and under the hands of workmen who are building or extending the north aisle and putting on a new roof.' The church was enlarged in 1818 and in 1869 by Edward Ashworth (Pevsner, *Devon*, 272). Six memorials are missing from the seventeen that Davidson recorded.

The whole structure is small and in the form of a cross with a small low tower at the western end containing 3 Bells. If not of recent erection the whole appears to have been modernised within the last century. The heads of the windows are semicircular and the interior is fitted up in the Roman style. The font is of stone octagonal but very small and painted – there is not a single monumental inscription visible within the walls but two or three tablets are said by one of the workmen to be deposited in the vestry during the alterations to belong to the families of Porcher and Porter. In the south aisle is a gallery with a barrel organ 1850 [missing].

The following particulars are gained from inscriptions in the Churchyard.
A Tomb. The revd Carolus Salter. Died 26 March 1773 aged 36. Anna Susanna Salter Died 10 April 1810 aged 75.
William Collibee Salter their son -- Elizabeth their daughter. Anna Susanna second daughter of Carolus and Anna Susanna S. Died 19 Jan. 1833. Marianne wife of John Pidsley esq eldest daughter of Carolus and Anna S.S. Died 8 Feb. 1837. Anna Susanna second daughter of John and Marianne Pidsley Died 16 Aug 1834
A Tomb. Edward Cotsford esq Died 25 May 1810 in the 70 year of his age. High Sheriff of this county in 1792. Arms (no colour) Argent 2 Bars gules within a Border engrailed sable impaling Gules a Cross fleury between 4 Trefoils ----
On the same tomb. Lydia Lady Ximenes daughter of the late Doctor Manning of Stoke, Devon, who first married Edward Cotsford esq of Winslade House and secondly Sir Morris Ximenes of Bear Place late high Sheriff of Berks Lieutenant Col. of Local Militia and Magistrate for the counties of Berks Wilts and Devonshire. Died 23 Dec. 1821.
A Tomb. Sir George R. Collier Bart K.B. Died 24 March 1824 aged 51. His widow Dame Maria Collier. Died Feb 1831 aged 46.

North wall. A Tablet. Maria widow of Charles Moncton O Neil esq Surgeon 52nd Reg. Foot. Died 4th April 1830 youngest daughter of George Tanner esq and Elizabeth his wife late of Winslade House in this parish. Arms (no colours) Argent 2 Bears or, on a chief of the last 3 cinquefoils --- [missing].

A tablet. – Mary relict of the revd. George Cooke of this parish Died 12 Oct 1803 aged 82. [missing]

Chancel floor, Catherine the wife of the revd George Cooke rector of this parish was buried March 17. 1748 Also the rev George Cooke died Jan. 20 1795 aged 85. [missing]

Nave Floor. Henrick Peck died at Exmouth Jan 7. 1817 aged 16 – (His father is said to be now the minister of an Irvingite congregation at Bath) [missing]
Here lyeth the body of James --- city of Exon-- Arms. Barry wavy of ten. On a Chevron embattled between three Sea Horse, five guttes. [missing]
In memory of John Olevent Colsworthy (or Golsworthy) of Mount Radford near Exeter who died July 1768 at 34. [missing]

South Aisle west wall. A marble tablet
Sacred to the memory of Thomas Dupre Porcher of the Honourable East India Company Service in Bengal and eldest son of Josiah Dupre and Charlotte Porcher He died at Calcutta Sept 25. 1812 Oct. 23.
He was endeared to his intimates by the most amiable manners, sweetness of temper which no change could ruffle, and an active benignity of disposition
of which few were long near him without experiencing the effects. His loss has been not less generally felt than deeply lamented. In him society has been deprived of one of its best ornaments and hopes, while those who were connected with him by closer ties have to mourn a friend of whom it may truly and emphatically be said that he was made to be loved.
A marble tablet. To the beloved memory of Rebecca Emma. Eldest daughter of Josias and Charlotte Porcher of Winslade House This tablet the last tribute of parental affection, is inscribed. She died on the 21 day of February 1816 aged 18 years in the full confidence of a glorious resurrection "when this corruptible shall put on incorruption, this mortal shall put on immortality".
A marble tablet. To the memory of Charlotte wife of Josias Dupre Porcher of Winslade House who died on the 29 September 1818 aged 48 years. this tablet the last tribute of an affectionate husband is inscribed. The Lord giveth and the Lord taketh away blessed be the name of the Lord.
A marble tablet. Sacred to the memory of Josias Du Pre Porcher Esq of Winslade House who died 25 April 1820 aged 59.
Arms Per pale argent and gules, barry of eight counter changed a cinquefoil of the first. Impaling Argent two Bards gules, in chief a Lion passant query of the field. Crest a Lion rampant holding in his paws a Cinquefoil. Motto. *Pro rege.*

Church Yard
A tomb. In memory of James Davy Esq late of the island of Jamaica who died Oct 19 1825 aged 60.
Other inscriptions with the name of Davy
A tomb. Beneath lie the remains of William Foulkes Esq of Medland in this county one of His Majesty's Justices of the peace and for many years an inhabitant of this parish who died the 7 of May 1773 aged 58.
Anna Foulkes relict of this above. -- June 9. 1797

SOWTON

Davidson (pp. 323–6) visited [St Michael and All Angels] Sowton on 15 July 1840 and noted it was 3½ miles east of Exeter. He observed that 'the church with its ivy mantled tower forms an interesting feature in the rustic scenery of this sweetly sequestered village'. The church was rebuilt in 1844–5 at the expense of John Garratt, the High Church patron and owner of Bishop's Court, by John Hayward. The church is important as a rare survival of an early Victorian Tractarian village church (Pevsner, *Devon*, 755–6). Nine memorials are missing from the eighteen that Davidson recorded.

It consists of a Nave about 33 feet long by 16 wide with an aisle on the north of the same length and a porch covering the south door a chancel about 15 feet long by 15 and a low embattled Tower at the west end containing 3 Bells.

The nave opens to the aisle by 5 low arches resting on columns formed of 4 shafts with intervening mouldings & capitals carved with the figures of angels & priests. The eastern window of the chancel aisle have 3 lights with cinquefoiled heads and perpendicular tracery and labels outside resting on corbels of human heads the other windows of the aisle have 2 lights finished at top in the ogee form of arch & cinquefoiled labels outside rest on grotesque heads of animals & monsters boldly carved in stone [now resting in the porch]. The western window in the Tower is of like design and date. There is a gallery at the western end of the nave with an organ [removed]. The pulpit is modern. The font is a modern marble basin but the upper part of an old one remains in the vestry it is of stone octagonal the sides carved in panels ornamented with quatrefoils and foliage. There is an oak screen across the east end of the north aisle [removed] and the old oak benches remain boldly carved in various devices among them are shields with the arms – a Saltire – 2 Chevrons with a crescent for difference – a rose – a Heart – Two keys in saltire with the letters T.C. – 3 Passion nails in pale and in saltire [all missing] – there are some fragments of old stained glass & some modern in the east window of the chancel & that of the tower in the former are 2 shields I a cross II the arms of the see of Exeter – Over the chancel door inside is a shield with the arms of the See impaling those of Buller [removed].

The monumental inscriptions give the following particulars.

Chancel

Floor – Margaret wife of Richard Beavis of Clist House esq and daughter of Sir John Davie of Creoy Bart. Died 4 1676 aged 49. Richard Beavis of Clist House esq her husband Born 9 August 1621 Died 20 Oct 1702 Arms – 3 Helmets – impaling Quarterly 1 & 4 – a Chevron between 3 Mullets 2 & 3 (azure) Three Cinquefoils (or) on a Chief (of the last) a Lion passant (gules)

William Beavis of Clist House gent. Born 29 August 1623.Died 12 Dec. 1703 aged 80.

Henry Beavis Merchant lived in Spain above 40 years. Died at Clist House 3 Aug. 1707 aged 80. Arms Beavis.

Antonia daughter of Peter Beavis of Clist House esq Born 20 Oct 1694. Died 6 Nov. 1695.

Peter Beavis e villa Clist armig. Obiit 13 Kal. Jan. Anno 1708.

Here also lieth Eliza relict of the said Peter B. Died 15 Dec. 1728 aged. --- Arms. Beavis impaling -- on a fess between 3 Fleurs de lis as many Mullets On a chief engrailed -- 3 lions rampant

Ann Wilcox. Died 11 May 1695 aged 13.

Nave

Floor. *Hic situs est Petrus Beavis de Clist House armig. Nuper comitat. Devon vice comes qui obiit 27° Octobris Anno dom. 1656 aet suae 67. Hic etiam sita est Susanna relicta dicti Petri B. quae obiit 22° die Marti AD. 1676 annos nata 78.* Also Mrs Margaret Beavis 30 Sept. 1717. Arms. Beavis – impaling – 2 Bars ---

Susanna wife of James Gayer of Rockbeare esq. Died 7 April 1760 aged 66. James G. esq Died 16 Nov. 1764 aged 70 [missing]

Roger Lee gent. Died 26 Jan. 1657. Elizabeth Lee his wife Buried 7 Dec. 1673. John Lee his son Buried -- Dec 1671 [missing]

Sarah his wife Buried 24 Feb, 1693. Roger Lee gent great grandson of the above John Lee Died 30 Sept 1712. John Lee son Died 17 June 1716. Elizabeth relict of the said Roger Lee Died 29 May 1717. Arms -- on a Fess cotised -- 3 Leopards faces [missing]

John Lee of this parish junior Died 2 Sept 1617 aged 39. Roger his son Died 17 Sept 1695 aged 33 [missing]

Nicholas Lee of this parish. Died 15 Oct 1696 aged 25 [missing].

John Hesketh of Exon gent a true son of the Church of England Died 22 June -- 3. also -- wife of the above John Hesketh. Died 4 April [missing]

North Aisle

Floor. Joyce Lee of this parish Widow & relict of John Forward. Died 16 June 1675. *Hic jacet corpus Johannis Forward medici qui nonis Novembris obiit Anno Dom. 1699 aetatis suae 66. Hic etiam jacet Agnes uxor supra defuncti Johannis Forward quae arbitrio omnipotentis Dei spiritum lubentissime reddidit pridie Idus Octo* [missing]

William Forward of this parish practitioner in physick Died 24 Oct 1724 aged 48. Mary his wife Died 1707 aged 25. Arms – a fess dancette [missing]

Against the north wall are 2 Hatchments for Lord Graves [missing]

Gules an Eagle displayed or ducally crowned argent on a canton of the last an anchor erect & corded sable. On an escutcheon of pretence – Gules a wolf argent issuant from a rock proper. – a Baron's coronet. Williams

II. Quarterly. 1&4 Gules an eagle displayed ducally crowned or. on a Canton argent an Anchor erect sable.

2nd Argent a Tower between 3 battle Axes erect sable.

3rd Gules a Wolf argent issuant from a rock proper impaling sable on a Cross engrailed between 4 Eagles displayed argent 5 Lions passant of the field.

Church Yard.

A Tomb The revd Edmund Granger B.D. Prebendary of Exeter. 26 years rector of this parish Died 25 Aug. 1777 aged 63. Mary Granger Died 25 Jan 1786 aged 20. Ann

Granger Died 4 Sept 1812 aged 82. Elizabeth wife of Thomas Granger esq Died 30 July 1835 in the 80 year of her age.

Tomb. *Infra dormit Gulielmus Stuart sacra licet. theologiae professor peccatorum maximus quondam Coll. Div. Joan. Baft. Oxon. socius nuper hujus parochiae rector dieceseos Cancellarius nunc pulvis et cinis et quicquid uspiam est recrementiti rei die 12 mens. Septembris anno 1734 Penitentium minimus animum Deo reddidit propitio.* Arms – a Fess checky in chief a Lion passant -- impaling -- 3 Crescents as many stars between their points.

Tomb. George Moore clerk 25 years rector of this parish Born 2 April 1772. Died 8 Oct 1821. Catherine daughter of Henry Christopher Wise of the priory of Warwick esq and Mary Scott his wife Born 2 March 1775. Died 3 July 1825. Tomb. Charlotte Mary eldest daughter of Henry Wise clerk of the Priory Warwick and Charlotte Mary wife. Born 23 Dec. 1802. Died at Torquay 9 Nov. 1820.

FARRINGDON

Davidson (pp. 329–32) visited [St Petrock and St Barnabas] Farringdon on 15 July 1840 and noted it was about 6 miles east of Exeter. The church was rebuilt in 1870 by William White re-using some of the old masonry (Pevsner, *Devon*, 447). Ten memorials are missing from the sixteen that Davidson recorded.

This retired village church consists of a nave about 35 feet long by 24 wide with an aisle on the north about 15 feet by 9 a Chancel about 16 by 14, and a Tower at the western end containing one Bell.

There is a gallery at the end of the nave [removed]. The windows are formed by four lights with low arches the pulpit is of recent date & the whole building appears to have been modernised. The Font is an interesting relic of antiquity being large circular stone basin ornamented with scroll, hatched, and cable mouldings around it, and resting on a cylindrical column of the same size.

The monumental inscriptions afford the following particulars.

Chancel.
North wall. A monument of black & coloured marble a pediment supported by Composite columns & a Tablet with a long inscription of which this is part. –
M. Cha. Con. S.
Hujusce sub introitu sacrarii jacent Francisca cum infantulo Ludovico cui moriendo quadrimestrem cum dederit vitam sibi adepta est immortalem Joannis Lethbridge de Bow in hoc comitatu clerici (nominis et familias (origine Danica) principis) filia natu minima et Ludovici Burnett S.T.B. hujus ecclesiae rectoris uxor dilectissima &c &c.
Nat. Fest Nat. 1651.
Nupt. 7° Idus Nov. 1682
Denat. Idibus Sept, 1683
23. die Julii Ano Dni 1704to. voti compos factus fuit Ludovicus Burnett eccl[esi]ae beati Petri Exon subdecanus et hujus eccl[esi]ae per 25 annos rector dignissimus.
Arms I. Argent a hunting Horn sable stringed gules garnished or, in chief 3 Oak leaves vert impaling Lethbridge. II as I – III Lethbridge [missing]
Tablet. Francis Rous Ellicombe only son of the revd William Rous Ellicombe MA. Rector of Clist St. George & of Esther Harriett his wife Commoner of Balliol College Oxford. Born 8 Nov 1811 Died 25 April 1834 Buried at St Mary Magdalens in that university.
Arms Quarterly
  1. Argent a Chevron engrailed between 3 Bucks courant sable.
  2. Azure 3 Bucks trippant or.
  3. Argent on a Pile vert 3 Griffons heads erased or
  4. Or an Eagle displayed sable [missing].

Tablet. – the revd Richard Rous MA. Rector of Clist St George. Died 2 Oct 1810 aged 57. Erected by his widow [missing]
Arms. Argent an Eagle displayed sable.
South wall. Tablet. The revd John Sleech Archdeacon of Cornwall Canon residentiary of the cathedral of Exeter Prebendary of Gloucester and Rector of this parish 52 years. Died 31 Jan 1788 aged 76. Mary his wife Died 28 Nov 1784 aged 66 – The revd Charles Sleech Died 18 Dec. 1785 aged 26 – John S. Died 13 Dec. 1780 aged 7. Anna S. Died 25 April 1758 aged 6 the son & daughter of the above John & Mary Sleech
Arms. Checky or and gules on a Canton argent, a crescent Azure impaling Per pale or and argent 3 chevrons sable, a label of three points gules.
Floor. Nicholas Hall D.D. Treasurer & Canon residentiary of the cathedral church of Exeter and rector of this parish Died 25 April 1709 [missing]
William Bartholomew rector of this parish 56 years Died 16 Nov. 1676. Catherine his wife Died 27 Dec. 1662 [missing]
Robert Rous of this parish gent. Died 13 Nov 1691 Catherine his wife Died 6 July 1700. Martha their daughter Died 18 Oct 1689. Bartholomew eldest son of Robert, R. Died 2 July 1682 aged nearly 19. Arms – an Eagle displayed
Drake or -- 1814 [missing]

Nave.
Floor. William Bone gent and Grace his wife, died 6 Oct.1658 & 18 Feb. 1653. Edith second wife of the same William Bone Died 26 Jan 1681. William their only son Died 8 Dec. 1679. Arms -- on a bend -- 3 Fleur de lis -- impaling -- 2 Bars -- on a Chief 3 Cinquefoils [missing]
-- chill esq of Dorchester who dep. -- (in old letters) 2& Churchill [missing]
Peter Trosse esq Died 1 June 1632 Peter son of Peter T. esq Died 10 Aug 1679. Elizabeth his daughter Died 22 Aug1672
Arms. (Gules) 3 Faulchions in pale their points to the dexpter side (argent) impaling Ermine on a Chief 3 Lozenges [missing]

North aisle.
East wall. A stone tablet. – Samuel Tanner esq Died 24 Dec. 1688. Mary his wife daughter of George Southcott of Dowleshays esq Died 19 Oct 1657 Isabella Tanner Died 21 Aug. 1684 and Frances Tanner Died 10 Dec. 1688 – their grandchildren Edith aged 2 years George T. buried 20 May 1664
Arms (not coloured) Barry of 6 -- & -- impaling Southcott
A large white marble tablet with weeping cupids and an urn. John Cholwick of Farringdon in this parish esq. Died 3 Oct 1714. aged 77 – Ann his wife daughter of John Cooke of Exeter merchant Died 9 April 1721 aged 68. – John Hornbrooke of Exeter merchant Died 27 March 1727 aged 67 – Philippa his wife daughter of John Cooke of Kentisbury esq and granddaughter of the said John Cooke of Exeter Died 24 August 1722 aged 47 – Philippa wife of the under named John Cholwich only daughter of the said John Horn Brooke and Philippa his wife Died 22 May 1736 aged 38 – John son of John Cholwich and Ann his wife Died 9 June 1765 aged 82 – John son of John Cholwich and Philippa his wife Died 24 May 1753 aged 35. – Elizabeth wife of the last mentioned John Cholwich daughter and Heiress of Samuel Burridge of Tiverton esq and Johanna his wife Died 15 Dec. 1760 aged 43 – Thomas son of John Cholwich and Ann his wife Died 14 June 1750 aged 59 – Elizabeth the daughter died 18 Jan. 1716 aged 4 months and Thomas the son of John & Philippa his wife

Died 11 April 1732 aged 11 and Richard died 25 Oct. 1746 aged 22 – William died 10 April 1800 aged 78 – Anne his wife Died 14 April 1813 aged 68. – Erected by John Cholwich esq and Philippa his wife

Arms Per pale or argent 3 Chevrons sable a Label of 3 points gules – On an escutcheon of pretence Barry wavy of 6 argent and azure 3 Crescents sable. Dated 1728. [missing]

A white marble Tablet. The revd William Cholwich Vicar of Ermington co. Devon long resident at Farringdon House in this parish Died 7 Sept 1833 in the 67 year of his age. Elizabeth his wife daughter of Sir John Duntze of Rockbeare House Bart Died 7 Sept 1836 aged 72 Arms Cholwich impaling Azure a Holy Lamb passant argent.

West wall. – Tablet. Frances Cholwich wife of John Burridge Cholwich esq of this parish Died 20 Jan. 1798 aged 39. Arms as before.

North wall a tablet a facsimile of the last. John Burridge Cholwich esq Died 14 May 1835 aged 82. Arms as the last.

Floor. *Hic situs est Georgius Taner generosus qui pie et placide e vivis excessit ad servatorem primo die Maii Ano Dni 1636 Sub hoc marmore etiam conduntur reliquiae Samuelis Taner armig, nepotis Georgii praedicti obiit nono die Novembris 1714 anno aetatis 63.*

Arms – 2 Bars -- on a chief 3 cinquefoils impaling -- on a Fess wavy -- 3 Lozenges barwise

HONITON CLYST

Davidson (pp. 337–9) visited [St Michael and All Angels] Honiton Clyst on 13 August 1834. The church was rebuilt by William White in 1876 (Pevsner, *Devon*, 270). Six memorials are missing from the ten that Davidson recorded.

This village church consists of a nave about 42 feet by 12 within the walls, a chancel about 9 by 12, north aisle 42 by 10, a tower at the western end and a porch over the south door. The building has been deprived by various alterations of every feature of antiquity. The nave is divided from the aisle by 4 low arches resting on piers composed of shafts & mouldings. The windows have been modernised as have also those of the chancel & aisle except one at the eastern end of the latter which has 3 lights with cinquefoil heads & perpendicular tracery. This aisle may be assigned to the 16 century. The tower is embattled & has a semicircular stair-turret on the north side. The belfry windows are square. The porch has a sun-dial on the gable. The pulpit is mean. A gallery runs across the western end of the nave in front of which are painted the arms. Of the Bps see and those of Yard, Argent a chevron gules between 3 water-bougets sable, impaling Sable 3 Alligators passant gardant in pale argent [removed]. The font is of ancient date and well worthy of observation, It is formed of granite or moor-stone, large, square, and low, lined with lead, and resting on a cylindrical pedestal with a shaft at each corner. The sides are cut into various rude ornaments, & one of them exhibits a range of semicircular-headed arches. It may with great probability be considered as ancient as the 12th century.

In the north wall of the chancel is a marble monument in a recess with a tablet thus inscribed.

Juxta conduntur reliquiae Francisci Webber A.M.
Hujus ecclesiae per XLIV annos pastoris
St. Petri Cathedralis Exon Praebendarii
Et parochiae de Stockly Pomeroy rectoris
Qui per integerrimam vitae probitatem
Per ingenii suavitatem eximiam
Per mores prorsus Christianos
Praecepta ista, quae concionibus tradidit
Exemplo illustravit
Obiit die 3° Novembris A.D. MDCCXXXVII aet. suae LXIX
Memoriam omnibus charissimam
Maerentibus viduae et octo liberis
Desiderium sui diutissime deflendum
Relinquens
Hoc marmor optimo parenti sacrum
Posuerunt filii pientissimi.

Above it are the arms. Gules on a chevron engrailed or. between 3 plate as many annulets sable query azure

Nave. Floor, here lieth the body of John ---- of this parish who departed this life the 20 day of August Ano Do 1653 [missing]

Aisle. N. Wall. A Tomb under an ornamented arch, the tablet thus inscribed. Here lyeth John Yarde Esquire who ended his lyffe the thirde of May and Jease his wyffe 1575. A shield above with these bearings.

Quarterly. 1 & 4 Argent a chevron gules between 3 water bougets sable. Yard & crescent for difference.

2 & 3 or on a Bend sable 3 Horseshoes of the field. Impaling Ferrers.

Quarterly of 5. 1. Argent 3 bars azure in chief as many a crescent for difference Torteaux. A label of 3 points.

2. Quarterly. 1 & 4. Or, a maunche gules

2 & 3 Barry of 6 Argent & azure 6 Martlets 3.2 & 1 gules (question as to colors)

3. Gules 7 Mascle, 3.3.1.or.

4. Azure a Cinquefoil or

5. As the first.

Above, a mural monument & Tablet.

In obitum Edwardi Yarde. (there follow some verses in English). Arms on 3 shields.

1. Yarde with crescents for differences

Crest viso of a ducal coronet a demi ostrich (query) holding in her beak an eel

2. (Sable) Three mantiques passant quadrant in pale (argent). 3.1 impaling 2. –

A loose stone leaning against the wall. – *In memoriam Johannis Short armigeri qui hic tumulatus erat vicessimo die 10bris Anno Dom 1657. Hoc monumentum posuit Johannes Short filius ejus primogenitus.* Arms gules a griffin segreant. A chief ermine.

Another lose stone – Hugh sonne of Charles Vaghan esq borne 26 April 1624, dyed 7 August 1631. Short though his life eternal yet his quest. God takes them soonest whom he loveth best. [missing]

Aisle floor. *Hic jacet Henricus Turney in agro Cornub. gen. filius perquam eximiae venustatis et juvenilis vltra aetatem acuminis prope 5 annos natus non procul ab hinc immatura morte correptus Xiij° die Septembris Ao Dni 1681.* Arms. Series of crosslets – a lion rampant.

Church yard – A Tomb – inscription illegible. Arms. 3 Lions passant in pale.

A Tomb. Sacred to the memory of Alice relict of Thomas Templer esq of the old abbey near Exeter who departed this life 8 Nov. 1829 aged 77 years [missing]

A Tomb. To the memory of Anna Crowther widow of the late Richard Crowther esq surgeon of Boswell court Carey Street London and Street court Herefordshire daur of John James esq Moor court Herefordshire. She died 18th May 1825 aged 68 [missing]

A stone against the East wall of the chancel. Sacred to the memory of John Hodge surgeon of this parish who died March 22. 1784 aged 68. James Hodge his son died 25 March 1775 aged 14. Ann wife of the above John Hodge died 10 January 1801 aged 82 and Hermon son of the above John and Ann who died 25 March 1797 aged 37 [missing]

AWLISCOMBE

Davidson (pp. 341–4) visited [St Michael and All Angels] Awliscombe on 26 June
1828 and noted it was 2 miles north west of Honiton on the road to Cullompton.
The church was remodelled in 1886–7 by R.M. Fulford who installed a wagon
roof in the chancel (Pevsner, *Devon*, 141–2). Seventeen memorials are missing
from the nineteen that Davidson recorded.

The church of this parish consists of a nave 40 feet long by 22 wide a chancel 24
by 14 A north aisle 56 by 14 and a projecting aisle or chapel on the south 14 by 17
adjoining to which is an elegant porch screen the south door – There is a square
embattled tower at the western end containing 5 bells.
The whole building appears to have been erected at one period although the column
and & arches dividing the nave from the north aisle are perhaps remains from a
former edifice – The date to which it may in all probability be assigned is about the
beginning of the 15th century, the windows in general have cinquefoil headed lights
and that of the south aisle is large & elegant it is divided by 4 mullions & a transom
into lights with cinquefoil heads & has been richly adorned with painted glass what
little remains is much defaced but 3 coats of arms remain visible, (Giffard) one is of
the Denham family Gules 4 fusilly in fess ermine – Another Argent a chevron between
3 Mullets sable the third too much covered with dirt to describe upon [missing]. This
so: window is richly adorned with panels in the hollow moulding of the arch and with
a niche on each side surmounted by tabernacle work, the arch which divided this aisle
from the nave is similarly ornamented. The remains of a beautiful stone screen exist
dividing the chancel from the nave, it is in the style corresponding with the other
parts of the church & has been ornamented with angels holding scrolls but these have
been mutilated and the whole is badly deformed with whitewash which has almost
obliterated the delicate parts of the work. The south porch is large & is a uniform style
beautifully adorned with tracery in the roof & with niches finished and tabernacle work
on the outside. To the abbey of Dunkeswell which property the manor of Gosford in
this parish may perhaps be attributed the rich embellishments which this village church
must have exhibited. The gable ends of the building are ornamented with cross.

The floor of the church presents several stones with ancient inscriptions but too
much worn to be deciphered, the principal monuments notices are as follows.
On the north side of the chancel a mural monument with a Latin inscription to the
memory of George Passemer clerk vicar of this church who died 1 May 1695. –
George his son buried 24 Aug. 1695. John his brother buried 10 April 1701 & Susannah
widow of the sd. George Passemer "*unica filia Alexandri Cheeke ar: Procuratoris
Generalis Serenissimo Carolo primo nec non Carolo secundo nuper regibus Angliae
&c infra curiam suam Admiralitatis quae sepelit. fuit 28 March 1722*. A coat of arms
in stone (Or) A pep (gules) between 3 escutcheons the last charged with a bend wavy
cinquefoils of the field all within azure bezanted a crescent for difference. Impaling
Ermine on a chief 3 fusil

Crest on a wreath a demi sea horse rampant changed with a crescent.

A flat stone in the chancel floor – Amelia widow of John Elphinstone Capt of the British & Admiral of the Russian fleet daughter of John Warburton esq. Somerset Herald at arms ob. At. Tracey House 16 Feb 1786 at 50 -- her grandson Hen Hartwell ob. 11 March 1786 at 8 months. [missing]

On the chancel floor – John Hassard -- of arts vicar of this parish & Elizabeth his wife which John ob. 16 Dec 1637 & Eliz ob. The 9 Jan following. [missing]

On the chancel floor Mary wife of John Smith of Honiton Gent daughter of the revd Mr George Passemer & Susanna his wife who died 15 March 1741 at 52. also John their son buried 6 Feb 1729 aged 8 months also William their son buried 24 Sept 1730 aged 6 weeks also Mary their daughter. buried 18 Jan 1733 aged 2 years. Also Susanna their daughter. buried 10 March 1735 aged 10 yrs. Arms 2 bars between 3 martlets impaling Passemer as above. – Crest a fox sejant [missing]

A flat stone in the nave – Eliz. Wife of John Mallack of Axminster Merchant & Nicholas their sonne which Eliz. Ob 7 May 1644 -- Rich ob. 19 of the same month [missing]

John Hussey ob. 25 July 1804 at 74 & his family for a cent & a half [missing]

Hannah daughter of Mr Fry ob. Sept 11. 1724 [missing]

--- wife of John Fry ob 16 Nov 1730 [missing]

In the N aisle. Thomas Charles buried June 16 1676

D⁰ a mural monument of white marble with a bust and the words Badajoz inscribed by a wreath in relief – to the memory of John Pring esq of Ivedon Capt in the 27th Enniskillen regiment of infantry died 2 May 1820 aet 38 – the monument erected by his only surviving brother Capt Dan Pring R.N.

Two hatchments are hung in the N aisle showing the following coats of arms

Quarterly Or & gules a labels of 3 points sable – impaling Gules 3 swords barwise in pale bladed proper hilted Or.

Sable a chevron between 3 trefoils or impaling Quarterly Or & gules a label of 5 points counter changed Az. & Or [missing]

A wooden tablet hangs against the wall of the nave with the following inscription in the old black letter

Benefactors to the poor

Peter Barton gave Ten Pounds to remain for ever to bind out apparently and keep the poor to work. John Borrow gave Ten Pounds the benefit there of yearly to be given to the relief of the poor

Forbeare not to use

This do not abuse

Forget not in need

But remember the deed

The font is large octagonal & adorned with quatrefoils resting on a low column ornamented with pointed arches. There are fragments of stained glass in several of the windows [removed] – The church plate consists of a silver flaggon chalice & paten with the following inscriptions on the latter Awlescombe parish R Martyn vicar 1729 T Bampfield & J Fry churchwardens.

The registers of Marriages Births & Burials commence in 1559 and are in very good preservation

The following are names of some of the vicars of this parish. –
John Hapard 1616/7 1634
James Burnard 1637
John Burrough 1695. 1721
R Martyn 1723, 1729
Thomas Roskelly 32 years buried 1873

Newspaper cutting, no name of newspaper, dated 8 May 1817
Mr. Urban, Awliscombe, May 8.
I send you a copy of the monumental inscriptions, &c. at Awliscombe in Devonshire, that they may be preserved, when the stones, like the persons they commemorate, are to be seen no more. 1817 Z.X.
On the chancel floor,
1. Here lieth -- of John Wa-- of Artes, late vicar of this parish, and Elizabeth his wife, which John dyed the 16th daye of December, Anno Dom. 1637; and the said Elizabeth dyed the 9th day of January following.
2. Here lyes the body of Mary, the wife of John Smith, of Honiton, gent. (dau of the Revd Mr. George Passamer and Susanna his wife), who dyed the 5th of March 1741, aged 52. Also of John Smith their son, who was buried the 6th of February. 1729 aged 8 months. Also of William their son, buried the 24th of Sept. 1730, aged 6 weeks. Also of Mary their daughter, buried the 18th Jan. 1733, aged 2 years. Also Susanna their daughter, buried the 10th of March 1735 aged 10 years.
3. Underneath this stone lie the remains of Mrs. Amelia Elphinstone, widow to the late John Elphinstone, esq. Captain of the British, and Admiral of the Russian fleet, and daughter of the late John Warburton, esq. Somerset herald at Arms. She departed this life at Tracy House in this parish, the 16th Feb. 1786, aged 50, sincerely regretted by her numerous family, who cherish with reverence and respect the memory of her virtues. Also near this place lie the remains of her grandson, Henry Hartwell, who died the 11th March, 1786, aged 8 months.
     On a marble slab against the chancel wall:
4. *Hic jacent Georgius Passemer cler. olim vicarius hujus Ecclesiae, qui sepelit. fuit primo die Maii, anno D'ni 1695. Etiam Georgius filius ejus qui sepelit. fuit 24° die Augusti, anno D'ni 1695. Etiam Johannes frater ejus qui sepelit. fuit decimo die Aprilis, anno D'ni 1701. Etiam Susannah, vidua et relict. praedicti Georgii Passemer, cler. unica filia Alexandri Cheeke, Ar' Procuratoris Generalis Serenissimo Carolo Primo necnon Carlo Secundo, nuper regibus Angliae, &. Infra Curiam suam Admiralitatis, quae sepelit. fuit 28 Mar. 1720°*
     In the church, on flat stones:
5. Here lie the bodies of Elizabeth, the wife of John Mallack, of Axminster, merchant, and Richard their sonne, which Elizabeth died the 7th daye of May, an'o Dom' 1644; and the said Richard died the 19th daye of the same month.
6. Here lieth the body of Anne, the daughter of William Pring, and of Joane his wife, who was buried the 2d day of February, 1704, aetatis sue the 6th.
7. William Pring, 1708.
8. Underneath this stone lieth the body of John Husey, who departed this life July the 25th, 1804, aged 74 years; and his family on his right for a century and a half past. Good people, do not remove this stone.
In the churchyard:

9. Francis Pring, serge-maker, departed this life Nov. 12. 1801, aged 82.

10. Mary Pring, departed this life April 27, 1799, aged 55. Also John Pring, of Chinestone Hill, her husband; died June 3, 1805, aged 74.

On an enclosed tomb:

11. Sacred to the memory
of Mary Anne Burges,
youngest daughter
of
George Burges, esq.
and of the Honourable
Anne Wichnoure Somerville,
his wife
She was born at Edinburgh
on the 6th day of Dec. 1763,
and died at Ashfield
in this parish
on the 10th day of August, 1813.

12. Sacred to the memory of William Pring, who departed this life July the 7th 1807, aged 72 years. Also four of his children: Anne died June 24th, 1765. William died June 9th, 1781. Jabez died May the 31st, 1782. Thomas Udy died June the 15th, 1785. There are four bells [now 6], on one of which is,

"T. Pen. 1627, John Smyth, Malachie Aishforde. Wardens.

I sound to bed – the sick repent,

In hope of life – when breath is spent.

T.,P. anno Domini 1670. I.M. I.C. C.W."

There are 10 windows in the church, one window in the chancel; one glass window, and six other ditto in the tower, There were in former days four windows in the chancel, but three of them are now walled up. There are four doors, and the principal entrance is on the South side.

Awliscombe is a parish in the hundred of Hemyock, Devon, and Archdeaconry of Exeter, two miles from Honiton, and 161 from London. It stands near the river Otter, on the Cullompton road, and contains 86 houses, and 429 inhabitants. It is a vicarage, value 12*l*. 10s. 10d, in the patronage of the Duke of Bedford.

"This was the birth-place of Thomas Charde, the last Abbot of Ford Abbey, who founded the hospital at Honyton (as fame hath). In the reign of King Henry the Third, Roger Gifford held lands in this parish, and the Abbot of Dunkeswell had a manor house here, whom Matthew Gifford, the son of Roger, impleaded, for hindering him to present to that church. By the marriage of Gifford's daughter Isabel to Mandervill, these lands came to Sir John de Stanton". – Risdon's Survey of Devon, p.40.

The Rev. Richard-Vyvyan Willesford, Chaplin in ordinary to the Prince Regent, is the present vicar.

Yours, &c. John Pring undated.

Sister of the present Sir James Bland Burges, bart. L.L.D. of Beauport, Sussex, and Knight Marshal of his Majesty's Household.

Book extract (?) Awlescombe Free Schools, March 1835

Printed by Mr. W Sawyer who then resided at the cottage called George Park in Awlescombe, which he afterwards sold to Sir Edmund Prideaux Bart.

1834. Received.	£.	s.	d.	1834. Paid.	£.	s.	d.
April Rev. W.E. Fitz-thomas	2	2	0	March Mrs Webber, for 27 boys	2.	18.	6.
H.B. Lott esq.	2	12	0	Mrs Morgan, for 28 girls	3	0	0
Capt. Pring, R.N.	2	12	0	June Mrs Webber, for 22 boys	2	7	8
Hon. Lady Head	2	12	0	Mrs Morgan, for 27 girls	2	18	6
Mrs. Dalrymple	2	12	0	Sept. Mrs Webber, for 22 boys	2	7	8
Miss Head	2	12	0	Mrs Morgan, for 26 girls	2	16	4
Mrs. A. Elliott	2	12	0	Dec. Mrs Webber, for 20 boys	2	3	4
Mr. W. Sawyer	2	12	0	Mrs Morgan, for 23 girls	2	9	10
E. Drew, esq.	1	12	0	1835			
Mrs. Drew, esq.	1	0	0	March Mrs. Webber, for 19 boys	2	1	2
Baroness de Milanges	0	10	6	Mrs. Morgan, for 25 girls	2	14	2
Mr. W. Banfield	0	2	6				
Mrs. Anning	0	2	6	Balance in the hands of the Treasurer	1	0	4
Mrs Brome	0	1	6		£26	17	6
Mrs. Granger	0	1	6				
Donation from Sir Edmund and Lady Prideaux	2	2	0				
1835 Donation from the rev. Jas. Duke Coleridge	1	0	0				
	£26	17	6				

BUCKERELL

Davidson (pp. 345–6) visited [St Mary and St Giles] Buckerell on 22 September 1829. The church was restored in 1838 (Pevsner, *Devon*, 221).

The church consists of a nave 35 feet long by 18 wide, a chancel 21 feet by 12 with a tower at the western end of the nave 10 feet by 8½ the basement of which is formed into a vestry [now the entrance], an aisle projecting from the nave on the north side 16 feet long by 13½ wide – the total length with the walls is about 66 feet. –
The arch which divided the chancel from the nave has been removed but the latter opens to the tower by a lofty pointed arch resting on corbels of mouldings. Two of the windows in the chancel have cinquefoil heads with perpendicular tracery in the arches but all the others have been despoiled of their tracery which has been badly supplied by a single mullion in each rising to the top of the arch. The ceilings are coved & ribbed with oak. a screen divides the nave from the chancel it is carved in oak & consists of a series of pointed arches and divided by mullions with 4 lights with cinquefoil heads, above the canopy of tracery are 4 mouldings carved in foliage fruit & flowers the whole painted. The pulpit is of oak adorned with small upright carved mouldings & varnished. The font is of stone octagonal & lined with lead the sides are carved in panels with quatrefoils & foliage, the measure across is 2 feet 3 inches – it rests on a plain octagonal column & is 3 feet 3 inches high – There is a gallery across the western end of the nave with an inscription "This church was new seated in the year of our Lord 1774" [the inscriptions are no longer there]. The tower is embattled & is 39 feet high to the top it contains a clock & 3 bells two of them inscribed †*est michi collatum I.H.S. istud nomen amatum* – the other illegible

The sepulchral monuments & inscriptions are as follow
On the chancel floor a stone without inscription but which has perhaps been larger. Arms in a lozenge a chevron Ermine between 3 pelicans vulning themselves (Culme).
Floor. Mary wife of Henry Fry & daughter of Richard Culme of Cannon Leigh esq who died June 4 16. – Arms 3 horses courant in pale (Fry) impaling (azure) between 3 pelicans vulning themselves. (or) Culme [too worn to read]
Floor. Susanna Culme daughter of Richard Culme of Cannon Leigh in the parish of Burlescombe in the county esq who died 24 May 1689.
Floor – Elizabeth the wife of Arthur Broughton of Warbrightsleigh in the parish of Stoodleigh in the county gent only daughter of John Baker of Hamwood gent died 18 Aug. 1720 aged 38. Arms a chevron between: 3 mullets pierced Impaling a saltier engrailed charged with 5 escallops on a chief a lion passant. – (*in the margin:* Argent a chevron between 3 mullets gules Argent on a saltier engrailed sable 5 escallops of the first. On a chief of the 2nd lion passant of the field) [too worn to read]
A tomb in the churchyard against the chancel wall John Baker of Hamwood in the parish of Trull in the county of Somerset gent who died -- Oct 1708. Elizabeth the wife of John Baker & daur of Henry Fry of Deane in this parish esq. who died 6

July 1688. Arms Quarterly in a saltier. 2 a chevron between 3 pears pendent. 3 a buck trippant. 4. 3 Horses courant in pale (Fry)

Hatchments in the chancel. I Quarterly & 4. Gules 3 horses courant in pale Argent. 2nd & 3rd. Three scimitars barwise points to the dexter side of the shield Argent hilted & pomelled Or an esquires helmet & crest on a wreath Gules and Azure a horses head erased Argent.

II Quarterly 1st Argent 4 bars wavy Azure. 2. Fry

3. Argent on a chevron Azure between 3 cross crosslets fitched Gules as many bezants. (*in the margin:* query Or on a chevron Crossing.) 4. Argent a lion rampant within a masculy Sable (Putt) [missing].

Nave. a white marble tablet with an urn & flowers Sacred to the memory of Elizabeth sole daughter & heiress of John Sedgwick of Staindrop in the county of Durham esq: & wife of Samuel Graves of Hembury fort in this parish rear Admiral of the Blue – married 17 years & died July 7. 1767 in the 39 year of her age erected by her husband Nave floor – C.M.B. May 22. 1829.

Against the west wall of the north aisle is a large mural tablet of white marble at the base of which is a concave medallion with a sitting figure in relief representing a weeping female holding a prostrate flag staff above is a wreath and an eagle with an olive branch in his beak the inscription is as follows. –

(This monument is by "Bacon R A London 1792")

Sacred to the memory of Samuel Graves esq. Admiral of the white who departed this life the 8 March 1787 in the 74 year of his age – A man of strict integrity and unsullied honour, distinguished for personal courage and a presence of mind superior to events. His own merit, raised him to the head of his profession without the support of Parliamentary interest and unassisted by splendid connections – He served and loved his country with a zeal seldom equalled, never exceeded. His loss is severely felt and deeply mourned by his widow and relations regretted by his acquaintances and lamented with tears unfeigned by the indigent and the distressed who emphatically styled him "the poor man's friend"

Against the east wall of the aisle is a white marble tablet with an urn by Blore London – inscribed as follows – Sacred to the memory of Joanna Philippa Griffith wife of Mr John Griffith of Stogumber in the county of Somerset and elder daughter of John Frances Gwyn of Combe Florey in the same county and of Ford abbey in the county of Devon esq. She departed this life July 18. 1801. born Dec 28. 1762. This monument was erected by her brother I.F. Gwyn from pure motives of affection and regard to her memory in the year 1808. Arms argent a chevron between 3 mullets Gules.

Against the north wall of the nave is a wooden tablet with this inscription

Left by the revd Thomas Howe deceased the sum of £300 in the 5 per cent to the parish of Buckerell Devon Dec 3rd 1817 in trust to the revd John Lee of Tiverton clerk Perry Dicken, & clerk John Wood to apply the clear amount and interest to purchase blankets and such necessary clothing for the poor persons resident in the said parish of Buckerell as the vicar & churchwardens for the time being shall think proper. The above donation is reduced by Legacy duty to £272.10.9 now in new 4 per cent this interest & ann amounting to £10.18.0¼ Revd Edward Colridge Vicar 1824 (Revd E Colridge of Ottery St Mary)

Newspaper cutting, no name of newspaper, dated 1851
W.M. Smythe., Esq., of Deerpark, has erected an obituary window, in Buckerell Church, to the memory of his wife, the Lady Isabella, sister of the Earl of Wicklow, and her three daughters.

Newspaper cutting, no name of newspaper, dated November 1851
Buckerell.- Two very beautiful obituary windows have just been placed in the chancel of the parish Church, by the Rev. Edwin E. Coleridge, the vicar, and the Rev. Barons Northcote. They are the work of Mr. Warrington, so justly celebrated for his skill and taste in stained glass. [no longer there]

DUNKESWELL

Davidson (pp. 349–57) visited [St Nicholas] Dunkeswell on 3 September 1828 and noted it was about 6 miles north west of Honiton. The church was rebuilt in 1868 by C. F. Edwards as an aisled cruciform structure (Pevsner, *Devon*, 343). The two memorials Davidson recorded are missing.

The church consists of nave chancel transepts & tower at the western end of the nave. The church is of recent erection the tower is ancient and the building presents nothing worthy of observation in its style of architecture. The nave is 34 feet long by 15 wide, the transepts 34 feet across by 14 wide the chancel 18.6 by 15, the tower 7 by 6 feet – a tablet of wood against the South wall of the nave informs us that "the church of this parish being ruinous was taken down in May 1817 and was rebuilt and enlarged the southern aisle at the expense of Mr. Simcoe the north aisle by subscription and the remainder by the church rates, and the church opened in the same year. The rev John Clarke curate Joseph Manley churchwarden." The tower which is 28 feet high to the top of the battlements contains 3 bells dated 2 in 1684 & the other in 1732.

The church plate consists of a Chalice Patten & dish of silver, not dated or inscribed. On the church door is a horse shoe fastened on with 10 nails which are said to represent the 10 churches within the rural deanery of Dunkeswell [removed]. The parish register commences in 1695. But the most curious & remarkable object here is the font which is placed at the western end of the nave. It is of stone circular or barrel shaped & in the earliest & rudest style of Saxon or Anglo Norman workmanship it is 2ft. 4in in height & 2 ft 1in in diameter & is lined with lead having a hole for the escape of the water. its circumference is divided into 8 panels or compartments by columns with circular bosses & hatched capitals in the Saxon or Anglo Norman style. The subject of the panels are as follows.

1st a man & woman with heads remarkably large – 2 a bishop or abbot with his right hand held up in benediction a crosier in his left - 3 a monk. 4. a warrior with a spear in his right hand & a shield in his left. 6. a man with a bow & arrow. 7. 2 figures scarcely intelligible. 8. destroyed. – below these compartments is a broad border entwined like a basket work & beneath it a finish to the base, of tiles with circular edges over laying one another, this relic of antiquity is in a state of apparent dilapidation & decay. –

The exterior of the church presents nothing remarkable, there are plain crosses on the gables of the transepts. The only inscriptions are these on the chancel floor "Here lieth the body of Edward Hill of Priory in the parish of Broad Hembury who died the 19 Sept. 16 -- aged --. Arms apparently (though much destroyed) on a chevron a trefoil slipped between 2 roses – impaling 1 Ermine a fess 2 gone [missing].
Here lieth the body of --- the relict of Edward Hill of Priory daughter to Richard Carey gent who died the -- of March -- aetatis suae 78 [missing].

A brass plate against the East wall partly covered by the commandments records 2 or 3 individuals named Vicary [missing].

The manor of Dunkeswell or Bowerhays is the property of Mrs. Simcoe widow of Gen. Simcoe of Wolford Lodge in this parish.

Miss Simcoe sent a drawing of Dunkeswell font to Lord Clifford. It certainly is not emblematic of the seven sacraments. Two of the eight sides have been injured – I have not considered the subjects sufficiently but suspect it to be allusive to St. Edmund King and Martyr

Rev: W. Oliver 1824.

Newspaper cutting, no name of newspaper, dated 21 September 1842

Sept. 21. The beautiful little Church erected on the site of the Old Abbey at *Dunkeswell*, near Honiton, co. Devon, chiefly at the expense of Mrs. Simcoe, of Wolford Lodge, who endows it, was consecrated, and dedicated to the Holy Trinity; an excellent sermon was preached by the Rev. Henry Addington Simcoe.

HEMYOCK

Davidson (pp. 353–5) visited [St Mary's] Hemyock on 9 September 1828 and noted it was about 10 miles north of Honiton. The church was restored in 1846–7 by Richard Carver of Taunton (Pevsner, *Devon*, 268). Six memorials are missing from the eight that Davidson recorded.

The church of this village consists of a chancel 28 feet long by 15½ wide a nave 42 by 21 with a tower at its western end 10 feet square within the walls a north aisle 41 feet by 11 a north aisle 16 feet by 25 wide and a porch protecting the door on the north side.

The nave is divided from the aisles by cylindrical columns with capitals in a sort of Roman style supporting flat areas which were erected on the repair of the church in 1771. The church is lighted by pointed windows each having 3 lights with cinquefoil heads, a screen divides the nave from the chancel [removed] which with the pulpit is varnished oak & in a Roman Doric style. The chancel window has 3 lancet shaped lights & on the eastern wall on the south side is a niche for a statue with a trefoil head. A door on the north side of the chancel leads into a vestry [hidden]. Against the eastern wall of the south aisle is a bracket for a statue and in the south wall a large piscina with a cinquefoil head. The font stands at the western end of the nave it is of dark coloured Devonshire marble large & square resting on an octangular column adorned with columns & standing on an octangular base, the sides appear to be enriched with quatrefoils but the whole is much obscured with whitewash – it is evidently of ancient date. The church plate consists of a flagon weighing 38oz 15 dct. Inscribed Hemyock 1763 & a chalice marked I.W. 1651. – Some fragments of painted glass linger in the windows [removed]. The tower which is 40 feet in height to the top of the battlements contains 5 bells inscribed "S. Pennington. Drawe neare unto God 1621" – "1624" – "We to the church the living call and to the grave we summons all 1793" "T. Bilbee 1811" – "Wm. Pannell Collumpton fecit. True hearts and sound bottoms"

On the south side of the chancel is a mural tablet "Sacred to the memory of Alexander Rayner MD. Fellow of Oriel collage in Oxford and for many years physician at Bath. He died the 18 September AD. 1746 aged 48. Underneath also lies the body of Elizabeth Rayner wife of Edward Rayner MA. who died the 17 June AD. 1769 Here likewise are deposited the remains of Edward Rayner MA. many years a fellow of Oriel collage in Oxford and also rector of this parish. This monument was caused to be erected to his and his brother's memory. He died 2 March 1775 aged 68." Arms. Quarterly 1 & 4. Azure a saltier engrailed Ermine. 2 & 3. Ermine o a chief Azure 2 stars fess Or. A hatchment with the same coat, Crest (or talbot dog) passant proper. On the N wall of the chancel a white marble slab on a black ground. Sacred to the memory of the reverend John Land who for 42 years faithfully and conscientiously discharged his duties as rector of this parish. He died 17 April 1817 in the 74th year of his age. Agreeably to his particular request his remains were deposited in the church yard in the midst of those who had been so long objects of his parental care.

On the floor of the chancel --- the bodie of Joan wife of Tristram Tooke -- Clayhidon here inte-- 7 Aug. 1633. [missing]

Here lieth -- Roger Kelly (apparently) the worthy pastor of -- 1643 [missing]

On the floor of the nave.

Here lyeth -- afford Clothier he dyed 13 March 1663 [missing]

Here lyeth the body of Alice wife of Clement Waldron who was buried 16 Oct 1673. [missing]

Here lieth Anthony the sonne of Clement Waldron junior who died -- Feb. 1668.

Here lieth Alice -- Waldron -- buried 11 day of December 1668.

-- Waldron -- [missing]

Floor of the south aisle. Here lieth the body of Mary the daughter of Thomas and Thomasine Clode who died 13 Jan. 1722 in the 19th year of her age. [missing]

A tablet against the south wall of the nave records as follows.

Nicholas Marks of Taunton gent: by his last will gave £5 to be yearly paid for ever by the owner of the land in Awliscombe in the parish of Hemyock for the binding out one poor child or children of the said parish their parents having no relief on this condition that no parish apprentice shall be bound to the owner of that estate for ever hereafter – AD. 1747 [missing].

A tablet against the wall of the north aisle, records – An account of money and lands given to the poor of Hemyock Charles Ford esq. gave 20/ to be paid yearly to the poor house keepers of this parish out of his lands called Strouds and Keen's meadow for ever – an estate called Holcombe purchased with money given to the poor now in the hands of feoffees in value about £5 p annum for ever – Nicholas Lack gave to the poor Housekeepers of this parish 5/ per annum to be paid out of his lands in Dunkeswell yearly for ever. Thomas Moore gave £5 the interest of it to be paid to the poor for ever – 1773.

There is an ancient yew-tree spreading from the ground in the church yard on the NW side of the church. – The iron gates of the church yard bear the date 1813.

The rev. Samuel Sparrow is the present rector, he resides at Clifton near Bristol. The rev. George Gale is curate. The manor of Hemyock is the property of Mrs Simcoe of Wolford lodge. –

A few remains of Hemyock castle exist on the north side of the village – a pointed arch in a mass of wall covered with ivy.

CULM DAVEY

Davidson (p. 357) visited the chapel of St Mary, Culm Davey, on 9 September 1828 and noted it was about 1½ mile north of Hemyock. He observed the chapel was dependent upon the church of Hemyock, and was restored in 1850.

The chapel consists only of a nave 37 feet long by 15 wide, lighted by 2 windows of 2 lights each with cinquefoil heads and an eastern window of larger dimensions divided by mullions & a transom into 6 cinquefoil lights & having tracery in its pointed arch. With some fragments of stained glass [removed]. The roof is open & the floor ornamented with several ancient tiles [removed]. In the south wall towards the eastern end is a piscina with a shelf and a trefoil head. The font which stands at the western end of the chapel is of stone, small, octagonal adorned with quatrefoils & resting on an octagonal column having panels with trefoil heads [now a plain stone font]. An oaken coffer bearing the date 1694 stands in the chapel [removed], the plate consists of a small cup and paten without a date a turret on the western gable covers 2 bells which are inaccessible. – The only monument is a tablet against the north wall "In memory of Alice wife of William Gervis of Ashculm who died 25ᵗʰ Feb. 1705 and lies interred in the western end of this chapel" the descendants of the above mentioned Mr Gervis lives in Goad House in the parish and ranks as a gentleman. The reputed manor of Culm David belongs to two persons named Pratt & Hallett brothers in law, but there are neither tenants nor services – the tything man is appointed at Hemyock court. –

CHURCH STANTON

Davidson (pp. 361–2) visited [St Peter and St Paul] Church Stanton on 9 September 1828 and noted it was about 12 miles north of Honiton. He observed that 'the church of this extensive parish is an ancient and very interesting edifice containing several remarkable vestiges of antiquity'. In 1830 there was a gallery supported on thin iron columns with 26 of the pew ends used as a gallery front; this has now been removed.[1] All four memorials that Davidson recorded are missing.

It consists of a nave 49 feet long by 17 wide Chancel 24½ by 12. South aisle 61½ by 11½ & a tower at the western end 15 feet square within the walls 52 feet high to the top of the battlements & having pinnacles at the corners. The nave is divided from the aisle by 3 columns & 2 halves of clusters shafts their capitals ornamented with foliage & supporting pointed arches of several mouldings. The chancel opens to the South aisle by a pointed arch resting on columns composed of shafts with plain circular capitals apparently of earlier date than those of the aisle. The chancel window is pointed comprising 4 lights with cinquefoil heads & having tracery in the arch as in the windows of the aisle. The windows of the aisle & nave have 3 lights with cinquefoil heads & tracery in their arches the whole are of early date. – The wall of the nave is supported by heavy buttresses between the windows. An oaken screen which supports the rood loft divides the chancel from the nave it is covered in open work with equilateral arches & tracery [removed] – the pulpit is of carved oak but much more modern. The font which stands at the western end of the nave is a very interesting relic & may perhaps be assigned to the Anglo Norman period, it consists of a rude heavy stone basin without sculptures or ornament 2 feet 4 inches square resting on a cylindrical column 1 foot high & having a small cylindrical detached shaft at each corner the base is square & the top is 3 feet high from the floor, the cavity is circular & lined with lead. – The ancient benches which are no doubt coeval with the church still remain & are very curious they are of oak the panels at the ends carved in finished style into a great variety of ornaments & designs no two of them being alike, they represent figures of men angels flowers grotesque fruit fleurs de lis & quatrefoils but many of them are now in a decaying condition [now low box pews]. An elegant little door leads from the W end of the aisle up the narrow stairs of the tower which contains 5 bells dated & inscribed as follow. – "NR. TB. Prayes yee the Lord Anno Domini 1660" – "NR. TB. CW. TB. AD, 1660" Dº Dº "I was made in hope to ring at the coronation of our King 1660. by Will: Richards of Paye. CW. TB.TP." – There are some fragments of ancient stained glass in the windows of the church representing churches – the letters JHS. in a cipher. The symbols of the 4 evangelists the Lion Angel Bulls & Eagle [removed]

[1] J. Orbach and N. Pevsner, *The Buildings of England: Somerset South and West* (New Haven and London: Yale University Press, 2014).

The floor is paved with small square tiles many of them ancient, glazed & figured with crosses [stone slabs]. –

The inscriptions in this church are as follow

On the floor of the nave – Thomas Hellier sonne of Hugh Hellier of Churchingford died 6 Dec. 1655. Here also lies Joshua North who was buried 4 Dec. 1694. On the floor of the aisle "John Southwood of Burnworthy died 10 July 1770- aged 56" [missing]

On the chancel floor. "Here lieth the body of Mr Peter Bond who was parson of this parish 40 years. he departed this life the 22 Oct. AD. 1632" [missing]

Chancel floor – "Here lyeth the body of Joshua North rector of this parish who was buried the 4 Dec. 1684" then follow some Latin verses – [missing]

Chancel floor – George Popham MA the last surviving son of Francis Popham of Wellington died 5 Feb. 1784 aged 64 years. his 3 brothers John Francis & Alexandra having died long before him and without issue. He married Catherine eldest daughter of Henry Gapper vicar of Pitminster by whom he had no issue. He was rector of the parish of Buckland St. Mary in Somerset & also of Bullington near Bristol the former he held the space of 39 years, the two latter some years only before his death [missing].

CLAYHIDON

Davidson (pp. 365–6) visited [St Andrew] Clayhidon on 9 September 1828 and noted it was about 11 miles north of Honiton. The church was restored in 1846 (Pevsner, *Devon*, 268). Five memorials are missing from the six Davidson recorded.

The church of this village consists of a nave 46 feet long 18 wide a chancel 24 by 14½ a south aisle 56 long by10 with a porch protecting the door & having a sun dial over its entrance. An embattled tower at the western end of the nave 10 feet long by 11 wide with a square turret for the stairs in the SE corner. The nave is separate from the aisle by 3 columns & 2 half columns consisting of alternate shafts & mouldings having plain capitals & supporting pointed arches. The windows have each 3 lights with cinquefoil heads. The chancel has a plain piscina in the south wall, its eastern window has 4 lights with cinquefoil heads. The tower is 52 feet in height to the top of the battlements & the pinnacles at the corners, it contains 5 bells cast by Bilbee of Collumpton in 1810 – one of them bears the inscription "Revd. T.E. Clarke Rector 1810" another "We was 4 cast into 5 in the year 1810" & a third "Religion Death and pleasure cause me to sound Revd. T.E. Clarke rector 1810".

The pulpit is of oak carved without much taste. The font at the western end of the nave is ancient, of stone, circular, 2 feet 1 inch in diameter 3½ feet in height resting on an octagonal column with a square plinth. There are a few fragments of ancient stained glass in the windows [removed].
A wooden tablet on the north wall records some benefactions but it is much defaced & the following only can be traced '--- gave to this parish out of a tenement called Hazele the sum of £5 to be paid every second year during all such term that he had therein --- bind children apprentices. John Channage (or some such name) gave unto the poor ancient people of this parish having no relief the sum of £10 to be paid yearly by the overseers the principal to be out of good security' [missing]

The following inscriptions are in the church –

On the floor of the chancel.
"Samuel Wilson the late lamented pastor of this church died 21 Feb. 1657 aged 63" [missing]
"Samuel Brown died 4 May 1794 aet. 79 he was rector of this parish 42 years" [missing] –
An inscription defaced & almost illegible to the memory of William --- curate---
-- eaves Marchant -- & of his -- March 1641 [missing]
On the north side of the chancel is a mural tablet stating "In a vault underneath the altar are deposited the mortal remains of Frances Lewis Clarke the beloved wife of

the Revd. John Clarke Rector of this parish who died 30 Nov. 1825 after an illness of a few hours in the 29th year of her age."
On the floor of the nave Thomas Crop of Hole in this parish died 6 May 1725 aged 76. Susanna wife of the above died 3 May 1738 aged 77. [missing]
Henry Hollway of this parish clothier died 17 June 1674 aged 86 years. [missing]

CULMSTOCK

Davidson (pp. 369–71) visited [All Saints] Culmstock on 9 September 1828 and noted it was about 10 miles east of Tiverton. The church was extensively altered in 1825 and the stone screen formerly placed across the entrance to the tower now forms the reredos carried out in 1835 (Pevsner, *Devon*, 307). Three memorials that Davidson recorded are missing.

This village church consists of a nave 48 feet long by 17½ wide, chancel 30 by 16 North & south aisles each 45 feet by 10 & a tower at the western end of the nave 63 feet high to the top of the battlements & 13 feet square within the walls at its base. The tower has an octagonal stair turret at the so: east corner & pinnacles at its 4 corners surmounted by vanes. –
The roof of the nave was raised at the time that the North aisle was built in 1825 and it is now lighted by 3 clerestory windows on each side it is separated from the aisles by 3 columns & 2 halves on each side consisting of each of 4 shafts with alternate hollow mouldings their capitals plain & circular & supporting pointed arches. A gallery without ornament extends across the western end [removed] & beneath it across the entrance to the tower are the remains of a beautiful stone screen which formerly separated the nave from the chancel it consists of a series of pointed arches divided by mullions & tracery into lights with cinquefoil heads highly enriched with tabernacle work & foliage, the doorway in its centre is ornamented with foliage in the mouldings & is surmounted by a highly enriched canopy. This ancient & elegant specimen of art was consigned to its present obscure station on the alteration of the church in 1825 [removed]. The font is stone ancient, low of octagonal form without ornamentation. The cloth which covers the communion table is a curious relic of antiquity and was in all probability the ancient altar cloth it is made of brown velvet enriched with a broad border of tapestry representing a series of saints & martyrs standing in niches adorned with canopy & tabernacle work [missing]. The aisles are lighted by pointed windows of 3 lights each having trefoil heads. The tower contains 5 bells inscribed respectively "*AVE MARIA GRATIA PLENA*" – "1639" – "Freely bestowed my voice shall sound their praise as freely who me found. Then grudge not a rope to me since others made me free I. P. 1652" This bell has 7 coins let into it 3 large & 4 small ones one of them is of K Charles 2nd coinage – "1661" – "1778". –

Against the wall of the north aisle is a tablet with the following inscription "This church was enlarged in the year 1825 by which means 250 additional sittings have been obtained and in consequence of a grant from the society for promoting the enlargement and building of churches and chapels 170 of that number are hereby declared to be free and un-appropriate for ever. William Karslake Minister."

At the time of the enlargement of the church several stones bearing inscriptions were used or destroyed, the following are all that remain visible.

On the floor of the chancel "Here lyeth the body of Robert Taylor of this parish gent: who died 18 Oct 1697 aged 38" [missing]
In the south porch are 2 stones which were removed from the chancel much defaced
Here lieth the body of John Wood who was buried 21 Nov. 1637" [missing]
-- "22 May 1644" [missing]

The registers of this parish commence in 1645. a memorandum in one of them was observed as follows
"1704 This year Henry Petit vicar died Sept succeeded by Nicholas Harris"
The great tithes of this parish with the manor belong to the cathedral church of Exeter

Against the south aisle of this church is a tablet bearing the following inscriptions
Charitable donations for the good of the poor of this parish of Culmstock
Henry Rainsbury of the city of London Factor gave to the poor £100 the interest of which to be equally distributed every year to eight poor old persons who do not receive parish relief – William Crosse of Lions Inn in the city of London gent gave £5 – Mary Wood gentlewoman gave £3.6.8 now come to £4 – Edward Wood gave £5 – Mary Wood relict of the above Edward Wood gave £5 – Benjamin Culme gent £5 – John Parsons of Samford Arundel in the county of Somerset merchant in Portugal £10 – Henry Butson of the parish clothier £5 –Thomas Hellings of this parish clothier £10 – George Melhuish of this parish gent £5 – John Wood of this parish gent £50 – John Were of this parish gent £5 – Edward Searle of this parish clothier £5 – Richard Thomas of this parish Sergemaker £3 – All these donations were probably made before the year 1674 - & 1675.
Nicholas Rowe of this parish gave £5 – in 1779 Jewel Collier of this parish gave £10 – and £3 a year to be distributed to them in bread during the present lives on the 3 leasehold estates of Tristrams Furzehouse and Nethercott in this parish £1 a year of each estate, the whole sum given exclusive of the £3 in bread s £190 it is vested in the church wardens for the time being and the interest of it distributed by them annually to the poor.

Newspaper cutting, no name of newspaper, dated 21 December 1859
Culmstock
An organ, built by Mr. Dicker, of Exeter, was opened with full choral service in this church, on Wednesday last. Several members of our cathedral choir assisted on the occasion. The anthem performed was 'Blessing and Glory' Bach, which was effectively sung. Mr Rice of Tiverton, presided at the organ, and an appropriate sermon, was preached on the occasion. After divine service, which was numerously attended, above one hundred of the influential inhabitants of Culmstock and neighbourhood sat down to an excellent dinner, the Rev. J.W. Karslake presiding. After the loyal toasts were given the health of the rev. Vicar was drunk with the usual honours. The health of the choir, who had this day so efficiently assisted was also drunk, after which the health of Mr Dicker was given. He was highly complimented, not only for the skill evinced in the construction of the Culmstock organ, which had given so much satisfaction, but it was forcibly contended that Mr Dicker's well-known ability enabled him to compete with any establishment in the metropolis.

FENITON

Davidson (pp. 377–9) visited [St Andrew] Feniton on 22 September 1829 and noted it was about 3 miles west of Honiton. The church was restored in 1877 by R.M. Fulford and the screen by Harry Hems in 1877 (Pevsner, *Devon*, 449). Five memorials are missing from the nine that Davidson recorded.

This church comprises a nave 37 feet long by 19 wide a chancel 26 by 16 south aisle 57½ by 10 & a tower at the west end of the nave 9 feet square, a porch protects the door on the western end of the aisle. The total length of the building within the walls is 74 feet.

The nave & chancel appear to be ancient, the south aisle and the tower of the 15th or beginning of the 16th century. The arch between the nave & chancel has been destroyed the ceiling of the latter has been covered & plastered & it is finished against the nave with a frame of wood – The nave & chancel open to the aisle by 5 low pointed arches resting on columns formed of 4 shafts with intervening hollow mouldings, the capitals which are angular are well carved in foliage and shields but are loaded with whitewash – the shield exhibit this coat of armour I 3 leaves (query Malherbe) II on a bend couped 3 horseshoes – The windows of the chancel & nave & of the aisle, except 2 have been despoiled of their tracery & a single mullion has been substituted at a much later date rising to the point of the arch & presenting a most tasteless appearance. Of the 2 windows remaining perfect in the aisle the one at the eastern end has an arch nearly flat the others pointed, the lights have cinque-foiled heads and the tracery above it is the perpendicular style, the inner arches rest of shafts with octagonal laminated capitals. The ceiling of the nave is coved, that of the aisle flat & both are ribbed with oak, a pointed arch opens from the nave to the tower which has a large window of similar design to those of the aisle, but it is hidden by a singers gallery of modern erection across the nave. The pulpit is modern. The font is of stone octagonal 2 feet across 7, 3 ft 4in: high it has projecting brackets on one side & the other are formed into panels with quatrefoils & foliage, it rests on a plain octagonal column. – Some fragments of stained glass remain in one of the windows of the aisle these represent in separate pieces the cross, the nails, the crown of thorns, the sponge & spear [missing] – Some oaken benches remain in the nave their ends formed into panels with cinquefoil heads and shields [5 remain along the south wall of the nave].

Between the chancel & the nave and across the aisle are the remains in good preservation of the screen which supported the rood loft – it consists of a series of pointed arches each divided by mullions into 4 lights with cinquefoil heads & having tracery above in the perpendicular style, the intervening shafts spread into a canopy of tracery ornamented with foliage knots & flowers, above in front of the rood loft is a series of 5 mouldings richly carved in foliage fruit & flowers the whole is of oak painted & gilt – a screen of similar design but without a canopy parts the chancel from the aisle. The tower is embattled & is 45 feet high to the top it has half an hexagonal turret on the north side for the stairs, Here are 5 bells on of them inscribed "3 cast into 5, 1707" –

The sepulchral monuments & inscriptions here are as follow. –
In the north wall of the chancel almost upon the floor is a low pointed arch of the 13th century which has doubtless covered a tomb perhaps that of the founder or one of the incumbents –
Against the south wall of the chancel is a stone altar tomb faced with quatrefoils 7 feet long 2ft 3in wide & 1ft.9in high upon which is the whole length effigies of a corpse in a winding sheet or shroud tied at the head and feet, this may probably be assigned to the 14th century & may represent one of the family of Malherbe.
Chancel floor, in the old letters. Here lyeth John Skinner yeoman father of George Skinner pastor of this church who died 9 Jan. 1582 [missing]
Do Here lieth Margaret late wyfe to George Wecham esquire daughter of Thomas D. – who died the 16 -- 1572 missing]
Do Kirkham -- *miserere mei amen.* [missing]
A marble tablet Mrs. Mary Bucknall died July 4. 1786 in the 58 year of her age.
Nave floor – Susanna the wife of Philip Wright of Curscombe who died 2 April 1712. Arms a bend between 3 fleurs de lis, a crescent for difference impaling a bend sinister. [missing]
Margaret the wife of Philip Wright of Curscombe gent – died Dec. -- [missing]
Tomb in the churchyard. To the memory of John Wright of Curscombe gent of this parish who died 12 July AD 1699.
Stone against the east wall of the chancel. Here lieth the body of Maximilian Wolcot rector of this parish who departed this life 22nd day of July in the 79 year (the remainder below the turf).
John Bytelesgate parson le englise de Fyneton 1378
Deed for Sparklaighes in Colyton & Branscombe 1388
William Tettewille pson ecclie de Fyneton 1374
Deed of this date for Axminster 1375

TALATON

Davidson (pp. 381–5) visited [St James the Apostle] Talaton on 10 July 1843 and noted it was about 6 miles west of Honiton. He observed that 'the church of this rural and sequestered village is a very picturesque object, of venerable and interesting character, standing in the midst of Scotch Pines of large and lofty growth.' The church was restored in 1859–60 by Edward Ashworth who added the north aisle (Pevsner, *Devon*, 777–8). Five memorials are missing from the eight that Davidson recorded.

It comprises a nave about 40 feet long by 18 wide, a chancel about 20 by 18 an aisle on the south about 40 by 12 and a porch covering the south door, and a square tower at the western end of the nave embattled, with pinnacles at the corners and a stair turret at the south east corner enriched with five canopied niches, containing statues which appear to have been of excellent design & representation, one of them remains in very good preservation representing the virgin crowned holding the child and below them a monk or priest in adoration another is a figure of St. George with the dragon. The corners of the tower are supported by buttresses having above them similar niches with statues. The tower contains 5 bells. –
The porch is large, embattled & ornamented with quatrefoil and pinnacles and a niche over the entrance which is under a pointed arch the moulding ornamented with a label rests on large corbels of angels. The north wall of the nave is propped by large heavy old buttresses. The chancel windows are of various dates one having two trefoiled two cinquefoiled lights under a horizontal head. The eastern window is modern, in the perpendicular style with three cinquefoil lights. The nave opens to the aisle by pointed arches on columns with foliage capitals the windows are formed by three lights with cinquefoiled heads and perpendicular tracery in the arches. There are some fragments of painted glass of old date representing the virgin and the symbols of the four evangelists [removed]. The ceiling is ribbed & has bosses of foliage at the intersections. The chancel screen remains formed by a range of open lights with shafts spreading into the capitals & tracery surmounted by several mouldings of foliage. There are ranges of benches of carved oak but not of extraordinary execution. The pulpit is modern & mean. A gallery at the west end of the nave [removed]. The old iron stand for an hour-glass formerly attached to the pulpit is now fixed to the screen [removed]. The font is very ancient, probably of the [word faded] century, formed of moorstone, large heavy and each side ornamented with a range of four semicircular arches, it is rested formerly on a low cylindrical column but has been raised & 4 additional shafts added under the corners.

The monumental inscriptions are as follow.
Chancel. North Wall.
A large marble tablet (*in the margin:* See Polwhele III.273)
En tibi viator

Subtus habes reconditum
Id totum quod mortale fuit
Caroli Harward
Juvenis (si quis alius) memorandi
In patrem habuit Carolum
Ecclesiae hujus rectorem venerandum
Matrem vero Katherinam
Ab antiquam Prideauxiorum de Netherton
(in vicinia hac) familia oriundam
Filius natu unicus nec minus natura ingenioque singularis
A prima usque pueritia
Tam vestitus quam corporis nitore non vulgare
Necnon indole suavissima spectabilis
Grandior jam factus mira erga parentes pietate et obsequio
Adeoque spei felicissimae
Tum deinde Ephebis excedens
Atque Danmonios suos apud Exonienses petens
Omnibus quibuscunque carissimus
Forma praeter caeteros honesta
Gestu animoque liberali decore comitatu modestia
Morum item innocentia
Nulla non denique cohonestatus
Variolae tandem (heu nimium juventuti inimice)
Fugientem patriusque Lares revisentem
Insecutae praependunt prehensumque opprimat
Annos natus nouendecim et quod amplius est
(purificata virgine Christum que in templo sistente)
Purus ipse Christi sanguine
Sese coram Deo sistebat
Anno post salutem humanam MDCCXVIII
Mireris licet viator aequare haud licebit. [now on west wall of south aisle]
Arms. Sable a Cross crosslet gules – with a label of three points for difference –
Against the wall a Hatchment with the same coat.
A black marble tablet.
To the memory of Mrs. Katherine Bradford widow of the revd George Bradford and daughter of the rev. Charles Harward both rectors of this parish. She departed this life 27th April 1785. An aetat. 83

East wall.
A tablet. Near this spot are deposited the remains of Thomas Phillips esq of Newport House co. Cornwall and of Collypriest House co. Devon who died at Sidmouth 19 Feb. 1806 aged 39 years.
A stone monument richly carved, consisting of an entablature & pediment supported by Corinthian columns with pinnacles &c. The slab thus inscribed.
The memmarie of John Leache Bachaler of Devennitie and chanssaler of the chath-thedrall cherche of Exon and persone of this paresh.
If ever virtues all in one were found
Of all this one doth yield that rare compound

Nimble wise grave lovinge soul curing leache
Not only taught to live but lived to teache
Leache was a lamp burning and shining bright
Empting himself to lend the world his light
All eating death determining to end it
Caught of mortality and so did mend it
Himself doth now himself surpass by farr
Earth lost a lampe heaven findes a glorious starr.
They that turne manie to righteousness shall shine as the starres for ever. Dan II. 3.
--- 1613. Arms – a saltire between 4 cross crosslets

Floor – here lie the bodies of Richard and Francis the two eldest sons, and Mary the
daughter of Richard Alford of this parish gent, and Ursula his second wife. [missing]
Here lieth the body of Bridgett wife of Charles Harward Mr. of Arts and rector of
this church. Died 21 Nov. 1696 [missing]
Arms – a fess wavy – between 6 Cross crosslets
The Dormitory of Robert Terry Mr. of Arts and rector of this parish. died 2 June 1677
at sue 44. Also Robert his son died 10 June 1695 aet suae 30. [missing]
Here lieth the body of Elizabeth Prideaux second daughter of Sir Peter Prideaux of
Netherton Bart by Elizabeth eldest daughter of Sir Bevil Granvill of Stow Knt who
died 31 March 1711
Hatchments against the wall.
I. per fess crenellee sable & or, in chief 3 Mullets fesswise of the last
II. Kennaway Argent a fess azure, in chief 2 Eagles displayed of the last, in an
annulet or though its base a sprig of laurel and another of palm in saltire proper. An
esquire's helmet.
III. Kennaway Argent a fess azure between 2 eagles displayed in chief and a amulet
in base gules, through the last a slip of olive and another of palm in saltire proper –
Executed for Bart. (Kennaway) impaling Per fess crenellee sable and or, in chief 3
mullets fess-wise argent. [missing]

South aisle. South wall.
A white marble tablet.
Near this tablet are interred the remains of James Amyatt esq. who departed this
life at Sidmouth 10 Jan. 1813 aged 78. He represented the borough of Totnes in one
parliament and the town and county of Southampton in four successive parliaments.
Also the remains of Maria his wife who departed this life at Sidmouth 21 Aug. 1804
aged 64. She was widow of Peter Amyatt esq second in council at Calcutta who
having been deputed on the public service of his country to the court of Cosseim
Ally Khan immediately after the nuptials ceremony was murdered by the officers of
that prince on his return to the residency. Likewise the remains of their three infant
grandsons George Ross, Amyatt Kyd; and Henry Kennaway. [missing]
South wall, A tablet.
Sacred to the memory of Lawrence third son of Sir John and Lady Kennaway. At
an early period of life he entered the civil service of the Hon. East India Company
in Bengal and died at Allahabad April 8th 1822 having just completed his 20th year.
West wall. A tablet. To the memory of Charles Harward esq. – Died at Exmouth 19
March 1816 aged 49. Erected by his widow [missing]

Against the front of the gallery a brass tablet of benefactors to the poor

1656	William Eveleigh senior esq	a field in Whimple 2½ acres.	
			£
1673	D⁰.		20
1706	William Eveleigh junior esq.		30
1710	Mrs. Elizabeth Prideaux for schooling of poor children.		33. 5. 6
1793	Jonah Pynsent esq.		100
1799	George Baker esq.		75

Messrs. Eveleigh 2 benefactions £20 and £30 purchased the poor house

Church yard.

A tomb. In memory of Charles Harward esq of Hayne House in this county, obit 19 March 1816 aet. 49.

A stone affixed to one of the buttresses. Here lieth the body of Nicholas Harries who died 4 Nov. 1700 at 66. and Petronella his wife.

"*Will– le Were rector ecclie de Talaton*" 1387 See deed for Axminster.

Newspaper cutting, no name of newspaper, dated 5 September 1860

Talaton.

Talaton Church was re-opened with a special service on Wednesday, after the re-con-struction of the old building with the exception of the tower. A small north aisle has been added to the original fabric, in which are the painted windows to the memory of the late rector, Rev. L.P. Welland. There is also a memorial window in the tower, representing the "last judgement", given by the family of the late J.P. Mathews, Esq, of Rydons. The windows are by Hughes, of London. A richly carved oak screen extending the whole width of the church has been restored with much labour, at the expense of rev. C.A. Hoggan, the present rector of Talaton: the passages are laid with Minton's tiles, and much old wood work in roofs and seats has been reinstated. The work has been carried out by Mr. Digby builder of Ottery St. Mary. The architect is Mr. Ashworth of Exeter.

ESCOT

Davidson (pp. 387–8) visited [St Philip and St James] Escot on 30 August 1843 and noted it was 5 miles west of Honiton. 'This neat and elegant structure is in the parish of Ottery St Mary but within the demesne of Sir John Kennaway Bart at whose expense it was erected. The architect was Henry Roberts of London – the cost about £2000 – and it was consecrated on the 1 May 1840.' It was built between 1838 and 1840 (Pevsner, *Devon*, 356). There are no memorials

It consists of a Nave about 43 feet by 24 wide and a Chancel about 20 feet by 14 opening to each other by a pointed arch resting on shafts with octagonal moulded capitals. The walls are supported by buttresses of two stages on the corners stone of one which at the eastern end all the following texts engraved "Not by night nor by power but by my sprit saith the Lord of Hosts" Zech. IV.6 "Other foundations can no man lay than that is laid which is Jesus Christ" 1 Corinthians. III.II. [both removed] – a porch covers the south door over which is the inscription "I am the door of the sheep" [missing] a turret on the western gable contains a bell. The other gables are ornamented with crosses except that of the nave which has a sort of canopy with trefoiled openings through it. The windows on the sides are of single lights with pointed arches. That in the eastern end was presented by the incumbent the revd P.W. Douglas & is formed by two lights and a quatrefoil above – It is filled with stained glass in chaste & elegant design with the letters J.H.S. in each light and a Dove in the quatrefoil. The western window is formed by three lancet lights, the centre the highest with a continuous label over them on the outside they are filled with stained glass & in neat and handsome scrolls, and were the gift of the Misses Kennaway sisters of the baronet, over the eastern window inside is a label resting on corbels of crowned heads of a man and woman. The roof the chancel is vaulted with ribs which spring from corbels of foliage and there are bosses of foliage at the intersections of the ribs. The ceiling of the nave is formed into panels without ornament. The communion table stands in the middle of the chancel and behind it is a lofty & handsome screen of carved oak formed in pointed arches a cornice of foliage ornamented with crocketted [word illegible].

The space between it and the eastern wall forms the vestry which is entered by the arch at the south side of the screen. This screen was presented by dowager Lady Kennaway. The pulpit and benches are of English Larch fir carved in panels and varnished. The Font is of stone of small size and octagonal in shape resting on an octagonal column ornamented with sunk panels under pointed arches. Around the font is this inscription "Suffer little children to come unto me and forbid them not". This font was presented by the rev. Charles Kennaway the baronet's brother.

This chapel will accommodate 220 persons and 100 of the sittings are free.

PAYHEMBURY

Davidson (pp. 389–91) visited [St Mary] Payhembury on 24 July 1843 and noted it was about 5 miles west of Honiton. The church was restored in 1895–7 by G. Fellowes Prynne (Pevsner, *Devon*, 625).

This village church consists of a Nave about 42 feet long by 15 wide, a chancel about 27 by 15, an aisle on the north about 56 by 12, a porch covering the south door and a tower at the western end of the nave on the north side of the aisle is a projecting half turret for the stairs to the rood loft. The entrance to the porch is a pointed arch enriched with foliage in the mouldings. The door is under a low arch under a horizontal label the moulding and the spandrels enriched with foliage. The tower is of oblong form being wider than it is long. It is embattled, has a turret for the stairs at the NE. angle and contains 6 bells.

The nave opens to the aisle by 4 low arches resting on columns formed by 4 shafts with entwining mouldings their capitals carved in foliage and shields charged with the following bearings viz.
I 3 Holly leaves II on a bend 3 Horse shoes III 3 Torteaux with a label of 3 points IV a Millrinds between 3 roundels 2 in fess and one in base. (I query Malherbe, II Farrers, III Courtenay)
The chancel opens to the aisle by a very low arch resting on similar columns the capitals carved in foliage and shields but loaded with whitewash. The windows of the nave are formed by 3 lights with cinquefoil heads, having perpendicular tracery above. Those of the chancel are similar but that on the east is modern. The windows of the north aisle are of the like character but that in the eastern end has 4 lights with fan tracery in the arch. The windows have been adorned with painted glass of rich and elegant designs. The figures of 5 or 6 saints remain, some architectural designs, flowers stars etc. but all more or less damaged among them appear the following coats of arms.
I Per fess azure and gules 3 Fleurs de les or
II Quarterly 1&4th Argent a bend wavy cotised sable 2nd & 3rd Argent 3 Escallops Impaling I
The ceilings are coved and ribbed with bosses of foliage at the intersections. There is a recess with a basin for holy water inside the south door. A chancel and aisle screen remain carved in oak formed by a range of arches with cinquefoil headed lights and mouldings of foliage above supported by fan tracery a ruinous altar of wood with painted heads of Moses and Aaron. The pulpit is modern. The old oak benches remain their ends richly carved in panels niches and foliage. The font is of stone octagonal, the sides carved in quatrefoils and foliage resting on an octagonal column. There is a gallery at the western end of the nave with a shield in front charged with the coat Azure fretty gules – it seems to be modern or very recently painted.
An ancient spreading yew tree stands on the north side of the church-yard.

The monuments and inscriptions furnish the following particulars.

Chancel.
North wall. A large marble monument, a canopy with drapery – two weeping cherubs holding 2 tablet busts of a lady and a clergyman. On a sarcophagus below this inscription. This monument is erected to the memory of Mrs. Dorothy Goswell late of the city of Exeter widow patroness of this place who by her late will bequeathed a set of communion plate for the use of this church as also a benefactor to the poor and likewise several benefactions to the poor in Exeter whose exemplary piety and charity caused her to be generally and very richly esteemed by all that knew her. She departed this life the 10th day of March 1745 in the 66th year of her age and was interred in a vault underneath. Also in memory of the revd. Mr Timothy Terry, vicar of this parish, son of the above said Mrs Goswell who by his also will gave Twenty pounds to beautify the chancel of this church. He departed this life the 16th day of April 1736 in the 30th year of his age and was interred in the same vault.
Arms in a lozenge – a Chevron or between 3 Garbs proper, with a bird (question a chough) standing on each sable. Impaling Sable
South wall a tablet.
The altar piece was erected and painted and the floor laid at the charge of the revd Mr Timothy Terry late vicar of Payhembury 1736.
Floor. *Hic jacit Robertus Terry vicarius de Pehembury qui obiit vicesimo die Octobris Anno Dom 1665, aetatis suae 65.*
Sacred to the precious memory of Mr Timothy Terry who died 16 April 1736 in the 30th year of his age.
Here lieth the body of William Potbury clerke son of Thomas Potbury vicar of this parish – died 27 July 1707 aetatis suae 31. Mrs. Elizabeth Saunders wife of Mr John Saunders of Uggaton in this parish sister of William Potbury died 22 Sept 1710 aged 42. Mary wife of Mr John Saunders died 31 Jan. 1735/6 aged 38
The revd. John Saunders of Uggaton in this parish died 26 July 1749 aged 76.
George Wescombe died 16 Feb. 1664, aged 24. Arms apparently – 2 Bars – on a quarter – bordered – 5 Billets in saltire

Nave.
South wall. A tablet. William Venn of Higher House in this parish died 24 June aged 86. Petronella his wife died 29 Oct. 1832 aged 92. Petronella wife of William Hex Venn of Whimple daughter of the above died 7 Aug 1820 aged 41 Petronella daughter of William Venn & Elizabeth Wright his wife of Upton in this parish granddaughter of W & P. Venn died 27 March 1819 aged 14 months.

North aisle
Tablet. Ann wife of John Venn of Lower House in this parish died 27 Nov 1795 aged 47 also John Venn died 25 March 1812 aged 77 also Gwen wife of John Venn died 12 Dec: 1819 aged 40 Arms Argent on a fess azure 3 escallops of the field.

A wooden Tablet dated 1606. Richard Venn gave to the poor of this parish £6.13.4. Thomasine Pigot gave to the poor £20. These two sums are vested in the parish stock and pay £1.6 yearly interest. 1669 Jane Saunders gave by will to the poor £8 yearly to be paid out of the late Palches estate

PLYMTREE

Davidson (pp. 393–6) visited [St John the Baptist] Plymtree on 24 June 1843 and noted it was 10 miles north east of Exeter. The church was restored in 1895–7 when the outer walls were extensively rebuilt by G. Fellowes Prynne and the rood screen and ceilure were repainted and gilded (Pevsner, *Devon*, 625–6). Five memorials are missing from the twelve that Davidson recorded.

This village church consists of a Nave about 48 feet long by 16 wide, a Chancel about 22 by 16 an aisle to the south 54 by 12, a porch over the south door, a tower at the western end of the nave, the nave & chancel open to the aisle by 5 pointed arches resting on columns formed by 4 shafts with hollow mouldings between them, having in each a niche for a statues and their capitals carved in foliage. The windows of the nave are of 4 lights with low arched heads in a horizontal frame, those of the chancel and aisle are formed into 3 lights with cinquefoiled heads and have perpendicular tracery in the arches. Some fragments of old coloured glass remain and in the eastern window some appears to have been introduced which is foreign and of modern date In the centre is a figure of the Virgin and child, and above an ancient coat of arms, viz. Azure 3 Garbs argent [now plain glass]. The south door is under a pointed arch adorned with foliage in the moulding over it a label resting on corbels of half angels holding shields and around the head of the arch a moulding of quatrefoils. The tower is of oblong form being wider than its length. It has been raised several feet in height, crowned in battlements pierced with quatrefoils & adorned with crocketted pinnacles, there is a turret for the stairs at the south eastern corner. In the western face of the tower above the windows is a large niche under a canopy with pinnacles in which the sitting figure of the Virgin crowned with the child on her knee. The ceilings are coved and plastered, a part in panels in the style of the 18th century. The chancel screen remains carved in oak, consisting of a range of pointed arches of four lights in each with cinquefoiled heads and perpendicular tracery in the head of the arch. Fan tracery spreading from shafts supports the rood loft in front of which is enriched with four various mouldings of foliage. The door way to the rood loft was in the south wall. The base of the screen is formed into a range of panels filled with painted whole length figures of evangelists martyrs bishops etc. in gaudy colours which have recently been restored. The chancel has been very handsomely fitted up and furnished with many of the showy and new steps accompaniments peculiar to Roman Catholic celebrations of worship. The eastern wall and the sides are covered in panels of old dark oak richly carved and representing various subjects in the history of our Lord etc, and in the centre above the altar the cornice of foliage is a cross with gilt nails in it as if it had supported a figure of the dying Saviour [removed]. The altar is also richly carved in oak in panels with figures of angels at the corners [now plain] above it against the wall is a white marble tablet partly gilt sculptured in bas relief representing the resurrection of our Lord with Roman soldiers etc [now at the western end of the south aisle] Upon the altar stands two large candlesticks richly carved and gilt with tall candles in them, and a large gilt metal dish for the offertory embossed in various devices in the centre the subject of the annunciation, the virgin kneeling at an altar and an eagle with a lily and a dove It has an inscription apparently in the Dutch language around it with the date 1739 [missing]. Books stamped with a cross in fold lie on the altar [missing]. On each side of it is an old carved oak chair partly gilt [missing]. In the south wall is a piscina under a trefoil-headed arch. Against the north wall outside of the altar rails are two large handsome sedilia of carved oak with elbows and turn up seats and above them two tablets well executed in base relief representing the history of the prodigal son, in one he appears indulging in riotous living and then as driven out by his companions, in the other he is as feeding swine, and meeting the embrace of his father. All these oak carvings are evidently of foreign execution [missing]. The floor of the chancel within the rails is covered with a carpet in pattern of encaustic tiles with figures of shields lions and other devices. In the nave and aisle are many of the old oak benches their ends carved in trefoiled panels etc. the font is of stone large & octagonal the sides sculptured in quatrefoils & foliage and its on a column of like shape ornamented with trefoil panels etc. The Font is of stone large & octagonal the sides sculptured in quatrefoils & foliage and rests on a column of like shape ornamented with trefoil headed niches. There is an alms box of old oak near the door. The pulpit is modern, the date 1697 with the letters J.L. are wrought on the pulpit cloth. There is a gallery at the west end of the nave built in 1719 in which is an organ [removed]. At the eastern end of the aisle was formerly an altar & there is a niche for a statue.

The monuments and inscriptions convey the following particulars.

Chancel.
North wall. A tablet. Beneath are deposited the remains of William James Arnold esq of Exeter collage Oxford who died the 21 June 1814 aged 21 years.
East wall. A tablet. To the memory of the revd Daniel Veysie B.D. late of Oriel college Oxford and for 20 years rector of this parish. He departed this life 7th of July 1817 aged 62.

Nave.
Floor. Here lyeth the bodie of Mr. Thomas. [missing]

South Aisle.
East wall. A tablet. Sacred to the memory of the very revd Charles Harward MA. Dean of the cathedral church of St Peter Exeter and of Hayne House in this parish who departed this life on the 15th day of July Anno Dom 1802 aged 79. also of Louisa his wife daughter of the Right Hon Sir William Yonge Bart of Escot in this county who departed this life on the 30th day of October An Dom 1811 aged 81 [missing]
Tablet. Sacred to the memory of Thomas Blake gent of Greenend. Obiit March 1. 1826 aged 63. [missing]
Floor. – --- Samford gent was buried Sept 2, 1621 [missing]
Roger Forde esquire was here buried July 21. 1631 [missing]
Abraham Webber gent died 11 October 1669 aged 84 Abigail his wife died 1 Dec 1670 aged 74 who lived together 57 years & 10 months. Mary the daughter of Walter Gale of Staplegrove Somerset and Granada child of the above died September 1671.

Thomasine Ford wife of Charles Ford of Plymtree esq and daughter of Abraham Webber gent died 20 Sept 1690 aged 69.

Here lieth the body of Richard Harward of this parish gent who was buried 5 Aug, 1685 & Rebecca his wife buried 16 July 1677. His eldest son John N. buried 18 Aug 1687. Mary his wife buried 21 Nov 1692 daughter of Edward Thrustone of West Buckland co Somerset gent. Rebecca daughter of Richard Harward buried 1673. – James son of Richard Harward buried 27 Nov 1695 George Harward of Langford son of Richard Harward gent died May 7 1762 aged 67.

Church yard

A tomb. John Pope of Woodbear Court gent died 31 Jan 1726 aged 79. William only son of the said John Pope died 14 Feb, 1764.

A stone. The revd John Fleming late fellow of Oriole College Oxford, rector of Plymtree 18 years died 26 March 1796 aged 51.

Extract from journal of the Exeter Diocesan Architectural Society, 6 June 1850

On Thursday last, the annual meeting of the Society took place at the Collage Hall, the Rev. Chancellor Harington in the Chair.

Mr. E. Ashworth, architect, of this city, then read an interesting paper on Plymtree Church. After some introductory remarks, Mr. Ashworth said the church is dedicated to St. Mary, and a rather rude representation of the virgin and child occupies a niche in the western face of the tower. In Domesday survey the place is Plumtrei, possessed by Bristrie in Edward the Confessor's time, and Odo Fitz Gamelyn in the reign of William the Conqueror. The church is wholly perpendicular, and consists of nave, south aisle, chancel and tower. The nave is lightened on the north side by three large square-headed windows, the arched heads of the lights being very flat. The angles of the splays and heads of these windows internally are disfigured by the architrave moulding of a classic building, plastered on, to correspond, it would seem, with the segment vault lining the roof, and partly panelled in octagons and diamonds which spring from two heavy dentil cornices, abutting most impertinently and obtrusively on the spandrels of the chancel arch, which itself appears to have been mutilated, through their western termination is countenanced by a little gallery [removed], whose swelling shafted columns reminds us of Sir Henry Wotton's animadversion on a practice "growne:" he says, "(I know not how) in certain places, too familiar, of making pillars swell in the middle as if they were sicke of some tympanie or dropsie, without any authentique pattern or rule to my knowledge, and unseemly to the very judgement of sight". The gallery chokes up a nicely panelled tower-arch. The pulpit accords with the gallery in style, and were it not recessed in one of the windows, would be much in our way, with is ponderous domed sounding-board, in taking a perspective view. The south aisle is separated from the nave by four pier arches, having a good point, and swept in a very quick curve near their springing on the expanding foliaged capital of the pillar. Two of the pier contain niches, much defaced, facing North.East. The pier opposite the jamb of the chancel arch is connected with it by a small arch, about ten inches wide, perhaps a hagioscope. The other jamb has on its west face an ornamental niche. This aisle is entered from a spacious porch, with a good double-moulded outer arch, and a band of quarter foils in circles on the parapet. The windows are good, having edge shafts to the splays, and the hood moulds springing from carved heads. One square-headed window over the porch is eclipsed by a large royal arms of George Iis time.

The rood screen is in a very perfect state. The fan tracery canopy is embossed with knots of foliage, the ribs are gilt, and the wedge-shaped panels shew traces of the original azure. It extends from north to south, the whole width of the church, unbroken by piers. All the cinque-foil headed panels in the lower part of the screen contain paintings, still very fresh, of saints, martyrs, and bishops; pre-eminent stands the Virgin saluting Elizabeth. The announcing angel, and the adoration of the Magi are also depicted here. Both south aisles and nave have very substantial old open benches. The twining foliage that edges the seat ends and the trefoil-headed panels are finely carved. There are, indeed, a few high pews, which hide part of the screen; and the south chancel aisle has an enclosure that would, with all decency, were it not a church, form a compartment of a dormitory in one of London model lodging houses [removed]. The font is situated close to the last pier westward, south of the nave. It is octagonal, boldly carved, and has an alms-box near it. A recess at the north end of the screen seems to have formerly contained a rood stair. The chancel is roofed with cradle ribs, and the plastered intervals are coloured blue. It is lighted by two square-headed windows on the north side. The east window contains some painted glass, and there is a window on the south side. The external quoins are without buttresses. The walls are lined with carved oak panelling. The altar reredos is composed of three ogees arched compartments, surmounted with a cresting. The central and widest of these contains a beautifully minute carving in alabaster, of the resurrection of our Lord. There is a piscina, its arch cinquefoiled, in the usual place. There are two carved stall seats, of late date, and the open seats of the chancel have good ends, surmounted by poppy heads, from a design, we believe, of Mr. Hayward, which stamps their merit at once. A parclose screen, with good carved gate, in one leaf, occupies the arch between the chancel and south aisle. The east window of this aisle is a made-up affair of two ogee-headed lights, braced by an arch outside. The priest's door is in the aisle, small, with depressed arch. Through this, we make our exit, to view the exterior of the church, and pause to admire the noble yew tree that shades the chancel, and seems, with its unfading greenery, an emblem of eternity itself.

The tower west of the nave is banded into three stages. Diagonal buttresses terminate near the top of the second stage, and here unfortunately the whole tower terminates, The upper story speaks for itself as having been entrusted to the tender mercies of a country builder for its restoration, (not very recently) the semi-hexagonal stair turret is stopped short, and finished off with a parapet and pinnacles of great pretensions. The windows of the bell chamber have imitation tracery executed in board. The pinnacles surmounting the tower are of a very composite character, and there is no cornice. Four spirited gargoyles, however, contrive to hang on without their usual resting-place.

There are five bells – the treble and second cast in 1826; the third has a legend, and is old, Ave Maria gratia plena; the fourth bell, 1669; and the fifth 1829.

BROADHEMBURY

Davidson (pp. 397–403) visited [St Andrew Apostle and Martyr] Broadhembury on 12 September 1828. He noted it was about 5 miles north west of Honiton. He observed 'the parish church of this village is a very interesting edifice as it contains several curious relics of antiquity and seems to have been adorned with some liberality of expense'. The chancel was rebuilt 1843 by John Hayward and restored in 1852–3 (Pevsner, *Devon*, 217). One memorial is missing from the thirteen that Davidson recorded.

It consists of a nave chancel south aisle & tower at the western end of the nave with a porch covering a door on the northern side, the entrance to which is by a pointed arch with several mouldings; above the entrance are three niches having canopies and the roof which is of stone is groined and adorned with tracery & foliage on the western side of the door is a recess or niche under which is a hollow basin evidently intended for holy water but the projecting part of the basin has been destroyed. The nave is 42 feet long by 18 wide, the roof lofty ribbed with oak & adorned with foliage at the intersections, it is divided from the tower by a lofty pointed arch & from the chancel by a flat arch also of considerable height against the aisle are 4 columns & 2 halves consisting of clustered shafts & alternate hollow mouldings having capitals of angular shapes carved into vine leaves grapes and foliage, these support pointed arches and in one of the spandrels on the side next the nave appears to be a niche supported by an angel surmounted by a canopy, but it seems to be covered with plaster or whitewash. On the north side is a very beautiful window with 3 lights having cinquefoil heads & tracery in the arch at the spring of the arches of the lights both within & without are 4 projecting corbels, those on the inside represent angels holding scrolls those o the outside are the figures of a man & woman the latter with the horned head dress the figures of two animals. –

A gallery crosses the western end of the nave in a most incongruous Roman style the pulpit is of wood & quite plain [now carved], some ancient tiles still remain in the floor [removed]. A modern screen of carved oak in the Roman style divided the nave from the chancel [removed], the door to the ancient rood loft with the staircase in a buttress against the north wall yet remain but the screen exists no longer on this side of the church. – The chancel is 21 feet long by 15 wide & has a door on the north side into the church yard – it is lighted by a pointed eastern window the tracery of which has been destroyed & replaced by 3 upright mullions & a transom. The south aisle is 64 feet by 12 wide and is lighted by 4 windows having each 3 lights with cinquefoil heads & tracery in their arches. A window at the eastern end is of larger dimensions having 4 lights with cinquefoil heads & tracery of elegant devices in the pointed arch. – In one of the columns against the nave is a niche with a tall canopy but much defaced & covered with whitewash. The eastern end of the aisle is elevated 2 steps above the level of the other parts and is separated from it by a portion of ancient screen with a rood loft, this consists of pointed arches carved in oak with tracery & tabernacle work but the old cornice has been replaced by some modern mouldings, this part of the aisle is also enclosed on the side next to the chancel by a lighter screen of similar devices [removed] – Against the south wall hangs an old iron helmet. – At the western end of the aisle stand the font which is a stone basin of octagonal form 2½ feet in diameter 3 feet high resting on a square column which is ornamented with shields and on 4 slender square pillars which are panelled & which stands one opposite to each face of the column – the whole rests on a square plinth, each of the eight sides of the basin is divided by sculptures into three compartments, the centre one a figure & on each side a panel with a trefoil head having shields in the middle one of the figures represents a bishop or abbot with his mitre and crosier, another a nun, the others cannot be ascertained as the whole of this beautiful specimen of taste and art is loaded with whitewash. The tower is 13 feet square at the base within the walls which are thick & strengthened by buttresses at the corners two on each side, there is an octagonal turret for the staircase at the North East corner which rises 5 feet above the battlements, on one of the faces of the turret about 20 feet from the ground is a niche with a canopy the western entrance to the tower is low under a pointed arch above it is a window of 4 lights with cinquefoil heads the belfry windows have 3 lights – The tower is 78 feet high to the top of the battlements and contains a clock & 5 bells which are dated and inscribed as follows "Sancta Thomas ora pro nobis" "God save the church. Mr Humphrey Lewis vicar 1714" – "1746" – "I to the church the living call and to the grave I summon all 1766" "T Bilbee 1767"

The monuments and inscriptions in Broad Hembury church are these. –
Against the north wall of the chancel at same height from the floor is a monument. consisting of a pediment supported by 4 Corinthian columns under which is a man in a robe and ruff kneeling at a desk, above the figure is a small tablet inscribed with some Latin verses and the date 1619, the name & was probably on another tablet below it which no longer exists there are 3 coats of arms with these bearings.
1. Quarterly. 1 & 4 (1) Sable a swan passant within a bordure engrails Or
2. (2) Barry of six Sable and Gules a canton of the first
3. (3) Barry of 7 Or & Azure a bend Gules a crescent for difference
    2nd (1) impaling (2)
    3rd (1) impaling (3)
At the eastern end of the aisle against the south wall is a marble monument consisting of a pediment supported by Corinthian columns the whole painted & gilded beneath which is inscribed Francis Drewe esq: died 24 Dec 1675 aged 71. Arms Drewe Ermine a Lion passant Gules impaling Waldron Crest on a small wreath Argent and Gules, a mound vert thereon a buck currant Or. –
On the floor at the eastern end of the aisle a stone to the memory of Thomas Drewe of Grange esq a deputy lieutenant & justice of the peace & some time knight of the shire for the county died 10th August 1707 – also Margaret his wife daughter of Sir John Prideaux of Netherton Bart by Susanna sister to John Lord Paulet late of Hinton St. George – who died 21 May 1695 – Arms Drewe impaling Prideaux – a chevron label of 3 points.

On the north side of the chancel a mural tablet thus inscribed In memory of Thomas Rose of Wotton Fitzpaine in the county of Dorset esq who died 9 Jan 1747 aged 68 and was buried in the family vault of that church. This was put up at the request of his only child Mary, the wife of Francis Drewe of Grange in the parish esquire, who died 7 Nov 1749 age 34 and was buried in this church. Above are the arms Rose viz. Sable on a pale le 3 roses in pale Gules leafed vert Crest on a wreath le & sable a rose Gules leafed vert. Below another coat Drewe impaling Rose.

On the north side of the chancel a mural tablet surmounted by an urn & bearing the inscription.

This monument is erected to the memory of Francis Drewe esq also of Grange in this parish who died 10 Feb 1773 aged 61 years. He was the eldest son of Francis Drewe esq: also of Grange who represented the city of Exeter in four successive parliaments & was lineally descended from Edward Drewe esq: Sergeant at law to Queen Elizabeth & recorder of the city of London in that reign – he was an upright magistrate – Having been twice married he had by his first wife 7 sons, 6 of who survived him, and by his second wife 2 sons and 3 daughters who all survive him. In the family vault of this church are also deposited the remains of Francis Rose Drewe esq his eldest son who died unmarried 29 April 1801 aged 63 years. There are also deposited in the same vault the remains of Edward Drewe his third son who died 26 April 1755 in the 14th year of his age also of Catherine his second daughter who died 13 April 1773 in the 15th year of her age Also of Harriet Maria daughter and only child of Richard Rose Drewe of the city of Exeter esq: his fourth son who died 31 August. 1792 in the 15th year of her age. Also the remains of the said Richard Rose Drewe esq: who died 29 Jan 1801 aged 58 years. Also the remains of Charles Drewe esq: only son of John Rose Drewe of the city of London esq: his sixth son who died 5 Nov 1801 aged 22. Arms Drewe impaling dexter Rose – sinister a chevron between 3 lions heads erased – crowned – Crest a buck courant. –

Against the north wall of the nave a mural tablet.
In memory of William Drewe of Cranmer in this parish who died 28 August 1759 aged 62 and Joan his wife who died 25 May 1809 aged 73. Also their issue William Drewe who died Feb 1766 aged 8 months. Margaret Drewe who died 19 Feb 1787 aged 21 years Susannah Drewe who died 17th April 1809 aged 38 years William Drewe who died 17 August 1810 aged 37 years. John Drewe who died 28 April 1818 aged 54 years and are all deposited in the north side of this church yard. This monument is erected by their only surviving son and brother Robert Drewe.

South side of chancel – mural tablet
In memory of Edward Drewe LLB late vicar of this parish died 25 June 1810 aged 53. Arms Drewe impaling Quarterly 1 & 4 Quarterly 1 & 4 a bend rompu between 6 martlets. 2&3 Three tablets heads erased 2&1. 2&3. Two barry of 4 surmounted by a crop charged with 5 talbots heads erased. Crest a buck courant
N wall of chancel a mural tablet
In the family vault of this church are deposited the remains of the revd. Herman Drewe AM rector of Wotton Fitzpaine Sheldon and Combrawleigh 7th son of Francis Drewe of the Grange esq. and Mary his wife daughter and heiress of Thomas Rose of Wotton in the co: of Dorset esq: who died 19 April 1818 aged 68 In memory of her beloved father this tablet was placed by Mary wife of the rev Lewis Way of Stanstead park Sussex.
On the floor of the aisle. Here lyeth the body of Susanna the relict of Andrew Davy of Boldhay in the parish of Zeal Monachorum in the co: of Devon esq: and daughter

of Francis Drewe of Grange esq: who died 27 Feb 1672 Arms – a chevron between
3 mullets & another for difference impaling Drewe.
Three hatchments hang in the aisle.1. Drewe. 2. Drewe. With the motto "*Delectare in
Domino*" 3. Drewe impaling dexter Rose. Sinister Argent a chevron Sable between
3 lions heads couped Gules crowned Or. On the centre 2 escutcheons of pretence
bearing the arms of his wives as in pale. [missing] –
On the floor of the nave. Here lieth the body of Mrs Grace Duck who was the wife
of Nicholas Duck rector of --- of Exon who departed this life 16 Sept 16-4. Arms On
a fess wavy 3 fusils impaling within a bordure engrailed a wyvern rampant Crest on
a wreath an anchor erect having a serpent entwined around the shaft.
On the floor of the aisle – Mrs Mary Seaward of Clist St George widow late of Priory
who died 15 March 1724 also Catherine Hill an infant her granddaughter also Edward
Hill son of Richard Hill of Priory esq: who died 13 July 1730 aged 30. Richard Hill
of Priory esq died 19 Nov 1737 aged 83. Mary relict of Richard Hill esq: died 15 May
1743 aged 66
South wall of the aisle a tablet of white marble
Richard Hill of Priory esq. second son of Edward Hill of Priory ninth son of Thomas
Hill of Hills' court in Shropshire esq. he married Mary only daughter of John
Seaward of Clist St George in this county elder brother of Sir Thomas Seaward of
Exon Kt. MP for that city by who he had on son Edward who died 17 July unmarried
and 4 daughters – Mary who erected this monument to his memory – Grace the wife
of Humphrey Sydenham of Combe in the parish of Dulverton esq. Hannah the wife
of Richard Nutcombe of Nutcombe in the parish of Clayhanger esq and Katherine
who died an infant. He died 19 Nov. 18773 aged 82 years. No arms but on the top of
the monument is a circular tower embattled
South wall of the aisle a mural tablet with an urn.
In memory of Ellery wife of St. Barb Sydenham esq: of Combe in the co: of
Somerset eldest daughter of Sydenham Williams esq: of Herringtone in the co: of
Dorset who died 26 March 1794 aged 67. Arms – Argent 3 coots sable armed gules 2
& 1 within a bordure engrailed Gules charged with alternate bezants & crosses patees
Or – impaling Argent 3 goats passant Sable 2&1.
On the floor of the nave. – William Pratt. Bridget his wife and Elizabeth their eldest
daughter" rest defaced

Against the south wall of the aisle is a tablet this inscription "1725 a person unknown
gave interest of £10 per annum: to poor labourers receiving no monthly pay.
1754 The rev. Hugh Lewis vicar of this parish gave by will the interest of £20 per
annum: to the poor honest industrious labourers who receive no monthly relief.
1755 Mrs Margaret Lewis gave by will the interest of £20 per annum: to poor honest
industrious labourers who received no monthly relief.
1756. Mrs Mary Hill by will a meadow in this parish (called butchers meadow) the
rent of which was to be expended in bread and distributed half yearly by the minister
and church wardens for the time being to the poorest families (clear annual rent
about £9) –
1759 Mr William Shiles gave by will the interest of £10 per annum: to poor labourers
who receive no monthly pay.
1771. Mr Peter Simons gave by will the interest of £5 per annum: to poor labourers
who receive no monthly pay.

Married 13 Oct. 1831 in Exeter, William Miles esq: of the 2nd regiment of Life guards, to Dorothea Rose, only surviving child of the late John Drewe esq of the Grange, in the co of Devon – Recorded newspaper

For a genealogy of the family of Drew of Ireland descended from that of Devon with many alliances see 'The Topographer and Genealogist' for March 1847. Vol. II. p 209 & seq.

KENTISBEARE

Davidson (pp. 405–12) visited [St Mary] Kentisbeare on 12 September 1828 and noted it was about 3 miles east of Cullompton. He observed that 'the church of this parish stands on the south western side of the village and is a very interesting edifice. It consists of a nave, chancel, south aisle and tower at the western end of the nave.' The church was restored in 1865–6 by John Hayward with reseating, re-flooring and new vestry (Pevsner, *Devon*, 514–15). Two memorials are missing from the fifteen that Davidson recorded.

The nave is 34 feet long and 17 wide and is entered by a pointed door way in the north wall having over it on the outside a niche with a canopy, the porch has also a similar niche with a canopy over the entrance. The nave is lighted by windows having 3 lights each with cinquefoil heads & their inner arches adorned with foliage, the roof was repaired in 1757. The pulpit is plain, in the Roman style & is dated 1738. The font is of stone octagonal 2½ feet in diameter & sculptured on the sides with alternative shields and quatrefoils, it rests upon an octagonal column & a square plinth. A gallery across the nave & the aisle at the western end, it is in an incongruous Roman style & is supported by Roman columns & is beautified with paintings and heads it bears the letters & date W.R.A. 1632 & 1704 when it was probably painted a fresh, with the following lines & coats of arms on the panels:
Anstice the wife of Robert Wiscombe here
Built this loft in the church of Kentisbeare
For the convenient hearing of the word
And praising of the true and living Lord
She also gave the profit of the same
Unto the poor in memory of her name
The donors are deceased and all wee
Who now survive them their good acts do see
Which if they should be quickly out of mind
Discourage 'twill some piously inclined
The reason why these lines are set to view
It is because the poor should have their due. WRA 1632
Arms. Azure a chevron between 3 Lions heads erased Or conjured Gules (Wyndham) – Argent 3 bulls heads caboshed Sable attired Or (Walrond) –

The ancient screen dividing the nave from the chancel and supporting the rood loft remains entire it extends also across the aisle the eastern end of which it divides & forms into a chapel called the Waldrons aisle it consists of a lines of pointed arches divided by mullions & tracery into openings with cinquefoil & trefoil heads & is enriched with shields tracery foliage and tabernacle work it has 4 cornices or mouldings carved into various foliage vine leaves grapes & flowers: a door in the south wall opens to a stair case in a projecting buttress which leads to the rood loft

above the screen & here are the mortises into which were fixed the cross and the various figures employed about the rood. There are 2 doorways in the screen one opening in the centre of the chancel the other to the Waldrons' aisle – The whole is of oak painted and gilded. The chancel is 30 feet long by 17 wide & has 3 windows in the north side having 2 lights each with cinquefoil heads, the eastern window is pointed having 4 lights with cinquefoil heads & tracery in the arches & retaining some fragments of painted glass, A door on the south side opens into a modern vestry, against the north wall is an ancient lectern with Fox's martyrs, Jewel's works & the Homilies chained to it but in a perishing condition [removed]. The south aisle is 43 feet long by 14 wide from the western end to the screen & when the Waldrons aisle is added which is 19 feet the total length is 62 feet. The aisle including the chapel is divided from the nave and chancel by 4 columns & 2 halves consisting each of 4 shafts with intervening hollow mouldings. The capitals are angular & some enriched by foliage and coats of arms & supporting pointed arches these are windows in the south wall each having 3 lights with cinquefoil heads & tracery in the arches which are acutely pointed, the eastern window has 4 lights & is otherwise similar to those on the south side. The roof is ribbed with oak having foliage at the intersections & the springers are supported by angels holding shields & each having a cross upon his head, at eastern end of the aisle on the south side of the windows is a rude painting on the wall representing 2 persons at the foot of a tree under a circular arch supported by Corinthian columns [removed] – a door in the south wall of the Waldron aisle leads into the churchyard. The arms upon the capitals of the columns between the nave & the aisle are these – a bend sinister wavy cotise – Quarterly 1&4 Argent a bend wavy cotised (Whiting) 2&3 & Gules within a bordure engrailed (angles) 3 escallops (argent) – Per fess azure & Gules 3 fleurs de lis Or – On the capital next the Waldron aisle appears alternately with wool packs 2 bars nebuly on a chief a lion passant gardant – a ship in the sea with a warrior armed in the bow The tower is 10 feet square within the walls at the base, & has an octagonal stair turret at the North East corner, the height is 60 feet to the top of the battlements 65 to the top of the turret, there are buttress & pinnacles at the corners – it contains 5 bells inscribed as follows
"Rev. Robert Tripp rector 1822"
"Mr. Roger Grubham Rector God save the church 1710" Arms 2 bars between 9 martletts. Crest a wyverns head.
"I.P. 1666" – "Leave thanks to God 1616" – "Mr. Roger Grubham rector gave three guineas 1710" arms as above.

An ancient yew tree stands on the NE side of the churchyard.

The Walronds chapel is divided from the Chancel by an open screen carved in oak it is finished with a square head & the arches are pointed but the door way into the chancel is under a flat arch & the whole is of later date than the screen already described – On the mouldings having shields exhibiting these bearings but several of them are defaced by time.
1) Quarterly 1&4 a bend wavy cotised (Whiting) 2&3 a lion rampant crowned
2) Quarterly 1&4 a bend cotised 2&3. Three fishes hauriant
3) Quarterly 1&4 a bend wavy cotised. 2&3. a cross Moline. A label of 3 points.
4) Quarterly 1&4 a bend wavy cotised. 2&3 defaced.
5) Defaced.

The chapel is fitted with panelling and pews in ancient carved oak painted & inscribed with numerous sentences from scripture and adorned with many coats of arms [removed]. On the north side against the chancel wall is an ancient marble altar tomb without ornamental sculptures – the inscription which appears to have been upon the brass fillet round the edge is gone – its length is 5 feet and width 2 feet 6 inches Two coats of arms remain one on the side the other at the end engraved brass shields & having the following bearings on both.
Quarterly of 6. 1. a saltier engrailed 2. on a chief a lion passant. 3. on a bend cotised 3 spread eagles 4.2 bends Or. 5, Barry bends of 10. 6. Gules a fess checky between 6 crosses patees fitched.

Against the eastern wall immediately over the end of the tomb is an oblong brass plate bearing the following inscription in the gothic letter
Here lyeth the body of Mary Guildford daughter of Sir Robert Wotton of Kent Knight first wife of Sir Henry Guildford Knight of the garter and controller of Household to the most noble & mighty prince Henry the VIII Kyng of England France & Ireland defender of the feyth & immediately under God of the churches of England & Ireland supreme head and one of Lys most honourable privy counsellor and late wyffe of Sir Gawyn Carew Knight who ended this life the XVII day of September M°CCCCC° VIII [missing]

On the south wall side of the chancel against the wall under a window is a large altar tomb of marble 6 feet long & 3 wide the side and ends sculptured in panels & quatrefoils having shields in their centres, on the slab are two small figures in brass representing a knight armour but without his helmet and his wife her hands in the posture of pray. The following inscription is on a brass label below them.
Orate pro animabus Johannis Whiting Armiger et Anne consort. sue qui obiit XV die Marcii Ano Dni m° CCCCCXXIX° Quorum animas propicietur Deo Amen. On the slab are 4 coats of arms in brass shields 2 above & below the knight with the same bearings viz. Quarterly 1&4 a bend wavy (Whiting) cotised sable 2&3 within a bordure engrailed 3 escallops (Erle) above and below his wife Party p fess 3 fleurs de lis
There are several shields on the side and ends of the tomb all shewing the same coats of arms singly and impaled –

There are not any other tombs or inscribed stones visible in this chapel but coats of arms affixed around the pews and panelling are numerous exhibiting the following bearings & alliances. [missing]
(Walrond. Argent 3 bulls heads caboshed Sable attired Or impaling) Per fess Azure & Gules 3 Fleurs de lis Or.
Walrond impaling Or fretty Azure.
Walrond impaling Argent within a bordure engrailed 3 lions rampant Gules
Walrond impaling Sable a chevron Ermine between 3 mullets Argent (Chamberlain)
Walrond impaling Per pale Gules & vert a lion rampant Ermine
Walrond impaling Argent 2 bars Azure over all an eagle displaying Gules (Speke)
Walrond Quarterly with Gules 3 holly leaves
Walrond impaling Or on a bend Gules 3 fess de Moulin Argent (Speedcot)
Vert on a bend cotised Argent (defaced) impaling Walrond
Argent a chevron between 3 peacocks in their pride impaling Walrond

Defaced/ impaling Walrond
Walrond impaling Argent a fess between 3 mans' legs couped Sable (Gambon)
Walrond impaling Argent a bend Sable wavy a bordure engrailed of the second
Walrond impaling a bend wavy cotised (Whiting)
A wyvern impaling Walrond
A saltier engrailed
Quarterly Whiting and Per fess Azure 3 fleurs de lis Or
Argent 3 ash keys between 2 chevrons (Ayshford) impaling Walrond.
On a fess cotised sable a crescent between 2 plates Argent impaling Walrond.
Whiting quarterly with 3 grey herons heads erased Or langued Gules.
Gules 3 fished naiant in pale Or impaling Walrond (Whiting)
Or a per as Moulin Gules impaling Walrond
Ayshford impaling Whiting (Ag. A Bend wavy)
A fish embowed Argent finned & tailed Or impaling Whiting
Walrond impaling 3 bars wavy Argent.
In a lozenge – Sable fretty Argent (Harrington)
Walrond impaling – Ermine on a chevron Azure 3 mullets
In a lozenge – Sable a saltier engrailed Argent
Walrond impaling Argent on a bend sable 3 cross crosslets fitchee Or in chief 3
martlets of the second
Walrond impaling Or a bend Sable 3
In a lozenge – Barry of 8 --- and sable
In a lozenge. Sable 6 mullets 32 & 1 Argent (Bonville)
Walrond impaling Or a bend Gules 3 fess de Moulin Argent (Speedcot)
Walrond impaling Argent on a chevron Sable 3 roses of the field. (Gilbert)
Walrond impaling masonry Argent Sable a chief indented of the first (Reynell)
Walrond quarterly with Or fretty azure
Walrond quarterly with Argent a bend wavy cotised Sable (Whiting)
Walrond quarterly with (Sable) 6 fishes hauriant 3. 2. & 1 Argent (Dishacre)
Walrond quarterly with Argent on a triangle Sable 3 bezants (per of couples & 27 a
chevron en-arched)
Walrond quarterly with Argent 2 irons glaziers in saltire Sable between 4 pears
pendant Gules (query or) (Keloways)
Or on a bend Gules 3 fess de Moulin Argent (Speedcot)
Gules 3 greyhounds courant in pale argent. (Whiting
Argent on a chief sable 3 -- (defaced)
Bendy -- and Or
Gules 3 cross crosslets Argent impaling Whiting
Whiting impaling Sable a bend ermine on a chief Argent 3 torteaux
Whiting impaling Argent a chevron between 3 fishes hauriant Gules (question Hake)
Argent a pair of wings points downwards Sable impaling Whiting
Ermine a cross fleury Sable impaling Whiting
Per chevron Gules and ermine
A fish hauriant argent finned Or between 3 mullets
Azure a chevron between 3 pears pendant Argent
Azure a bend wavy Argent
Gules a cross patonce Argent
Sable a cross engrailed Argent

Gules on a bend engrailed Argent 3 coots Sable
Barry of 6 Gules and Ermine
On the floor of the south aisle is a stone on which a whole length figure has been engraved but whether male of female cannot now be discovered these letters of the inscription only remain '--*lrond - ppiciet Deus Amen'*

In the church yard on the south side of the chancel are 2 altar tombs thus inscribed Mrs Mary Walrond daughter of Henry Walrond esq: of Bradfield died at Topsham 7 Sept 1743 & was here interred pursuant to her own age 64.
Joseph Lyons Walrond esq of Montrath died 16 Jan 1815 aged 63. Lyons Walrond esq: son of Joseph Lyons Walrond esq: died from his horse falling with him 21 May 1819 aged 19.

On the floor of the chancel --- body of Richard -- the pastor of this parish and Mary his --- Mary died May 26: 1652 Richard April 10, 1656.
Floor of chancel. *In spe vitae resurrectionis requiescit depositum desideratissimi juvenis -- eri Rogeri Grubham hujus ecclesiae rectoris secundo genito qui obiit 16 Sept AD. 1699 aet suae 18. Etiam Rogeri Grubham patris hujus ecclesiae per 44 annos rectoris qui obiit 19 May 1726 aet: 76. Atque ---ae uxoris supra dicti Rogeri Grubham rectoris 10 May 1727.*

Against the north wall of the nave is a black marble tablet under an entablature supported by 2 Corinthian columns inscribed – In memory of William Eveleigh gent: who died 23 June 1671 and of Johan his wife who died -- and also of Elizabeth their daughter wife of the rev. Dr. Nicholas Hall Treasurer of the cathedral church of St Peter Exon who died 28 Feb. 1697 and of William Eveleigh their son MA & rector of Woolbrough who died 29 Jan 1700. Lastly of Mary their daughter wife of John Were of Culmstock gent who died -- Arms. Per pale Or & Sable 2 chevrons between 3 griffons passant all counter charged.
Crest a unicorn's head erased per chevron Or & Sable holding in his mouth a branch vert. 2 coats on the sides both – Sable 3 talbots heads erased Argent collard Gules a crescent for difference (Hall)
On the floor of the nave. here lyeth the bodies of William Eveleigh gent: who dies 23 June 1671 and of William his son who died 22 Jan 1700.
Floor of So aisle Here lieth the body of Robert Wiscombe who died 5 May AD 1630.
Floor Nave. – Here lieth the body of Thomas Butson of the par. – who died the -- of May.
Here lieth the body of -- Butson
Floor S. aisle – here lieth the body of Mrs. Mary Hurley

Against the wall of the south aisle is a tablet thus inscribed [missing]
Robert Wiscombe of this parish clothier gave to the poor here of £110 the £100 to be bestowed in lands. Anstice his wife to further his intent added to it £14 with which is purchased £6 a year out of Berry Parks parcel of Pool farm to remain for the use of the said poor for ever. She founded this loft and devised the annual profit thereof with the profit of the £30 more now by her last will devised to the use of the said poore for ever She purchased the church house for the term of 3 lives for the impotent poor of this parish to dwell in.
Tis not of glory vain these things are brought to view

Its thus recorded here the poore may have their due
Without obscuring of the founder's will
Which in some places is a custom ill
He departed this life May 3. 1630
We hope his soul to heaven is gone
Through Christ his saviour's mercy
She persevered in pious works in charity and devotion
Heaven to attain for evermore through Christ his death and passion.

Against the north wall of the Nave a tablet thus inscribed
Edmund Crosse of this parish clothier hath given to the use and -- of the poore and
impotent people of this parish the sum of £100 to be employed for the best use and
benefit of the said impotent poore the profit where of arising to be yearly distributed
to such of the said pore as have most need by and with the approbation of my
executor and overseer the principal to remain for ever or land in foe simple there
with purchased by and with the consent of my overseers or 5 of the most sufficient
inhabitants of the aforesaid parish of Kentisbeare for the time being

Against the south wall of the nave is a tablet with this inscription Anstice Westcombe
gave the sum of £30 the interest there of to remain to the use of the poor of the said
parish for ever
Armond Butson gave the sum of £10
Oliver Buston his son gave £10
John Berry gave £10
John Facie gave £10
William Walrond gave £6.13,4
Ann Hake gave 40/-
Ane Willy of Willand gave £6
John Bale gave £20
Agnes Helfield gave £50
Thomas Butson gave £40
Henry Butson gave £10
William Everleigh gave £10
William Eveleigh jun. gave £4
Robert Merson gave £5
John Westlake gave £10
There is £6.10 more given for the use of the poor by whom the same was given cannot
be remembered. The sum total is £454.3,4 the interest there of is to be distributed by
the churchwardens and overseers for the poor of the said parish to such poor as have
no monthly pay £3 of the said interest money is to given in bread yearly.
Robert Westcombe gave £100 to be laid out in land & for the better improvement
there off Anstice his wife did freely contribute £14 & with the same did purchase £6
per annum: for ever to be paid out of 2 fields called Berry Parks being part of Pool
farm to be distributed the approbation of the churchwardens for the time being and
the heir of Bradfield for ever.
Anstice Wescombe did also erect the loft in the parish church of Kentisbeare & gave
the profit of the same to the poor of the parish for ever
Edmund Cross gave £100 the interest thereof to remain to the use of the poor of this
place for ever to be distributed yearly by the approbation of the executor & trustees

of his last will & testament or 5 of the most sufficient inhabitants of the said parish to such poor as have no monthly pay.

John Sanders of this parish gave £3 to be paid every year to the poor to be distributed yearly on Christmas day the money to be paid out of an estate called Sheppards' rally lying in the parish of Dunkeswell.

The waste lands in Kentisbeare were enclosed under an act 41 Geo: 3 the Honourable Charles Percy Wyndham then lord of the manor, the map and awards are preserved in the church chest.

Newspaper cutting, Trewman's Flying Post, *dated 5 March 1857*
Monumental Brasses: Ten Guineas Reward
Stolen from a tomb within the Church of Kentisbeare, near Cullompton, two Flat Monumental Brass Figures of an Esquire and his Wife. Of about two feet in length. The brass inscription, left untouched, bears the date of 1520. Whoever will restore these figures to J. W. Walrond, Esq., of Bradfield, Cullompton, Devon, will receive five guineas reward; and whoever will give such information as may convict the offender, shall also receive five guineas reward.

(*In the margin:* Amongst the names of churchwardens is Pratt a family of this name inhabited an old house called Kingsmill in a room of which is a coat of arms the same as that by Lord Camden. Memo: coll memo book W.w. p 32)

SHELDON

Davidson (p. 413) visited [St James the Greater] Sheldon on 25 September 1828 and noted it was about 7 miles north of Honiton. He observed that 'the extent of this parish is only about 600 or 700 acres of which about half is enclosed and half remains waste or common. The manor is divided among the freeholders.' The church was rebuilt on the old foundations in 1871 by John Hayward (Pevsner, *Devon*, 726).

The church consists only of a nave 28 feet long by 13 wide a chancel 16 by 13 and a tower at the western end 7 feet long by 8 wide. The chancel is parted from the nave by an open screen carved in oak it consists of 15 arches or openings divided by mullions into lights having cinquefoil heads & is adorned with quatrefoils above them – the chancel window has 2 lights with cinquefoil heads & is square on the top finished with a label on the outside [now pointed arches]. The nave has one window of 3 lights with flat heads. there is a niche for holy water on the east side of the porch – The font is of stone rude and ancient it is circular basin 2 feet diameter resting on a cylindrical column, the whole is 3 feet high & without ornamentation. – The church plate has only a cup of silver inscribed Sheldon 1809. The registers commence in 1721. The tower which is 38 feet high to the top of the battlements contains 3 bells one of them is dated 1620 but the two others are much more ancient & have both the same inscription in the gothic letters something like the following: *Est nuda --- collatum JLS istud -- nomen amatum. –*

Between the battlements in the centres of the north & south sides of the tower are niches & the southern one seems to have contained a statue in relief – The living is a rectory & this is held by the revd. CE Band who also holds Comberaleigh & is resident there, the sum paid as a composition for tithes does not amount to £100 a year. There is not a single monument or inscribed stone in the church.

CULLOMPTON

Davidson (pp. 417–29) visited [St Andrew] Cullompton on 25 July 1843 and noted it was 12 miles north east of Exeter. He observed that 'the large and handsome church of this parish which attests the former opulence of the town and the prosperity of its manufacturers is a highly interesting object to the architect and antiquary'. The church was restored in 1848–50 by Edward Ashworth (Pevsner, *Devon*, 303–4). Twenty-seven memorials are missing from the fifty-six that Davidson recorded.

It consists of a nave Chancel, three aisles, one on the north and two on the south, a Tower at the western end of the nave and a large porch covering the south door. The Nave is about 70 feet long by 24 wide within the walls, the chancel about 30 by 21 and they open to the north and south aisles by 6 low pointed arches on each side resting on columns formed by shafts with intervening mouldings their capitals boldly carved in foliage cherubs and grotesque figures. They are lighted by 6 clerestory windows in each side of 3 lights with cinquefoiled heads under low pointed arches having 8. foiled openings and between the lights. The chancel eastern window has been modernised in the most unseemly style, two other windows are made by 3 lights with cinquefoiled ogee heads under pointed arches with perpendicular tracery. The roofs are coved and divided by ribs into quarter panels and again into angular compartments by mouldings having bosses of foliage at the intersections the whole enriched with foliage painted and gilt. The ribs are supported by whole length figures of angels with crosses on their heads holding some crosses, other shields charged with a cross, and others open books, and these stand upon corbels beneath the cornice which is carved in foliage and gilt.
The north aisle is lighted by 6 windows on the side one at each end under pointed arches divided by two subarches and mullions into 4 lights with ogee arched & cinquefoiled heads and perpendicular tracery above. Two of these windows have a transom & therefore are made into 8 lights. In the eastern window are some fragments painted glass in architectural designs. The north aisle 85 feet long by 15 wide. Externally the walls supported by buttresses of three stages on the tops of which are gargoyles of uncouth animals around the roof core a parapet and battlements ornamented with quatrefoils.
There is a half turret for the stairs to the rood loft embattled in the same manner at the western end is a door under a pointed arch with foliage in the mouldings.

(In the margin: Cutting, no name of newspaper, dated 26 November [1843]
Mr Urban,
In repairing the church of Cullompton, Devon last year, the workmen, scraping the mortar off the walls and door, laid open many paintings both of landscapes, buildings, and figures, all of them sacred subjects, and emblems of the Passion, &, surrounded with interlaced borders, and explained by scrolls in black letter. Some of your correspondents in the neighbourhood may, perhaps give up a fuller account of

these paintings, which the ignorance of russicks whited over immediately. If these were of the same of John Lane, who built an aisle or chancel adjoining to the church, 1526, they are of the 16th century. Mr Polwhele (II.254, 255) ascribes the nave to the same time of Edward I. B.)

The south aisle opens to Lane's aisle except at the eastern end which is lighted by 2 windows one east and one south, of the same design as those of the north aisle. The roofs of both aisles are nearly flat, ribbed and divided into panels with bosses of foliage at the intersections all gaudily painted. Externally the walls of the south aisle are crowned by a parapet and battlements ornamented with quatrefoils, a small door opens into the aisle from the church yard under a low arch of several mouldings the spandrels richly carved in foliage. This aisle is about 87 feet long by 14 wide. The porch covering the door into the south aisle is 12 feet by 8 wide, its walls are supported by buttresses of two stages at the angles having gargoyles above them. The door way is under a pointed arch with foliage in the mouldings, the walls are finished with a parapet & battlements ornamented with quatrefoils. There is a room over the porch with a window formed by two cinquefoiled lights in a quadrangular frame.

Lane's aisle is south of the South aisle and is about 57 feet long by 18 wide within the walls. The aisle opens to each other by low pointed arches on columns of clustered shafts & mouldings their capitals richly carved in foliage. The columns are strengthened by buttresses on the north side in several stages relived with niches containing statues of ecclesiastics saints holding scrolls and surmounted by canopies and crocketted pinnacles. This aisle is lighted by 5 windows on the south, one at the eastern and one at the western end under pointed arches varying in their form but divided by two sub-arches into four lights with ogee cinquefoiled heads and perpendicular transoms. The roof is vaulted with stone and elaborately ornamented with fan tracery springing from corbels, over the capitals of the columns and in the side walls between the windows, of angels holding shields charged with mercantile marks and centring in foliated pendants bosses beautifully sculptured in figures of angels holding shields charged with mercantile devices.

On the floor is a stone which formerly bore the brass figures of John Lane and his wife but these have been carried off. The inscription remaining legible. *Hic jacet Johannes Lane Mercator hujusque capellae fundator cum Thomasina uxor sua qui dictus John obiit XV die. Februarii ano Dom millo ccccc°xxviij°* [missing]

Externally the walls of this aisle are supported by buttresses of three stages ornamented by stones cut in various designs of relief – the letters J.L. – ships – anchors – merchants marks – and other devices. Above the buttresses is a cornice ornamented with sculpture in relief of foliage woolpacks & various devices, and over them are gargoyles of grotesque figures. The walls are finished by an open embattled parapet enriched with quarter foils their centres ornamented with foliage roses etc.

Below the windows on a course of white stone is engraved & painted black in old letters the following inscription which commences at the north western corner & extends the whole length and breadth of the aisle to the north eastern corner. "In honour of God & his mother Mary remember the souls of John Lane *wapnt. custos lanarius* † and the sowle of Tomsyn his wife to have in memory † with all other their children & friends of your own ch'ryty † which were founders of this chapel & here lyeth yn sepulchre † the yere of owner Lord God a thousand fyve hundredth six and twynti † God of his grace on the both soules to have mercy † and finally bring them to the eternal glory amen for charity" [missing]

The tower of this church is the most highly ornamented part of the structure though the perishable nature of the stone of which the parts are composed has occasioned many of its beauties to be defaced by time & weathering. It is 17 feet long by 15 wide within the walls which are 7 feet thick at the base, and 100 feet high to the top of the battlements: the total height to the summit of the vanes is 120 feet. The face of the structure is divided by string courses into 5 stages, the angles are supported by heavy buttresses diminishing in size at the string courses. The battlements are ornamented by what appears to be the remains of an earlier building, viz pinnacles and gargoyles of rude figures worked onto the face of the wall. The west front has a door way under a pointed arch with a horizontal label and quatrefoils in the spandrels, above it a window under a pointed arch made by sub arches and mullions into 4 lights with perpendicular tracery above. On each side of the window is a panel of richly carved stone, on the north side the Royal arms with crown and supporters on the south the arms of Bishop Vesey supported by two men, with the name "John Vesey" Below these panels are the words sunk in the stone "In the year of our Lord a. M.D.X.L.V. we began to build" over the windows are the remains of a large piece of Sculpture representing the crucifixion viz the cross surmounted by a canopy and on each side the mutilated figures of women. Above it may be traced a part of an inscription viz "John Manning & Katherine his wyfe" – on each side are ornamented niches, that on the north containing a standing figure of K Edward the sixth holding the sceptre and orb, and above the words "K. Edward VI", that on the south St. George and a dragon with the letters "St. George"

The belfry windows are filled with stonework richly carved – In the north face of the tower is a panel supported by columns and ornamented as the others the subject of which appears to have been the resurrection of our Lord but it is much defaced. On each of it is a large fleur de lis [all the ornamentation is degraded]. On this side of the tower is a half hexagonal turret for the staircase. On the south side are similar panels and columns one representing Adam and Eve with a tree between them much defaced. Two others contain shields charged apparently with these coats of arms.
I A Chevron 3 leopards faces impaling a Bend
II Quarterly 1st & 4th a Fret with a chief 2nd & 3rd 3 pairs of pincers (question) impaling Quarterly 1st defaced 2nd a Lion rampant 3rd on a chevron --- 4th 2 Bends indented. (question reguardant)
The summit of the tower has an embattlement parapet with open quatrefoils a crocketed pinnacles at each corner supported by smaller ones at its base, all terminating in finials and gilt vanes.
Returning to the interior. A rich and handsome chancel screen remains extending across the nave and both aisles. It consists of a range of 11 pointed arches of 4 lights with cinquefoiled heads and perpendicular tracery above, between them are shafts from which springs the fan tracery which forms the base of the rood loft, in front of which are five series of mouldings of various foliage all richly carved in oak painted

and gilt. The whole forms a splendid specimen of art. At the western end of the church repose on the floor some huge blocks of oak which formed a portion of the holy rood (so called) itself, these are carved in the representation of rocks & stones on which lie sculls & bones & on the top are the holes for the feet of the crosses & the figures of saints. A side screen between the chancel and the south aisle is not so rich and more in decay. One between the chancel and the north aisle is of later date and in a debased style. on the upper part of it is a range of 6 shields on each side, charged with the following coats of arms repeated [shields removed].

I Ermine on a Chevron azure 3 Cinquefoils or. (Moore)
   impaling Argent a Fess between (Gambon) 3 Men's legs couped sable
II Moore impaling --- on a Chevron between 3 Barnacles – 5 Guttes de sang.
III Moore impaling Argent a fess between 3 Escallops gules
IV Moore impaling Gules a Cross of lozenges argent (question) chief 3 bends within A bordure.
V Moore impaling Argent a Chevron gules between 3 sprigs of oak fructed proper. (Boys)
VI Ermine 3 Lions rampant gules, impaling Moore (Chudleigh)
VII Argent 3 Bulls faces horned or impaling Moore (Walrond)
VIII Moore impaling Argent a bridge of two arches gules (Trobridge)
The principal screen is affixed a shield with the coat
Argent 3 Bulls faces horned or. (Walrond)

Against the east wall of the chancel below the window is a very large painting of our Lord in the garden of no great merit [removed]. The communion table & the rails are without ornament. On one side stands a modern carved oak chair in bad taste with a shield on the back charged with a Dove rising between 3 Fountains and on a Canton a Caduceus [removed]. The Font which stands at the western end of the north aisle is of stone, small, octagonal, ornamented with quatrefoils, on an octagonal column carved in trefoiled niches, with an octagonal base. A gallery extends across the nave and aisles within an organ. The pulpit is of carved oak in the style of the 17th century. The pews are in modern style and there are some remains of old carved oak benches [removed].

The monuments and inscriptions are these.

Chancel
North wall. a marble monument, an entablature supported by Corinthian columns painted gilt with the inscription in capital letters
Here lyes deposited in trust
With the cold earth what one day must
Return refined from the dust.
With tears thou mayest & greife dispence
For Southcott (Reader) who went hence
Vested with youth and innocence
But kinder heaven hath granted to survive
His Sister who alone doth keep alive
All that on earth imbellished the fame
Of Southcote's family except the name.
Arms Quarterly I Argent a Chevron between 3 Coots (Southcott)

II Argent a Bull passant within a border sable bezanted (Cole)

III Gules a saltire between 4 Lions rampant or.

IV Gules on a Bend or between 2 Escallops argent a chough between 2 Cinquefoils azure, on a Chief of the second a Rose between 2 Demi Fleurs de lis of the field. (Peter)

A marble tablet with an urn and a weeping figure. Sacred to the memory Alice wife of Henry Brutton of this parish gent. who died 1 June 1817 in the 67 year of her age and is interred underneath. Also to the memory of Henry Brutton esq of this parish husband of the above named Alice Brutton who died 19 March 1821 aged 87. Arms. Argent 3 Horseshoes sable, impaling Argent a fess between 3 Leopards faces ducally crowned or.

Floor. A stone partly covered by a pew
    -- who died the --- in the 75ye --
Arms 2 shields. I Ermine on a pale --- 3 -- impaling -- 3 Bars wavy.(Brutton)
II – on a Fess between 3 Elephants heads & necks erased -- as many Mullets -- impaling Ermine on a pale --- 3

Here -- Humphrey Parys merchant who deceased the third -- [missing]
Here lieth the body of Philipp the wife of Richard Dene of Collompton -- 17 day of November A.D. 1637. Here lieth also the body of Eliz. Mother of the said Richard who died 9 April 1641 aged 90. [missing]
-- the late wife of Richard English of Collompton gentleman who deceased the XXII day of -- the body of the aforesaid Richard English gentleman who departed this life 30 day of October A. D. 1623. [missing]
Hic jacit Roger Stocma quondam --- obiit XVII die decebr cui ppiciet deu Amen. 1585.

Nave

Floor. *Hic jacit Johannes Smythe qui ---*
Here lyeth also Winifred the wife of Daniel Cockram gentleman & grandchild of the above named John Smith.
Here lieth the body of Mellase Cockram the wife of George Cockeram gent. who deceased the 13 day of April 1637. [missing]
Here lyeth -- Cockram of this parish gent. M of Arts & some time fellow of Oriel college in Oxon & Profess -- who died the -- of March Ano Dom 1695. [missing]
Here lieth the body of James Crosse of Venn in the parish died 11 Dec. 1714 aged 89 Elizabeth his wife died 17 Aug 1678 aged about 86 Their 2nd daughter Elizabeth wife of Mr Thomas Sumpter died 6 Oct. 1695. Jane Cross died 24 Dec. 1714.
Richard Cockram sonne of -- gent.
Eliz. wife of Simon Albin of Venn died 19 June [missing]
Hic tumulatur Johannes Trot mercator & Johana uxor ej-- V die Feb. A.D. M---
Under these two adjoining stones lie the bodies of Hugh Speed the son Richard and Joan Speed virgin daughters of Hugh and Margaret Speed of Newlands in the parish of Collompton who lived singular love and so died within the compass of four days and were here buried together on the 3rd day of July in the year 1678 where they are silent under and secure from the scandalous and reproachful tongue waiting for the second and last glorious coming of the Son of God from heaven who is able to raise their mortal bodies to immortality to live with him in unchangeable glory for ever. Aged 20, 22 & 24 years. 1658.

Margaret wife of Hugh Speed mother of the 3 children buried 5 Sept in the year of our Lord 1671. Hugh Speed interred April 1 1685. Thomas Speed his son died 28 April 1708 aged 69. [missing]

North Aisle
North wall. a tablet. Sacred to the memory of Jemima wife of Francis Colman esq who died 28 July 1807 aged 66
A Tablet. Sacred to the memory of William Colman youngest son of Francis Colman esq and Jemima his wife of Hillersdon in this parish killed in a naval engagement 14 March 1795 aged 15. Augustus Colman their eldest son Captain in the 29 regiment of foot died of a fever in the island of Grenada 16 Dec. 1795 aged 21 Francis their second son Lieutenant of Dragoons died 30 July 1799 aged 21.
Tablet. David Sweet esq late of Hillersdon in this parish died 20 Dec. 1807 in the 57 year of his age. David second son of David and Lucinda Sweet died 10 Feb. 1808 aged 9. Arms. Gules 2 Chevron between as many Stars of 6 points in chief and a Rose in base argent.
Floor. *In memoriam Richardi Peche hujus ecclesiae pastoris – uxor ejus charissima Susanna posuit obiit 14th Aug. A.D. 1637.* [missing]
Orate pro animabus Johannis More armigeri et Elizabethae uxoris ejusdem qui quid. Johes obiit VII die Mch. A. Dni. MCCCCCII praedicta uxor Elizabetha obiit -- die March AD. MD – cujus animabus ppiciet Deus amen. [missing]
Here lieth the body of George More of Morehays esq who departed this life the 5 day of February AD, 1669 also here lieth the body of George son of James son of the above George More of Morehays esq who died 5 Nov 1711.
Arms Ermine on a Chevron 3 Cinquefoils impaling 3 Fireballs blazing. –
Hic jacet Mast. Humbrid. More armiger dominus de Morehem hujus ecclie liberalis benefactoris & Agnes uxor ejus qu. quid-- Humfrid. obiit 20 die Augusti 1537 qua animabus ppicietur deus (Arms defaced.) [missing]
Hic jacit Willm. More -- ac Mauric. More frater ejusdam necnon Dorothea aux. predicti Willi. ac --- Willi. & Dorothee liberi qui quidem Will. ab ac luce migravit 6o die Decris A.D. MCCCCCXIIV quorum animabus ppicuit deus amen. Here lieth the body of John son of Richard More gent of this parish who died 30 June 1650 also Richard More gent died 8 June 1674. (Brass figures of a man woman & 4 children lost)
Here lieth the body of Elizabeth the late wife of Anthony Salter of this parish esq who departed this life 30th June 1677 in the 42 year of her age. Elizabeth his daughter died 18 July following. Anthony his son aged near 6 died 2 Dec 1678. John Salter of Kingsmill in this parish gent died 18 April 1724 aged 48. Ann Fry his daughter wife of William Fry died 2 June 1737. [missing]
John Kerslake of Collumpton gent. died the 26 day.--- [missing]
Hict jacit Johannes Kaileway de Cullompton armiger et mercator --- Elizabeth --- die Februarii Ano Dni MDXXX quorum animabus ppiciet Deus.
Here lieth Henry Blackmore of Rull in this parish died 20 Aug 1666 aged 30. Henry B. his son died 26 Nov. 1683 in 21 year of his age. [missing]
--- brother unto Mary James died 2 Sept 1659.
Orate pro animam Joannis Tanner junioris cujus animae ppiciet Deus Amen.
Orate pro animabus Johannis Hyll et Amicta uxoris ejus qui obierunt 250 die Julii Ano Dni MCCCCCXXIX. [missing]

South Aisle.

Tablet. Sacred to the memory of the revd. John Veryard Brutton upward of 40 years vicar of this parish who died 1 April 1821 aged 80. Arms Argent 3 Horses hooves sable. [missing]

Floor. – Here lieth -- Henry Blackmore of Newland yeoman who -- day of July Ano Dom 1590 [missing]

Hic jacet Johannes Kyng quondam de Collumpton mercator et Johanna uxor ejus aellta.--- obierunt nono die mensis Octobris Ano Dni MCCCCLXXXV (a cross on the stone) [missing]

Here lieth the body of Mary James late wife of --- Leen James of this parish gent.

Here lieth the body of George Babidge of Collumpton clothier who gave to this church one silver cup for Communicant for ever and died 24 June 1628.

--- Babidge widow the wife of -- the 24th day of April. [missing]

Francis Colman esq second son of Francis Colman esq and Jemima his wife of Hillerdon in this parish died 30 July 1799 aged 21.

Here lieth the body of George Saffyn gent who deceased the 20 day of June Ano Dom 1612. [missing]

Here lieth the body of Robert Hill of this parish Tanner who died 29 May 1658 and gave to the poor of the parish fortie pounds and likewise to the poor of the parish of Chawley fortie pounds also to the poor of the parish of Childon twentie pounds to be bestowed in land and remain to the use of the said poor for ever.

Here lyeth Thomas Froche merchant which departed this present life the XXIV daye of July AD 1549 Also the body of Thomas Atkins of Cullompton gent who died 23 June 1655. [missing]

Here lieth the body of Mr Ralph Fowler of this parish Clothier who died 2 Nov. 1676. John Joan Elizabeth and Ann the son and daughters also Ralph Fowler and Mary his wife Also William son of Ralph and Mary Fowler died 28 October 1771 aged 74. [missing]

Here lieth the body of Mary Fowler daughter of William and Joan Fowler of Collumpton who departed this life 17 June 1649.

Lane's aisle

East wall. tablet and urn. Sacred to the memory of Anthony Heathfield gent who died 30 March 1753 & Alice his wife who died 23 Feb. 1764. Susanna their daughter died 7 Oct 1783. Erected by their son Anthony Heathfield esq of Lympstone in this county. Judith daughter of James Hubert esq of Guernsey and wife of the above Anthony Heathfield esq died Jan 20. 1816 also the above Anthony H. esq of Lympstone died 19 Jan 1836 aged 92.

South Wall. tablet. Capt. Elias Jarmin of the Collumpton Volunteers died 31 Oct 1795 in the 39 year of his age Erected by his widow.

Tablet and urn. Mary Cross of Charlton Musgrove co Somerset died in this parish 7 Nov. 1785 aged 29 Erected by her sister.

Tablet. Anthony John only son of R. Forster esq of Jardinefield Berwickshire born 3 July 1808. died 19 March 1813.

Floor. – Stone for John Lane, before mentioned p.418.

Here lieth the body of Richard Stone of this town clothier died 9 Dec. 1680 aged 56. [missing]

Henry Skinner gent of this parish died 15 Sept 1828. Susan his wife died 12 June 1805. [missing]

Here lieth Ede the wife of George Cokram merchant who deceased the XXXI day of Januarii ano 1572 *Hic jacet Robt' Cokeram Artium Magister et filius Georgii Cokeram mercatori et Edith uxoris ejus qui obiit 28 die Aprilis AD. 1632*. [missing]

Tower.

Floor. In memory of James Huish of this parish who died 25 May 1784. Amy Huish his widow died 18 June 1807 aged 86. [missing]

Church yard.

Stone – here lieth the body of Mr William Skinner Mr. of Artes sometime pastor of this parish who departed this life 1643

Tomb. In memory of Christiana Burn relict of Major General Burn of the Hon East India Company's service who died 1 June 1824 aged 60.

Tablet. The revd Thomas Harris a native of Rugby co Warwick died 9th April 1811 in the 26 year of his age.

Tomb. Sacred to the memory of John Henry youngest brother of the rev Thomas Harris. Died 29 May 1814 in the 21 year of his age.

Stone. Sacred to the memory of Jane daughter of the rev. John Eddy vicar of Toddington Gloucestershire and of his late wife Catherine daughter of the revd William Hughes vicar of all saints Northampton who died at this place on her return from Hot Wells Bristol 7 Aug 1803 in the 13th year of her age.

Tomb. Sacred to the memory John Hole gent of Winham Park House in the parish of Bradninch – Died 14 Dec. 1826 aged 63 years.

Tomb. Here lieth the body of Thomas Flaye of Chaldon in this parish gent. died 30 March 1679.

Stone. Here lieth the body of Mary wife of Thomas Flay of Chaldon in this parish gent who died 24 Feb. 1691 in the 82 year of her age,

Newspaper cutting, no name of newspaper, dated June 1849.
Collompton. – The restoration of our church is commenced, and the whole of the Pewing taken down. The works are instructed to Mr. Ashworth, Architect, and to Mr. John Mason, Builder, of Exeter.

Newspaper cutting, no name of newspaper, dated July 1849.
The walls of Cullompton Church, Devon, now being restored, are found upon partially scraping off the white liming, to be covered interiorly with paintings in distemper. In the north aisle is a figure of St. Christopher, nine feet high, with fishes and a mermaid at his feet, and his green twisted palm staff: other figures, on an equally gigantic scale, are sadly cut up by marble monuments; one of these is St. Michael, weighting departed spirits; a demoniacal horned head is grinning between the cords of the lighter scale. There is another figure with a sort of pontifical crown, and bearing a wand, cruciform at its termination. On the north side of the nave clerestory is St. Clara in an orange coloured robe, with a mitre terminated by a ball, her name is on a ribbon beneath. There are other specimens of the colourist's art in foliage adapted to spandrels, which, as well as the pier arches, are chiefly of an Indian red colour. It is a matter of regret to many that our antiquaries do not

unveil more of these figures and their inscriptions, before the decayed plastering is renewed, which it necessarily must be very shortly. – Builder.

Newspaper cutting from Exeter and Plymouth Gazette *dated 9 August 1849.*
Mediaeval Wall Painting in Collumpton Church.
To the Editor of the Exeter and Plymouth Gazette.
Sir, - Since the last notice of wall paintings discovered in Collumpton Church, the following lines inscribed in the spandrels of the pier arches in the north aisle, have been brought to light: - "Though I spake with tonges of men and angels and have no love, I were even as sounding brasse or as a tynkelyng Cimball, and though I could prophesy and understand all secretes and all" – (in the next spandrel the sentence is continued) – "knowledge, yea if I had all faith no love, I were nothing;" further than this the whitewash is not scraped off. In the south aisle spandrels, white foliage on a red ground encircles a panel, containing a text scarcely legible; the characters are of sixteenth century. The arches opening into the florid monumental chapel and aisle of John Lane, have their mouldings beautifully figured with foliaged patterns in vermillion and white, the splayed linings of the windows were dark red, also the external spandrels of the pier arches.

The subject in the nave clerestory are not well defined, they consist of shields encircled by twisted wreaths of leaves. These vestiges of mediaeval art will all of necessity be swept away in a few days, which is my reason for troubling you with this communication.
Yours, &., E. Ashworth.
High-street, Exeter, Aug., 9. 1849.
Su mention of a visit to Cullompton church in Madam D' Anblay's Diary vol V p 206 – N & Q. vol X p 216

BRADNINCH

Davidson (pp. 441–7) visited [St Disen] Bradninch on 2 August 1843 and noted it was 2½ miles south of Cullompton. He observed that 'the church of this very ancient town and borough presents no remarkable feature of antiquity but is interesting on account of the perfect condition of the chancel screen with its superstitious memorials'. The church was restored in 1889 by Hayward and Tait, when the roof was replaced, the screen was re-coloured and restored by Bradley of Exeter, and the pulpit was executed by the stone mason Harry Hems (Pevsner, *Devon*, 200–1). Twenty-two memorials are missing from the thirty-seven that Davidson recorded.

The building underwent considerable repair in 1841 the columns and arches being taken down and rebuilt and the roofs considerably heightened It was opened again for divine service in 1842. It consists of a nave about 58 feet long by 22 wide a chancel about 30 by 14 Aisles north and south 70 by 12 and a tower at the western end embattled with square pinnacles at the corners, containing 6 bells and a clock. The nave and chancel open to the aisles by 6 pointed arches on each side resting on lofty columns formed by shafts and several mouldings their capitals richly covered in foliage. The nave opens to the Tower by lofty pointed arch exhibiting the western windows which has 4 cinquefoiled lights with perpendicular tracery in the arch all the other windows are formed by 3 lights with quatrefoils above. The eastern window has some modern coloured glass. The side windows of the chancel are surmounted by labels resting on corbels of angels holding shields thus charged A saltier charged with a Fleur de lis impaling 6 crosses patties fitchees 2 and 2. – (Precentor of Exeter cathedral)
Quarterly 1st a saltier charged with a Fleur de lis (Persecutor
2nd & 3rd Six Crosses patties fitchees 2 2 and 2.
4 a Lion passant gardant.
The ceilings are coved and plain. [now wagon roof in nave and plain ceiling in north aisle]

The chancel screen which crosses the nave and aisle has been repaired & restored and is now remarkable perfect and handsome being richly painted and gilt It consists of a range of 12 open pointed arches each divided by mullions into 4 cinquefoil headed lights, the arches above are filled with tracery. Shafts between them support the fan tracery below the rood-loft which is rich in quatrefoils trefoils bosses of foliage etc. In front is a series of 4 various mouldings of foliage and a handsome cornice. The basement is formed into a long range of panels each occupied by a painted figure of an apostle evangelist saint or angel some from scripture but most from legendary history, each with an appropriate emblem or designation At the back of the screen, next the chancel, along the cornice is the following restored inscription "*Beati qui ambulant in viis ejus x Cantate Domino canti – cum novem x Laus ejus in ecclesia sanctorum x Laudate nomen ejus in choro in tympano et pratterio x Laudate Deum in sono tubae x Laudate eum in cymbalis benesonantibus x Laudate eum in cymbalis jubilationis x Omnis Spiritus laudet Dominium. Amen A.D. 1528.*" A gallery extends across the western end of the nave and aisles [removed] and underneath it across the opening in the basement of the tower is a similar screen to that above mentioned. Removed from the north aisle; the openings glazed and the whole painted and gilt anew. The lower part exhibits most offensively in 12 panels the figures of saints the recorded in the living legends of the Romanish church among them that of a monk probably St Francis of Assisium or St. Dominick receiving the Stigmata or marks in his hands feet and the side of the wounds of our Lord. The altar screen is not yet provided. The communion table is of carved oak & there are 2 old carved oak chairs [missing]. The pulpit & pews are of oak & of recent date. In the church yard are the shaft and base of an ancient cross.

The monuments and inscriptions are these.

Chancel
North wall. A large monument of black and white marble carved in the Grecian Style. 2 Tablets.
I. Sacred to the memory of Peter Sainthill esq well known in this place for his piety charity and justice sonne of Peter Sainthill esq and grandson of Peter Sainthill esq all inhabitants of this ancient borough (the two last lying in a vault under the communion table in the chancel) who having served King Charles I in honourable changes both civil and military according to the obligation of his path, to reserve himself for more successful service to his King and country in the 1646 withdrew into Italy to his brother Robert Sainthill esq then agent with: the great duke of Tuscany from King Charles the 1st where having spent the remainder of his life in the experiences of virtue and devotion, and lamenting the miseries a civil war had brought upon his county He resigned his spirit to God who gave it in the year of Grace 1648 and the 54th year of his age.
II Samuel Sainthill esq his son and heir both of his fidelity to his prince and estate though impaired & lessened by his Father's loyalty dedicate this Marble & desire the memory of the reader for the piety of the act which he caused to be done in the year of grace 1679. *Caetera memorent Posteri.*
The above mentioned Samuel Sainthill esq who erected this monument lyes also buried under the communion table of this church. He departed this life the 14 Nov. 1708 in the 83 year of his age. Arms
Or on a fess engrailed azure between 3 Leopards faces gules as many Bezants, each changed with a Fleur de lys of the second: in chief on a pile azure 3 Fleurs de lys of the field.
Floor. The Honourable. L.G.K. Murray died 4th Jan 1835 aged 65 years. [missing]
Here lieth the body of Winifred the wife of Mr Thomas Harrcourt who departed this life the XIX of April anno Domo 1628. Here lieth the body of Winifred wife of Mr John Taylor which deceased the -- day of November anno Domini 1658. [missing]
In memoriam Petri Sainthill armigeri et Elizabethae uxoris ejus et Marcia --- vivunt in ecclesia -- in grandior. Gloria [missing]
Thomas Warren thrice mayor of this borrow who departed this life the 16 day of July 16-- aged 85 years. [missing]
Here lieth the body of Giles English gent twice mayor of this town and parish who died the 24 daye of September Anno Dni 1647. [missing]

Here lieth the body of Elizabeth wife of Walter Kelland of this parish gent who departed this life 22 October Anno Domino 1722 aged 53. Here also lieth the body of the above mentioned Mr Walter Kelland whose unspotted integrity and unoffensive conduct both in public and private life made him to be loved whilst alive by all that knew him and much lamented when dead. He exchanged this life for a better on the 5 day November 1728 aged 59. "Behold an Israelite indeed in whom there was no guile" reader go and do thou likewise. [missing]
Here lieth the body of Mr Edward Martyn of Hele Payne --- Anthony [missing]
Here lieth the body of William Beales 1683 also Ann his wife died April 1. 1722. Also Mary Beales [missing]

Nave
Floor. Here lieth the body of Samuel Salter parish clerk died 8 Sept 1694 [missing]
Here lie the bodies of Thomas and Richard sons of Peter Warren gent. Thomas died 2 April 24 Richard died Jan. 31.1766 both children. Here also lieth the body of Thomas Warren gent who for his faithful services to the public was thrice elected mayor of this ancient borough & corporation & died 12 day of July 1711 in the 53 year of his age. Here also lieth the body of Thomas son of Peter Warren gent who died 1 Aug 1711. [missing]
Here lieth the body of Robert German of this parish gent. once mayor of this town and corporation who departed this life -- day of May Anno Domino 1715 & in the -- year of his age Also here lieth the body of Mary German wife of the above. [missing]
---ne the wife of Mr: Anthony Martyn was buried Nov. 23 1711. Also the above Mr Anthony Martyn being 3 times mayor of this corporation buried 16 Oct A.D. 1732 aged 60 Also Anthony the son of Mr. A. M. aged 9 weeks was buried 2 April 1737.

North Aisle
North east corner a marble sarcophagus tablet.
In a vault underneath lie the remains of Thomas Pearse esq rear admiral in H.M. Royal navy who departed this life 10 day of April 1830 aged 71 years. Elizabeth Margaret widow and relict of the above named Thomas Pearse daughter of Edward Sainthill esq. formerly of this place died on 21 March 1845 in the 79 year of her age. Arms Gules a Bend embattled between 2 unicorns heads and necks erased or.
North Wall a tablet. In memory of John Podger 70 years schoolmaster of this town died 2 Nov 1829 of his life aged 95. This tablet was erected by a subscription of his numerous pupils.
An elegant mural tablet richly carved in quatrefoils niches shields and foliage with a handsome cornice Sacred to the memory of Richard Martyn of this parish who departed this life April 10 1830 aged 84 years. Also of Charlotte his wife who departed this life Dec. 14 1828 aged 49 years. Also of Samuel Linnington son of the above who died Dec. 17. 1824 aged 6 months Also of Susan Linnington daughter of the above who died April1 1835 aged 21 years Also of Emma daughter of the above who died Nov 23. 1842 aged 24 years. On the cornice are the words "I know that my Redeemer liveth".
A Tablet In a vault near this place are deposited the remains of Mr Samuel Linnington of Bradninch who departed this life 20 Nov 1792 Three times mayor of this ancient borough who closed a valuable life the 59th year of his age. [missing]
Floor. Here lieth interred Henry Shapcott of this parish gent also Margaret his daughter y' wife of Mr. Christopher Samford of Exon merchant who died 13 day of

Jan 1689 also the body of Vrith Shapcott wife of Francis Shapcott who died the 27 day of April A.D. 1704 in the 53rd year of her age. Here also interred Oct 18. 1707 the above said the foresaid Francis Shapcott esq in the 55th year of his age Arms (sable) a Chevron (or) between 3 Dove cots (argent).

--- died May the 4 1719. Also here lyeth the body of Wilmot Marshall who died March 14 1727. Here also lieth the body of Mary Marshall who died 30 June 1746 aged 38 years Also here lieth the body of Humphrey Marshall who died 22 Aug 1748 aged 38 years.

Here lieth the body of Henry vicar of this parish [missing]

Here lieth the body of -- wife of Abraham Quick physician who departed this life 31 July A.D. in the 60 year of her age. Here also lieth the body of the said Mr. Abraham Quick who departed this life 20 day of August 1732 aged 69 years.

South Aisle

East wall. A tablet. Sacred to the beloved memory of John Charleton Tanner Yeatman the pious and exemplary son of John Charleton Yeatman esq physician to his late Royal Highness the Duke of Gloucester and Sarah his wife daughter of the revd Thomas Tanner also of Sarah the amiable young sister of the above.

South Wall a stone tablet under an ogee arch crocketted, with pinnacles and a cornice of foliage in good taste. Sacred to the memory of John Drew who departed this life May 18. 1833 aged 72 Susanna wife of the above John Drew died 27 Oct 1828 aged 65 The sons of the above – Robert died Sept 13 1832 aged 42 Thomas died 17 Aug 1837 aged 39. merchants – Mary Jane daughter of Charles and Elizabeth Drew and granddaughter of the above John and Sarah Drew died 1 Dec 1836 aged 10 months.

Floor. Here lieth the body of Mary Garnsey daughter of Mr Anthony Martyn who died 21 day of March 1764 Also here lieth the body of Thomzaney wife of Henry Martyn who died Feb. 12. 1732. [missing]

Here -- body of -- daughter of Phillip -- dyed the 10 of Oct? 1621. Here lieth the body of Henry Moore son of John Moore and grandchild of the said Philip Moore who died the 7 of Sept 1622. Here lieth the body of ------

Here lyeth Joan Marshall wife of Humphrey Marshall son who died April 6 1701 also here lieth the body of Humphrey Marshall, Mercer who departed this life on his birthday Nov 17. 1732 aged 66 years.

--- 1669.

Here lyeth the body of Mr Robert Taylor twice mayor of this town who deceased the 6 of Julie A.D. 1652

Here lieth the body of Elizabeth Martyn [missing]

Here lieth the body of Robert Martyn who was – twice mayor of this borough and died standing justice March 18 1747 in the 78 year of his age. [missing]

Here lieth the body of Mr John Saunders who died July 30 1718 also Elizabeth his wife. [missing]

Grace wife of Philip Moore [missing]

Here lyeth Elizabeth daughter of James Ross who died 27 June 1684. Mary daughter of Jane Force who died 27 June 1711 also John son of John Gercus died Sept 1. 172- – in the 2nd year of his age. [missing]

Here lieth the body of William Dodge senior. Buried 2 Nov. – Joan D. wife of the said W.D. buried 1771. [missing]

Here lieth the body of Mary Forde wife of John Forde builder of Tiverton deceased 5 day of Aug.

Elizabeth wife of Peter Brice died 2 March 1770 [missing]

Joan and William children of William and Elizabeth -- 1712. [missing]

Newspaper cutting, no name of newspaper, dated 1841

The Churchwardens of Bradninch, Devon, are soliciting contributions for the restoration of the screen or rood-loft in their parish church. It is a most curious relic of Bygone days, and when restored would be an ornament to any church in the kingdom. The panels of the lowest part of the screen contain no less than forty-six ancient paintings (of the period of Henry VII.) of Romish saints &.

Newspaper cutting, no name of newspaper, dated 1842

The venerable church of Bradninch, Devon, has during the last 18 months undergone a thorough and substantial repair, and was re-opened on the 20th April, when the Very Rev. the Dean of Exeter preached. The restoration has been so accurately effected, and the tracery of the windows, together with the columns and arches, have been so ably imitated, that it is in many instances very difficult to distinguish the new parts from old. A carved oak screen or rood-loft is a curious and remarkable relic. There is a date on it (A.D. 1520), but it is supposed to be the work of an earlier period. The panels of the lower part contain no less than forty-six ancient paintings of the saints &. We have great pleasure in being enabled to subjoin from the Report, lately read before the Exeter Diocesan Architectural Society, the following record of the part taken by that Society in procuring this most laudable restoration. "The first opportunity which presented itself", says the Report, "of extending the usefulness of the Society, was at Bradninch, where an attempt having been made to remove – and by so doing probably to destroy – the magnificent screen of Bradninch Church, an attempt sanctioned (we are sorry to add) by some members of the Incorporated Church Building Society in London; your Committee stepped in to the aid of the Venerable the Archdeacon of Exeter, who with his accustomed vigilance, resisted the proceedings, and finally succeeded in inducing the Committee at Bradninch to hold out a hope that the screen should not only be retained in its proper place, but that it should be thoroughly repaired, re-gilt, and re-painted in its original colours. On condition that this be done to their satisfaction, the Committee voted the sum of 21*l*. towards the restoration, a sum which, though small in itself, procured the Bradninch Committee a further sum of 13*l*. from various subscribers, besides aid from the Cambridge Camden Society."

SILVERTON

Davidson (pp. 453–9) visited [St Mary the Virgin] Silverton on 1 August 1843 and noted it was 7 miles north of Exeter. The church was restored in 1861–3 by Edward Ashworth (Pevsner, *Devon*, 743). Four memorials missing from the twenty-nine that Davidson recorded.

The church of this town consists of a Nave about 60 feet long by 18 wide, a chancel about 14 by 16, aisles on the north and south each 60 feet by12, a porch on the south wall, and a Tower at the western end of the nave supported by buttresses at the corners crowned with battlements and pinnacles. The walls of the south aisle the porch and a vestry on the south side of the chancel are embattled over the south door is a cinquefoiled ogee arch with buttresses on the sides carved in mouldings, terminating above in pinnacles & a canopy. The nave opens to the aisle by 4 wide and high arches on each side resting on lofty columns formed by shafts with intervening mouldings their capitals boldly carved in foliage & scrolls & angels holding shields labels and devices. A similar arch between the nave and chancel. The windows are all of four lights with cinquefoil heads and perpendicular tracery with quatrefoils in the arches. The upper part of the east window is occupied by gaudy modern stained glass with two figures of our Lord, one as bearing a lamb on his shoulders. The ceiling of the nave is coved and ribbed, with bosses of foliage at the crossings of the ribs: in one of them is the head of a bishop. The ceilings of the aisles are flat – The ceiling of the chancel is ribbed in oak with bosses of heads and foliage the openings painted in imitation of clouds [removed]. A modern balustrade of carved wood work divides the chancel from the nave [removed]. A large and lofty altar screen reaching almost to the ceiling hides all the lower part of the eastern window. It is of old dark oak handsomely carved in pilaster fluted, supporting an entablature and large scrolls. On the face are two medallions representing the agony in the garden and the resurrection, in the centre a transfer with the letter J.H.S [removed]. The communion table large and heavy, of oak carved and panelled although on each side of it is an old carved oak chair. The Font is modern octagonal black marble basin on a pedestal and has a pipe with a stop cock to convey the water from it to the ground, over it in a corner of the wall is fixed the figure of an angel holding a cross carved in oak [removed]. The pulpit and pews are modern. There are two galleries one above the other at the west end of the nave, the upper one for the choir, on the front of the lower one is the date 1734. There is also a gallery over the eastern end of the south aisle [all removed]. In the church yard are the remains of a cross, a part of the shaft on two stages the base ornamented with quatrefoils – also a very ancient yew tree.

The monuments and inscriptions convey the following particulars.

Chancel
North wall. A tablet. In memory of the revd John Rashleigh second son of Jonathan Rashleigh of Menabilly in the co of Cornwall esq 22 years rector of this parish and

of Catherine his wife and daughter of William Stackhouse of Trevone in the same county. D.D. also of five of their children Margaret Helen born 7 Jan 1780 buried 7 March 1787 Martha born 22 May 1785 buried 15 Feb. 1787 John born 2nd April 1787 buried 26 April 1788 Philip born 8 Oct 1774 buried 6 April 1795 and of Catherine born 29 April 1778 buried 18 June 1799.

South wall a tablet. Sacred to the memory of the revd Mr Richard Troyte who was during six years rector of this parish and died March the 20th 1733 aged 79. as also to the memory of Mary his wife who died May 4 1734 aged 74. He was a gentleman of politeness and hospitality piety and charity honour and integrity She was a woman of prudence and economy virtue and civility strictness and fidelity – Both now happy to eternity. *Hoc bene merentibus nepos fecit monumentum. A.D. 1736.* [missing]

Floor. *Depositum pentecostes Gulielmi Wrayford generosi --- qui obiit sexto die Februarii an Do 1650*

Arms – a chevron between 3 arrows pointed downwards

Hear lyeth the body of Katherine late the wife of William Co(tton) -- ed the second of June an Do 1649. Arms Quarterly 1&4 (argent) a Bend between 3 Pellets. 2&3 -- Semee of Escallops a Lion rampant -- impaling Ermine on a (qy Strode) Cauton -- a crescent

Here lyeth the body of John Were of Dunmore who died in the year of our Lord 1666 also of Grace his wife daughter of the late revd William Cotton chancellor of St Peters in Exon rector of this parish who died the 9 day of April Ano Dom 1694. Arms (Sable) a Bend between 6 Cross crosslets fitchee (argent) (Were) impaling (Argent) a bend between 3 (Pellets) (*in the margin:* Cotton)

Ille patrem elapso caelesti morte secutus
Ipsa que post ferme bis tria lustra virum
Ille orbos praemature tres patre reliquit
Matre quot ille tamen dicere nemo potest .

Here lieth the body of Marie Trott ye
-- esq who died the 15 April. 1623,
Here lies her cross for who we grieve
But yet her soul with Christ doth live.

Here lyeth the body of Mary late the wife of
-- gentleman who died the -- day of August an do. 1659.
--tum Gulielmi
--oniae Were) qui
-- Octobris anno
--sexto salutis
-- 1662
-- Shibbeare qui – vicessimo octavo die September – anno domi 1636.

Hear lyeth the body of Francyis Snellinge of the parish of Plimpton St Mary esq who dyed the 7th of Sept 1649. Arms defaced. [missing]

Here lieth the body of Joan wife of John Land gent who died 13 May in the 31 year of her age Anno Dom 1697. Here lieth the body of Thomas Land of this parish gent who departed this life the 3 day of April A.D. 1731 in the 65 year of his age.

Nave

Floor. -- wife of Roger Richards of Upex in the parish of Rew who departed this life the -- day

Hic jacet corpus Marthae uxor Gulielmi Land gener. quae obiit vicesimo octavo die Mariae anno aetatis sue 51. 1696. Arms Quarterly – 3 Leopards faces (qy) 2&3 --- a Hoopoe
Here lieth also Francis son of the said William who was buried the 11 day of April 1673.

North Aisle
North wall. A large marble tablet. M.S. To the memory of Mr. Frances Brown who died June the 11 Ano Dom 1769 aged 45 late wife of Henry Langford Brown esq of Combe Satchfield in this parish and third daughter of William Tucker esq of Corryton in the co of Devon the virtuous mother of eleven children two of whom were buried underneath viz Philippa who died Jan. 1753 aged 3½ years Dolly in March 1758 aged 6 years. Whilst nine survived to lament with a disconsolate father their mutual and irreparable loss in the best of wives and parent. *Vivit post funera virtus.* Arms a shield on which the charges are intermixed contrary to the rules of blazon apparently attempting the impalement of these two coats viz.
Argent on a Chevron gules between 3 Bears heads erased sable as many castles field – impaling Argent 3 Human hearts in chevron gules between 2 wreaths of foliage vert. (Brown)
A white marble tablet. To the memory of Dorothy Ayre Brown who died Jan 11. 1831 widow of Henry Langford Brown esq of Combesatchfield in this parish. This tablet is erected to record her true heart and full assurance of faith in the gospel promise of God her regular and joyful attendance in this Holy House and her deeds of charity to the sick and poor and also in token of affectionate sorrow and lasting gratitude by her only surviving sister Francis Duke Coleridge. Arms in a lozenge (argent) on a Chevron (gules) between 3 Bears heads (Brown) (Sable) as many castles (of the field) impaling – 3 Chaplets -- (Duke)
A large white marble tablet.
In grateful acknowledgment of the pastoral services of the rev. William Barker MA. thirty two years rector of Silverton this memorial is raised by his parishioners of every class.
He was a diligent labourer in the vineyard of the Lord
devoting the energies of a vigorous understanding
the resources of most varied and extensive knowledge
with great judgment and experience in the affairs of men
to the temporal and eternal welfare of his flock
in gentleness wisdom and ever considerate kindness
informing counselling assisting comforting
under all their difficulties wants and sorrow
the many who sought him in the hour of need
leading their hearts and minds to the knowledge and love of God
and all their hopes and fears to the cross of Christ
whom above all he preached and in whom alone he trusted
he ministered to his congregation in seeming health
on the first Sunday in advent December 2. 1838
and very early in the morning of the following day
was suddenly called hence in the 66th year of his age
yet even so to use his very last words from the pulpit
did not "that day come upon him unawares"

for he was prepared to meet his God.

A marble tablet. Near this place lies the body of Juliana Rashleigh daughter of the rev. Peter Rashleigh rector of Southfleet Kent and wife of the rev George Cumming Rashleigh fellow of St Mary's college Winchester on the 6th day of December 1831 at the age of 39 years her mortal put on immortality Juliana Frances Rashleigh their only child who was born April the 14th died Dec. 20th 1834 and was buried in the cloisters of the college chapel Winchester.

Floor. Here lyeth the body of Elizabeth daughter of Mr John Suke was buried the 8 day of June 1804.

Here lieth the body of John Russell of this parish yeoman who died 7 July 1690. Arms (Argent) a Lion rampant (gules on a chief (sable) 3 escallops (of the field) also lieth the body of Mrs. Catherine Hammond widow who died the -- day of February 1731 in the 78 year of her age. Here also lieth the body of John Russell late of this parish esq who died the 7th day of Nov. 173 - in the 88 year of his age.

Here lieth the body of William Scibbowe who died 20 April 1634. Sarah Scibbowe who died the -- of June 1641 and daughter to Henry Scribbowe of this parish gent [missing].

South Aisle

South wall. A tablet. Sacred to the memory of William Land of Hayne in this parish esq who died on the 1 day of Nov 1821 in the 72 year of his age. He was for more than 20 years a most upright magistrate for the county and was son of Barton Land esq of the same place who died 31 Dec 1787 aged 67 Also in the same vault under-neath the family seat are interred Ann, Williams Barton and Leticia Ann three infant children of the above mentioned William Land esq & Ann his relict who has caused this monument to be erected. Arms. Argent a Cross composed or & gules in the 1st quarter a Lion passant of the last: impaling Argent a Chevron gules between 3 water bytes sable (Bussell or Yarde)

A tablet. In a vault adjoining this wall are deposited the mortal remains of William Cleve of Ash in this parish who died May 10 1811 aged 74 also of Betty Cleave his wife who died Jan 17 1832 aged 88 years.

Your children grieved when you were doomed to die
Yet faith replied the awful path once trod
Heaven lifts its everlasting portals high
And bids renewed souls behold their God.

Thanks be to God who giveth us the victory through our Lord Jesus Christ. 1 Cor. XV.57.

A Tablet. Sacred to the memory of Charles Richards of Roach and Pitt in this parish who died Feb. 11 1805 aged 78, also of Hannah his wife who died June 10 AD. 1807 aged 77 Also of Mary daughter who died Feb 7. 1822 aged 70. [missing]

Floor. William Barton gent son of Thomas and Mary Barton of Hayne died August -- (a coat of arms quite defaced) -- William Barton -- 8 of June 1696 -- who was the son -- Barton son of -- Barton – Arms -- a fess between 3 Bucks heads caboshed Lawrence Vicar of Dunkeswell in the ---

Here lyeth the body of William Barton the younger gent who died at Rattery 10 Jan 1619- aged 31 years. Here lieth the body of Elizabeth Barton wife of William Barton of this parish gent who died 21 day of March in the year of our Lord God 17.6/7 in the 71 year of her age.

-- Broadmead junior of this parish -- departed this life 6 day of March 1715 aged 21 years. Here lieth the body of Philip Broadmead who died the 5 day of --- 1730 aged 84. There are other stones to the memory of Broadmead, partly covered by pews.

Church yard.
A tomb. Thomas Langford Brown esq of Combsatchfield in this parish died Jan 27. 1833 aged 74 years.

Newspaper cutting, no name of newspaper, dated 27 June 1863:
Silverton: Re-opening of the Church
On Saturday the parish church, now handsomely restored, was re-consecrated by the Right Rev. Bishop Tower (the newly-elected Bishop of Gibraltar), acting for our venerable Diocesan; and at the same time the large piece of ground added to the churchyard was consecrated. The chancel which was ruinous and fitted up in the style foreign to the character of the edifice, has been rebuilt, with enlargements. The whole interior has been fitted up with low seats of red deal. A new rail and illuminated standard enclose the sacrarium [removed], and a gallery deforming the east end of the south aisle has been removed, the improved light admitting the extinction of some ugly skylights in the nave roof. A new pulpit of Bath stone and reading desk of wainscot are placed at the entrance to the chancel. The Decalogue, Creed, and Lord's Prayer are executed with illuminations on four tables on the east wall of the chancel [removed]. The north aisle has been newly roofed and covered with lead, and part of the nave roof renewed. New battlements and pinnacles have been supplied to the tower, and other repairs. Amongst the embellishments bestowed on this church, in an age antagonistic to Gothic architecture, we may enumerate in the chancel a high wainscot panelling of the Ionic order, hiding a good part of the east window with a quality of painted drapery of theatrical character. In the place of the rood screen a post and rail fences, adorned with gilt pine apples, extended across the church. It is almost needless to add these inconsistent features have been removed. The appearance of the edifice, which is of the perpendicular style, is much improved by the addition of a piece of ground added to the churchyard on the east side, given by Lord Ilchester and the trustees of the late Lord Egremont. The portion is enclosed by new walls and gates. The work has been carried out by Messrs. S. Moass and Sons; the Bath stone work by Mr. T. Mitchell and Sons; the architect is Mr. Ashworth. The cost of the work, exclusive of £150 spent in enlarging and levelling the churchyard, will be about £1,500.

Columbjohn

Davidson (p. 461) visited Columbjohn chapel on 2 August 1843 and noted it was 5 miles north east of Exeter. He observed that 'an arched gateway only remains of the mansion house which formerly stood here. The chapel which is situated a short distance from the western extremity of Killerton park still exists but is in a state of great dilapidation.' 'The building was erected in the year 1608.' Davidson recorded no memorials here. The chapel was rebuilt by Arthur Acland in 1851.

The walls are shored up and the windows in ruins. A luxuriant growth of ivy has almost covered the western end of the structure and entirely conceals the bell turret on the gable and the evergreens which surround the little chapel yard have been suffered to grow to luxuriance, the only apparent feature of antiquity about the building is the door in the south wall which is a moulded arch and piers in the Early English style, though perhaps of more recent date. The walls have been almost covered with texts of scripture painted in the Old English letters on the plaster in large panels bordered with scrolls etc [now plain walls]. The ceiling is coved and the plaster worked in panels with a cornice of scrolls and heads in the style of the 16th century & there are heavy carved pendants in the centre of the ceiling painted in human faces & knobs [wood rafters]. A heavy beam remains across the western end which supported a gallery [removed]. There is not the vestige of a single monument or inscribed stone.

The building was erected in the year 1608.

KILLERTON

Davidson (pp. 463–5) visited [the proprietary chapel of The Holy Evangelist] Killerton on 2 August 1843 and noted it was 6 miles north east of Exeter. He observed that 'this splendid edifice stands a short distance from the high road and within the grounds of Killerton, having been erected as a private chapel by Sir Thomas Dyke Acland Bart in the year 1841 and consecrated to divine service on the 21 September in that year. Mr Cockerell of London was the architect.'

It has been erected on the model of the chapel of St. Joseph at Glastonbury Abbey but is in the English Norman style and has a semicircular apse at the eastern end. It is a parallelogram bounded at each corner by a rectangular turret crowned by a square pinnacle relieved by open lights and highly enriched. The doorway is at the western end and under a deeply recessed semicircular arch with numerous mouldings, above it is a splendours circular window richly ornamented with appropriate sculpture and mouldings, the windows on the sides have semicircular heads the arches resting on shafts with capitals both within and without highly decorated with foliage and mouldings in appropriate style. The roof is open, supported by semicircular arches of oak, carved in mouldings, and the whole is ceiled beneath the slate with boards of cedar grown in Killerton park – The various chevron cable rosette and other mouldings throughout the building are boldly and appropriately carved in the Anglo Norman style, but it may be doubted whether the corbel tables are in accordance as to their design with the architecture of that period. The crosses on the gables are beautifully executed and in very good taste. The walls are finished internally with ranges of intersecting semicircular arches and the floor ornamentally inlaid with tiles. The open seats which are carved in oak & are arranged longitudinally by the walls in the form of stalls and benches in the manner of a cathedral choir. The windows are filled with painted glass of chaste and elegant colours and designs, excepting those at the eastern end and for which the glass is not yet finished. The communion table is only a temporary provision, as a magnificent stone altar is said to be in preparation. On each side of it is a carved oak chair designed from one belonging to Glastonbury Abbey and like it they bear the following inscription on the sides and backs "*Sit laus deo Johannes Arthurus monacus glastonie saluet ecc Deus. Da pacem dne*" There is a heavy carved oak gallery across the western end of the building for the use of a choir beneath which on either side the western door is a vestry and a baptistery. The font is an octagonal stone basin without ornamentation. The doors of oak are fine specimens of workmanship and are oriented with hinges and fastenings of ancient design admirably executed. The whole building within the walls is about 65 feet long by 26 feet wide. The ground around the chapel is laid out with great taste and newly planted and when the shrubs have advanced in growth the effect of this splendid building among them will by highly interesting and beautiful.

Newspaper cutting, no name of newsaper, dated 21 September 1841
The Bishop of Exeter consecrated the new chapel erected by Sir Thomas D. Acland, Bart. M.P. in Killerton Park, Devonshire. The Bishop of Barbados and a large congregation of the clergy of the county were present. This building is constructed on the model of St. Joseph of Arimathea, at Glastonbury. The ground plan is a parallelogram, bounded at each angle by a tower; but at Killerton a circular apse completes the east end; and whereas a north and south door exist at Glastonbury, here there is but one entrance, at the west, and this sole doorway recedes deeply, with mouldings, intended to be sculptured. Above the doorway is a circular window richly ornamented; the outer rib, ten feet in diameter, has the chevron moulding, while within is carved the cable, and within that hollow carved with roses. This wheel-window was copied from that lately discovered at the Temple Church in London, and engraved in our Magazine for January last. Over the window is an enriched cornice, and above, a lofty gable, surrounded by a Norman Cross. The four windows on the south side are of freestone moulded and carved; those on the north are plain, except the corbels to the window labels. The whole wall between the windows is hewn stone, dressed on the beds and face and laid in courses; while the tower and buttresses are worked in courses of ashler. The apse is more richly and elegantly worked, the stone being rubbed and sanded, so as to approach somewhat to a smooth and polished surface. It contains five windows, while a gallery above exhibits five more, which communicate with the roof, all of slender proportions. Externally the roof is unbroken; it is surmounted by a ridge of freestone, and covered with Bangor slates of different hues. The end of the ridge eastwards is surmounted by a cross. Within the chapel is 64 feet 5 inches long, 25 feet 7 inches broad, and 37 feet 6 inches high. The front doors are of solid oak, 3 inches thick, ornamented by wrought hinges and bolts of ancient design and exquisite workmanship. Another door, six feet within, with carved panels, closed by plate glass, admits to the body of the building, while on the other side of the space between these doors is a baptistery to the right, with a small but massive font, and a vestry on the left. Over these, a gallery of original and chaste design. The interior is fitted up in the style of a college chapel, with substantial seats of oak and walnut timbers; the floor of the body is a perfect lime-ash; and the chancel is ornamented by a design composed of cruciform flowers, the pattern of which was brought by one of the family from the ruins of a Christian church at Ephesus. Seven steps lead to the altar; two rising from the body to the chancel, two to a platform before the rails, two to the rails themselves, and one on which the Communion-table itself stands. This is of stone from Caen. The walls are stuccoed with hard composition. The windows have columns on the inside with carved capitals and enriched mouldings in their circular heads. On either side of every window are lofty columns which support the roof. The roof is worthy of great attention; it is a pure conception of the architect, Mr. Cockerell. Circular principals carved with a zigzag ornament rest on the capitals just named, and, not-withstanding that they are elegant in form, support, without lateral pressure, the whole weight of the roof. These principals are of oak, but the ceiling between is of cedar of Lebanon grown at Killerton. The painted glass is not yet quite complete; nine windows are fixed, and of these eight, together with one or two others things, were the tribute of Sir T. Acland's children, and other friends.

NETHEREXE

Davidson (p. 473) visited the chapel of St John the Baptist, Netherexe on 2 August 1843 and noted it was 5 miles north of Exeter. He observed that the chapel stood 'in a low and secluded, but fertile, spot near the river Exe, having only a single house near it'. The church was restored in 1890 (Pevsner, *Devon*, 582). Two memorials are missing from the three that Davidson recorded.

The building consists only of a nave and chancel the former about 22 feet long by 13 wide and the latter about 10 by 33. A porch covers the south door which is under a pointed arch of early date. The eastern and western windows are also ancient being formed by 3 and 2 trefoiled lights with quatrefoil above. The other windows are modern. There is a turret on the western gable containing one bell. The pulpit is of carved oak panelled [changed] and the pews and benches are of oak [now chairs]. The font is of stone square and very low resting on a cylindrical column, the under part of the basin hatched in the Norman style. The ceiling is coved and without ornament [now wooded rafters].
The inscribed stones are these.

Chancel
Floor. – here lieth the body of Elizabeth Andrews wife of Anthony Andrews who was buried 17 of May Anno Dom 1641. Here lieth the body of William Andrews of this parish who died the 6 March 1741 in the 69 year of his age [missing].

Nave.
North wall. A marble tablet gilt.
To the memory of Miss Mary Young the beloved daughter of Mr. Peter and Salome Young who died Oct. 18. 1771 in the 11 year of her age. Also Thomas Martyn the son of the above named Peter and Salome who died August 6. 1817 aged 63 years. The poor man's friend.
Arms. Vair on a chief gules 3 Lioncel rampant barwise or.
Floor. Here lyeth the body of Thomas Cole of this parish gent who departed this life the 12th day of May Anno Dom 1684. Here lieth also the body of Susanna his wife who departed this life the 22 of Feb. 1714 [missing].

THORVERTON

Davidson (pp. 477–81) visited [St Thomas of Canterbury] Thorverton on 1 August 1843 and noted it was 7 miles north of Exeter. He observed that 'the body of this church was rebuilt about the year 1834 and it is now a large handsome and commodious structure, though many of its features are incongruous with the pointed style of architecture'. The church piers were raised in 1834 to accommodate the galleries which have since been removed, and the church was restored in 1864 (Pevsner, *Devon*, 803). Eleven memorials are missing from the fifteen that Davidson recorded.

It consists of a nave about 70 feet long by 18 wide, a chancel about 6 by 18 Aisles on the north and south side each 70 feet long by 12 wide a porch covering the south door and a low embattled tower at the western end containing a clock and 5 bells. In the north wall is an old door way walled up with a trefoiled niche over it and traces of a porch. The porch is a very interesting specimen of art, it is vaulted and ribbed with stone, springing from plain corbels. There are bosses of foliage with curiously carved figures of a monk and a priest preaching and in the centre a figure much mutilated perhaps of our Lord or of the Virgin Mary. There is a room over the porch not used. The nave is open to the aisles by 6 pointed arches on each side resting on lofty columns formed by shafts with intervening mouldings their capitals sculptured with angels holding shield scrolls and foliage. The eastern window is new, formed into two subarches divided by mullions and a transom into 10 lights with cinquefoiled head. The others are all of 3 cinquefoiled lights with six foils above, The ceilings are coved and plain. The chancel is panelled with old dark oak in the Roman style [removed]. The communion table is of oak and on it stands two large candle sticks carved and gilt with tall candles which are lighted at evening service [removed]. On the sides are 2 old carved oak chairs [missing]. The Font is an octagonal stone basin resting on a cylindrical and four shafts without ornament. The pulpit and pews are modern. There is a heavy gallery at the western end of the nave containing an organ [both removed].
The monuments and inscriptions convey the following particulars.

Chancel
North wall. A tablet, a female figure with a cross, sickle and some ears of corn sculptured in marble. "Blessed are the dead which die in the Lord. Sacred to the memory of Elizabeth Tuckfield spinster of Little Fulford in the county of Devon who departed this life Nov. the 10th 1807 in the 92nd year of her age.
Sincerely regretted by her numerous friends and justly lamented by the poor, to whom during a life unusually extended, and by her last will and testament she was a great and liberal benefactor Francis Lord de Dunstanville erected this monument in testimony of his gratitude affection and esteem for a women whom he loved and admired whilst living and whose death he deeply deplored.

South Wall. A tablet with Ionic columns and an entablature. *In memoriam Rogeri Tuckfield de Raddon Court armigeri et Mariae uxoris qui Deo vocante feliciter ex hac vita. Illa 22 Januarij 1677 aetat 72 Ille 22 Januarii 1683 aetat 78 in meliorem transmigrarunt. Hic etiam dormit Johannes Rogeri filij natu maximi et de Raddon Court armigeri primogenitus qui trimestris praepropera morte raptus tutissimus in tumulo invenit cuna 15° Julij 1681.* Arms 3 Shields
I. Argent 3 Fusils in fess sable (Hamlya or Holway)
II. I impaling Sable 2 Swords in saltier, points upwards argent hilted or.
III. I impaling Argent a Chevron sable between 3 mullets pierced gules. (Davie)

Nave
Floor. *Hic jacet Rogerus Tuckfield de Raddon court Armiger qui post vitam piam fe -- die Octobris Anno Domino 1686 aetatis suae 51.* Arms Tuckfield impaling -- a chevron between 3 Mullets
Here lieth the body of Nicholas son of Nicholas Thomas of this parish who died 26 Nov. 1668 aged 43 years.
Here lieth the body of Mary wife of Roger Tuckfield of Raddon Court esq who departed this life 22 Jan. anno 1677 being in the 72 year of her age.
Here also lieth the body of Walter Tuckfield their son who departed this life 19 day of Feb. ano 1668 in the 23 year of his age, Arms. Tuckfield impaling 2 swords in saltier.
Here lieth the body of Roger Tuckfield the elder of Raddon court esq who departed this life the 22 Jan 1663 aged 77 also here lieth the body of John son of said Roger Tuckfield esq who died 27July 1705. Arms. Tuckfield impaling 2 swords in saltier.
Here lieth the body of Elizabeth wife of Richard Mallack of Axmouth esq and daughter of Roger Tuckfield of Radon Court esq who departed this life Sept. 17. 1682 Arms Per chevron engrailed (or stable) in chief 2 (Sellet) each charged with a Fleur de lis (of the first) in base a (Bezant) charged with a Fleur de lis (of the second) impaling Tuckfield.
Here lieth the body of Thomas Sandford vicar of this parish who died Sept 29 1716 also Anstice his wife who died Feb. 17 1707 and Edward their son who died March 26 1711. [missing]
-- Depositum reverendi viri ac gravis theolog. magistri Johanni Preston --

North Aisle
Tablet. Underneath are deposited the remains of Charles Pugh esq who died Jan. 30 1787 aged 56 also of Sarah his wife who died May 31. 1793 aged 50 and their children Nicholas Thomas died Sept 1784 aged 17. Henry died Feb. 11 1807 aged 33. John died March 13 1809 aged 36 Charles Dally died July 19 1826 aged 56 Hugh died Feb. 2 1829 aged 52 Also Mary Sanders wife of the above John Pugh died April 29 1837 aged 63 [missing]
Floor. Here lieth the body of George Barne esq of Chapple St Martin in this parish who departed this life 16 June 1789 aged 47 Mary B. relict of the above died 4 Nov.1823 aged 82. Dinah Arabella daughter of Thomas & Frances Kingdom of Chapple St Martin in this parish died Dec. 19. 1830 aged 2 years [missing]
Here lieth the body of Thomas the son of Thomas Pennington of this parish who departed this life 8 April 1680 also George the son of --- [missing]
--nth day of March An Dom 1638 [missing].

James Thomas of Bidwell in this parish died 5 Sept. 1782 aged 41 years Grace his wife died 17 April 18-- aged 79 years [missing].
Here lieth the body of John Rackcliffe of this parish who died 1734 also of Elizabeth his wife who died 22 Jan. 1761 aged 76 years [missing].
--- of Chapple in this parish who was buried the 22 day of March 1759 aged 51 years [missing].
Richard Thomas of this parish yeoman died 25 March 1705 in the 57 year of his age [missing].

South aisle
Floor. Here lieth the body of Richard the son of -- October 1730.
Hic juxta dormiunt Petrus West de Yellowford armiger. Et Elizabetha uxor filia Georgii Fursdon de Fursdon armig. qua morte rapia 25 Septembris 1673 conjugium ita solutum mors denuo junxit Janua. 28. 1694. Also here lieth the body of George West their son who departed this life 26 day of July 1664 aged 26 years. Arms semi of Billets a Lion rampant. -- impaling -- a lion passant between 3 Fleurs de lys
Here lyeth the body of Elizabeth Richards daughter of Ralph Richards yeoman departed this life 20 day of October Ano Dom 1643 [missing].
Underneath are deposited the remains of Thomas Kingdom of Lynch in this parish who departed this life 7 day of May 1833 aged 72 years. Also George son of the above who died May 9 1836 aged 31 years [missing].

Church yard.
A tomb. Sacred to the memory of Catherine Potbury wife of the revd Brian Beauchamp who departed this life Nov. 16. 1832 aged 67 also the rev Brian Beauchamp rector of Hawkridge and Withypool Somersetshire who departed this life June 15. 1834 aged 58.
William Crosse of London departed this life 20. Dec. 1825 aged 31 years.
Against the East wall of the church are Tablets thus inscribed.
Infra situs est Lucas Hermannus Coleridge chirurgus qui aetate al nimium nova vitam obiit periti peritum egeni humanum cuncti honestum laudabunt quod compro-bavit vita obsignavit mors Christianams amplexus est fidem et hancce (absit invidia) tam cari capitis memoriam inscuim voluit veritas et domesticus dolor. Ob. tredecimo die cal. Feb. A.D. 1790 aetat 24.
Underneath are deposited after a widowhood of 40 years the mortal remains of Sarah wife of Luke Herman Coleridge of this parish surgeon and daughter of Richard Hart of Exeter who died on the 4 Feb. 1830 aged 69 years. This tomb was erected over the tomb of both his parents by William Hart, bishop of Barbados and the Leeward islands.
Sacred to the memory of William Rennell Coleridge son of William Hart, bishop of Barbados and the Leeward islands and of Sarah Elizabeth his wife daughter of Thomas Rennell D.D. Dean of Winton. Born at Barbados 16 Aug. 1826 and died 13 June 1827 and was buried in the churchyard of St. Michael in that island.

BUTTERLEIGH

Davidson (pp. 485–7) visited [St Matthew's] Butterleigh on 28 July 1843 and noted it was 4½ miles south east of Tiverton. He observed a church in a 'secluded village'. The church was rebuilt in 1861 by John Hayward (Pevsner, *Devon*, 240). Three memorials are missing from the five that Davidson recorded.

The church of this secluded village consists of a nave about 24 feet long by 12 wide a chancel 12 by 9, an aisle on the north side about 22 by 12, a porch covering the south door and an embattled tower at the western end of the nave containing 3 bells. The door is under a lancet arch of early date pointed arch divides the nave from the chancel. The windows of the nave & chancel are small, of two lights with trefoiled heads, those of the aisle are formed by three small lights in a rectangular frame that of the tower has 3 lights with cinquefoiled heads and 6 foils in the arch above. The ceilings are flat [now coved and ribbed]. There is a piscina with a shelf in the south wall of the chancel under a trefoiled arch. The font is ancient, a rude low circular stone basin on a column ornamented with rude mouldings. The pulpit and pews are of oak are modern. On one side of the nave is a curious alms box on a pillar both of oak carved in scrolls & devices and painted with an ancient lock; the date 1629 is carved among the scrolls and below is painted "This boxe is freelie given to receive alms for ye poore" There is a gallery at the western end of the nave [removed]. The monuments and inscriptions afford the following particulars.

Chancel
Floor. "Here lyeth the bodie of John Sampson rector of this parish who died ye 14 of August 1644 and also Gresey Porter minister of this parish who died ye 9 th of March 1650" On three sides of the lower part of the stone are these inscriptions
This stone upon These did bestow
A wife to both as some did know
Learning with virtue meet together
In these teachers to teach other
Arms. (Sable) 3 Church bells (argent) a canton ermine [this stone is now located in the porch]
In the tower lie the fragments of 2 monuments which were formerly affixed to the wall of the aisle and which seem to have been handsomely painted & gilt, among them were discovered two tablets which the following inscriptions were with great difficulty and long investigation deciphered [both missing]
1. *Memoriam sacrum venerablis viri Petri Mudeni ex Hagacomitis Belgica oriundi in medecina doctoris Padua apud Italos creati A.D. 1597 hujus insula in qua jacit fundator qui una cum uxore ejus Elizabetha (Philippi Courtenay e Molandia Damnoniorum armigeri) sub vicino marmore placide in Domino obdorm -- cu firm -- fretus fiducia beatificae resurrectionis.*
Epicedium.
Petra tegit vicina Petrum cum conjuge Muden

Qui celebris medica doctor in arte fuit
Vir probitatis, amans, puraeque ac clarus amicis
Sed quos odit, eis hostis acerbus erat
Natus apud Belgas, apud Anglos vixit, et inter
Coelicolas foelix regnat in arce poli.

II To the memory of Elizabeth the wife of Dr. Peter Muden & eldest daughter of Phillip Courtenay of Molland esq who departing this life exchanged it for a better the fifth day of February. Anno Domi 1624.
Quid --- promeritis conjux fidissima praestem
Quo satis extremo fiet et officio
Fundo gemens lachrimas ac te sequor ut bene paris
Jungamur Christi sanguine coelicolis.
Abi et bonis cum vivere
Discito cum piis mori
Fide, sed vide.
Arms in a lozenge. Or 3 Torteaux, a Label of three points azure charged with 9 plates.

Nave
Floor: here lieth the body of Christopher Leigh of the parish of Bradninch who departed this life the 5th June 1715 in the 57 year of his age.
On the south site lieth the body of Alice the wife of Nicholas Chattey of this parish who died 2 Aug 1652 Elizabeth his daughter died 16 Nov1643. Ann the wife of John Uppington of this parish died 27 July 1651 aged 30. Married 10 years [missing]

BICKLEIGH

Davidson (pp. 493–8) visited [St Mary's] Bickleigh on 28 July 1843 and noted it was 4 miles south of Tiverton. He observed that 'the church of this village which is seated in so beautiful a spot contains some interesting relics of ancient time'. The church was rebuilt in 1847–8 (Pevsner, *Devon*, 170). One memorial is missing from the twenty-two that Davidson recorded.

It comprises a nave about 27 feet long by 16 wide, a chancel about 25 by 14, an aisle on the south side about 45 by 8, a porch over the south door, and a tower at the western end of the nave embattled and containing 4 bells and a clock, The south door is under a semicircular arch with a label over it, and above a niche for a statue, but all is loaded with whitewash. The chancel and nave open to the aisle by 4 low ogee arches on columns formed by 4 shafts with intervening mouldings, their capitals boldly carved in foliage with shields & devices, but thickly loaded with whitewash. The eastern window of the chancel may be assigned to the 13th century; it is formed by three lancet lights without sweeps under one arch the other windows are of various dates, some of lancet trefoiled & others of lights with low arched heads in a horizontal frame. The western window in the tower is of unusual form having 3 lights the centre one highest with semicircular heads under one arch, with triangular openings above them. There is no painted glass nor any chancel or altar screen. The ceilings are coved and that of the nave is ribbed, with bosses of foliage at the intersections of the ribs. The Font is of stone and very ancient, a low basin circular at top and octagonal below, with a kind of lozenge & beaded moulding near the upper edge. Some of the old oak benches remain, the ends boldly carved in trefoiled panels and foliage, on one of them is the figure of a husbandman in high relief done with great spirit. The pulpit & some of the pews are modern. On a pew in the chancel are the following coats of arms carved in oak & painted.
I Quarterly 1 & 4 Or 3 Lions passant gardant in pale Sable (Carew)
2 & 3 (argent) 3 Chevrons sable. (archdeacon or Ercedeene)
II Quarterly 1 & 4 Carew. 2 & 3 (argent) 3 Bends sable
III Quarterly 1 & 4 Carew, 2 & 3. sable 6 Bezants
IV Carew impaling vert a blazing Star or. 3. 2 & 1.
V Carew impaling -- a blazing star
VI Carew impaling Or a cross engrailed sable (Upham) [missing]
Near the door is an old alms box of oak [missing]. The floor is paved with red tiles among those in the aisle some are ornamented with quatrefoils & fleurs de lis [stone floor]. There is a gallery across the western end of the nave [removed].

The monuments and inscriptions convey the following particulars.

Chancel
North wall. Under an ogee with six sweeps an altar tomb, on the slab this inscription.

Here lieth the body of John Carew of Bickleigh esq who died the 5th day of
December 1588
Marmora nec tumuli grandesve ex aere colossi
Nec genus aut proavi nobile nomen habet
Buccina nobelium virtus sit claraque vitae
Postera transacta gens canat acta bene.
Arms -- 3 lions passant in pale, impaling -- a Blazing star
Arms on the wall under the arch Quarterly 1 & 4 Carew
2 & 3. Or 3 torteaux
Above the last a marble monument Corinthian columns supporting an entablature
with figures, painted and gilt on the base the effigy of a man in half armour kneeling
with a book in his hand, a tablet behind him adorned with scrolls is thus inscribed
Reader as thou walk by this vault here under thou viewest my tomb shed for ---a tear
now are I was blest with sweet ioyes on----- as well as in heaven.
Arms Carew. Two loose shields which appear to have belonged to this monument
are thus charged
I Carew impaling Carew
II Carew impaling Or a Cross engrailed sable
A small tablet which appears to have been a part of a ruined monument, thus inscribed.
Here under lieth -- of Thomas Carew -- it son of
Floor. *Hic jacet Johannes Drue quondam Rector de Byelegh obiit xviii die mens*
Januarii a. dni MCCCCCXXXI.
On the same stone here lieth the body of Mr. George Carew late parson of Bickley
who died ye eight daye of April 1610.
Hic jacet Thomas Carew filius Theodo-- Carew -- M Rectoris de Bickl-- et Cadeleigh
et Alice uxoris ejus ob 28 die Octobris -- Domini 1693 ter--
Here lieth the body of John Deuenish rector of this parish who departed this life 6
day of April 1678 Here also lie his three daughters Katherin Dorothe and Dorothe
[missing]
In memory of Timothy Smallwood esq of Cumberland who died 23 Dec. 1794 aged 34.
In memory of Lydston wife of the revd John West Carew who died 25 day of Nov.
1795 aged 39. Charles Smallwood son of John West and Lydston Carew died 13
day of March 1706 aged 19 months. The revd John West Carew died 5 Jan 1826
aged 70 years.
Underneath lieth the body of Mrs. Ann Samford who departed this life 4 Sept 1752
aged 75.
--- year of his age. Christ's mercy is my merit
---- *Carew quondam archipresbyter de Haccombe et vicarius de Harberton obiit 25*
die Novembris A.D. 1681.
A stone with a cross bonus standing on a base on one side of the stone "*Hic jacet*
Matheus Carew archipresbyter de Haccombe et rector de Bickleigh qui obiit primo
Aprilis Domini 1684."

Nave
North Wall. A tablet. Near this tablet lie the remains of Agnes Waldron who died 30
Aug. 1796 aged 80 also of Elizabeth Gammons who died 28 June 1799 aged 85 also
Susanna Morse relict of Mr John Morse of Halberton who died 18 March 1807 aged
88 also Elizabeth Pitman only child of the above John and Susanna Morse and wife

of the revd John Pitman M.A. Rector of Porlock in the co of Somerset, who died
Feb. 2. 1824 aged 62.
Floor. Christopher Gill of Chederleigh was buried A.D. 1654 also Margaret wife of
John Gill of Chederleigh was buried here Sept 20. 1687. Here lieth the body of John
Gill of Chederleigh the elder who died 23 Aug 1693.

South Aisle
East wall. A large handsome stone altar tomb carved in pilasters vases and flowers,
upon it the whole length recumbent effigy of a man in armour without a helmet
by his side lying on her side against the wall his wife with a book in her hand. At
his head and feet the kneeling figures of two daughters, against the wall is a tablet
but the inscription is totally defaced and above it a shield with the following coats
of arms
Quarterly of 20
I or 3 Lions passant gardant in pale sable (Carew)
II Per pale sable and Gules a Saltire counter-charged (&)
III Gules ---
IV --- 3 Serpents nowed
V Gules a Maunche (ermine) (Mohun)
VI Or 3 Eagles displayed gules
VII Vair, a chief compony or and gules
VIII Gules 2 Bends wavy or (Brewer)
IX Or 3 Torteaux (Courtenay)
X (argent) 3 Chevrons sable (Ercedeene or archdeacon)
XI (argent) 3 bends sable (Haccombe)
XII Azure a Bend or a label of 3 points gules (Carmino)
XIII Gules 4 Fusils conjoined in fess ermine (Dinham)
XIV Or a Cross engrailed sable (UpHam)
XV (Gules) 3 door arches argent (capitals & pedestal or) (Arches)
XVI Or 3 Torteaux a label of 3 points azure (Courtenay)
XVII --- 6 ----3, 2 & 1
XVIII --- a fess between 3 rams (question) passant sable
XIX Or, Crusily of cross crosslets patees fitchees and a Lion rampant azure.
XIV Or a cross engrailed sable.

South wall. A large handsome stone monument, an altar tomb richly carved in scrolls
and devices, upon it a smaller tomb, and on the table the effigy of a women lying on
her side, her right hand holding a book, her head resting on a skull, over the whole a
semicircular arch, the soffits and back enriched with scrolls & foliage on the side two
fluted Corinthian columns supporting an entablature with figures and obelisks, and
below the female the effigy of an infant in a cradle. A tablet at the back thus inscribed
Carew's daughter Erisey's wife her name Elizabeth
By pleasure of Almighty God in child bed found a death
With sad & unexpected chance with grief did kill ye joy
Of gladded parents and her mate in bringing forth a boy
To God she lived in God she died young years in vertus old
And left until it rise again this tombe her corps to hold.
Vixit annos 23 et mortua est 8° die Augusti Anno Dni 1616.
Arms. Sable a Chevron argent between 3 Griffins sergeant or.

In this wall is a lofty ogee arch with several mouldings and 4 sweeps. The tomb, if ever any below it, no longer remains.

On the wall above the last mentioned arch are two panels occupied by half length portrait figures in relief of a man in armour and his wife and below them this inscription. Here under lieth the body of Peter Carew esquire who died the 18th day of September 1654 aetatis suae -- also Elizabeth his wife daughter of Sir Christopher Chidly who died the 17 day of August 1619 aetatis suae 56.

Here lies our bodies God hath our spirits

Not for our owne but Gods' owne merrittes

Arms. Carew impaling Ermine 3 Lions rampant gules (Chidleigh)

It is stated that the notorious vagabond Bampfylde Moore Carew was buried in this aisle but that his uncle the revd John Carew then rector of this parish would not allow his body to remain there and caused the coffin to be taken up and interred in the church yard at the eastern end of the aisle.

Church yard.

An altar tomb. Here lyeth the body of Simon Pidesly who dyed the 16th day of August Anno Domino 1609. Here near adjoining lyeth buried ye bodie of Joan ye wife of Simon Pidesly who died ye 2 daye of June Ano 1624

An altar tomb. Here lyth the body of John Lovell of Bickleigh who died the 25 Nov. 1690 aged 68 years who gave one parte of four of the land of Collacy to the poor of Puiles quarter in Tiverton, two parts in -- cloth other in money to ye poor of this parish to be distributed yearly by ye overseers of each parish on the 25th day of March

Here also lieth the body of Mary wife of the above John Lovell who departed this life the 10 day of -- 1707.

CADELEIGH

Davidson (pp. 501–3) visited [St Bartholomew] Cadeleigh on 28 July 1843 and noted it was 4 miles south west of Tiverton. He observed that the church 'presents no remarkable features of antiquity'. Seven memorials are missing from the fourteen Davidson recorded.

It consists of a nave about 45 feet long by 15 wide a chancel about 18 by 5 an aisle on the north side about 54 feet by 14 a porch covering the south door and a tower at the western end embattled & contains 5 bells – In a half turret on the north side of the tower, for the newel stair, is a niche with a statue much mutilated. The south door is under a lancet arch of an early date. The nave and chancel are open to the aisle by 5 low arches of many mouldings resting on columns formed by shafts & mouldings with capitals boldly carved in foliage heads and shields all loaded with whitewash. The ceilings are coved, that of the aisle ribbed and ornamented with bosses of foliage at the intersections of the ribs gilt. The western window is of 3 lights with ogee trefoiled heads and perpendicular tracery in the arch. The windows of the nave and chancel are of 2 and 3 lights, one is large with perpendicular tracery the others modernized. Those of the aisle are of three pointed lights under low arches. There is an altar-screen of plain wood painted. The pulpit & pews are of oak and a recent date. The Font is a low square stone basin with corners cut of standing on an octagonal column. The floor is paved with red tiles and there are a few ornamented with knots & devices. A gallery across the western end of the nave [removed].

The monuments and inscriptions afford the following particulars.

Chancel
North Wall. A marble monument – an entablature supported by Corinthian columns.
Juxta hunc locum jacent reliquiae Jacobi Battin gen. et Katharinae uxoris ejus ambo erga pauperes eximie liberales – ut utriusque testamentis constat constabitque –
Prior obiit 15° Julii Anno Dni 1669
Posterior obiit 3rd Jun Anno Dni 1691
Floor. Here lye the bodyes of James Batten gent who gave ye poore of this parish four pounds yearely for ever out of his farm of Langleigh & Dame Katherine his wife who after his death married Sir Benjamin Oliver Kt. After his death married Nicholas Dennys esq & gave to ye poor of this parish twenty pounds for a stock to employed for ever and ye yearely profit thereby raised to be annually distributed amongst the poor & died the 3rd of June 1691.
The wicked like a wasted candle sink
Within ye socket & there lye & stink
But godly men dissolved do yield a sent
Like pretious odours went their box is rest
Even so did they at their departure giving
Large and lasting guiftes to refresh ye living.

Here lie the bodies of two sonnes of John Fursdon of Cadeleigh gent each of them named John, dying in their infancy ye 1 was buried 1649 ye other 1651.

Lo what a fatal change is this
The youngest death doth not dismiss
The best beloved of their friends
Must hence away for whom death sends
Mortalitie behold & look
Read here thy fate as in a book
Tis not the aged hence must go
But youth and children die also:
Punctum est quod via -- us et puncto minus. [missing]

Nave
Floor. Here lyeth the body of Mary ye wife of Thomas Mogridge of this parish who departed this life ye 24 of August 1692. [missing]

North aisle
East wall. A large Grecian altar of white marble on which is an urn, painted and gilt, a tablet within a scroll in front is this inscription.

In memory of ye Lady Bridget Higgins daughter of ye Hon Sir Bevill Granville Baronet first wife to Simon Leech esq mother to ye Honourable Sir Simon Leech Knight of the Bath afterwards ye wife and relict of Sir Thomas Higgins Knt. Who died the 7 March aged 62 in ye year 1691 (painted over a former inscription in Latin filled up with plaister but apparently to the same person)

North wall. A large and splendid stone and marble monument 12 feet long and reaching to the ceiling, in the Roman style carved painted and gilt, a tomb under a lofty canopy supported in front by 4 Corinthian capitals, the roofs and back filled with scrolls figures cherubs etc. On the tomb lie the recumbent effigy of a man in armour and his wife in a large ruff; at their head a man in plate armour kneeling, at their feet a woman and in front of the tomb 4 males & 5 females all kneeling. At the back above the tomb is a tablet thus inscribed. "Here lye the bodyes of Sir Simon Leach Knight son of Simon Leach of Crediton blacksmith and ye lady Katherine Leach his wife daughter of Nicholas Torberville esquire whose true affection in religious wedlock caused there desire to make there bed together in the dust."

Coniugis a fato cedo incurvatus ad unam Qui vitae consors fuuceris ibo comes.

Tablet on the right side. *Gualteros filius et haeres*

Simonis Leach militis medicis occubuit fato

Sistas care pater citius mea corrit arena

Ut possim voti nuntius esse tui.

Below it

Simon leach Gualter. militis filius et haeres Regis Caroli secundi exulis assertor strenuus obiit desideratissimos Junii 25 Ano Dom 1660 aetatis sue 28.

Tertius en sequitur nulli tamen ille secundus.

Pudicis rarus rarus et ingenio

Tablet on the left side M. S. Sir Simon Leach Kt. of the Bath son of Simon Leach esq buried 30 June 1708. Arms

I.   Ermine on a chief indented gules 3 ducal Coronets or (Leach)
II.   I impaling Argent a Lion rampant gules (Turberville)
III.   I impaling Argent a Saltire engrailed between 4 cinquefoils or (false)

A shield loose – question whether belonging to this monument
Gules 3 Falchion barwise in pale argent hilted or.
Floor -- lieth ye -- Philip Shoridge of Tiverton -- the 5 day --1646. [missing]
Here lyeth the body of Eliz. Helmore wife of Ambrose H. who departed this life the
23 day of November 1670 [missing]
Here lie the bodys of Tristram & Sarah son and daughter of Thomas Helmore &
Sarah his wife of this parish who departed this life June 14th 1685 [missing]
Here lieth the body of -- wife of -- Helmore of Cadbury who dep. this life 20 Sept.
AD 1695 aged 69 [missing]

CADBURY

Davidson (pp. 505–11) visited [St Michael and All Angels] Cadbury on 28 July 1843 and noted it was 6 miles north east of Crediton. The church was extensively restored in 1856–8 by William White (Pevsner, *Devon*, 240).

The church of this parish consists of a nave about 32 feet long by 15 wide a chancel about 15 feet square an aisle on the north side about 42 feet long by 12 wide, a porch over the south door and a tower at the west end of the nave embattled & contains 4 bells, with a square turret on the north side rising above the battlements. The south door is under a pointed arch of early date with a niche over it. The nave and chancel open to the aisle by 4 wide arches of numerous mouldings resting on columns formed by alternate shafts and mouldings with capitals boldly carved in foliage and shields. The windows of the chancel and the west window in the tower are new and are of the same design as the old east window in the aisle of 3 lights with cinquefoiled heads under ogee arches with perpendicular tracery above. The windows of the nave are of 3 lights with low arched heads in rectangular frames. Those of the aisle are 3 pointed lights under low pointed arches. In the eastern window of the aisle is a large figure in old painted glass of a saint with his hands uplifted. Against the east wall of the chancel is a new free stone altar screen recently erected in very good taste, consisting of sunken panels under trefoiled ogee arches supported by attached shafts with capitals of foliage. The side panels are higher than the others, under cinquefoiled canopies supported by buttresses terminating with crocketted pinnacles and finials. There is a small square piscina in the south wall. The communion rails are new and in good taste formed by open cinquefoiled arches and mouldings of foliage, carved in oak. The Font is a small modern marble basin on a pedestal. The pulpit & pews are of oak & not of ancient date. There is a gallery across the western end of the nave. In the church yard remains the base and part of the column of an ancient cross.

The monuments and inscriptions afford the following particulars.

Chancel
North Wall. A marble tablet with a long laudatory inscription to George Sydenham Fursdon of Fursdon esq who died Feb. 8. 1837 aged 65. Charles Fursdon the eldest much beloved and deeply lamented son of George Sydenham Fursdon and Harriet his wife died July 16 1824 aged 26.
Floor. Here lyeth ye bodye of George Fursdon second sonne of George Fursdon of Fursdon esquire who died the first day of July 1610.

North aisle
North wall. A marble monument and sarcophagus. Sacred to the memory of Charles Hale esq late of Fursdon in this county who died 28 Oct 1795 aged 76
(then follows a laudatory inscription)

Underneath is the body of Ann Hale the affectionate wife and disconsolate widow of the above Charles Hale who survived him near ten years, aged 78

Arms Azure 3 arrows points downwards – a chief or impaling

Per pale indented or and azure an Eagle displayed

East wall. A tablet, Lucy Fursdon a dutiful child died on the 29 Oct 1838 in the 8th year of her age.

South wall. A tablet. Harriet Fursdon eldest daughter of George Sydenham Fursdon and of Harriet his wife closed a life twenty two years and two weeks July 24. 1820. affectionate meek gentle diligent dutiful and holy.

North wall. A tablet and urn. Near this place are deposited the remains of Elizabeth wife of John Lyon esq; she was daughter of George Fursdon esq by his first wife. She died 30 June aged 26. Erected by her husband.

Nave

Floor. Here lieth the body of Henry Tucker of this parish yeoman -- Anno Dom 1628.

WHIMPLE

Davidson (pp. 513–19) visited [St Mary] Whimple on 29 July 1840 and noted it was 8 miles east of Exeter. The church was rebuilt by Hayward in 1845, when the nave was extended and the south aisle was added (Pevsner, *Devon*, 905). Four memorials are missing from the eight that Davidson recorded.

This village church consists of a nave about 24 feet long by 21 wide, a chancel about 24 feet by 21, an aisle on the north, a porch on the south and a large heavy low tower at the western end relived by 2 Buttresses on each face & crowned by battlements and a pinnacle at each angle There are 4 Bells. The nave opens to the aisle by 5 low arches resting on columns formed by 4 shafts with mouldings between them and capitals carved in foliage & flowers but loaded with whitewash one of them next the chancel has been restored but not in good taste. The ceiling is coved and divided into compartments by mouldings with bosses of rude faces at their intersections [now a wooden ceiling]. In the south wall is a window of unusual character, wide & large & divided by mullions into 4 lights with trefoil heads with openings above them under a very low arch. The eastern window is formed by mullions and a transom into 6 lights which have cinquefoiled heads but the arch above is hidden by a flat ceiling to the chancel [flat ceiling removed]. The windows of the aisle are in the perpendicular style having 3 lights with cinquefoiled heads. The pulpit is of oak but in modern taste. Many of the old oaken benches remain the ends carved in panels with various devices, among them a shield charged with a saltire a Bird bolt, and a heart pierced by arrows [old pew ends removed]. In the south wall of the nave near the chancel is a small piscina or a locker under a cinquefoil arch. The Font is of stone, octagonal, the sides carved in panels divided saltire well into trefoil with a moulding with trefoil headed panels but the whole is heavily charged with whitewash. There are some remains of a chancel screen the base of which was ornamented with a range of saints painted on panels, among them may be traced St. Apollonia holding a tooth in a pair of pincers – St. John the Baptist with a lamb. and St. Sebastian pierced with many arrows [removed]. The Porch is covered by a large heavy arched roof in front of which is a stone with the date of name "1718 John Fort, minister" [removed]

The monuments & inscriptions afford the following particulars.

Chancel
In the S.E corner a handsome marble monument, an entablature supported by Corinthian columns, ornamented with cherubs and scrolls painted & gilt- In memory of the revd John Hickes D.D. late rector of this parish who departed this life aged 55 on the 14 day of January AD. 1707 with the just & universal commendations of all that knew him for a constant & painful performance of all the duties of his holy functions with true and unaffected piety towards God justice towards his neighbour charity to the poor, inviolable affection to his loving wife & unmovable fidelity to his friends. This monument was caused to be erected by Sarah his mournful relict.

Arms 2 shields I Gules a chevron between 3 Fleurs de lis or. II I impaling Argent a Crofs between 4 Rose gules.

East wall. A Marble tablet. – Anna Maria Newcome daughter of Norah Neale of Stamford Baron co Northampton Esq wife of Daniel Newcome DD. Dean of Gloucester & Rector of this parish. Died 20 March 1732 in the 44 year of her age. Arms. Argent a (Lions head erased sable) between 3 Crescent gules, impaling Per pale -- & gules -- (defaced)

Floor – memorial of Dr Hicks as above, then "Sarah his wife died 9 April 1750 in the 83rd year of her age." Arms as above [missing].

Master William Showers of the city of Exeter Merchant son of Mr. William Showers of Soppesham deceased Died 7 Oct 1661. Thomasine S. wife of W.S. of Topsham & Mother of W.S. of Exeter Died 1 Sept 1663.

Daniel Newcome M. A. Rector of this parish. Died 2 Feb. 1781 aged 65.

Mary wife of Samuel Walker of this parish Died 20 Dec. 1703 – Samuel W. gent of this parish Died 23 July 1719 [missing]

Nave

Floor. Abraham Smith of this parish gent. Died 21 Oct. 1764 aged 35. (or 85).

Mary wife of William Perryman Died 22 --- 1613 [missing].

William P. Buried 26 Sept 1643 [missing].

Aisle

Floor. Richard Newbery gent. Died 9 Oct 1769 aged 63. Susanna N. his wife. Died 7 Aug 1774 aged 79.

Newspaper cutting, no name of newspaper, dated 1846

The late Canon Heberden, - A very handsome monumental tablet, in memory of the late Canon Heberden, has been executed by Mr. S. Rowe, statuary, of this city, from a design by Mr. Harward, architect, for the purpose of being erected in the church of Whimple, of which parish the rev. gentleman was rector. The tablet is of jet black marble, and bears the following inscription in gold letters, of the early English character: – In memory of Thomas Heberden, M.A., nearly 55 years rector of this parish, and 55 years canon residentiary of the cathedral Church at Exeter, where his body is interred; born at Overbury, in the county of Worcester, Sept. 28; 1754; died at the rectory in this parish, Oct. 17, 1843, aged 80 – "Like a shock of corn in his season!" The tablet is crowned by a canopy and pinnacles of Caen stone, carved elaborately in the decorated English style of architecture; and at the sides are narrow panels, supporting scrolls, wreathed around leafless branches, and bearing the inscription, – "Blessed are the dead which die in the Lord; even so saith the sprit, for they rest from their labours." The plinth consists of compartments with quatre-foils, having the arms of the family in the centre. The tablet is erected by the family of the deceased, who was much beloved and esteemed.

CLYST ST LAWRENCE

Davidson (pp. 521–2) visited [St Lawrence] Clyst St Lawrence on 24 June 1843 and noted it was about 8 miles north east of Exeter. Three memorials are missing from the four that Davidson recorded.

This village church consists of a Nave about 32 feet long by 20 wide, a chancel about 18 by 12, a large embattled tower at the western end containing 5 bells and a porch covering the north door which is entered by a pointed arch of several mouldings. The western door in the tower is under an elegant pointed arch enriched with foliage in the mouldings. A stair turret at the north-east corner of the tower has a niche with a crocketted canopy and pinnacles in which is a statue of the Virgin and Child. The windows are of three lights with cinquefoiled heads and perpendicular tracery in the arches. The ceilings are coved and ribbed with bosses of foliage at the intersections of the ribs, but all coated with whitewash. The chancel screen remains. It is formed by a range of open pointed arches with fan tracery above them carved in oak and mouldings of foliage above which is the rood loft apparently perfect. It is entered from a door way with stairs in a projecting turret in the south wall. The pulpit and pews are modern. The Font is very ancient, a large circular stone basin with a rude moulding under it, very low but raised on a block of stone. A gallery at the western end of the nave with the date in front 1652 and a shield with arms – on a Bend 3 Pheons [removed]--- In the church yard are the remains of a handsome cross a quadrangular pillar on an octagonal base about 12 feet high. It has a niche with the remains of a statue in it and on the upper part what appears to have been sun dial. It has been richly sculptured but it much decayed.

The inscriptions convey the following particulars

Chancel.
Floor. Here lieth the body of the revd Mr David Mechinsham rector of this parish and vicar of Salcombe who died the 23 Nov. 1751 in the 75 year of his age. also Dorothy his wife. [missing]
Joseph Elliot late of Exeter died April 1. 1829 aged 72 years. [missing]

Nave
Floor. Here lieth the body of Robert & Elizabeth son and daughter of Nicholas and Margaret Eveleigh died 8 Jan 1650 and 9th Sept. 1751. [missing]
Here lieth the body of Joan wife of Mr Robert Baker died 28 Jan 1736 in 62 year of her age. – The said Robert Baker died 17 Jan 1752 aged 87. Robert Baker gent their son died 19 Jan 1774 aged 69. Dorothea wife of the said Robert Baker and daughter of Humphrey Blackmore of Rull in Collumpton gent, died 6 June 1776 aged 50 Elizabeth Blackmore Baker daughter of Robert Baker of Collumpton esq and Alice his wife died 3 May 1763 aged 13 months Elizabeth Baker daughter of the said Robert Baker and Alice his wife died 25 Jan 1792 aged 5 years.

CLYST HYDON

Davidson (pp. 525–7) visited [St Andrew] Clyst Hydon on 24 July 1843 and noted it was about 8 miles west of Honiton, where he observed a 'rustic village'. A north aisle was added in 1856 (Pevsner, *Devon*, 270–1). Three memorials are missing from the ten that Davidson recorded.

The church of this rustic village consists of a Nave about 33 feet long by 16 wide, a chancel about 18 by 16 an aisle on the south about 48 by 12 a porch covering the south door and a Tower at the western end of the nave embattled and containing 5 bells. The nave and chancel open to the aisle by 4 low arches resting on columns formed of four shafts with intervening mouldings, their capitals carved in foliage shields and heads all coated with whitewash. Of the windows some are modernized, others are formed by 3 lights with cinquefoil heads and perpendicular tracery. The western window in the Tower is of unusual design being divided into two lights by a mullion which is continued to the head of the arch and branches off forming arches on each side. The porch is embattled and supported by buttresses & the roof is vaulted & ribbed with rich fan tracery far too handsome to be covered as it is with whitewash. The doorway is under a low arch with several mouldings. The ceiling of the nave is coved and plain, that of the aisle coved and ribbed with bosses of foliage at the intersections of the ribs. The altar screen [removed], the pulpit and pews are all of plain panelled oak. On the vicarage pew are carved the arms of Huyshe and on another those of Huyshe impaling Newte. The Font is of stone octagonal and plain. A gallery extends across the west end of the nave and another along the south aisle [both removed], the entrance to the latter is by a doorway & stairs in a projecting turret in the south wall formerly the way to the rood loft. In the church yard are the remains of a cross; a part of an octagonal shaft on a base of the same shape. An ancient yew tree stands on the north side of the chancel.

The monuments and inscriptions comprise the following particulars.

Chancel.
North Wall, a marble monument, thus inscribed.
On the north side of this church lie the remains of Francis Huyshe MA. who was almost 61 years rector of this parish and died in the 92nd year of his age Feb. 9. 1764 It was his particular request to be interred not within these walls nor with his ancestors in the vault of his family in the church of the parish of Sidbury but in this church yard in the midst of his departed flock and near the spot where he had deposited the bodies of Richard his eldest son who died June 24 1736 in his 27th year and of his beloved wife Sarah the daughter of Richard Newte esq, of Duvale in the parish of Bampton in this county who died March 19 March 1748 in the 70th year of her age. Arms Argent, on a Bend sable 3 Fishes naiant proper, impaling a Chevron between three Hearts transfixed with arrows and vulned argent.

Tablet. The revd Francis Huyshe MA. many years rector of this parish. Born at Pembridge in Herefordshire 29 Feb 1768. Died 28 Aug. 1839. Arms. Huyshe impaling Or a Pile engrailed sable.

South Wall. Tablet. Wentworth Huyshe only son of Francis Huyshe second son of that name rector of this parish and Harriet his wife daughter of John Waterhouse of Halifax Yorkshire Born 29 May 1812 died in the Island of Madeira 22 Nov: 1829. His death though awfully sudden to those around him had been long expected by himself and was met with a smile that spoke his sure and certain hope in the merits of his saviour His life will be best told by the monument which the unexampled feelings of his schoolfellows have erected in the church of Harrow to record his attainments in literature and virtues and their own veneration and affection for his memory. Arms Quarterly 1st Huyshe. 2nd Argent 5 Fusils in fess sable 3rd Argent a Cross engrailed gules between 4 Water bougets sable 4th Masonry argent & sable Chief indented sable.

North Wall a Tablet thus inscribed
Bodleio Mnema
Tres hic in terris habit Bodleius hostes
Hostes tres grandes mundum carnem Satanamque
Tres charitesque ipsi armas vos queis vicerit hoste
Tres natura benigna dedit patruos tria mundi
Virtutum specula & tanquam tria sidera coll--
Tresque academia grata gradus tria pignora honoris
Tres pariter gestat Bodleii insigne coronas
Hae tres sunt fragiles mani ipsum quarta perennis.
Arms. Or 5 Martletts in saltire sable, on a chief of the last 3 Ducal Crowns of the field. [missing]

Floor. Here lieth the body of Elijah Dene late rector of this church who died 10 May A.D. 1703 and also the body of Mary his wife who died 26 Sept. 1701 also Dorothy, John, Thomas and Elijah their children.

Here resteth in the Lord William Gifford Bach. in Div. some time fellow of Exceter college in Oxon & late rector of Clayhidon where he lived XVIII years ---- are elder & ---ble preacher --- holy keeper & an exemplar --- & --- saint & so died on ye XIII of Nov. Ano Dom 1651.

Here rested Rebecca the wife of Mr Elijah Dene rector of this parish the daughter of James Huish of Sand esq who was buried July 27 Ano Dom 1870.

-- body of -- Pyne of this parish gent who died the -- day of February

South aisle
Floor. Here lieth the body of Robert Culliford of this parish gent who died -- 21. Ano 1678. [missing]

Against the wall of the nave a wooden tablet thus inscribed
25 April 1667 Dr. Robert Hall gave by will a rent charge on his manor and lands in Broadwoodkelly and Monk Okehampton of £15 for a schoolmaster and £5 for binding apprentices 1751 Revd. Francis Huyshe gave by deed a field called highlands in this parish the rent of which is to be applied from the benefits of the schoolmaster and poor labourers [missing]

Church yard
North side a large vault with iron rails. On one of the stone. The revd Francis
Huyshe. Died 28 Aug 1839.
Stones. Milborugh Arm Huish
Martha wife of the revd Peter Mann Osborne of Pinhoe in this county died Sept
8. 1834.
Frances third daughter of the late revd George Greaves rector of Stanton-by-bridge
in the county of Derby died at Sidmouth 4 Jan 1843 aged 63 years.

BROADCLYST

Davidson (pp. 529–35) visited [St John the Baptist] Broadclyst on 30 August 1843 and noted it was 5 miles north east of Exeter. He observed that 'the noble church of this village with its lofty and handsome tower which is so great an ornament to the beautiful county around it was repaired and the ruinous parts restored in the style in which they had previously existed in the year 1833, a new roof of cast iron being at the same time put up'. This was done by Edward Ashworth (Pevsner, *Devon*, 215). One memorial is missing from the thirteen that Davidson recorded.

It consists of a Nave and Chancel without apparent division about 106 feet long by 18 wide within the walls, an aisle in the north 95 feet by 15, and aisle on the south about 90 by 12 a porch covering the south door and a square tower at the western end of the nave and chancel open to the aisles by 6 wide painted arches on each side of similar design resting on columns formed of shafts and intervening mouldings their capitals boldly carved in foliage fruit scrolls & other devices with shields one of which against the south aisle bears the date 1576. Over the arches on both sides are labels resting on large corbels of angels holding shields charged with crosses books etc. & on two of them Acland family.

The ceilings are coved and ribbed, formerly with oak, now with plaister of the same design as before The intersections of the ribs are ornamented with bosses of foliage but among them are several representing a sow and pigs, 3 rabbits, 3 fishes, human heads & scrolls – At the western ends of the aisle at the corners are octagonal turrets for stairs to the roofs which are all embattled. The porch is also embattled and ornamented with pinnacles. The south door way and that of the porch are under pointed arches the later covered by a label resting on corbels of human heads. The nave opens to the tower by a lofty arch exhibiting to view a part of the western window. The Tower is 100 feet high and contains a peal of 6 bells & a clock. It is supported by buttresses at the angles their set offers enriched with pinnacles and sculptured figures. The western doorway is handsome under a pointed arch with a rectangular labels resting on corbels of mitred heads, and quatrefoils with shields in the spandrels. The battlements are enriched with sculpture in quatrefoils and immediately below on each face is a coat of arms carved in stone. Those on the east and western sides are evidently the Royal arms, on the north & south they are not readily distinguishable but the latter is a coat quarterly of which the 2nd appears to be 2 Bends and the 3rd a Lion rampant. The summit of the tower is finished by 8 pinnacles, those at the corners larger and very handsome crocketted and enriched with sculpture. One window of the church is of early English date, that at the east end of the north aisle the mullions spread into branch tracery, the openings being filled with quatrefoils. The east window of the chancel is formed by 5 lights the others by 4 lights all cinquefoiled under low arches with perpendicular tracery. The western window in the tower has some modern showy coloured glass amongst which are the arms of the See of Exeter & those of Bishop Phillpotts, a mitre, a harp, bells, an hour glass, etc. There was formerly a chancel screen but it no longer exists. The altar screen is of free stone handsomely carved in sunken panels with crocketted canopies pinnacles and a cornice of foliage – It was designed by Hayward an architect of Exeter and executed by Rowe a sculpture of that city. In the south wall of the chancel is a piscina under a pointed arch. The communion table is modern, in the form of an altar richly carved in oak, having a range of trefoiled arches with canopies and pinnacles, the slab inlaid with strips of rosewood [changed]. On each side of it stands an ancient carved oak chair. The pulpit is modern of carved oak, the panels ornamented with shields charged with the following arms and figures.

I a Saltier Sable on a chief of the last 5 Scallops
II Quarterly. 1 & 4 Checky sable and argent a Fess gules (Ackland)
      2&3. Or 3 Cinquefoils --- with an Escutcheon for Bart. Impaling Sable a
      Spread Eagle (argent) within a Bordure of the last (Hoare)
III. St. John the Baptist holding a Lamb and a book
IV. Gules a Sword erect in pale surmounted by 2 Keys in saltire within a Bordure or.
      (For the See of Exeter)
V. Gules a Cross between 4 Swords erect. – (Bishop. Phillpotts) [removed]

The pews are of oak and modern. The font is of stone octagonal and plain on a column of similar form [changed]. A new one of more elegant design is in preparation. There are modern galleries one above the other at the western end of the nave, the fronts carved in oak in trefoil panels [removed]. In the other one is an organ [removed]. The church yard is entered by a lych-gate at the north east corner and immediately before it is a lofty cross elevated on several stages but quite plain. On the south side of the church is a very ancient yew tree.

The monuments and inscriptions are these.

Chancel.
North wall. a small but handsome marble monument. Two Corinthian columns supporting an entablature beneath which are figures of a man and woman kneeling at a desk & on a tablet below the following inscription "The tomb and monument of Henry Burrough gent who dyed the XII of December. 1605 and Elizabeth his wife (daughter of George Reynell of Malston esq.) who founded XII alms houses in Broadclyst and gave weekly maintenance to the poore and for repayraton thereof and provided VIII sermons should be there yerely preached for their better instruction."
Arms 3 shields
I Ermine a Falcon's head erased azure beaked and collard gules between 3 Fleurs de lis of the second
II Quarterly 1. Masonry Argent and sable, a chief indented of the last.
      2. Argent on a bend Sable 3 Bezants
      3. Azure on a Fess engrailed argent 3 Lozenges gules.
      4. Per pale argent and gules on a Chevron azure 3 Cross-
             crosslets or.
III. I impaling II.
Below on a large brass plate let into the wall.
Here lyeth Henry Burrough Gentleman who died the XII day of December Anno Dni MDCV [missing].

A tablet. In memory of Thomas Theophilus Cock esquire of Messing in the county of Essex who departed this life on the 12th day of April A.D. 1811 aged 57 As a small testimonial of his excellence in every relative duty of life this tablet is erected by his truly afflicted widow Eliza Cock.

As Husband Father, public, private, Friend,
all own his worth and all lament his end.
His thoughts to universal good allied
In early life, and thinking so he died!
His bright example lost my hopes I raise
In God my confidence, in God my praise!
South wall. a tablet with an urn.

In memory of Mary Ann Vigors Thomas daughter of Major General Thomas and Neville his wife who departed this life the 22 Feb. 1810 aged 1 year.

In the south wall is a monument which seems to combine a tomb with 3 sedilia. It is an open screen formed by 4 panelled rectangular shafts finishing in crocketted pinnacles & supporting ogee arches with canopies adorned with heavy crockets of foliage above them is a cornice with shields and foliage. At the back is a range of 5 panels under trefoiled arches & in them shields of the peater form. On the tomb is an effigy of a knight in plate armour with his sword by his side and a close cap on his head. His hands are uplifted in prayer angles support his head which rests on his crest which is out of a ducal coronet an arm and hand habited & the first clenched. His feet rest on a couchant lion. There are neither arms or inscription visible but as the surcoat is said to have been charged with lions the monument probably belongs to one of the Chudleigh family and may be assigned to the early part of the 16th century or late in the 15th. (See Lysons cccxxxiii)

On the floor of the nave are fragments of two stones formerly in the chancel thus inscribed.

Here -- of Richard Chidley -- Jhu have merc. – 1526.

--- *armiger qui obiit XXIX -- cum animae propicietur deus* – arms defaced – but 3 animals.

North aisle

North wall. East end. – A splendid monument to the memory of Sir John Acland knt, formed of stone & 20 feet in height consisting of a large altar tomb with a canopy supported by Corinthian columns beneath which is the whole length effigy of the knight in armour except his head, and at either side the figures of his two wives kneeling at desks. The whole structure is richly carved with scrolls and devices in the style of the period. Above the principal figure is a tablet without any inscription. On a label over the arch above are the words "*Caro mea requiescit in spe. Post tenebras sparo lucem.*" On the summit is a shield charged with these coats, and the date 1614. Quarterly of 6.

1. Checky argent sable a fess gules with a crescent for difference
2. Argent a bend wavy sable in sinister chief a gloved hand holding a hawk or.
   (false)
3. Argent a Bridge sable water proper on the bridge 3 --- (question pennons) or.
4. Argent 2 Bends wavy sable (Stapleton)
5. Argent a bend engrailed sable with a crescent for difference gules
   Charged with a trefoil (question) (Radcliffe)

6. Or on a Fess dancetty between 3 Delves azure each charged with a Lion
    rampant of the field as many Bezants (Rolle)
Motto. *A Deo omnis victoria*
Two other shields below
I Acland impaling Rolle.
II Acland impaling Or a Fleur de lis azure. (Portman)
Over the figure of one woman with the date 1613 are 2 shields with the arms of
Acland and Rolle. (Portman)
A tablet. Here layeth the body of Thomas Chappelle of Inholder of the city of Exon
who departed this life the 31 day of July Anno Dom 1637.

South Aisle
South wall. eastern end. A stone monument, an altar tomb with a flat canopy
supported by several columns beneath which on the tomb are the effigies of a man
and his wife in the costume of the 17 century. On a tablet at the eastern end against
the wall are the figures of their 4 sons and 3 daughters kneeling at a desk. The
inscription no longer exists. It recorded Edward Drew of Killerton who died in 1662.
No shield of arms.
A tablet. This tablet is erected to the memory of Paul Voysey of this parish who
departed this life March 5 1833 in the 69 year of his age. also of Thomasine his wife
who died July 22. 1820 aged 60 years.
Floor. *Hic jacit corpus Clementis Bear sepultum IX die Septembris ---.*
Hic jacit corpus -- Bear sepultum ---

In the church yard, a tomb. – John Ratcliffe died April 9. 1838 aged 75 Edward son
of John and Jane R. died 29 May aged 39. Arms. Argent 2 Bends engrailed sable.

WILLAND

Davidson (pp. 541–2) visited [St Mary the Virgin] Willand on 25 July 1843 and noted it was 2 miles north of Cullompton. Seven memorials are missing from the eight that Davidson recorded.

This village church consists of a nave about 32 feet long by 16 wide, an aisle on the north side about 44 by 14 a chancel about 16 feet square, a small Tower at the western end, and a porch covering the south door. The porch is entered by a very low arch, above which some letters are carved on a sort of label, the following may with difficulty be traced "mogryge dns" above them is a cornice ornamented with quatrefoils. The nave and chancel open to the aisle by 4 low arches resting on columns formed by 4 shafts with intervening mouldings having capitals carved in foliage and shields on which the following changes may be traced though loaded with whitewash
I Ermine on a Chevron (azure) 3 cinquefoils (or) (Moore)
II a spread eagle
III a fess between three ---
IV 3 Swords in file question Powlet.
The eastern window of the church is formed by 3 lights with cinquefoiled heads & perpendicular tracery above them. It contains a few fragments of old coloured glass. The nave has a window formed of 2 trefoil headed lights. The north aisle windows are of 3 lights with cinquefoiled heads in quadrangular frames, but the two at the east end & the west ends are under pointed arches with 3 cinquefoiled lights and perpendicular tracery above. The ceiling is coved and plain. There is a chancel screen of very late date and not worthy of notice. The Font is a modern octagonal stone basin. There are some old Tiles in the floor of the north aisle [removed] – a gallery at the western end of the nave [removed] The pulpit and pews are of recent date except for a few in the chancel called the Walrond pew around which are applied shields bearing the following coats.
I Quarterly 1 & 4 Argent 3 Bulls faces sable horned or 2 & 3 Gules 3 Mulberry leaves. (Walrond) Cogan
II Or fretty azure
III Argent 3 Bulls (or rams) passant sable horned or (Wilbey)
IV -- 3 Bulls faces sable
V Or on a bend gules 3 Millrinds argent. (Speccot)
VI Argent 3 bars wavy azure. (Sampford)
VII Argent a bend wavy cotised (sable) (Whiting)
VIII per fess azure and gules 3 Fleurs de lis or [now used as bench ends].
The Tower is low and small and contains 2 bells the openings in it are loop-holes with trefoiled heads

The monuments and inscriptions are these.

Chancel.
Floor. Here lyeth the body of William Wood who was buried the 2nd day of June 1641 [missing]
Here lyeth Joan Hartknoll the daughter of Thomas Hartknoll Clarke who departed this life the 27th day of July 1668 being aged 22 years & nine months [missing]

Nave
North wall. A wooden tablet. Memorandum Thomas Tymewell of Ashbrittle upon the desire of Susanna Lerman once of this parish gave ten pounds to this parish the interest of it to be given every St. Thomas day for ever to four poor labouring people that have no relief at the discretion of the Minister and three or four sufficient men of the parish: the relations to have it first as long as they shall remain [missing].
Floor. Here lyeth ye body of James Osmond of this parish yeoman who departed this life ye 3rd day of December Anno Dom 1684 in the 61st year of his age Here also lyeth the body of Thomas Osmond gent son of the above said James and of Grace his wife Hee left this life ye 17 day of March Anno Dom 1704 in the 33 year of his age Here lieth also the body of Grace Osmond wife of the above said James Osmond who departed this life the 23 day of July An Dom 1706 in the 75 year of her age [missing]
Here lieth the body of Joane daughter of James Osmond of this parish who died 3 May 1691 aged 11 years [missing]
Here lieth the body of -- Chave of Uplowman widow of William Chave gent who died 4 March 1728/9 aged 63 [missing].
Here lieth the body of -- Osmond wife of -- Osmond died 1 day of -- 1709 in the 44 year of her age [missing]

North aisle
North Wall. A tablet. Sacred to the memory of John Binford late of Burn Rew in this parish who died 5 April 1835 aged 75. The last of the family resident in Willand for 5 centuries. Sarah wife of the above died 16 October 1840 aged 71.

SAMPFORD PEVERELL

Davidson (pp. 545–7) visited [St John the Baptist] Sampford Peverell on 25 July 1843 and noted it was 5 miles north east of Tiverton. He observed that the village church presented some rather interesting features of the early English style of ecclesiastical architecture. The north wall of the church was rebuilt in 1861–4 by Edward Ashworth (Pevsner, *Devon*, 715–16). One memorial was missing from the four that Davidson recorded.

This village church comprises a Nave about 54 feet long by 20 wide, a Chancel about 24 by 20, an aisle on the south side about 50 by 10, a porch at the western end of the aisle and a heavy square Tower at the western end of the nave, recently repaired and containing 5 bells and a clock. The chancel is most ancient part of the building & was erected probably in the 13th or 14th century. The eastern window is formed by 3 lancet lights of unequal height under one arch the centre light being the highest the three side windows are formed of 2 lancet lights under one arch with a quatrefoil above. They have all been despoiled of their sweeps. The inner sides of the openings for the windows are formed into pointed arches resting on cylindrical shafts with circular capitals. In the south wall is a handsome double piscina under pointed arches on short cylindrical columns with circular capitals and in the north wall is a locker under two arches with trefoiled heads. The windows of the nave are of the same date & form as those of the chancel and in the north wall is a doorway walled up with a pointed arch resting on shafts with circular capitals bands and bases. There are a few bits of modern coloured glass in the windows but not one of the ancient coats of arms remains which once adorned them. The aisle was built by Margaret Countess of Derby mother of King Henry VII. It opens to the nave and chancel by 5 pointed arches on columns of alternate shafts and mouldings with plain capitals. The windows are all of 3 lights with cinquefoiled heads and perpendicular tracery. The ceilings are coved and ribbed & have bosses of foliage at the crossing of the ribs [removed]. The floors are paved with red tiles [removed]. The communion table is of carved oak and very neat & bears in front the date 1827. The pulpit and pews are modern. The Font is a modern stone basin in the Grecian style. The ancient Font lies neglected in the garden of the old parsonage house near the church. It is a low circular basin carved in stone with a rude moulding round the under part but it is much defaced. A gallery extends across the western end of the nave [removed].

The most ancient monument is a huge stone effigy of one of the family of Peverell cross legged with sword and shield which was formerly recumbent on a tomb against the north wall of the nave now set up on end against the east wall of the aisle [now against the east wall of the chancel]. It is much defaced and the armorial bearings on the shield can no longer be traced. The other monument and inscriptions are as follow.

Chancel
North wall. A stone monument carved and gilt Sacred to the memory of the pious
Mrs. Margaret Collyns wife of Thomas Collyns rector of this place grandchild of
William Cotton Lord Bishop of Exon. Died June ye 7th 1655. Arms Gules a Chevron
engrailed between 3 martletts argent [missing]
East wall a marble tablet with a brass plate in the upper part on which is engraved
a lady at her devotions with 4 sons before and 3 behind her all kneeling, below is
this inscription.
In obitum Pientissimce Heroinae D. Margaretae Povlett conjugis D. Amiciae Povlett
Equitis Aurati Epicedium
Felix prole parens, felix et sponsa marito
Margareta fui, dum superesse datum;
Ut qui contigerant, quae nil potuere beare
Omnia, vir, soboles, stirps generosa, decor,
Fundus, opes, famulumque, greges, domus hospita egenis
Magnificusque animus munificaeque manus.
His dotata bonis, populo dilecta Deoque
Vixi, et quam sortem, fata dedere tuli.
Nunc moriens animam domino cui serviet uni
Reddidi, et hoc tumulo, corpus inane jacet.
Franciscus Vincent Miles et Georgius Poulett Armiger Filii et Executores Dominae
Margaretae Poulett defunctae XXVIII die Maii 1602 Hoc monumentum posuerunt in
obsequium et grati animi testimonium. Arms in a lozenge.
Quarterly 1 & 4 Gules on a bend argent 3 Trefoils slipped (2nd Harvey)
2. – a Lion rampant
3. Per pale gules and azure 3 Lioncels rampant or within a border gobony of the
second and argent
Floor. Here lies the body of Ann Wills of this parish widow who died 7 Sept 1750
aged 68.

Nave
Tablet and urn. Sacred to the memory of Elizabeth wife of Henry Daubeny of
Landside esq who died Aug 30. 1809 aged 57.

HALBERTON

Davidson (pp. 549–55) visited [St Andrew] Halberton on 25 July 1843 and noted it was 3 miles east of Tiverton. The church was restored in 1847–9 by John Hayward (Pevsner, *Devon*, 466). Twenty-five memorials are missing from the forty-two that Davidson recorded.

The church of this parish consists of a Nave about 60 feet long by 20 wide, a Chancel about 25 by 20 aisles north and south both 74 feet by 10 a Porch over the south door and a Tower at the western end of the nave. the nave and chancel open to the aisles by 5 pointed arches on each side resting on heavy octagonal column, their capitals ornamented with small shields and foliage but all whitewashed, the windows are of 3 cinquefoiled light with perpendicular tracery in the arches – there is no stained glass. At the eastern end of the south aisle formerly stood an altar as there is a piscina in the south wall under a trefoiled arch. The south door is under a pointed arch with foliage in the mouldings and over it a cinquefoiled niche for a statue. Over the entrance porch is a coat of arms with helmet crest and supported of two animals all whitewashed and unintelligible. There is a small doorway with an elegant lancet arch in the south wall of the chancel. The ceilings are coved and modernized [now a wooden roof with bosses]. The walls of the nave and porch are embattled. The tower is also embattled and has a half hexagonal turret for the stairs on the north side. It contains 6 bells a clock and chimes.

A chancel screen of carved oak extends across both nave and aisles consisting of a range of 11 pointed arches with 6 cinquefoiled lights in each, fan tracery above them supports the rood loft which had door into it both on the north & south sides, the stairs on the south side yet remaining in a loft turret. There is no altar screen [now a wooden screen] and the communion table is quite plain. In the south wall of the chancel is a piscina under a cinquefoiled head and horizontal moulding. The Pulpit is very handsome, of oak carved in sunk panels filled with trefoiled and cinquefoiled niches, crocketted pinnacles finials, quatrefoils etc. but spoiled by being painted white [now plain wood]. The pews are modern. The Font is very ancient of stone & square and low the under part hatched in the style of the capital of an Anglo Norman column. It rests on a short cylindrical column. There are a few old tiles in the chancel floor. A gallery at the western end on the nave bears the date 1736.

Newspaper cutting, February 1852
The Right Hon. Viscountess Downe, has presented an excellent organ to the church of Halberton, built by Mr. H.P. Dicker of this city. The performance commenced on Sunday last, to a large congregation who expressed their high approbation of this brilliant instrument.

The monuments and inscriptions convey the following particulars

Chancel

1. Floor. Here lye John Were and Thomasine his wife who had issue Humfrye Were counsellour at law & Johan maryed John Bere of Huntsham esquire. This John Were in his life time gave XX pence weekly to be distributed in bread amongst poor labourers of Halberton for ever & dyed the XXVII day of June Ano Dni 1621. *Christus nobis vita* [missing]

2. H.S.E. Tho. Gul. Barlow MDCCCXXI [missing]

3. *Hic jacent Francis – de orchard et -- embris Anno Dni 1632 haec 30 D-- Dni 1633.* [missing]

4. Here lyth the body -- dyed the 29 day of January Ano Dni 1625 – Here also lyeth Elizabeth wife of the above John Minif -- who dyed the -- day of -- Ano Dni 1612. [missing]

5. -- body of Margaret Chamberlyn the wife of John Chamberlyn who died 31 day of August 1650. Also John C. yeoman died 8 Jan 1667. [missing]

6. -- *Mannitree* (query) *hujus ecclie quondam pastoris qui vitam deposuit quinto die Maii A.D.* [missing]

Nave

7. Tablet. This monument is humbly dedicated to the name of Henry May late of this parish who died Nov. 9. 1791 aged 53 years by his disconsolate daughter Sarah Baker. [missing]

8. Table and urn. Due to the merit and unassuming worth of Edward Cross gent of Corham in this parish who died 15 Nov 1723 and Susanna his wife who died 8 Nov. 1717 Also Richard Cross esq of Rawridge son of the above who died 15 June 1750 Erected by their grandson A Heathfield esq.

Floor. *Hic jacet Johannes Weare de Corham qui obiit primo die Martii Anno Dni Millessimo quinquagentes nonogesimo. Hic jacit etiam Julyana uxor ejusdem Joannis Were quae ex hac vita migravit tertio die --- 1608.* Here also lieth the body of Thomasine Were daughter of the said John Were and Johan who gave to the poor 45 pounds & she dyed the 23 day of August Anno Dni 1629.

Here lieth the body of Nicholas Turn -- of Rawridge gent who gave to the poor of this parish £20 year for ever. He died 23 day of January Ano Dni 1628.

Here lieth the body of Thomas Were of Corham in this parish gentleman aged 87 – 24 day of -- [missing]

Here lieth the body of Robert Chowne of this parish yeoman who departed this life the 28 Jan. An Dom 1653 Anno aetatis 70. [missing]

Sacrum hoc saxum cineres tegit Gulielmi in artibus magister filii natu maximi Joannis Ham de Widhayes generosi qui temperantia unica uxore felix vita sancta felicior morte beata felicissimus sicut gratus omnibus vixit ita deploratus obiit 15° die Septembris Ano Domini MDCLXXXIII annoque aetatis suae 37.

Terram terra capit melioris originis autem

Caelum animam dominum sic voluisse... [missing]

Here lieth the body of Ermine Cummins of this parish spinster who gave to 20 poor labouring persons of this parish 20 shillings a year yearely for ever to be paid to churchwardens of ye parish for the time being out of profits of -- in this parish called Mountstephens & by the said wardens with overseers to be equally divided yearly at Xmas amongst 20 such poor labourers of the parish as they shall think most fit to receive the same She departed this life 1 March 1702 in the 21 year of her age [missing].

Here lieth the body of James Osmond who dyed 25 March 1644 aged 36.

16. Here lieth the body of Ann May widow, wife of Richard May gent and sister to Nicholas Turner of Rawridge gent. She departed this life the 19 day June A.D. 1641. [missing]

17. Here lieth the body of John Crosse who died 21 March A.D. 1635 aged 28.

18. Here lieth Elizabeth relict of Robert Chowne of this parish yeoman died 20 Oct 1658 in the 75 year of her age which two had issues Margaret their eldest daughter who married John Ham gent since deceased & next adjacent buried and Agnes the youngest daughter yet living. Come Lord Jesus

19. *Hic jacet Petronella uxor Johannis Ham in parochia de Uplowman generosi qui vicessimo quarto Decembris 1658 anno aetatis 34. Johannes Ham generosus praedictae Margaretae --- amantissimus qui obiit -- die Augusti --- aet 56* [missing].

20. Here lieth the body of Mary the wife of Thomas Hartnoll clerk and daughter of -- Crosse [missing]

21. Here lieth Mary the daughter of John Ham gent & Margaret his deceased wife who died [missing]

North Aisle

22. A marble tablet. Here lieth the body of Richard Clark of Breedwell in this parish gent who died 30 July 1728 in the 35 year of his age Arms. Argent on a bend Gules between 3 Pellets as many Swans proper. (Clark)

A Hatchment for baron. Argent on a Bend between 3 Pellets as many Swans proper: On an escutcheon of pretence Argent on a Bend azure between 6 Crosslets Gules 3 Crosier or. (Clark)

23. A tablet with a female figure weeping over an urn. Sacred to the memory of John Chave esq of Nemberton House in this parish who departed this life 29 July 1796 aged 63 Cecilia his wife who departed this life 29 July 1796 aged 63 Cecilia his wife eldest daughter of the late William Troyte esq of Huntsham. She died 1 Aug 1807 aged 49. Erected by her mother

24. Floor *Orate pro aia Johannis Sambon de Mouston qui obiit XVIII die mens Octobri ano Dni millo quadragentesimo octogesimo primo.* [missing]

Floor. Here lieth the body of Agnes Clarke the daughter of Richard Clarke who dyed 24 daye of January A.D. 1633.

Here lieth the body of John Sheere gentleman who died the 2 and 20th day of Sept. in the year of our Lord 1646 Here also lieth the body of Rose his wife who dyed 26 Oct A.D. 1603 Here also lieth the body of Ambrose Sheere of Halberton gent son of the above John Sheere and Rose his wife who departed this life 8 May A.D. 1676 aet suae 73 [missing].

Here lieth the body of Richard Clark gent of Breedwell of this parish who departed this life May 30. A.D. 1728 in the 34 year of his age.

Here lieth the body of Richard Clarke yeoman late of Bridwell who departed this life 16 day of Oct A.D. 1635 here also lieth the body of Agnes Clarke wife to the foresaid Richard who departed this life 27 Sept A.D. 1648.

Richard Clarke son of the aforesaid Richard C. died 19 July 1671 aged 65.

Here lieth the body of Margaret wife of John Carpenter of Manley in this parish yeoman daughter unto Peter Warren of Broadwidger gent who departed this life 19 April 167-aged 50. John Carpenter died 21 July

South Aisle
South Wall. A marble monument. An entablature with Corinthian columns.
Here lieth the body of Humphrey Were esq Bencher of the Inner Temple deceased 27 day of March 1625 who had issue John Were his only son and Mary his eldest daughter who married Henry Copplestone of Bowden gent and Elizabeth his youngest daughter who married John Bourne of Wiveliscombe esq he lived religiously died virtuously and now we hope he reigneth with God everlastingly through Christ
Arms on 4 Shields.
I.   Sable a bend between 6 Crosslets fitchees argent (Were
II.   Sable a bend --- between 2 Lions rampant ---
III.   As I
IV.   I impaling II [missing]

An old wooden tablet with a coat of arms in a lozenge
a Bend between 6 Cross crosslets fitchees – impaling a chevron between 3 Trefoils slipped [missing] (Were)
Floor. *Hic jacet corpus Elizabethae uxor Joannis Were armigeri filiaeque Henrici Hawler militis quae obiit quinto die Decembris 1636 Hic jacit corpus Joannis Were armigeri et nuper pro republica Anglicani Chiliarchi qui obiit vigesimo quarto die Octobris Anno Domini 1658.* Arms on 3 shields.
I.   a bend – between 6 Cross crosslets fitchees impaling a Chevron between 3
        Trefoils slipped (Were
II.   -- impaling -- a Saltire engrailed
III.   In a lozenge -- a Saltire engrailed [missing]

--- 1675 leaving her sole issue married to Richard Rose of Wotton Fitzpaine in Dorset gent. (see Lysons ccxxii 3/a)
32. A tablet. Henry Manley of Manley in this parish died 1 Dec. 1819 aged 68 Mary his wife died 4 Feb 1820 aged 68. Erected by their 5 children.
33. A tablet. Sacred to the memory of Mrs. Rebecca King of Ballylinch King's County Ireland who died 18 May 1824 aged 74 Also her grandchild Harriet Eagles daughter of the revd John Eagles of Halberton died 27 June 1824 aged 15.
34. A tablet. Sacred to the memory of Henrietta Balfour Wemyss eldest child of the late Colonel Balfour Wemyss of Wemyss Hall Fifeshire N.B. and Mary his wife. She died at Torquay April 1828 aged 30.
35. Stone Tablet. Joan wife of Hugh Pullin of Swetton of this parish gent died 6 August 1774 aged 47. – left husband and 10 children – James her son died 8 Sept 1776 aged 2. Hugh Pullin her husband died 12 Oct 1818 aged 88.
36. Floor. Here lieth the body of Welthian the wife of Thomas --- daughter of Abraham Turner who deceased the 13 day of June A.D. 1617 Here lieth the body of Welthian daughter of the said Thomas and Welthian who deceased 21 day of May An Dni 1619 Here lieth the body of Thomas Maunder husband of the said Welthian who died 22 day of Feb. A.D. 1627 [missing]
Here lieth the body of Capt. Thomas Carter of this parish who departed this life 12 April 1712 in the 77 year of his age Also Mary wife of John Morse of this parish gent and widow of the said Thomas Carter died 25 Dec. 1759 aged 75.
Here lieth the body of Sarah wife of Thomas May of this parish gent daughter of John Thorne of Kings Nympton yeoman. Died 19 May [missing]

Here lieth the body of Thomas May son of Thomas May of Halberton gent. Died 31 Aug. 1677 aged 23. [missing]
Here lieth the body of Elizabeth wife of Thomas Pullin died 24 Dec 1719. [missing]

Newspaper cutting, no name of newspaper, dated November 1816
Halberton.
A memorial window to the family of Trist has just been erected in the church of this parish, by Mrs. Wynne Pendarves, of Tristford, which for the beauty of its designs and richness of colour, reflects great credit on the artist, Mr. Alfred Beer, of St. Bartholomew's-yard, Exeter. The window, a four-light perpendicular, contains figures of St. Agnes, St. Margaret, St. Catherine, and St. Barbara. Below are coats of arms of different families' alliances, and above richly coloured foliated canopies. In the tracery is the sacred monograms and angels bearing scrolls with appropriate texts.

Cutting labelled 'Gents. Mag.', dated February 1849
The church of Halberton has lately been completely restored, the whole, with the exception of the four walls, being new, at an expense of about 1,400*l*., of which 350*l*. was contributed by the ratepayers, and a considerable portion by the Rev. G.C. Newcomb, the Vicar, and his friends. The whole area has been reseated, and the whole area of the nave has been given up for the use of the poor in free and open sittings. The piers and arches have been taken down and rebuilt, and a fine open roof put over the chancel. The windows have all been restored, and that over the Communion table has been enlarged, whereby its proportions have been greatly improved. The alterations have been completed under the superintendence of Mr. Hayward, architect of Exeter.

UFFCULME

Davidson (pp. 557–61) visited [St Mary] Uffculme on 9 September 1828 and noted it was 8 miles east of Tiverton. 'At the time the cloth manufacture flourished in Devonshire the town of Uffculme had a considerable share of that business and of other trades connected with it, and to the prosperity which then attended it is to be attributed the respectable appearance of the church in what is now so inconsiderable a place'. The church was rebuilt and refitted and a south aisle added in 1847–9 by John Hayward (Pevsner, *Devon*, 877–8). Three memorials are missing from the five Davidson recorded.

The building consists of a nave chancel north and south aisles, a vestry on the north side of the chancel and a tower at the western end of the nave – the nave is 48 feet long by 16 wide and is separated from the north aisle by 3 cylindrical columns with laminated capitals which support pointed arches without ornamentation and of an early date, it is parted from the south aisle by columns consisting of 4 shafts with intervening hollow mouldings having angular capitals adorned with foliage & supporting pointed arches. the nave is divided from the chancel by a magnificent screen supporting a rood loft which extends entirely across the church dividing the eastern ends of the 2 aisles into chapels, it is of carved oak and consists of a series of low pointed arches with mullions & tracery forming openings having cinquefoil heads between the arches are clusters shafts which divide into tracery & tabernacle work beneath the rood loft which projects considerable out in front & the intervening space of the groining are filled with cinquefoils trefoils & foliage clusters & detached. It is finished in front with 3 lines of mouldings beautifully carved in foliage, the whole painted & gilt & on the top of the mortises remain in which the figures were fixed which composed the rood and its accompaniments – the northern end of the screen being decayed 3 arches have been restored at the cost of about £50 one half defrayed by the parish and the other by the revd. James Windsor the rector. The work has been done in most capital style by John Beales Carver & Joiner & the clerk of the parish of Uffculm in 1828 – The door to the rood loft remains at the north end of the screen in the wall & open to the stair case in a projecting buttress the upper door way is also visible level with the rood loft.

A gallery across the south aisles & the nave bears the name and date Humphrey Steare vicar 1631, it is adorned with carving and grotesque figures in a very interesting style and the panels are painted with the follows coats of arms, but the colours seem to have been altered – Sable a chevron between 3 eagles displayed Sable (query Bluett) argent 3 leaves between 2 chevrons sable (query Ayshford). Sable a fleur de lis Argent on a canton the arms of Ulster Argent on a cross engrailed between 4 water bougets Sable. – (Bouchier)
The gallery continued across the north aisle was "erected in 1721 John Windsor vicar" [removed] – the pulpit was presented to the parish by the Waldrons of Bradfield and was the work of an Italian artist it is carved and enriched with foliage, flowers & has

in front the arms of Waldron impaling a chevron between 3 arrows with their points downwards. The chancel is 29 feet long by 14 wide & opens to the chapels on each side at the ends of the aisle by wide & flat arches resting on clustered columns with foliage capital similar to those of the south aisle, a door on the north side opening into a vestry has a flat pointed head & is finished above in an angular compartment with cinquefoil head panels – a similar door opens on the south into the churchyard. The eastern window is divided by mullions & has a transom into 8 lights with cinquefoil heads & has tracery in the arches. In the south wall is a plain piscina.

The north aisle is 47 feet long by 18 wide, the chapel at the eastern end is 16 by 18 making the total length 63 feet. The south aisle is 47 by 9 the chapel 16 by 9 total length 63 feet, all the windows are similar in style having each 3 lights with cinquefoil heads and tracery in their arches, that at the eastern end of the S. aisle has 2 bases on the side apparently for statues. The font which is at the western end of the nave is of stone large heavy & low of octagonal shape & without ornament resting on an octagonal column. There are some ancient tiles still remaining on the floor of the church some of them bearing devices [removed]. The gable end of the chancel on the outside has an open cross enriched and on the eastern side of the churchyard stands a very fine yew tree. The tower is 11½ square within the walls at the base & 49 feet high to the top of the battlements it contains 5 bells inscribed & dated respectively as follows.
"Rev. James Windsor vicar" – "God preserve the church and King T. Bilbee 1801" – "1801" – "Rev J. Windsor we were five cast into 6" – "1801" –

The register books commence in 1542 & are in good preservation. The revd. James Windsor is the present vicar he succeeded his brother the revd. John W whose predecessor was their father revd. John Windsor. – The register book mentions "Richard Matthew Clerke MA inducted to the vicarage 25 Oct 1660". Over the south door beneath the porch is a coat of arms with foliage round it but the bearings are quite defaced & gone the clerk states that it is proposed to replace them by the ones of the early Kings of England.

The eastern end of the N aisle is as before stated enclosed by principal screen & also on the S side by a lighter screen returning to the corner of the chancel & is called the Waldron's aisle as appropriated to the burial place & the monuments of that family who reside at Bradfield in this parish. Over the door of the screen in a coat of arms Quarterly 1&4 Walrond. 2&3 a bend wavy

Against the north wall is an altar tomb of stone adorned on the side and ends with medallions having portraits in relief with intervening figures of faith hope and charity with fruit flowers and coats of arms. – 5 shields remain with the following bearings.
1st Quarterly 1&4 Argent 3 bulls heads caboched 2&1 sable attired Or (Walrond) 2&3 two irons in saltier between 4 pears pendant – (2nd Kelloway)
2nd Walrond
3rd Defaced
4th Or on a bend gules 3 hens de Moulin (argent) (Speedcot)
5. Quarterly 1&4 Walrond 2&3. Or 3 annulets or wreaths

On the edge of the tomb is this remainder of an inscription "*1663 Fallax saepe fides testata vota per--- constitues --- si sapis -- tuam 1663*" On the surface slab is inscribed
"This lowe built chamber to each obvious eye
Seemes like a little chapel where I'll lye
Here in this tombe my flesh shall rest in hope
When ere I dye this is my aim and hope"

On a shelf against the eastern wall are 3 stone busts painted in high colour in rich dresses, they are said to be Sir William Walrond his wife and son, they have each a book and the hands of the two last rest on skulls.
Under an arch in the north wall is a whole length figure the size of life on his right side on a mat & pillow his hands supporting his head he has a flowing wig and is attired in armour, a book lies beside him and his left arm rest upon his sword – The inscription is gone but it is said to represent the son of Sir William Walrond [now resting on the window sill]. On a tablet above the figure are the following lines.
Here lyeth one whom had you living seen
His posture in this house had kneeling been
Oft by the word awakened heretofore
Now (till the great trump sound) shall wake no more
Reader make use of tyme while tyme you have
For there's no worshiping within the grave.

Two hatchments are hung against the wall, one bears a coat – Quarterly of 16. –
1. Argent 3 bulls heads caboshed Sable armed Or (Walrond)
2. Argent 2 irons in saltier sable between 4 pears pendant (Kellaway)
3. Argent 2 chevrons sable (De Esse or Ash)
4. Argent on a fess sable 3 cross crosslets fitchees Or, in chief 3 martletts of the second.
5. Defaced apparently 6 fishes 3. 2&1 (Fissacre)
6. Argent 2 Bars Azure over all an eagle displayed Gules (Speke)
7. Gules 3 greyhounds courant in pale Argent
8. Argent a bend wavy coloured Sable (Whiting)
9. Azure 3 grey griffon's heads erased Argent
10. Argent 3 escallops Gules
11. Per fess Azure & Gules 3 fleurs de lis
12. Or fretty Azure
13. Sable a crop engrailed Or
14. Or a trivet Sable
15. Azure semee of fleurs de lis Or a bend compound Azure and Gules
16. Azure the sun in the fess point Or

Helmet mantle & crest on a wreath Argent & Azure a griffin sejant crined Or. Motto.
Sic vos non vobis
The other hatchment shows a coat bearing Walrond with the crest. On a wreath Argent and sable, a griffon sejant Sable. [both missing]

On the floor of the south aisle – here lieth the body of John Windsor vicar of this parish who died 19 May 1725 aged 42 also the body of John son of John Windsor vicar of this parish & Elizabeth his wife who died 29 March 1759 aged -4 years.

Against the south wall of the aisle a mural tablet with an urn. In memory of the revd. John Windsor AM 26 years vicar of this parish who died 13 Feb. 1793 aged 70 he was the son of John Windsor MA vicar of this parish and Anna his wife. This monument is erected by his son James Windsor the present vicar 1810. Arms. Argent an escutcheon bearing sable 2 swords in saltier points downwards Of the field hilted Or, surmounted by an esquires' helmet with a crest a demi lion rampant Sable langued Gules holding a bezant

On the floor of the nave. – Here lyeth the body of Joan the wife of Nicholas Holway of this parish clothier, she was his wife for 46 years. – Here lieth the body of Peter Holway of Dunkeswell and more of his brothers. [missing]

S wall of the aisle a painted stone slab. Here under lieth the body of Mr James Holloway of this parish clothier who departed this life the 17 Dec. 1639 who gave to the poor of this parish £40 and £20 to the poore of the parish of Hemyock where he was borne – aetat: suae 53. Here also lieth the body of Mrs. Joan Holloway who departed this life 18 June 1645 she gave to the poore of this parish £40 – To Ottery St. Mary where she was born £10 and to Honiton £10.

Against the south wall of the aisle a tablet with an urn. In memory of Humphrey Blackmore gent: of Rull in the parish of Cullompton who died 8 Oct. 1788 aged 74 years. descended by the maternal line from the family of Hollway. The revd. James Windsor erected this stone. Arms Or on a fess Sable between 3 blackamoors' heads filleted Argent, as many crescents as the last.

On the floor of the south aisle. Here lyeth the body of Robert of Borro who was husband to Wilmott Borro who died the 7 day Dec & was buried the 9 day of Dec. 1601. [missing]

D⁰ Here lieth the body of Wilmott Borro widow who died [missing]

BURLESCOMBE

Davidson (pp. 565–8) visited [St Mary the Virgin] Burlescombe on 10 September 1828 and noted it was about 9 miles north east of Tiverton and 5 south west of Wellington. The church was restored in 1844 (Pevsner, *Devon*, 239). Three memorials are missing from the eight that Davidson recorded.

The church of this parish consists of a nave 38 feet long by 15½ wide a chancel 25 feet long by 14½ wide a north aisle called the Ayshford aisle 40 feet by 12 a south aisle 38 by 11 & a tower at the western end of the nave 12 feet by 10 within the walls. The nave is divided from the north aisle by 2 columns & 2 halves consisting of 4 shafts with intervening hollow mouldings the capitals are angular carved into foliage & these support pointed arches having no ornament. The columns & arches adjoin the S aisle are similar in number & design except that the shafts have small circular laminated capitals – The chancel is lighted by a window with a pointed head having 4 lights with trefoil heads & tracery. There is a small plain piscina in the south wall & an altar screen in a debased Roman style disfigures the eastern end [now a picture of The Last Supper]. A screen carved in oak with arches & tracery divides the chancel from the nave this formerly stood across the South aisle. On the south side of the church at the western end is a porch with a vestry room over it & from this a door walled up in 1827 led into the South aisle – this aisle has 3 windows of 3 lights each formed by sweeps into cinquefoil heads. In the south wall of this aisle a door way now stopped led up a staircase in a large buttress to the rood loft, the door way above remains & a communication was probably made by this means across the church by the rood loft. The north aisle was without doubt built by the Ayshford family, the entrance to it is by a north door protected by a porch which has over the entrance 3 shields bearing 1. Three ash keys between 2 chevrons (Ayshford) impaling a chevron between 3 roses. 2. Ayshford – 3 Ayshford impaling a chevron between 3 escallops beneath them in a niche with a canopy which as the church is dedicated to St. Mary probably contained an image of the Virgin.
(*In the margin:* The western end is said by Mr Tanner to have been built at the cost of the parish)

The roof of this aisle is adorned with a cornice of foliage the springers supported by figures of priests holding shields bearing the arms of the family – one of them is Ayshford impaling 3 swords in file points downwards the whole carved in oak. (*In the margin:* At the SE end is a small plain piscina the windows contain some fragments of painted glass [removed] – Arms Ayshford impaling Sable 3 swords in pile argent points down (Paulet) & Ayshford impaling argent on a bend Sable 3 roses of the field (Cary).)

There are 4 windows in the aisle of 3 lights each with trefoil heads & tracery in pointed arches. the tower has a pointed window of 3 lights with cinquefoil heads beneath on the outside is a tablet with Roman moulding round it – the inscription is

defaced but what remains legible is "--- 1637 – 1638 which ware --" This is said by the revd. Thomas Tanner the vicar, to have recorded the date of the erection of the tower there having been previously only a bell turret but this seems doubtful judging by the style of the upper windows & the masonry of the tower. The western door of the tower is under a Roman arch & piers, this with the tablet above are of Ham hill stone which the tower is of the stone of the neighbouring – The tower is 68 feet high to the top of the battlements & contains 5 bells thus inscribed
"Draw near to God & God will draw near to you 1636"
"New cast into five" 1637
"*Soli Deo Gloria*" 1637
"When I call follow me all 1637"
"Henry Ayshford – new cast 1642" a shield with the Ayshford arms

The pulpit is modern of oak, hexagonal, with a heavy sounding board [removed] – The font is large octagonal 4 feet 3 inches wide adorned with quatrefoils resting on an octagonal column ornamented with panels & surrounded by 8 detached square columns having pendant ornaments above them. The communion table bears the date 1637. The church plate is valuable consisting of 2 large silver flagons, 2 plates, & a chalice inscribed "*Donum Philippi Culme*" another flaggon bearing the Ayshford arms which came from the chapel at Canonsleigh & was given on its destruction – a smaller chalice inscribed "The parish of Burscome"

There are several remains of ancient benches in different parts of the church, the panels at their ends carved in oak with various devices & ornaments of foliage.
The register books commence in 1579.
The most ancient monument is an altar tomb against the north wall of the chancel having at the ends & side 10 niches adorned with canopies & pinnacles between them – In each stands a priest supporting a shield all of which have been painted with the arms of the Ayshford family but are now defaced the slab on the top bears the inscription in the Gothic letter as far as legible –
Hic tumulantur Nicholaus Aisheford armig. Isabella Margareta uxores ejus -- 93 – obiit – die -- AD MCCCCC -- q animabus propicietur Deus.
On the floor of the N aisle – Here resteth in death by the Grace of God Nicolas Ayshford Esquire Elizabeth and Margaret Lys wyves. M.A.E. Christ Jesus have mercy upon us. Amen E.M. 1503.
In the NE corner of the N aisle a mural monument, under a pediment the kneeling figure of a man & woman, on a tablet of black marble below – "*In mortem et memoriam Roger Ayshford Armigeri epitaphuim qui obiit – die Januarii AD 1610 Anno aetatis sue 76*" then follow some lines in English.
3 coats of arms.
1. Ayshford –Argent between 2 chevrons 3 ash keys best.
2. Per fess Gules & sable – a pike between 3 swans argent – query Mitchell
3. Quarterly of 24.
1. Ayshford
2. Azure a chevron between 3 fess de Moulin Or
3. Argent a chevron between 3 moors heads couped Sable pelleted Gules – query Jewe
4. Argent on a bend Sable 3 horse shoes Or in chief a mullet Gules – Ferrers.
5. Gules a chevron between 3 roses Argent, a mullet for difference – Wadham
6. Argent on a chief Gules 2 Stags faces Or – Popham

7. Gules a chevron Argent between 9 bezants, 5 in chief 4 in base.

8. Or on a chevron Gules 3 martlets Argent (question of the field if so Chiseldon)

9. Sable 6 Lions rampant or 3. 2&1.

10. Argent 2 bars Azure, over all an eagle displayed Gules – Speke

11. Gules 6 fusils in bend Ermine

12. Quarterly 1&4 sable. 2&3 Argent a bull passant Sable.

13. Or semee of cross – crosslets fitchees Gules a lion rampant of the second.

14. Or a lion rampant Ermine debruised by a fess of Gules

15. Argent a bend wavy cotised Sable – Whiting

16. Azure 3 griffins heads erased or langued Gules –

17. Argent a crop Moline Gules a label of 3 points Azure

18. Argent 2 bendlet wavy Sable – query Stapleton

19. Sable 3 fishes hauriant Argent – query Hake

20. Ermine 3 escallops Argent – Keppel

21. Or a lion rampant sable crowned Gules

22. Gules 3 escallops Argent

23. Per fess Azure & gules 3 fleur de lis Or

24. Gules 3 lions rampant Or

Floor of N aisle – Here resteth the body of Nicolas Ayshford of the family of Ayshford gent who died at Taunton St Mary Magdalene 19 August 1701.

N wall of N aisle – A marble monument painted & gilded – Under pediment supported by two Corinthian columns 2 kneeling figures of a man & woman – on a black marble table below them. "To the memory of Elizabeth Ayshford wife of Arthur Ayshford eldest son of Henry Ayshford only daughter to the right honourable Charles Lord Wilmot Viscount of Athlone late General of His Majesty's forces in the Kingdom of Ireland now a privy counsellor both of England & Ireland she died the 23rd year of her age AD. 1635. June 13th."

Arms 3 coats

  1. Ayshford

  2. Ayshford impaling Argent on a fess Gules 3 escallops (2nd) between 3 griffins
      heads (2nd) Sable.

  3. Ayshford impaling Sable on a bend 3 Mullets Azure (2)

Floor of nave – Here lieth the body of Edward Chave who departed the world 9 Feb. 1609 who had issue Thomas Edward Jane Agnes & Elizabeth [missing]

Floor S. aisle. Here lieth the body of John Upton son of Henry Upton gent; who died 10 Dec 1633. aged 36 [missing]

NW column So aisle. A wooden tablet. Near this place in the church yard lieth the body of William Sheppard of this parish. died 4 Sept 1733. Dorothy his wife who died 28 May 1753 & Hannah their daughter who died 28 Feb. 1750 [missing]

Burlescombe is a vicarage endowed in 1326 with the usual vicarial tithes except that the tithe of Hay is also reserved to it. – The rectorial tithes belong to Ayshford Sanford esq of Ninehead the representative of the Ayshford's.

The registers mention

John Warren vicar prior to 1660

Thomas Clarke MA of Queens College Cambridge inducted to the vicarage 5 June 1735

Thomas Tanner is now vicar 1828.

The mansion house of Canonsleigh in the parish was destroyed in 1824 & the

materials sold in that year to a Mr. Heathcote who made use of them erecting a factory in Tiverton – the wings remain and are now converted into farm houses. This information was given me by the vicar the revd. Thomas Tanner.
See notices of Ayshford chapel

AYSHFORD CHAPEL

Davidson (pp. 569–71) wrote that Ayshford chapel was 'in the hundred of Halberton, Devon & Parish of Burlescombe'. It was restored to use as a chapel in 1847 (Pevsner, *Devon*, 146).

This was the private chapel attached to the very large mansion of Ayshford court, the residence of the Ayshford Family, supposed to have been settled there at least as early as the conquest – The mansion after the death of the last heir male of the name in 1689 was dismantled and now, 1828, only the inferior offices are standing, a date of I believe 1609 appears on one of the chimneys, belongs to the Farm house into which these remains were converted. The ancient approach to the Buildings are destroyed by the grand western canal, which bisects the Lands – the whole of this manor of Ayshford together with the manor of Burlescombe passed to the Sanford Family by Will, in consequence default in male ipse; the head of the Sanford family having married a female Ayshford about the year 1642 – The Sanford's have been settled at Nynehead court near Wellington Somerset about 2 centuries
But to return to the Chapel –
This building to the best of my knowledge appears an erection of the fourteenth century the timbers of roof are ponderous; and the twenty three arched principals, give the appearance of reuse, keel up wards – I imagine it to be the original Roof, slated – The interior length of nave to the Screen is 24 feet the length of chancel is 12 feet- Breadth 14½ feet. Formerly within the memory of a man, there were five Bells within a cupola of Wood – At present there is only one Bell [no bell] – Three windows tracery good, on the south – & three on the opposite to each other – and a window at the east end of the chancel – The Screen is plain, but ornamented by quatrefoils & oak leaves carved & gilded – Some remains of painted glass, but only two pieces can be distinguished are armorial Devices – but not the Ayshford arms [missing] – These I have been informed, were long ago taken from their places & removed to the painted windows in the Sanford Pews at Nynehead Church – There is in the chancel a plain oak communion Table within strong oak rails – on the north side of the Table is a Bracket affixed to the wall, on which I presume the Basin of Holy Water was kept – A large Font with vent at the Bottom was last summer fixed in the Chancel, it was restored to the chapel, after lying In the farm yard for common use many years, about twenty years since, but not before fixed [font removed] – the pulpit is modern of Wainscot oak; but I have been informed that the old one was rich with carved work – where it now is I cannot say [pulpit removed] – There were six priests with wings affixed to the arches of the Roof within the Chancel – 4 now remaining – an altar, a mural & a floor monument are to be seen – The altar Tomb by the screen in the nave is under the north wall – arms engraved (3 ash keys between 4 Chevrons) a date 1666 for Henry Ashford aged 7 years 9 months departed this life in 17 day of January 1666 son of Arthur A: – some verses on the side but partly obstructed by the Boards of the Desk – The mural, very gaudy similar to those in Burlescombe church – on the south corner near the communion Table – Richly

ornamented with armorial bearings, cherubs & to John Ayshford Esquire died Feb. 24th 1689 aged 49 – I believe he was the last of the line – & Susanna – his wife – daughter of Lucy (a singular name for a man) Knightley of London; Merchant – He died Dec. 6th 1688 aged 24

The floor stone with armorial Bearings at the lower end is a plain face stone within the Communion rails – to Henry Ayshford Esq. he Died in 1649 aged 73 – and to Amie his wife – she died 31. Oct. 1659 – these inscriptions on the floor are in Latin. John Ayshford above, bequeathed the sum of £15 per annum, for the maintenance of the chapel not off the Barton Estate – divine services performed here on Sunday evening during the Summer – and the vicar of Burlescombe is the chaplain – A crucifix of iron is on the top of east wall, & it seems that image was once affixed to it – like some Catholic Tiles remain on the floor

The communion plate, said to have belonged to chapel is gone – but a Flaggon in Burlescombe church, having the Ayshford arms is believed to have belonged to the chapel, --- Bewhill farm in the tithing of Ayshford & Parish of Burlescombe pays Rectoral & Vicinal Tithes to Halberton the hundred Town – but church Rates & then parochial Dues to Burlescombe –

There may be a piscina behind the mural.

Monument at chapel –

Dear Sir the above is a hasty account of chapel If you wish it I will refer to Register for the Ayshford names since 1578 their commencement by Mr. Todd thinks you will be induce to come over – if so make this your home – Or I am ready to send you any further information in my power

I am dear sir

Yours truly

Thos. Tanner

Burlescombe

Vicarage house Dec. 30th 1828

[Further notes added 19 August 1850] Ayshford Chapel is now in course of repair 22 July 1847 and restoration at the cost of Ayshford Sanford esq – The new stone windows are in the perpendicular style formed by two and three lights with cinque-foiled heads. The Font is an ancient large circular stone basin without ornamentation. The monuments are removed for a time.

This chapel has been left till now in an unfinished state, without doors or floor and the new windows without glass. It is about 32 feet long by 14 wide – the ancient Font lies neglected on the ground amidst unfinished stone work – Cattle and sheep take shelter in the building.

Against the north east corner stands an altar tomb the slab thus inscribed. Here lyeth the body of Henry Ayshford son of Arthur Ayshford Esq who departed this life the 17 day of Jan. A.D. 1636 aged 1 year and 9 months. Arms Ayshford. On the south side of the tomb are some lines of verse.

There is no other monument within the chapel but in a room over the old gateway among the outbuildings at the back of the adjoining farm house are preserved the fragments of a mural monument, perhaps more than one, formerly in the chapel. The only inscription to be seen among them is on a tablet of stone, viz, – "Near this place lies entered the body of John Ayshford of Ayshford in the county of Devon esq who departed this life the 24 day of Feb. 1689 in the 49 year of his age, as also the body of Susanna Ayshford his wife daughter of Lucy Knightley of Fawsley in the county of Northampton Esq who departed this life the 6th day of December 1688 in the 24th year of her age"

Shields of arms detached exhibit the following coats of arms

I Argent, three Ash keys vert between two Chevrons sable – Ayshford

II. I impaling Quarterly 1st & 4th Ermine 2nd & 3rd Paly of six or and gules Knightly

III. I impaling Argent three bars wavy azure Ayshford

IV Quarterly of 28

    1. Ayshford as I – Ayshford

    2. Gules a Fess between sic Cross – crosslets argent – Beauchamp

    3. Barry wavy of six argents and azure. – Sanford

    4. Argent three Bulls' faces Sable – Walrond

    5. Azure a Chevron or, between three question Millrind or cotton Hanlis argent

    6. Or on a Bend sable three horse-shoes argent – Ferrers

    7. Gules a Chevron between three roses argent – Wadham

    8. Argent on a Chief gules two Bucks' faces or – Popham

    9. Gules a Chevron or between 9 Bezants, 5 in chief and 4 in base.

    10. Or on a Chevron gules three martletts argent – question Chisldon

    11. Sable 6 Lions rampant, 3, 2, 1. or

    12. Argent 2 bars azure all on an Eagle displayed with two heads gules. – Speke

    13. Gules 6 Fusils conjoined in bends argent on each an Ermine spot – Hele

    14. Quarterly argent and sable on the first and fourth quarters a Bull passant of the second

    15. Or a Lion rampant gules – Pomeroy

    16. Gules three Lions rampant or.

    17. Barry of eight argent and gules, on a Canton of the first 4 Fusils in bend of the second

    18. Argent a Chevron sable – question Prideaux or Raplihill

    19. Argent 2 bends wavy sable – Stapleton

    20. as 18 – Trelawney

    21. argent a bend wavy sable cotised of the last – Whiting

    22. Azure three Lions heads erased or – Prodhome

    23. Argent a Millrind gules

    24. ----

    25. Argent 3 Escallops gules

    26. Or a Lion rampant sable crowned of the field

    27. Per fess azure and gules three Fleurs de lis or.

    28. as 1. – Ayshford [now restored and placed on the north wall]

Among the fragments preserved in the same chamber is a Bell of small size thus inscribed "This Bell is Henry Ayshford's T.P. 1657" [missing]

HOLCOMBE ROGUS

Davidson (pp. 573–80) visited [All Saints] Holcombe Rogus on 10 September 1828 and noted it was about 8 miles north east of Tiverton. He observed that 'the church of this parish is situated on the north side of the village and at a short distance from the mansion of Holcombe court the residence of the Bluett family for many centuries'. The church was restored in 1858–9 by John Hayward, with further restorations in 1881, and 1875 when the chancel was restored by J. Mountford Allen. The south parclose screen was brought from St Peter Tiverton to match the north parclose screen in 1854. The reredos was designed by Allen and executed by Harry Hems in 1875 (Pevsner, *Devon*, 486–7). Two memorials are missing from the twenty-two that Davidson recorded.

It consists of a nave chancel north and south aisles and a tower at the western end of the nave. The nave is 40 feet long by 15 wide and is separated from the north by 3 columns and 2 halves composed of shafts and intervening hollow mouldings having capitals variously sculptured into foliage which supports high pointed arches. The columns against the south aisle are similar but the shafts have circular laminated capitals & support triangular arches, one of them at the western end has a niche for a statue. The chancel is 31 feet by 15 having 3 pointed windows of 3 lights each with cinquefoil heads, a door into the church yard on the south side and in the south wall a plain square piscina, the screen which divides the chancel from the nave and supported a rood loft has been removed, but the door way remains in the south wall with a stair case in a buttress lighted by a small window having a cinquefoil head a door in the wall remains open on a level with the rood loft which extends across the aisles & the nave as there are openings in the spandrels of the arches on each side to admit a passage along it. The south aisle is 55 feet long by 10½ wide & its windows have each 3 lights with cinquefoil heads. the porch which covers the entrance into the aisle has a groined roof enriched with quatrefoils and over the pointed door way is a niche with panels on each side having cinquefoil heads. The north or Bluett aisle is 59 feet by 13 at the eastern end is a window with a low pointed arch having 5 lights with cinquefoil heads the other 3 windows have 1, four lights & 2 three lights with cinquefoil heads. The roof is open, ribbed with oak having knots of foliage at the intersections, the springers rest upon a cornice of foliage & are supported on the north side by angels holding shields. In the north wall at the eastern end is a piscina. The tower is 12½ feet square within the walls at its base and is 70 feet high to the top of the battlements it has a stair turret at the SE side & contains a clock & 5 bells – one of them has a † with a Latin inscription in the gothic letter almost entirely illegible – the others are dated & inscribed as follows – "1625" – "Cryspyan Sanders Warden 1626" this bell has some coins let into it – "Anthony Sticker vicar. Thomas Wroth made me 1691" this bell has also some coins of the reign of Charles 2nd – "Thomas Bilbee Cullompton fecit 1763" –

The pulpit is of oak modern & without ornament. The ancient font has been removed & its substitute is a pewter basin kept in a movable wooden closet [now an octagonal stone font with carved panels]. The pew occupied by the family of Holcombe court is on the north side of the nave and extends across the north aisle it is enclosed by a screen of oak in the style of Queen Elizabeth's period and its cornice is adorned with angels at the corners and in the centre of the front by a figure of David the King with his harp. The cornice itself is formed of a series of oval medallions rudely carved in oak representing the following subject from scriptures to begin at the NW end the first represents a priest with a pitcher in his hand leading a bullock, behind him is a warrior with a sword & shield & having a human head at his feet – 2nd Adam & Eve in the garden with the serpent in the tree. – 3rd Adam & Eve driven out of paradise by an angel. 4. A man at the plough with 2 yoke of Oxen 5, – Adam & Eve clothed in skins, he with a mattock, she nursing a child, some turnips & carrots at their feet and a cock & hens in a tree. – 6 Cain murdering Abel – thus respective altars and offerings – 7 Abraham offering Isaac, the ram in the thicket & the servant waiting with the ass – 8 David kneeling to Nathan, his sceptre on the ground – behind the prophet a poor man with a dead lamb – 9 The brazing serpent surrounded by the Israelites – 10 Mosses & the burning bush. – 11 Aaron & Hur supporting Mosses hands during the battle with Amalek 12 Balaam with his axe, an angel in the way. 13 Mosses on the mount with the tables of the law, the people worshipping the calf. –

The monuments and inscriptions in this church are these beginning with the Bluett aisle
On the floor a stone with an inscription in the gothic letter but too much defaced to be legible.
DoDo --- *Joanna Poyntz olim Arthure Bluet armigeri et nuper Philippi Poyntz generosi conjugis charissimae obiit 19 Junii 1641.* Her younger son Connell Francis Bluett and Joan his wife lye interred also. He was killed before Lyme 1644. Arms 2 coats 1st Bluet impaling – 2 Bars a canton a lion passant – 2nd Barry of 6 crescent for difference impaling 2 Bars as above. 2 Crests 1st a naked arm and hand 2nd a squirrel. Against the north wall at the eastern end is a magnificent monument composed of a variety of marbles painted and gilded consisting of an altar tomb on the sides of which are Corinthian columns supporting a circular arch highly enriched and ornamented beneath it are two recumbent whole length figures of a man and his wife dressed in full costume with ruffs round their necks, she lays on her back with her hands in the attitude of prayer, he a little elevated above her reclines on his right side with a book in his hand. A tablet above inscribed "Mary the only wife of Richard Bluet of Holcombe Rogus esq: the daughter of Sir John Chichester of Raleigh Knt. and sister to the right honourable the Lord Chichester Lord Deputy of the Kingdom of Ireland who had issue 6 sonnes viz Arthur Roger Walter Charles Francis and Charles the younger and five daughters Gertrude Amy Joane Anne and Dorothy. She departed this life 11 Feb. 1613 aged 65 years." Another tablet bears the following inscription
To the dear virtuous memories of Richard Bluet late of Holcombe esq: who died 3 March 1614 & lieth here interred.
Nor goodness nor desert must hope to have
A privilege of life against the grave
For these lie here in-tombed, death did his best

It changed but houres of toyle for houres of rest
Which the good man hath found, his faith made way
To heaven before his works, still day to day
Now follow him, such grace doth mercy give
As who lives well to dye dyes well to live.
Nascendo moriar Moriendo renascimur.
On another tablet
A modest matron here doth lye
A myrror of her Kynde
Her husband and her children's good
Her lyke is rare to finde
Godly chaste and hospitable
A housewife rare was she
Ye poore she often would relive
Yet would not wasteful be
Her death a paterne was to die
Her life was good likewise
Her life and death assure her friends
that she to joy shall ryse
Vixi in freto Morior in portu
3 Coats of arms adorn this monument
1 Bluet. Or a chevron between 3 eagles displayed vert impaling Chichester Checky
Or and gules a chief vairy
2 crests 1 Bluet a squirrel argent proper. 2 a heron with a fish in his beak
2. Bluett. 3. Chichester.

Against the north wall adjoining the before mentioned monument on the western side is another magnificent altar tomb surmounted by a canopy in the Roman style supported by Corinthian columns the whole composed of a variety of marbles. On the tomb is the white marble effigy of a knight with his head bare and his hands in the attitude of prayer, at his feet his crest, a squirrel segreant proper eating a fruit Gules. At his left hand a little more elevated lies his wife in full dress with large sleeves & her hands in prayer, at her foot a crest a talbot dog segreant. – The inscription on a tablet above "*Memoriae sacrum viri nobilis at generosi Johannis Bluet armigeri et charissimae illius conjugis Elizabethae Johannis Portman militis et Baronetti filiae. Ille quidem fato cessit 29 die Nov: Anno aet: suae 31 et salutis 1634 Haec 7 die Julii Anno aetatis 32 et salutis 1636.*" Below the tomb are the figures of 5 daughters of which the 1st 4th 5th & 6th have skulls in their hands which seems to denote their previous decease. This monument exhibits 4 coats of arms. 1 Bluett impaling Portman Or a fleur de lis Azure. 2 Bluett. 3 Portman. 4 Quarterly of 9.
(1). Bluet
(2) Azure 3 bends Argent a bordure Gules
(3) Argent a chevron Sable, a label of 3 points Gules (Prideaux)
(4) Argent a chevron between 2 crosses patees in chief and a saltier in base sable
(5) Argent 3 coots sable
(6) Or on a bend Gules 3 martletts Argent
(7) Azure a chevron between 3 fess de Moulin Or
(8) Azure 2 bars between 8 martletts Or 3.2.&3

(9) Barry of 6 Argent & Gules on a canton of the second a lion passant gardant Or.
On the floor Francis Bluet younger son of Francis Bluet esq: died 21 Oct 1691 aged
53. Arms Bluet a crescent for difference
On the floor Elizabeth wife of John Bluet esq: daughter of John Buckland late West
Harptree co: Somerset esq. died 14 July 1692. Arms Bluet impaling Quarterly 1&4
Three lions rampant a canton fretty --- 2&3 a chevron between 3 roses.
On the floor – John Bluet late of his Holcombe Rogus died 30 Sept. AD 1700 aged
62. Arms. As the last mentioned Crest a squirrel sergeant.
On the floor – Robert Bluett esq: formerly of Little Colan in Cornwall late of
Holcombe court ob: 30 Nov. 1725 at 72. also Kerenhappuch his wife who died 27
Oct 1759 at 94. also Isabella and Mary their daughters who died unmarried Isabella
23 August 1732 at 28 Mary 7 Oct 1739 at 29.
Against the north wall of the chancel a marble monument representing a sarcophagus
with an urn & 2 female sitting figures – To the memory of Robert Bluett esq: formerly
of Little Colan in Cornwall afterwards of Holcombe court and Kerenhappuch his wife
daughter of Robert Wood LLD of Sherville in Essex who had 2 daughters named
Martha who died young and 3 sons and 5 daughters who survived the father viz John
distinguished for settling the affairs of the South Sea Company in 1720 & 1721 He
married Anne daughter and heir of Perceval Hart esq: of Lullingstone castle in Kent.
Robert who married Jane daughter of Sir Thomas Webster bart. of Battle Abbey in
Sussex. – Buckland who by act of parliament took the surname of Nutcombe Bluett
on his marriage with Hannah Nutcombe of Nutcombe daughter of Richard Hill of
Priory in this county. 5 daughters Elizabeth Frances Catherine Isabella and Mary.
Buckland Nutcombe Bluett the survivor of all his father's children and heir after
six descents of Francis brother of Sir Roger Bluett of Holcombe court who married
Elizabeth daughter of Tristram Colan esq: of Little Colan in Cornwall and by her
had 13 sons and 9 daughters erected this monument in the year 1783. Arms Bluett
with the crest.
On the floor of the aisle. Robert Bluett clerk vicar of this parish and rector of Berry
Narbor died 18 Dec 1749 aged 48 [missing]

Against the wall of the north aisle a monument of marble with a medallion representing the good Samaritan & surmounted by an urn between 2 Roman Doric
columns, underneath the following inscription. In a vault near this place is the
remains of the late revd. Robert Bluett of Holcombe court in this parish who died
18 Dec 1749 in the 48th year of his age. Also of John Edward Robert only child of
the above Robert Bluett & Jane his wife (3rd daughter of Sir Thomas Webster bart
of battle Abbey in Sussex) died 21st Nov. 1766 aged 17 years also in memory of Jane
Bluett who died 2 Nov. 1772 aged 64 years
Arms. Bluett impaling Azure a bend between 2 demi lions rampant erased argent
charged with a rose gules between 2 boars heads couped sable.
Against the north wall of the nave a marble slab Sacred to the memory of James
Bluett who died 16 July 1809 aged 6 months
3 Hatchments are hung in the Bluett aisle, One of them exhibits a shield Quarterly
of 46.
1. Bluett
2. Azure 3 bends within a bordure Argent
3. Argent a chevron sable a label of 3 points of the second

4. Argent a chevron between 2 crosses patees & a saltier of sable
5. Argent 3 coots sable
6. Or on a bend gules 3 martletts Argent
7. Azure 2 bars between 8 martletts Or 3 2 & 3
8. Azure a chevron between 3 fess de Moulin Or.
9. Argent a chevron between 3 coots sable
10. Defaced
11. Sable 6 martletts 3 2 & 1
12. Argent a wolf or dog at bay in fess sable
13. Per fess indented quarterly Or & gules
14. Azure 3 -- Or
15. Azure 3 fishes naiant in pale Argent
16. Ermine a saltier Gules
17. Azure a bend Or a label of 3 points gules – Carminow
18. Azure a Staple face Argent – Trethirf
19. Azure a lion rampant Argent
20. 21. 22. 23. & 24 defaced
25. Gules a lion rampant Or – Northmore
26. 27. 28. 29. 30. 31 defaced
32. Gules fretty Or – Audley
33. Gules 3 lions passant gardant argent
34. Argent 2 bars Gules – Martin
35. Gules a Maunche Argent (question Ermine) the hand proper Holding a fleur de lis Or – Mohun
36. Or a mans leg couped at the thigh Azure
37. Argent 3 cups Gules
38. Argent 3 cinquefoils Gules within a bordure engrailed
39. Argent 3 fleur de lis Sable – Curtoyse
40. Azure 6 martletts Argent 3 2 & 1
41. Gules 4 fusils in fess argent on each an ermine spot – query Dinham
42. Gules 3 bezants a label of 3 points Argent – Hidon
43. Gules 3 arches 2 single in chief 1 double in bas with their capitals & pedestals Argent
44. Argent a cross sable
45. Gules a chevron Or between 3 lobsters Argent
46 Defaced.
Hatchment. Bluett impaling Webster – viz Azure on a bend Argent cotised Or between 2 demi lions rampant of the second a rose Gules 2 boars heads couped Sable langued of the 4th
Hatchment. Quarterly 1&4. Or a chevron embattled Gules between 2 escallops sable. 2 & 3. Bluett. On a escutcheon of pretence Ermine on a fess Sable 3 towers Argent. Crest On a wreath Gules & argent a squirrel sergeant eating on a leafed all proper.
Floor N aisle – here lieth the body of -- Kerslake son of this parish who died -- Dec. 1700 aged 78. -- lieth the body of Sarah -- Kerslake who died 19 day of --- 1706 aged 79.
D⁰ – In memory of Mrs Hannah Kerslake daughter of Robert Kerslake of this parish gent who was buried 19 day of Oct AD – at 50.
Floor of the nave. – Here lieth the body of Mary wife of Robert Kerslake of this

parish eldest daughter of John Clarke of this parish gent died 27 May 1713 aged 57 years – also the body of Sarah daughter of the said Robert and Mary Kerslake who died 2 April 1714 aged 28 years. also the body of the above mentioned Robert Kerslake who died 2 June 1722 aged 67 also the remains of Elizabeth daughter of the said Robert Kerslake and wife of Samuel Walker of Pugham gent: with her infant the innocent cause of her death 2 July 1731 aged 31 – Robert Kerslake of Wellington grandson of the above Robert Kerslake died 2 March 1771 aged 39.

Wall of N aisle a mural tablet. In memory of Faith Clarke daughter of John Clarke of this parish who died 24 June 1711 aged 49. also of Hannah Kerslake daughter of Peter Kerslake sen. of this parish who lies buried under a stone inscribed H.K who contributed to the expense of erecting this monument

Floor N aisle. H.K. obit 7 June 1752 aetatis: 87.

Floor S. aisle Here rested the body of Mrs Joan the wife of Richard Gardner gent died 19 Jan. --- also the body of Richard Kerslake.

Floor of Chancel. In memory of the revd. Samuel Wills late vicar of this parish ob: 16 June aged 63 years.

In memory of the revd. Joseph Wills ob: 17 Sept 1787 at 35

The revd. Mr. Wills is the present vicar 1828.

S. wall of chancel a mural tablet. To the memory of the revd. Tristram Whitter MA 47 years vicar of this parish who died 9 May 1824 aged 81 years eldest son of the revd. Tristram Whitter rector of Pitt portion in the parish of Tiverton also of Elizabeth wife of the above who died 5th April 1813 aged 71 years. Arms Ermine a bull passant sable horned & hoofed Or impaling Argent a cannon in fess Sable. Crest on a wreath argent & Sable a dexter arm armed holding a battle axe proper. Motto. *Esto fidelis.*

Wall N aisle. A slab between 2 Roman Doric column surmounted by an urn – To the pious memory of Mrs. Mary Baynard daughter of Thomas Baynard of Clift in the co: of Dorset esq. who died 6 Sept 1718 aged 59 & lies buried in the co: of Dorset esq who died 6 Sept 1718 aged 59 & lies buried in the adjacent ally this monument is erected by her nephew George White of Stafford in the co: of Dorset esq: Arms Sable in a lozenge. Sable a fess between 2 chevrons Or.

S. aisle a mural tablet surmounted by 3 urns. In a vault underneath lieth the body of Anne wife of Oliver Peard of Tiverton esq: who died 4 August 1756 aged 52. also the body of the said Oliver Peard esq. who died 18 Dec. 1764 aged 64 years. Arms Argent 2 wolves passant in pale proper. Crest a wolfs' head erased proper.

Floor N aisle half hidden by a pew. Here -- ye -- body -- Phillip -- gent -- who -- August -- Dom

Floor nave. Here lyeth the body of Amos Needles of this parish gent who died 12 March 1698.

A tablet against the wall of the N aisle states as follows.

A charity school on Dr. Bell system was endowed by Mrs Susannah Webber a native of Bampton in June 1823 for the education of 30 poor girls and 20 poor boys of the parish of Holcombe Rogus with the sum of £1000 invested in the new 4% cents in the name of the 4 trustees under mentioned viz

Tristram Whitter clerk vicar of Holcombe Rogus

Thomas Tanner clerk vicar of Burlescombe

James Parker clerk vicar of Oakford

Stukeley S. Lucas esq: of Barons Down [missing]

HOCKWORTHY

Davidson (pp. 581) visited [St Simon and St Jude] Hockworthy on 10 September 1828 and noted it was about 8 miles north east of Tiverton. He observed that 'the church of this retired little village presents but little worthy of notice'. The church tower was rebuilt in 1848, and the remainder of the church in 1864 by Charles D. Greenway (Pevsner, *Devon*, 483).

It consists of a nave 39 feet by 14 a chancel 16 by 13 having a door in the south wall, with a tower at the western end 8 feet square within the walls and 40 feet high to the top of the battlements & having an ancient appearance its belfry windows being rude in character – they have each two lights with trefoil heads. the church is lighted by 4 pointed windows 2 of them having 3 lights & 2 two lights but their mouldings have been destroyed, on the side of one of them is a niche which has probably contained a statue. A gallery at the western end was erected in 1822 [removed]. The remains of a screen which separated the chancel from the nave still exists [removed] as do the door & staircase which led to the rood loft above it. The font is ancient and rude, of stone 1 foot 2in: square resting on a circular column with a square base but destitute of ornament. The tower contains 3 bells cast by Bilbie of Collumpton & all bearing the date 1808.
Stones on the chancel floor record
Joane Catford the wife of William Catford who died the 18th June 1624
William Catford died -- Jan. 1625 [missing].
Dorothea Catford wife of John Catford late of Hockworthy who died 27th --- 1645 [missing].

CLAYHANGER

Davidson (pp. 585–8) visited [St Peter] Clayhanger on 11 September 1828. The church was restored in 1879–81 by Hine and Odgers (Pevsner, *Devon*, 267–8).

The church consists of a nave chancel & tower at the western end. The nave is 39 feet long by 18 wide within the walls and is lighted by 2 windows one of them of early date having a lancet shaped arch & divided into two lights with cinquefoil heads the other with a square head & 2 lights also with cinquefoil heads. A gallery cross the western end which seems to have been erected about the time of Queen Elizabeth it is adorned with rude sitting figures between the panels and is ornamented below with a moulding of foliage carved in oak of more ancient date which probably belonged to the screen or rood loft perhaps removed at the time the gallery was put up [removed] – The pulpit is of oak in the Roman style. Against the wall on the right hand side of the door which is in the south side is an ancient alms box secured by 2 locks but now disused, as the frame work of a pew covers its edifice [still there and now accessible]. The font stands at the western end of the nave, it is of stone and unusual form being a circular basin of small size resting on a cylindrical pedestal & carved on the outside with a fluted ornament surmounted by a band or fillet – it is 2½ feet high & lined with lead. – Several ancient benches remain in the nave their oaken panels curiously carved in figures & devices & foliage. The chancel is 20 feet long by 12 & has 2 windows of 2 lights each with trefoil heads.

The tower is 8 feet square within the walls at its base and 57 feet high to the top of the battlements, containing 3 bells inscribed "BN Bluett esq. Edward Beadon Rector 1749" "B Nutcombe Bluett esq 1750" "Edward Beadon Rector: T Bilbee GP 1761"

The church plate consists of a cup & paten of small size dated 1574

The pulpit cloth is of red velvet & dated 1720.

The inscriptions in this church are these.

On the floor – Here lieth the bodie of John Nutcombe of this parish esq: born 21 May 1627 died 4 March 1657 aged 30 years 10 months & 11 days. Arms a fess embattled between 2 escallops.

Nicholas Nutcombe of this parish gent: died 3 June 1650 aged 6 – Christian his wife died 8 May 1673 daughter of John Dob--- of Ashbrittle gent: aged 75.

Christian daughter of Nicholas Nutcombe gent: died 22nd Sept. 1656 – Arms Nutcombe in a lozenge

Rebecca Christian and Mary the wife and daughter of Richard Nutcombe of Nutcombe gent: Christian the eldest daughter died 5 Oct 1660. Rebecca the mother and Mary the youngest daughter both died 22 May 1671

Arms. Five fusils in saltier between four cross crosslets.

Anne eldest daughter of Richard Nutcombe of this parish esq. by Anne his wife died 4 July buried 7th 1717 aged 20.

John Nutcombe son of Richard Nutcombe died 22 Sept 1685 aged 17.

Richard Nutcombe of Nutcombe in this parish gent died 3 Nov. 1680 aged 52. Arms Nutcombe

Anne Nutcombe wife of Richard Nutcombe of this parish esq: third daughter of Robert Seymour of Handford esq: in the co: of Dorset by whom he had only two daughters Anne and Rebecca. She died 4 July & was buried 10th aged 48 AD. 1718. Arms Nutcombe impaling. A pair of wings, on a chief 3 martlets in pale.

Against the north wall is a marble monument consisting of a tablet under a pediment supported by 2 Ionic pilasters, thus inscribed.

Here lieth Richard Nutcombe of Nutcombe in this parish esq: who in an age both in principles and practice corrupt kept his faith entire and his morals untainted. He was sheriff of this county in the 2nd year of George 1st and served King and country as a Justice of the peace. By his first wife Ann daughter of Robert Seymour of Hanford in Somerset esq: he had 2 daughters Ann who died unmarried and Rebecca the wife of John Quick esq: by who she left 3 sons John Nutcombe and Andrew: His second wife was Hannah daughter of Richard Hill of Priory in this county esq: by who he had no issues who erected this monument to his memory. He died 13 Nov. 1766 aged 76 and in memory of Hannah, Buckland Nutcombe Bluett esq; her second husband inscribed this – She died 30 May 1747 aged 48

Arms in 3 coats

1. Or a fess embattled between 2 escallops Gules. Nutcombe
2. Nutcombe impaling Ermine on a fess Sable a castle Argent a mullet for difference
3. Quarterly.
1. Nutcombe
2. Sable a chevron engrailed between 3 arrows downwards Argent
3. Sable on a fess between 3 bells Argent on a doe trippant
4. Azure 5 fusils in saltier between 4 cross crosslets Or.
Impaling Quarterly of 6
1. Ermine on a fess Sable a castle Argent a mullet for difference
2. Sable a lion rampant or between 3 crosses patience fitchees Argent
3. Argent a crop importance between 4 martletts gules a canton Azure.
4. Azure a lion rampant argent gules
5. Argent a crop patience Azure
6. Gules 3 pheons Argent an escutcheon of pretence

Quarterly 1 7 4 on a fess Or between 2 chevrons Ermine 3 leopards faces Azure 2 & 3 Quarterly Ermine and Sable on a cross Or 5 torteaux – Seward

The manor of Clayhanger with the estate of Nutcombe as also the manor of Ashbrittle co: Som. Formerly the property of the Nutcombe's have now descended to 3 daughters co heiresses Wife Nutcombe of Exeter & her 2 sisters married to the revd. Mr Oxenham residing near Exeter & the other to -- Gould esq.

On the floor of the nave. Richard Southele of this parish gent: buried 6 June 1661 at 40. Mary his wife died 2nd July 1710 at 86. Mrs Joan Southele daughter of Mr Richard & Mrs Mary Southele of this parish died 27 Feb. 1733 aged 73. Susanna wife of John Southele of this parish gent: and Thomas Southele their son she died 11 March 1710 aged 58 & their son was buried -- Nov 1692 aged 2 years. The above mentioned John Southele gent: died 4 Feb. 1717 aged 68 Mary daughter of Henry Bonner of Watson esq. in Somerset who married John Southele of Southele gent: died 18 Jan. 1722 leaving 1 daughter named Mary.

Also on the floor of the nave. Ann Burge widow of this parish buried 21 May 1675 John Milton son of Edward Milton of Bampton died 26 August 1736 aged 26.

The registers of this parish commence in 1538
The following list of rectors is extracted from them
Robert Chalacombe Rector buried 18 Sept 1602
Emanuel Maxey Rector buried 23 May 1633
Hugh Pym Rector buried 24 May 1671
Thomas Seagar Rector buried 17 May 1706
William Wood Rector buried 4 September
George Lewis (Mariduniensis) Rector buried -- Oct 1816
--- Harrison Rector succeeds & is now living

A tablet against the N wall records as follows
Mrs Mary Sayer of this parish widow by her will proved at Exon 16 Oct 1701 gave a yearly rent charge of 20/ for ever issuing out of a moiety of Perry tenement in this parish in trust to bestow the same yearly in bread amongst such poor people of this parish as the major part of the trustees shall think to be in most need within one week next after 2nd February for ever. Also Mrs H Nutcombe Bluett wife of B. Nutcombe Bluett of Nutcombe esq: by her deed enrolled in the high court of chancery 9 May 1747 gave a clear annuity of £3 for ever payable out a moiety of West Clayhanger tenements in the trust for teaching as many of the poorest children of this parish to read & for buying books for them as the annuity shall be sufficient to answer and in case there shall not be sufficient number of such children then any other poor children in any neighbouring parish are to have the benefit as appears by the deed kept with the parish records – Mr. John Norman of Tiverton apothecary by his will proved at Tiverton 27 April 1749 gave to the rector & principle rates payers to the poor of this parish £50 in trust to be placed out at interest and to pay the interest annually for ever for teaching the children of such poor inhabitants as they shall deem least capable of paying for their instructions.

BAMPTON

Davidson (pp. 589–90) visited [St Michael and All Angels] Bampton on 11 September 1828 and noted it was 7 miles north of Tiverton. The church was restored in 1872 and again in 1896–8 by R.W. Sampson of Taunton (Pevsner, *Devon*, 146–7). Four memorials are missing from the seven that Davidson recorded.

The parish church of Bampton consists of a nave chancel north aisle and tower at the western end of the nave. The nave is 68 feet long by 22 wide within the walls & is divided the aisle by columns formed of alternate shafts and mouldings having angular capitals carved in various devices of angels shields foliage etc, the windows have each 4 lights with cinquefoil heads, the roof is ribbed with oak & divided into rectangular parts having foliage at their intersections. A gallery at the western end in the Roman style was erected in 1731 [removed] and the pulpit in the same style is of oak the upper panels adorned with foliage & flowers a screen carved oak in the pointed style divides the nave from the chancel it is formed of a range of pointed arches having openings with cinquefoil heads & adorned above with tabernacle work quatrefoils & foliage, this screen was formerly of greater length and before the repairs of the church in 1812 extended across both of the nave & the aisle where the door way was placed which leads to the rood loft, it is now walled up but the stair case remains in a buttresses, another screen returned eastwards from this to the corner of the chancel & enclosed the eastern end of the aisle which perhaps dedicated as a chapel [removed].
The chancel is 31 feet by 17½ it is lighted by the head of a large window of 3 lights but its mouldings have been destroyed as have those of the eastern window – a door in the north side of the chancel leads into a vestry of modern erection [no longer a vestry]. An altar screen covers the eastern end it is in a kind of Roman style and in very bad taste [removed] & over the altar is a picture the subject of which is our Lord bearing the cross, this was painted by R. Cosway ARA. Who was a native of Oakford about 3 miles distant from Bampton & present by him in 1816 [removed] – In the south wall is a large piscina with cinquefoil head and mouldings.

The aisle on the north side of the nave is 67½ feet long by 12 wide, the windows have each four lights but the mouldings in their heads have been destroyed the inner arches rest upon corbel heads – the eastern window of this aisle is perfect & is filled with painted glass of brilliant colours but it has evidently been formed from a heap of broken materials & now presents a confused assemblage of saints & martyrs coats of arms & architectural ornaments part of one coat may be traced but that is placed upside down, it is a tower impaling Gules partly pale on the dexter side 3 arches with their columns 2 in chief & one in base Argent – sinister Gules a fess of 4 fusils Ermine [removed].
The tower is 14 feet square within the walls at the base it contains a clock and 6 bells inscribed "Rev. B. Davey vicar Bilbee 1800" "Five into six 1800" – "I the church the

living call and to the grave I summon all 1800" "1800" –"1800" – The tower is 80 feet high to the top of the battlements. –

The font is stone octagonal 2 feet 2 inches in diameter & 3½ feet high adorned with quatrefoils & resting on a octangular column with panels & a capital carved in foliage. The church plate consists of a chalice and paten with the date 1664, a plate and a small cup together with a magnificent service presented by Miss Davey the sister of the present vicar in 1823 comprising a flagon chalice plate and paten embossed in modern style & the whole of silver weighing more than 9 pounds.

The monumental inscriptions in this church are but few in number and it is stated that when the pews were newly put up in the year 1812 a large number of stones many of them with ancient inscriptions & coats of arms were buried underneath them. The chancel presents a most interesting & beautiful specimen of a tomb in the altar style this consists of black marble monument 10 feet 6 inches long and 3½ high which formerly stood across the open area of the chancel but with a most barbarous want of taste the surface slab has been destroyed while the sides have been separated and removed one to each side of the chancel where they are fixed against the wall & partially hidden by the altar screen, enough however remains visible to attest its original magnificence & to show the beauty of its workmanship, the sides are elaborately carved into panels enriched with tracery & having shields in their centres, these are relived with niches surmounted by canopies and adorned with pinnacles. The coats of arms which were probably brass have been removed nor does any figures or inscriptions remain which no doubt were upon the surface slab but some smaller shields remain amongst the borders & scrolls which fill every part, these exhibit the letter T the monogram IHE and the armorial bearings the water-bouget & the fret, which two last enable us to ascribe this beautiful tomb to one the Bourchiers Earls of Bath [now both sides of the tomb are placed against the north wall of the chancel].

Against the south wall of the chancel is a slab "In memory of the truly pious and virtuous Dorothy the daughter of Sir George Farewell knight & wife of Frances Fullwood DD & archdeacon of Totnes who dyed the 27 day of July 1669" [missing] Slabs in the church also record the following "Hereunder lyeth the body of John the son of John Bowbeare of this town yeoman who died 12 May 1676" "Arthur son of John Bowbeare of this town yeoman who died 17 Dec. 1675" [missing] "Grace wife of Henry Pengelly of this town & daughter of John Allen gent of the same who died 8 Nov 1670" [missing] Revd. Thomas Wood MA resident vicar of this parish 13 years died 5 Oct 1784 aged 78. Alice his wife died 12 June 1779.

Against the east wall of the nave is a tablet recording. "John Tristram esq: of this town died 28 June 1722 aged 34. He married Mary daughter of Scipio Stukeley in this county esq: & widow of Michael Arundell esq: by whom he had issue John & Mary. John died at a year old and Mary his only daughter and heiress has erected this monument. His second wife was Gertrude daughter of Lewis Southcombe Rector of Rose Ash." – Arms Argent 3 torteaux on a chief gules a label of 3 points vert 7: impaling in chief Azure

3 pears Lewant (Stukeley) Or in base argent a chevron Ermine between 3 roses Gules (query Southcombe) [missing]
On the south side of the nave a tablet – "Sacred to the memory of John Webber serge maker & native of this place who died in London 1 Jan 1764 in the 43 year of his age. Also of Jane Webber his wife granddaughter of William Chamberlain of Doddiscombe who died in London 20 March 1778 in the 60th year of her age. Susannah Webber & Elizabeth Penton their daughters erected this monument".

Against the north wall of the aisle a table states.
"The donation of Susanna Webber spinster is as follows £300 new 4 per cent for the benefit of 6 poor women of this parish of Bampton widows or spinsters of the age of 50 or under that age if blind or bedridden 3 of whom are to received from the vicar for the time being 1 shilling a week for life and the others 6d a week. Also the interest of £50 in the same fund to keep in repair the tablet of John and Jane Webber & the board for the charity. The deed of trustees is in the care of the vicar & enrolled by the clerk of the peace for the county"

A tablet against the south wall of the nave records
John Tristram gent: by his will gave to the poor of this parish 40/ a year to be paid out of Little Pilemore to the wardens and by them to be distributed to the poor. Sir John Ackland knt gave to the poor a dozen of wheaten bread called Cheat bread to be delivered every Sunday after morning prayers weekly for ever by the churchwardens. In Lieu of this donation the parish now receives 26/ a year Robert Mogridge gave to the poor of this parish £5 yearly to be paid out of his lands in Hillbishop to the present churchwardens and also 20/ to the same for their pains in fetching and distributing the same for ever. A donation of £2.4.0 annually for ever was bequeathed by the will of Mrs Elizabeth Lucas for the poor of this parish as her deed in the hands of the vicar. In the year 1807 a vane was erected in the tower a gift of Daniel Badcock. A dial plate was also affixed to the clock at the joint expense of Daniel Badcock & Thomas Newte in the year 1812 this church was newly seated & paved by faculty lodged in the parish chest. Mrs. Elizabeth Penton a native of the parish generously contributed £450 towards it in consequence of the woollen trade failing in the town. In the year 1816 an altar piece the gift of R Cosway a native of Oakfield was erected in the chancel by the parish. In the year 1821 a free school on Dr. Bell's system was erected and endowed by Elizabeth Penton for the purpose of educating 100 poor children 50 of whom are to be annually clothed viz 25 boys and 25 girls the funds to arise from the interest of the sum of £2200 vested in the navy 5% cents in the names of the following gentlemen as trustees. Sir Thomas Dyke Acland Bart. Revd. B. Davey. Stockley Tristram Lucas esq: John Nicholas Fazakerly esq: Daniel Badcock esq: the clergyman to be the treasurer, £5 from the above mentioned interested money to be extended every year in bread for the poor in the month of February by the clergyman and church wardens The manor of Bampton is the property of the Honourable Newton Fellowes. The rectorial tithes belong to Mr. Chichester of Calverleigh who presents to the vicarage which is said to be worth about £100 a year.

SHILLINGFORD

Davidson (p. 593) visited the chapel of St George, Shillingford on 11 September 1828 and noted it was 2 miles north east of Bampton.

This hamlet is in the parish of Bampton and here is a small chapel which was formerly served by the curate of this place and for which he is said to receive the stipend at the present time although service has not been performed there for about 14 years. The chapel is now a ruin almost covered with ivy, it was last repaired in 1813 when a rate was levied on the estates which are charged with its support and which are 17 in number. The building was originally about 36ft long but the eastern wall has fallen in consequence of the ground having sunk away the present wall has been built which reduces its length to 29ft & it is 13ft 9in wide. The eastern window no longer exists but is supplied by a wooden frame, on the south side there is a small window of 2 lights with trefoil heads. The eastern end was separated from the other by a screen carved in oak with pointed arches & tracery, some portions of this remain but in a state of great decay. There was formerly a piscina in the south wall near the east end and with a trefoil head – a single bell hung in the gable of the roof at the western end but having fallen down it was taken into the possession of Mr Robert Capron the chapel warden. it is of small size and was cracked by its fall it. It is without date or inscription. There was never a burial place attached to this chapel nor any font
Lord King has large estates in the immediate neighbourhood.

PETTON CHAPEL

Davidson (p. 595) visited the chapel of St Petrock at Petton on 11 September 1828 and noted it was about 4 miles north east of Bampton. He observed that 'this is a chapel of ease to the church of Bampton and divine service is performed here once a month by the curate of that place'. Rebuilt in 1846–8 by Gideon Boyce of Tiverton (Pevsner, *Devon*, 628).

The building consists of a nave 25ft long by 13 wide a gallery across western end – and a chancel 12 ft by 13. The eastern window is pointed having 2 lights with cinquefoil heads. There are 2 windows at the south side one of 3 lights with flat heads and the other 2 lights with trefoil heads – the doorway also on the south side is modern. The chancel has a plain piscina in the south wall. There are remains of a carved oak screen with low arches dividing the nave from the chancel. The font is of stone small and rude, in shape octagonal without ornament & resting on an octangular column [now round and dated 1848]. A turret at the western gable contains 2 bells but they are inaccessible. The floor has some ancient tiles – the only monument is a slab against the north wall. "In memory of Francis Wilson of this parish buried 2 Dec. 1719 at 60". –

Newspaper cutting, no name of newspaper, dated 8 May 1848
Petton Chapel, Bampton. – This chapel having been rebuilt was opened by the bishop's permission on Monday last. Prayers were read by the Rev. E. Rendell, vicar of Bampton, and a sermon was preached by the Rev. Mr. Richie, of Stoodleigh. The edifice which is in the Norman style, and contains accommodation for 170 persons with 100 pew sittings, was designed by Mr. G.A. Boyce, architect of Tiverton, and built by Mr. Gale, of Bampton.

MOREBATH

Davidson (pp. 601–3) visited [St George] Morebath on 11 September 1828 and noted it was about 2 miles north of Bampton. The church was restored in 1875–82 by Butterfield (Pevsner, *Devon*, 575–6).

This village church consists of a chancel nave north aisle and tower at the western end. The chancel is 22ft long by 16 wide, its west window is pointed and has three lights with cinquefoil heads but the upper part if it is hidden by the ceiling which has been lowered. A pointed arch open to the north aisle the staircase which formerly lead to the rood loft still remains in a buttress against the wall. The nave is 44ft long by 15 wide its windows each have 3 lights but the mouldings in their head and in the tracery have been destroyed. three columns and 2 halves divide the aisle from the nave. they are composed of 4 shafts with intervening mouldings the former having plain circular capitals and supporting pointed arches with mouldings; a porch covers the south door – the pulpit is heavy in the Roman style with a cumbrous sounding-board [removed], a gallery across the western end is equally incongruous [removed]. The north aisle is 56ft long by 11 wide the roof is pointed, ribbed with oak and ornamented with foliage at the intersections which are rectangular the windows have low arches mutilated. The tower is 8ft sq within the walls at the base it is 41ft high to the top of the buttresses it contains 5 bells which are inscribed "1742" "Richard Sharpe Rector 1742" – "William Evans cast us all 1742" – "Peace and good neighbourhood 1742" – "Prosperity to our benefactors W.E. 1742."

The font is placed at the western end of the aisle & is an interesting relic of antiquity it is of stone, square 2ft across standing on a cylindrical column with a detached shaft at each corner with a circular capital & base the whole standing on a square plinth, the basin is circular lined with lead which has been marked all round with the letters H.C. The upper part has been surrounded with a band of iron to preserve it entire but it is so much loaded with whitewash that the ornaments if any cannot be traced – it may be attributed to the Anglo Norman period [now black marble]

The church plate consists of a small chalice & paten dated 1593 and a larger paten 1698. On the floor of the church are some ancient glazed tiles of various devices, some of them with portions of an inscription in the gothic letter on a circular pattern [removed].

Against the north wall of the aisle is a tablet under a pediment supported by Corinthian columns inscribed to Mr Nicholas Sayer who died 13 Nov 1732 aet 70 Mary daughter 23 Jan 1704 died aged 13, Sayer Bere grandson 26 May 1737 aged 1 year, Mary wife of the above Nicholas Sayer died 1 Dec 1740 aged 69 – Arms Azure 3 cinquefoils Gules impaling Gules a cross Or. Crest a man's head & shoulders in front covered with whitewash
North wall. A tablet & urn. Davy Bere esq died 12 Feb 1774 aged 61. Ann his wife daughter of Nicholas Sayer of Ashtown in this parish died 26 Nov 1773 aged 70. their son John died of a consumption 30 Jan 1766 aged 24. Arms Argent 3 greyhound's

heads erased Sable muzzled Or impaling Argent 3 cinquefoils Gules Crest on a wreath Argent & Sable, a greyhound's head & neck Sable muzzled Or.

North wall mural tablet with an urn. Thomas Frederick Musgrave esq of Exford in the county of Somerset died 21 Oct 1780 aged 60 years. He was descended from a younger branch of the ancient family of Musgrave of Eden hall in the county of Cumberland which settled in Somersetshire in the reign of Henry the 8th. This monument was ordered to be erected to his memory by the last will of Mary his widow daughter of Davy Bere esq. of this parish, she died 14 Jan 1784 aged 50 years. Arms. Azure 6 annulets Or 3 2 & 1 impaling Bere. Crest on a wreath Or & Azure two arms armed & embowed holding an amulet Or.

North wall. a mural tablet with sitting female figure weeping over an urn. Ann wife of Montague Bere Baker Bere esq of Rill house in this parish who died 7 Nov 1802 in the 26th year of her age. Arms: Argent 3 greyhounds heads couped sable impaling on a bend Gules between 3 bezants 3 swans of the first. Crest on a wreath Argent & gules a greyhound's head and neck sable.
Mem: Mr M. B. B. Bere died not long after his wife but left a son a barrister on the western circuit who is married and has a child.
South wall. a mural tablet monument erected by the co-heiresses of Robert Pearse esq and Elizabeth his wife to the memory of the best of parents. He died 27 July 1777 aged 53 she 7 Feb 1787 aged 62. Arms Azure 2 bars between 6 mullets argent 3. 2 & 1 impaling Azure a chevron between 3 pelicans vulning themselves Argent
South wall of the nave – a tablet thus inscribed
1688 John Brooke by deed gave to trustees 2 cottages and gardens and charged his estate called Ashtown in this parish with £100 for building & £4 per ann. to repair an alms house for two poor persons with a chamber over for a school room £10 per annum to the master for teaching the children of Moorbath and Skillgate 12/- per month to the 2 poor of a gown of 20/- value to each once in 3 years the interest of £45 is distributed, yearly on the Sunday after Easter to the resident labourers of the parish. NB when or by whom given not known [missing].

The vicarage which is estimated at about £150 a year clear is held by the revd. Richard Bere. The great tithes belong to Mr Montague Bere who is Lord of the manor.

For Pedigree of Musgrave wherein 2 of the family of Bere are mentioned, the Gent's Magazine 1825 I. p 389 & page 610 of this book

UPLOWMAN

Davidson (pp. 605–8) visited [St Peter] Uplowman on 25 July 1843 and noted it was 5 miles north east of Tiverton. He observed a church 'in a retired and rustic village'. The church was almost completely rebuilt in 1863–6 by John Hayward (Pevsner, *Devon*, 881–2). All eleven memorials are missing that Davidson recorded.

The church of this retired and rustic village consists of a nave about 36 feet long by 10 wide, a chancel about 25 by 13, an aisle in the south about 46 by 12, a vestry at the west end of the aisle, an embattled tower at the western end containing 5 bells, and a porch covering the south door it is entered by a low pointed arch of several mouldings & has over it a niche for an image. Over the doorway of the porch is a sundial [removed]. The nave opens to the chancel by a lofty pointed arch resting on columns formed by shafts with mouldings between them their capitals carved in foliage on one of them is a shield but the arms are defaced. To the aisle the nave opens by 3 pointed arches on similar columns, their capitals carved in foliage and shields all painted but exhibiting no armorial bearings. The chancel is divided from the aisle by a double arch of similar design but in the space between the 2 arches on the west is a cinquefoiled opening through the columns under an open arch, opposite to it against the pie on the east side between 2 arches is a bracket for an image on a half·octagonal column ornamented with trefoiled panels. In front of the bracket is a wide shield coated with whitewash but evidently charged with the arms of Courtenay – 3 Torteaux with a label of 3 points impaling 6 mullets 3.2&1 (Courtenay) with supporters dexter a Dolphin sinister a Swan (Bonville). The capital of the columns above exhibit the following coats
I Courtenay impaling II
II -- 5 Fusils in bends, a label of 3 points
III Courtenay with a Mullet on the lower Torteaux
IV as III but painted or 3 Torteaux the lower one charged with a Mullet argent. a label of 3 points azure.
V – IV impaling Barry of 6 Argent and gules 8 Bells 3 & 2 on the Argent painted or
VI. as V
VII as IV.
The windows are of 3 lights with cinquefoiled heads & perpendicular tracery. There are some fragments of ancient stained glass among which is a shield the arms of Courtenay impaling [removed]. The ceilings are coved & ribbed with foliage at the intersections & shields charged with the arms of the Courtenay [removed]. – below the ceiling cornices have been put up in plaister with Grecian mouldings [removed]. The Font is a low octagonal stone basin the sides carved in foliage and quatrefoils. The pulpit [now stone] & pews are modern. A gallery at the western end of the nave [removed].

The monuments and inscriptions convey the following particulars.
A tablet on the wall states. This church was repaved and floored 1816 [removed].

Chancel
North wall, a Wooden Tablet. *In memoriam Seymori Kyrton A.M. huius parochae nup. Rectoris fidelissimi qui mortalitatem magis quam vitam exiut Octobris 8th die Anno Salutis 1661 Aetatis 54. Amoris ergo maerens uxor posuit.*
Come Reader view with fixed eye
What worth here underneath doth lye
One that did preach & lived peace
That studyed God not man to please
To birth renowne that did prefer
To be sent as Christ minister
Who in worst times undaunted stood
Patient tow'rd God to foes kind, good
Pleasant yet grave His love was high
To nature's and faith's family
When burning feavers flam'd the nest
His phoenix soul flew to her rest
In Christ he liv'd in him he dy'd
By Christ he shall be vivified.
Arms Argent a Chevron between 3 Cross crosslets gules impaling Argent a Chevron gules between 3 Coots sable [missing]
South wall a Tablet. Sacred to the memory of the rev. Simon Pidsley rector of this parish and of Sampford Peverell who died 7 of September 1821 aged 47.
Also of Mary his eldest daughter who died June 25th 1822 aged 16 Arms Sable 3 Lozenges argent on a chief or 3 Fleurs de lys gules [missing]
Floor. Here lieth John Southcott gent who died October X 1648 aged 20
A spark of fire that flies about
Is quickly in and quickly out
Thy fate o man in strength of breath
Soe thy life is – then waite for death
Life will not flourish – still for mine
I'th' bud was nippt with saints to shine.
In obitum venerabilis viri Ludovici Swete (archidiaconi Totton -- et hujus ecclesiae (rectoris)
Here lies -- pastor once without compare
Patient laborious and exceeding rare,
Who for his love, life, hospitalitie,
The heavens raft up into eternitie
Obiit 3° die Decembris An Dni 1615
A matron rare as husband joyntlie lye
Who brought 17 to life & so they dye
Alicia Ludovici uxor obiit Ano Dni 1631 [missing].
Here lyeth the body of Anthony Clarke rector of Charland -- Enmore in the county of Somerset who dyed -- 20th 1689. Arms – 2 Bars, in chief 3 Escallops -- Martletts, for difference [missing]

Nave
Floor. Here lyeth Henry Collamore of the Court place who deceased the XX day of May Dni 1598. [missing]

Here lyeth the body of Mr Christopher Collamore of Court place who changed mortality for immortality the 16th daye of June in the 67th year of his age of our redemption 1622. I know that my redeemer liveth [missing]

Here lyeth Ro -- more of the -- who deceased the XX date of August anno Dni 1594

Here also lieth John Collamore the wyfe of the above named Robert Collamore who deceased the XX daye of August A/D. 1599 [missing]

Aisle

Floor. Here lieth Edward -- Osmond of Stag -- who deceased the XXIII of July Ano Dni 1592 [missing]

Here lieth Edward Buketon of Stagmill who was buried 4 day of April AD. 1608 [missing]

Here lieth the body of Philip Chase who deceased May 31. 1624 and Joane his wife who died Sept 10 1633. This was laid at the charge of James Knight her executor [missing]

Here lieth the body of Bridgett Crudge daughter of Henry and Joan Crudge died 13 Jan 1674 aged 3 years and half [missing]

Churchyard.

A tomb. To the lasting memory of William Chase of this parish of Uplowman gent who departed this life the 10 September in the year of our Lord God, 1719 and in the 50th year of his age. He gave in and by his last will and testament to the use of the poor of this parish the sum of Four Pounds a year yearly

HUNTSHAM

Davidson (pp. 609–10) visited [All Saints] Huntsham on 11 September 1828 and noted it was about 6 miles north east of Tiverton. He observed that 'the church of this village is situated within the grounds on the south side and at a short distance from the mansion of the rev. Dr Troyte Rector of the parish. It has a venerable appearance and is a picturesque object, the tower & other parts being clothed in ivy.' The church was restored in 1854 by Benjamin Ferry (Pevsner, *Devon*, 497). Two memorials are missing from the five that Davidson recorded.

It consists of a nave 34 feet long by 16 wide a chancel 17 by 14 and a tower 8 feet square inside & 52 feet high to the top of the battlements a part of the ancient roof of the nave remains, it is carved in oak ribbed & adorned with foliage at the intersections & stars in the spaces between the ribs [removed]. A screen carved in oak with 3 foil headed openings under pointed arches divides the nave from the chancel & supports a rood loft which was entered by a door in the south wall leaving by a stair case in a buttress [removed]. The font is ancient, it is of stone heavy octagonal shape & ornamented with quatrefoils [changed in 1856]. Several of the old benches remain in the nave the panels at the ends of them elaborately carved in oak with various devices, warriors heads in armour eagles & one of them represents an angel holding a lozenge with the letters AC (AC.) [three remade into the pulpit] The south door is protected by a porch & the entrance are by pointed arches. Several ancient glazed tiles remain on the floor. – The church plate consists of a chalice and paten inscribed Huntsham 173½ .

Against the south wall of the church is a tablet with an inscription which is defaced & illegible below it is a medallion with the bust of a female capitally executed in relief & painted
There is a coat of arms but those on the dexter side of the escutcheon are defaced they Impale Party of fess in chief argent 3 mullets 2 &1. in base Sable a chief Gules. [missing]
On the chancel floor is a flat stone inscribed. Here lieth the body of Charles Bean cleric who died 2nd day of Nov 1607 [missing]
Arms. 3 heads couped 2&1
On the floor of the nave – Mary Donne wife of Christopher Donne died 6 Jan 1642 aged 78. they lived man & wife together 42 years 4 months & 14 days. – [now in the porch floor]
On the floor of the nave --- G --- *filia Johannis Dean de Huntsham armigeri & uxor Tomae Collins de Off--- obiit 26 Feb 16* – Arms, a chevron between 3 martletts impaling 3 heads --- Arms in a lozenge – a chevron between 3 martletts [now in the porch floor]
The tower of this church contains 3 bells thus inscribed

Deo detur Gloria IMP. 1667.
† AVE MARIA.
† AVE MARIA.

Johannem Bere dominum de Honeshm – 1378 See deeds for Musbury.
Robtus Scotte or Scut dns Bere 1378 D°.D°.

George Musgrave of Nettlecombe co Som: married Juliana daughter of Thomas Bere of Huntsham co Devon & had issue. See Gent's Mag. 1824 II. pp 98: & 1825 [III] p 290. & 389 at which last there is a pedigree.

TIVERTON

Davidson (pp. 613–43) visited [St Peter] Tiverton on 28 July 1843 and noted it was 15 miles north of Exeter. He observed that 'the church of this ancient and populous town is a large and interesting building and though it now exhibits no features of great antiquity it is well worthy of notice especially as regards the munificence of one individual who expended so considerable a part of his wealth on its enlargement and decoration'. In 1853–6 the northern aisle was doubled in width to balance with the Greenway chapel carried out by Edward Ashworth (Pevsner, *Devon*, 808–9).

It comprises a nave a chancel and Aisle on the north side with an additional aisle on the same side, a vestry adjoining the last, a south Aisle an additional aisle Chapel, a large Porch and a Tower at the western end of the nave. The only vestige of a building of an early date is a doorway now in the north side in the Anglo-Norman style it is under a semicircular arch with an outer arch formed by mouldings of zigzag design from the ground.

The nave is about 84 feet long by 25 wide, the walls externally are finished by battlements and plain pinnacles. It is lighted by 6 clerestory windows on each side. Those on the south are formed by 3 trefoil headed lights under low arches, those on the north are 3 lights with cinquefoiled heads and quatrefoils above under low arches. The nave appears to have formerly opened to the chancel by a lofty arch which has been destroyed and the roofs or ceilings lowered, another low arch of modern date has been erected in its place, panelled in the soffits and having a window in its head. The nave opens to the aisles on each side by 6 low arches of numerous mouldings resting on columns formed by clustered shafts and mouldings their capitals carved in foliage angels animals birds and shields some plain others charged with mercantile marks and devices. In the western side of each column next the nave is a large niche supported by an angel below and ornamented buttress in the sides under a crocketted canopy with a finial. These niches now contain no images but the backs of 8 of them are painted with shields charged with the following coats of arms [now plain].
I Gules a Bend between 6 Cross crosslets fitchees argent (2nd for Were)
II Argent a Fess gules, in chief 3 Torteaux (2 & 1 for Mules or Wake
III Argent a Cross engrailed gules between 4 Water bougets sable (Bourchier)
IV Per pale vert and argent 3 Lions rampant counter charged within a bordure compo or and gules.
V Gules a Lion rampant within a bordure engrailed or.
VI Argent a Lion rampant gules, in a chief sable 2 Escallops of the field.
VII: Azure a Cross or between 4 Birds (Doves) argent
VIII. Barry of 6 or and azure, a Chief quarterly 1 & 4 Azure 2 Fleurs de lis in fess or 2 & 3 Gules 2 Lions passant gardant in pale or.
The ceiling of the Nave is modern mainly flat but ribbed with bosses at the

intersections of the ribs, apparently cast in plaister of various devices – some appear to be Grecian figures. [now wood rafters]

The Chancel is about 34 feet long by 24 wide. Externally the roof is surrounded by large battlements & there is a pinnacle at each of the two eastern corners one of which is finished with a crown the other with a mitre. The battlements which are said to have been erected about 1709 sculptured in panels and shields bearing inscriptions portions of which may be deciphered thus.

I *Primo quaerite regnum caelorum*
II a shield with arms – a chevron between 3 Hearts transfixed with swords impaling – on a Bend 3 Fleurs de lis. (Newte Bone)
III The arms of Newte impaling a Bridge with water below and a flag upon it (Trowbridge)
IV An open book inscribed *In verbo tuo spes mea.*
V a skull and bones
VI a radiant crown and the words *Vincente dabito.*
VII. as II
VIII. a tablet inscribed *MEMENTO Quatuor NOVISSIMA.*
IX Dᵒ. Inscribed *D.O.M.H.P.S. John Newte hujus Ecclesiae rector 1709.*

The chancel opens to the aisles by two low arches on each side resting on columns of alternate shafts & mouldings their capitals carved in foliage. The ceiling is flat, ribbed and boarded with wood, and painted white [now wood rafters].
The eastern window of the chancel is divided into two sub arches forming 5 lights with ogee arches and cinquefoil heads, and perpendicular tracery the side windows are 3 cinquefoil lights with small triangular openings in the low arches above. The north Aisle, independently of the eastern part is about 70 feet long by 12 wide & the wall is supported on the outside by heavy buttresses & finished by an embattled parapet. The windows are under wide pointed arches formed by 2 sub-arches into 4 lights with cinquefoil heads & perpendicular tracery above. There are some fragments of old painted glass in some of them [removed]. The ceiling is flat and plain [now wood rafters]. The eastern end of the north aisle, which has had a projecting portion added to it is about 48 feet long by 22 wide. The walls are crowned by an embattlement parapet and at the eastern end to the battlements are ornamented with quatrefoils and shields charged with foliage and devices. The windows are 4 lights with cinquefoiled heads under low arches, except one which has 5 lights and perpendicular tracery above. The roof of this aisle is ribbed with fan tracery springing from the capitals of shafts attached to the wall, and is ornamented with bosses of foliage and devices at the intersections of the ribs.

The south aisle or Greenways aisle which was rebuilt by John Greenway about 1517 is about 120 feet long by 22 wide. It is lighted by 6 windows on the south and one at each end. Those on the south are under pointed arches divided into 2 sub-arches forming 4 lights with cinquefoiled heads and perpendicular tracery. The eastern window is of similar design but has 6 lights. The western window is under a low arch and is divided by mullions and a transom into 10 lights with trefoiled except the middle which are cinquefoiled, the arch is filled with perpendicular tracery and quatrefoils. Externally the walls are supported by buttresses of three stages & surmounted by a close embattled parapet. The buttresses terminate in quadrangular pinnacles rising above the parapet carved in panels and enriched with crockets and finials. The faces of the walls, its buttresses and the parapet are all richly adorned with sculpture of various devices, quatrefoils and foliage – the letters J.G. variously deposed and conjoined – Greenway mercantile marks – ships – shields charged with a cross, others with 3 Beehives – tuns – woolpacks – animals – and cross fleury – 2 keys in saltire – angels – monkeys – griffins with a fish upon it – a tun and a cats face – etc. The part of the aisle towards the east appears to have been rebuilt lately in which is an elegant doorway under a low arch supported by numerous mouldings with a horizontal moulding above and an embattled cornice, the rose and thistle in the spandrels of the arch. In the south east angle of the wall of this aisle is the figure of an angel holding a scroll on which is the date anno Dni MCCCCCXVII. The ceiling at the western end of this aisle is flat and without ornament at the eastern end it is relieved by ribs which spring from large handsome corbels of foliage and fruit against the south wall and the spandrels of the arches on the opposite side [now wood rafters].

Greenway's chapel projects in front of the south aisle & is about 22 feet long by 12 wide within the walls lighted by two windows on the south under low pointed arches divided by 4 sub arches into as many lights with trefoiled headed and quatrefoil above one window at the eastern end divided by a transom & mullions with sub arches into eight lights with quatrefoils above. The walls externally are supported by buttresses of three stages surmounted by pinnacles rising above the parapet enriched by sunken panels crockets and finials. The bases of the pinnacles are relieved by small flying pinnacles resting on corbels richly sculptured in grotesque figures and animals. The walls the faces of the buttresses are most richly ornamented with sculpture of the greatest variety of design in panels niches quatrefoils and shields. There is a rich cornice above it a range of panels and on top an open parapet embattled & super-embattled. Amongst the devices may be enumerated various incidents in scripture history and the life of our Saviour – shields supported by dragons and charged with a cross – a plain shield – grotesque animals – couchant lions – monkeys – figures of the evangelists seated in niches – the letters J.G. in various forms – Ships and boats of various shapes and size some sailing on the sea – anchors – woolpacks – merchants marks open books – bones – tuns – fruit – flowers – shields monkeys nursing their young – lions supporting shields etc –

On the range of panels is a series of shields supported by angels and dragons thus charged
I a Cross – II a Chevron between 3 covered cups, in chief as many Eagles heads erased. – III 3 Bars wavy a chief quarterly 1 & 4 a Lion passant gardant. 2 & 3 2 Roses fess wise – IV. 3 Beehives V The monogram.
In the south east angle of the walls is an elegant niche with a canopy and crocketted pinnacle supported by an angel holding a scroll thus inscribed
"Of yr charity pray for the souls of John Greenway & his wyfe" On the wall by the side of it "God sped J.G" and above it "O Lord ye all may grant to John Greenway good fortune & grace & in heyven a place." Under the east window is a low arch and beneath it the front of an altar tomb carved in four panels with shafts and pinnacles between them. The panels are occupied by angels holding shields thus charged. I The monogram, II a chevron between 3 covered cups on a chief 3 Eagles heads erased. III 3 Beehives IV The mercantile mark

Of John Greenway. Above the panels & under the slab this inscription "Whilst we think well & think t'amend Time passeth away & Death's the end".
Below the arch above the tomb. "John Greenway founded this chapel A.D. MDXVII. Died A.D. MDXXIX."

Internally this chapel opens to the south aisle by two low pointed arches resting on a column and two half columns formed by 4 shafts with intervening mouldings with octagonal capitals richly carved in two tiers of foliage with the monogram J.G. The faces of the column and half columns next the aisle are relieved with niches under handsome canopies supported by buttresses & finished with crockets and finials, over all are cornices of foliage. Across the openings beneath the arches is a low screen of stone carved in panels with trefoil heads and pendants of foliage and at the base next the floor a range of quatrefoils with shields devices and monograms. A doorway under a low pointed arch leads into Greenway's porch at the western end of this chapel. The soffits of the windows and their arches are filled with trefoiled panels.
The roof is of stone covered and filled with rich tracery in circular compartments filled in with trefoils and quatrefoils the centres finished with bosses of foliage and rich pendants. Under the roof is a cornice carved in relief with anchors bales and angels holding shields charged with the monogram J.G. and his mercantile mark. Under the cornice is the inscription "John Greenway built this chapel Anno Dom MDXVII the porch aisle and ends of the same and an almshouse at the east end of the town for V poor men and finished the same XII years before his death and was interred underneath with his wife." Against the south wall in the pier between the windows is a niche supported by buttresses resting on angels holding shields on which are
I the mercantile mark of John Greenway impaling 3 Beehives
II The monogram
Above is a rich canopy with tabernacle work finished with crocketted pinnacles and finials surmounted by a cornice of foliage. No image in it but on the back is painted this inscription "This chapel founded A.D. 1517 by John Greenway a Merchant of this town and a great benefactor to it having gone to decay. The churchwardens of this parish who were by his appointment charged to preserve all the buildings connected with his charitable bequests caused it to be restored from the funds arising from them A.D. 1829. Francis Pratt. William Baker. Wardens. Rev. John Pitman. Rev. John Blundell. Rev. William Pager. Rev. C. O. Ossmond. Rev. William Page Richard D.D. Rev. John Pitman jun. B.B. Dickenson esq. Henry Dunsford esq. George Barne esq John Ware esq. Feoffees. G.A. Boyce architect. J. Watkins Mason."

On the floor is a stone about 12 feet long by 4 wide with whole length brass figure of the founder and his wife their hands uplifted in prayer, a large plate and label over their heads are gone as also one shield, a shield over her remains charged with these arms [now located on the wall]
Nebuly a chief quarterly 1 & 4 a Lion passant gardant 2 & 3 2 Roses in fess, and about it the words "pray for John Greenway --" (the rest under a pew) a brass fillet once along the outer edge of the stone is also removed.

Against the western wall of this chapel is a fixed a painting which was formerly the altar piece of no great merit; the subject is the angel delivering St. Peter from Prison [removed].

At the west end of the chapel is Greenway's porch projecting a little. It is entered by a low pointed arch of several mouldings with a label over it resting on corbels of angels holding shields charged with monograms J.G. and his mercantile mark. The corner and the western side are supported by buttresses of three stages terminating in pinnacles and ornamented with panels and sculptures of various devices boldly executed niches with figures standing and sitting – shipping – quatrefoils – monograms – mercantile marks etc. The set of the buttress are encircled with animals boldly carved lions monkeys etc. The face of the porch is richly sculptured in panels etc on each side of the arch is a niche supported by angular shafts resting on corbels of angels under canopies of tabernacle work with crockets pinnacles and finials. Above the arch is a canopy under an ogee arch supported by twisted columns terminating above in a large cross rising above the parapet under the canopy is a shield with three arms

Quarterly 1 & 4 3 Roundels. 2 & 3 a Lion rampant impaling – intended for Courtenay & Redvers

Quarterly 1st Quarterly France and England

2nd & 3rd a Cross

4th Barry of 6 on a chief – a pale between (Mortimer)

2 Bar – esquire. An escutcheon.

Crest a dove standing on a bundle of rods. Supported dexter a man in armour with a dragon at his feet sinister a woman habited.

On each side are trefoiled panels containing shields supported by Angels thus charged. I. 3 Beehives II 3 Beehives and in chief the monogram J.G. impaling 3 Beehives and in base Greenways mercantile mark. Below these coats is a label thus inscribed in old letter. "In tyme & space God send grace John Greenway to perform yt y haste be gone." On the upper part is a cornice ornamented with shields foliage birds woolpacks monograms J. G. & below it an embattled parapet carved with numerous figures in high relief the subjects apparently scriptural and legendary. Within the porch the side walls are plain on the east side a richly carved oak door opens into Greenways chapel. The roof is coved and carved in modern Gothic style in quatrefoils enriched with devices of great variety, monograms, birds, ships anchors foliage wool-packs fish fruit a cat cordage etc below the roof is a cornice with similar devices. The principal doorway into the south aisle is under a semicircular arch with rectangular mouldings and foliage in the spandrels. On each side is a niche with a canopy enriched with crockets pinnacles & finials. Over the door is an elaborate piece of sculpture presenting the apotheosis of the Virgin Mary as Queen of heaven standing on the moon & surrounded by angels. Above is the half length figure of a venerable man crowned to represent the Almighty. The whole is under an ogee arch & resting on twisted columns finished above with pinnacles and finials. On one side is the figure of a man kneeling at a desk, above him the monogram J.G. on the other side his wife also kneeling at a desk and above her letters which appear to be BH or WH or WB. Below the figure of the virgin is a small shield with the charge 3 Beehives. Over the doorway inside is this inscription. This Porch erected in MDXVII was taken down and rebuilt in MDCCCXXV James Somers and Thomas Haydon churchwardens.

The Tower is 27 feet square and is supported by buttresses at the angles of four stages the set offered ornamented with lions or grotesque figures of animals. The face of the tower is divided by string courses into four stages above the basement. The western door is under a pointed arch with a rectangular label and carvings of foliage & fruit in the spandrels on either side is a vacant niche under a canopy. The western window is under a pointed arch and is formed by two sub-branches into four lights having cinquefoil heads and perpendicular tracery above. The belfry windows are divided by a mullion and transom into four lights with trefoiled heads and are filled with open quatrefoils. The tower is crowned with battlements beneath which are gargoyles of rude figures and above them rises eight crocketted pinnacles four of them at the angles finished will vanes. The height of the tower is 100 feet to the top of the battlements and 16 more to the top of the tower. It contains 8 musical bells a clock & chimes.

A carved oak screen said to have been erected in 1517 divides the nave from the chancel consisting of a range of 5 pointed arches containing four open lights with cinquefoiled heads and perpendicular tracery above. Shafts between them rise into fan tracery below the rood loft, which is now appropriated as a gallery and is fronted by four series of mouldings carved in foliage. There are side screens to the aisles of later date & inferior execution [removed]. There is a low altar screen of carved oak supporting a large picture said to be by Rubens presented to the church by the rev. Mr Hole. The subject is the offering of the wise men to the infant Jesus, it is finely painted and is excellent preservation [removed].

The communion table is of plain oak, covered by a plain crimson velvet cloth with the date upon it 1777. Tables with the commandments are affixed to the north & south walls of the chancel. The pulpit with its canopy are in wood carved in the style of the 17th century and painted – on the under part of the latter is a painting of an angel with a trumpet attended by cherubs and on the back the text "Cry aloud spare not lift up thy voice like a trumpet and shew my people their transgressions and the house of Israel their sins. Isaiah 58.1" [now stone]. About the pulpit are shields painted with the following coats of arms [removed].
Courtenay. I. Or 3. Torteaux II. Argent on a bend sable a Mullet between Garbs of the field
Bishop Cotton. III. the arms of the See of Exeter impaling Argent a Bend Sable between 3 Pullets
Greenway. IV. Gules a Chevron between 3 Covered Cups or, on a chief Argent as many Eagles heads erased azure
Query Bourdon. V Argent a Chevron sable between 3 Trees vert. VI Gules a Lion rampant argent within a bordure engrailed sable Entoyre of Billets or.
Stretch or Ashenden or Downing. VII Argent a Lion rampant gules.
Newte. VIII Gules a Chevron argent between 3 Heart of the last transfixed by Swords azure hilted or.

The desks and pews are modern of oak in panels with mouldings in form of pointed arches. In front of the pews in the south aisle appropriated to the mayor and corporation are 2 carved figures a Lion and a Unicorn holding shields, one charged with a Rose & crown the other with a Thistle and crown. The doors of the pews in the south aisle are ornamented with the following coats of arms capitally carved in oak in modern style. (Carew) Or 3 Lions passant in pale (sable) with an Escutcheon for

Bart Crest a Demi Lion rampant between 6 Spears erect. Supporters two Antelopes – Motto. *Nil conscire sibi* [removed].
The font which stands at the western end of the nave is a new octagonal stone basin ornamented with quatrefoils on the sides, on an octagonal column carved in sunk niches trefoiled.

A gallery erected 1659 the front of which is of carved oak crosses the western end [removed] of the nave in which is a large and handsome organ in a carved oak frame with numerous gilded pipes in front. This inscription appears on the front of it "Built AD 1696 by Johann Suetzler" There is a plain mean gallery in the south aisle erected 1708 and a similar one at the east end of the north aisle both removed]. A large and handsome brass chandelier of 30 lights hangs from the roof of the nave.

The numerous monuments and inscriptions of this church convey the following particulars.

Chancel
East wall a handsome marble Tablet. With the arms Gules a chevron between 3 Hearts argent (Newte) transfixed with swords sable hilted or impaling Or on a bend azure 3 Fleurs de lis of the field (Bone)
In memory of the rev. Mr John Newte MA son of the right worthy and revd. Richard Newte B.D. late rector of the parish of Tidcombe and Clare in this parish. He was sometime fellow of Balliol college in Oxford and for three years member of convocations for the clergy of the diocese. He maryed Edith the daughter of Mr William Bone of Farringdon in this parish gent. He was a person of exemplary piety diffusion charity remarkable meekness and generous hospitality a diligent and faithful pastor a laborious preacher a strenuous asserter of the rights and dues of the church and tender father and defender of the poor and oppressed after being 37 years rector of Tidcombe and 36 of Pitt in this church he patiently bore the pains of a lingering sickness & cheerfully resigned his soul to God March 7. 1715 aged 60 years. Peter Newte his only surviving brother & executor thus expressed his more than equal share of a generous loss.
East wall. A marble tablet and an urn and foliage. Near this place are deposited the remains of the revd. John Newte MA. rector of Tidcombe in this parish he was eminently distinguished for his extensive learning brilliancy of wit cheerfulness of disposition amiable manners and unbounded charity. He died Dec. the 9th 1792 aged 37. Arms – a Chevron between 3 hearts transfixed – (Newte) impaling – a Fess between 3 Crosses patees --- (esq Northcote)
North Wall. A handsome stone monument with Corinthian columns and entablature above it a tablet and plasters on which are these arms
Quarterly   1 (sable) 3 Fusils in fess ermine (Gifford)
                  2 On a Bend engrailed between 2 Swans or Pelicans holding
                        Swords or Trefoils slipped in their beaks 3 Roundels.
                  3. (azure) Three pears pendants (or)
                  4. Three Bugle horns stringed
Underneath.
Sacrum memoriae monumentum generissimo viro Rogeri Giffard armigero
Armigeri quondam Giffardi membra Rogeri
Haec tegit, in Cineres, terra; soluta suos

Miles erat Genitor, Dominus, de Brightleigh Rogerus
Quintus et ipsius filius iste fuit.
Consors prima Thori, Nati Genitrixque Georgii
Nata, Equitis de Afton, Andrea Stocla fuit
Corporis externo multum spectabilis ore
Mentis at internae gratia maior erat
Cultores amicitiae constans et cultor agrorum
Summus Egenorum cultor amansque fuit
Ex triplici binos generavit conjuge natos,
Nec vidit stirpis gemina plura suae
In conis annos moritur remanesque secundus
Hoc patri sacrum conficiebat opus
Septuaginta, senex postquam compleverat, annos
Ecce animam caelo reddidit, ossa solo.
Obiit, sepultus Tyvertonii Octobris 8° 1603.
Tablet. Near this tablet are deposited the remains of the Revd. John Pitman MA. Formerly fellow of Oriel college Oxford Prebendary of Cutton in Devon Rector of Porlock in Somerset and for 48 years a zealous and indefatigable officiating Minister of this church, who died 29 Dec. 1830 in the 81 year of his age.
South wall. Tablet of marble with a wreath – near this stone are deposited the remains of the revd. John Newte MA. who died 9 Dec. 1792 of Sarah Crosse her daughter who died 4 June and of Elizabeth the only other daughter of the first named Sarah Crosse who died 9 Sept 1822 having been married first to the above named John Newte and secondly to the rev John West Carew MA.

A large stone monument with Corinthian columns with an entablature painted and gilt.
Richard Newte A.M. – annos – rector serenissimo Carolo 20 sacris, vir prudentia pietate et doctrina insignis qui juventutem schola Blundelliana provectiorem aetatem studiis versatus Oxoniae excoluit Coll. Exon socius Theologia linguis. omnique politiori literatura-difficu--- Astu arte bello intestino non nisi Regis hortatu exteras gentes pelagiavit Patria reditus pastor vigilantissimus gregique -- pestilentia --prce--- Regi ad extrema fidelissimus – quae expecta --- meritus Pater Dominus et amicus optimus vitaeque in omnibus admirendum exemplar D.--- senectute quam morbo labora correptus --- inchoavit vitam 10 die Augusti aetatis suae 66 --- liberos suscepit et -- Henricus Katherina & Susanna --- succubuere Richard – ob--- Pet & Hen. & Christianam superst --- maerentes tanto parente --- pietatis et amoris ergo Johannes in eccl. condignus successor --- poni curavit Juxta situs est – Arms Quarterly 1 & 4 Newte.2&3 Argent a Bridge gules, flag or, water proper. (Newte. Trobridge.)

Floor. Subtus jacent exuviae mortales Isabellae Samuelis Taner de Farringdon in com. Devon armigeri filiae natu tertiae, Quae per duodecim plus minus annos viro consors; febre tandem correpta, vitam suis maxime desideratam, Deo, a quo prius grata recepit, non invita reddidit 1° Octobris AD 1728 aetat 42° Conjugis adamatae reclamantis Memoriam pie colens, et claros juxta cineres, suos etiam quandocunque Deo Opt. Max. visum fecerit sepeliendo esse statuens marmor hoc Samuel Newte M.P. Ipse etiam voli compos. podagra aliisque morbis diu vexatus et per totos menses ne dicam annos (supra forsan quam quodcunque credibile fuerit) vix unquam somno oculos declinans paralysi tandem lassatus pie requiem invenit 27° Mar 1742 aetat 57

A crown supported by two angels with the motto *Mortuorum in Christo Corona. In pace beataeque resurrectionis spe hoc conseruantur sepulchro cineres Edithae charissimae conjugis Johannis Newte portionum de Pitt & Tidcombe in hanc ecclesiam Rectoris, Filiae Gulielmi Bone de Farringdon gen. quae apoplexia correpta usque tamen Dominum expectans ad mortem parata, obiit Feb:13 1704 aetat. suae 46. Vigilate et orate quia nescitis horam. Hic etiam jacet Samuel Newte A.M. Collegii Novi Oxoniensis Socius et ecclesiae de Alphington Rector. Filius natu maximus Samuelis Newte hujus ecclesiae rectoris vir pro pietate erga Deum & parentes, pro ingenii acumine & Doctrina et prae omnibus pro felici indolis amoenitate et morum urbanitate merito omnibus carus, suis carissimus. Qui febre putrida correptus quam paucus tantum laborans Dies vitam talibus auspiciis insigniter inchoatam! Heu! nimis celeriter finivit. 3° die Dec 1772 aetat 28.* Arms 2 shields. I Newte. II (or) on a Bend (ar) 3 Fleurs de lis (field)

Here lieth the body of Elizabeth daughter of Thomas Leigh gent four times mayor of this towne married to Mr John Chishull rector of the portion of Pitt to whom she bore 3 sons who fell with her under the blessing of the couenant, and one daughter yet living. She departed September the 9th 1656. She was naturally week, constitutionally tender and gratuitously humble. Her life was full of doubtings her sickness fuller of patience & her death fullest of consolations. Reader, thou shall know that she was all this and more, at the great day when the story of her life shall be told. *Hic jacet Richardus Newte hujus ecclesiae rector qui obiit Aug 10 1678 aetat 66. Filius fuit Henrici de hoc oppido generosi. Prope hunc tumulum jacent etiam Henricus Newte opt. spei juvenis praedicti Richardii filius natu maximus variolis correptus: occubuit Sept 15. 1663 aetat 12. Susanna filia natu minima eodem morbo laborans brevem vitam terminavit Oct 1. 1663 aetat 4. Et Katherina natu maxima caelum appetens mortalitatem exuit Junii 18. 1668 aetat. 20: Thomas Newte variolarum fatali morbo correptus valde deploratus Londini e vivis excessit Oct 3. 1683 aetat. 23. & sepultus jacet in ecclesia St Michaelis Cornhill. Hic jacet Thomasina reverendi Richardi Newte relicta filia unica et haeres Eduardi Trobridge de Brushford in agro Somersetensi generosi quae quum assidua pietate constantia temporibus infaelicissimis plusquam foeminea et industria laudabili vitam adornavit serenamque taedio licet morborum Arthritidis et nephritidis lassarum diu seruavat faelicissime in Domino obdormivit Maii 19 aetat 72. 1697. -- corpus animale spirituale resurrecturum Sarae charissimae conjugis Richardi Newte generosi et filiae. Rogeri Colman armigeri feminae spectata in Deum pietate exemplari in maritum fide materna in filiam charitate (quam unicam et ejusdem nominis reliquit) singulari vitae et morum probitate, ad priscae virtutis gloriam ad surgentis; quae omnibus amata vixit at caelo matura eam luctu variolis --- rata in Caelum ad festum Epiphaniae evocata Jan 6. 1678 aetat suae 21. Tegit etiam hoc saxum cineres praefati Richardi Newte de Duvale in parochia de Bampton generosi qui quam acutissimum diu arthritidis dolorem patienter sustulerit hinc ad feliciorem vitam migravit Aug. 18° Anno Domini 1697 aetat 37. Richardus Newte filius natu maximus praedicti ---* W.R. 1817.

Beneath this stone lyes intered Frances the wife of Edmond Gibbon gent. & Elizabeth their daughter to whose memory the monument opposite to this vault was erected. Buried here Mary and Thomas son & daughter of Robert London the former Aug. 10

1695 aged 18 months the latter Sept 27 1705 aged 4 years & 2 months. Also the said Robert who died Dec 5 & was buried 12th 1728 aged 55 years 8 months & odd days also William his son who died Jan 15th .
Here lieth the body of Eleanor the wife of Marmaduke John -- of Tiverton Goldsmith and daughter of -- John Sprat D.D. sometime Canon Subdean of Exon – departed this life 2° day of Aug, -- Arms in a lozenge -- 3 Quatrefoils slipped ---
Deposita sunt hoc tumulo mortales reliq-- Thomae Monck de Potheridge armigeri in spem beati resurrectionis 1649.
M.S. Gulielmi Lee Medici Gulielmi Lee de Wincellade in com. Devon armigeri filii qui quatuor lustris in -- anelo humani generi quam feliciter incubuit cum morbis vix plures congressus habuit quam triumphos quibus solis infensus aegrotantibus vero gratus infirmorum tam animis quam corporibus contribuit --- obiit A.D. 1679 aetat suae 42. Arms – A Fess cotised – impaling Ermine. A Chevron.

North Aisle
East wall. a Tablet with an urn.
In memory of Richard Blundell esq of this town who died 25 April 1811 aged 82 years. Also to the memory of Mrs Mary Shapleigh daughter of the above R Blundell esq died 21 Jan 1823 aged 70. Arms
Gules 2 Pales argent. An escutcheon of pretence
Azure a Chevron or between 3 Mullets argent (Query Chattey)

Stone monument, an entablature supported by twisted Corinthian columns – painted and gilded.
This was erected to the just memory of Frances wife of Edmund Gibbons of this town gent who was the oldest daughter and one of the coheirs of William Amory late of Bishops Nympton in this county gent deceased by Cecile his first wife the only daughter of Roger Molford of the same parish esq also deceased. She died 17 Feb. 1688 in the 28th year of her age being the happy mother of one son and two daughters viz Edmund Frances and Elizabeth. The said Elizabeth died in the first year of her age on the 1 Feb. 1682 and lieth interred with her. *Vivit post funeral virtus.* Arms 3 coats
I Sable a Lion rampant gardant ducally crowned or between 3 Escallops argent
II Barry nebuly of 8 argent and gules a bend sable
III I impaling II.
A tablet with an urn. Sacred to the memory of Elizabeth Pomery wife of Thomas Phillipps esq of Collipriest. She departed this life the 29 Jan 1800 in the 39 year of her age. also Thomas son of Thomas & Elizabeth Pomery Phillips who died the 25 May 1796 aged 4. Arms. Quarterly. 1st & 4th or a Lion rampant sable langued gules chained and collard of the field holding in his paws a shield gules charged with a stag's head couped or. 2nd & 3rd Quarterly 1st & 4th or a Lion rampant sable langued gules collared argent 2nd & 3rd per pale indented or and azure an Eagle displayed and counter-charged, impaling quarterly the last 2 coats.

North Wall. A marble monument – Corinthian pilasters supporting a pediment on which are two angels holding a skull and an anchor – a tablet under a canopy. In memory of Mr Nathanael Thorne of this town merchant who died 23 Nov 1734 in the 63rd year of his age and Elizabeth his wife who died 28 Sept 1716 aged 40 by whom he had seven children George Nathaniel Eliza Margaret. Mary George and James. Margaret died in the 22 year of her age 1738. The rest (excepting Eliza and James who only survived their father) in their infancy James died in the 22nd year of his age 1735 surviving his father one year only. Arms. Argent a Fess gules between 3 Lions rampant sable impaling Gules a Lion rampant argent, on a chief of the last a Pheon between two 2 Bulls heads and necks erased or.

A tablet under the last monument.
In the same vault like wise lyeth interred Mr John Newton, Merchant who died 8 Feb 1731 aged 33. He was married to Elizabeth who being now the only surviving child of Mr Nathanael Thorne caused this monument to be erected. A.D. 1737. Arms. Argent on a Chevron azure 3 Garbs or impaling Argent a Fess gules between 3 Lions rampant sable.
A marble monument. An entablature supported by Corinthian columns with urns etc. In memory of the venturous and most ingenious Mr John Lane merchant and his most pious and charitable wife Elizabeth (only daughter of no less pious father Mr Giles Barry) who having lived most lovingly together twenty one years dyed both in this town he having given by his last will an estate of about £500 for the benefit of the poore besides several other considerable gifts for pious use to other places and persons. She died three days after him and both of them were in one day interred underneath this monument
The turtle dove can't long survive the fate
Or sad divorcement of her dearest mate
Soe he first dead: She stayed a while and tried
To live without him, liked it not and died
Arms 3 shields I Per pale Argent and gules 3 Saltier counter charged. II as I. III Barry of 6 Argent & gules
A stone – here lieth the body of Catherine wife of Richard Spurway of this town who died 12 Oct 1707, Richard, Richard, Robert, Thomas, John and William six sons of the said R. S. who all died in the lifetime of their said mother and before they attained the age of 3 years. Here also lieth the body of the above said Richard Spurway who was three times mayor of this town & died 2nd Feb 1718 in the 66 year of his age Below this is a large stone defaced to the memory of several of the family of Spurway.
A tablet. Edward Gatchill of this town merchant brother in law to the above John Lane died 24 June 1722 Mary his wife died 25 June 1726. Rebecca their daughter died 24 July 1744 aged 63.
A Tablet. Thomas Gilbert surgeon of this town died 3 Feb, 1770 aged 50. Margaret G. his wife died 12 March 1807 aged 52.

South Wall. a Tablet and urn. Benjamin Gilbert of the city of Exeter merchant and native of this town a liberal benefactor to it and an honest man died 31 July 1790 in the 68 year of his age. In gratitude this memorial is erected by John Blackmore his executer.
North wall. a tablet and urn. Sacred to the memory of Joanna Lewis who died 24 March 1790 aged 75 erected by her daughter. – Arms Azure 3 Fleurs de lis or.
A large marble monument, Corinthian columns pediment and entablature – painted and gilt. In memory of Robert Chattey merchant who departed this life 19 June 1679 aged 68 years having been twice mayor of this town. He gave to the poore at his death forty pounds and ten pounds yearly for ever. He had 4 sons and 4 daughters which with his former wife died before him, they are all interred in the middle alley

of this place in hope of a glorious resurrection. (here follow some verses) Also his second wife Priscilla daughter of John Skinner gent who died 10 April 1680 aged 59 years. Arms Azure a Chevron between 3 Mullets or. impaling Sable a Chevron or between 3 Eagles heads & necks erased argent.
A tablet. George Sweet esq died 14 Dec. 1809 in the 86 year of his age. also his son Specot Long Sweet died -- Sept 1775 aged 19 His daughter Elizabeth Sweet died 13 April 1814 aged 45. – raised by his surviving family.
A Tablet. John Halsey third beloved and lamented son of Richard and Maria Budden died 24 April 1817 aged 9 years.

A large marble monument – entablature & pediment supported by Corinthian columns – angels etc. painted and gilt.
In memory of the virtuous Mary second wife of Samuel Foote esq and daughter of William Keate gent who had by her 4 sons and 7 daughters of whom only 4 daughters survived them namely Mary Sarah Dorothy and Elizabeth. She departed this life 17 Jan A.D. 1677 in the 44 year of her age
Arms gules a Chevron between 3 Doves argent impaling Argent 3 mountain cats passant gardant in pale sable.
A white marble tablet. Sacred to the memory of Philip Blundell of The Lodge in this parish son of Philip Blundell of Collipriest and Agnes his wife born 10 May A.D. 1744 died 26 Feb 1822. Arms Gules 2 Pales argent.

A large marble and stone monument Corinthian columns with an entablature and pediment. In memory of Thomas Thomas of this town and Joan his wife who died in the 86th and 79th year of their age. Their issue were eight, of whom one only survived them, all the rest dying in their minority. Margaret the survivor was married to John Upcott of this town merchant by whom she had seven children John Thomas Mary, & Catherine who died before her, William Margaret and Joan who out-lived her and died the 11 Jan 1717 and was buried the 22nd in the 77 year of her age. All interred near this place – a shield but no arms visible.

Between the north aisle and the chancel a large stone tomb about 8 feet long by 4 wide and 4½ high. The sides sculptured in pilasters, scrolls, plain shields and devices, on top a heavy black marble slab thus inscribed. Hereunder lieth buried the body of George Lee merchant, who departed this life the 1st day of September Anno Domini 1615. He gave by his will to be distributed to the poorest people of Tiverton fifty pounds to the parish church and church yard of Tiverton ten pounds to and for the building of an alms house for six poor & honest women and for to purchase rents for their maintenance at twelve pence every week to each of them five hundred pounds to fifty poore craftsmen of good name and fame in Tiverton one hundred pounds to the poorest honest and painful labourers in husbandry in Tiverton ten pounds to the parish of Colridge for the relief of keeping on work the poorest people there ten pounds to the poore of the parish of Halberton forty shillings to the poore of the parish of Uplowman forty shillings. He left behind him living two sonnes and three daughters.

Floor. Here lieth the body of Mr John Denham of Hayparke yeoman once mayor of the town who departed this life the 12 day of Feb. 1654 aged 83 years. Here lieth the body of Agnes the wife of the said Mr John D. who departed this life the 20 day of

Aprill 1665 being the age of 94 years. here lieth the body of Mr John Denham son of the above said Mr J.D. once mayor of this town who died 25 day of June 1684 aged 84.

Cunae novissimae Joannis Carel Roberti Minstri filii unici qui sesquiannarius occubuit.

Here lieth the body of Richard Cross of Lowman Cleave of this parish yeoman who died in the faith of his Redeemer 6 Feb. 1648 aged 70. Elizabeth his wife died 8 June 1683 aged about 97 year.

Here lieth the body of Mr John Lane of this town merchant and Elizabeth his wife he dying 26 July 1680 she 29th of the same month were interred in one day, to whose memory this tomb and monument were erected by their administrators.

Surreptos moesto depleret haec marmore fato
Virtute ingenio conjugioque pares
Vir tristis primo recubuit, mox flebilis uxor
Tanquam anima eiusdem corporis ipsa cadit
Ille equidem perit invitus sine conjuge caelos
Despicet it terras haec viduata viro.

Arms as on monument

Here lieth the body of Agnes the wife of John Forse of this town mercer daughter of Mr Walter Deble of Exon merchant who departed this life the 11 day of Dec. anno 1673 aged 35. Here also lieth the body of Elizabeth the third wife of the above said John F. daughter of Mr Seymour Kyrton lately rector of Uplowman who departed this life Sept 25 1683 aged 34 years.

Here lieth the body of Judith late wife of Giles Barry of Uffculm who died 20 Sept. 1669.

Here lieth the body of Richard Powell gent who died 5 day of Oct. 1608.

Here lieth the body of John Blundell son of Richard Blundell of Collipriest esq deceased who departed this life 6 Nov. 1696 aged 14.

Mrs Mary Shapleigh died 21 Jan. 1823 aged 70.

Orate pro animabus Johannis Hodge et Johan uxoris ejus alter -- Anno Domini 15--
Here lieth the body of Mr George Parrett of this town clothier sometime mayor of this town who departed this life the 9 July 1673 aged 72. Here lie the bodies of 2 sons and 3 daughters of the said G.P. Here also lieth the body of Prudence daughter of the above G.P. who departed this life the -- day of Jan 1677.

Ann daughter of William Wood of this town merchant born 5 April 1696 died 24 Sept 1705. Mr William Wood her father, merchant and one of this corporation died 30 April 1713 age 52. Roger Wood of this town surgeon his son died 4 Nov 1721 aged 24 Susanna wife of the above William Wood mother of the above children died 13 March 1736 aged 73.

M.S.M. Johannis Chishull Medicinae professoris doctissimi qui felici morborum curatione vim artis expertus est suaque tandem morte impotentiam confitebatur. Obiit vicessimo tertio die Decembris Anno Domini 1717 aetat sue 54.

Here lieth the body of Alexander the son of Mr Zachary Bidgood of this parish who departed this life 24 Oct 1687.

Nave

Floor. --- Thomas Prowse gentleman daughter unto Humphrey Barlow of Silverton gentleman being the age of XXXVIII who departed this life the XIIIJ daye of March

A.D. -- insurrection who was the first mayor of this town after the miraculous restitution of King Charles the second and was the first that began a reformation in it according to the ancient fundamental laws of this nation and dyed in the Lord August the seventh 1661 aged 55 years.
-- gent and Isabella his wife daughter of Henry Atkins in this parish gent who died 6 June 1711 in 12th year of his age. Also the body of the said Isabella who died 3 Oct 1723 aged 63. Also the body of the said John Richards one of the capital burgesses of this town. He died 25 July 1734 aged 65 Also the body of Ann daughter of the said John Richards who died 11 Oct 1755 aged 53,
Here lieth the body of Mary daughter of Richard Chattey of this town merchant who departed this life 11 July aged 7 years. Here also lieth the body of the said Richard Chattey who having been twice mayor of this town departed this life 19 June 1679 aged 68 years, in honour of whom his wife Priscilla erected this monument. Also the body of the above said Priscilla daughter of John Skinner of this parish gent who departed this life 10th April 1680 aged 79.

Rev. C. O. Osmond.

Here lieth the body of Willmot wife of Mr Peter Bere jun. clothier and daughter of Mr John Skinner of this p[ar]ish who departed this life 7 Jan 1659 aged 36 Here also lieth the body of Elizabeth wife of Nathanael Cleaveland of this town merchant and daughter of the above said Peter Bere who died 21 Feb 1684 aged 27. Eliz. Cleaveland daughter of the above Nathanael and Elizabeth died 14 April aged 7 weeks Nathanael Cleaveland merchant of this town departed this life 3 Jan 1714 Ann wife of the above Nathanael and Frances their daughter were likewise interred here 1736 Sarah C. daughter of the above Nathanael and Ann departed this life 20 June 1691 aged 2 years & 4 months Here lieth the body of Thomas son of the above Nathanael C. and Ann his wife who departed this life 27 March 1699 aged 10 months. Here also lieth the body of William son of said Nathanael. & Ann his wife who died 4 June 1700 aged 9 months.
John son of Nathanael Cleaveland of this town merchant died 30 Jan 1687 aged 34 weeks. Nathanael C. son of the above N.C. died 4 March 1689 aged 10 weeks.
Here lieth the body of Peter Bere jun. of this town merchant who died 7 April 1701 aged 42. Also Peter Bere his father of this town clothier who died 26 Dec. 1709 aged 80.

South Aisle.
East wall. a tablet. Henry Osmond esq died Oct 5th 1792 aged 81. Henry Peard Osmond esq died June 11th 1801 aged 47 Henry Fortescue Osmond esq died March 29 1827 aged 19 Charles Osmond Osmond clerk died Sept 17. 1830 aged 44. Margareta Fortescue Osmond widow of Charles O. Osmond clerk died 24 May 1841 aged 52. Arms Sable a fess dancette ermine, in chief an eagle displayed or.

A monument with a tablet and an urn.
Near this place are deposited the remains of Samuel Newte M.A. rector of Tidcombe in this parish who died Feb. 18. 1781 aged 63 Erected by Thomas and John N. surviving sons of the deceased. Arms Newte with an escutcheon of pretence. Quarterly 1 & 4 Argent a greyhound courant between 3 Martins sable 2 & 3 Ermine in a chief argent 3 Lions rampant in fess sable.

North wall a tablet. Near this stone lie the remains of the rev. Philip Atherton M.A. vicar of Ninehead in Somerset and one of the ministers of this church who died 19 March 1777 in the 59 year of his age He was master of Blundell's school in Tiverton 18 years –

A tablet below the last – Betty the wife of the rev Philip Atherton died 29 Jan 1784 aged 75 years – according to her request she lies here interred. This inscription to the memory of their beloved benefactor was added by her grateful nephew and niece Richard and Elizabeth Tucker. Arms. Gules 3 Hawks argent impaling Argent a Chevron azure between 3 Griffins heads & necks erased sable.

A white marble tablet. Sacred to the memory of Caroline Jane Coles the beloved daughter of the rev James Coles and Marcella Coles his wife and granddaughter of Sir Thomas and lady Carew who died at Staplake cottage Dec 20 1838 aged 20 years Arms. Quarterly 1 & 4 Gules a Chevron ermine between 3 Leopards faces or. 2 & 3. Or 3 Lions passant gardant in pale sable.

South wall. a stone and marble monument with an entablature and Corinthian columns.

In memoriam Henrici Newte generosi qui summa industria aequitate per biennium hujus oppidi praeturam egregie gessit et obiit anno aetatis suae 62° A.D. 1670 Octobris die 29° et Aloisiae uxoris suae probatae virtutis matronae.
Principis et juris non observantior alter
Utque suum regi sic dedit ille Deo

A stone monument with twisted Corinthian columns and an entablature.
In memory of Jane wife of William Colman of Gornhay esq and daughter of Sir Edmund Fortescue of Fallopit bart who departed this life 7 Sept 1682 in the 21 year of her age. Also in memory of the above Edmund William Colman esq who departed this life 18 Dec 1733 and of William Colman esq his son who departed this life 3 Sept 1744 and of Jane his wife (daughter of Sir Edward Seymour Bart and sister of Edward Duke of Somerset) who departed this life 24 March 1757. Arms 2 coats I 6) Per fess argent and Sable a Cross fleury between 4 Mullets pierced and counter charged impaling (2) Azure a Bend indented on the lower side gules between 6 escallops sable each charged with another or. (Colman)
II impaling Ermine a Lion passant gules. (Drewe)

A marble monument with Corinthian columns and an entablature – painted and gilt. Samuel Foote esq of this town and corporation and several times one of their representatives in parliament departed this life 26 March AD. 1691 aged 66 years and lies buried in this church. William Foote his only son and child by Martha (his third wife) daughter of Thomas Mompesson of Newham in the co. of Somerset esq who departed this life the 5th of 9th 1696 aged 14 yeres lies buried the same grave. Arms 2 coats. I Gules a Chevron between 3 doves argent II. I impaling – (defaced)

White marble tablet. In a vault near this spot are deposited the remains of George Davey esq of this parish who departed this life 17 Dec. 1784 aged 70 – Erected by his grandson John Hamilton esq Colonel Coldstream guards. In the same vault are deposited the remains of Alice wife of George Davey esq & sister of William Rich esq of Chief Lowman in the parish of Halberton. She died 2 Oct 1773. Arms Azure 3 Cinquefoils – on a Chief gules a Lion passant --

Tablet. Near this place are interred the remains of Mrs Agnes Down who departed this life 25 June 1775 in the 72 year of her age. Also Mr Richard Down who departed this life 10 April 1792 in the 83 year of his age Erected by their children. Arms Gules a Stag's head caboshed ermine impaling – 3 mullets or.
West wall. a stone tablet with cupids cherubs & drapery etc. painted and gilt.
Margaret wife of Robert Burridge lies under interred and daughter of Samuel Foote esq by his first wife who was the daughter of Thomas Leigh gent mother of 13 children of which 8 survived her. Obiit Dec. 7. 1700 in the 45 year of her age. Arms defaced
A hatchment for two wives
Azure 3 Dolphins naiant imbrued argent, on a chief or as many in fess sable (Burridge). Impaling Dexter. (Foote) Gules a Chevron between 3 Doves argent Sinister Argent a Lion rampant sable (or azure) (Mompesson)

A large stone on the floor, against the west wall
Here lies interred the body of Margaret wife of Robert Burridge of this town and in the chancel of this church Matthias the elder, here also lie the bodies of Robert and Robert Matthias and Christopher in all 5 sons of the said Robert Burridge who all departed this life before they attained the age of 5 years Also under-neath lieth Martha second wife of the above said Robert B. esq daughter of Thomas Mompesson of Brewham esq who died 8 Feb. 1715 in the 59 year of her age. Here also lieth the above said Robert Burridge esq one of the representatives in parliament of this town in the first year of 2. Anne & likewise in the parliament of the union of England & Scotland who departed their life August 25. 1717 in the 61 year of his age Also the body of Samuel Burridge son to the above said R.B. who died the 31 of Jan 1734 aged 56.
Between the chancel and the south aisle a large heavy stone altar tomb about 8 feet long by 3½ wide carved in pannels quatrefoils and shields with merchants marks devices the initials J.W. and the date 1579. On the slab is engraved. Here lyeth -- & which deceased the XXVIII daye of July Ano Dni 1579.

South Aisle
Floor. -- John -- who departed the 3 Sept 1585 and Alice his wife which lyved in marriage 47 years who died the 13 day of April Anno Dom 1583 & who had 6 sons and 6 daughters and also Elizabeth the wife of George Clarke mayor in the army of King Charles the first during that late war. She was daughter of Richard Prowse of Hayne gent. She departed this life 10 Nov 1663.
Here lieth the body of James Cornish gent who at the age of 24 years departed this life the 22nd day of January 1628 and left behind him 2 sons and 1 daughter. He took to wife Dorothy widow of Richard Prowse gent of Hayne Here also lieth James son of the said James Cornish who died 25 Sept 1655 aged 20 years.
Of yor charyte ye yt be on lyfe pray for the soul of --- Syllyak & Jone hys wyfe founder of our ladymass as hys last will was AD. MDXXIIII XXXJ day of Aug.
Here lieth the body of Robert Waldron Spanish merchant sonne unto John Waldron merchant who departed life the XXIIII day of April anno domi 1635 being about the age of 55. Here also lieth the body of Richard the wife of the aforesaid R.W. who departed this life the 7th day of December 1687 aged 88 years.
Here lieth the body of Robert Chatty sone of Robert Chatty jun. of this town merchant who departed this life the 6 of August AD. 1674 aged 2 years & 10 months.
Here lith the body of the said John C. -- dd 9 -- 1678.

Here lieth the body of Alice the wife of Henry Newton of this town gent who departed this life the -- day of Oct.

Here lie the bones of Mr John Skinner & Wilmot his wife She died Dec 12. 1627 he died June 5. 1636 aged 60 Also the bodies of Mr. Peter Land who died 26 March 1653 aged 46 & Elizabeth his wife oldest daughter of the said Mr. Skinner she died Jan 5 1681 aged 71. Of Margaret Land their daughter who died Oct 8. 1669 aged 18 years & of Peter Land their son who died February 10. 1671 aged 26 years also Mary their daughter wife of Mr. George Stukeley. She died Jan 5 1700 aged 52 years & 9 months. -- in the year of our Lord 1682 and of -- her only daughter surviving.

Here lieth the body of Francis Nott gent sometime one of the capital burgesses of this corporation son unto John Nott of Prishcome gent & Bridgett his wife daughter of Francis Colman sometime of Gornbay esq. who departed this life May 1 1687 at 20 Here also lieth John his son who died -- Aug. – Arms -- a Bend between 3 Escutcheons

-- William Colman gent who married with Mary the daughter of -- Also lieth the body of Francis Colman gent brother of the said William who married Bridgett the eldest daughter of James Cruys esq & dyed the 16 day of June A.D. 1650 aged 59. Also the said Bridgett who departed this life May 1659 aged 61 also here lieth Margaret daughter of Roger Colman also died Aug 13. 1676.

Here lieth Margaret -- Richard son of Robert Henley of Lee in the co Somerset esq who departed this life -- 1603 -- of -- children

Here lieth the body of Mr John Cogan mercer sometime mayor of this town who deceased Feb17. -- 76 at the age of -- Here also lieth the body of Charity wife of John Cogan who deceased 22 day of May 1635 aged 72.

Here lieth the body of Mr. Valentine – sometime mayor of this -- departed this life the 14 March A.D 1644. Here also lieth the body of Anne Hartknoll wife to the said Valentine who deceased 11 June A.D. 1649.

Here lieth the body of Mr George Hucklen merchant sometime mayor of this town who departed this life the 20 day of Aprill A.D. 1632 and left behind him a wife one son and one daughter.

Here lieth the body of Mr Ellis Bennet merchant sometime mayor of this town who departed the 28 day of Feb 1637 being 77 years of age.

Hic requiescit in pace et spe beate resurrectionis Richardus Webber de Halberton filius Ricardi Webber de Manley occidentali hujus parochiae villa qui annos agens XXIX obiit Aprilis nono A.D. MDCLXXVIII

Thomas Haydon of this town was buried here 24 March 1762 aged 80.

-- Elizabeth and Rebekah – daughters of -- Cockram of this -- bachelor in Physick -- departed this life -- them attaining -- one year -- Dorothy --- of the said George -- died 20 --- 1708 in the 38 year --- Here also lieth -- George Cockram who -- 17 Dec 1710 --- years of his age.

Church Yard.

On the south side, in front of Greenways aisle, is a square stone obelisk with an urn on the summit. The sides are thus inscribed.

North side. Martin Dunsford of Tiverton Serge maker a truly wise sincerely good man died October the 30th 1763 aged 52. Reader, his mouldering remains beneath bid thee remember thy own dissolution apply therefore thy heart to wisdom and learn the importance the eternal truth which he often articulated that wisdom and virtue lead

to peace and permanent happiness vice and folly to present and future misery. A.D. 1783. Anne daughter of the above lived an amiable pattern to the young under a long and painful disorder awaited the wise disposal of future immortality 13 February 1771 aged 25 years. Ann widow of the above Martin Dunsford after a long life of her age July 21. 1804.
West side Anne the beloved wife of Martin Dunsford of Tiverton merchant died Oct 8. 1782 aged 23
Take venerable earth the lovely frame
That for a while contained a lamb like soul
Lately the happy gift to me from God
To crown the joys to soothe the cares of life
But oh! how soon required! Torn from my soul
Rent from my love and numbered with the dead
Preserve inviolate the sacred change
Till the last trump shall raise the sleeping dust
And call her to her native air and home
Lasting abode of innocence and love. A.D.1783.
Her infant daughter Elizabeth died Dec. 20 1782 aged 4 months
Beneath this pillar raised by himself are also deposited the remains of the said Martin Dunsford merchant author of the Historical Memories of Tiverton who died March 13 1807 aged 63 years. He was a man of respectable abilities possessed of a liberal and well cultivated mind which rendered him a judicious instructor and pleasant companion He bore the numerous ills of life with steady forming of soul in submission to the Divine will. His afflicted widow who had ample proofs of the truth and excellence of the character here recorded deeply laments her heavy loss.

South side. This inscription is a tribute to the memory of Gideon Acland many years a respectable draper and grocer in Tiverton. He married Sarah daughter of Martin Dunsford serge maker, died 7 March 1799 aged 55 years and was buried in the vault below. Beneath also are deposited the remains of his widow Sarah Ackland who died on the 13 July 1809 aged 60 years.

East side.
Omnibus his piis cognatis juxta hunc locum sepultis Hoc marmor quorum reliquiae intus sepulchro una composita jacent M.D. 1783.
Floret amabiliter justorum fama perennis
Turpiter at vitii nomen inane perit.
Edward eldest son of Edward and Sarah Boyce died October 3rd 1793 aged 8 months. Sarah Acland --- daughter of Edward and Sarah Boyce died --- 27th 1811 aged 11 years. Edward second son of Edward and Sarah Boyce died Dec. 23rd 1817 aged -- years. Edward Boyce father of the above, many years a respectable bookseller of this town died Oct. -- 1823 aged 56 years. Sarah relict of Edward Boyce and eldest daughter of Gideon and Sarah Acland died Nov. 26. 1834 aged 62 years. George Boyce bookseller of this town 4th son of Edward and Sarah Boyce died Jan 13th . 1841 aged 36 years.

Newspaper cutting, no name of newspaper, dated 12 September 1856
St. Peter's Church – A magnificent stained glass window. By Wailes of Newcastle, has been placed in the chancel of St. Peter's church, this week. It is the gift of the rev.

Mr Rayer, rector of Tidcombe Portion, who has also contributed liberally towards the restoration of the church and chancel. The subject is "The Ascension."

Newspaper cutting, no name of newspaper, dated April 1856
St. Peter's Church. – A splendid glass window by Wailes, of Newcastle, in memory of the late Mr. John Barne, who died whilst the restoration of this church, of which he was one of the chief promoters, was in progress, has just been placed in the tower of that venerable building. The subject is the rebuilding of the Temple at Jerusalem. There are four figures, David, Solomon, Ezra, and Nehemiah. It is generally understood that the church is to be reopened about Midsummer next.

Newspaper cutting, no name of newspaper, dated 26 June 1856
Re-opening of St. Peter's Church
This interesting ceremony took place yesterday (Thursday), under the most favourable auspices. More than three years ago it was thought expedient that the services of the church should be discontinued, in consequence of the dilapidated state of the building, and measures were taken with a view to its restoration. The call for subscriptions was liberally responded to, and although the cost was computed at between £6,000 or £7,000, nearly the whole of that amount has been collected. The church which was probably built about the middle of the 15th century, consists of a spacious nave, chancel, aisles and western tower. It has on the south side a remarkable and beautiful monumental chapel to the memory of John Greenway, one of the wealthy wool merchants of the olden time, who completed this mausoleum, and the adjoining porch, and south aisle, in 1517, and they exhibit in their architecture excellent examples of the florid gothic of Henry 7th's and Henry 8th's time. Modern galleries and ceilings had much concealed the decay of the roofs and walls of the church, and after years and years of repairs of expediency, it was with difficulty that many constant church-goers and influential townsmen of Tiverton, would believe that a restoration was necessary, when the rebuilding a great part of the edifice was proposed in 1852. A committee was formed chiefly through the exertions of rev. J.B. Hughes, head master of the Tiverton Grammar School, consisting of F.O. Patch, Esq. (Chairman), T.L.T. Rendell, Esq., Dr. Paterson, W.N. Row, Esq., Rev. J.B. Hughes, secretary, T. Aldred, Esq., - Radford, Esq., T. Parkhouse, Esq., W. Reed, Esq., and others. The works, which were undertaken after a survey by Mr. Ashworth, architect of Exeter, and from drawings furnished by him early in 1853, consist of rebuilding entirely the nave and north aisle, with considerable enlargement of the aisle, and constructing an organ chamber opening from it on the north side. A great portion of the south aisle has been rebuilt, and the whole church substantially roofed with oak, with carved tracery in the open parts, covered with oak boarding, and lead, and enclosed with battlements parapets. The tower, a lofty and commanding one, has had much of its exterior ruin repaired; and the pleasing varieties of material, in native stone, Thorverton trap, and Hamdon Hill dressing, are shewn with admirable effect in the renewed surfaces. Within the last six months the chancel has been rebuilt, introducing a large east window, which is to be filled with painted glass by Wailes, the gift of the Rev. Mr Rayer – the subject, the Ascension. The refitting the interior is carried out in Wainscott oak, some of the old fitting being made use of. There is a pulpit of Caen stone. The lofty richly carved rood-screen has been taken down, it being in a very ruinous condition; it is replaced by a low partition of carved oak, separating the chancel from the nave. A simple rail divides

the chancel eastward, and within it there is a paving of Minton tiles and a brilliant "reredos" of encaustic tiles against the east wall. Otherwise the church is rebuilt to correspond as much as possible with the old. The singular panelled oak roof of the south (Greenway's) aisle has been reproduced, and the piers and pier arches throughout; with their niches and ornamentation (sadly mutilated in the original) strictly imitated from the old work.

The windows are in part glazed with Cathedral glass, and the west window of the tower is of painted glass, a memorial to the late J. Barne, Esq., who as church-warden commenced the restoration of the church. The subject comprises figures of David, Solomon, Ezra, and Nehemiah, and scenes concerning the building of the temple.

Admission to the church at the morning service was by ticket, and upwards of 1,200 were disposed of to the gentry and other respectable inhabitants of the town. At about eleven, a procession was formed at the Guildhall, and proceeded to the Church.

St George's Chapel, Tiverton

Davidson (pp. 645–9) visited St George's chapel, Tiverton, on 26 July 1843. He observed that 'this building, which was commenced in 1714 but not finished till 1733, is in the Grecian style of architecture'. St George's was designed by John James and begun in 1714–16 with the intention of accommodating Dissenters. The church was restored in the late nineteenth century (Pevsner, *Devon*, 810). Eight memorials are missing from the twenty that Davidson recorded.

This building is about 85 feet long by 58 wide, the roof is supported by two rows of columns of the Ionic order, and at the western end is a turret in which is a clock & bell. At the eastern end is a heavy carved altar screen above which is a shield with arms of the See of Exeter [the arms are now situated on the front of the west gallery}. The windows and doors are under semicircular arches. The monuments and inscriptions are as follow.

Chancel

East Wall. A marble tablet with an urn & weeping figure.

This monument is erected to the memory of Benjamin Dickinson esq of this town who departed this life the 23 day of October 1806 aged 69 His death deprived society of a truly upright and just and religious character. His qualities as an affectionate husband an anxious parent and a constant friend can only be estimated by those who best knew the possessor. The short but painful illness which terminated his existence he bore with a manly and Christian fortitude. His surviving wife inscribes this marble an unfeigned testimony of his worth and of her affection. Also to the memory of four of their children who died in the following order

Maria died Feb. 17. 1769 aged 9 months
Sarah died Aug 11. -- aged 5 years
Elizabeth died Oct 11. 1779 aged 7 years
Benjamin Peard died Feb. 18. 1800 aged 30 years.

Sacred also to this monument to the memory of her who raised it. Mary the widow of the above mentioned Benjamin Dickinson on whose well spent life terminated most serenely 13 May 1810 aetatis sue 80. Arms

Or 2 Foxes passant in pale sable.

A white marble Tablet. John Davy Foulkes of Moreland in this county died April 26 1813 aged 56. Elizabeth Fortescue Foulkes his wife died March 25 1827 aged 85 Erected to the memory of their beloved parents by 8 surviving children. Arms. Azure 3 --- passant in pale argent impaling Azure a Bend (engrailed) argent cotised or.

North wall. A white and black marble tablet & urn. In memory of Mrs Mary Peard, a worthy lady of this town whose piety towards God, her charity to the church by a gift of £1000, etc. her bountiful distributions to her acquaintance friends and relations and

universal benevolence pronounce her amiable character. Having completed 82 years in the practice of Christian duties she was summoned to receive her reward Dec. 31. 1780. As a most grateful testimony of respect this monument was erected by her cousin Benjamin Dickinson esq. Arms Argent 2 wolves passant pale sable impaling vert, 3 Trefoils slipped or, on a chief indented gules 2 amulets of the second. –
South wall. A large marble tablet with an urn Sacred to the memory of Mr. Henry Blagdon of this town, merchant a great example of piety temperance justice and industry both in his private and public affairs etc. Towards the building of this church he gave in his life time £500 and by his will £1000 more after a short but well spent life, he died, with hopes full of immortality April 21 1716 in the 36 year of his age. Mrs Mary Peard out of pious regard to the memory of her excellent uncle. Erected this marble. Arms gut 3 trefoils slipped or, in a chief undented gules 2 amulets of the second.

In the body of the church.
South wall. A tablet to the memory of Henry Dunsford of this town who died 10 March 1812 aged 72. This strict integrity and great benevolence will long under his name to those that knew him. Also of Elizabeth his wife who died 11 Oct 1785 aged 42 and Sarah their infant daughter.
A tablet. In this church yard lie interred the remains of Edward William Langslow fourth son of Richard Langslow M.D. A.M. and Sarah his wife of Clifton in the co of Gloucester who expired at this place on the 14th Dec. 1807 aged 19. His sufferings were only equalled by his patience.

West wall. A black marble tablet with sculpture in relief of white marble, representing a fortress and the sea with a ship, on one of the towers is the Portuguese flag and on another below it the English ensign.
Sacred to the memory of Priscilla wife of Benjamin Dickinson esq Major of the royal Marines who departed this life at Fort St. Julian near Lisbon in Portugal on the 13 day of Sept 1811 aetat suae 50. She was an invaluable wife and fell victim to an unbounded love for her husband whose long and repeated intervals of absence on his country service she deeply deplored. In the beginning of this year he was again ordered on service to command a battalion of his corps under Lord Viscount Wellington in Portugal. She could no longer bear to be separated from the object of her affection therefore regardless of danger she determined to visit him but her delicate frame enfeebled by sickness and anxiety was incapable of supporting the change of climate and on the 24th day after her arrival on that fatal shore she calmly yielded up her immortal soul in resignation and prayer to him who gave it. Her afflicted husband inconsolable for the loss of all he held most dear in this world in compliance with her request accompanied her remains to England deposited them in a vault near this place and caused this monument to be erected as a tribute of grateful esteem and tender regard to her memory. Arms Or, two Foxes passant in pale sable.

A marble tablet. In memory of the rev. William Walker M.A. Rector of Broughton Gifford Wiltshire, Swainswick and North Stoke Somersetshire and Prebendary of the Cathedral Church of Wells who died March 23. 1811 in the 67 year of his age. Also of Jane his relict who died July 23 1825 in the 80 year of her age. In grateful recollection of their worth and parental affection, this monument is erected by their surviving children Margaret Louisa their youngest daughter died April 10. 1798 in the 11th year of her age. Arms azure a Griffin segreant within a border ermine.

Tablet and sarcophagus. Sacred to the memory of John Baptist Questel esq student of the Inner Temple whose remains are deposited near this place. He died universally regretted after a short illness while on a visit in this town on the 2 June 1825 aged 24 years.
Adieu blest shade too early from us fled
I loved thee living and lament thee dead
Thy mother's trembling hand with grief sincere
Inscribes this stone and drops the tender tear.

Chapel yard.
A tomb. In a vault underneath lieth the body of Mrs. Alice Peard daughter of Oliver Peard merchant by Elizabeth his wife sister of Mr. Henry Blagdon of this town merchant who was a very liberal benefactor to the charity school in this town and contributed largely to the erecting of the new church as likewise to several other charities. She died 15 Aug. 1747 aged 50 years.
Also here lieth the body of Mrs. Elizabeth Peard sister to the above Alice who departed this life 23 Feb. 1760 aged 52 years. Here also lieth the body of Mrs. Mary Peard sister of the above ladies who departed this life Dec. 31.1780 aged 82. Arms Peard impaling Blazon as before. [missing]
Underneath in a vault lie remains of Mary wife of Leonard Blagdon of this town who died 25 Nov 1739 aged 49 years. Also the said Leonard Blagdon twice mayor of this town who died May 7 1763 aged 77 years. Also of James son of John Blagdon of Puddington died Oct 3. 1747 aged 21 years. Henry son of the said John B. died Dec. 6. 1750 aged 26 years. Also the remains of Mrs. Mary Sharland of this town who died March 20 1783 aged 69 years.
A Tablet. Mrs. Cowley widow of Capt Cowley of the Hon. East India Company service died 11 March 1830 aged 66. [missing]
Tomb. To the memory of the rev. Henry Land late Rector of Clare quarter in this parish who -- died 9 Dec. 1793 aged 62. Erected by his son John Land, surgeon [missing].
Tomb. Arabella Land wife of the rev. Thomas Land died 10 Oct 1829 aged 44. Their two children Edward Pyott Land and Louisa Land died in their infancy. Also the revd Thomas Land – died 12 Jan 1835 aged 68. Erected by their son Thomas Land esq of Spanish Town Jamaica. [missing]
Tomb William Pusey Hayley esq a native of the island of Jamaica died 7 Jan 1822 in the 63rd year of his age. [missing]
Stone. – Near this place are deposited the remains of Tristram Whitter. L.L.D. rector of Pitt Lorton in this parish who died Nov. 2. 1776 aged 64. Erected by his two sons. Near him lie buried his wife and their mother, Katherine daughter of Thomas Ackland MA. rector of South Brent in this county. [missing]

Against the east wall a tablet.
Here lye interred the remains of the rev. Mr. Samuel Wesley MA. sometime student of Christchurch Oxon, (a long laudatory inscription) first for 20 years one of the ushers of Westminster school afterwards for near 7 years Head master of Blundell's

school in this town – resigned his Soul to God 6 day of Nov. 1739 in the 49th year of his age.

Tablet. The revd. Samuel Dolly MA. Died 7 Nov. 1645 aged 45. [missing]

A tomb. Oliver Peard, merchant, died 22 April 1767 aged 48. Honour Peard his wife died 18 Nov. 1761 aged 31. [missing]

CHEVITHORNE

Davidson (pp. 651–2) visited the chapel of St Thomas, Chevithorne, on 30 September 1844 and noted it was about 1 mile north east of Tiverton. He observed that 'this chapel was erected in 1843 by voluntary contributions to accommodate the inhabitants of the hamlets of Chettiscombe, Chevithorne, Craze Lowman and East and West Rose in the parish of Tiverton and was consecrated on the 13 June 1843. It is in the decorated style of Old English architecture.' Built in 1843 by Benjamin Ferry (Pevsner, *Devon*, 257). There were no memorials when Davidson visited the chapel.

It consists of a Nave about 47ft long by 21 and a Chancel about 17 by 13. A porch covering the south door. There are crosses on the gables and a Turret with a bell on the western gable. The walls are supported by buttresses at the angles. The windows on the south side are of two lights with trefoil heads. That on the east side has three lights with quatrefoils in the arch above. It is filled with stained glass and is handsome but there are figures are of the Virgin Mary, the adoration of the Wise Men etc [removed]. The western window is a circular divided by tracery into triangles and also filled with stained glass in which are symbols of the Evangelists a Pelican, a Lamb, Angels etc. The rood is open & is of dark coloured wood relieved with gilt bosses of foliage [removed] – The pulpit and the open benches are also of dark wood. At the east end is an altar of Caen stone richly carved enriched in front with quatrefoil in which appear the monogram J.H.S. A Pelican, a Lamb, on an altar, and under the slab the words "whose who eateth my flesh and drinketh my blood hath eternal life" [now wood]. On the south side of the chancel is a stone Credence table. The font is also of Caen stone enriched with sculptured trefoils and standing on a column sculptured in trefoils panels. Around it, carved in relief is the text 'By our spirit are we all baptised into one body' Cor XII XIII

The entrance to the porch has a label over it resting on corbel heads, one intended to represent Queen Victoria and the other Bishop of Exeter but certainly they are no portrait, and as unlike these personages as the whole structure is to a Protestant place of worship.

COVE CHAPEL

Davidson (p. 653) visited the chapel of St John the Baptist, Cove, on 27 July 1843 and he noted it was 5 miles from Tiverton. He observed 'this is a chapel of ease in the parish of Tiverton'. Rebuilt by Edward Ashworth in 1855 (Pevsner, *Devon*, 293). The chapel became a private residence in 1987.

The chapel consists of a nave about 34ft long by 16ft wide, & a chancel about 15ft by 16ft with a Turret near the western gable containing two bells, but the whole structure is in a very ruinous condition and must shortly be rebuilt.
The western window is of early date under a pointed arch form with two trefoiled lights with a quatrefoil above, the other windows are modernised. The pulpit and pews are of oak, quite plain. The font is ancient is a large circular stone basin set on a short elliptical doric column without ornamentation. There is a gallery at the western end, and a few glazed tiles on the floor.
The only inscribed stone is one in the chancel floor but the following is all that can be deciphered. -- body of -- Arthur -- and of -- who departed this life the 5th day of -- 1659.

Newspaper cutting, no name of newspaper, dated 13 December 1855
Cove Episcopal Chapel. – On Thursday se'nnight the foundation stone of a new chapel to be erected at Cove village, about five miles from this town, was laid by T. Daniel Esq., the High Sheriff of Devon, with the usual formalities. The chapel at present standing in the village has for some years past been in a very dilapidated condition, but no active steps were taken to build a new one in its stead until a few months ago, when several gentlemen formed themselves into a committee, and collected a sum of money large enough to warrant them in commencing the undertaking. The contract for the construction of the edifice has been taken by Mr. T. Parish, stonemason, of Tiverton, who has, we are informed, engaged to complete it by the latter end of September, or the beginning of October, 1856. Mr Ashworth of Exeter is the architect employed to superintend the work.

Newspaper cutting, no name of newspaper, dated November 1856
St John's Chapel Cove. – This pretty edifice was opened on Saturday, the 1st instant. Morning prayers was impressively read by the Rev. R.B. Carew, rector of Bickleigh, and an excellent and appropriate discourse was preached by the Rev. P.L.D. Ackland, vicar of Broadclyst. About £40 was collected after the service. The chapel has been substantially built by Mr. T. Parish, of Tiverton, from plans drawn by Mr. E. Ashworth, of Exeter, who superintended the erection of the works.

CALVERLEIGH

Davidson (pp. 657–60) visited [St Mary the Virgin] Calverleigh on 27 July 1843 and noted it was 2½ miles north west of Tiverton. He observed that 'the church of this parish is situated in a lovely and sequestered spot very near to the ancient manor house which a number of workpeople are now in the act of taking down for entire destruction'. The chancel and north wall were rebuilt in 1883–7 (Pevsner, *Devon*, 243).

It consists of a nave about 28 feet long by 16 wide a chancel 15 by 15 a south aisle 40 by 12, a porch over the south door, and a tower at the western end with a large battlement containing 3 bells & a clock. The porch is entered by a pointed arch with a label resting on corbels of human heads. The doorway is in the early pointed style. The western door in the tower is also under a lancet arch. The nave & chancel open to the aisle by 3 low pointed arches resting on columns and half columns formed of shafts with intervening mouldings their capitals enriched with foliage & shields. The ceilings are coved and ribbed that of the aisle has bosses of foliage at the intersections of the ribs. Of the windows some have three lights with cinquefoil heads and perpendicular tracery others are 3 lights with low arched heads in rectangular frames. The eastern window of the aisle contains some fragments of old stained glass among which is a figure of St. John the Baptist [removed]. A chancel screen extends across the nave and the aisle formed by a range of arches under horizontal heads divided into lights with ogee-arched heads. It is most richly carved and is furnished above with three mouldings of foliage painted and gilt. On the plaister above it on the chancel side is a rude painting but executed with great spirit representing in the centre a tree laden with fruit and below it the text "Herein is my father glorified that the bear much fruit" on each side of it another tree, one living but without fruit and two men cutting it down – with the text "Every branch in me that beareth not fruit he taketh away and every branch that beareth fruit he fungith it that it may bring forth more fruit" the other tree dead and an angel cutting it Down and the devil pulling at it with a rope, with the words "Cursed be the tree that beareth no fruit" Another text also viz "Every tree that bringeth not forth good fruit is hewn down and cast into the fire" [removed]. Against the east wall a wooden table thus inscribed "This chancel was sealed plastered painted and paved by Edward Serridge parson of Calverleigh 1662" On the plaister above the screen in the western side are the Royal arms with the date 1660 and 2 shields with these coats [removed]
I Argent a Cross engrailed gules between four Water-bougets sable (Bourchier)
II Argent a Bend sable between 3 Pellets. (Bishop Cotton)

There is no altar screen and the communion table is of plain oak. The pulpit and pews are of oak and deal of a modern date, on the back of the former is inscribed "He that hath ears to hear let him hear" [removed]

The font is an ancient stone octagonal basin without ornament on a low column of the same shape. The floor is paved with red tiles [now black and red tiles]. There is a modern gallery across the western end of the nave [removed].

The monuments and inscriptions convey the following particulars.

Chancel.
Floor. Here lyeth the body of John Prouz late rector of this parish who dyed the last day of July Ano Dni 1646 Here lyeth also near adjoining the body of Elizabeth Prouz daughter of George Prouz of Collumpton who dyed the XV day of July afore said aetat suae ---. Arms defaced
-- Charity -- & Robert -- da -- two sons of -- Furlong of Palmers -- Edith his wife -departed this life – 30th 7 1693 ob 5. -- the 17th 1700 aged -- July the 1st 1700 – ob. 12

Nave
Floor. Here lyeth the body of John Crooke clothier sonne of Humphrey Crooke. He deceased the XXV day of October 1616.

South aisle
East wall a stone monument painted and gilt Ionic columns with an entablature and pediment on the base the figure of a woman in a black gown and ruff kneeling at a desk and above her three medallions portraits of 2 men and a woman. On the upper part of the monument this inscription George Southcott married one of the daughters and coheirs of -- Robinson alderman of London by whom he left issue --- He died AD 1589 and was here buried "on small tablet appears the names Thomas Annise Robert Humphrey Mary Thomasine Margaret Mary and Cicely their tablets are thus inscribed Thomas Southcott esq married Mary the daughter of John Crocker of Lynam esq he deceased August the 21 A.D. 1621 & was here interred." He left issue two sons Richard and George and two daughters Mary and Elizabeth by Mary his wife who died Anno 1603 here also buried. Arms on 4 shields.
I II & III Argent a Chevron gules between 3 Coots sable (Southcott)
IV Sable a coup fleury between 4 Mullets argent impaling I
Round the medallions are these mottos "*Crux Christi nostra corona est*" "*Spes mea passio Christi*" "*Finis ab origine pendet*" "*Soluit mea debita Christi*"
Underneath this monument a medallion portrait of a man holding a book above it the arms of Southcott and round it the motto "*Hi mihi principium sed virtus det mihi finem.*" Above it a tablet thus inscribed In memory of George Thomas and Mary Southcott as also of Mary their daughter the wife and widow of William Colman of Tiverton gent She dyed March the 13 An Dni 1636.
Here in one bed of earth asleep doe lye
Three generations for they did not dye
Nor lose a being but exchanged and must
At the trumpets sound awake out of this dust
Here but their cross in heaven their souls doe dwell
Live here so to live with them farewell.
Funus virtute famis.
Georgius Southcott nepos in piam parentum memoriam. H.M. F. F. Ano Dni 1638.
South wall a tablet. † Here lies interred the body of Ann Throckmorton daughter of

George Throckmorton of Western Underwood in the co: of Bucks and of Anna Maria Paston of Horton in the co: of Gloucester. She died 6 Nov. 1783 aged 32 years. R.I.P. A tablet. – † beneath this stone are interred the remains of David Nagle esq of Ballygriffin in the co of Cork, Ireland who died 4 June 1800 aged 81. R.J.P. Arms. Ermine on a Fess azure 3 Lozenges or impaling Azure a Hay fork argent flory at the points, between 3 Mullets or.

A tablet with an urn. Sacred to the memory of Joseph Nagle esq who died 29 Jan and was interred here Feb. 8th AD 1813 anno aetatis 89. R.I.P.

Floor -- the 6 day of March 1654 being in the 15 year of his age.

Under this tomb stone know there lies

A dainty youth of richest price

(The rest of the inscription and the coat of arms concealed under a pew)

LOXBEARE

Davidson (pp. 665–6) visited [St Michael and All Angels] Loxbeare on 27 July 1843 and noted it was 4 miles north west of Tiverton. The chancel was rebuilt in 1850 and further restorations carried out in 1896 by E.H. Harbottle (Pevsner, *Devon*, 540–1). Two memorials are missing from the nine that Davidson recorded.

The church of this parish comprises only a nave about 27 feet long by 13 wide, a chancel about 18 feet by 13, a porch covering the south door and an ancient low tower at the western end, square and not embattled containing 3 bells. The south door is under a semicircular arch the head and the sides ornamented with zigzag moulding and are probably of Anglo Norman date. The western door in the tower is also under an arch of the same early date formed by two and three lights with trefoiled heads. There are some fragments of ancient stained glass among which is the monogram J.H.S. [removed]. The ceiling is coved and plain. There is a small piscina under a low arch in the east wall of the chancel [removed]. The Font is a small octagonal stone basin standing on a square column with the angles cut off. The Pulpit and the pews are of oak and quite plain. There are some ancient glazed tiles in the floor ornamented with fleurs de lis, quatrefoils etc [removed]. – A gallery at the western end of the nave [removed].

The monuments and inscriptions convey the following particulars.

Against the eastern wall a tablet painted with the inscription. This tablet presents the courteous spectator with the monument of Zachary Cudmore esquire who in the 47th year of his age and of our Lord 1657 the 28 day of May to the great grief of all his acquaintance and relations departed this life and lieth interred in the underneath vault.
-- *"ibi tu caelum*
Debita sparges lachryma favillam
Dulcis amici
Ita maerens posuit uxor eius et relia Maria Cudmore.
--- *nec mihi vesper*
Surgente decedunt amores
Nec rapidum fugiente solum"
Underneath also lyeth the body of Mary Cudmore wife of the above said Zackry Cudmore who departed this life the 25 day of March Anno Dom 1666 aged 47.
Arms of 2 shields
I Argent a fess nebuly gules between 3 Eagles displayed (Sable) impaling (Cudmore)
--- 3 Bulls heads caboshed (Walrond esq)
II The same impaling Argent on a Bend gules between 6 Quatrefoils slipped, 3 Garbs or.
A marble tablet. Sacred to the memory of the rev. Richard Abraham MA. and rector of this parish for the space of 52 years who died 22 days of April 1802 aged 87.

North wall. A stone tablet with pilasters.

Underneath sleepeth in hope of the resurrection the body of Daniel Cudmore gentleman who departed this life the 30 day of November in the year of grace one thousand 6 hundred thirty seven and in the year of his age sixty and eight. He gave to the use of the poore of this parish twenty pounds to remain for ever and the benefit thereof to be distributed every good Friday among the poor people by the owners of Loxbeare and the parson. *Beati morti qui in Domino mortuntur.* Underneath also lyeth the body of Joan Cudmore wife of the above said David Cudmore who departed this life the sixth day of May Anno Dom one thousand six hundred and forty five.

Floor. Here under lie the bodies of Catherine Cudmore Elnor Togood & Elizabeth Cudmore daughters of the above said David Cudmore. Catherine Cudmore died the 14 day of February 1630 Elnor Togood died the 13 day of December 1635 Elizabeth Cudmore died the 5 day of April 1636. [missing]

Mary daughter of Alexander Marshall rector of this church was buried 31 July 1642. [missing]

Nave floor. Here lyeth the body of Richard Coles of this parish who departed this life the sixth day of April 1637 He gave to the poor of this parish ten pounds to remain to the use of the poor for ever. This stone was given unto Jane Cole sister of the said Richard in remembrance of him and doth intend to lie here to sleep when God shall call them out of this life. Ano Dom 1640

Here lyth the body of Rose the wife of Bernard Voysey who departed this life the 3rd of Nov. 1721 aged 47.

WASHFIELD

Davidson (pp. 669–72) visited [St Mary the Virgin] Washfield on 27 July 1843 and noted it was 2½ miles north of Tiverton. He observed that this was a 'beautifully situated village'. The church was extensively restored in 1875 to the designs of the rector, the Rev. William Lloyd Jones (Pevsner, *Devon*, 889–90).

The church of this beautifully situated village consists of a nave about 33 feet long by 14 wide, a chancel about 19 by 12 an aisle on the north 50 by 12 a porch covering the south door and an embattled tower at the western end of the nave supported by buttresses at the corners and containing 5 bells. On each side of the western window of the tower is a niche under a low arch with a label over it. The nave and chancel open to the aisle by 4 pointed arches resting on columns formed of alternate shafts and mouldings with plain capitals except those of the eastern arch which are carved in foliage. The windows are 3 lights with cinquefoiled heads under low arches with quatrefoils above. There are some fragments of painted glass which have formed figures of saints, etc [removed]. A screen covers the nave and aisle of very early date. A range of semicircular arches with Corinthian columns and mouldings of scrolls & figures in Grecian style. In front of it is a shield with the date 1624 and the name Bernard Seridge W. another with the King's arms and another with the Princes feathers and the letters C.P. the altar screen is of wood with tall Corinthian pilasters and semicircular headed panels reaching to the ceiling and partly gilt. The ceilings are coved and ribbed and whitewashed [now plain]. The door to the rood-loft is in the north wall of the aisle. The pulpit and pews are of oak but not ancient. – The Font is a very ancient square stone basin each of the sides ornamented with 6 semicircular headed arches resting on a short cylinder with four shafts at the angles. The floor is paved with red tiles. A gallery at the western end of the nave [removed].

The monuments and inscriptions afford the following particulars.

Nave
South wall a tablet. Sacred to the memory of Jane Ann Terrill Gibson relict of Francis Gibson squire who was born in the island of Barbados Feb 13. 1756 and died at Washfield Sept 17. 1836. Raised by her sole surviving child Jane D Gibson & Thomasine A Thornhill.

North Aisle
A large marble monument an entablature and pediment supported by Corinthian capitals & richly gilt
Henry Worth of Worth esq who died in 1630
The cle's his Monument. Another is
The tombe that he built this son of his
He well provided for building of his owne
That builds a place where seed of life is sowne

The eagle wings may make a lofty flight
But gracious souls mount higher out of sight
Worth of his owne in man there can be none
Our worth is all in the most Righteous one.
And Elizabeth his wife daughter of Nicholas Fry of Yarty esq who dyed 1626,
Also Elizabeth Worth daughter of Sir Thomas Moulins Knight first wife of Henry
Worth the son of John Bampfield of Poltimore esq;
His second wife who died 1660.
Also Simon, Henry, Arthur, Garthrude, and Sarah, sons and daughters of the said
Henry and Dorothy,
Also Henry Worth of Worth esq who erected this monument and died April 21 1680
aged 75.
Lye here interred.
Arms 3 shields
I Argent a Spread eagle sable beaked & numbered Or impaling Gules 3 Horses
currant in pale argent (Worth)
II The same impaling Argent a Millrind sable (Moulins)
III The same impaling Or on a bend gules 3 Mullets pierced argent. (Bampfield)

North wall. A stone monument. Corinthian capitals supporting an entablature with
pediments and pinnacles painted in gilt. On a brass tablet the figures of a man and
women kneeling at prayer and below them this inscription.
Armiger Henrycus curat hoc sub semate Worthus,
Worthus clarus avis sicla tricena suis,
Cujus digna micat virtus, constantia digna
Digna fides, dignus religionis amor,
Integrior quo nemo fuit nec amantior aequi
Egregium meritus, nomine reque decus,
Non oriens periit, tantum disparuit atque
Caelitibus saperis annumerandus abit.
Vivit in Henrico nato, Henricoque nepote.
Ne cadat antiqua stirps recidiva domus
Obiit Aug. 3. Ano Dni 1606 aetatis suae 72.
Arms on 4 shields
I Argent a Spread eagle sable remembered or
II as I
III I impaling Azure 3 escallops or a crescent for difference
IV I impaling Gules 3 Horses currant in pale argent.

Brass tablets thus inscribed (the u's all v's)
Al'ce daughter unto William Frye and Phillip Styning's wyfe
(Both squires) with her husband led a long and loving lyfe
Nyne sonnes & daughters five she bare and then a turtle true,
(He dying first she lyved sole and would not choose a new)
Birth beauty personage good grace court breedinge gravitye
Chast love trueth virtue constant faith and sincere piety
Lyfe made her belov'd and bless'd yea dead though every burst
And malice selfe can speake but well if they would speake the worst
Aged seaventie two she yielded heere body to the dust

Her soul into her Saviours hands in whom was all her trust
By whom in sorrow sickness health lyfe death she still was bless'd
With whom she now in heavenly joy hath everlastinge rest
Her birth place Yarty was her life in Holnicot she led
In Worth amongst her dearest friends she made her fatall bed.
Adiew deere Mother we must part although wee lov'd dearely
Yet spyte of death lyfe once again I hope shall enjoy us nearely
And for thy love whilst thou didst live I vow though dead thou lye
Thy sonne Montgomeriis love to thee & thine shall never dye
Obit 8th Aug 1615 aetatis suae 72 Georgius Montgomerius gener. posuit. Arms 2
shields.

I. Quarterly   1 – a Remorque displayed (Steyning)
                    2 – a chevron gules between 3 leaves slipped
                    3 – On a Bend 3 Fishes
                    4 – 2 bars and in chief a Chevron gules impaling
       3 Horses currant – 2&1 for Fry

II – a tilting spear and sword in saltine between 3 Fleurs de lis and as many Gem
rings – impaling – a rare moult displayed – Montgomery

A tablet. This marble is erected to the memory of the two children of John Francis
Worth of Worth esq and Lucy his wife Henry who died 23 April 1829 aged 1 year
John Henry who died 30 April 1829 aged 3 years. They were buried in one grave on
the same day.
A Hatchment. Arms.

Quarterly   1st & 4 Argent a Spread Eagle sable remembered gules
                   2 & 3 Gules 2 Bars and in chief an Eagle displayed or, over all a
Bend vair.

North Aisle
In memory of Lucretia the daughter of Theodore Luders esq. of Bath. She was married
first to William Light esq. of Baglake in Dorsetshire and after his death to Robert
Anstey esq. Died April 7th AD 1794 aged 43 years and was buried in this church

A tablet with an urn
James Langford Nibbs esq. late of Beauchamp Hall in this parish and her 5 children.
Mary N. died 5 April 1769 aged 7 months
Jane N. died 4 June 1769 aged 1 year & 10 months
Samuel N. died 4 July 1771 aged 5 years & 3 months
Thomas N. died 27 January 1791 aged 18 years
J. L. Nibbs esq. died 17 December 1795 in his 58th year
Be it remembered that the relics of Barbara Nibbs who died 22 August 1813 aged 73
and her son Samuel Nibbs esq. who died 4 September 1805 are interred in the Abbey
church at Bath
A Hatchment for baron
Azure a Chevron engrailed ermine, on a chief argent 2 Bucks heads caboshed Jules
impaling Gules a Barnacle argent

Floor. Here in one grave were buried John and Alice Buckleigh aged John 5 years 8
months, Allis 3 years. Both died 29 Sept 1699.

APPENDIX: LIST OF JAMES DAVIDSON'S MANUSCRIPTS IN DEVON HERITAGE CENTRE, WITH DHC SHELFMARKS

A corographicall description of Devonshire (1690?) sfDEV/0001?RIS 5 volumes ms. unpublished

An account of some noble families in Devonshire and of some of the parliament in the year 1640 (1856) 929.3/DEV/DAV 5 volumes

Appendix to literary collections of Devon (1850?) S016?DEV?LUK 5 volumes

Axminster during the civil war in the seventeenth century (1851) sB/AXM3?1645?DAV

Bibliotheca Devoniensis; a catalogue of the printed books relating to the county of Devon (1852) 016?DEV/DAV

Bibliotheca Devoniensis: supplement (1861) 016?DEV/DAV

Biographical collections for a literary history of the county of Devon. Begun 4 Decr 1821 (1821–) George Sercombe Luke s016?DEV?LUK 5 volumes

Biography of Exonians (1849–) Notes from Trewman's *Exeter Flying Post* collected by James Davidson sB/EXE/920.02/OLI

Cartulary of Newenham Abbey, Devon (1827) s255.12?AXM/NEW

Catalogue of Sektor House, Axminster (1886) s018.2/WES/CAT

Catalogue of James Davidson's library auctioned after his death

Catalogue of Devon MSS. (1830) Z19/8/25

Church notes: Dorset (1835?) s726.5/DOR/DAV

Church notes on Devon: volume 1, East Devon (1843–) G2/11/15/2

Church notes on Devon: volume 2, South Devon (1843–) G2/11/15/2

Church notes on Devon: volume 3, Exeter (1843–) G2/11/15/2

Church notes on Devon: volume 4, West Devon (1843–) G2/11/15/2

Church notes on Devon: volume 5, North Devon (1843–) G2/11/15/2

Church notes on Devon PDF: volume 1, East Devon (1843–) DAVCHU1843

Church Notes, West volume s726.5/DEV/DAV

Cliffordiana, transcribed by J. Davidson (1830) s929.2/CLI

Collection for Axminster and District (1830) Z19/21/2

Collections for Devon (1850?) sxDEV/1830/DAV scrapbook of cuttings

Collections for Devon topography (1860?) Formerly Ms.10 newspaper cuttings: a Brooking Rowe bequest 1908EV/0001?DAV

Collections for Membury and Kilmington (1861?) sxB/MEM/0001?DAV

Collections for pedigrees and family history: mostly relating to Devonshire (1854?) s929.3?DEV/DAV

Collections on family history (1850?) s929.3?DEV/DAV

Collections relating to Colyton (1840?) sB/COL7?0001?ANS

Collections relating to Colyton (1850?) sB/COL7?0001?ANS

Collections towards a history of the medical worthies of Devon (1855–)

Cuttings from the *Western Times* (1855) s610.922?DEV/MUN

Collections of letters and printed posters relating to Bideford Z19/21/5

History of Axminster (n.d.) In Axminster parish File Box 1 Typescript taken from Davidson's 'History of Axminster'

A History of the Town and Parish of Axminster (1832) Z19/21/1

Index to Jenkins's History of Exeter, 2nd ed., 1841. From a ms. compilation (n.d.) B/ EXE/0001?DAV
Indexes to Westcote's View of Devonshire in 1630 (1895) DEV/1630?WES
Indexes to Polwhele's History of Devonshire (1790–1800)
Create New Feoffees (for Axminster charities) (1828) 406A/2/PF/36
Create New Feoffees (for Axminster charities) (1853) 406A/2/PF/37

BIBLIOGRAPHY

Unpublished Sources

Cresswell, B. 'Notes on Devon Churches. The Fabric and Features of Interest in the Churches of the Deanery of Honiton', vol.1, DHC S726.5/Dev/cre (1920b).

Davidson, J. 'Collection for Axminster and District', DHC Z19/12/1 (1830).

Davidson, J. *A History of the Town and Parish of Axminster*. DHC Z19/21/1 (1832).

Davidson, J. 'Church Notes on East Devon', vol.1, DHC G2/11/15/1 vol.1 (1843).

Davidson, J. 'Church Notes on South Devon', vol.2, DHC G2/11/15/2 (1843).

Davidson, J. 'Church Notes on Exeter Devon', vol.3, DHC G2/11/15/2 (1843).

Davidson, J. 'Church Notes on West Devon', vol.4, DHC G2/11/15/2 (1843).

Davidson, J. 'Church Notes on North Devon', vol.5, DHC G2/11/15/2 (1843).

Harding, W. 'Harding Collection', Athenaeum NDA hrd/H.

Hutchinson, P. *The History of the Restoration of Sidmouth Church*. DHC DRO 4584. 3 (1880).

Incledon, B. 'Monumental Inscriptions', North Devon Athenaeum d2 929 5/NC.

Milles, J. 'Devonshire Parochial Collections', Oxford, Bodleian Library MSS. Top. Devon b. 1–6.

Milles, J. 'A Parochial History of Devonshire 1747–1762', DHC (microfilm).

Oliver, G. 'Common Place Book', NDHC, Athenaeum, File H43, 1828.

Williams, M.A. 'Medieval English Roodscreens (with special reference to Devon)', Unpublished Ph.D. Thesis, University of Exeter, 2008.

Published Sources

Anon., 'Obituary of James Bridger Davidson', *Transactions of the Devonshire Association* 18 (1886), 58.

Addleshaw, G.W.O. and Etchells, F. *The Architectural Setting of Anglican Worship* (London: Faber, 1948).

Aston, M. *England's Iconoclasts. Volume I: Laws Against Images* (Oxford: Clarendon Press, 1988).

Barnwell, P.S. 'Seating in the Nave of the Pre-Reformation Parish Church', in T.H. Colvin (ed.), *A Biographical Dictionary of British Architects 1600–1840*, 3rd edn (London: Yale University Press, 1993).

Bligh Bond, F. 'Devonshire Screens and Rood Lofts', *Reports and Transactions of the Devonshire Association* 24 (1902), 531–50.

Brandwood, G.K. 'Anglican Churches before the Restorers: A Study from Leicestershire and Rutland', *Archaeological Journal* 144 (1987), 383–408.

Brown, S. 'Introduction: Pews – Understanding Significance, Recognising Need', in *Pews, Benches and Chairs*, ed. Cooper and Brown, 1–8.

Cann-Hughes, T. (ed.) 'Sir Stephen Glynne's Notes on the Churches of Devon', *Notes and Queries* 163 (1932): 328–31, 363–5, 400–2, 437–41, 471–5; 164 (1933): 21–6, 57–60, 95–6, 130–2, 169–71, 200–4, 236–9, 277–80, 313–15, 348–51, 416–17, 454–6; 165 (1933): 20–2, 63–5, 96–8, 130–2, 168–70, 204–6, 241–3, 274–7, 314–16, 349–51, 382–4, 420–2, 456–8; 166 (1934): 24–7, 63–5, 93–5, 131–3, 168–70, 200–3.

Cann-Hughes, T. (ed.) 'Sir Stephen Glynne's Notes on the Churches of Cornwall', *Notes and Queries* 167 (1934): 363–6, 400–2, 438–9; 168 (1934): 5–7, 42–5, 74–7, 111–13, 151–3, 182–4, 219–20, 255–60, 295–7, 329–31, 366–8, 399–41, 437–9; 169 (1935): 6–8, 43–5, 78–81, 112–15.

Chanter, J.F. 'Fifth Report of the Church Plate Committee,' *Transactions of the Devonshire Association* 45 (1913), 93–116.

Chapman, G. *A History of Axminster to 1910* (Honiton: Marwood Publications, 1998).

Cherry, B. and Pevsner, N. (eds). *The Buildings of England: Devon* (London: Yale University Press, 1991).

Clarke, K.M. 'The Baptismal Fonts of Devon', *Reports and Transactions of the Devonshire Association*. Part I, 45 (1913), 314–29; Part II, 46 (1914), 428–36; Part III, 47 (1915), 349–56; Part IV, 48 (1916), 302–19; Part V, 50 (1918), 583–8; Part VI, 51 (1919), 211–21; Part VII, 52 (1920), 327–35; Part VIII, 53 (1921), 226–31; Part IX, 54 (1922), 216–22.

Collinson, J. *The History and Antiquities of the County of Somerset, Collected from Authentick Records and an Actual Survey Made by the late Mr. Edmund Rack* (Bath: R. Cruttwell, 1791).

Cooper, T. 'How Many Seats in Church?' in *Pews, Benches and Chairs*, ed. Cooper and Brown, 37–66.

Cooper, T. and Brown, S. (eds) *Pews, Benches and Chairs. Church Seating in English Parish Churches from the Fourteenth Century to the Present* (London, Ecclesiological Society, 2011).

Courtney, W.P., revised by Maxted, I. 'Davidson, James (1793–1864)', *Oxford Dictionary of National Biography* (Oxford: Oxford University Press, 2004).

Davidson, J. *The British and Roman Remains in the Vicinity of Axminster, in the County of Devon* (London: J. B. Nicholls and Son, 1833).

Davidson, J. *The History of Axminster Church in the County of Devon* (Exeter: W.C. Pollard, 1835).

Davidson, J. *The History of Newenham Abbey in the County of Devon* (London: Longman and Co., 1843).

Davidson, J. *Notes on the Antiquities of Devon which Date before the Norman Conquest* (Exeter: W. Roberts, 1861).

Ellacombe, H. *A Detailed Account of the Bells in the Old Parish Churches of Devonshire* (Exeter: W. Pollard, 1872).

Esdaile, K.A. *English Church Monuments 1510–1840* (London: Batsford, 1946).

Fletcher J.M.J. (ed.) 'Sir Stephen Glynne, "Notes on some Dorset Churches"', *Proceedings of the Dorset Natural History and Antiquarian Field Club* 44 (1923), 86–104; 45 (1924), 12–74.

Friar, J.S. *A Companion to the English Parish Church* (Frome: Alan Sutton, 1996).

Gilbert, C.S. *An Historical and Topographical Survey of the County of Cornwall, to which is added a complete Heraldry of the same* (Plymouth-Dock: J. Cogdon, 1817–20).

Gray, T. and Rowe, M. (eds) *Travels in Georgian Devon: The Illustrated Journeys of the Reverend John Swete, 1789–1800*, 4 vols (Tiverton: Halsgrove, 1997–2000).

Hutchins, J. *The History and Antiquities of the County of Dorset*, 3rd edn, 4 vols (London, 1861–73).

Lindley, P. *Tomb Destruction and Scholarship: Medieval Monuments in Early Modern England* (Donington: Shaun Tyas, 2007).

McGarvie, M. (ed.) *Sir Stephen Glynne's Church Notes for Somerset* (Taunton: Somerset Record Society, 1994).

Newman, J. and Pevsner, N. *The Buildings of England. Dorset* (Harmondsworth: Penguin, 1972).

Orbach, J. and Pevsner, N. *The Buildings of England. Somerset South and West* (New Haven and London: Yale University Press, 2014).

Polwhele, R. *The History of Devonshire*. 3 vols (London: Cadell & Davies, 1793–1806).

Pulmans Weekly News, 8 March 1884.

Roffey, S. 'Deconstructing a Symbolic World', in *The Archaeology of Reformation 1480–1580*, ed. D. Gaimster and R. Gilchrist (Leeds: Maney Publications, 2003), 341–55.

Scott, J.G.M., Mack, F.D., and Clarke J.M. *Towers and Bells of Devon*, 2 vols (Exeter: The Mint Press, 2007).

Spreat, W. *Picturesque Sketches of the Churches of Devon* (Exeter: W. Spreat, 1842).

Stabb, J. *Devon Church Antiquities: Being a Description of Many Objects of Interest in the Old Parish Churches of Devonshire* (London: Simpkin, Marshall, Hamilton, Kent, & Co., 1908–16).

Wainwright, T. 'An Index to the Names of Persons Found on the Monumental Inscriptions in Devonshire Churches', *Reports and Transactions of the Devonshire Association* 36 (1904), 522–42.

Webster, C. 'Patterns of Church Seating from Waterloo to 1850, and the Role of the Cambridge Camden Society', in *Pews, Benches and Chairs*, ed. Cooper and Brown, 197–210.

Webster, C. and Elliot, J. (eds), *'A Church as it Should Be': The Cambridge Camden Society and its Influences* (Stamford: Shaun Tyas, 2000).

Yates, N. *Buildings, Faith and Worship* (Oxford: Oxford University Press 2000).

Index of Subjects, after Davidson

Index of People and Places,
after Davidson

DEVON AND CORNWALL
RECORD SOCIETY PUBLICATIONS

Previous volumes are available from Boydell & Brewer Ltd.

A Shelf List of the Society's Collections, ed. S. Stride, revised 1986

36 *The Local Customs Accounts of the Port of Exeter 1266–1321*, ed. Maryanne Kowaleski, 1993

37 *Charters of the Redvers Family and the Earldom of Devon 1090–1217*, ed. Robert Bearman, 1994

38 *Devon Household Accounts, 1627–59, Part I: Sir Richard and Lady Lucy Reynell of Forde House, 1627–43, John Willoughby of Leyhill, 1644–6, and Sir Edward Wise of Sydenham, 1656–9*, ed. Todd Gray, 1995

39 *Devon Household Accounts 1627–59, Part II: Henry, Earl of Bath, and Rachel, Countess of Bath, of Tawstock and London, 1639–54*, ed. Todd Gray, 1996

40 *The Uffculme Wills and Inventories, 16th to 18th Centuries*, ed. Peter Wyatt, with Introduction by Robin Stanes, 1997

41 *The Cornish Lands of the Arundells of Lanherne, Fourteenth to Sixteenth Centuries*, ed. H. S. A. Fox and O. J. Padel, 1998

42 *Liberalism in West Cornwall: The 1868 Election Papers of A. Pendarves Vivian MP*, ed. Edwin Jaggard, 1999

43 *Devon Maps and Map-makers: Manuscript Maps before 1840*, ed. with Introduction Mary R. Ravenhill and Margery M. Rowe, 2000

44 *The Havener's Accounts of the Earldom and Duchy of Cornwall, 1287–1356*, ed. Maryanne Kowaleski, 2001

45 *Devon Maps and Map-makers: Manuscript Maps before 1840*, ed. with Introduction Mary R. Ravenhill and Margery M. Rowe, 2002

46 *Death and Memory in Medieval Exeter*, ed. David Lepine and Nicholas Orme, 2003

47 *The Survey of Cornwall by Richard Carew*, ed. John Chynoweth, Nicholas Orme and Alexandra Walsham, 2004

48 *Killerton, Camborne and Westminster: The Political Correspondence of Sir Francis and Lady Acland, 1910–1929*, ed. Garry Tregidga, 2005

49 *The Acland Family: Maps and Surveys 1720–1840*, ed. with Introduction Mary R. Ravenhill and Margery M. Rowe, 2006

50 *Cornish Wills 1342–1540*, ed. Nicholas Orme, 2007

51 *The Letter Book of Thomas Hill 1660–1661*, ed. June Palmer, 2008

52 *Collecting the New, Rare and Curious: Letters Selected from the Correspondence of the Cornish Mineralogists Philip Rashleigh, John Hawkins and William Gregor, 1755–1822*, ed. R. J. Cleevely, 2011

53 *Robert Furse: A Devon Family Memoir of 1593*, ed. Anita Travers, 2012

54 *The Minor Clergy of Exeter Cathedral: Biographies, 1250–1548*, Nicholas Orme, 2013

55 *The Chancery Case between Nicholas Radford and Thomas Tremayne: the Exeter Depositions of 1439*, ed. Hannes Kleineke, 2013

56 *Elizabethan Inventories and Wills of the Exeter Orphans' Court*, Vol. 1, ed. Jeanine Crocker, 2016

57 *Elizabethan Inventories and Wills of the Exeter Orphans' Court*, Vol. 2, ed. Jeanine Crocker, 2016

58 *Devon Parish Taxpayers, Vol. 1, Abbotskerkwell to Bere & Seaton*, ed. Todd Gray, 2016

59 *Devon Parish Taxpayers, Vol. 2, Bere Ferrers to Chudleigh*, ed. Todd Gray, 2017

60 *Stratton Churchwardens' Accounts, 1512–1578*, ed. Joanna Mattingly, 2018

61 *A Lord Lieutenant in Wartime: The Experiences of the Fourth Earl Fortescue during the First World War*, Richard Batten, 2018

62 *Sir Francis Henry Drake (1723–1794): Letters from the Country, Letters from the City*, ed. Charity Scott-Stokes and Alan Lumb, 2019

63 *The Exeter Cloth Dispatch Book, 1763–1765*, Todd Gray, 2021

Devon Maps and Map-makers: Manuscript Maps before 1840. Supplement to Volumes 43 and 45, ed. Mary R. Ravenhill and Margery M. Rowe, 2010

Extra Series

1 *Exeter Freemen 1266–1967*, ed. Margery M. Rowe and Andrew M. Jackson, 1973

2 *Guide to the Parish and Non-Parochial Registers of Devon and Cornwall 1538–1837*, ed. Hugh Peskett, 1979, supplement 1983

3 *William Birchynshaw's Map of Exeter, 1743*, ed. Richard Oliver, Roger Kain and Todd Gray, 2019